Colonial America

Colonial America

Ronald P. Dufour

Professor of History
Rhode Island College
Providence, Rhode Island

West Publishing Company
Minneapolis/St. Paul • New York
Los Angeles • San Francisco

Compositor: *Parkwood Composition*
Cover Design: *Diane Beasley*
Text Design: *Melinda Grosser*
Front and Backmatter Design: *John Edeen*
Copyediting: *Marilynn J. Taylor*
Index: *Sandi Schroeder, Schroeder Indexing Service*

West's Commitment to the Environment

In 1906, West Publishing Company began recycling materials left over from the production of books. This began a tradition of efficient and responsible use of resources. Today, up to 95 percent of our legal books and 70 percent of our college and school texts are printed on recycled, acid-free stock. West also recycles nearly 22 million pounds of scrap paper annually—the equivalent of 181,717 trees. Since the 1960s, West has devised ways to capture and recycle waste inks, solvents, oils, and vapors created in the printing process. We also recycle plastics of all kinds, wood, glass, corrugated cardboard, and batteries, and have eliminated the use of Styrofoam book packaging. We at West are proud of the longevity and the scope of our commitment to the environment.

Production, Prepress, Printing and Binding by West Publishing Company.

Cover Credit: Detail of "Penn's Treaty with the Indians" by Benjamin West. Courtesy of the Pennsylvania Academy of the Fine Arts, Philadelphia. Gift of Mrs. Sarah Harrison (The Joseph Harrison, Jr. Collection).

Photo Credits:
12 Copyright British Museum; *13* Copyright British Museum; *15* The Newberry Library, Chicago; *26* Musees Royaux des Beaux-Arts de Belique, Bruxelles (Photo by G. Cussac); *29* The Metropolitan Museum of Art, Gift of J. Pierpont Morgan, 1900. (00.18.2); *37* Staatkiche Museen Zu Berlin, Munzkabinett, East Berlin; *39* Reproduction by permission of the Syndics of the Fitzwilliam Museum, Cambridge; *44* William L. Clements Library, Ann Arbor, Michigan; *45* Courtesy of The Hispanic Society of America, New York; *58* By permission of The British Library; *59* By permission of The British Library; *88* Reproduced by permission of The Huntington Library, San Marino, California; *89* The Mansell Collection; *93* Reproduced by permission of The Huntington Library, San Marino, California; *117* Courtesy, American Antiquarian Society; *138* Smithsonian Institution Photo Number 75-5850; *160* Eno Collection,

Photo credits continued on p. 524

TEXT IS PRINTED ON 10% POST CONSUMER RECYCLED PAPER

PRINTED WITH SOY INK

COPYRIGHT © 1994 By   WEST PUBLISHING COMPANY
610 Oppperman Drive
P.O. Box 64526
St. Paul, MN 55164–0526

Library of Congress Cataloging-in-Publication Data

Dufour, Ronald P. (Ronald Paul), 1947–
    Colonial America / Ronald P. Dufour.
        p. cm
    Includes index.
    ISBN 0-314-02749-1
    1. United States–History–Colonial period, ca. 1600–1775.
    2. United States–History–Colonial period, ca. 1600–1775–Sources.
    I. Title
    E188.D84   1994
    973.2–dc20
                                    93-37278
                                        CIP

To my parents

Contents

❧ *Chapter Four*

The Settlement of New England   106

❧ *Chapter Five*

England Pursues An Empire   146

Preface

Over the last few decades, historians of colonial America have produced a seemingly inexhaustible stream of creative scholarship. The sheer mass of new research threatens to outpace our ability to keep up. This text is an attempt to provide a thematic synthesis of this material. It treats the standard topics and includes as much of the basic factual material as space allows; in this sense, it will, I hope, serve as a useful introduction to the principal events of the period. But it also strives to introduce students to a world of astonishingly varied personal and cultural experiences. Indians, Europeans, and Africans lived in a world shaped by constant change and conflict, and their struggles with these forces transformed their lives.

I have sought to weave several broad themes through the story that follows. It has become increasingly clear that American Indian culture, and its interaction with the cultures of Old World migrants, is an essential component of the colonial experience. The American colonies matured, moreover, within an international context marked by the ongoing contest for empire between European nations. Early American historians can no longer ignore the Spanish and French colonial empires, and organized warfare and random violence were ever-present elements of life in the New World.

Cultural conflict was as common as the clash of arms. Men and women of all backgrounds found themselves divided by race, gender, wealth, religion, and region. Economic growth and the growing intrusion of the Atlantic market economy heightened tensions still further, even while bringing prosperity to many. Ordinary Americans sought to make sense of these changes through belief systems that were themselves being transformed and through the daily comforts of family and community. The eighteenth-century British colonies were rapidly entering the modern world, but with considerable reluctance.

In bringing this complex and fascinating story to life, I have included many maps and a number of charts, graphs, and illustrations. Each chapter also contains several selections from primary sources, chosen to illustrate themes delineated in the text. Wherever possible, I have retained the original idiosyncratic spelling and language of the originals, hoping to provide a more colorful sense of the style and culture of a distant age.

This book would not have been possible without a good deal of help along the way. My colleagues in the history department at Rhode Island College have provided an atmosphere of collegiality and intellectual stimulation that has been a constant source of support. Norman Smith and especially George Kellner, chairs during these years, have been generous in granting my scheduling requests and in many other small, but essential, ways. Stan Lemons read early versions of several chapters and greatly improved the end result with his perceptive historical and stylistic criticisms. Peter Piccillo, Bob Cvornyek, Leslie Schuster, Joanne Schneider, Don Sippel, Armand Patrucco, and other members of the department, along with anthropologist Terry Hays, provided encouragement or assistance at various times. Myra Blank of the Adams Library interlibrary loan office proved a marvel at acquiring obscure publications on short notice, and Lei Chang served as an invaluable research assistant for a semester. The Rhode Island College Faculty Research Fund provided financial support twice during the early stages of writing.

I owe an incalculable debt to three other groups. The historians of early America have produced a body of scholarship unmatched in breadth and quality, and it is they who have made this project such an exciting challenge. My students have added to the challenge; their persistent searches for understanding have pushed me to make this the best book possible. Finally, my own teachers never let me forget the importance of communicating the excitement of history to a broader audience. Ed Roddy, Peter Ford, Paul Hudon, Richard Maxwell Brown, Bruce McCully, Ed Crapol, and Mike McGiffert taught me what it means to be a scholar *and* a teacher.

West has been all that an author can expect of a publisher. My editor, Clark Baxter, encouraged me to attempt this project, and he has provided constant and understanding support. Amy S. Gabriel has been a model of efficiency as production editor, while copy editor Marilynn J. Taylor's suggestions significantly improved the style and clarity of the manuscript. The historians who reviewed the manuscript for West greatly improved the end result by their criticisms and suggestions; I am grateful to David Ammerman; Ross W. Beales, Jr.; Robert A. Becker; Richard Buel; Clive R. Hallman; Robert L. Hatzenbuehler; Owen S. Ireland; Jessica Kross; Glenn M. Linden; Daniel W. Markwyn; Robert W. McAhren; Sharon V. Salinger; Thomas P. Slaughter; and Darold D. Wax.

As always, my greatest debts are more personal. My son, Matthew, and my wife, Anne, have put up with my endless preoccupation with writing and research yet again. Their understanding has made it all possible.

Colonial
America

❧ *Chapter One* ❧

Worlds Apart: Americans and Europeans in the Fifteenth Century

Fifteenth-century Europe was an aggressive, technologically advanced society poised on the brink of economic and geographic expansion. Its people measured wealth in gold and silver and worshipped a Christian god who assured them they were at the spiritual center of the universe. Unknown to them, three thousand miles to the west, cultures as diverse and as complex as their own populated North and South America. These continents were neither an uninhabited, savage wilderness nor the Edenic paradise many Europeans sought, but their people did embrace material and spiritual values markedly different from those of the Europeans. When European explorers reached this world, they saw not difference but inferiority. The dramatic clash between these two worlds offers compelling insights into the origins of early American society.

First Settlement

Nomadic groups of people first wandered from Asia into the Americas between 30,000 and 20,000 B.C., crossing the Bering Strait when that area became an exposed land bridge during the most recent ice age. These hunters were probably following game and did not notice they were moving onto a different continent. Once here, they continued to move south and east, and over thousands of years, hundreds of splinter groups settled the length and breadth of North and South America. The process of dispersal could be casually simple: a family group might decide to move off from the larger group, perhaps seeking better game or tastier plants. From such movements, new cultures proliferated. Twelve distinct linguistic stocks developed in North America alone, with as many as two thousand different languages by the time of European contact.

Significant Dates

30,000–20,000 B.C.	Indian migrations across the Bering Strait
8000–1000 B.C.	Agricultural revolution among American Indians
2000 B.C.	Algonquians begin to arrive in New England region
1500 B.C.–1 A.D.	Preclassic period in Mexico
300–900 A.D.	Classic era; Mayan civilization flourishes
c. 900 A.D.	Toltecs emerge
	Pueblo cultures emerge
c. 1000 A.D.	Vikings reach Labrador and Newfoundland
1095 A.D.	Europeans initiate the Crusades
c. 1100 A.D.	Inca culture begins to flourish
1200s A.D.	Aztecs arrive in the Valley of Mexico
1271 A.D.	Marco Polo begins his journey to China
1420 A.D.	Portuguese discover and settle Madeira
1420s A.D.	Prince Henry begins to send mariners to explore the African western coast
1440 A.D.	Portuguese settle the Azores
1458–59 A.D.	Frau Mauro map
Fifteenth Century	Time of the Hiawatha legend
1469 A.D.	Ferdinand and Isabella wed
1471 A.D.	Portuguese sailors reach the African Gold Coast
1474 A.D.	Toscanelli map
1481 A.D.	Bristol fishermen possibly reach North America
1485 A.D.	Henry VII establishes the Tudor Dynasty
1487 A.D.	Bartholomew Diaz rounds the Cape of Good Hope
1492 A.D.	Spanish troops enter Granada
	Columbus reaches the New World
1493–96 A.D.	Columbus's second voyage
1494 A.D.	Treaty of Tordesillas
1497–98 A.D.	Voyages of John Cabot
1498 A.D.	Vasco da Gama reaches India
1498–1502 A.D.	Columbus's third voyage
1500 A.D.	Cabral lands on the Brazilian coast
1502–04 A.D.	Columbus's fourth voyage
1507 A.D.	New World named after Amerigo Vespucci
1517 A.D.	Martin Luther protests the sale of indulgences
Sixteenth Century	Iroquois establish the Great League of Peace and Power

About fourteen thousand years ago, improved weapons and new hunting techniques led to more settled living arrangements. During the Archaic Era, from about ten thousand to twenty-five hundred years ago, an agricultural revolution further transformed the lives of many tribes. The domestication of food plants created a more sedentary culture, leading to dramatic population growth, more complex political and religious institutions, and greater interest in artistic expression. A broader sexual division of labor began to evolve, as women became increasingly responsible for agricultural work, childcare, and home-related duties, while men continued to engage in hunting, warfare, and other tasks requiring heavy physical labor. Indians on both continents were at different stages of this mixing of hunting, farming, and gathering, depending on geography and ecology. By 1500 A.D., there were between 50 million and 100 million Indians in the Western Hemisphere, from 7 million to 18 million north of Mexico, and at least 5 million in what is today the United States.

Mesoamerican Cultures

The area between North and South America, known as Mesoamerica, covers approximately 350,000 square miles and possesses more geographical and ecological diversity than any similarly sized region on earth. The oldest human remains from the area date to about 9000 B.C. The population began to move toward agriculture about 5000 B.C., and by the second millennium B.C., Indians were living in permanent villages and had begun to grow maize, beans, and other plants. Larger urban communities began to appear in the preclassic period, stretching from about 1500 B.C. to 1 A.D., most noticeably around present-day Vera Cruz on the Gulf of Mexico. Here, the Olmec tribe developed sophisticated writing and mathematical systems and constructed substantial building complexes for religious use, without the use of the wheel or any knowledge of metallurgy. The Olmecs are best known, though, for their impressive stone sculptures. Some of these are male heads carved from boulders six to eight feet high, highly individualized and complete with ornamental hats or bands; they are most likely portraits of dynastic rulers.

Several large urban centers dominated Mesoamerican culture during the first millennium A.D., known as the classic period. About fifty thousand people lived in the most important of these cities, Teotihuacan, which embraced an urban center and suburbs spread over eight square miles and included temples, pyramids, schools, paved streets, and a drainage system. A monarch who served as both king and high priest ruled the city, which was physically dominated by a pyramid about 210 feet high and 690 feet square at the base. The city was destroyed around 800 A.D., probably after being set afire by enemies.

Mayan culture was the most highly developed of all those to appear during this period. The Mayans lived in an area that today comprises the Yucatan Peninsula, Guatemala, and Honduras. They built large urban centers and complex religious structures decorated with friezes, paintings, and sculptures. Their precise mathematical system allowed them to develop four separate calendars: a lunar calendar, another based on Venus, a sacred calendar that marked times of religious significance, and an annual calendar of 365 days. All were precise and accurate, telling the Mayans when to plant crops and predicting eclipses years in advance. The Mayans alone among American Indians had a written language and books.

Mayans combined hunting and agriculture, growing corn, beans, and squash and pursuing turkeys, wild pigs, and fish. Their clothing was simple and minimal—loin cloths for men, tunics for women, and capes for colder weather. The upper classes owned more jewelry and decorative items. Some marks of status undoubtedly seemed bizarre to Western eyes: kings pierced their penises with stingray spines, and queens ran barbed ropes through their tongues.

Mayan society was highly stratified politically and economically. The king ruled, advised by a council of royal family members. Nobles occupied administrative offices and served as the government's connections to localities. Priests held considerable power and used their mastery of the calendars to advise on political and military decisions; they also treated the sick and conducted sacrifices (sometimes human) to the Mayan gods. Merchants held high economic status and engaged in extensive trade with Indians throughout the region in cotton, skins, pottery, and textiles for cocoa, beans, feathers, and highly prized jade. Peasants were forced to pay heavy taxes in produce and labor and to serve in the army. Slaves were drawn from prisoners of war or peasant children sold to pay their parents' debts. The system was designed to perpetuate royal authority and to maintain the traditional use of wealth—ostentatious display by the ruling classes.

The Maya truly distinguished themselves from their neighbors in the realm of aesthetics. Like other Mesoamerican societies, they grouped their buildings around central courtyards, placed temples on high platforms, and were skilled in such crafts as ceramics, weaving, and stone carving. But within these shared patterns, they developed a unique style, preferring baroque ornamentation to severe geometric lines, steep temple pyramids to massive hulks, and vaulted rather than flat roofs.

Mayan society began to decline as early as 700 A.D., ravaged by internal social struggles, peasant revolts, and invasion. By 950 A.D., the classic period of civilization in Mesoamerica had passed, and when the Spanish arrived in the New World, all that remained of the Mayan empire were a few modestly sized cities.

The Aztec Empire

The Toltecs briefly succeeded the Mayans as the region's dominant tribe. Centered in Tula, some fifty miles north of Mexico City, they were already in decline by the middle of the twelfth century. Extensive population movements marked the following centuries, but one group eventually emerged as the dominant force in the Valley of Mexico—the Aztecs. The Aztecs arrived in the area during the thirteenth century and increased their power under a series of fierce and expansionistic leaders. By the time of their first contact with Europeans, their empire stretched west to the Pacific, east to the Gulf of Mexico, south almost to the Yucatan, and north to the Rio Grande River. Their leaders held absolute power and claimed direct descent from the Toltec god Quetzalcoatl; although the chief priest, the chief justice, and the chief of markets advised them, they ruled without restrictions.

The Aztecs traded extensively throughout Central America, exchanging cloth, blankets, knives, jewelry, herbs, and dyes for unfinished goods, such as skins, feathers, and pearls. They exacted tribute from the tribes they conquered and imposed a brutal system of military control. Their capital, Tenochtitlan, was in the middle of Lake Texcoco on the site of present-day Mexico City, connected by a causeway to the mainland. It was a city of three hundred thousand (only six European cities had as many as one hundred thousand people), graced with whitewashed homes of adobe or stone and numerous public and private gardens. Cortes later called it "the most beautiful city in the world."[1]

From here, Aztec rulers collected tribute in gold, silver, cotton, food, and jade and sacrificed human victims by the thousands to their gods. At one temple dedication, at least twenty thousand victims lost their lives. Montezuma II, the Aztec ruler who confronted Cortes, was descended from a Toltec royal family through his mother. He actively pursued the Aztec policy of expansion and suppression of tributary tribes, but he was also renowned for his devotion to art, learning, and his religious duties, marking him as perhaps the greatest of Aztec rulers.

Both the common people and the nobility were organized into clans based on kinship connections. Elders allocated resources, enforced laws, and represented their clans at national councils. Clans ran local schools, where boys studied martial arts, law, and an occupation and girls learned the skills necessary to become good wives. Nobles' sons attended school at temple locations and received extensive training in reading, writing, religious and ritual practices, and a wide variety of other subjects. Merchants wielded much economic power. They worked through special guilds that regulated trade and often engaged in diplomacy with other tribes. Strong families were essential to the stability of this society, and marriage was one of the most important social rituals.

A combination of religious belief and terrorism held the Aztec social structure and empire together. The nobility created their own image and history, going so far as to destroy all written records of Toltec civilization. Aztec religion was based on a belief in the cyclical destruction of the earth, and Aztecs hoped they could forestall the next cycle of destruction through ritual sacrifice. They also believed the sun required nourishment or it would die. The priests fed the sun by slicing open sacrificial victims[3] chests with razor-sharp knives, tearing out the hearts, and offering them to the giver of life. This was, of course, much easier for the nobility to accept than it was for the common people. The combination of tribute and human sacrifice fostered deep resentment against Aztec rule, and the Spanish would later take advantage of this discontent to speed their conquest of Mexico.

The Inca Empire

The Incas, centered in present-day Peru, were the other powerful people European invaders confronted. Like the Aztecs, the Incas greatly expanded their influence during the last quarter of the fifteenth century under the leadership of a series of powerful rulers also known as Incas. The Tupac Inca Yupanqui succeeded his father to the throne in 1471 and created an empire that stretched from the present Colombia-Ecuador border to central Chile—more than twenty-five hundred miles. More than seven thousand miles of roads and a highly efficient postal system united these lands, which were divided into four regions, eighty provinces, and 160 districts.

Authority in this society was hierarchical. Inca leaders solidified their rule by claiming descent from the sun, and they maintained royal family dominance through a tradition that required the eldest son of royal families to marry his eldest sister. They possessed a strong army and required all males between the ages of fifteen and twenty-one to serve. The Inca claimed all gold and silver collected through conquest or trade, and each tribe had to pay him a quota of other products.

The economy was centralized and prosperous; trade extended down the west coast of the continent over the extensive network of roads and bridges. Inca artisans produced superb pottery, cloth, and metal work. Inca society was as structured as others in the area: priests, merchants, and artisans were all part of closed classes, and most people were farmers. Common people had some compensations, however. Upon marriage, couples received a plot of land and a house form the village; in old age, they were freed from tax and labor payments and given food and clothing if necessary. The Inca upper classes had a greater sense of social responsibility than other societies in the area, even if it was designed to ensure their continued dominance.

North American Cultures

Farther to the north, Indian life evolved in dramatically different directions. Indians throughout continental North America shared certain common traits. For all tribes, the natural world was holy; the secular and the sacred were not separated. Indians believed that many beings inhabited this world and that animals, plants, and even rocks had their own spirits, all related to the sacred whole. If humans harmed the land or killed an animal unnecessarily, the spirits would strike back. Killing too much game, for instance, destroyed the relationship of mutual trust between animal and human spirits and could result in animals leaving the area for more hospitable environs. All North American tribes had political structures that governed their secular affairs, kinship customs that regulated social life, and economic systems that defined modes of subsistence and were based on a sexual division of labor. These structures contrasted sharply with those of their Mesoamerican neighbors and of the future European invaders.

West and Southwest Tribes

American Indian cultures were at least as diverse as their European counterparts, and a discussion of those that had the most extensive contact with Europeans is essential to an understanding of early America. At the time of European contact, the Hopi and Zuni tribes, Pueblo Indians, had been practicing agriculture for some four thousand years in the area north and northwest of Mesoamerica. By 900 A.D., they had begun to build apartment-like residences, often on ledges and cliff sides; these large, terraced buildings with many rooms were designed to offer protection from their more war-like neighbors, the Apaches. One such structure, the Pueblo Bonita, had up to eight hundred rooms. Both tribes depended on growing maize and developed extensive systems of irrigation canals and terraced cultivation methods. They also had sophisticated ceramics and basket-weaving industries. The Pueblos had sacred spaces that radiated out from them and holy caves or ceremonial rooms called *kivas* that were believed to be connected to the source of all life, the underworld. Religious figures known as *caciques* preserved the spiritual knowledge essential to Pueblo rituals. Like European peasants, these Indians lived by the seasons and performed rituals that guaranteed the success of planting, irrigating, harvesting, and hunting.

Farther east, two distinctive cultures dominated the central portion of the continent. The Mound Builders in the Ohio River valley are best known for their geometric earthwork constructions, shaped like humans, birds, and snakes and reaching as high as seventy feet. Ancestors of the Creeks, Choctaws, and Natchez tribes, these people left ten thousand mounds in southern Ohio alone. Apparently used as burial sites, the mounds were located near large, earth-walled enclosures that served as residences. More than one thousand of these enclosures have been discovered; the largest had a circumference of three and a half miles, enclosing one hundred acres—the equivalent of fifty modern city blocks. The Mound Builders also established an extensive trading network covering the eastern half of the continent. For reasons still unclear, the culture was in decline by 500 A.D.

About this time, another culture was beginning to flourish in the broad area stretching from Wisconsin to Louisiana and Oklahoma to Tennessee, centered in the area of modern St. Louis. Known as the Mississippian culture, its people prospered in an intensive agricultural system. They too constructed large burial and ceremonial mounds. One such mound, built between 900 and 1100 A.D., had a rectangular base that covered fifteen acres. It was located in a region with more than one

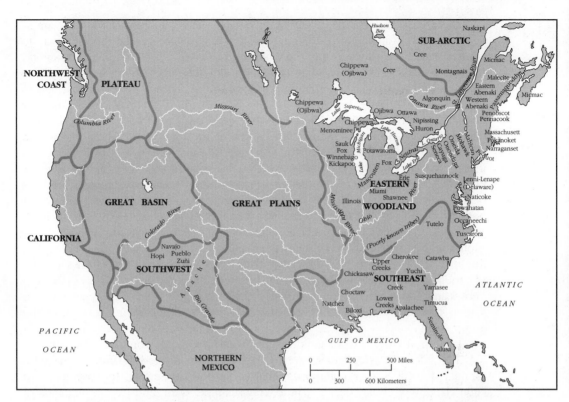

MAP 1.1: North American Indian Groups in the early 1600s The map designates primarily those tribes that had contact with European settlers during the colonial period. ❧

hundred burial mounds and a palisaded city, Cahokia, inhabited by about thirty-five thousand people. Archeologists have uncovered a wealth of ornaments from this site, including fine ceramics, sculptured stonework, embossed and engraved copper and mica sheets, and a funeral blanket made from twelve thousand shell beads. Cahokia was truly an urban center, with markets, clustered housing, toolmakers, potters, weavers, and artisans of all sorts. Though this culture disappeared in the early sixteenth century, its influence continued to be felt in Indian cultures throughout the southeast.

Eastern Woodland Tribes

Indians who lived east of the Appalachian Mountains shared many common characteristics and, with a few exceptions, had remarkably similar cultures. All of these tribes perceived and understood the world largely in religious terms. They believed that spirits of varying significance and strength suffused the natural world, including powerful "guardian" spirits *(manitou)*, the master or creator spirit, and an active and destructive evil spirit *(matchemanitou)*, whom they spent much time trying to pacify. Every plant or animal had its own "boss" spirit. Indians developed complex creation myths to explain their origins. Matrilineal cultures, such as the Iroquois and the Huron, believed that life began when a woman fell or was pushed from the sky and gave birth to good and evil twins; the good twin created humanity and other life forms and struggled with his evil brother for control of the earth and its inhabitants. Patrilineal tribes that relied on hunting, such as the Ottawas, believed that the creator spirit (the Great Hare) drew the first men out of the bodies of animals and then created women from men.

These Indians performed a variety or rituals to maintain contact with this super-natural world. Propitiation of the appropriate spirits often seemed the only way to control nature, disasters, crops, the hunt, and anything else that seemed beyond rational explanation. Dreams served as an important source of knowledge for these peoples—knowledge of supernatural wisdom and of individual desires that had to be fulfilled to achieve happiness. In all of these tribes, shamans had particular importance. These religious figures, who were both revered and feared, were believed to possess a mysterious connection with the spirit world. Their duty was to maintain contact with the supernatural, to cure disease, to drive out evil spirits, and in general to insure that the tribe stayed on the right side of the spiritual balance. Only they could cure one of the greatest of Indian fears, bewitchment. Indians believed that they all had some degree of spiritual power that could be used for both good and evil and that any individual could bewitch another by introducing a small object, such as a lock of hair or piece of fur, into their body or perhaps by capturing their soul in a dream. Only the shaman (for a fee or gift) could counteract this spell and even then only if his own power was greater than that of the witch.

Indians' attitudes toward authority differed markedly from those of western Europeans. Individuals jealously guarded their autonomy, and they expected their leaders to exercise their authority wisely and with restraint for the survival of the group. Thus, Indians rarely recognized an authority greater than that of the band, a small group of villages that shared resources and people. Beyond this, the clan sys-tem helped unify widely dispersed tribes. Clans consisted of individuals who claimed descent from a common animal ancestor. The Seneca, for instance, had eight clans: Wolf, Bear, Beaver, Turtle, Hawk, Snipe, Deer, and Heron. Members of different clans lived in each village; though they could not marry other members of the same clan, they could claim hospitality from them.

Indians encouraged cooperation in every possible way. They owned land com-munally, with village leaders granting individuals usage rights for specific periods of time. They "possessed" only those items they made themselves or the food they cultivated. House sites, gardens, hunting territories—all were assigned to individuals and families by tribal leaders and recognized as belonging temporarily to the indi-vidual but ultimately derived from the group. Indians shared their wealth willingly. They praised men who were successful in the hunt but expected them to share their bounty with those who were less fortunate.

Indian justice was retributive—a life for a life. In Europe, murder was an offense against the state. Among American Indians, it was a crime against the fami-ly; the victim's kin sought vengeance, though the obligation was often commuted to a payment of valuable goods. War was a common extension of this justice sys-tem, but Indians fought for vengeance or prestige, not for gain. War parties were small, their goals limited and relatively easy to achieve. Warriors snuck up on the targeted village and frightened their foes with cries and screams, attacking in a sort of free-for-all; a single death or two would usually end the battle immediately. Unlike their European counterparts, most Indians did not kill women or children and did not fight to subjugate other tribes. After a successful attack, they plundered the village and took prisoners if possible. Occasionally, they exacted tribute to establish dominance over a neighboring tribe, but even this was a two-way street. The losers paid a tribute, and the victors confirmed the relationship with a gift of wampum. The defeated Indians deferred to the conquerors and allowed them free passage through their territory, but they could also claim protection against their enemies and did not always give up the use of their lands. Indians regularly used gifts in dealings between equals to guarantee that promises would be carried out and reciprocal obligations and duties observed.

This world could be as cruel and violent as its European counterpart. Torture was not universal, but it could be horribly sadistic. Captors often scalped and burned their victims to death, and even old women would "satisfy some horrid lust by thrusting firebrands at his [a captive's] genitals or chewing off the joints of his fingers."[2] Captives were expected to show only contempt for their tormenters, and any expression of fear would bring derisive laughter from their captors. Such stoicism should not be surprising. American Indians inhabited an environment that could quickly turn from a source of natural bounty to one of scarcity or destruction. Indian justice and warfare reflected the harshness and unpredictability of their lives.

Spiritual beliefs and values were evident in Indian life from birth to death. Taboos marked pregnancy; Indians believed that women acquired heightened spiritual powers at this time (and during menstruation) that could both harm and heal, so males sought to insulate themselves from danger by limiting contact with women during such times. Women had to abstain from sexual relations until weaning. Father, mother, and the entire community treated newborns and older children with love, affection, and indulgence. A few months after a child's birth, the community held a formal initiation rite to welcome the child into the community. Children of both sexes spent the first years of their lives strapped into a cradle board, which did nothing to lessen the care they received. As the Jesuit Pierre de Charlevoic later noted,

> The care which the mothers take of their children, whilst they are still in the cradle is beyond all expression, and proves in a very sensible manner, that we often spoil all, by the reflections we add to the dictates of simple nature. They never leave them, they carry them every where about with them; and even when they are ready to sink under the burthen with which they load themselves, the cradle of the child is held for nothing . . .[3]

Physical punishment of children was unknown; Indian parents rebuked their children by withdrawing affection. They shaped behavior by encouraging their children to casually explore the tasks they would pursue more seriously when older. Boys played at hunting, for instance, and girls helped their mothers make clothes and prepare food. Parents encouraged children to question authority even while they imbued them with a strong sense of loyalty to the group. Those who trespassed against group norms would be barred from the company of their people until they showed repentance.

Boys and girls passed through rites of passage at puberty. Boys formed close friendships that would last a lifetime, and they were welcomed into the tribe with a new name when they killed their first big game or performed some particularly courageous act. Young men often went on vision quests, where they sought instruction from a guardian spirit that would become their personal helpmate for life. Girls withdrew from the village for a time at puberty, so that the spiritual forces released within them by menstruation would not harm themselves or others. Most Indian youths engaged in sexual exploration without guilt, though public displays of affection were not encouraged (Europeans introduced kissing). Young lovers met secretly at night or in cornfields during the day.

A young man would seek consent to marry from the woman's parents, who would consult other clan members. The couple often lived with the woman's parents during the first year or two, while the man showed he was capable of supporting his family. In some tribes, the couple even abstained from sex during this time. Divorce was virtually unknown after the first children were born, another reflection of Indians' implicit understanding of the critical nature of the family in their harsh environment.

Labor was clearly divided by sex among these Indians. Women were responsible for domestic and agricultural duties, men for warfare, hunting, and heavier

❧ *Documents* ❧
Childhood Among the Indians

Samuel de Champlain, one of the most perceptive of European observers, described the Indian practice of cradling.

> As to the nurture and bringing up of their children, they place the child in the daytime on a little wooden board, and clothe and wrap it in furs or skins and tie it to the said board which they stand upright, leaving a little opening by which the child does its little business; and if it is a girl they put a leaf of Indian corn between its thighs which presses against its privates and they turn the end of the said leaf and bring it outside, and by this means the child's water runs off on this leaf without soiling the child. . . .

H. P. Biggar, ed., *The Works of Samuel de Champlain*, 6 vols. (Toronto: Champlain Society, 1922–35), 3:41. Reprinted with permission of The Champlain Society, Toronto, CANADA.

Indian children enjoyed a kind of freedom that contrasted dramatically with European practices. The following account of childhood among the Delaware describes typical attitudes.

> Children, especially boys, are not held to work; the latter are to become hunters. They are allowed their own way, their elders saying "We did not work ourselves in the days of our youth." They follow their own inclinations, do what they like and no one prevents them, except it be that they do harm to others; but even in that case they are not punished, being only reproved with gentle words.

Archer Butler Hulbert and William Nathaniel Schwarze, eds., *David Zeisberger's History of the Northern American Indians* (Columbus: Ohio Archeological and Historical

domestic chores. Women tended the fields, raised the children, and made baskets and other utensils from bark and wood. In addition to hunting and conducting war, men made snowshoes, sleds, and canoes, the latter framed with cedar, covered with strips of birchbark, and made watertight with a coating of pitch.

At death, the individual remained as much a functional part of the community as during life. Indians believed the dead remained in their lodge for a while after death, so that friends and relatives could say good-bye. Survivors were regarded as impure as a result of their contact with the dead person (and the spirit world), and they remained isolated for a time before they were reunited with the community through feasts and celebrations. Widows could remarry after a period of mourning, generally a year or two.

While all eastern Indians shared these general personal and social characteristics, many particular regional variations existed. To understand the complexity of

Society, 1910), 16; reprinted in James Axtell, ed., *The Indian Peoples of Eastern America: A Documentary History of the Sexes* (New York: Oxford University Press, 1981), 41–2.

The vision quest was an essential rite of passage for many Indian boys. The following description of the Huron practice offers an example.

> Now this is the way in which they create the Divinity. When a child has reached the age of ten or twelve years, his father gives him a lesson, imparting to him the necessary instructions for finding out what will be his God thenceforth.

> First, he has him fast for several days, in order that, with his head empty, he may the more easily dream during his sleep; for it is then that this fancied God is bound to reveal himself to him. . . .

> Accordingly, when morning has come, the father questions his son, very seriously and with great secrecy, on all that has occurred during the night. If nothing has appeared to him, the fast must be begun again, and followed up until finally something is formed in the empty brain that represents to him either the Sun, or Thunder, or something else about which he has often been talked to; and, immediately upon awaking, he tells the good news to his father, who confirms the image in his thoughts. . . .

Reuben Gold Thwaites, ed., *The Jesuit Relations and Allied Documents,* 73 vols. (New York: Pageant, 1959), 54:141.

Indian culture, we must look a bit more closely at the customs and beliefs of some of the tribes with which the English settlers would have contact.

Chesapeake and Carolina Cultures The principal tribes along the mid-Atlantic coastal plain—the Powhatans, Tuscaroras, Piscataways, Roanocs, and others—shared certain basic cultural characteristics. All were in the late Woodland Period of development and practiced a mixed economy typical of coastal Woodland tribes, extensively cultivating maize, squash, beans, and tobacco and making seasonal migrations to hunting areas. The growing season could be as long as 240 days on the coast or as short as 180 days inland; tribes adapted by engaging in more or less extensive hunting. Coastal Indians also relied heavily on the sea and foraged for nuts, berries, and roots. All villages burned away underbrush to make way for new crops, thereby releasing nitrogen in the soil, creating park-like areas around villages, and destroying such pests as ticks, lice, mosquitoes, and particularly fleas. The entire village moved on to new areas when the land began to lose its fertility.

Indians moved inland during the summer months to avoid coastal heat and humidity. In autumn, they moved back to the coastal areas to protect their crops from crows and scavengers. After the harvest, they spent much of their time hunting for deer, bear, and turkey. The hunters moved silently by water, in canoes built from large pines or yellow poplars. They felled the trees with fire and then hollowed out the trunks to make canoes up to forty feet long and two or more feet wide. Such canoes could carry up to twenty people, were easily maneuverable, and were much larger and heavier than the northern birchbark canoes. They also helped connect the region's extensive trading networks. The Carolina tribes, for instance, traded with Creek, Cherokees, and most of the major tribes from the southern Appalachians to the lower Mississippi valley.

These Indians lived in semipermanent villages often densely concentrated along major waterways. The Powhatan empire extended throughout most of the coastal plain and included as many as fourteen thousand Indians and three thousand warriors. About seven thousand Indians lived in North Carolina alone, and almost two thousand lived along a mile-long strip of coast land between the Santee and Savannah Rivers. Inland, the Cherokees numbered as many as thirty thousand around the time of European contact. The interior in particular was quite diverse linguistically and was home to a number of tribes: Iroquois, Cherokee, Tuscarora, Sioux, Catawba, Musjoge, Creek, Chickasaw, and Choctaw. The material culture of most of these people was similar to that of more northern groups. Women wore deerskin or woven grass aprons, men loincloths made of leather, grass or leaves; both wore outer garments of animal skins or furs during cold weather. Women

The Indian Village of Secoton, drawn by John White about 1590. ❧

John White's painting of a North Carolina Algonquian Shaman (1585). ❧

built dwellings from frames of green saplings set in rows, bent over, and tied at the top with bark and roots. The frames was covered with bark or woven grass, and a hole in the roof allowed smoke from the fire to escape.

Like all American Indians, the coastal tribes had elaborate belief systems. Their religions centered on a complex polytheism respectful of the forces of nature. The Powhatan Indians believed in a benign god, Quioquiascache, who appeared as a Great Hare, gave good things to everyone, and harmed no one. They sought to placate the evil god Okee with regular offerings. The Powhatans also believed in an afterlife, a place of happiness with plentiful hunting grounds. Those whose lives warranted punishment went instead to a stinking, hot lake. Indians followed careful guidelines in hunting, so as not to anger the animal spirits through overkilling; they prayed for an animal spirit's forgiveness when they did make a kill. They engaged in various rituals that reaffirmed their own proper place in the natural universe. The fall Green Corn ceremony, for instance, involved fasting, dancing, housecleaning, and forgiveness of transgressions committed by community members during the preceding year; the intent was self-purification and celebration of the ripening of the maize.

Descent and inheritance in these tribes were generally matrilineal. Indian leader Powhatan's line of succession passed not through his sons but to his brothers, his sisters, and then to the sons and daughters of his eldest sister. There were, in fact, several female tribal leaders in the region, and women in general held considerable power—they could speak in council meetings and own houses, and they had much sexual freedom before marriage. Women ran the households and were responsible for planting and harvesting, cooking, making clothing, gathering wood and tending fires, making pottery and baskets, and raising the children. Men performed the more physically demanding labor, such as making canoes and preparing gardens, conducting war, and fishing and hunting.

As in most Indian cultures, political structures maintained order without coercion. A council of village elders and warriors selected chiefs from among eligible kin groups; these leaders could advise, but not coerce, their followers. Special war chiefs led their tribes into battle. Regional alliances were formed based on cultural loyalties and common defense needs against attacks from Sioux or Iroquois on the western borders. The Powhatan empire, though, was an exception, unusual both in its extent and in the power of its ruler. Each tribe in this confederacy had its own chief, but Powhatan appointed other chiefs, known as lesser *werowances,* to rule over several tribes collectively. Powhatan himself, as the great *werowance,* exacted tribute from each member tribe and presided over the entire structure, aided by a council of relatives, *werowances,* and spiritual leaders. While custom was the principal form of law in other tribes, Powhatan made his own will law. He inflicted terrible retribution on his enemies through torture, mutilation, and murder. But he was also careful to cultivate the loyalty and gratitude of his subjects, redistributing food from his vast stores to earn their allegiance. He succeeded in maintaining a political and military force powerful enough to challenge the English settlers.

Iroquois   The Iroquois confederation consisted of five tribes: Mohawk, Oneida, Onondaga, Cayuga, and Seneca. It embraced ten thousand people, and its origins provide insight into the function of myth and the importance of communal values in Indian life. Around 1300 A.D., Iroquois from the mid-Mississippi valley migrated to the eastern Great Lakes region in search of new hunting grounds. By the fifteenth century, however, blood feuds and chronic violence had seriously eroded Iroquois strength. According to legend, sometime around 1450, an Indian named Hiawatha lost several of his relatives through such violence and wandered into the woods in sorrow and grief. There, he had a vision, and a supernatural creature revealed to him a plan to revitalize Iroquois society. Hiawatha recruited followers and formed the Iroquois confederation called the Great League of Peace and Power, which prohibited blood feuds and allowed vengeance only through ritual bereavement. A council of fifty sachems, or chiefs, made all decisions for the tribes, lessening the temptation to engage in destructive warfare with other tribes. Each of the five nations had only one vote, and responsibilities were clearly divided. The Mohawk, Onondaga, and Seneca, for instance, were the more powerful tribes and thus were assigned war responsibilities. The league's system of checks and balances ensured that despite their power, these tribes could not dominate affairs.

Iroquois culture bore little resemblance to the popular image of a society of fierce, destructive warriors. Warfare was ritualistic. Warriors retreated in battle if their party suffered even a few casualties; an Iroquois who died in battle was doomed to spend eternity seeking vengeance. Participation in a war party was indeed a critical experience for young Iroquois males, and success in battle heightened individual prestige and improved a warrior's chances for marriage or leadership. But war served primarily social purposes. An individual's death lessened the power of the clan, so the person had to be replaced. Iroquois of ordinary stature could be replaced by war captives—hence, the phenomenon known as mourning wars. The mourner's grief at the loss of a loved one had to be assuaged, so a clan matron would ask a war captain from her own clan or that of her husband's to lead a raid to capture a member of an enemy tribe.

The Iroquois treated the captive with ritual cruelty, old women leading the abuse. The assaults were designed primarily to humiliate the victim; blows to the body, hands, and feet inflicted much pain but usually did little permanent damage. The woman who had initiated the raid would decide the fate of the captive. If her loss were recent and her pain still great, she might demand his death; if she needed someone to help in the hunt and provide emotional support, the clan would adopt him and treat him as a blood relative, dressing his wounds and lavishing attention on him. At times, captives were tortured and executed to vent the rage and pain of the villagers, who then feasted on their remains.

The Iroquois built their towns on hilltops and bordered them with log palisades. In the surrounding fields, they grew maize, beans, squash, and sunflowers. They lived in longhouses, which were long, relatively narrow buildings framed with saplings. Women and children of the same clan lived together, with paired family quarters facing each other across a center aisle that contained a shared cooking hearth. Iroquois culture was matrilineal. A typical family consisted of a woman, her daughters, and their families; sons joined their wives' families after marriage. Women initiated divorce simply by placing their husbands' belongings outside the door. Divorce was relatively common among the Iroquois, and many men lived apart from their wives although they remained married. Though fathers were close to their children, the mothers' brothers served as the primary male role model.

Several matrilineal kinship groups formed an *ohwachira*, which were grouped together to make up clans. A dozen or so clans comprised a village, and a group of villages made up a nation. Women held extensive political power in this society, particularly the old women who headed the *ohwachiras*. They chose the men to

Iroquoian longhouse, details from the Plan du Fort Frontenac ou Cataraouy, circa 1720. ❧

represent the clans at councils and also named the fifty chiefs of the confederacy. At meetings, they openly gave counsel to the male representatives, and they simply removed from power men who strayed too far from their will. Perhaps most indicative of female power was the fact that compensation for a woman's life was twice that for a man's.

The division of labor was similar to that of other woodland societies; women performed agricultural duties and were often in command of the village when men were away hunting for long periods. The Iroquois also made seasonal migrations. At the end of February, families left their villages to camp near sugar maple groves, where men helped the women make sugar and hunted and trapped. In the spring, everyone fished and women planted crops while men and boys repaired old dwellings or built new ones. Summer was the time for socializing, politics, and diplomacy; autumn for the harvest, the Green Corn festival, and the thanksgiving dance. During the late fall and winter, men again spent most of their time hunting.

One particularly interesting aspect of Iroquois culture (common to many other eastern tribes) was their belief in dreams as "the language of the soul." Individuals carefully studied the content of their dreams, believing that they expressed desires that had to be fulfilled or fears that required soothing and that ignoring such messages could bring serious illness. Individuals often recounted their dreams so the entire group could discuss them.

Hurons The Hurons lived at the southwest corner of Georgian Bay at Lake Huron, on a strip of land only thirty-five miles wide east to west and twenty miles north to south. They were united in a confederacy akin to that of the Iroquois, though more loosely structured. Huron villages held as many as several thousand inhabitants, and wooden palisades surrounded the largest. These settlements contained fifty or more longhouses, each inhabited by ten or so closely related families. Families marked off their own private living areas, but all shared the food stored in large casks in a communal area.

Hurons were an Iroquoian people and their lives and beliefs followed similar patterns. The Huron creation myth, for instance, closely resembles that of the Iroquois. They believed that Aataentsic, the mother of all humans, fell through a hole in the sky one day. The great tortoise, swimming in the primeval ocean below, ordered the ocean's animals to pile up dirt from the ocean bottom on his back so she would land gently. When she fell, Aataentsic was pregnant and she later became the mother of two boys: Tawiscaron and Iouskeha. Iouskeha created the lakes and rivers, controlled the weather, taught humans the secret of fire, and released all earthly animals from a cave where they had been hidden. Unfortunately, his mother had an evil side to her nature and spent much time working with Tawiscaron trying to undo Iouskeha's good works; she brought death to humans and caused disease and epidemics. Iouskeha eventually defeated Tawiscaron, and the two thereafter lived together in a bark cabin, competing for control of human destiny.

The Huron economy was agricultural. Women used wooden spades to form hills of soil a foot high and three feet in diameter in which they planted corn, beans, and squash; they also gathered acorns, walnuts, and grapes. Men cleared the fields and fished for trout, pike and sturgeon. Hurons could clear as much land as they desired, so long as they cultivated it; once abandoned, anyone could claim and cultivate a field. Fall hunts often kept the men away from the village for months at a time. Hurons traded extensively with Algonquian peoples to the north, exchanging corn, tobacco, and wampum for dried meat, fish, skins, and clothing. Trade was so important to them that they distrusted tribes with whom they did not have a reciprocal trading relationship. Like other Indians, Hurons made every effort to keep warfare to a minimum. They were particularly careful to stop blood feuds from developing with their trading partners, and they often exchanged children with other tribes to encourage cooperation and friendship.

New England Woodland Indians As the ice sheet covering the New England area began to recede around 15,000 B.C., the large Pleistecene mammals, such as mammoths and caribou, began to enter the region, and the so-called Fluted Blade Hunters followed them from the south and west around 10,000 B.C. The Algonquians began to arrive in the area after 2000 B.C., probably in search of new hunting grounds. Over time, these societies remained unified by language but distinguished by regional economic specialization. Indians in southern new England became relatively more tied to agriculture, those further north to hunting, and those on the coast on the abundance of the sea. Dialects followed waterways. The Micmacs dominated the regions farthest to the north, while Eastern and Western Abenakis populated northern and central areas of what is now Maine, New Hampshire, and Vermont. There were four language groups in the south, each with several dialects: the Massachusetts, on the lower Merrimack River and the coast, the Wampanoag of southeastern Massachusetts, the Narragansett on the western shore of Narragansett Bay, and the Mohegan-Pequot of eastern Connecticut and Quinnipiac of western Connecticut.

Culturally, these tribes had much in common. In warm weather, Algonquian women wore a wraparound skirt, men a breech cloth, and children nothing; all wore skins and furs during the winter. They took particular pride in their appearance. Men and women alike painted their faces and wore embroidered headbands and decorative wampum, and even the men decorated their hair, trimming it to leave only a narrow scalp lock.

Individual identity and village (band) groupings were based on kinship lineage. Indeed, members of one band or village could join their kin group in another band if they became dissatisfied with their own group. Individuals known as sachems in the south and sagamores in the north led the bands, attaining power through marriage, gift exchanges, kinship connections, or personal charisma. They were responsible for conducting war, trade, and diplomacy and for maintaining the territorial integrity of the group. They ruled through consensus, and though many of them lived quite lavishly, they generously shared the wealth with their followers. Sachems' power also depended on their demonstrated ability to commune with and affect the spiritual forces of their area. They were careful, therefore, to maintain close relations with the shamans, or spiritual leaders. They also worked closely with other powerful figures in the village. All the villages would meet to discuss major decisions, often debating the issues for days. Political unity beyond the band or village level was common mostly in northern New England.

Village life was similar to that of other woodland tribes. These Indians lived in wigwams of birchbark or woven grass mats placed over frames of bent saplings, with a smoke hole in the center. All New England tribes moved according to the season. In spring, the northern tribes moved to the coast, where they fished and gathered birds' eggs. Summer was a time of plenty, as the Indians continued to fish and gathered fruits, berries, and a variety of wild plants. Toward the middle of September, they moved inland again, feeding off the abundance of eels returning to the smaller creeks from their spawning runs. In September and October, the tribes broke into smaller family bands that hunted large game—bear, moose, deer—in preparation for winter. Men hunted, while women dressed the game and maintained the campsite. The winter months could be difficult; it was not unusual for the men in particular to spend several weeks seeking game and eating little.

❧ *Documents* ❧
Life Among the
Hurons and Micmacs

French explorer Samuel de Champlain was more perceptive than most early European observers, but even he injected his own values into the following description of women's and men's duties among the Huron.

> Among these tribes are found powerful women of extraordinary stature; for it is they who have almost the whole care of the house and the work; for they till the soil, sow the Indian corn, fetch wood for the winter, strip the hemp and spin it, and with the thread make fishing-nets for catching fish, and other necessary things they have to do: likewise they have the labour of harvesting the corn, storing it, preparing food, and attending to the house, and besides are required to follow and accompany their husbands from place to place, in the fields, where they serve as mules to carry the baggage, with a thousand other kinds of duties and services. . . . As to the men, they do nothing but hunt deer and other animals, fish, build lodges and go on the war-path.

H. P. Biggar, ed., *The Works of Samuel de Champlain,* 6 vols. (Toronto: Champlain Society, 1922–35), 3:136–7. Reprinted with permission of The Champlain Society, Toronto, CANADA.

Hunting could be a long and arduous experience, particularly in winter. The following description of beaver hunting among the Micmacs offers an example.

> Having found them [beavers], the Indians cut through the ice and made a hole large enough to let through a Beaver. Then they made another hole twenty-five or thirty paces away, on the open surface of the lake. In this place an Indian or two took their stand with a bow and an arrow which has a harpoon of bone at the end. . . . Everything being ready, another Indian went to the other hole near the house of the Beavers. Lying down on his belly upon the ice, he placed his arm through the hole to find the Beaver's opening. . . .

The pattern in the south was somewhat different, illustrating once again that regional variations among tribes could be considerable. Here, agriculture shaped seasonal movements. In the spring, tribes moved to their summer fields and prepared the ground for planting. Women tilled the earth with clamshell hoes and grew corn, beans, and squash all together. The result may not have looked pretty (at least not to European eyes), but the method created high yields, discouraged

> Having found them, the Indian passed his hand very gently along the back of one several times, and, approaching little by little to the tail, tried to seize it.
>
> I have heard it said by the Indians that they have kept the arm so long in the water that the ice froze all around the arm.

Nicholas Denys, *The Description and Natural History of the Coasts of North America (Acadia)*, William F. Ganong, trans. and ed. (Toronto: Champlain Society, 1908), 431–2.

Hurons, like the Iroquois and other North American Indians, believed that dreams revealed wishes and desires that had to be fulfilled. As this account makes clear, the Jesuits were both aware of this belief and appalled by it.

> Now they belive that our soul makes these natural desires known by means of dreams, which are its language. Accordingly, when these desires are accomplished, it is satisfied; but, on the contrary, it it be not granted what it desires, it becomes angry, and not only does not give its body the good and the happiness that it wished to procure for it, but often it also revolts against the body, causing various diseases, and even death. . . .
>
> In consequence of these erroneous ideas, most of the Hurons are very careful to note their dreams, and to provide the soul with what it has pictured to them during their sleep. If, for instance, they have seen a javelin in a dream, they try to get it; if they have dreamed that they gave a feast, they will give one on awakening, if they have the wherewithal, and so on with other things. And they call this *Ondinnonk,*—a secret desire of the soul manifested by a dream.

Reuben Gold Thwaites, ed., *The Jesuit Relations and Allied Documents,* 73 vols. (New York: Pageant, 1959), 33:189–91.

weed growth, and preserved soil moisture. After planting, the villages dispersed and moved eventually to the coast, from where men often embarked on lengthy hunting or fishing trips. The fall harvest was celebrated with rituals and festivals, often including ceremonies in which individuals gave away much wealth to maintain reciprocal relations with other village members. During the late fall, villages broke up into smaller bands, the men hunting and the women processing the game. When the snows came sometime in December, villages reassembled in protected valleys, seeking wood for fuel and shelter from the harsh winter winds. The men continued to hunt, often spending weeks away from camp.

A value system based on reciprocity and maintained through regularly practiced rituals bound village members to each other. The redistribution of family wealth, for instance, was an important component of the harvest festivals of the southern New England tribes. Male members of the village danced before the group and gave their wealth away to a poorer Indian, who begged for it as part of the ritual. Those Indians who gave away the most gained the highest status. This rivalry and competition thus benefited the entire community.

This society had little sense of exclusive ownership. People owned only what they made with their own hands; they claimed control only of the fields that they used. They saw no need to prevent other village members form trespassing or gathering goods from that land, and different groups could make different claims upon the same piece of land. Even the hunt was subject to the needs of the village or band. Abundance and success was shared, and only in the winter were individuals justified in keeping for themselves what they killed in their immediate area. New England Indians, like most of those in North America, did not hold the acquisition or accumulation of material goods as a goal in itself. They were about to confront a people and culture, though, that certainly did.

European Culture

American Indian society was based upon the ethic of cooperation and reciprocity. It was a world where religion and nature were one, where humans had to respect the rights of their environment or suffer the potentially fatal consequences. Europe, on the other hand, was in the midst of a long capitalist revolution that fostered competition, prospered from the subjugation of nature, generated wave after wave of new technology, and was moving toward a social ethic that stressed the individual accumulation of wealth. European society was organized to engender and support competition. Countries fought wars to control others and to gain the upper hand in the search for wealth and power. But it was not always so. The feudal society that preceded the early modern period was far smaller and less expansionistic, even resembling in small ways the contemporary society of the American Indian.

Medieval and Renaissance Europe

From the fifth to the twelfth century, a small number of Europeans controlled most of the continent's wealth while the vast majority lived in poverty. This society was static, with little sustained geographic or economic expansion; nobles accumulated wealth only for display or consumption. A group of small states constantly involved in warfare dominated the political landscape. The kings were only one of many political forces and relied on nobles for military and financial support. Nobles controlled the economic and legal systems, possessed extensive hereditary and legal privileges, and dominated legislative institutions where they existed. They lived in comfort and leisure, and many remained provincial and ignorant of the wider world. The Catholic church controlled still more wealth and wielded considerable political authority. The pope, in fact, was the most important unifying force in the Christian world.

Sixty million people lived on the European continent in the sixteenth century, with another 4 million or so in the British Isles. Most lived in isolated manors and villages concentrated on coasts and rivers. It is difficult to generalize about so many people over such a large area, but there are certain clear patterns. On the whole, peasants and serfs spent their lives in small villages on the lord's estate or manor, more or less completely under his control. Serfs in particular had little freedom of choice or movement. They were bound to the land, inheriting their status from their parents and passing it on to their children.

For the peasants, the weather and the rising and setting of the sun determined the rhythm of their days, the passing of the seasons the nature of their work and play. Farm labor began in March. On Lady Day, March 25, peasants commemorated the annunciation and, in one of many annual rituals, prayed to the Virgin Mary for a fertile crop. During the spring, the men sowed the fields and sheared their sheep; women washed the wool and spun it into cloth. Everyone worked in the fields through the summer and performed a variety of required duties for the manor lord. Harvest occupied most of the autumn, followed by often riotous celebrations that reflected the need for emotional release after periods of strenuous labor. Winter, finally, was a season for indoor tasks and preparing for the spring planting. Strenuous labor, together with periodic famines, short life expectancies, and high infant mortality rates (up to 20 percent for the first year of life), meant that most peasants' lives were brief and filled with suffering.

Religion was an essential component of this society. The church played a crucial political role, preserved the few remnants of classical culture in western Europe, and remained a powerful and wealthy landlord in most areas of the continent. Christianity functioned as all religions do, offering explanations for personal and natural disasters and for the inequities of the secular world. It gave meaning to a world that seemed to have none, promising joy in the next life for those who suffered in this one. The church itself provided a sense of stability in a world of the unexpected. Peasants could pray to saints, take comfort in relics, and in general gain some small feeling that there was a force in the universe that saw their plight and sympathized.

The disruptive economic changes of early modern Europe gradually transformed this society. Cities, towns, and markets existed in medieval Europe, but trade was primarily local, and products were generally made and sold in the merchant's own home. Even the Italian city-states that traded with the Near East during this period had little exchange with northern and western Europe. Merchant communities began to emerge in small towns on rivers and coasts as early as 1000 A.D. The Crusades stimulated economic activity. Knights and nobles fighting in the east helped spread knowledge of goods produced there, and economic activity quickened. Italian merchants set up trading houses in a number of ports and began to distribute these goods throughout Europe. Chinese silks, spices, Indian cottons, and jewels began to make their way into European society.

By the thirteenth century, clear signs arose of economic expansion and a capitalistic spirit as merchants began to seek new markets and opportunities and to diversify their activities to protect their investments. This activity created new wealth, and with the availability of spices and other exotic goods, dietary habits began to change and tastes became more sophisticated. Improved cultivation techniques, an expanding food supply, and greater political stability combined to fuel significant population growth. Trade began to draw people into the cities and increased the value of gold and silver in comparison to land. Feudal duties were increasingly commuted into cash payments, as landed aristocrats sought to maintain their wealth and living standards and peasants sought greater freedom to explore the new opportunities the towns offered. By the fourteenth century, economic isolation was rapidly disappearing, and the great merchant had become a common sight on the European economic landscape.

The Renaissance encouraged the transition to a more secular society through its emphasis on individualism, humanism, and curiosity. Italian city-states in particular heralded a new interest in materialism and business. The secularization of political thought, particularly in the works of Niccolo Machiavelli, opened the door to the growth of state power. The Renaissance emphasis on knowledge encouraged developments in medicine, astronomy, and mathematics, while the invention of the printing press made possible the wide dissemination of the new wave of scholarship.

The rise of early nation-states played a crucial role in this process of secularization and economic growth. The feudal nobility lost much of its economic power, and many nobles lost their lives in the constant warfare that ravaged the continent. Weakened by corruption, internal divisions, and heresies, the church also lost much of its political influence during these years. In France, England, and Spain, kings began to strengthen their control over both the nobility and the church and to create a new sense of national purpose and pride.

Early Nation-States

The pace and nature of political consolidation varied throughout Europe. French kings in the fifteenth and sixteenth centuries strengthened the country's finances, reformed the justice system, promoted industry, and won the right from Rome to appoint bishops and abbots within France's borders. In England, the Crown ruled through a Royal Council and Parliament and controlled the population through local officials, such as justices of the peace. The English nobility, seeking order and social stability above all else, supported the Crown's efforts. Henry VII (1485–1509) established the Tudor dynasty and fully restored royal power. He also won the backing of the English merchant community through his support of the cloth industry and the merchant marine; as the wool trade increased, royal tax revenues went up and merchants' profits grew.

In Spain, the monarchy initiated the Reconquista to rid the peninsula of its Muslim conquerors. By mid-fifteenth century, the kingdoms of Castile and Aragon dominated the weaker ones of Navarre, Granada, and Portugal, and except in Granada, Christianity was once again dominant on the Iberian peninsula. A major step toward reunification came with the 1469 marriage of Isabella, the heiress of Castile, to Ferdinand, the heir of Aragon. Still, Spain remained for sometime a loose confederation of states that shared only a foreign policy; each kingdom had its own parliament, courts, and coinage and taxation systems. Isabella and Ferdinand set out to change this. They established a Royal Council, excluding aristocrats and reducing the influence of the nobility on policy, to supervise local authorities. The council was staffed by middle-class bureaucrats trained in Roman law, which perceived the monarchy as the embodiment of the state. The monarchs also established a diplomatic alliance with the papacy and won the right to appoint bishops in both Spain and their New World territories. On January 6, 1492, Ferdinand and Isabella entered Granada, marking the end of the Reconquista and the final consolidation of Spanish royal power.

The Reformation

The growth of commercial activity and the emergence of Renaissance humanism created a sophisticated urban elite throughout Europe. Many of these individuals became increasingly disillusioned with the corruption that continued to plague the Catholic church. The turning point came October 31, 1517, when Martin Luther posted his ninety-five theses on the castle door in Wittenberg. Luther's forceful attack on church corruption, particularly simony (the sale of church offices) and the sale of indulgences, struck a responsive chord in hundreds of thousands of European Christians. He contended that salvation came not as the result of good works or earthly activities and religious rituals but rather solely from faith and divine mercy. Religion, he argued, should be accessible to any literate person, and he encouraged all to search the Bible, the source of Christian truth, for answers to their religious questions. He abandoned the Roman emphasis on ritual, translated the Bible into the German vernacular, and greatly lessened the significance of the institutional church for European Protestants.

Luther was not a social rebel; he supported the ruthless repression of the Peasants Rebellion in Germany in 1524. But his doctrines and those of his many followers furthered the dismantling of a medieval, religiously centered world view by substituting a personal religious outlook for an institutional one. Salvation for Protestants became an individual concern, a matter separate from the secular affairs of state. Luther's success opened a wellspring of radicalism in European religious circles. The French lawyer John Calvin (1509–1564), for instance, stressed the power and omnipotence of God and the weakness and depravity of humans even more than Luther did. He established a theocratic government at Geneva, Switzerland, requiring all members of the community to lead a good life, participate in the remaining sacraments (baptism and communion), and offer a public profession of faith. A consistory of five pastors and twelve lay elders governed the moral life and daily behavior of Genevans.

The Reformation eventually spawned a variety of religious movements that played a decisive role in the settlement of the British North American colonies. It also shattered European religious unity and introduced a powerful competitive element. First, since it rejected the pope and lessened the power of church institutions in general, Protestantism strengthened the political power of kings. Second, the Reformation promoted individualism by encouraging a direct relationship with God and, in its more radical expressions, individual interpretation of the Bible. Finally, the Reformation and the Catholic Counter-Reformation had a profound effect on the European settlement of America. As Protestants and Catholics competed for souls, they took seriously their responsibility to Christianize New World inhabitants. European nations, in fact, explicitly claimed this duty as a primary motivation for the establishment of both the Spanish and French empires. One may question the sincerity of such claims, but there can be no doubt that religion raised the stakes of expansion.

European Exploration And Discovery

There had long been myths and legends about the existence of a world somewhere west of Europe. Old Irish tales, the story of Atlantis, legends about seven Portuguese bishops fleeing the Moorish invasions and founding the Seven Cities on a western island, even parts of Homer's poems that spoke of a distant land separated from Europe by the ocean—all these stories were popular in Europe during the fifteenth century. While no evidence exists that such legends had any influence on explorers, they did create a certain climate of thought concerning new lands. The legends always depicted a land of plenty where one did not have to work to survive. Food grew for the picking, the climate was ideal, there was no disease or poverty, and the inhabitants were simple and peace-loving. The state of mind such expectations created undoubtedly had much to do with European reactions to their new discoveries. It is no accident that America has always been regarded as the land of boundless opportunity.

Early Explorations

The Vikings were probably the first Europeans to land on the American continent. They crossed from Norway to Iceland sometime in the late ninth century, motivated by a sense of adventure and a population explosion in their Scandinavian homeland. Erik "the Red," exiled from Iceland for manslaughter, settled in Greenland with his family in the late ninth century and founded a colony that lasted until the fifteenth century. By the end of the tenth century, more than twenty thousand Norse people lived in Iceland and several thousand in Greenland.

Erik's oldest son, Leif Eriksson, sailed west in the year 1000 and discovered Helluland (flatland), Markland (timberland), and Vinland (land of pasture). The three locations correspond to Baffin Island, Labrador, and Newfoundland. Leif may also have landed at Cape Cod. His Vinland landfall was likely at the present site of L'Anse aux Meadows in northern Newfoundland; there, archeologists have uncovered artifacts that are similar to those used by the Norse. Settlement attempts soon ended, however, despite follow-up ventures. *Skraelings* (screechers, and presumably Eskimos) killed Leif's brother Thorvald during one such expedition. Norway lost systematic contact with Greenland sometime after the mid-fourteenth century, and active exploration of the area temporarily came to an end.

Contemporary European events, however, were beginning to lay the groundwork for the long period of exploration and discovery that changed the course of world history. Contact with products from the Near and Far East during the Crusades first stimulated European demand, and the actions of adventurous individuals soon furthered interest and knowledge. In 1241, Pope Innocent III sent the Franciscan monk John of Plano Carprini as an envoy to Genghis Khan, and Louis IX of France sent a similar envoy in 1253. Both traveled along the famous Silk Road that extended from Europe through central Asia to Cathay (mainland China), reopened by the 1200s as a result of Genghis's success in pacifying and controlling the largest land empire in history. The most famous of the new travelers was Marco Polo, the Venetian trader who ventured through the East from 1274 to 1295. Polo gained the confidence of the Mongolian emperor Kublai Khan and traveled throughout his empire. Upon his return, Polo evocatively described the wealth of China, India, and Persia and what he had heard of Japan, Zanzibar, and Madagascar. His information had a profound impact on the European mentality, and the first printed edition of his work, published in 1477, was widely circulated.

Italian merchants had always maintained some trade with the Near East. After the Crusades stimulated European demand, the merchants began to accumulate ships and capital and to bring textiles (silk, satin, velvet, taffeta, damask), spices (pepper, cinnamon, ginger, nutmeg, cloves), and a great variety of other desirable products (including rugs, tapestries, gems, china, glassware, perfumes, dyes, and steel weapons) to northwestern Europe. Such exotic fruits as cherries, melons, apricots, peaches, and dates, previously unknown or rarely available, became common in wealthy homes. Europeans developed a craze for spices, which helped preserve food and enliven its taste. Columbus often wrote of gold and spices in his log as if they were of equal value.

These goods traveled thousands of miles, and Italian city-states, particularly Venice, Genoa, and Pisa, dominated the trade with the East. They imported the goods and then reexported them to the rest of Europe at much higher prices. Traders from the Low Countries, Iberia, France, England, and the Hanseatic League (an economic alliance of Baltic and North Sea cities) exchanged hides, furs, tin, lead, woolens, and leather products for goods from the East. These areas soon became the banking and industrial centers of western Europe. Merchants also began to support monarchs in the latters' attempts to break free from the control of the nobility in their individual countries. Their financial backing allowed kings to hire mercenaries and subdue nobles, to engage in various military adventures, and to finance explorations in the New World. In return, the monarchs supported the merchants' desires to end medieval trade restrictions and to supplant the landed aristocracy in economic and political power.

At the same time, the high cost of imported goods from the East created a serious balance of payments problem. This drove the rest of Europe to seek ways to bypass the Italian stranglehold on the eastern trade. The crucial figure in this search for an alternative route to Asia was Prince Henry the Navigator (1394–1460) of Portugal. Henry, a devout Christian, was motivated by a variety of factors. He hoped to find a mythical Christian king called Prestor John, who supposedly had established a large empire in northwest Africa, and to form an alliance with John against the Moors. Henry also wanted to reach Guinea, on the African west coast, where caravans from central Africa were reported to regularly deliver gold, ivory, and slaves. Finally, he sought to discover a passage through or around Africa to the Far East. Systematic searches soon led to the discovery of Madeira and the Azores. Henry endowed a naval observatory at Cape St. Vincent on the southeastern tip of Portugal and brought in astronomers, mapmakers, and navigators, sending expeditions down the African coast for almost forty years. Local tyrants and the Turks, meanwhile, had begun to threaten the established trade routes. Genoa in particular now turned to the west and provided much of the financial support for Iberian exploration.

By 1471, the Portuguese had reached a point south of the equator. By 1484, they had discovered the mouth of the Congo River, and in 1486, Bartolomew Diaz rounded the Cape of Good Hope and sailed into the Indian Ocean before his crew forced him to turn back. In 1498, finally, Vasco Da Gama completed the journey to India and returned with pepper, cinnamon, cloves, nutmeg, and a variety of gems. By that time, of course, the stakes of the game had changed. The Ottoman Turks captured Constantinople in 1453, blocking the growth of European trade with the East and lending greater urgency to the search for a route that would bypass North Africa and the Near East. Dramatic improvements in technology and advances in mapmaking further encouraged efforts by other European powers to seek an alternative route to Asia.

Until the mid-fifteenth century, there were certain natural hindrances to western exploration. The Atlantic Ocean was the greatest barrier. A northern crossing route was known, but economic incentives were not strong enough to overcome the dangers of the North Atlantic. Even the southern route presented formidable difficulties. Few ships could sail in any direction without the wind behind them. Sailors had to rely on sight, sound, smell, experience, and their interpretation of wind, currents, moon phases, the color of the water, and changes in the weather to tell them where they were. The compass (borrowed from the Moslems) and effective rudders were the first innovations to assist mariners, and the practice of taking soundings with lead also helped. Improved marine charts, systematically updated with each new discovery and exploratory voyage, expanded the base of information available to sailors. The astrolabe could be used at noon to take observations of the height of the sun and thus determine approximate latitude. Longitude remained difficult to figure. Long voyages, where supplies could give out, remained particularly dangerous; calculating east-west distances remained largely a matter of dead reckoning. Improvements in ship design were a particularly helpful advance. Spanish caravels were larger, longer, narrower, and higher than previous ships, had multiple decks and three masts, and were speedier and more maneuverable. Spain had an advantage in being closest to the newly discovered Canaries Current and the northeast

Two masted-ocean going ship of sixteenth century, detailed from a painting by Pieter Brueghel. ❧

trade winds, which made crossing in tropical and subtropical latitudes the fastest and easiest route to the west.

The English, on the other hand, faced potent barriers from the start. British sailors had a difficult time making any progress at all against the prevailing westerly winds. Ships tended first to go far to the southwest and then turn northward, or they would wait for more easterly winds before sailing. Thus, there were few direct voyages to continental North America before the early seventeenth century. Mariners either followed a more southerly route or crossed to Newfoundland and sailed down its eastern coast.

Advances in mapmaking also spurred western voyages. Marine charts gradually extended knowledge of the eastern Atlantic. Yet for some time, both scholars and the general population accepted the information portrayed by late medieval maps, which showed a round earth with Jerusalem at its center and a single land mass in one hemisphere. There seemed little need to explore the other hemisphere, since it was believed to be only water. Even with the information provided by marine charts, only the picture of the known land mass became more detailed and complex.

The Fra Mauro map completed this process. Compiled in Venice from 1458 to 1459, this map put all available knowledge about the world on a single surface. Using newly recognized Arab sources, it also gave Europeans an authoritative portrait of Africa and the Indian Ocean. The map was quite accurate as far as it went, but it tended to discourage western exploration. The world it portrayed was about twenty-four thousand miles in circumference, with about twelve thousand miles of ocean separating Europe from Asia to the west.

Then in 1474, Paolo dal Pozzo Toscanelli, a member of a Florentine merchant-banking family, produced a map that differed significantly from the Fra Mauro map. Toscanelli accepted some of Marco Polo's contentions that Asia extended much farther east than was commonly believed and that Cipango (Japan) lay beyond this. He thus reduced the distance between Asia and Europe to between six thousand and sixty-five hundred miles. He even argued that a ship could sail approximately twenty-five hundred miles to the west, put in at the mythical island of Antilia, and then cover the same distance to reach Japan, leaving only about fifteen hundred more miles to China.

The English, meanwhile, were making significant western explorations of their own. Bristol fishermen began fishing heavily around Iceland after the 1420s, and they apparently started venturing farther west in their new longer, narrower, and more seaworthy vessels. While definite proof is lacking, there is a real possibility that they reached Newfoundland and Cape Breton Island by the 1480s. A 1481 voyage, for example, went an unknown distance to the west, returning after seventy-five days at sea. The time is adequate for a North American landing, and during this period, the English government allowed Bristol men to sail westward without the restrictions commonly imposed on fishermen. It is unlikely, though, that we will ever know whether these adventurous sailors did indeed beat the Spanish to the prize.

It was Christopher Columbus who eventually stumbled upon the America continent. Born in 1451 in Italy, Columbus spent his early adult years sailing the Mediterranean. He was probably on a Portuguese ship that sailed to Ireland and Iceland in 1476. In 1477, he settled in Lisbon, married the daughter of a Portuguese navigator, and worked for a while in his brother Bartholomew's chart-making shop. Columbus began to collect strange timber that washed up on European shores and sailed on trading voyages to Guinea. By 1485, he had copied the Toscanelli map, studied most of the known cosmographic theories and maps, and read a work by Cardinal Pierre d'Ailly, *Imago Mundi,* which maintained that the Asian continent could be reached by sailing west from the Azores for only a few days. By the late 1480s, he had developed a theory based on Toscanelli's work that he would find Antilia fifteen hundred miles west of the Canaries on the twenty-eighth parallel and then Cipango only a thousand miles farther on. From there, he contended, it was only a thousand miles to Cathay. The grand total was only forty-five hundred miles!

When Columbus approached John II of Portugal in 1486 with a proposal to sail west to Asia, John quickly rejected it. He simply did not believe that such a trip was possible, hardly surprising since few other experts agreed with Columbus's optimistic assessments of distance. Columbus then worked with his brother on a new plan, one that involved sailing to an imagined new island somewhere in the North Atlantic. Several European courts, including the Spanish, rejected this proposal as well. In 1492, he approached the Spanish once more and was again rejected. But as soon as Columbus left, some court advisers began to argue that though his demands for a title and handsome commission seemed extravagant, they would cost little. First Isabella and then Ferdinand reconsidered and agreed to finance the voyage. They negotiated a detailed contract, and the monarchs accorded Columbus the hereditary ranks of admiral, viceroy, and governor over all territories he might discover, as well as one-tenth of all gold, silver, and other commodities produced or traded for in those lands. Ironically, in that same year, Martin Behaim of

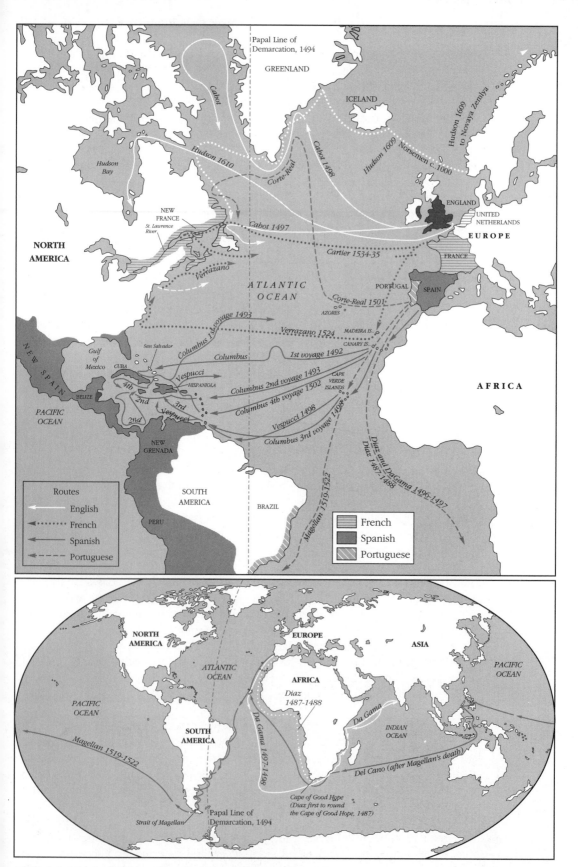

MAP 1.2: Major Voyages of Exploration and Territorial Claims in the Fifteenth and early Sixteenth Centuries

Nuremberg published a globe showing Antilia, Cipango, and Cathay just where Toscanelli and Columbus said they would be. It was to be one of the shortest-lived cartographical advances in history.

Columbus sailed with three ships—the *Nina, Pinta, Santa Maria*—on August 3, 1492. Favored by the winds and weather, the tiny fleet spent only thirty-three days at sea. On Thursday, October 11, a lookout sighted reeds and a carved stick floating by the ships; flocks of sea birds had already been passing overhead for several days. Then, on October 12, the little fleet sighted land. Columbus made his first landfall at San Salvador (Watlings Island) in the Bahamas. He unfurled the royal banner and flags, led a prayer of thanksgiving, and took possession for the king and queen of Spain, declaring the inhabitants to be Spanish subjects. Of the natives (Taino Indians), his comments reveal Spanish assumptions of religious and secular superiority: "I think they can easily be made Christians. . . . they ought to make good and skilled servants, for they repeat very quickly whatever we say to them."[4]

Continuing his search for gold, Columbus next landed on Hispaniola and then on the north coast of Cuba. He identified the first as an outpost of Asia and the second as part of Cathay. He subsequently established the first Spanish settlement in the New World on Hispaniola; he ran the *Santa Maria* aground and left thirty-nine men on the island to build a fort and establish a colony. Columbus returned home, arriving at Lisbon in March 1493. He had brought back tobacco, corn, sweet potatoes, and coconuts but little gold. Nonetheless, he declared he had discovered a direct route to Asia, a claim he continued to make until his death.

Portrait of Christopher Columbus, attributed to Sebastiano del Piombo (1519). Although we do not know what Columbus looked like, this painting is probably a reasonably accurate depiction. ❧

❧ *Documents* ❧
Columbus in His Own Words

Columbus's description of his encounter with the Tainos on Hispaniola reveals how much his expectations were shaped by the legends of innocent, friendly people in Edenic lands to the west of Europe. The passage is taken from Columbus's report of his first voyage to Ferdinand and Isabella.

> The people of this island and of all the other islands which I have found and seen, or have not seen, all go naked, men and women, as their mothers bore them, except that some women cover one place only with the leaf of a plant or with a net of cotton which they make for the purpose. They have no iron or steel or weapons, nor are they capable of using them, although they are well-built people of handsome stature, because they are wondrous timid. . . . It is true that after they have been reassured and have lost this fear, they are so artless and so free with all they possess, that no one would believe it without having seen it. Of anything they have, if you ask them for it, they never say no, rather they invite the person to share it, and show as much love as if they were giving their hearts.

S. E. Morison, trans. and ed., *Journals and Other Documents on the Life and Voyages of Christopher Columbus* (New York: Heritage Press, 963), 183.

The second voyage (1493 to 1496) involved a much larger expedition, with seventeen ships and fifteen hundred colonists, including two hundred gentlemen adventurers. Columbus found his earlier colony destroyed and all its inhabitants dead. He established the new settlement of Isabella and continue his exploration of the Caribbean area. It was Columbus's changed attitude toward the Indians, though, that was perhaps the most significant outcome of this voyage. Writing to Isabella and Ferdinand, he proposed to enslave captured Caribs, whom he believed to be cannibals, and to send them back to Spain "for the good of the souls of the said cannibals. . . . "[5] In February 1495, he sent five hundred captured Arawaks to the monarchs. His new policy introduced a heightened level of violence to Hispaniola, and during 1495 and 1496, the Spanish completely subjugated the island. He also imposed a gold quota on the natives, to be delivered under penalty of death.

On his third voyage (1498 to 1502), Columbus landed on the South American continent at the mouth of the Orinocco River. But he also faced a mutiny in Hispaniola and was returned to Spain in chains. On his final voyage (1502 to 1504), a poorly equipped effort, he landed on the coast of Central America, still unsuspecting of what he had actually discovered. He died on May 21, 1506, insisting he had reached Asia but having found few of the jewels, gold, or spices that would have proven he had landed in Cathay. He believed that he had discovered a vast new land that was part of Asia but insular and separated by a sea channel from the mainland.

Columbus's letter concerning his fourth voyage reflects both his fixation with the search for gold and his persistent unwillingness to believe that he had, in fact, discovered a new world.

> When I discovered the Indies, I said they were the world's wealthiest realm. I spoke of gold, pearls, precious stones, spices and of the markets and fairs. But, because not everything turned up at once, I was vilified. . . .
>
> The Genoese, the Venetians and everyone who has pearls, precious stones and other things of value, they all carry them to the ends of the earth to barter and convert into gold. O, most excellent gold! Who has gold has a treasure with which he gets what he wants, imposes his will on the world, and even helps souls to paradise.

S. E. Morison, trans. and ed., *Journals and Other Documents on the Life and Voyages of Christopher Columbus* (New York: Heritage Press, 1963), 382–3.

Columbus's perceptions of his discovery should not be surprising. Unique perhaps in his courage and vision, he was in most other ways a man of his times. He believed that the Indians should adopt Spanish customs and religion. Like most Spanish explorers, he was obsessed with gold and sought it every place he landed. His observations of the land reflect the typical fifteenth-century European's fascination with animals and nature. "The singing of little birds," he noted, "is such that it seems like a man could never wish to leave this place; the flocks of parrots darken the sun, and there are large and small birds of so many different kinds and so unlike ours, that it is a marvel."[6] Most interesting of all, perhaps, was his obsession with this new land as an earthly paradise, evident in his fanciful speculation that the earth was like "a very round ball, and on one part of it is placed something like a woman's nipple, and that this part. . . . is the highest and nearest to the sky, and it is beneath the equinoxial line in this Ocean sea at the end of the Orient. . . ."[7] To Columbus and to his many successors, the New World served personal and emotional fancies as much as political and economic ones.

Columbus did not even have the honor of having the new continents named after him. Amerigo Vespucci claimed that distinction. Vespucci was a Italian businessman turned explorer, an amateur geographer and navigator who sailed for Spain and Portugal and explored much of the Brazilian coast in 1501 and 1502. An Italian collection of materials dealing with the new discoveries, published in 1507, contained one of Vespucci's letters entitled "Mundus Novus"—the first reference to the New World. In 1507, Martin Waldseemuller, a professor of geography, published a book containing maps that identified the new discoveries as America. The name was applied only to the southern hemisphere until the end of the sixteenth century.

The discovery of the New World also engendered a conflict between Portugal and Spain over exactly who owned the new lands. The Treaty of Alcacovas, signed in 1479, had given the Portuguese a monopoly of trade and settlement on the west African coast and title to all Atlantic islands except the Canaries. Spain then asked Pope Alexander VI to recognize Spanish authority in the New World, and a 1493 papal bull did exactly that. A new bull was issued several weeks later that drew a demarcation line one hundred leagues west of the Azores and Cape Verde Islands, giving the Spanish control over all territory to be discovered west of that line. The Portuguese asked that the line be moved to 370 leagues (1,175 miles) west of the islands; Spain agreed, and the two signed the Treaty of Tordesillas in 1494. Neither country realized that the new territory was an entirely new continent, and Portugal did not expect to have control over the area that was to become Brazil. In 1500, Pero Alvarez Cabral discovered the Brazilian coast and claimed the region for Portugal, though a colony was not established there until the 1530s. It was to be some twenty years before Spain began to fully exploit its new territories.

Over the next century or so, Spain, France, and England established major empires in the New World, and Portugal, Sweden, and Holland undertook smaller ventures. Columbus and the other great explorers who preceded and followed him, though, were not the only figures who made the exploitation and European settlement of the Western Hemisphere possible. Ordinary Europeans, Africans, and Americans made contributions of equal significance to early American history. The first of these were the sailors who labored on the caravels and other ships of the fifteenth- and sixteenth-century explorers. Life was hard for these men. All ships provided at least the necessities of life for their crews; many, for instance, gave sailors clothing (though only a single change). Food was abundant during most normal voyages, or at least it seems so from the accounts of the Englishman Martin Frobisher's second voyage in 1577. On this voyage, each sailor's daily ration included one pound of biscuit, one gallon of beer, one pound of salt beef or pork (on fast days, one dried codfish for four men), a quarter-pound of butter, and a half-pound of cheese. While the diet seems adequate, the lack of vegetables resulted in high rates of scurvy and malnutrition. On smaller ships, the cook-box (galley) was only a hooded box with several inches of earth as a base for the fire. A few pots and pans and some firewood rounded out the entire range of kitchen supplies. None dared drink the water until the wine, beer, and cider were all consumed or spoiled. Even the staples of the diet were far from predictable in quality; the hardtack usually became moldy and full of maggots before the end of a transatlantic voyage.

The ship itself provided even less comfort. Sailors slept where they could find space, and they had to spend a good deal of time keeping the ship clean, especially if there were passengers. All the hold space not used for stores or cargo was generally filled with ballast—sand or cobblestone, perhaps. A great variety of material made its way into this hold, including water, urine, vomit, and leftover food, and there were only two square pumps available to suck up this disgusting mix. In time, the ballast and bilge water began to stink, so much so that the ship often had to be grounded on a beach, the ballast thrown out to be cleaned by the tide, and the entire inside of the hold scraped down and sprayed with vinegar. One final element added to the discomfort of the passengers living in such circumstances—rats.

Every ship carried at least one cat to keep them under control, but little could be done about the cockroaches and other vermin.

The men who sailed these ships were making a living in the only way they could. They may have hoped for booty and plunder from enemy ships or gold and silver from the shores of the New World. Those who fished the Newfoundland banks—French, Spanish, and English—also faced danger from huge icebergs. When they returned home, whether to large cities or small villages, they brought tales of adventure and wonder, of strange peoples and rumored riches. It was they as much as anyone who spread news of the New World throughout the old It was ordinary men and women like them who ultimately populated the American continents.

The first Indians that the Europeans met, the Aztecs and the Incas, were perhaps most similar to the Europeans in their political, social, and economic structures. They were adventurous, conquering people with clear and repressive class and status divisions. The rest of the American peoples were largely agricultural, village oriented, and closely connected to nature and the supernatural. Indian population was stable, and Indian cultures lacked any sort of technological impetus. Indians acted upon and changed the land but with less impact than their European counterparts. They lived in communal villages that shared wealth as a necessary aspect of survival in a harsh environment.

Late-medieval Europe was still a society based largely on status. The church and the nobility presided over a relatively insulated world, and ordinary peasants lived less comfortably and had far less control over their lives than their Indian counterparts. But Europeans gradually developed greater confidence in their ability to control and shape nature. Economic growth and the centralization of political power created an expansionist impulse that eventually led Europeans to the New World. The Protestant Reformation and the Catholic Counter-Reformation injected a righteous desire to proselytize that would give the coming clash of cultures spiritual urgency. In Europeans' eyes, conquests was both desirable and right.

৯৯ *Chapter Two* ৯৯

Fire and Ice: Spain and France Settle the New World

Spain, France, and England dominated European involvement in colonial Central and North America. Enemies they were, but the three shared certain problems during the first two centuries of colonization. Each had to deal with the expense and risk of exploration and settlement, to develop an imperial structure of governance, and to confront and resolve the near-fatal gap between Old World settlement plans and New World reality. The three nations were forced to make endless decisions, conscious and unconscious, about how much of their Old World culture would be transferred to the New World. In every case, the settlers faced opposition to their invasion and had to decide how to deal with that resistance. Even this early in the colonial period, the home countries faced the disturbing reality that their offspring inevitably were moving further and further away from their constricting control. The colonies were settled primarily for the economic benefits they could bring to their European founders. From the beginning, however, they developed their own needs and goals.

First Contact: "Strangers and a Strange Land"

Indians and Europeans expressed amazement and astonishment at the first sight of each other. Neither had a reliable frame of reference that would help them categorize these new beings, who seemed truly mysterious. European explorers had grown up with stories of innocent beings living in the west, and they absorbed the Renaissance fascination with the strange and different and tales of monsters with eyes in the middle of their heads. For them, the "other" was usually (though not

Significant Dates

1500	Cabral claims Brazil for Portugal
1501	Spain authorizes the first shipment of black slaves to the Caribbean
1513	Balboa becomes the first European to see the Pacific
	Ponce de León reaches Florida
1519	Cortes invades the Aztec empire
1519–22	Magellan circumnavigates the globe
1521	Tenochtitlan surrenders to Cortes
1524	Verrazzano expedition
1528	Narváez expedition
1531–33	Pizarro conquers Incan empire
1534–35	Cartier explores the St. Lawrence River valley
1528–36	Cabeza de Vaca wanders through the southwest
1539–42	De Soto expedition
1540–42	Coronado expedition
	Cartier's third voyage
1542–43	The New Laws
1552	Las Casas publishes
1555	French colony off the coast of Brazil
1562–64	French settlement attempts in Carolina
1565	Spanish establish St. Augustine
1598	De Onate founds the colony of New Mexico
1603	Champlain publishes *Les Sauvages*
1604	De Monts and Champlain sail for New France
1609	Champlain accompanies Algonquian war party on raid against Mohawks
1625	First Jesuits arrive in New France
1629	English capture Quebec
1632	First publication of the *Jesuit Relations*
1635	Champlain dies
1638	Jesuit mission headquarters established at Sillery
1649	Iroquois defeat the Huron and scatter the survivors
1663	New France becomes a royal colony
1673	Jolliet and Marquette explore Mississippi River
1680	Pueblo revolt against Spanish rule
1682	La Salle reaches mouth of the Mississippi
1683	Colbert dies

always) inferior by definition, an impression they believed was confirmed by their contacts with Middle Eastern and African peoples. Indians knew only other Indians, gods, and mythological figures. They saw Europeans either as others like themselves and accorded them traditional hospitality or as spirits or gods, in which case they treated the newcomers with even greater care and respect. The Delaware, for instance, believed that their manitou lived in the first Dutch ship they saw. Indians had stories or myths about white-skinned or bearded men who would visit or conquer them; a Powhatan shaman predicted that bearded men would one day conquer their land. This forewarning made little difference. The outcome was symbolically predicted by Columbus's first contact with the Tainos, when he "showed them swords and they took them by the edge and through ignorance cut themselves."[1] American Indians would indeed cut their own cultures to the very bone in touching European civilization.

The Spanish Empire

Spain established the first European empire in the Americas. Two hundred and fifty thousand Spaniards came here in the sixteenth century, and another two hundred thousand arrived in the first half of the seventeenth century. Until recently, the dominant historical view of this empire centered on the "Black Legend," a stark, one-dimensional picture of Spanish exploitation of land and Indians. Drawn in particular from the works of the Franciscan Bartolomé de Las Casas, this view contains a strong element of disturbing truth. The English, however, did much to popularize this interpretation and to distort the Spanish experience for their own purposes. New Spain was a far more complex place than popular legend allows.

The Spanish had great hopes for the Caribbean islands, based in part on their initial belief that they had established contact with the Far East. They set up outposts on Cuba, Hispaniola, Jamaica, and Puerto Rico in the late 1490s and early 1500s. Most of the early settlers were Spanish commoners who hoped to better their lives; they expected the natives to work for them and to provide them with the wealth they thirsted after. Queen Isabella declared that the Indians were Spanish subjects, and the government introduced the *encomienda* system. Officials assigned *encomenderos* (Spanish settlers) a village or villages of Indians and gave them the power to exploit residents in any way they desired. Other Indians were simply enslaved. Consumed by their search for gold and instant wealth, the adventurers had little incentive to plan permanent settlements, and by 1509, they had mined what little gold there was. Up to ten thousand Spaniards now inhabited the islands, their prospects increasingly dim. The Indians were virtually wiped out by the invasion, felled by European diseases against which they had no protection or simply worked to death. The Tainos, inhabitants of Hispaniola and Puerto Rico and the first people Columbus encountered, declined from about one hundred thousand in 1493 to only three hundred in 1570. Indians on other islands suffered a similar fate.

Discouraged by the dwindling opportunities the islands offered and hungry for more adventure, the Spanish turned to the continental mainland. Francisco Balboa was a poor Haitian colonist who stowed away on a ship bound for Panama. There, he married the daughter of an Indian chieftain and became close friends with the son of another. In 1513, he led an expedition of two hundred men, of whom only sixty survived, across Panama to the South Sea (Pacific Ocean) and claimed the sea for Spain. During his trek, he found just enough gold and pearls to spur the Spanish on in search of more. In the same year, Ponce de León, governor of Puerto

Rico and a veteran of Columbus's second voyage, went north looking for gold, Indian slaves, and the legendary fountain of youth. He landed on the Atlantic side of the Florida coast and bathed in all the springs he could find, but he found no gold and continued to grow old. He returned for another try in 1521 and met his death by an Indian arrow. At first, the Spanish did little to follow up the Florida expedition. Spanish slavers sailed the Carolina coast in 1521, and in 1526, Lucas Vasquez de Ayllon founded the town of San Miguel de Gualdape in present-day Georgia; the town quickly disappeared, the settlers discouraged by illness, poor weather, and a lack of food. Only in 1565, with the founding of St. Augustine, would the Spanish establish a permanent presence in the region.

Hernando Cortes led the first significant Spanish attempt to conquer the mainland. Cortes arrived on Hispaniola at the age of nineteen in 1504. He served the monarchy in a variety of capacities over the next fifteen years, for which he received two *encomiendas*. Then in 1519, the governor of Cuba sent Cortes to establish a trading post on the Mexican coast. The ambitious Spaniard had his own agenda. Stirred by the rumors of great Mexican wealth that had been sweeping the Spanish community in Cuba, Cortes and others began to dream of riches, glory, and adventure—little of which they had been able to find on the islands. Upon landing on the Mexican coast—and after being greeted by four thousand Aztecs laden with gifts—he scuttled his ships and made his way slowly through the interior, seeking to win over the Indians he met either by diplomacy or warfare.

Cortes had a force of more than six hundred Spanish troops and two hundred Cubans. Montezuma II, the Aztec leader, was undoubtedly impressed and acted cautiously, at first sending Cortes messages of welcome and offering him gold and whatever supplies he might need. The Spaniard would not be so easily satisfied, and he continued to advance through Aztec territory. His most difficult battle came against the Tlaxcaltecs, a powerful independent tribe that assumed that the invaders were allies of the hated Aztecs. They resisted ferociously for two weeks. The Spanish suffered numerous casualties in the struggle and lost some of their sixteen horses, but they prevailed in the end and convinced the Tlaxcaltecs to join them as allies. Cortes and his men next entered the tributary town of Cholula and killed six

Portraits of Cortes, as minted on a medal. ❧

thousand of the inhabitants when the Spanish heard rumors of a surprise attack. At this point, Montezuma stopped his efforts to keep Cortes from entering the capital.

Montezuma may have feared Cortes to be the Toltec god Quetzalcoatl returning to seek revenge, as legend predicted, or he may have simply decided to welcome Cortes as an ambassador in established Aztec fashion. Whatever the reason, his hesitation in reacting to the invaders proved fatal. The Spanish marched into the capital and took Montezuma prisoner. Though shaken, the Aztec leader hoped to lull the Spanish into complacency. He opened his personal treasure to his captors and even called in gifts from the empire, including gold, silver, pearls, and such exotic items as golden nose crescents and blowguns inlaid with silver. Bernal Diaz del Castillo, a companion of Cortes, later recounted his first impressions of the city:

> And when we saw all those cities and villages built in the water, and other great towns on dry land, and that straight and level causeway leading to Mexico, we were astounded. Those great towns and temples and buildings rising from the water, all made of stone, seemed like an enchanted vision . . . , indeed, some of our soldiers asked whether it was not all a dream.[2]

At that point (May 1520), Cortes received word of a Cuban force dispatched to capture him for exceeding his orders. Leaving a small force to guard the Aztec leader, he departed to confront this new threat. While he defused the danger and in fact recruited many of the new soldiers to his cause, events in Tenochtitlan took a fateful turn in his absence. Montezuma was both a secular and religious leader. Though Cortes tried to establish him as a front man for Spanish rule, his capture was a blow to the Aztec belief system and a direct threat to the priestly caste. The Spanish greed for gold, now clearly evident, further encouraged resistance. When Cortes returned, he discovered that his troops had massacred hundreds of Mexicans celebrating a religious festival and that war had subsequently broken out. The Spanish fought their way out of the city on the night of June 30, 1520. Montezuma himself was killed, but Cortes lost half of his men. The Tlaxcalans gave the Spanish safe haven, and Cortes recruited more allies from other tributary states; in April 1521, he lay siege to Tenochtitlan. Though the Spanish were unyielding, the Aztecs met their defeat at the hands of a different Old World invader. Smallpox had appeared on the mainland even before Cortes, and an epidemic now devastated a people who had no immunity to European diseases. On August 21, 1521, Cortes retook the city.

Who was Hernando Cortes? Who were the men who accompanied him on the daring expedition? Cortes was one of a number of Spanish adventurers known as *conquistadores,* men shaped by a tradition of Castilian frontier warfare that developed during the Reconquista. This tradition combined principles of honor, cruelty, religion, and greed; it embraced both individualism and a strong sense of community. *Conquistadores* never acted alone but always as part of a group with a *caudillo,* or leader, whose power hinged on success in battle. They were driven by a personal, feudal sense of honor that was won by the sword and ensured them a place in honor in their king's eyes. They willingly faced privation and death, and they were capable of immense cruelty. Some were younger sons of noble families, but most came from humbler backgrounds. They all expected not only to conquer the New World but also to exploit its land and wealth and to establish lordship over their new vassals, the Indians. In the end, they subjugated everything, including their faith, to the desire for instant wealth.

Cortes was successful because he quickly understood how to exploit the centralization of the Aztec empire. He courted the tributary tribes and gained the support of hundreds who had long chafed under repressive Aztec rule. Without their assistance,

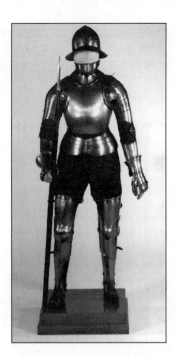

A suit of armor similar to the
type worn by the Spanish
conquistadores. 🖝

he and his men would not have lasted long. The Spanish won their victory with
almost unseemly ease, relying heavily on the impact of disease, the weaknesses of
the Aztec empire, the mobility their horses provided, and the technological advantage of steel swords and muskets, against which the Mexicans were defenseless.

The other major Spanish conquest during these early decades came in Peru. In
1523, news of the Incan empire had reached Panama and Francisco Pizarro, a veteran of Balboa's expedition who had spent years fighting Central American Indians.
Pizarro spent from 1528 to 1530 in Spain negotiating with the crown for the governorship of the area he planned to conquer. He launched his search for greater fame
and glory in January 1531, when he left Panama with 180 men and thirty horses.
Disease weakened his small force even before he sailed, but he pushed ahead in
true *conquistadore* fashion.

The Incan empire was even more tightly organized than that of the Aztecs,
but its internal strains were also greater. Measles and influenza epidemics cut a
deadly path along the trade routes to the northern part of the empire during the
late 1520s. The popular Incan ruler Huayna Capac and one of his sons died, and
the two remaining sons fought with each other for control of their father's
domain. Atahualpa won the struggle and ordered his brother, Huascar, executed.
He then established his court at Cajamarca in the northern Peruvian mountains
and allowed Pizarro to land uncontested, believing he could easily control him as
he ascended from the coast. Atahualpa underestimated his enemy, and on
November 16, 1532, Pizarro defeated the Indian armies and captured their leader.
Almost a year to the day later, on November 15, the Spanish captured the capital
of Cuzco. Atahualpa made the rest of Pizarro's task easier when he used his still-
considerable prestige to collect his ransom rather than to order an attack on his
captors. The ransom amounted to 13,420 pounds of twenty-two carat gold and
26,000 pounds of silver! Nevertheless, Pizarro decided to execute the Incan leader
by burning. He relented when Atahualpa agreed to be baptized, allowing him to
choose execution by garroting.

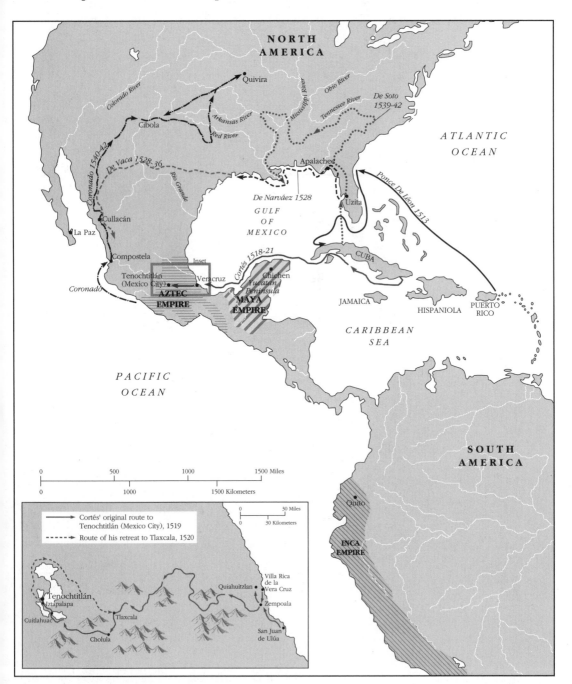

Map 2.1: The Spanish Empire in the New World ❧

Pizarro proved less perceptive than Cortes in consolidating his victories. He built a new capital on the coast at Lima, but this location weakened his control of the interior. He sent expeditions into Ecuador, Chile, Argentina, and Bolivia, but when his men found no gold, they tortured the Indian leaders, assuming they were hiding their wealth. Only in 1572 did the Spanish eliminate the last military resistance in the outlying areas of the empire.

The Spanish were even less successful in extending their control over other parts of South and Central America. Drawn by prospects of gold and instant wealth, ambitious *conquistadores* followed Indian rumors wherever they led. Many of the tales featured an Indian prince who covered himself with gold dust—the legendary El Dorado. A number of Spaniards searched in vain for this mythical figure, one even navigating the length of the Amazon River. Other explorers were no more successful in their search for wealth. In 1528, Pánfilo de Narváez landed on the west coast of the Florida peninsula with four hundred men. Eight years later, four men, the only survivors of the expedition, appeared in northern Mexico. They included Cabeza de Vaca, a Spanish nobleman who had been Narváez's second in command and later wrote a book about his experiences. He and his companions had wandered through the harsh Texas coastlands, living in semislavery, going naked like the Indians, and sharing their meager diet of spiders, worms, lizards, deer dung, and ants' eggs. In 1534, the four started a westward trek from an area near present day San Antonio, almost reaching the Pacific Ocean. With prayers and the power of suggestion, they cured many Indians of various illnesses and developed a reputation as faith healers, and Indians willingly provided them with food and lodging. In the spring of 1536, a group of Spanish slave traders finally picked them up and brought them back to Mexico City. De Vaca portrayed the country as the hard and unforgiving land that it was, but he also stimulated the Spanish imagination with reports of buffalo herds and large towns further to the north, leading explorers to renew their hopes of discovering the Seven Cities.

Fernando De Soto, who had served with Pizarro, landed in May 1539 near Tampa Bay, Florida, with about six hundred men, several hundred horses and dogs, and a herd of pigs. As he traveled, he added Indians to his force as slaves or aides. De Soto moved from Florida through present-day Georgia and the Carolinas, where he met (and briefly held captive) the Lady of Cofitachequi, leader of a South Carolina chiefdom. He then moved west to Tennessee and back down through northwest Georgia, where he killed twenty-five hundred Indians in a pitched battle, and finally turned northwest to Mississippi and Arkansas. Throughout his trek, the arrogant De Soto casually looted graves and temples. In the spring of 1542, he died of a fever, and his army tried to find a land route through Texas back to Mexico but ran short of supplies. In June 1543, the 311 surviving Spanish and Indians sailed down the Mississippi River to the Gulf of Mexico. They had found no gold or any other instant wealth, but the survivors spread stories of a place they called *coosa,* a land of milk and honey that existed somewhere to the north of Florida. Later expeditions spent much time searching for this mythical world, and in 1538, Fray Marcos de Niza roamed through the southwest in search of the Seven Cities, returning with unsubstantiated claims that he had in fact glimpsed them.

The explorations of Francisco Coronado remain the best known of the Spanish expeditions. Coronado left Mexico in 1540 with several hundred soldiers, servants, and slaves and more than one thousand friendly Indians. He wandered through present-day Arizona, New Mexico, Colorado, and the Great Plains before he returned in June 1542. He was likely the first European to see the Grand Canyon, but for the most part, he found not gold, silver, or jewels but a hard, inhospitable, and sparsely inhabited land. He did discover the fabled Cibalo, the greatest of the Seven Cities, but it proved to be only a small pueblo of two hundred people who responded with arrows when Coronado approached them. His journal also indicates his wonder at the abundant wildlife of the American interior:

> There are many animals, bears, and tigers, lions, porcupines, and some sheep as big as horses, with very large horns and little tails. I have seen some of their horns, the size of which was something amazing. There are wild goats, whose heads I

have also seen, and the paws of the bears and the skins of the wild boars. For game they have deer, leopards, and very large roebucks. They inhabit some plains eight days' journey toward the North Sea. The natives here have some very well-dressed skins, and they prepare and paint them where they kill the cattle [buffalo], according to what they tell me.[3]

Settlement of this region proceeded slowly. Between 1529 and 1536, Nuño de Guzman established the kingdom of New Galicia in northern and western Mexico, but it remained an underpopulated and undeveloped area until the Spanish discovered rich silver deposits there in 1546. The Spanish turned to the California region still later. Cortes sent out ships that cruised along the coast in the 1530s, and in 1542, Juan Rodríguez Cabrillo sailed as far north as present-day Oregon. It was only in the eighteenth century that Spanish Jesuits began to establish missions, and until mid-century, there were only fourteen of them in all of southern California. In 1767, the Spanish government expelled the Jesuits and replaced them with the Franciscans, who proved more energetic in expanding the Spanish presence. Father Junipero Serra founded twenty new missions as far north as San Francisco.

The Spanish also moved to counter a French attempt to establish a presence in the southeast region of North America. In 1565, Pedro Menéndez de Aviles attacked a French Huguenot settlement in present-day South Carolina, killing all the male residents. In the same year, the Spanish founded St. Augustine and a series of small coastal bases, hoping to protect their shipping in the Florida channel from hurricanes and privateers. Only St. Augustine lasted, and it remained an isolated outpost until the Jesuits expanded their missionary efforts in the next century. In 1598, finally, Juan de Onate founded the colony of New Mexico, consolidating the work of earlier expeditions. The extent of Spanish ignorance about this region is revealed by Onate's belief that he could supply New Mexico by sea, from either the Atlantic or the Pacific Ocean!

Both Florida and New Mexico differed from earlier Spanish settlements. They attracted relatively few settlers, and they cost Spain far more than they generated in revenues. The exploration and settlement of these colonies also reflected the importance of the Spanish missionary impulse in the borderlands. From 1526 on, royal regulations required that at least two priests accompany all explorations, and in 1573, the Spanish monarchy issued the Royal Orders for New Discoveries, giving missionaries a central role in the exploration and pacification of new lands. Priests relied on the military for security, and they quickly concluded that they would succeed in their efforts only if they obliterated Indian culture.

Administration

After the initial blush of conquest, Spain had to confront the administrative requirements of its new empire; post-conquistador rulers were bureaucrats. Spain established two principal bodies to govern the New World territories. The House of Trade regulated all aspects of the colonies' economies. It granted the merchant guild of Seville (later Cadiz) a monopoly over all trade with the colonies, and to facilitate tax collections, it required ships to sail in convoys and to land only at designated ports. The government also sought to prevent the colonies from trading with foreign countries, though this became impossible by the seventeenth century because of the decline of the Spanish navy and merchant marine, the bureaucracy's growing inefficiency and corruption, and the colonists' desires for cheaper goods from abroad.

Spain also established the Council for the Indies, which promulgated all laws for the colonies, approved major expenditures, and heard judicial appeals. The council divided the Americas into four kingdoms: New Spain, which included Mexico, the West Indies, and Central America; New Castile, which embraced Peru and Chile; La Plata, which governed Uruguay, Paraguay, Bolivia, and Argentina; and New Granada, which controlled Venezuela, Colombia, and Ecuador. A royal viceroy headed each kingdom, endowed with full military and political powers and subject only to Spain and to the advice of regional councils *(audiencias)*. Antonio de Mendoza was New Spain's first viceroy. Like all viceroys, he was born and raised in Spain. A member of one of Castile's most influential noble families, he possessed both the proper aura of authority and the necessary connection to the patriarchal figure of the Spanish king. He lived in a luxurious palace, attended by several Spanish gentlemen and sixty Indian servants. His duties and powers included control of all taxes and the submission of revenues to Spain, maintenance of public order and defense, and support of the Catholic church in all its activities.

For the most part, this was a top-heavy system. *Cabildos,* or municipal councils headed by two judges, governed the towns, but the monarchy also appointed special inspectors *(visitadores)* to supervise these and other local officials. Spain required every official to forward written reports to the Council for the Indies, and the king himself read many of them closely. In practice, though, officials often took the law into their own hands, altering or even disregarding it as they saw fit. Crown authority may have been absolute in principle, but interest groups and individuals competed with one another for power and influence, both in Spain and in the New World. Viceroys found their actions officially limited by laws and decrees and their authority constantly challenged by political enemies. As the sixteenth century progressed, officeholders increasingly viewed their positions solely as opportunities for personal gain.

Spain's King Philip II himself was torn between conflicting obligations. He needed New World silver to pay for his northern European wars, but the same silver had to stay in America to finance protection for the colonies against attacks by Spain's enemies. By the early seventeenth century, moreover, the supply of silver was diminishing, and the Spanish government began to pursue a much tighter fiscal policy in the New World. It put colonial offices up for sale and struck bargains with local elites that further weakened royal control. With Spain's power in decline in Europe, the colonies increasingly found themselves relying on their own resources for defense. Spanish visions of imperial glory were dim indeed by the end of the century.

Labor and the Economy

The Spanish instituted the *encomienda* system in the West Indies in 1503. The system granted a Spanish overlord, called an *encomendero,* control over all the Indians in a certain area, and required the Indians to work part-time for the Spaniard and to pay him a portion of their crops. In theory, it also obligated the Spaniard to Christianize and civilize the Indians. The *encomiendas* varied enormously in size; there were thirty in the Valley of Mexico alone that had an average of six thousand Indians, far beyond the legal limit of three hundred workers. Most commonly, though, they included only a single *cacique* (a local Indian leader) and his people. Predictably, the system quickly became an exploitative one. *Encomenderos* bought and sold Indians, forced them into virtual slavery, and often worked them to death. They seized property and women and killed those who resisted. Income was always the central concern, and the Spanish used Indian labor in the most profitable way they could, forcing them to work in cacao and textile production and later sending them to their deaths in the mines.

Illustrations from Bartolomé de Las Casas showing native Indians being tortured by the Spanish. ❧

Father Bartolomé de Las Casas was the most significant opponent of this system. Las Casas contended that the Indians were rational beings who should be converted without force. In 1520, his arguments convinced King Charles V to abolish the *encomienda* system on the Caribbean islands, but Cortes's conquest of Mexico changed the king's mind before the decree could be put into effect. Cortes himself initially resisted the use of the system in Mexico, but he soon saw that soldiers would not settle down unless they could be guaranteed free labor from the Indians.

In the long run, though, church attacks on the system took their toll. In 1542 and 1543, the "New Laws" forbade the creation of any new *encomiendas,* imposed stricter regulations on those remaining, and made them nonhereditary. Though the colonists got the ban on inheritance postponed for another generation, the laws now strictly limited the amount of labor the Spanish could require Indians to perform. The high death rate among the Indians, together with the declining profits under the new regulations, doomed the system long before additional legislation finally abolished it in the eighteenth century.

None of these measures stopped the Spanish from exploiting and enslaving the Indians. They often demanded payment for taxes in services or agricultural products, allotted Indian workers to Spanish landowners, and encouraged settlers to force rural Indians into villages and to take over their lands. A small number of Spaniards came to control more and more of the land, forging estates known as haciendas; Indians living on or near these tracts became virtual peons. The most dramatic incitement to continuing exploitation came in the 1540s, when the Spanish discovered large silver deposits in Mexico and Peru. As Spain began to more strictly regulate *encomiendas,* in fact, it actually became easier to forcibly mobilize Indians for "public" service in the mines. In the end, the decimating impact of disease and suicide combined with frequent escapes, to make Indian slavery uneconomical and eventually illegal. When Cortes landed on the shores of Mexico, there were twenty-five million Indians in the Aztec empire. Within fifty years, there were a tenth that many—about 2.5 million.

Disease was the silent, unpredictable killer, while the effect of working in the mines was more visible and certain. The Spanish made two major ore discoveries near Mexico City in 1530 and several more in the 1540s and 1550s. A network of urban centers and rural dependencies sprang up around the discoveries, providing food, fuel, and labor. Potosi, in Peru, was the most famous of these centers. The Potosi mines were producing 220 tons of silver annually by the end of the sixteenth century. Potosi itself was like a European city, with thirty-six silver-paneled churches and an equal number of gambling houses, ballrooms, and saloons. The descendants of the Indians who labored there, though, called it "the mountain that eats men."[4]

At first, most Indians lived far from the mining centers, so the Spanish forcibly relocated them through labor drafts *(repartimentos)*. They then required Indian communities to fill quotas, usually amounting to several months of labor a year for each Indian. In time, the declining Indian population made such solutions impractical, so the Spanish simply hired Indians to work for low wages. In Peru, the state supplied workers through forced drafts known as *mitas,* but even here, about half of the Indians working in the mines were free wage laborers. These Indians may have escaped forced labor, but they found few of the benefits of freedom. At Potosi, they commonly hauled loads of more than one hundred pounds in straw baskets or cloth or leather bags up steep ladders and through narrow tunnels with only a candle for light.

As Indians became less numerous, the Spanish turned to an alternative they were already familiar with, African slave labor. By 1500, slavery had become well established on the Iberian peninsula and the sugar plantations on the Canary Islands. Both black slaves and black freemen accompanied the Spanish to the New World, the latter sometimes holding positions of authority. A free black was second in command of Pizarro's artillery, while another distinguished himself in the expedition against Chile and was rewarded with an *encomienda.* The Spanish king approved the first slave shipments from Spain to the West Indies in 1501, and slaves began to enter the colonies in large numbers; they worked in fields and mines as laborers and in cities as servants and artisans. But most of the blacks who came to the colonies during the earliest years came directly from Europe. The Indians regarded them as "black white men," fully acculturated to Spanish civilization. The Spanish even used slaves to supervise Indian workers.

Work at the mines at Potosi, Bolivia, 1584. 🙶

Except in the few cities, black slaves lived in harsh conditions; they were whipped or mutilated for even the smallest violations, and they frequently revolted. As blacks imported directly from Africa came to outnumber those from Europe, racial stereotyping increased and conditions worsened. Though clerics themselves often owned slaves, the church did have some success in improving conditions. The government allowed slaves to be baptized and acknowledged them to be human beings with souls; it recognized slave marriages and allowed blacks to earn their own money and to buy their freedom and that of their families. Manumission was particularly common in urban areas, where slaves were better fed and clothed and were able to take advantage of greater economic opportunities. Since interracial marriage was also relatively common in Spanish America, by the end of the colonial period, free blacks actually outnumbered those who were enslaved.

The Church and Spanish-Indian Relations

From 1512 to 1556, Spain required its commanders to read a document known as the Requirement *(Requirimiento)* to the Indians before attacking them. This described the basic beliefs of Christianity and ordered the Indians to accept them and to acknowledge the authority of both the pope and the Spanish king or lose their land and freedom. The Spanish could thus justify their conquests by pointing to the Indians' refusal to heed this warning. This assumption that no rational person would refuse to convert typified Spanish ethnocentrism. The Franciscan friar Tomas Ortiz urged that the Indians be enslaved; the ones he had met "were like donkeys, dumb, crazy, and without sense. . . . They did not have the makings or skills of men."[5]

But while the church did not question the superiority of Spanish religion and culture, it did offer substantial resistance to the cruelties practiced upon the Indians. And not all priests agreed with Ortiz. The Spanish church as a whole was committed to spreading the Gospel in the spirit of the Catholic Counter-Reformation, though certain factors limited the nature of the church's response. The Catholic hierarchy realized that Rome could not finance its conversion efforts, so it had to rely upon the Spanish monarchy—and this inevitably entailed some acceptance of the settlers' treatment of the Indians.

Bishops were crucial to the church in New Spain, responsible for missionary work and for training local parish priests. Yet the clergy was almost entirely white. Despite its sympathy for the Indians, the church remained ethnocentric and did not believe that most Indians were capable of becoming priests. By mid-century, the clergy had lost all faith in the Indian ability to recognize the truth of Catholicism, and they did everything possible to destroy the remnants of Indian religion.

The individual priests who traveled to the New World represented a wide range of attitudes. The Franciscans were first in both Mexico (1524) and Peru (1534), followed by the Dominicans, Augustinians, Mercedarians, and Jesuits. In later years, such orders as the Hospital Brothers of the Order of St. John of God devoted themselves to pastoral work, caring for the sick and poor and establishing hospitals. Among these hundreds of clergy, many were dedicated in their defense of the Indians. The Dominican Fray Anton Montecino attacked the colonizers of Santo Domingo, striking at the heart of Spanish motivation: "Your greed for gold is blind," he warned them. "You are in mortal sin. And you are heading for damnation. . . . For you are destroying an innocent people."[6]

Bartolomé de Las Casas remains the most famed of those who attacked Spanish greed and cruelty. As an eighteen-year-old in Seville, Las Casas had seen Columbus pass through the town on his return from his first voyage in April 1493. That same year, Las Casas's father and two uncles sailed with the admiral on his second voyage. Las Casas himself traveled to the New World with the Spanish governor in 1502 and became an *encomendero*. Guilt over the treatment of the Indians, though, ate away at his conscience, and in 1523, he became a Dominican priest. He devoted the remaining fifty years of his life to defending the Indians. He pressured administrators to protect their charges and urged friars to stop giving absolution to *encomenderos*. He argued that the Indians were not beasts or barbarians and that the monarchy had an obligation to protect them from exploitation. "All the people of the world," he contended, "are one men and there is only the definition of each and every man, and that is that he is rational."[7] Las Casas's publications were widely influential, particularly his *Brief Account of the Destruction of the Indies,* first published in Spain in 1552. Despite his crusading zeal against atrocities, however, Las Casas differed from others essentially in his belief that the Spanish mission should proceed by peaceful rather than coercive means. He never questioned the assumption that the Indians should accept Christianity or that the Spanish had political jurisdiction over the New World. His value as an historian is minimal, since he wrote about places he never saw and made up statistics to fit his case.

How did the Indians react to all of this? The upper classes adopted Spanish culture most readily, often affecting European clothes and customs. Commoners maintained their traditions for a much longer period of time. In both Mexico and Peru, most Indians refused to accept Spanish customs; they never did more than integrate a few appealing elements into their own cultural practices. While the conversion rate was spectacular, the quality was poor. Indians continued to practice their own religious rituals in secret. They resisted such moral dictates as monogamy, since they regarded women as servants and the accumulation of wives as a sign of wealth. The vestments, music, and ceremonies of Catholicism attracted many at first, but they cooperated only when they had something to gain—access to a new spiritual power, for instance, or simply protection from the hostile soldiers who so often burned their villages.

The interaction of Spanish and Indian culture in central Mexico passed through three main stages. From 1519 to about 1550, little changed in Indian ideas, customs, or social organization. From about 1550 to about 1650, Spanish elements began to dominate most aspects of Indian life, though often as additions to a still unchanged core of Indian beliefs. After 1650, Spanish customs began to transform the basic framework of Indian culture. The 1540s and 1570s were both critical decades in this process; devastating epidemics during these years created dramatic shifts in the ratio of Spanish settlers to Indians and seriously weakened Indian institutions.

Resistance was most successful in the northern periphery of the Spanish empire. Indians here welcomed missionaries at first, assuming that, as in their own society, spiritual leaders were the moral leaders of Spanish society. They also eagerly adopted the agricultural technology the friars brought with them. But they balked when the military tried to draft them into forced labor. The Indians grafted Spanish forms and labels onto their own political and cultural traditions. They incorporated the new Christian god and rituals, for instance, into their existing forms of worship. Pueblo Indians had long used bodily movement and ritual sound in their worship, so the Franciscans created boys' choirs and emphasized the church's tradition of chanting to attract converts. The Pueblos also saw similarities between crucifixes and their prayer sticks and between the Catholic use of incense and their own smoking rituals. But the Franciscans tried to destroy any practices they viewed as idolatrous or pagan, and Pueblo traditionalists resisted. They warned their fellow villagers against baptism and commented on the Franciscan practices of self-flaggelation, "You go through the streets in groups flagellating yourselves, and it is not well that

❧ *Documents* ❧
The Spanish View

Most Spaniards in the New World never doubted the righteousness of their cause. The following excerpt from the Requirement makes Spanish assumptions clear.

> So their Highnesses are kings and lords of these islands and land of *tierra firma* by virtue of this donation [from the pope]: and some islands, and indeed almost all those to whom this has been notified, have received and served their Highnesses, as lords and kings, in the way that subjects ought to do, with good will, without any resistance, immediately, without delay, when they were informed of the aforesaid facts. . . . and you too are held and obliged to do the same. Wherefore as best we can, we ask and require you that you consider what we have said to you, and that you take the time that shall be necessary to understand and deliberate upon it, and that you acknowledge the Church as the Ruler and Superior of the whole world . . . and the high priest called Pope, and in his name the King and Queen Doña Juana our lords, in his place . . . and that you consent and give place that these religious fathers should declare and preach to you the aforesaid . . . .
>
> But, if you do not do this, and wickedly and maliciously make delay in it, I certify to you that, with the help of God, we shall powerfully enter into your country, and shall make war against you in all ways and manners that we can, and shall subject you to the yoke and obedience of the Church and of their Highnesses; we shall take you and your wives and your children, and shall make slaves of them. . . .

Arthur Helps, *The Spanish Conquest in America and Its Relation to the History of Slavery and to the Government of the Colonies*, vol. 1 (London: J. W. Parker & Sons, 1855–1861), 265–6.

The following excerpt from Las Casas's *The Devastation of the Indies* portrays the Indians as innocent victims and the Spanish as cruel aggressors.

> And of all the infinite universe of humanity, these people are the most guileless, the most devoid of wickedness and duplicity, the

the people of this pueblo should commit such madness as spilling their own blood by scourging themselves."[8] Moreover, the Franciscans could do little to stop the Spanish governors from enslaving mission Indians.

In the 1660s and 1670s, drought and a series of Navajo and Apache raids further threatened Pueblo villages. In response, the Indians increasingly turned to their traditional religion and ceremonies for solace. They had already revolted several

most obedient and faithful to their native masters and to the Spanish Christians whom they serve. They are by nature the most humble, patient, and peaceable, holding no grudges, free from embroilments, neither excitable nor quarrelsome. These people are the most devoid of rancors, hatreds, or desire for vengeance of any people in the world. . . . They are very clean in their persons, with alert, intelligent minds, docile and open to doctrine, very apt to receive our holy Catholic faith, to be endowed with virtuous customs, and to behave in a godly fashion. . . .

Yet into this sheepfold, into this land of meek outcasts there came some Spaniards who immediately behaved like ravening wild beasts, wolves, tigers, or lions that had been starved for many days. And Spaniards have behaved in no other way during the past forty years, down to the present time, for they are still acting like ravening beasts, killing, terrorizing, afflicting, torturing, and destroying the native peoples. . . .

Bartolome de Las Casas, *The Devastation of the Indies: A Brief Account,* trans. Herma Briffault (Baltimore, MD.: The Johns Hopkins University Press, 1992), 28–9.

Juan Gines de Sepulveda, writing in *Democrates Alter* in 1547, presented what was likely the majority Spanish view.

Those who surpass the rest in prudence and intelligence, although not in physical strength, are by nature the masters. On the other hand, those who are dim-witted and mentally lazy, although they may be physically strong enough to fulfill all the necessary tasks, are by nature slaves. It is just and useful that it be this way. . . . And so it is with the barbarous and inhumane peoples [the Indians] who have no civil life and peaceful customs. It will always be just and in conformity with natural law that such people submit to the rule of more cultured and humane princes and nations.

Frederick B. Pike, *Latin American History: Select Problems,* trans. J. L. Phelan (New York: Harcourt, Brace, Jovanovich, 1969), 47–8.

times against Spanish dominion, and the governor was fearful of another uprising. In 1675, the Spanish began to suppress the use of kivas, confiscate sacred masks and prayer sticks, and imprison and execute medicine men. In 1680, the Pueblos revolted. Their leader, El Pope, told the Indians that their god was stronger than the Spanish one, and they burned churches, defaced statues of the Virgin Mary, and destroyed chalices. El Pope succeeded in uniting most of the villages and forcing the Spanish to abandon the town of Sante Fe. The Europeans did not regain control of the area until the 1690s, and the revolt taught them a lesson in humility. They backed off from their exploitative labor practices, and the Franciscans ceased trying to completely stamp out Pueblo religious practices. But in the end, the Spanish god was stronger.

Society and Culture in New Spain

From the beginning, Spain saw overseas conquest in part as an outlet for the energies of the unruly unemployed. And indeed its migrants to the New World were mostly young males seeking adventure and quick profits. Only a few of them struck it rich as miners, ranchers, or manor holders. Yet the population of New Spain was remarkably diverse in some ways. Colonists worked as government officials, landowners, traders, doctors, lawyers, artisans, farmers, and clergy, and by the end of the sixteenth century, they numbered one hundred thousand. Racial distinctions were even more important than those based on occupation. Whites born in

---

❧ *Documents* ❧
Through Indian Eyes

The following accounts by Inca and Zuni sources reveal both Indian amazement at the Spaniards' powers and a realistic understanding of their actions.

> They resembled the Viracochas [one of two chief deities], that name by which we referred, in times gone by, to the Creator of all things. Thus they named them, first because they were very different from us, in face and costume, second because they saw them riding on the backs of huge animals with silver feet (this from the sparks struck out by the iron shoes). Another reason was that they saw the strange beings converse with one another, silently, by means of pieces of cloth, just as easily as one man speaks to another by word of mouth (this from their reading of letters and books).

Quoted in Nathan Wachtel, *The Vision of the Vanquished. The Spanish Conquest of Peru Through Indian Eyes, 1530–1570* (New York: Harvester Press, 1977), 22.

> They wore coats of iron, and warbonnets of metal, and carried for weapons short canes that spit fire and made thunder . . . these black, curl-bearded people drove our ancients about like slave creatures.

Quoted in David J. Weber, *The Spanish Frontier in North America* (New Haven: Yale University Press, 1992), 14.

Spain held all the highest positions and considered themselves superior to creoles (whites born in the colonies). All whites viewed themselves as better than the mestizos (those of mixed Indian and white descent) and the mulattos (those of mixed African and white heritage). All of these considered themselves far superior to the pure-blooded Indians and Africans.

The Spanish sought to recreate, as far as possible, the society they had known in Europe. They constructed towns on the Spanish model, with a central plaza and intersecting streets. The urban wealthy lived in richly decorated, plushly furnished homes that contained musical instruments, silk curtains, and even some libraries. The working class, in contrast, lived in single rooms divided by blankets. Single men and women often lived in the back rooms of stores. Even in rural villages, homes generally had only a single room and perhaps a separate kitchen; the more prosperous added rooms as they needed or were able to. Few of the settlers showed any appreciation for or understanding of Indian culture, destroying artifacts, records, and buildings and constructing churches on the sites of destroyed temples.

In other ways, this new Spanish society differed significantly from its Old World counterpart. Women often enjoyed a higher status in New Spain, particularly economically, since few families could survive on the husband's income alone. Women helped out during the harvest, and many worked profitably as artisans. Women with property enjoyed considerable freedom of action and retained complete control over their dowries during marriage and one-half of the wealth they and their husbands acquired. They often owned and operated mines and businesses. It was in the church, though, that women attained their highest status. During the Counter-Reformation in Europe, the Catholic Church emphasized anew the medieval worship of the Virgin Mary, and it encouraged men and women alike to withdraw from society and seek a mystical union with God. These developments had a powerful affect on women's religious orders.

Although some women enjoyed new freedoms, many others found themselves increasingly marginalized. Even the daughters of *conquistadores* often fell into poverty; they could not marry men in the lower social orders and lacked the financial means to attract wealthy husbands. The church offered a viable alternative. Around 1550, the Conceptionist order established a convent for the daughters of *conquistadores* and other Spanish settlers. Other orders quickly followed suit, and over the next two centuries, they trained hundreds of nuns born in the New World, though they excluded the poor and Indians until the eighteenth century. Late in the sixteenth century, though, the church established lay branches of the various orders, in which women professed simple vows only. Known as the Third Order, these groups accepted women from all social classes and even admitted blacks and Indians. They also provided the only female saints from the colonial period—Santa Rosa de Lima (1586-1617) and Santa Mariana de Jesus (1618-1645).

The Spanish did all they could to establish a healthy intellectual life in New Spain. They founded schools that provided courses in the humanities, philosophy, theology, and languages. By 1551, Spain had authorized universities in Mexico City and Peru. Over twenty colleges granted 150,000 degrees during the colonial period, and ten universities offered doctorates. During the second half of the sixteenth century, nuns began to teach the daughters of the elite in boarding schools and opened public schools for girls of all social classes. Yet New World settlers produced few great literary works. Cortes, Coronado, and other *conquistadores* have left us with accounts of their explorations. Cortes's *Letters from Mexico* reveal his high intelligence, while Bernal Díaz's *True History of the Conquest of Mexico* remains both a readable narrative and a valuable source of information on the activities of the first conquerors. By 1572, various religious orders, particularly the Franciscans, had written more than one hundred books to aid in their missionary work.

Only one resident of New Spain produced work that rivaled that of the best writers of Europe: Sor Juana Ines de la Cruz (1651-1695). The illegitimate child of a modest family, de la Cruz came under the patronage of a viceroy's wife and entered a Carmelite convent at fifteen, later leaving to join the Jeronymite order. Acclaimed during her lifetime, she wrote love poems, religious songs, plays, and symbolic poetry. She was a master of the lyric form. Her work communicated both emotion and intelligence and reflected the conflicts between reason and emotion, science and revelation that plagued so many other great church figures. Not surprisingly, her religious superiors found her writing too secular. De la Cruz ultimately renounced all her possessions, including her cherished library and musical instruments, and turned to fasting and meditation. She died an obedient daughter of the church.

Spanish culture in the New World reflected its unique colonial status in at least one other way—the conflict between popular and elite values. In theater, music, and the mascara (a parade of men and women in costumes), people made fun of the pretensions of metropolitan culture. One mascara included a float on which celebrants beat effigies of the viceroy and his wife. Such tensions would characterize almost every culture that colonized the New World.

Ironically, Spanish successes in the New World brought disaster to Spain itself. Charles V and Philip II spent most of the income from America on Spain's ambitious European wars; under Philip, an average of 2 million ducats a year poured in from America, but the monarch spent over 12 million ducats annually to support his military ventures. The influx of gold and silver also stimulated inflation, which in turn caused Spanish products to become overpriced and thus uncompetitive in the international marketplace; textiles and other industries collapsed. Several times in the late sixteenth and early seventeenth centuries, the government was forced to repudiate the state debt. When the output of New Spain's mines began to decline by the mid-seventeenth century, the Spanish economy simply collapsed. It had relied too long on an easy influx of wealth from the American colonies. Weakened by its overextended political and military ambitions in Europe and unwilling to develop a diversified, solid economic structure at home, Spain became a second-rate power.

Portuguese Settlement

During the early sixteenth century, Vasca da Gama and other Portuguese explorers solidified their small country's foothold in the Middle East and India by establishing trading posts around the Arabian Sea, the Bay of Bengal, and the South China Sea. At the same time, the Portuguese turned westward, hoping to exploit any lands they might discover under the Treaty of Tordesillas. Portugal would eventually realize it had made a bad bargain in this treaty, but for now, it was more than happy with the sugar islands in the eastern Atlantic and with the added bonus Pero Alvarez Cabral provided when he discovered and claimed Brazil in 1500. The complacent Portuguese did not attempt to establish a colony in the area until the 1520s.

Relations between the Indians and the early Portuguese explorers were peaceful, and the Europeans were quickly able to uncover and exploit the new colony's natural resources. They exported tropical birds, animals, and some Indians to Europe, but the most profitable discovery was the red dyewood, Brazilwood. Portuguese and French ships anchored offshore and traded tools, weapons, and other goods to the Indians, who cut and hauled the logs to the shore. The natives' willing involvement in this trade soon ended, though; like all American Indians, they had only a limited desire for European goods, and they resisted work that would drastically alter their economy by drawing them into the Atlantic trading network. When the Portuguese established settlements and introduced sugar cultivation in the 1530s, they began to enslave the Indians, tapping into the ready supply of captives generated by the warfare that was widespread among the indigenous peoples. Divided among themselves, the Indians could offer no effective resistance.

Early Portuguese settlement concentrated on the coast, but the colony remained disorganized and relatively undeveloped for some time. Communication was a constant problem, particularly between the northern and southern settlements. The Portuguese had no equivalent of the *conquistadores* to provide a dynamic of conquest. The monarchy at first treated Brazil as part of the system of trading outposts it had already established in Africa and Asia; it granted individuals hereditary captaincies with control over defined areas and required them to colonize and defend their grants. In turn, the recipients could keep most of the revenues their grants generated and enjoyed full governing powers. The monarchy retained control over only a few taxes and a monopoly over the dyewood trade.

The system was a failure, and the monarchy gradually reasserted control over the colony and began to actively promote colonization. It appointed governors-general and granted them powers similar to those of the Spanish viceroys; municipal councils controlled local government, again functioning like their Spanish equivalents. In 1642, the monarchy created the Overseas Council, with governing powers analogous to the Spanish Council of the Indies. By the end of the seventeenth century, the Portuguese empire in the New World had finally acquired a stable, definable shape.

Like all Old World countries seeking to exploit their new discoveries, Portugal had to find a reliable source of labor. Like the Spanish, the Portuguese eventually found Indian labor inadequate because of resistance and the impact of disease. So when they established sugar plantations, the settlers turned to a familiar source of forced labor, African slaves. The typical Brazilian sugar plantation had sixty to one hundred slaves, compared with the thousands that labored on many Caribbean plantations. These blacks lived in terrible conditions, in stifling barracks with minimal diets; many had only rags for clothes, and few had even a bed to sleep in. The brutal work schedule and the prevalence of tropical diseases led to a very low average life expectancy. Since slave owners could recover their initial investments in only two years, they simply worked the Africans to death.

African slaves did resist. They feigned illness, broke tools, and ran away by the thousands. Some who escaped formed free communities in remote jungle areas, often joining with local Indians; the colony had up to twenty thousand of these escapees by the 1670s. Most, though, suffered through a cruel life in the New World and died young. Africans and Indians were the major victims of the contact of cultures between the New World and the Old.

The French Empire

The French delayed their involvement in the New World for a variety of reasons. During the late fifteenth and early sixteenth centuries, the Valois dynasty was more interested in the Mediterranean world than in the lands affected by the Treaty of Tordesillas. French seamen and merchants, though, were very much aware of the potential wealth the North American continent held. From 1500 to 1502, the French-born Corte-Real brothers explored the Newfoundland and Labrador southern coasts and claimed the area for Portugal. The French and Spanish were constantly at war from 1521 to 1559, and French King Francis I came to see colonial expansion as a way of challenging Spanish hegemony in Europe. Francis engaged Giovanni de Verrazzano to explore for the French in the northern hemisphere. In 1524, Verrazzano sailed up the coast from Charleston to Maine and was the first to prove that North America was indeed a vast land barrier. At the same time, Breton and Norman seamen became increasingly involved in the Brazil trade, at least until Portugal captured and executed some of them as pirates.

Ten years later, in 1534, Francis sent out Jacques Cartier, a sea captain from St. Malo, to discover mineral wealth and a route to Cathay. Sailing with two sixty-ton ships, he entered the Gulf of St. Lawrence and explored the Labrador coast. Perhaps the most significant event of this first voyage was Cartier's encounter with Indians summering in the area, a group from Stadacona (near the future site of Quebec City) led by the chief Donnaconna. The Indians' eagerness to trade furs for metal goods (suggesting an earlier French trading presence) and their open friendliness intrigued Cartier, as did the land itself: "There is not the smallest plot of ground of bare wood, and even on sandy soil, but is full of wild wheat . . . as well as of pease, as thick as if they had been sown and hoed; of white and red currant-bushes, of strawberries, of rasberries, of white and red roses and of other plants of a strong, pleasant odour. Likewise there are many fine meadows with useful herbs, and a pond where there are many fine salmon."[9] He did not see that the Indians had planted the wheat and peas.

The St. Lawrence River seemed to offer promise as the fabled Northwest Passage the French were seeking, and Cartier planned to return soon. Before he left, he placed a thirty-foot cross on the shores of the Gaspé peninsula with the inscription, "Long Live the King of France," thus claiming the land for his country. He kidnapped Donnaconna's two sons, intending to train them as interpreters and guides and undoubtedly to show them off at the French court.

Cartier returned in May 1535 with a more ambitious expedition and plans to winter in the area, though the French king did not envision a permanent settlement. The French were still expecting to discover an alternate route to Cathay and did not yet view the region as a source of wealth. Donnaconna greeted Cartier warmly after he saw that the Frenchman had brought his two sons back alive. This time, though, Cartier found himself in over his head in dealing with the Indians. Two groups of Iroquoian tribes were living in the St. Lawrence region at this time. The first, Donnaconna's Stadaconians, consisted of a dozen or so small communities. The second, the Hochelagans, resided in the upper part of the valley (at present-day Montreal), living in at least one large town surrounded by extensive cornfields. Cartier expressed his desire to visit the Hochelagans when he heard of them, but Donnaconna and his people did all they could to prevent him from making the voyage, arguing that the trip was too dangerous and not worth the effort. In reality, they probably did not want him to make a separate alliance with a people who were their rivals. Cartier never did understand the situation, and by insisting on making the trip, he lost a golden opportunity to establish friendlier relations with Donnaconna.

In their visits to both Stadacano and Hochelaga, the French also discovered that the Indians did not possess the instant wealth they had hoped to find. Instead of jewels, they had crude weapons of wood, stone, and bone, houses and canoes of wood and bark, and fur clothing. Wintering at Stadacona, the French also confronted other cruel realities of the New World. By spring, twenty-five Frenchmen had died, and disease and malnutrition had weakened the others. The survivors alienated the Indians by their ruthless search for food and their fumbling attempts to convert the natives to Catholicism. Meanwhile, Cartier developed a consuming interest in a mythical kingdom to the northwest, along the Saguenay River. From the Indian descriptions of the area, he became convinced that he was on the fringes of Asia and that Saguenay wealth would rival that of the Spanish empire. He returned to France that spring with ambitious hopes for the future. Donnaconna, his two sons, and several other Indians accompanied him; they never saw their homeland again.

War with Spain delayed a third expedition until 1541, when Cartier sailed as navigator under the command of Jean Francois de la Rocque, Sieur de Roberval. The expedition contained eight ships and several hundred colonists equipped with livestock and farm equipment. This first attempt at permanent settlement, near Stadacona, was a complete disaster. The group spent only one winter in Canada, and again the French alienated the friendly Stadaconians by occupying land without asking permission, an affront the Indians interpreted as a challenge to their authority. The French also abandoned their search to locate the fabled "Kingdom of the Saguenay," and the gold the expedition brought back to France turned out to be fool's gold. Francis I now abandoned his efforts to establish an overseas empire. His only consolation, and undoubtedly one he found little solace in, was that his principle of sovereignty by occupation had become the ruling doctrine in the settlement of the New World. By now, moreover, maps had begun to clearly detail the North American coast, and Canada itself was identified.

The first French settlement success, short-lived though it was, came in South rather than North America. Henry II, at the urging of the Huguenot leader Gaspard de Coligny, devised a plan to establish a refuge for Huguenots and a French base for future expansion off the coast of Brazil in 1555. But volunteers were scarce, and as before the settlers were drawn from the streets. Both proper planning and intelligent leadership were sorely lacking, and the Portuguese captured the base in March 1560. Coligny persisted and briefly established a colony at Port Royal in South Carolina in 1562, again as a Huguenot refuge, but the colonists soon abandoned the settlement. Two years later, the French built a fort further south on the St. John's River, but the Spanish governor, Menéndez, captured and executed the colony's inhabitants. The French king then lost interest and turned his attention to the more pressing demands of continental warfare.

French fishermen continued to travel to the Grand Banks, Acadia, and the Gulf of St. Lawrence to trade with the Indians as the European demand for beaver felt hats rose; the Indians were eager to receive European metal goods in return. Only in 1603, though, did political conditions in Europe improve sufficiently to allow France to mount a substantial settlement effort. Henry IV commissioned Pierre du Gua, Sieur de Monts, vice-admiral and lieutenant-general of all lands claimed by France across the Atlantic and granted him a ten-year monopoly over the fur trade. The king also required de Monts to explore for mineral wealth, establish settlements, begin converting the Indians, and continue the search for the elusive Northwest Passage. De Monts's most fateful decision was to hire Samuel de Champlain as his navigator. Champlain had already made one trip to the area in 1603, and his published report, *Les Sauvages,* gave the French public a vivid picture of the geography and Indian life of the St. Lawrence valley. He described in admiring detail the physical perfection of the Indians, their cheerfulness and readiness to laugh, their enthusiasm for speechmaking, their amazing endurance, and especially their intelligence. None of these qualities, however, made them the equals of the French, either in Champlain's or most other French eyes.

The expedition sailed in March 1604 and established a base at Port Royal, in present-day Nova Scotia. De Monts accomplished little, though, and lost his trade monopoly in 1607. Champlain, however, proved that cereal grains and vegetables

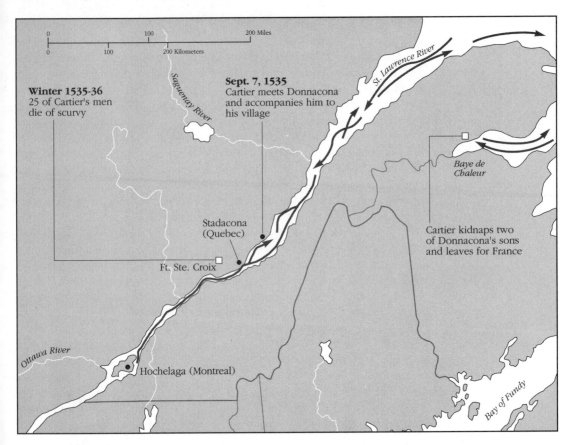

Map 2.2: Cartier's path up the St. Lawrence River during his second voyage, 1535–36 ❧

could be grown in the area and established a successful working relationship with the Micmac and Abenaki Indians, now dominant in the lower valley after the mysterious departure of the Iroquois Cartier had dealt with earlier. He made detailed marine charts and learned how to survive a Canadian winter. His most important contribution came when he convinced de Monts to establish a new base on the upper St. Lawrence River at Stadacona. This was a more defensible location than Port Royal, and here the French traders would have first pick of the furs that arrived each spring from the interior. The move convinced the king to grant de Monts and Champlain a new trade monopoly for one year. He also required them to establish a permanent settlement; the French were now there to stay.

Only eight of twenty-eight men survived the first winter at Stadacona, but Champlain solidified his good relations with the local Montagnais Indians, Algonquians who had replaced the Iroquois. The settlers learned how to slaughter animals when winter set in and to hang the frozen meat in an icy cellar. During the second summer, Champlain accompanied an Algonquian war party on a raid against a Mohawk village; French firearms carried the day in the ensuing battle, and his new allies rewarded him with the head of one of the enemy chiefs. He also established trade relations with the Huron confederacy, whose members would soon become the middlemen of the French fur trade system.

The French-Huron relationship prospered despite initial Algonquian resistance, largely due to Champlain's own perseverance. The Frenchman understood little of

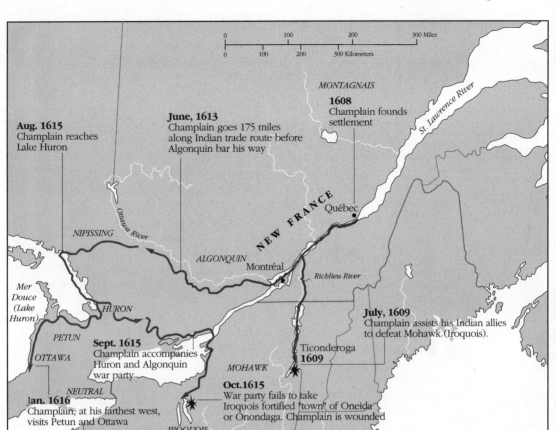

Aug. 1615
Champlain reaches
Lake Huron

June, 1613
Champlain goes 175 miles
along Indian trade route before
Algonquin bar his way

MONTAGNAIS

1608
Champlain founds
settlement

St. Lawrence River

NIPISSING

Ottawa River

NEW FRANCE

Québec

ALGONQUIN
Montréal

Richlieu River

*Mer
Douce
(Lake
Huron)*

HURON

July, 1609
Champlain assists his Indian allies
to defeat Mohawk (Iroquois).

PETUN

OTTAWA

Sept. 1615
Champlain accompanies
Huron and Algonquin
war party

Ticonderoga
1609

MOHAWK

NEUTRAL

Jan. 1616
Champlain, at his farthest west,
visits Petun and Ottawa

Oct.1615
War party fails to take
Iroquois fortified "town" of Oneida
or Onondaga. Champlain is wounded

IROQUOIS

Map 2.3: Champlain in New France ❧

Indian ways and remained too inflexible to learn; he criticized Huron customs and constantly threatened to take his business elsewhere if the Indians did not agree to his terms. But he visited all the major Huron villages personally, and he gained the right for Frenchmen to live freely among the Indians. Champlain's men also aided their hosts in warfare, and Champlain maintained the relationship through the repeated exchange of gifts and other expressions of good faith. He impressed the Indians with his courage, shooting the dangerous Lachine Rapids with them even though he could not swim. His implicit understanding of Indian values made him the right man for the situation.

Champlain had a number of clearly defined goals: to maintain his trading alliance with the Indians, to further explore the interior in the hope of finding a passage to Asia, to establish permanent settlements deeper in the interior, and to provide religious instruction for the Indians. He succeeded to some degree in achieving all four. Trading fairs, for instance, became well-established rituals during these years, marked by formal speeches of welcome by both sides, conferences and private meetings, and a full assembly to discuss the trading program for the coming year.

Scarce capital, though, continued to frustrate his larger ambitions. In 1617, he submitted a report to the French Chamber of Commerce in hopes that it would support a substantial colonization program. The report emphasized both the country's wealth and the possibility that the English or Dutch would exploit the area if the

French did not. But the private business community was not interested, and Louis XIII was preoccupied with his attempts to suppress the nobles resisting his rule. So Champlain turned to the church, hoping to use missionary and church funds to solidify his relations with the Hurons. The first order to arrive, the Recollects (a Franciscan order), failed miserably. They could not overcome their constraining ethnocentrism and stayed in Quebec most of the time.

At first, the Hurons seemed to be ideal candidates for conversion, "for they have a really noble carriage and bearing, occupy themselves only with hunting and war, do little work and always have something to live on."[10] When the Recollects failed to convince the Indians to abandon their culture and embrace that of the French—that is, to live as farmers and tradespeople under European law—the priests retreated into the common European perception of Indian culture as innately evil, shot through with superstition and savagery. They argued that the Indians were "stupid and dull," a people "without subordination, law, or form of government or system, gross in religious matters, shrewd and crafty for trade and profit, but superstitious to excess."[11] In 1625, the first Jesuits arrived in the colony, and over the next decade, they developed a dramatically different approach to Indian relations.

French officials came to realize that support for the Jesuit effort to save souls would help ensure greater profits in the fur trade. Crucial financial backing came from a group of one hundred French investors who, moved more by religious devotion than by the desire for profits, formed the Company of New France. In exchange for land and trading rights from the French monarchy, the company promised to settle four thousand inhabitants in New France within fifteen years,

Samuel de Champlain's first fort at Quebec (engraving published in Champlain, *Voyages de Sieur de Champlain*, Paris, 1613). ▲

Battle at Ticonderoga in 1609, between the Iroquois and Champlain and his Indian allies (Montagnais, Algonquian, and Huron), from *Voyages de Sieur de Champlain.* ❧

and in May 1628, it sent four hundred settlers to Quebec. The timing could not have been worse; England and France were now at war. English privateers immediately captured the settlers, and in 1629, Champlain surrendered Quebec. Even after the French regained the territory in 1632, they remained in a weak position. An expedition from Boston captured Port Royal in 1655, and the English did not surrender their claims to Acadia until 1670. Champlain was appointed governor of the region in 1632, and he returned to New France equipped with supplies, soldiers, workers, and some families. Growth was slow; thirty years later, the population was only about twenty-five hundred, and the French government had contributed little to help the tiny colony along. Fearing the king would revoke its charter, the company granted large tracts of land to lords *(seigneurs)* and required them to bring in the settlers that the company could not.

Champlain died on Christmas Day 1635 at Quebec at age sixty-eight. His accomplishments in New France were impressive, but the demands of the Canadian environment and the lack of full support from the French government kept the colony from establishing more than a precarious foothold. And despite his success in developing friendly relations with the Algonquians and Hurons, Champlain never moved beyond his limiting, ethnocentric views of Indian culture. One group of French colonists, however, realized they would have to make some compromises if they were to achieve their goals.

The Jesuits and the Indians

The first Jesuits arrived in New France in 1625, their position guaranteed by a generous grant of land from the king. These priests were among the best-educated individuals in Europe, and they began to establish control over Indian relations almost immediately. Rather than rely on the company's traders to help them in their work, for instance, they used their own servants *(donnés),* who were bound to the missions by vows and lived with the priests. This allowed the Jesuits to control their treatment of the Indians.

Initially, the Jesuits had no more success than the Recollects. Hoping to shield young Hurons from French vices, they established a boarding school north of Quebec. But Indian boys proved unenthusiastic about the French regimen of restrictive clothing, 4 A.M. risings, and separation from their families. Illness and escapes doomed the project. The Jesuits then decided to recruit the prominent old men and heads of families from among the tribes. The arrival of a group of Ursuline nuns, who offered medical care and staffed a hospital, aided these efforts. The priests also realized that the Indians were quite intelligent and began to treat them with much more respect.

As the Jesuits struggled to establish themselves, they found their position endangered by the epidemics of 1635 and 1637. Until this time, the Hurons had regarded the church as just another of the many "curing societies" they eagerly joined. But when the onslaught of measles or smallpox seemed unaffected by Jesuit intervention, some Indians began to claim that the priests themselves were causing the illness and accused them of witchcraft. By 1637, fear and hatred of the Jesuits had become general, and the tribal headmen were finding it difficult to control the young men. But in the end, the Hurons did not want to threaten the fur trade upon which they had become so dependent. The headmen in particular had strengthened their own position through the trade, and they actively used their influence to protect the priests.

The Jesuits now began to expand their missions under the leadership of a new superior, Father Jerome Lalemant. Lalemant established a single mission headquarters at Sillery, near Quebec, in 1638, including a seminary to train older Hurons as priests; he set up four subordinate village stations the following year. By now, there were thirteen Jesuits in Canada. Yet success remained elusive. The seminary and missions still worked to turn Indians into French people, and the Jesuits continued to underestimate the centrality of the Indians' cultural practices to their religion and identity.

When smallpox returned in 1639, hostility to the Jesuits reemerged. But the epidemic also cut the Huron population in half, and the Indians' involvement in the fur trade continued to protect the priests from harm. After 1640, the Jesuits finally began to understand the limitations of their approach and to implement more effective policies. In 1641, for instance, the order initiated "flying missions" among the Montagnais, in part to remove them from the corrupting influences of French civilization and alcohol, "the general perdition of all the Indian missions."[12] The Indians lived at these mission locations for a few months a year, speaking their own languages and wearing their own clothing. As long as they prayed and used the sacraments when they were available, the Jesuits were satisfied. Louis XIV and Jean Colbert, France's minister of finance, were not particularly pleased with this approach, since it kept the Indians from purchasing large amounts of French goods, and they persistently tried to undermine Jesuit policy. But by 1672, when the Comte de Frontenac arrived as governor, it was clear that the Jesuits had won the battle; he had explicit instructions not to restrict their activities.

After 1643, the priests averaged 150 baptisms a year, and by 1646, there were about five hundred Christian Hurons. Many undoubtedly converted to obtain guns or to establish better trade relations, but others joined the church to ensure they would be with dead relatives in the afterlife or simply because the Christian god seemed to offer a better explanation for what was happening to them than did their traditional deities. Still, the majority of Hurons continued to be troubled by the breakdown of their traditional way of life, and opponents taunted and ridiculed Christians and accused them of witchcraft.

Continued Indian resistance to conversion likely influenced the Jesuits to make one final adaptation in their policies, this one the most successful of all. Beginning in 1647, the priests began to relax some of their requirements for baptism and became more tolerant of traditional Indian practices. The new superior, Father Paul Ragueneau, supported this reassessment, arguing that the Jesuits had in fact asked more of their Indian converts than of ordinary Christians. The Jesuits began to encourage rather than require converts to abandon their "pagan" practices, with immediate success. In 1647 alone, the priests baptized five hundred converts, and from 1648 to 1649, after a devastating famine, more than seventeen hundred. By 1649, half of the Hurons were Christians.

Other developments were also pushing the natives toward embracing Christianity. During the 1620s and 1630s, trade had not altered the basic nature of Huron and Algonquian society. Headmen had continued to redistribute wealth, and the greater need for furs had simply reinforced matrilineal values by requiring the men to stay away from home for longer periods of time. Then disease began to take its toll, and the survivors became increasingly dependent on European goods. Finally, and perhaps most important, the Iroquois began to raid Huron villages with devastating frequency and savagery. They won a major battle in the spring of 1649 and scattered the Huron survivors, burning their villages. Historians disagree on the motives for the Iroquois attacks; some argue that they were trying to redirect the fur trade from Montreal to their Dutch allies at Albany, while others contend that it was an unthinking extension of their annual efforts to gather enough furs for their share of the trade. It made little difference to the Hurons, who lost their identity as a separate tribe.

Despite their success in establishing a working relationship with the Indians, the Jesuits never abandoned their belief in their own cultural and ethical superiority, or their basic goal of destroying the Indians' religion. Only their methods changed. The Indians, of course, made the process more difficult because they believed their own culture to be superior. They saw how Jesuit clothing slowed the priests' movements through the woods and how their pants hindered bodily functions. They believed that the priests' beards and hair reflected both low intelligence and limited sex appeal (they thought the Jesuits were incredibly ugly). The Jesuits did little to help their own cause in the early years. They had great difficulty in learning the Indians' language, though most did pick up at least a few of the rudiments. They baptized only the seriously ill at first, and these often died; the connection seemed most forbidding to the Indians.

The priests gradually realized they would have to change their approach to reach their goals. "A Missionary does not fear to make himself a Savage, so to speak, with them, in order to make them Christians . . . ," the Jesuits argued, and they believed priests must be willing to "follow them to their homes and adapt . . . to their ways, however ridiculous they may appear, in order to draw them to ours."[13] They displayed oratorical skills, generosity, and moral integrity in abundance to lure the Indians back for a second and third hearing of their message; all of these qualities were highly valued in Indian culture. They called the shamans' work child's play and insulted them. They gained prestige from their own immunity to the European diseases that so often ravaged Indian villages. They earned the loyalty of many when they cared for the sick during epidemics. Most important, they used such disasters to their own ends, blaming them on the anger of the Jesuit god at the failure of the Indians to worship him. For many Indians, common sense seemed to indicate this to be the case. A 1635 incident illustrates the power of such events. The Hurons were suffering through a drought, and they asked Father Jean de Brébeuf to make it rain—as they believed the Jesuits had done before. Brébeuf told them that if they resolved to abandon their traditional behaviors and become Christians, he and the Jesuits would say a novena of masses and march in procession to ask for divine assistance. Nine days later, as the priests paraded through the village, it began to rain, and the showers continued for a month.

The Jesuits' stubbornness also served them well, since the Indians were amazed at the amount of public humiliation they were willing to put up with; they themselves avoided such embarrassment at any cost. The ability of the priests to predict

❧ *Documents* ❧
Bringing the Church to the Indians

The French, like the Spanish, believed they were bringing civilization and salvation to the Indians. Champlain's introduction to the third volume of his voyages, addressed to the king, reflects this belief.

> And since they are by no means so savage but that in time and through intercourse with a civilized nation, they may be refined, you will likewise see here what a great hope we entertain of the result of such long-continued and painful toil as for fifteen years we have sustained, in order to plant in this country the standard of the cross, and to teach them the knowledge of God and the glory of His holy name. . . . And although many have no such purpose but may be said to be urged on by the lust of gain, nevertheless we may believe with some assurance that these are the means which God employs to give more scope to the holy desire of others. . . . This is a reason for increasing our long-cherished desire to send out yonder communities and colonies to teach those peoples, along with the knowledge of God, the glory and triumphs of your Majesty, so that with the French speech they may also acquire a French heart and spirit, which, next to the fear of God, shall breathe nothing but the desire to serve you.

H. P. Biggar, ed., *The Works of Samuel de Champlain,* 6 vols. (Toronto: Champlain Society, 1922–35), 3:3–6. Reprinted with permission of The Champlain Society, Toronto, CANADA.

The following vivid description provides interesting detail about the function of shamans in Huron society, but it also shows that even the ordinarily perceptive Champlain understood little of Indian religion.

> These scamps [shamans] also counterfeit a loud, distinct voice, and speak a language unknown to the other Indians. And when they speak in an old man's voice, the rest think that the devil is speaking, and is telling them what is going to happen in their war, and what they must do.

> Yet out of a hundred words all these scoundrels, who pretend to be wizards, do not speak two that are true, and go on deceiving these poor people to get things from them, as do many others in this

natural phenomena, such as eclipses, seemed to prove that they had a special connection to the spirit world. The simple skills of reading and writing, finally, seemed magical to members of an oral culture who could only communicate ideas and information in person.

At first, the Jesuits expected converts to give up many superstitions and to abandon such practices as adultery, nudity, premarital sex, torture, and cannibalism.

world who resemble the gentry. I often pointed out to them that what they did was pure folly, and that they ought not to believe in such things.

H. P. Biggar, ed., *The Works of Samuel de Champlain,* 6 vols. (Toronto: Champlain Society, 1922–35), 2:88. Reprinted with permission of The Champlain Society, Toronto, CANADA.

The Jesuits were certainly ethnocentric and often self-righteous, but they were also dedicated and sincere. There can be no other explanation for their bravery in the face of the sort of torture that men such as Father Jean de Brébeuf (and his colleague Gabriel L'Allemant) suffered at the hands of the Iroquois.

They tied both of their hands together. They tore the nails from their fingers. They beat them with a shower of blows from cudgels, on the shoulders, the loins, the belly, the legs, and the face.. . .The savages told us further, that, although Father de Breboeuf was overwhelmed under the weight of these blows, he did not cease continually to speak of God, and to encourage all the new Christians who were captives like himself to suffer well, that they might die well, in order to go in company with him to Paradise. While the good Father was thus encouraging these good people, a wretched huron renegade . . . , hearing him speak of Paradise and Holy Baptism, was irritated, and said to him . . . "thou sayest that Baptism and the sufferings of this life lead straight to Paradise; thou wilt go soon, for I am going to baptize thee, and to make thee suffer well, in order to go the sooner to thy Paradise." The barbarian, having said that, took a kettle full of boiling water, which he poured over his body three different times, in derision of Holy baptism.. . . . After that, they made him suffer several other torments. The first was to make hatchets red-hot, and to apply them to the loins and under the armpits. They made a collar of these red-hot hatchets, and put it on the neck of this good Father.

Reuben Gold Thwaites, ed., *The Jesuit Relations and Allied Documents,* 73 vols. (New York: Pageant, 1959), 34:27–9.

They were more successful when they imaginatively synthesized traditional and Indian practices with the more formalistic rituals of Roman Catholicism. They substituted religious sacramentals for traditional stone amulets and charms, for example, and the Indians soon found themselves bejeweled with crucifixes, medals, and rosaries. One priest might put a rosary around the neck of an ill child to restore her health, while another might hang a crucifix above a sick boy's bed, replacing the father's medicine pouch. They hammered their message home with graphic descriptions of the terrors of hell, often dramatized by the apparently magical way the priests produced fire from sulfur.

Many of these priests were also intellectuals and produced significant works of literature during and after their stays in New France. Father Paul Le Jeune began the *Jesuit Relations* in 1632. Invaluable resources for historians today, these lengthy, detailed annual reports served to stimulate interest in the missions in France and to raise funds. Father Christian Le Clercq arrived in Canada in 1673 and served on and off for eleven years among the Indians on the Gaspé peninsula. He devised a hieroglyphic system for writing Micmac, composed a dictionary of the language, and in 1691 published his *New Relations of Gaspesia* in France. Father Pierre de Charlevoic worked in Canada from 1705 to 1709 and 1720 to 1722. An explorer as well as an intellectual and a missionary, de Charlevoic spent his second tour searching for a route to the Pacific, traveling with others from the St. Lawrence valley to the Gulf of Mexico. He also published a three-volume *History and General Description of New France* in 1744. Although they are limited by religious and ethnocentric biases, these works and many others provide fruitful insight into the history of French settlement in Canada.

A Colony under Siege

The Jesuits' success meant the French would succeed as well, despite the loss of their Huron allies. By 1650, the French had explored Canada to the western end of Lake Superior, and the Ottawas quickly stepped in to replace the Hurons as middlemen in the fur trade. Montreal prospered and became a microcosm of French society. By 1665, it had 605 residents, including nobles, clergy, and commoners, and a church, a school, and a hospital. But life remained dangerous everywhere in New France. Iroquois continued to roam the region and to inflict heavy casualties in sporadic raids, religious enthusiasm among French supporters of the colony had faded, and the Company of New France was facing bankruptcy. As early as 1645, settlers took matters into their own hands and negotiated a monopoly on the fur trade in exchange for annual payments of one thousand beaver pelts to the company. But they too failed, and the French government was forced to intervene. For the remaining years of the company's existence, power was diffused in a confusing way between the king, the company, the governor, and the council. Internal conflicts continued to curse the settlements as well. The Jesuits, for instance, succeeded in prohibiting the sale of liquor to the Indians, much to the dismay of the civil authorities, who saw it as a means of striking better deals in the fur trade. Alcohol was new to the Indians, and they drank to get drunk, believing they would thereby be transported to the spirit world. In May 1663, Louis XIV decided he had had enough of these disputes, and he made Canada a royal province.

Despite its ignominious demise, the company had accomplished a good deal. The fur trade, basic crops, and farm animals provided a solid economic base for future growth, and the colony was almost self-sufficient in food. The generous land policy meant that the colony's farmers were much better off than French peasants. And despite the early difficulty in recruiting settlers, the colony had not become a dumping ground for the French jails. Many migrated to escape religious persecution in France (though Huguenots were not allowed to settle), others to seek economic opportunity. The church provided all settlers with a strong link to French society. Thus, the groundwork was already in place when Jean Colbert began to reorganize the French colonial empire.

Colbert's Canada

Colbert established the government-controlled Company of the West to overseas French settlements in the New World. He believed that the French colonies should make the same sort of contribution to France as the English colonies did to England. At first, he hoped that Canada would provide food for the West Indies and take in sugar, molasses, and rum in exchange, but the long distance between the colonies and the small size of the Canadian population made such a trade unprofitable; New England, in fact, provided West Indian products for Canadians at a much lower cost.

Colbert reorganized the colony itself along military lines, with the king at the top. The minister of marine oversaw daily affairs and reported directly to the king. The minister's assistant read all colonial dispatches and thus determined what information reached both the minister and the king. In New France, a governor-general, always a soldier, headed the government and was responsible for Indian relations, while local governors held power in Acadia, Montreal, and Trois Rivieres. In both New France and the West Indies, intendants ran the civil administration, administered justice, and supplied the needs of the military. They also appointed delegates from the towns to assist them and oversaw the activities of the numerous minor officials. A Sovereign Council, whose membership ranged from five to twelve over the years, served as a judicial court of appeal and enacted minor legislation; it was not, however, a representative body.

Local government functioned through the militia. All males between the ages of sixteen and sixty served in the militia, and every parish had a company. The captains were habitants, or ordinary citizens (not nobles), and reported directly to the intendants. The governor sometimes consulted the people in the three principal towns by calling an open assembly, but he did so only to gather information. Though it did seek to serve the needs of the people, this was an authoritarian government.

In structuring the economy, Colbert sought to achieve self-sufficiency. He expanded the fisheries and agricultural production, broadened the search for minerals, and attempted to establish shipbuilding and naval stores industries (with minimal success). The fur trade continued to be the colony's commercial backbone. Colbert allowed the company to retain a monopoly over the trade at Tadoussac, located at the mouth of the Saguenay River, and he set a fixed price that allowed the company a healthy profit. So profitable did the trade remain, in fact, that many Canadians abandoned farming for the fast profits furs seemed to guarantee. Colbert tried to confine the trade to the three main towns, but he was never able to stop this drain on the colony's other resources.

Colbert also opposed westward expansion, but Governor-General Louis de Buade, comte de Frontenac countered his efforts and worked to extend French power into the interior. In 1673, he built a new trading post on Lake Ontario (Fort Frontenac) and another at Niagara. Jesuits bravely took their message to Indians deep in the interior throughout the century, and in 1669 missionaries reached the western end of Lake Superior. The *coureurs de bois* (literally, runners of the woods, or French traders who spent most of their time among the Indians) began to travel to the headwaters of the Mississippi River and to bring more and more tribes into the French trading orbit. In 1673, trader Louis Jolliet, Father Jacques Marquette, and five others traveled down the great river as far as the mouth of the Arkansas River, only seven hundred miles from the Gulf of Mexico, before they turned back in fear of the Spanish. In 1681, Colbert tried to impose a restrictive licensing system under which only twenty-five canoes were allowed to trade with the west annually, but the attempt failed. And in 1682, Robert Cavalier de La Salle explored the Mississippi River all the way to its mouth.

On the whole, the minister's economic policy was a success. He recruited large numbers of farmers, mechanics, landless men, and poor women to settle in the New World, as many as five hundred men and 150 women a year, and encouraged them to marry as quickly as possible. The population began to increase through natural growth by the end of the century. The birth rate was five or six children per family (compared to four to five in France), and women married at an average age of twenty-two (two to three years younger than in France). Twice as many children survived to marriageable age in Canada than in France. By 1680, the colony held about ten thousand French inhabitants, and the habitants were markedly better off than European peasants. Ironically, it was the Canadian upper class *(seigneurs)* who often experienced difficulties. While the king granted concessions to the *seigneurs,* they faced a persistent labor shortage, and high fees prevented them from selling off their land for speculative profits. The government could confiscate their property if they did not find enough tenants to work their manors.

Colbert died in 1683, leaving behind a mixed record of achievement. He had certainly stabilized the colony, although the economy remained underdeveloped and heavily dependent on the fur trade. Under his somewhat reluctant leadership, the French had taken dramatic steps to open the interior of the continent to European exploitation, and Canada had become powerful and wealthy enough to present a real threat to the growing English colonies. Indeed, the success of both empires had significantly raised the stakes of European conflict. In a few short years, England and France would begin a protracted struggle that would shake the Western world for almost a century.

The Old World and the New affected each other in both obvious and subtle ways. Disease devastated American Indian society to an extent that Europeans could scarcely comprehend; not even the plague had killed people on such a scale. The exchange was more equitable in other areas. Foods and plants of the New World forever changed the dietary habits of the Old: sugar, potatoes, coffee, corn, tomatoes, tobacco, dyes and vanilla are only a few of the products that were scarce or unknown before Columbus's discovery. The Aztecs grew dozens of varieties of tomatoes, a vegetable Europeans devoured with delight. The Old World also eagerly adopted the potato. Though some peasants at first believed potatoes might be poisonous (the city of Burgundy banned them in 1619 for fear they caused leprosy), others embraced them as aphrodisiacs. Europeans brought chicken, sheep, goats, and horses to North and South America, and they introduced new strains of vegetables, wheat, chickpeas, and other crops.

Expansion also deepened European political rivalries, as various countries competed for control of New World wealth. The Portuguese and Spanish were the principal contenders for most of the sixteenth century, but the French, English, Dutch, and even the Swedes soon joined them. Perhaps the most startling transformation was in Old World perceptions of the earth itself. Magellan's circumnavigation of the globe from 1519 to 1522 finally proved that Columbus had indeed discovered a new continent. This realization promoted renewed debate over the moral and legal validity of the conquest of strange and different peoples. The Spanish confronted this problem most directly, with intellectuals exchanging views openly and often bluntly. Certainly ethnocentrism and the religious dictates of the Reformation limited the ability or desire of most to consider their actions unwise or immoral. Yet Spanish intellectuals were profoundly influenced by the Renaissance sense of discovery and curiosity, and they brought a wide range of views to the debate. Juan Gines de Sepulveda was typical of many of the participants, an Aristotelian scholar and a fervid nationalist who believed that the Spanish represented the peak of civilization and that the Indians were mere barbarians. The Spanish, he argued, should train these unfortunates in "virtuous and humane customs," and they in turn should gratefully provide the Spanish with free labor.

Las Casas stood at the other extreme of this debate, and at times his arguments actually prevailed. In addition to the "New Laws" of 1542–1543, Charles V ordered in 1550, that conquests in his name stop until the Council of the Indies met to decide whether the conquest was just. He appointed a special committee of fourteen officials, scholars, and theologians to consider the matter. But while the king prohibited Sepulveda from publishing his views and in 1573 established strict conditions for future expeditions, the committee never produced a final report. The impact of the controversy on New World exploration was minimal. Spanish soldiers and landholders continued to behave as they would, and the English were about to initiate a series of settlements that in many ways would continue the traditions of the *conquistadores*.

❧ *Chapter Three* ❧

> # England and the Chesapeake:
> # Trouble Within,
> # Disaster Without

Like other European countries in the early modern era, England shaped its foreign and colonial policies around the doctrine of mercantilism. Theorists of mercantilism contended that the world held only a finite supply of wealth, and European monarchs recognized the urgency of gaining control over these limited resources. Countries sought to decrease foreign imports and increase their own exports, thus creating a favorable balance of trade, enlarging their store of bullion, and stimulating domestic manufacturing. Monarchs also sought to foster strong merchant communities that could serve as their political allies and provide added financial resources. Colonies had a clearly defined and potentially essential function in this structure. They could provide substantial amounts of bullion, serve as a steady source of raw materials, and guarantee markets for finished goods produced in the home country.

Spain, France, and England all founded their colonies with these principles firmly in mind. In England's case, domestic concerns delayed the search for suitable colonies until late in the sixteenth century. And the first English colonies were serious missteps, confounded by the misleading example of the Spanish colonies and by the unrealistic expectations of the Crown, the London Company, and the settlers. For two decades, the land, climate, and people of the New World held the Old World invaders at bay.

The Roots Of The English Empire

Early Exploration

England was the last of the European powers to seriously explore the New World. Giovanni Caboto, a Venetian known to the English as John Cabot, was the only fifteenth-century explorer to voyage westward for England. Cabot arrived in

Significant Dates

1485	Henry VII establishes the Tudor dynasty
1498	John Cabot explores North American coast
1509	Henry VIII becomes king
	Henry marries Catherine of Aragon
1534	Act of Supremacy
1549	First *Book of Common Prayer*
1547	Edward I becomes king
1552	Second *Book of Common Prayer*
1553	Mary I becomes queen
1558	Elizabeth I succeeds Mary
1560s	Irish rebellion
1578	Sir Humphrey Gilbert receives patent to settle in New World
1584	Sir Walter Raleigh receives extension of Gilbert patent
	Richard Hakluyt's *Discourse on Western Planting*
1585	Defeat of the Spanish Armada
	Ralph Lane and Sir Richard Grenville attempt to establish colony on Roanoke Island
1587	John White establishes the first permanent English settlement at Roanoke
1590	White returns to find the colony abandoned
1606	London Company patent
1607	Jamestown settled
1609	Revised Virginia charter
1609–10	"Starving time"
1611–16	Gates and Dale governorships
1612	New Virginia charter
	John Rolfe introduces tobacco into the colony
1613	Dale kidnaps Pocahontas
1618	The Great Charter
1619	First Africans imported into Virginia
	First meeting of the House of Burgesses
1622	First Indian War
1624	Virginia becomes a royal colony
1632	Cecilius Calvert receives charter for Maryland
1634	Maryland settled
1635	Counties established in Virginia
	First meeting of the Maryland Assembly
1644–46	Second Indian War
1649	Maryland Act of Toleration
1655	Battle of Severn

Bristol sometime between 1493 and 1495, and Henry VII gave him permission to seek new lands in England's name. Cabot sought the northern version of a western route to Asia, the northwest passage that would lure European explorers for two centuries. In May 1497, he sailed from Bristol on the *Matthew* with a crew of eighteen. He returned several months later with a story of an island with tall, straight trees suitable for English masts and surrounded by shallow seas teeming with codfish. The land Cabot discovered was most likely Newfoundland, though he may have sailed as far south as Cape Cod. In 1498, he outfitted five ships and sailed again in search of the northwest passage. He was never heard from again, and the English subsequently abandoned serious exploration efforts. Cabot's son Sebastian explored the Hudson Bay area a few years later, but for several decades, English presence in the New World consisted largely of fishermen regularly visiting the Newfoundland Grand Banks. Any colonization attempt might have threatened English-Spanish relations and the limited rights English merchants had won to trade with Spain's American colonies.

The Tudor Dynasty

Instead of seeking wealth in the Western Hemisphere, the English concentrated on resolving a series of domestic problems and crises. Henry VII (1485–1509), the founder of the Tudor dynasty, faced continued resistance from nobles who refused to accept royal authority. He had no standing army and only a small navy, so he brought commoners into the government to help check the nobles' power. He ruled through the Royal Council, a group of twelve to fifteen lesser landowners who possessed some legal training, and he called a meeting of Parliament several times during the early years of his reign to confirm laws. Locally, Henry and the other Tudor monarchs relied heavily on unpaid members of the gentry, particularly justices of the peace, to ensure public order. These members of the local land-owning class punished criminals, enforced laws, fixed wages and prices, supervised weights and measures, and enforced appropriate moral behavior among villagers. Henry established a profitable alliance with the commercial middle class and supported the development of the cloth industry and the merchant marine. Finally, he married his eldest son, Arthur, to Catherine of Aragon, the daughter of Spain's Ferdinand and Isabella, establishing a strategic alliance against England's traditional enemy, France. The young, sickly Arthur died before the marriage was consummated, but England at Henry's death was at peace and prosperous and had a new and enhanced status in the world of European nations.

The English Reformation   Henry VIII (1509–1547) succeeded his father to the throne and continued to pursue the centralization and stabilization of English governmental administration. Two minor exploratory voyages took place during his rule. John Rut sailed along the North American coast in 1527, and Richard Hore further explored the Newfoundland region in 1536. These events pale in significance, though, beside Henry's break with Rome and the Catholic church.

The English laity, beginning with the Lollards in the fourteenth century, had begun to demand church reforms. Lollards stressed individual reading and interpretation of the Bible and found particularly strong support in the cloth-making regions of eastern England. They were forcefully anticlerical, opposed such rituals as the sacraments and veneration of saints, and stressed the individual soul's relation with God. The humanist William Tyndale (1494–1536) later continued the tradition of religious reform by printing an English translation of the New Testament. By the early sixteenth century, many of the English laity were disillusioned with the low level of education and uninspired preaching of the English clergy. The shepherds of the church seemed to concentrate on accumulating land, wealth, and offices, while their flocks were spiritually starving. Despite such abuses and widespread feelings of anticlericalism among the laity, Protestants failed to make serious headway in the kingdom. Henry himself earned the title "Defender of the Faith" for writing a pamphlet attacking Lutheran doctrines.

Henry had married Catherine of Aragon (the deceased Arthur's wife) in 1509. Since Spain controlled the Netherlands, a critical partner in England's growing cloth trade, a Spanish alliance was essential to English economic health. But Catherine failed to bear Henry a son; only one child, Mary, survived from Catherine's six conceptions. Henry desired a male heir more than anything else, and by 1527, he had become convinced that Catherine could not produce one. When Henry married her, he had insisted (unnecessarily, since her marriage to Arthur had not been consummated) on a dispensation from Pope Julius II granting permission for the marriage. About 1527, he began to quote a passage from the Bible's book of Leviticus that prohibited a man from marrying his brother's wife, and he insisted that God was denying him a male heir as punishment for his sin. Though his argument had no validity, he aggressively pursued his case. He petitioned Pope Clement VII for an annulment, but Clement had his own problems. He was confronted with the Lutheran revolt in northern Germany and the Hapsburg-Valois struggle for Italy, and any such dispensation would have seemed proof of papal corruption to the reformers. Then in 1527, the Holy Roman Emperor Charles V, Catherine's nephew, sacked Rome. Charles's subsequent control over Clement negated any possibility of Henry achieving his goal through legitimate Catholic channels.

At this point, Henry ran into a bit of luck. The archbishop of Canterbury died, and the king appointed Thomas Cranmer to succeed him. Cranmer heard the divorce case and granted the annulment. Henry married Anne Bolyn, who had captured his eye while he was still married to Catherine, on May 28, 1533. Elizabeth was born in September. Over the next several years, Henry, acting through Parliament, finalized his break with Rome and established a national English church. The Act of Supremacy (1534) recognized him as the new church's spiritual head.

The English Reformation was essentially imposed from above, and church doctrine changed little under Henry. He retained many of the traditional Catholic ritual practices, such as confession, clerical celibacy, and the belief in transubstantiation. Bishops remained in control of church government. But Henry did authorize the use of an English translation of the Bible in 1539, and the break with Rome catalyzed important administrative changes in English government. Henry seized all church lands and dissolved the monasteries, for instance, bringing about one-sixth of the total land in England under his control. He established a more centralized royal bureaucracy to administer the property. First through rent and then through long-term lease and sale, the English government reaped a financial bonanza from church lands, most of which ended up in the hands of nobles loyal to Henry.

Ironically, Henry failed to achieve the immediate goal of his break with Rome. Anne failed to bear him a son; Henry charged her with adulterous incest in 1536 and had her beheaded. His third wife, Jane Seymour, finally gave him the male child he so ardently desired—the future Edward VI—but she died in childbirth. Henry had three more wives, and before he died in 1547, he had Parliament relegitimize both Mary and Elizabeth.

When Edward VI (1547–1553) ascended to the throne sickly and still a minor, Cranmer presided over the true reformation of the church. He established contacts with John Calvin and other continental leaders of the Protestant movement, and he invited reformers to Oxford and Cambridge to help train future English clergy.

Radical Protestant ideas swept through the country. Clerical marriage was approved, the first *Book of Common Prayer* was published in 1549, followed by a second book, still more reformed, in 1552. Images were removed from the church, and communion tables replaced altars. Shortly before he died, Edward endorsed the Forty-Two Articles, a thoroughly Protestant codification of church doctrine.

Edward's successor, Mary I (1553–1558), swung the pendulum in the other direction. Mary had never forgotten the treatment her mother, Catherine of Aragon, had been subjected to, and she vowed to restore Catholicism to England. She executed several hundred Protestants during her reign and forced hundreds to flee to radical Protestant centers on the continent. Henry's divorce and England's growing economic and political rivalry with Spain had poisoned relations between the two countries, and Mary now moved to restore good feelings. Her marriage to the future Philip II of Spain and her alliance with that country only served to further arouse the antipathy of the English people, who were understandably ready for a religious respite when Elizabeth I (1558–1603) acceded to the throne.

England under Elizabeth   Elizabeth realized that her most important task lay in resolving the religious uncertainty that had plagued the country since Henry's break with Rome. She thus sought to travel a middle road, establishing what has become known as the Elizabethan Settlement of 1559. The church under Elizabeth was Protestant in doctrine but retained much of the ceremony and structure of Catholicism. The queen's main concern was not religious issues but rather the need to bring stability to English public life and to retain the loyalty of the majority of the people. Most of the Protestants who returned from exile were willing to work within the confines of the settlement, but the few who were not provided the impetus for a religious revolution that profoundly affected English domestic and foreign policy in the late sixteenth and early seventeenth centuries.

These dissidents sought to return the church to its original, purer form, ridding it of such popish remnants as clerical vestments, various rituals, all of the sacraments save baptism and communion, and the observance of saints' days. Elizabeth's attempts to suppress this dissent only caused it to spread. The Puritans, as the dissenters became known, first emerged as a force to be reckoned with in the 1566 dispute over the use of vestments during church services. They argued that such a practice was too close to Catholicism; in response, Elizabeth ordered the archbishop of Canterbury, Matthew Parker, to enforce the use of the vestments. The reformers subsequently turned to their many allies in the House of Commons for assistance. Major efforts in 1566, 1571, and 1572 produced no success, however, as Elizabeth cut off debate and imprisoned those who introduced reform bills. Angered by the Puritans' actions, she ordered Parker to launch a more widespread campaign of suppression.

Parker died in 1575 and was succeeded by Edmund Grindal. Grindal's theological beliefs were more sympathetic to Puritan views. He relaxed the enforcement of anti-Puritan measures and turned his efforts instead against the remnants of Catholicism in the English church. Grindal, in fact, encouraged the development of a preaching ministry, and prophesying among the dissenting clergy began to increase during the 1570s. Regional ministerial conferences began to meet in some areas, focusing on the ongoing education of the clergy and even allowing lay attendance. Once again, though, Elizabeth intervened. In 1576, she ordered such meetings to end; Grindal dissented, and she suspended him.

Grindal's suspension lent a degree of urgency to another innovation in dissenter thought, the idea of a church without bishops, governed by a group of ministers and lay elders. This theory of church structure first became popular among a group known as Presbyterians, and it was introduced to England by Thomas Cartwright in 1570. Cartwright's advocacy cost him his job at Cambridge University, but he and others organized a series of ministerial conferences and a correspondence network. Archbishop of Canterbury John Whitgift's attempts to counter the movement by enforcing conformity to the *Book of Common Prayer* only increased sympathy for the Presbyterians, and a shadow church gradually began to emerge, giving dissenters a growing sense of fellowship and providing an extensive network of religious and social support. Lay patrons, moreover, had appointed many dissenting ministers to private positions attached to property they had acquired when Henry VIII had dissolved the monasteries, and other ministers received strong support and protection from sympathetic noblemen and local officials. The movement peaked in the late 1580s and then faded. Leaders died, sympathizers in government circles lost their enthusiasm, and the government forced Cartwright and ten others, under threat of imprisonment, to pledge to stop their efforts to convert Anglicans to their point of view.

Puritans now turned to developing their theology, emphasizing an essentially Calvinist view of the relationship between God and humankind. Certain characteristics of English Puritan theology are worth pointing out here. Such theologians as William Perkins stressed the importance of the sermon and the Bible as the most essential sources of the word of God. Puritan congregations, meeting secretly and often in private homes, tended to embrace a relative equality between minister and laity, and ministers themselves emphasized the pastoral nature of their work. Apart from their religious protests, finally, English Puritans deplored the rampant individualism of English society. Order and morality seemed to be crumbling before their eyes, and chaos appeared imminent as modern economic values and divisiveness in social relations increasingly permeated their daily lives.

Sixteenth-century England was certainly a sacralized landscape, with church buildings, chapels, and shrines everywhere and religious disputation common. But the poor in particular were far less involved in church affairs than the gentry or prosperous freeholders and artisans. For most English men and women, the magical power of secular rituals and signs offered a more coherent explanation of reality than did the systematic theology of Christianity. Many of the laity understood the world around them in supernatural terms; magic, astrology, and divination continued to thrive. Literacy was uncommon, and the Bible remained inaccessible to the majority of the population; even devout dissenters seemed to need more than theological pieties to help them fathom the mysterious world around them.

English Society in the Sixteenth Century Order and hierarchy obsessed the members of Tudor society. In 1550, the poet Robert Crowley offered the following advice to freeholders:

> Have mind, therefore, thyself to hold
> Within the bounds of thy degree
> And then thou mayest ever be bold
> That God they Lord will prosper thee.[1]

Men and women were expected to keep their place, ensuring stability and security for everyone. Some social rankings were clearly etched in this world, others less precisely so. The peerage was tiny, containing fewer than one hundred individuals in 1600. Lords were born to their positions or annointed such by the Crown, which also selected knights from favored families. Below them were a mixture of esquires, justices of the peace, and other gentlemen, who with their families made up only around 2 percent of the population but controlled most of the country's wealth.

These people possessed enough landed wealth to allow them to pursue a life of leisure and conspicuous consumption. In this, they were far different from the majority of English men and women.

The famed English yeoman was clearly below the country gentlemen in status, but his precise position in the English social structure has always been difficult to pin down. The best indication that a farmer held yeoman status was the amount of land he held, whether by ownership or lease—generally fifty or more acres. Only these freeholders could survive price and harvest fluctuations, and substantial yeomen could even profit during hard times. Smaller farmers lived at the mercy of larger economic trends, while landless laborers fought a constant battle of survival, eking out an existence in one-room cottages. Village crafts- and tradespeople could belong to any of these three categories, depending upon their income and wealth. The status of town inhabitants was somewhat less clear. Even though these people owned no land, they could intermarry with the gentry or gain substantial profits through trade; some of them were as wealthy as the gentry. Great contrasts in diet, clothes, housing, and education helped remind everyone of these differences. The rich wore silks and linen, the poor leather and rags; the wealthy lived in mansions, the landless laborers in hovels.

Merchants and the gentry had personal and social ties that reached beyond their region and across the nation. Yet even they retained a strong sense of place, an identity with their town or county. Ordinary English men and women had few ties beyond their own locality. The typical rural family was a nuclear household, relatively isolated even from kin outside its own village. Neighborhoods were the central social group for most people, creating communities that relied on reciprocal economic obligations and a consensus of acceptable social behavior. It was a moral community, one that placed the needs of family and the group above market and economic standards of value. It was also a strongly paternalistic and deferential community. As long as the wealthy fulfilled their traditional duties and did not exploit the dependent relationship of freeholder and laborer, they received the respect and deference they expected from their positions. All members of this society came together in seasonal celebrations, marriages, church services, and other ritualistic observations characteristic of rural life.

People married relatively late in this world, generally in their mid- to late twenties. The community had to be able to provide a place for them before they could create their own families; only access to land would guarantee that they could support themselves without becoming a burden on others. Parents allowed their children considerable freedom in choosing a mate, and the bond between husbands and wives often went deep. Most families did their best to care for their children and were deeply attached to them emotionally. Infant mortality was high; about one-fourth of all children died before they were ten. But children did not work until they were placed in service or apprenticeship in their early teens, and even this separation was designed primarily to help prepare them for adulthood. Still, their lives could be frustrating and unsatisfying. Most children became servants, not apprentices, and had little control over their lives. Employed by masters who frequented the hiring fairs that took place all over England every fall, they were bound by contract for a year. Masters were obliged to feed, house, and clothe their charges, but they could also punish them with a whipping if the youths tried to leave before completing their term or committed any one of a number of indiscretions.

Violence was an unavoidable part of this world. Armed gangs prowled the countryside, while violent crime and even homicide were common. The Tudor preoccupation with order stemmed in part from the constant fear of rebellion, both by ambitious nobles and discontented rural laborers. There were two major rebellions

MAP 3.1: England in the Sixteenth-Century ❧

in 1549 alone, while in 1596, Oxfordshire villagers rioted against enclosure of their farmland.

Less dramatic but equally disruptive were a variety of long-term changes that shook English society to its very roots. The most obvious transformation was demographic: England had about 2.5 million inhabitants in the 1520s and more than 4 million by 1603. In Leicestershire County, the population increased by 58 percent between 1563 and 1603. This phenomenal rate of growth prompted a significant and disruptive movement of people across the countryside. Many left older agricultural areas for more pastoral regions with extensive commons, areas that were to become centers of the emerging putting-out system of household manufacturing.

Others flooded into London, which grew at a phenomenal rate. In 1520, only about seventy thousand people lived in the metropolis; by 1600, there were more than two hundred thousand. Englishmen complained that London was swallowing up other towns and cities; James I observed that "soon London will be all England."[2] At the same time, the rise in population and the influx of Spanish silver into the European economy promoted spiraling inflation. Between 1500 and 1600, the cost of goods and services rose up to five times in England.

Elizabeth's government embarked on a significant effort to diversify the economy, encouraging the growth of such industries as coal, lead, copper, and iron. The most important component of economic growth, though, lay in the small, idyllic creatures that increasingly graced the English countryside—sheep. The expansion of wool production and trade placed new strains on the English agricultural system. Landlords took advantage of the growing demand for clothing and used their political influence to force small farmers off the land and abridge the customary, long-term rental rights of open-field villages. Enclosure acts passed during the sixteenth century consolidated larger and larger areas of land that were subsequently fenced in for use as sheep pastures.

The "putting-out system" was the next step in this process, and it provided a modicum of security to many who had lost part of their livelihood as a result of enclosures. The system incorporated thousands of families in Yorkshire, East Anglia, and the West Country into the wool production industry. Merchants gave families raw wool, women and children spun the wool into thread, and men wove the thread into cloth. Other men dyed and shaped the cloth before it was finally sold. But the government tightly regulated even this alternative to poverty. The 1563 Statute of Artificers gave justices of the peace the power to fix wages and threatened imprisonment to those who paid or received higher amounts than the law allowed.

Demographic changes and inflation threatened landlords' positions, but they could just as easily profit from the growing need for land and from rising prices. The same changes forced freeholders to carefully evaluate their market opportunities at every turn and to optimize their economic opportunities; like the gentry, they bought and sold land with an eye to profit, and as a group they prospered. Small farmers did less well, hurt by inflationary rent increases and their precarious susceptibility to market influences; many of them fell into the ranks of landless wage laborers. The majority of the population, landless laborers and cottagers, experienced little but disaster throughout this period. They simply did not have the wherewithal to adapt to the fluctuations of the market.

Poverty now became a constant problem, no longer restricted to certain times in the life cycle—such as youth or old age—or to being the result of illness or natural disaster. Though it is impossible to generalize for the entire country, the years 1580 through 1630 saw a variety of events that adversely affected English men and women: periodic harvest failures, rent increases, government war taxes, and alternating periods of scarcity and abundance that pushed small farmers deeper into debt. Vagrants became a common sight on country byways. For weavers and town inhabitants in particular, the 1620s were the worst decade; angered as well by Charles I's interference in local affairs, many of these people left their homeland and joined the Puritan migration to New England. Social commentators lamented the worsening plight of the common English man and woman. Parliament passed Poor Laws in 1552, 1597, and 1601, confirming the parish as the unit of poor law administration and empowering justices of the peace to levy poor rates (taxes) to help support the growing number of unfortunates.

Indeed, the justices bore the greatest burden of governance in this society. They were the essential link between the local and central governments. Though gentlemen sought the office as an honor and it provided useful training for future membership in Parliament, its responsibilities were increasingly onerous. About all the central government could do was oversee their efforts through inspections by regional councils and such officials as assize judges, who visited the councils twice a year. Justices focused their efforts particularly on pauper, bastardy, and vagrancy cases and the regulation of unlicensed and disorderly alehouses. Many people resisted the expansion of governmental authority, often assaulting constables, bailiffs, and tax collectors. It is a tribute to the persistence of local authorities that by the 1640s, communities accepted the imposition of the poor rates as a way of raising funds to care for the displaced.

England was beginning to feel the effects of this transformation by the late sixteenth century, just as the Crown was identifying Spain as the national enemy and just as the country was about to embark upon its first serious efforts at American colonization. The juxtaposition of the three developments made it inevitable that they would influence and shape each other. Both the Spanish example and the shifting internal needs of English society inspired the first efforts to establish permanent settlements in the New World, and these early attempts suffered greatly from the inability of English colonizers to move beyond these initial limiting factors.

England and Europe Very much aware of the hostile world of nation-states that dominated sixteenth-century affairs, Queen Elizabeth formulated a foreign policy that preyed on the weaknesses of England's enemies but was cautious and moderate in its formal relations with France and Spain. Elizabeth's fears were firmly rooted. The confrontation between Catholicism and Protestantism was a reality in the world of the Counter-Reformation; Pope Pius V excommunicated the queen shortly after her accession to the throne. Elizabeth's greatest achievement, perhaps, was her merging of a moderate English Protestantism with a growing English nationalism. As the two became one, Elizabeth and the English people grew determined to end Spain's hegemony over the Western world. The queen secretly commissioned mariners John Hawkins and Francis Drake to prey upon Spanish shipping in the New World during the 1560s, 1570s, and 1580s. Drake in particular achieved considerable success in his ventures, terrorizing Spanish settlements and leading a twenty-five hundred-man invasion of the colonies in 1585. He also circumnavigated the globe from 1577 to 1580, acquiring enormous amounts of gold and silver for the Crown and receiving a knighthood from Elizabeth as a reward.

Philip II, king of Spain and Portugal, decided to bring the confrontation to a head. In 1588, he assembled a massive invasion fleet in Lisbon, the so-called Spanish Armada. He believed the fleet to be invincible and hoped English Catholics would rise against Elizabeth and support his invasion of the island. A combination of bad luck, poor weather, and England's smaller and more maneuverable ships conspired to wreck Philip's plans. Spain's power was already fading, but after this venture, it was clearer than ever that its position of world dominance was ending. England, on the other hand, was soon to emerge as the world's largest and most powerful empire.

England Moves Outward

A mid-century depression pushed England to reconsider its policies toward overseas colonies. To this point, regulated companies had conducted English overseas trade. In these organizations, merchants contributed to a common fund and shared in trading ventures, remaining free to pursue additional trade on their own without sharing their profits. Such activities often worked at cross-purposes to the interests of the company. The formation of the joint-stock company dramatically altered this situation. This new investment structure allowed merchants to share both risks and profits, but with limited liability. The companies bought and sold shares and paid dividends. The Crown also granted these groups of merchants-investors monopolies on certain areas of trade, rewarding loyal supporters. The government chartered the first such effort, the Muscovy Company, in 1555, giving the company a monopoly over the trade with Russia. The Crown also granted the Levant Company a monopoly over the spice and silk trade in the Mediterranean in the late 1570s and chartered the East India Company in 1599, granting it exclusive control over trade directly with Asia by sea.

These companies also provided a workable structure for colonial enterprises in the New World and freed the Crown from the burden of financing such ventures. A joint-stock company sent the fierce Yorkshire soldier and privateer Martin Frobisher on three voyages to North America in 1576, 1577, and 1578, all in search of a northwest passage. Though he sailed as far inland as the Hudson Strait, he was distracted by his search for gold and silver. He brought back several Eskimos and tons of black rock to England, but the Eskimos died and the black rock turned out to be fool's gold. From 1585 to 1587, John Davis followed up Frobisher's voyage to the Arctic region, also seeking a northwest passage with no success.

More important to English colonization than such expeditions was the massive promotional and propaganda effort for colonization mounted by a variety of individ-

❧ *Documents* ☙
Supporting English Colonization

Richard Hakluyt's *A Discourse on Western Planting* (1584) was one of the most influential of the many pamphlets supporting English colonization of the New World. This excerpt highlights both English concerns with unemployment and the anti-Spanish, anti-Catholic thrust of Elizabethan foreign policy.

> This enterprise may staye the spanish kinge from flowinge over all the face of that waste firme of America, yf wee seate and plante there in time. . . . Howe easie a matter may yt be to this Realme swarminge at this day with valiant youthes rustinge and hurtfull by lacke of employment, and havinge goodd makers of cable and of all sortes of cordage, and the best and moste connynge shipwrightes of the worlde to be Lordes of all those Sees, and to spoile Phillipp's Indian navye, and to deprive him of yerely passage of his Treasure into Europe, and consequently to abate the pride of Spaine and of the supporter of the great Antechriste of Rome. . . .

E. G. R. Taylor, ed., *The Original Writings & Correspondence of the Two Richard Hakluyts* (London: The Hakluyt Society, 1935), 314-5.

uals during the last decades of Elizabeth's reign. The two Richard Hakluyts, elder and younger (they were cousins), were the most successful of these pamphleteers, publishing a number of extremely influential pamphlets during the last twenty years of the century. The elder was an unsuccessful lawyer with a particular acute understanding of England's social and economic situation and substantial connections in the merchant community. The younger, a clergyman, apparently found the uncharted regions of the New World worthier of exploration than those of the soul; he spent his career publishing essays and collections of sailors' narratives that are the best source for an understanding of England's motives for colonization. Among the most important are several masterpieces of propaganda: the *Discourse on the Western Planting* (1584); *Divers Voyages Touching the Discovery of America* (1582); and *The Principall Navigations, Voyages and Discoveries of the English Nation* (1589).

Hakluyt published *Western Planting* in support of Sir Walter Raleigh's plans for a New World settlement; its arguments offer a vivid summary of England's expectations for prospective colonies. Norumbega, or the New World, would offer a reliable source of cheap raw materials and new crops, including timber for masts and ships and naval stores. Settlement there would provide a bulwark against Spanish expansion in North America, strengthen the British navy and bolster the shipping industry, and generate new jobs and businesses in England itself. New World settlement would also help solve the country's persistent struggles with poverty, offering new opportunities for soldiers, beggars, and surplus labor. Colonies would, finally, "inlarge the glory of the gospell . . . "[3] and spread English liberty as a counterforce against the repression of Spanish tyranny. As practical as many of these goals were, however, such expectations were unrealistically high. And England's only experience with colonization did little to leaven them.

Ireland

While Hakluyt provided justification for and spurred interest in settlement, Ireland gave England its concrete experience in colonization—with unfortunate results. The English viewed the Irish as a wild and barbaric people, a million inhabitants scattered in small villages practicing backward pastoral farming who had no intention of acceding to the ancient British claims to the island. According to one English commander, the Irish were "more uncivil, more uncleanly, more barbarous and more brutish in their customs and demeanors, than in any other part of the world that is known."[4] The English controlled a small area around Dublin and established semimilitary colonies in Ulster and Munster in the north. When the Irish began to rebel in the 1560s, the English responded with brutal force. The Crown appointed Sir Humphrey Gilbert military governor of Munster in 1569, and when rebellion broke out, he began to execute all the Irish he captured. On one occasion, he decapitated the enemy soldiers killed in battle and laid their heads on the ground leading up to his tent. His intent was to "bring great terror to the people when they saw the heads of their dead fathers, brothers, children, kinsfolk and friends, lie on the ground before their faces. . . ."[5] Lord Grey of Wilton, another English commander, ordered all captives of a captured Irish fortress killed despite a promise of clemency if they surrendered. This policy of occupation and repression, together with a profound ethnocentric sense of cultural superiority, helped shaped a North American colonial policy that bred disaster in its early years. Gilbert and Sir Walter Raleigh, both involved in the suppression of the Irish rebellion, were themselves the leaders of the first serious English colonization attempts.

Roanoke

In 1578, Queen Elizabeth granted Sir Humphrey Gilbert a patent to explore and occupy any lands in the New World not already occupied by Christian peoples; the charter also made him proprietor of all lands between Florida and Labrador. Gilbert's interest in America began in the 1560s, when he became convinced of the existence of a northwest passage to Asia. Like other Englishmen who sought to settle the early colonial south, he was influenced by the Spanish example and motivated by the prospects of easily recoverable mineral wealth. Unlike the Spanish, he hoped from the start to establish a colony that would serve as an agricultural refuge for the English poor, who would live as tenants under his feudal, manorial guidance. Gilbert sailed from England with seven ships and almost four hundred men in 1578, but storms forced the expedition to turn back without ever sighting America. Plagued by a lack of funding, he was not able to try again for five years. He left England in June 1583 with five ships and more than 250 men, pledging his family fortune to finance the project. He reached St. John's harbor in Newfoundland in August and then drifted southward, seeking a suitable spot for an outpost. Caught in a violent storm at sea, his ship, the *Squirrel,* sank beneath the waves with Gilbert on deck shouting to his men, "We are as near heaven by sea as by land . . . ," a paraphrase of a line from Sir Thomas More's *Utopia,* "The way to heaven out of all places is of like length and distance."[6] It seems unlikely that the terrified sailors found any solace in Gilbert's aristocratic faith.

Sir Walter Raleigh, Gilbert's half-brother, took up the cause of colonization with enthusiasm. Raleigh was a court favorite and a wealthy man. Elizabeth had granted him monopolies on sweet wines and the export of cloth, and he lived comfortably in a mansion, Durham House, which he made into a center for experts in cartography and exploration that attracted the most skilled names in England. Thomas Hariot wrote a text on navigation and Hakluyt the younger produced his most famous works under Raleigh's sponsorship. One central problem remained, though: sufficient capital to finance a settlement. To attract investors, Raleigh proposed an American base that would serve as a center for British attacks on Spanish ships. Elizabeth did not want to antagonize Spain unnecessarily by openly supporting the venture, but she did grant Raleigh a patent similar to that given to Gilbert.

In April 1584, Raleigh sent Philip Amadas and Arthur Barlowe with two ships to reconnoiter his proposed area of settlement. Amadas and Barlowe reached present-day North Carolina early in July and decided that the outer banks region offered an ideal settlement site. Barlowe described Roanoke Island and its inhabitants in almost Edenic terms: "We found the people most gentle, loving, and faithful, void of all guile, and treason, and such as lived after the manner of the golden age. The earth bringeth forth all things in abundance, as in the first creation, without toil or labor."[7] Such statements tell us more about the English and their expectations than they do about the Indians or Roanoke. The only English to make any real attempt to understand the natives were John White and Thomas Hariot, two of the experts chosen to accompany the expedition. They befriended two of the local Indians, Wanchese and Manteo, whom Raleigh brought back to London for the edification of the court gentry. White and Hariot also spent the 1585–86 winter living among the Indians of Chesapeake Bay. There, White sketched the scenes of Indian life that have since become so famous. Raleigh named the area Virginia, after the Virgin Queen, and she rewarded him with a knighthood. Encouraged, Raleigh commissioned Hakluyt to memorialize the queen in his *Western Planting,* but Elizabeth was not ready to provide further financial assistance for expensive colonization attempts.

Again forced to fall back on his own resources, Raleigh put together a group of specialists in botany, mapmaking, drawing, and other skills to further explore the area. He sent them to Roanoke in 1585 under the leadership of Richard Grenville and Ralph Lane. His choice of leadership could not have been worse. Both men were veterans of the Irish campaigns; both had deserved reputations for pride, greed, and violence. Grenville, for instance, had an amazing habit of breaking wineglasses with his teeth and swallowing the broken glass. Other factors also helped seal the fate of the expedition. The island lacked fertile soil and deep-water harbors, and Raleigh's plans envisioned a military settlement of young males, modeled on the Irish expeditions with which he was so familiar.

Disaster courted the expedition from the beginning. The provision ship ran aground, ruining many of the supplies. The colonists arrived too late in the season to plant crops. They had to rely on the Indians for food. The Indians had not planned for such a drain on their resources, and their own limited supplies became depleted. Grenville did not hesitate to use force against the Indians from the beginning, fearing that any show of weakness would only invite retribution. When he lost one of his silver cups, he accused the Indians of stealing it and burned one of their villages in retaliation. When Lane sought the cooperation of an Indian leader, he kidnapped the leader's favorite son as a hostage.

An expected April 1586 shipment of supplies failed to arrive, while Lane became convinced that he faced a growing threat from the Roanoke tribes. At the same time, familiarity with Europeans made the influential Wanchese increasingly suspicious of English motives, and he convinced the chief, Wingina, to let the English starve. Fearing the Indians were planning to attack, Lane decided to launch a "preventive" strike in June 1586. The English killed Wingina and displayed his head on a post. The colony thus succeeded in destroying its relations with the Indians, and its food was all but gone. The supply ships finally arrived a few weeks later, but the settlers had already deserted the colony, sailing back to England with Francis Drake, who had landed at the colony hoping to restock his ships after a series of privateering raids on the Spanish.

But Raleigh was not ready to give up. In 1587, he named John White deputy governor and prepared to try again. This time, the settlers included men, women, and children and promises of five hundred acres of land for each family and a borough form of government for the colony. Raleigh instructed White to find an appropriate spot further north, in the more suitable Chesapeake region. But when the expedition reached Roanoke Island, the pilot, Simon Fernandes, refused to take them farther; he hated White and preferred to be free to continue his privateering. Wanchese, witnessing their return, swore they would not be permitted to settle there.

The new colonists included White's own daughter, Eleanor Dare, and her husband, Ananias; their daughter, Virginia, was the first English citizen born in the New World. White decided to return to England to inform Raleigh of the undesirable turn of events, leaving just after his granddaughter was born. On hearing the news, Raleigh authorized a new fleet to be assembled, but the threat of the Spanish Armada led Elizabeth to stop all ships from leaving the realm. Raleigh became involved in other projects, and only White remained concerned enough to continue to fight for a relief expedition. It was 1590 before he was finally able to return. On August 18, he landed on the island and found the settlement deserted, the only sign of English habitation being the word *CROATAN* carved on a tree. A Maltese cross would have been the sign that the colonists had left the island in distress. There was no cross, and the settlers had carefully buried their belongings, suggesting that they had expected to return. *Croatan* was the name of Manteo's village on Croatan

Island, the last remaining group of Indians in the area friendly to the English. But when White prepared to sail to the Indian village, a storm came up and forced his ship to return home. The fate of the "lost colony" remains a mystery. The best guesses of modern scholars are that the colony's survivors moved to the Elizabeth River near the friendly Chesapeake Indians, intermarried, and learned Indian ways but were eventually wiped out by Algonquians led by Powhatan, along with the entire Chesapeake tribe, on the eve of English settlement at Jamestown.

Hiatus And Renewal

While two decades passed before the English would make another colonization attempt, the New World was not forgotten in London. Roanoke, and the Chesapeake region in general, had impressed the English with its natural beauty and its plentiful fish, game, and natural resources. Dozens of streams and rivers ran into the bay, many navigable. The bay's waters were rich in nitrogen and phosphorus and filled with plankton, bacteria, and the fish that fed off them. The James River was larger than the Thames, and the Potomac longer than the Seine. The tidewater was lush and green, with trees that rose seventy feet before a single branch appeared. Wild fruit trees abounded, and fields were filled with wild raspberries and strawberries.

So the English maintained contact. Captain Christopher Newport explored the area during the 1590s, Bartholomew Gilbert and Martin Pring visited it in 1602 before going on to New England, and Capt. George Weymouth cruised the coast in 1605. All reaffirmed the potential for great profit, the abundance of fish and timber, the healthful climate, and the high expectations for raw materials. The Indians were even viewed as a potential labor force.

The continued interest in the region finally reached fruition in 1605, when Richard Hakluyt, Sir John Popham (Lord Chief Justice of England), and Sir Thomas Smythe drafted a charter that proposed a "venture" to Virginia; the petitioning group included merchants from London, Plymouth, and Bristol. The king granted the charter on April 10, 1606. The Virginia Company, as it was called, consisted of two privately funded joint-stock companies. One, dominated by Plymouth and Bristol merchants (the Plymouth Company), was granted the land between thirty-eight and forty-five degrees latitude, from the Potomac River to Maine. The other, comprised of the London merchants (the London Company), received rights to the area between thirty-four and forty-one degrees latitude, or the Cape Fear River to New York Bay. The overlapping area, present-day Pennsylvania, New Jersey, Delaware, and Maryland, was open to settlement by either group, provided they did not locate within one hundred miles of each other. The charter granted future colonists all the rights and liberties of citizens living in England. These were more than just joint-stock companies, however. The king retained the power to appoint a royal council of fourteen to maintain overall control over the enterprises, while each company would establish a council of thirteen, headed by an elected president, to control affairs in America.

The Virginia Company immediately set about planning its first settlement, trumpeting its intentions in sermons, broadsides, and ballads all over the country. It issued instructions to the first group of settlers to establish themselves on an island in a navigable river, for protection against the Spanish. They were also to construct a town, to clear land and prepare for planting, and to explore the general region. The directors chose Bartholomew Gosnold and Christopher Newport to lead the expedition at sea, and they ordered that the names of the seven councillors who were to rule the colony remain secret until the group landed. The goals and expectations for the colony were hopelessly optimistic, reflecting the curse of early English colonies—the gap between vision and reality in the New World.

On December 20, 1606, three ships set sail—the *Susan Conant,* the *Discovery,* and the *Godspeed.* A total of 105 adventurous souls were on board; about half were gentlemen, the others a mix of laborers, craftsmen, and artisans. The voyage was typically unpleasant for the early seventeenth century, and the gentlemen quarreled constantly among themselves. The legendary John Smith, in fact, was arrested and confined for the duration of the trip for pushing one future councillor a bit too far. The small fleet reached Cape Henry on the southern point of Chesapeake Bay on April 26, 1607. On the very first day, the colonists had a brief skirmish with a group of Chesapeake Indians, though the inhabitants of another village later welcomed them. After searching for a suitable settlement site and rejecting at least one other alternative (Archer's Hope), they finally landed at Jamestown peninsula on May 13. Surrounded by water on three sides with a deep channel offshore, the peninsula seemed easily defensible and an ideal location. The settlers immediately constructed a fort and a triangular stockade. Unfortunately, they had chosen a low, swampy area that was deep within territory the Paspakegh Indians considered their tribal hunting grounds and so unhealthy that the Indians would not live there. The names of the councillors were revealed, and among the seven were John Smith and Edward Wingfield, Smith's chief accuser during the voyage. The group elected Wingfield president.

The group settled in quickly, clearing trees and unloading the ships. They commented favorably on the environment, noting the waters full of fish and seafood and the abundance of birds and animals, including flocks of five hundred turkeys and strings of ducks seven miles long flying overhead. Smith observed, "The mildnesse of the aire, the fertilitie of the soile, and the situation of the rivers as so propitious to the nature and use of man as no place is more convenient for pleasure, profit, and mans sustenance."[8] But there was one part of this landscape which the English were not so well prepared to deal with—the Indians.

Indian-English Contact

Rejecting the Spanish approach, the Virginia Company hoped to bring the gospel to the Indians, to civilize them and "to cover their naked miserie, with civill use of foode, and cloathing, and to traine them by gentle meanes, to those manuall artes and skill, which they so much affect, and doe admire to see in us."[9] But the colonists had gotten off on the wrong foot by settling in Paspahegh territory. They claimed the Indians had given them the land through signs, but the Indians themselves had left that meeting clearly very angry, and they soon began harassing the young settlement. Since there were at least two hundred Indian villages in the tidewater at the time, the Indians had the initial advantage. The English settlements were tiny outposts surrounded by Powhatan and his allies.

In 1607, Powhatan was a healthy, active chief in his sixties who dominated the members of his confederacy and controlled some thirty territories and fourteen thousand Algonquians. He undoubtedly regarded the whites with some caution, but he soon came to value their trading goods and their potential assistance as allies against his enemies. He was not easily cowed, and he always received the English at his own capital, surrounded by a bodyguard of forty bowmen, some of his one hundred wives, and his chief councillors.

From the beginning, Powhatan and the other Indians believed the English were inferior. These strange foreigners did not seem to hunt or fish, had arrived without

❧ *Documents* ❧
Utopian Expectations

European expectations of the New World remained unrealistic almost throughout the colonial period, but the London Company was perhaps the most naive of all. The first selection below reflects the company's utopian views of both Indians and the land. The second document is a listing of the first settlers at Jamestown. Study this list closely. Who is included? Who is not?

> The country it selfe is . . . commendable and hopefull in every way, the ayre and clymate most sweete and wholsome, much warmer than England, and very agreeable to our Natures: It is inhabited with wild and savage people, that live and lie up and downe in troupes like heards of Deare in a Forrest: they have no law but nature, their apparell skinnes of beasts, but most goe naked . . . they are generally very loving and gentle, and doe entertaine and relieve our people with great kindnesse . . . the land yeeldeth naturallie for the sustentation of man, aboundance of fish, both scale and shell: of land and water fowles, infinite store: of Deere, Kaine and Fallow, Stags, Coneys, and Hares, with many fruits and rootes good for meate.
>
> There are valleyes and plaines streaming with sweete Springs, like veynes in a naturall bodie: there are hills and mountaines making a sensible proffer of hidden trasure, never yet searched: the land is full of mineralles, plentie of woods (the wants of England). . . . But of this that I have said, if bare nature be so amiable in its naked kind, what may we hope, when Arte and Nature both shall joyne, and strive together, to give best content to man and beast?

Robert Johnson's *Nova Brittania* (1609), in David B. Quinn, ed., *New American World: A Documentary History of North America to 1612,* 5 vols. (New York: Arno Press and Hector Bye, 1979) 1:238–9.

THE VIRGINIA COMPANY LIST OF ADVENTURERS, 1607

The names of them that were the first planters, were these following.

Councel

Master Edward Maria Wingfield.	Captaine John Ratliffe.
Captaine Bartholomew Gosnoll.	Captaine John Martin.
Captaine John Smith.	Captaine George Kendall.

Gentlemen

Master Robert Hunt *Preacher*.	Robert Fenton.
Master George Percie.	Robert Ford.
Anthony Gosnoll.	William Bruster.
George Flower.	Edward Harrington.
Captaine Gabriell Archer.	Dru Pickhouse.

Thomas Jacob.

John Brookes.

Ellis Kingston.

Thomas Sands.

Benjamin Beast.

Jehu Robinson.[1]

Thomas Mouton.

Eustace Clovill.

Stephen Halthrop.

Kellam Throgmorton.

Edward Morish.

Nathaniell Powell.

Edward Browne.

Robert Behethland.

John Penington.

Jeremy Alicock.

George Walker.

Thomas Studley.

Richard Crofts.

Nicholas Houlgrave.

Thomas Webbe.

||John Waller.

John Short.

William Tankard.

William Smethes.

Francis Snarsbrough.

Richard Simons.

Edward Brookes.

Richard Dixon.

John Martin.

Roger Cooke.

Anthony Gosnold.

Thomas Wotton, *Chirurgian*.

John Stevenson.

Thomas Gore.

Henry Adling.

Francis Midwinter.

Richard Frith.

Carpenters

William Laxon.

Edward Pising.

Thomas Emry.

Robert Small.

Labourers

John Laydon.

William Cassen.

George Cassen.

Thomas Cassen.

William Rodes.

William White.

Old Edward.

Henry Tavin.

George Goulding.

John Dods.

William Johnson.

William Unger.

James Read, *Blacksmith*.

Jonas Profit, *Sailer*.

Thomas Cowper, *Barber*.

William Garrett, *Bricklayer*.

Edward Brinto, *Mason*.

William Love, *Taylor*.

Nicholas Scot, *Drummer*.

William Wilkinson, *Chirurgian*.

Samuell Collier, *boy*.

Nathaniell Pecock, *boy*.

James Brumfield, *boy*.

Richard Mutton, *boy*.

With divers others to the number of 100.

John Smith, "The Generall History of Virginia, New-England, and the Summer Isles . . . ," (1624), in Philip L. Barbour, ed., *The Complete Works of Captain John Smith,* 3 vols. (Chapel Hill, NC: IEAHC, The University of North Carolina Press, 1986), 2:140–2.

women, and died by the scores while settling on land the Indians themselves had little use for. Powhatan launched a small attack after the English built a palisade at Jamestown, sending almost four hundred warriors to assault the still-unfinished structure on May 26. Ships' cannon and guns drove the Indians off. Two Englishmen died in the attack, and both sides were frightened by what they learned about each other from the encounter. Powhatan turned to diplomacy in mid-June, informing the English of his desire for an alliance and providing them with food throughout the summer. Even with this assistance, half of the colonists died from illness during the summer. At the same time, Powhatan had not completely abandoned his more aggressive policy. Three Englishmen died in Indian ambushes during those months, and on December 12, the Pamunkeys killed two more, capturing

MAP 3.2: Early Settlement in the Chesapeake ❧

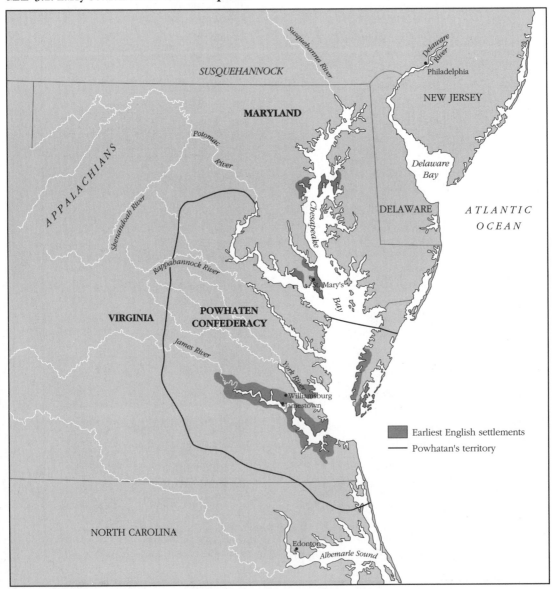

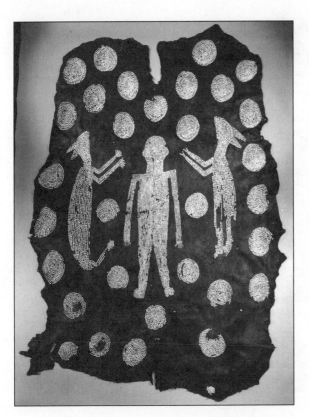

Powhatan Ceremonial cloak, given to Captain Christopher Newport in 1608 (Courtesy, Ashmolean Museum, Oxford). ❧

Smith in the process. Powhatan took advantage of the circumstances to ritually adopt Smith and make him *werowance* of his newest allies—the English!

The English countered with their own ceremonial assertion of hegemony in October 1608. Capt. Christopher Newport sailed up the James River to the falls at present-day Richmond. Powhatan met Newport and warned him to travel no further, or he would be attacked by Powhatan's enemies, the Monacans. At Powhatan's capital on the north bank of the York River—Werowocomoco—the two negotiated an agreement for revenge against the Chesapeake, the tribe who had attacked the English when they first landed in April 1607. Newport then gave Powhatan a basin, a bed, and a scarlet cloak, but Powhatan would not kneel to accept an offered crown, by which Newport hoped to claim him (and his territory) as a subject of the king. "At last by leaning hard on his shoulders," Smith noted, "he a little stooped, and Newport put the Crowne on his head."[10] In exchange, Powhatan gave the Englishman a pair of his old moccasins and his own fur mantle. After plying the Indians with the staples of English trade—glass beads, pocket knives, and scissors—Newport then planted a cross on an island in the river, claiming the area in the name of the king. When queried on the nature of this suspicious ceremony, he told Powhatan that the two arms of the cross represented their own two persons, the joining of the arms a symbol of the friendship between them.

Powhatan's policy during the first decade of English settlement seems fairly clear. He had, first, to limit English expansion and movement and to keep them out of his own political affairs. But he also needed their friendship for the trading goods he desired and as allies against both his enemies west of the fall line and the more obstreperous members of his confederacy. Thus, as historian James Axtell has noted, he "vacillated between killing and kindness."[11] Those tribes nearest white

Captain John Smith (1580–1631), engraving by
Simon Van de Passe. ❧

settlements had mostly negative experiences with the newcomers and were generally the least friendly. But either from kindness or for their own ends, the Indians
often gave the colonists food—for free or for desirable trading goods, such as
hatchets, copper, and highly sought-after blue glass beads. They also taught them
basic Indian agricultural techniques, perhaps hoping the English would stop draining their own finite resources if they could provide for themselves. Powhatan
ordered the Paspahegh to stop harassing Jamestown and to give the inhabitants
much needed food, and on one occasion, he sent his daughter Pocahontas to the
settlement to heal some of the wounds between the two groups. He also asked that
an English-style house be built for him, undoubtedly a request that greatly pleased
the ethnocentric settlers. Yet the old chief was just as capable of seeking control in
other, more violent ways. When seventeen colonists deserted to the Kecoughtans
seeking food, Powhatan had them killed and their mouths stuffed with bread—just
to make sure the English got the point.

Powhatan's only true equal among the English was Capt. John Smith. The son of a
West Country tenant farmer, Smith ran away from his position as an apprentice at age
sixteen to go to war. He became a professional mercenary, fighting duels in
Transylvania and Turks in Hungary, and escaping to Russia from several years of slavery in Istanbul. He was also a skilled cartographer. All of these qualities made him a
much-sought-after recruit for the Jamestown expedition despite his difficult personality. Smith had little patience with gentlemen who knew nothing of real work or fighting. During the colony's first year, while others sought instant wealth and did little
else, Smith explored the James, York, and Chickahominy rivers. He also pursued an
aggressive policy toward the Indians, training soldiers in their language, customs, and
style of fighting. He and his commanders were ruthless in their dealings with the local
tribes. On one occasion, near the town of Pamunkey, Smith and fifteen soldiers found
themselves surrounded by several hundred Indians. Challenging their leader

Opechancanough to hand-to-hand combat, Smith grabbed the Indian by his scalp lock and held a gun to his chest. The Indians got the message, and the English had no trouble during the rest of the day's trading. Opechancanough, though, would not forget Smith's humiliating treatment; it was he who organized and led the 1622 uprising.

Gold, Disease, and Starvation

While the English and the Indians were working out their perceptions and expectations of each other, the fledgling settlement was teetering on the brink of disaster. The first group of colonists contained no farmers, and the many gentlemen spent most of their time looking for gold rather than growing food. They were not used to work of any kind. Many others during the first years came from an England, were a depressed agricultural economy and a population explosion forced laborers to share what work there was. These people were simply not used to working very hard. The company, too, apparently expected that the colonists would live like their counterparts in England's woodland and pasture regions, spending only a portion of their time tending small garden plots and caring for their cattle and sheep. They would devote the remainder of their efforts to spinning, weaving cloth, and extracting the valuable ores assumed to lie just beneath the surface of Virginia's rich soil. There were, unfortunately, no riches to extract, and the settlers devoted precious little time to farming.

John Smith captures King of the Pamunkeys, from John Smith, *Discovery of Virginia* (1609). The didactic scene depicts a smaller Smith using English technology (his pistol) and, presumably, English intelligence, to capture the physically more imposing Indian. ❧

❧ *Documents* ❧
The Struggle to Survive

Early Virginia settlers faced seemingly insurmountable difficulties even in simply surviving. The first selection below is John Smith's famous description of the "starving time." The document tells us as much about John Smith, though, as it does about the terrible conditions that plagued the colony during the winter of 1609-1610. The second document, from Richard Frethorne's letter home to his parents in 1623, shows how little things had changed over a decade later.

> Now we all found the losse of Captaine *Smith,* yea his greatest maligners could now curse his losse: as for corne provision and contribution from the Salvages, we had nothing but mortall wounds, with clubs and arrowes; as for our Hogs, Hens, Goats, Sheepe, Horse, or what lived, our commanders, officers and Salvages daily consumed them. . . till all was devoured; then swords, armes, pieces, or any thing, wee traded with the Salvages, whose cruell fingers were so oft imbrewed in our blouds. . . , there remained not past sixtie men, women and children, most miserable and poore creatures; and those were preserved for the most part, by roots, herbes, acornes, walnuts, berries, now and then a little fish: they that had starch in these extremities, made no small use of it; yea even the very skinnes of our horses.
>
> Nay, so great was our famine, that a Salvage we slew and buried, the poorer sort tooke him up againe and eat him; and so did divers

Provisions spoiled quickly in the damp climate, and throughout the early years, malnutrition was a persistent problem. Despite the frequent gifts of food from the Indians, most of the English suffered from niacin and protein deficiencies. Disease was rampant; typhoid, dysentery, and saltwater poisoning were near-universal afflictions. The brackish water of the James poisoned the shallow wells the settlers dug. By September 1607, half of the original colonists were dead. Newport returned with new settlers and provisions in January 1608, but none of the recruits was a farmer, and only thirty-eight settlers remained alive from the first group. Fire ravaged the fort shortly thereafter, and rats consumed much of the new food.

Almost in desperation, the council elected a somewhat reluctant John Smith president. Smith's success was such that, had he remained in the colony, the suffering and failures of the coming years might have been avoided. He imposed military discipline on the settlers, organizing them into work gangs and drilling them in the use of firearms. He had them build new housing and gather corn for the winter. When the supply proved to be rotten, he dispersed the settlers across the landscape, preventing malnutrition and another famine by moving them closer to healthier, fresh-water streams. Though many hated him for it, Smith established order and kept the settlers alive. He lectured the reluctant from the Bible, remind-

one another boyled and stewed with roots and herbs: And one amongst the rest did kill his wife, powdered [i.e., salted] her, and had eaten part of her before it was knowne; for which hee was executed, as hee well deserved: now whether shee was better roasted, boyled, or carbonado'd [i.e., grilled], I known not; but of such a dish as powdered wife I never heard of.

John Smith, "The Generall History of Virginia, New England, and the Summer Isles . . . ," (1624), in Philip L. Barbour, ed., *The Complete Works of Captain John Smith*, 3 vols. (Chapel Hill, NC: IEAHC, The University of North Carolina Press, 1986), 2:232.

Loving and kind father and mother, my most humble duty remembered to you hoping in God of your good health, as I my self as at the making hereof, this is to let you understand that I your Child am in a most heavy Case by reason of the nature of the Country is such that it Causeth much sickness, as the crurvy and the bloody flux [dysentery], and divers other diseases, which maketh the body very poor, and Weak, and when we are sick there is nothing to Comfort us; for since I came out of the ship, I never ate any thing but peas and loblollie (that is water gruel). . . [we] must Work hard both early and late for a mess of water gruel, and a mouthful of bread, and beef. . . people cry out day, and night, Oh that they were in England without their limbs and would not care to lose any limb to be in England again, yea though they beg from door to door, for we live in fear of the Enemy every hour. . . .

Susan M. Kingsbury, ed., *The Records of the Virginia Company*, 4 vols. (Washington, DC: Government Printing Office, 1906–1935), 4:58.

ing them that "he who does not work shall not eat."[12] Even Smith, though, expected only four hours of labor a day. In October 1609, he was injured in an accidental gunpowder explosion and forced to return to England; he never saw Virginia again.

The winter and spring of 1609 were relatively healthy times for the colony. By mid-August, after six ships brought 250 new settlers, the colony reached the apex of its early population—381 colonists. But the new arrivals also brought plague and typhus with them, and the summer heat brought a renewal of disease and the death of fifty more Jamestown inhabitants. The colony also began to pay the price for Smith's aggressive Indian policies. The Indians had by now acquired several muskets, metal hatchets, and some fifty swords. From late summer until Smith's final departure, Powhatan's warriors killed about one hundred settlers. From November to May, the Indian leader essentially lay siege to the tiny settlement at Jamestown. This was the colony's infamous "starving time," when the entrapped settlers were driven to desperate measures to survive. One-hundred colonists died from famine and disease, another thirty-three were killed by Indians, while thirty-seven deserted for better climes. In May, there were only ninety Englishmen left alive in the colony. Late that month, Sir Thomas Gates arrived with 134 new recruits, already weakened from being shipwrecked in the Bermudas. Gates reluctantly decided to abandon the colony.

Commitment Renewed

On June 10, 1610, as the survivors set sail down the James, the newly appointed governor, Thomas West (Lord De la Warr) hove into view, his ship carrying 150 new colonists and a new charter. He ordered the group to turn back and put the colony under martial law. The Charter of 1609 implemented a complete reorganization of the Virginia Company. The Crown was eager to lessen its own involvement, and the charter abolished the Royal Council and replaced it with a council elected annually by the stockholders. The company could now make its own laws and regulations, provided they did not contradict English law. It also became a true joint-stock venture; shares were sold to the public for as little as twelve pounds, or about a year's wages for an unskilled worker. The directors anticipated the first distribution of profits would take place in 1616, and they initiated a widespread publicity campaign to attract prospective shareholders.

Gates, meanwhile, began a military counteroffensive, drawing his tactics from the Irish occupation—deception, surprise, ambush, the murder of captives, and the destruction of entire villages. In August, he led an assault on the Paspahegh town, killing eighteen Indians, burning houses, cutting down the corn, and putting the chief's children to death—"which was effected by Throweinge them overboard and shoteinge

Table 1 ⅍ Population growth in early Virginia

Date	Population
May 1607	104 (first landing)
October 1608	200 (from new arrivals)
Summer 1609	131 (death from disease)
August 1609	381 (from new arrivals)
October 1609	280 (death from Indian attacks)
May 1610	90 ("starving time")
June 1610	375 (from new arrivals)
December 1610	250 (death from disease and Indian attacks)
Late March 1611	152 (departures; death from Indian attacks)
Early May 1611	482 (from new arrivals)
August 1611	752 (from new arrivals)
December 1611	600 (death from Indian attacks)
May 1615	400
1619	700 (approximate)
1619–22	Sandys sends out 3,570 settlers
1622 (before Indian Attack)	1,240
1625	1,300
1629	2,600
1632	3,200
1634	5,200
1644	8,000

Adapted from information in J. Frederick Fausz, "An 'Abundance of Blood Shed on Both Sides': England's First Indian War, 1609–1614," *Virginia Magazine of History and Biography*, 98 (1990), 55–56, and Edmund S. Morgan, *American Slavery, American Freedom: The Ordeal of Colonial Virginia* (New York: W. W. Norton & Company, 1975), 404.

Pocahantos (1595–1617), painted while she was living in London. ❧

outt their Braynes in the water."[13] Captain George Percy was barely able to stop them from burning the chief's wife at the stake; instead, she was put to death by the sword, regarded as a more humane way of execution. There were many such scenes, as the English continued to expand their settlements and lay out new plantations.

Yet success continued to elude the colonists. By the end of the year, disease had taken the lives of one hundred of the new settlers, and the Indians had killed another twenty-five. Fighting continued throughout 1611. De la Warr left in March 1611, and almost six hundred new colonists arrived that spring and summer. The new governor, Sir Thomas Dale, implemented a military code that meted out severe punishment to those who refused to work. He ordered everyone to work in the fields from 6 to 10 A.M. and 2 to 4 P.M. and to devote the rest of the day to repairing their cottages and cultivating their own garden plots. The *Lawes Divine, Morall and Martiall* (Dale's Laws) introduced the death penalty for rape, adultery, lying, blasphemy, and a variety of other crimes, including killing any domestic animal. Dale also began to expand the settlement, sending three hundred men up the James to establish the town of Henrico, with fifty houses and a church. He understood that more extensive dispersal of the population would help prevent future health problems and serve as a better defense against the Indians. Still, another 150 colonists died during the last six months of the year, felled by disease or Indians. And in the spring of 1612, Dale punished a group of settlers who had run away to live with the Indians, hanging some and shooting others.

The next two years were relatively quiet. Dale's policy of dispersing settlements began to pay dividends in improved health conditions, and a shaky truce remained in place between whites and Indians. A new charter in 1612 allowed the company to run an annual lottery to raise money and granted it a seven-year exemption from customs duties. But once again, the colony's governing board in London intervened. The directors still viewed the Chesapeake as an earthly paradise, blaming all the colony's problems on lazy settlers and a few intemperate Indians and whites. In early 1614, they demanded a new offensive against the Indians. In March, Dale led a force of 150 into Pamunkey territory in the most ambitious campaign yet. Luckily, both sides realized the dangers of continued conflict, and negotiations prevented further deaths.

The 1614 marriage of John Rolfe and Powhatan's daughter Pocahontas finally brought an end to the war. After Dale kidnapped Pocahontas in 1613, the young Indian woman converted to Christianity. She later went to England with her husband and son in 1616. A court celebrity, she stimulated interest in and financial backing for the company's venture, but she died in England and is buried at Gravesend in London. The wedding failed, moreover, to cement an alliance between whites and Indians. Indeed, Powhatan viewed the marriage as a "gift" of his favorite daughter to the enemy, the terms for peace as a surrender of the English to his own authority.

By 1614, the colony's original servants had worked off their terms of indenture, and they needed an inducement to remain. Dale gave all those who had settled prior to 1612 three acres of land in exchange for an annual rent of twelve bushels of corn and a month's service to the company. To encourage families to migrate to the colony, he offered them twelve acres of improved land rent-free for a year. It was not enough to better the colony's situation. Most of the new settlers grew tobacco, not food, and by 1616, death and remigration had reduced the population to 350. The company could not grant the stockholders the promised divided of one hundred acres of cleared land; instead, it offered them fifty acres—but only if they bought additional stock.

Tobacco

Virginia's salvation did not come from company reorganizations or new ways of attracting settlers. In the end, the English found their own version of Spanish bullion, and organic equivalent of gold and silver. Tobacco had been widely used in Europe as a mild narcotic since it had first been brought to Portugal from Florida in the 1560s. Sir Francis Drake brought a boatload of what was referred to as the "jovial weed" to England from the West Indies in 1586, and it became more than just a "medicinal" drug. Tobacco use became a social addiction among the English upper class, and young gentlemen learned such smoking tricks as the "Ring," the "Whiffle," the "Gulp," and the "Retention." Tobacco's popularity persisted despite the opposition of King James I himself, who published an anonymous pamphlet, *Counterblast to Tobacco,* in which he described smoking as "a custom loathsome to the eye, hateful to the nose, harmful to the brain, dangerous to the lungs, and in the black stinking fumes thereof, nearest resembling the horrible stygian smoke of the pit that is bottomless."[14]

In 1612, John Rolfe introduced a Trinidad strain of tobacco to Virginia that was more palatable to English tastes than the native variety. He shipped the first four barrels of cured leaf to England in 1614, and within three years, the colony was shipping fifty thousand pounds annually. Planters now organized their lives around tobacco, isolating themselves on plantations scattered along the colony's rivers to provide easy transportation of their crop to market and reinvesting profits into tools, labor, and land so they could grow still more. The "jovial weed" consumed everyone's energy as tobacco prices rose to dizzying heights in the 1620s. Any planter who could stay alive and acquire a few servants could get rich in a year. Such men paid little attention to physical luxury; their homes were ramshackle hovels, and they spent their free time in the many taverns that appeared in private houses. This was, in one historian's view, a "boom town" mentality—instant wealth was the goal, at any cost. The village-centered, close-knit communities that dotted the New England landscape were nowhere to be seen in early Virginia.

Tobacco rewarded the planter with a high yield per acre, could be stored for a long time if properly cured, and could be grown fairly easily. Planters made their initial labor even easier by acquiring already cleared Indian fields through purchase or other means and by adopting the Indian method of slashing and burning wooded areas as they expanded westward. Virginians possessed few plows, and those they had could barely scratch the soil's surface. Hence, they relied on servants using broad hoes to prepare and cultivate the soil, though even these could penetrate only to a depth of about six inches. Once planted, the seedlings required constant attention for nine months of the year. The essential repeated turning of the light, alluvial soil fostered erosion, and the lack of fertilizers or crop rotation—aside from an occasional fallow period—hastened soil exhaustion. Virginians sowed the average field (three to five acres) with tobacco for only three or four years, then grew wheat and corn for a few more years, and finally moved on to new land, allowing the original field to return to forest and lie fallow for twenty years. Planters also faced dangers from disease and weather. But the rewards were great. Most planters sent four or five hogheads of tobacco a year to London, each weighing six hundred to nine hundred pounds. Prices were extremely high at first, then stabilized at lower levels in the late 1630s, holding their own until the depression of the 1660s and 1670s, when chronic overproduction began to take its toll.

Sandys and the Charter of 1618

By 1618, a group of smaller investors, led by Sir Edwin Sandys, had grown frustrated with the lack of progress and moved to completely reorganize the company. The Great Charter of 1618 reflected Sandys's realization that the colony needed to be set on firmer economic and administrative footing. To attract more settlers, Sandys relaxed martial law and promised a representative assembly. He sent more than one hundred women and hundreds of artisans to the colony; from 1618 to 1622, the company sent out about thirty-five hundred new colonists, mostly young, single males in their teens and early twenties. The company set aside lands to support an Anglican ministry, raised money to build a school for Indians, and made plans to establish a university. Sandys announced that all "Old Planters," those who had arrived in the colony before the spring of 1616, would receive one hundred acres each when their terms of service expired, and those who were shareholders would get an additional hundred acres for each share. Colonists who had arrived after 1616 received fifty acres, and anyone who arrived henceforth and paid their own way would receive a "headright" of fifty acres, along with fifty more acres for each person they transported at their own expense. Sandys also offered an alternative to servitude; those who migrated at company expense would work as tenants for seven years and would receive fifty acres at the end of that term.

Sandys also poured his efforts into economic experimentation. He sent over experts to develop an iron industry, Germans to build a sawmill, Italian glassblowers, shipbuilders, and even a Frenchman who claimed he could extract salt from seawater. Tenants working on company land experimented with growing cotton, sugar cane, oranges, lemons, pineapples, potatoes, and even silkworms from Italy. Sandys assumed that the colonists had learned enough to at least provide themselves with food, and he went out of his way to discourage tobacco production. He forbade company tenants to plant it, and he stipulated that the colony allow no more than one hundred pounds per person to be produced annually.

The results of this enormous outpouring of energy were mixed at best. The promised representative assembly did meet during the summer of 1619 and did enact a variety of laws. But the colony failed to show any signs of growth or economic health. The artisans and craftsmen the company sent were ill prepared to cope with the disease-ridden environment, and Sandys and his associates had failed to provide adequate housing and food for the new settlers. Only about a quarter of the settlers sent over between 1618 and 1622 survived. Company officials used tenants to work on their private lands rather than on the company plantations they had been recruited to develop and the colonists continued to grow tobacco, ultimately destroying any hope of a stable, orderly community. A competitive, materialistic culture in which profit was sought above all else continued to dominate the Virginia landscape. Frustrated with the lack of progress and angered at the internal squabbling that dominated company affairs, James revoked the lottery in 1621, depriving the group of a critical source of income.

The Indians Strike Back

Appropriately, the Indians delivered the death blow. As settlement expanded and the need for land grew, the company made one final attempt to deal with the Indians peacefully. In 1619, George Thorpe implemented the plan to establish a school for the Indians that would help turn them into acceptable versions of English people. But the Indians proved reluctant to entrust the English with their children, fearing they would be used as hostages, and the personnel employed by the company were ill-equipped to deal with this resistance. Rev. Jonas Stockham, reflecting the majority view, complained in 1621 that "till their Priests and Ancients have their throats cut, there is no hope to bring them to conversion."[15] Unlike the French, the English never considered the possibility of cultural accommodation or converting those "Priests and Ancients" rather than killing them.

Each side unable to find peaceful accommodation with the other, the War of 1622 was all but inevitable. Powhatan had retired in 1617 and died the following year, succeeded by his kinsman Opechancanough, who became convinced of the necessity of military resistance and of spiritual revitalization for his people. The whites had taken their land and decimated their numbers through battle and disease. Openchancanough relied heavily on Nemattanew, a war captain and religious prophet who convinced his tribesmen he was immortal and that they would be immune to musket fire if they rubbed their bodies with a special ointment. In the midst of the Indians' preparations for attack, the colony executed Nemattanew in March 1622 for murdering a planter and openly wearing the deceased white's clothing. His death only increased Openchancanough's determination to seek revenge against the invaders.

March 22 was Good Friday. As morning dawned, the Indians rose to their attack throughout the colony. They killed the settlers as they stood next to them in the fields or sat with them at the breakfast table. There had been no indications of the Indians' plans in the preceding days, nothing unusual in their behavior as they continued to guide and trade with the English. A total of 347 settlers out of 1,240 lost their lives; the dead included the well-intentioned George Thorpe. Incensed, the whites vented their rage with two years of reprisals. There was no need now to balance the positive and negative views of the Indians that had competed for primacy in the early days. Hereafter, Virginians viewed Indians as inhuman savages. In May 1623, the English killed almost two hundred by toasting peace with them with poisoned sack (sherry). They lured fifty more into an ambush, taking their first scalps. In July 1624, sixty settlers killed eight hundred Pamunkeys in just two days of fighting.

🌸 *Documents* 🌸
Justifying English Conquest

The 1622 Indian uprising was among the most devastating of the colonial era. As the following excerpt suggests, Virginians reacted to the Indians' attack by further dehumanizing the natives and thus justifying English conquest of Indian land.

> And by this means that fatal Friday morning, there fell under the bloody and barbarous hands of that perfidious and inhuman people, contrary to all the laws of God and men, of nature and nations, three hundred forty seven men, women, and children. . . . Secondly, because our hands, which before were tied with gentleness and fair usage, are now set at liberty by the treacherous violence of the savages, not untying the knot, but cutting it. So that we, who hitherto have had possession of no more ground than their waste, and our purchase at a valuable consideration to their own contentment gained, may now, by right of war and law of nations, invade the country, and destroy them who sought to destroy us. Whereby we shall enjoy their cultivated places, possessing the fruits of others' labors. Now their cleared grounds in all their villages (which are situated in the fruitfulest places of the land) shall be inhabited by us, whereas heretofore the grubbing of woods was the greatest labor.

Susan M. Kingsbury, ed., *The Records of the Virginia Company,* 4 vols. (Washington, DC: Government Printing Office, 1906–1935), 3:556–7.

Not even this paroxysm of destruction, though, could save the company. The Crown revoked its charter in 1624, and Virginia became a royal colony. Sir Francis Wyatt arrived in the colony in 1625, the first royal governor. The king now appointed the members of the council, and the new charter made no mention of the assembly. Though assembly members met twice unofficially, the Crown did not recognize the body's authority until 1639.

Virginia as a Royal Colony

Governors tried to control expansion throughout the 1620s and 1630s with little success, as plantations proliferated out from the tidewater, up the James and York rivers, and along the Rappanannock and Potomac river systems. Food production did increase, but when Gov. John Harvey tried to convince the colonists to move away from tobacco production in early 1630s, the more powerful planters seized him and sent him back to England. Harvey returned and shipped the planters off to England for trial, but they won their case and had the governor dismissed in 1639.

The colony established a county system in 1634 to serve the growing need for local government. The assembly created eight counties (there were twenty by 1668) governed by justices of the peace. Individual justices dealt with minor controversies and issued warrants, while all of the justices in a county sat in monthly sessions to hear civil cases that involved amounts below a stipulated figure. Quarter courts, consisting of the governor and the council, heard criminal cases for which the penalty was a loss of life or limb. Sheriffs, chosen from among the justices, served warrants and made arrests, conducted assembly elections, executed court sentences, organized the militias and church vestries, and collected taxes. Overall, these courts had much broader authority than their English counterparts, a necessity if this far-flung, atomized society was to retain any sense of true community.

By 1640, Virginians numbered eight thousand and settled much of the land west to the fall line. Only one brief incident temporarily halted their expansion westward. In 1644, Opechancanough, old and watching the once-great Powhatan empire wither away into obscurity, decided to make one last effort to rid his people of their nemesis. Though the Indians killed five hundred English, they failed in their objective. Virginians returned to their plantations after only six months, and only those on the frontier were seriously threatened. The colony responded to the attacks forcefully, burning Indian towns and crops and bringing the old chief to Jamestown, where he was jailed and then shot in the back by a colony soldier. In a treaty signed in 1644, the Indians surrendered all their claims to land and recognized English sovereignty. In return, the English granted them a reservation north of the York River, where whites could enter only by special license. A second treaty in 1646 erected a defensive perimeter on the frontier and sought to further control contacts between the two groups. The colony constructed a series of forts, and in 1649 it created new reservations for two additional tribes. But the Virginians could not control their hunger for land. Encroachment continued, along with scattered violence, throughout the 1650s. The colony would have to wait for Bacon's Rebellion for a final, tragic solution to its Indian "problem."

Life in Early Virginia

Life in early Virginia was hard for all Europeans, regardless of sex or social status. The colonists' diet contained little variety, relying heavily on pork and corn; salting, drying, and smoking did not always prevent winter spoilage. Most houses had only the basics—farm tools, beds, cooking and eating materials. Life expectancy during the entire century was only about forty-three; one-quarter of the children died in infancy and another quarter before the age of twenty. Families were small and short-lived, particularly compared with those of New England. The average woman bore only one to three children, and only about one-third of Chesapeake marriages lasted ten years or more. In one county, more than three-quarters of the children lost at least one parent by the time they were twenty-one or had married. Even those who survived their initial contact with the Chesapeake climate and the spartan living conditions often remained sickly all of their lives. Life expectancy was only in the low forties.

This situation had a profound effect on sex roles as well. Men predominated among the early settlers; as late as 1640, there were six men to every woman. Single women obviously had much better opportunities for marriage than their counterparts in England, and women in general showed greater resistance to disease and lived longer than men. Almost all women married, and with the high death rate among men, many widows remarried in less than a year. While women continued to be viewed as inferior, they possessed significantly greater economic power in the seventeenth-century Chesapeake than did their English counterparts. The life of Elizabeth Willoughby provides an excellent example. Willoughby was the sister of Thomas Willoughby, an immigrant who arrived in Virginia in 1610 and died a prominent member of the gentry class in 1658. Elizabeth first married the Dutch merchant Simon Overzee, a man with extensive trading contacts in the Chesapeake region. Overzee died in 1660, and within a year, Elizabeth married again. This time, the lucky man was George Colclough, a merchant, the younger brother of a wealthy London grocer, and a member of the House of Burgesses. Colclough died in 1662, and, Elizabeth again remarried within a year. Her new husband was Isaac Allerton, son of a Plymouth, Massachusetts merchant, a justice of the peace, and a future member of the House of Burgesses and the governor's council. Through Elizabeth, the Willoughbys had become one of Virginia's elite families.

The majority of Virginians were not, of course, gentlemen or members of the English gentry. Tobacco required constant and extensive labor, and for most of the seventeenth century, white indentured servants provided that labor. Most of the men and women who arrived in Virginia between 1634 and 1674 voluntarily sold themselves into labor. Generally, they were from the middling spectrum of English society, farmers and laborers, and more than three-quarters of them were men and boys, usually in their late teens or early twenties. Their decision to come to America were simply an extension of their relentless search for opportunity in a rapidly changing English economy that still offered few alternatives to farm labor. Servants contracted to work specific periods of time for their masters, generally four to seven years. The masters agreed to pay the cost of transportation to America and to provide them with food, shelter, and other essential needs during their term of indenture. Masters also agreed to grant freedom dues of corn, clothing, tools, and sometimes land when the servants had completed their terms. The written document that contained this agreement, the indenture, could be bought and sold like any other form of property, the individual along with it. Those who could read or write were able to negotiate shorter terms of indenture.

During the middle decades of the century, those who survived their terms often became middling planters and freeholders and, occasionally, justices of the peace or militia officers. Even those who lacked land could work as wage laborers for planters who could not afford servants, or they could lease land in exchange for a portion of their crop. The shortage of women meant that female servants had no difficulty making a good marriage, often to men several years older than themselves who had substantial estates. If their husbands died, women could then be even choosier in seeking another. All of these prospects were to disappear during the century's final decades.

Even during the "good times" for servants, these young men and women faced truly appalling conditions. Up to 40 percent did not survive their terms of service, dying from disease, overwork, and abuse. Planters believed they would die soon anyway, so they saw no point in treating them well. They worked them as hard as possible and then replaced them with new emigrants, maximizing their return on their investment. Though the legal elements of indentured service were ostensibly modeled on the English apprenticeship system, the laws were far harsher than those that governed the lives of servants in England. Even in the early decades of the settlement, servants received more severe treatment than their social superiors. Gentlemen who were found guilty of capital crimes, for instance, were shot or hanged, while servants were often mutilated before and after their execution. For lesser crimes, the wealthy were allowed to pay fines, while others were whipped, branded, or suffered the loss of an ear, nose, tongue, or limb.

The courts punished infractions that trespassed on the masters' rights by adding years onto the terms of service; one indentured servant who killed three of his

❧ *Documents* ☙
The Hard Lives of Indentured Servants

These two documents provide powerful evidence of the conditions indentured servants had to endure in the early Chesapeake settlements. The first, testimony from a court case, shows that servants often were in physical danger from their masters. The second, an excerpt from a rare example of a literary effort by a servant (in this case, a transported felon), is a moving commentary on the generally deplorable conditions Chesapeake laborers endured.

> That Deborah Fernehaugh, the Mistress of this deponent, did beate her mayd Sarvant in the quartering house before the dresser more Liken a dogge than a Christian, and that at a Certaine time, I felt her head, which was beaten as soft as a sponge, in one place, and that as there shee was a weeding, shee complayned and sayd, her backe bone as shee thought was broken with beating, and that I did see the mayds arme naked which was full of blacke and blew bruises and pinches, and her necke Likewise. . . .

Testimony by Joseph Mulders, 31 July 1649, from the 1649 Lower Norfolk County Order Book, reprinted in Warren M. Billings, ed., *The Old Dominion in the Seventeenth Century: A Documentary History of Virginia, 1606-1689* (Chapel Hill, NC: IEAHC, University of North Carolina Press, 1975), 136.

> At length, it pleased God I sick did fall
> But I no favour could receive at all,
> For I was Forced to work while I could stand,
> Or hold the hoe within my feeble hands.
>
> Much hardships then in deed I did endure,
> No dog was ever nursed so I'm sure,
> More pity the poor Negroe slaves bestowed
> Than my inhuman brutal master showed.

master's hogs had six years added to his term. Unmarried female servants who became pregnant during their term of service (and about 20 percent of them did, often as a result of assault by their master) also had their indentures lengthened by one year, and some had their children taken away from them and bound out. Masters could legally administer beatings, and many maimed or mauled their servants. Elizabeth Abbott and Elias Hinton, servants of John and Alice Proctor, both died after such beatings. When a court representative examined Abbott, she found

Oft on my knees the Lord I did implore,
To let me see my native land once more;
For through God's grace my life I would amend
And be a comfort to my dearest friends.

Helpless and sick and being left alone,
I by myself did use to make my moan;
And think upon my former wicked ways,
How they had brought me to this wretched case.
. . . .

Thus twelve long tedious years did pass away,
And but two more by law I had to stay:
When Death did for my cruel Master call,
But that was no relief to us at all.

The Widow would not the Plantation hold,
So we and that were both for to be sold,

A lawyer rich who at James-Town did dwell,
Came down to view it and lik'd it very well.

He bought the Negroes who for life were slaves,
But no transported Fellons would he have,
So we were put like Sheep into a fold,
There unto the best bidder to be sold.

James Revel, "The Poor Unhappy Transported Felon's Sorrowful Account of His Fourteen Years Transportation at Virginia in America," John Melville Jennings, ed, *Virginia Magazine of History and Biography,* 56 (1948), 192; reprinted in Warren M. Billings, ed., *The Old Dominion in the Seventeenth Century: A Documentary History of Virginia, 1606-1689* (Chapel Hill, NC: IEAHC, University of North Carolina Press, 1975), 140–1.

that the servant "had been sore beaten and her body full of sores and holes very dangerously raunckled and putrified both above her wast and uppon her hips and thighes."[16] English courts took pains to control such cruelty, but the Proctors received no punishment at all. Such treatment added only more pain to a life that was often short, devoid of any real hope, and all too typical for the ordinary Virginian during the seventeenth century.

own stripped the Virginia Company of its New World claims after Virginia me a royal colony, opening up the remaining areas to new grants by the king. eorge Calvert, Baron of Baltimore, was a court favorite of James I. Born in Yorkshire, he had been a member of Parliament and a principal secretary of state who converted to Catholicism in 1624. As part of a group interested in founding a colony in Newfoundland, he received a patent for the southeast coast of that region in 1623. In 1628, he led an expedition to found a colony he hoped to call Avalon; one Newfoundland winter was enough to dissuade him of the viability of this plan. But on his way home, he stopped off in Virginia and was impressed enough to apply for a charter to settle the northern region of the area that had been part of the original grant. Though Baltimore died on April 15, 1632, the Crown granted the charter to his son Cecilius on June 20.

Perhaps the principal motive behind the Calvert family's growing interest in the New World was their sympathy with the plight of their fellow Catholics in England. There were about fifty thousand Catholics in England, and during the late Elizabethan period, they had suffered persecution, torture, and death. Between 1588 and 1603, sixty-one priests, forty-seven laymen, and two women were executed. Some Jesuits had been hung, drawn, and quartered, having been convicted of high treason simply by virtue of their being Catholic. Catholics who refused to declare their allegiance to the Church of England were fined twenty pounds a month or had most of their property confiscated. The situation remained far from comfortable even after Charles I married the French princess Henrietta Maria and relaxed enforcement of the anti-Catholic laws.

The Calverts named their chartered land Maryland, after Henrietta Maria. The charter granted the Baltimore family authority based upon the feudal powers of the Bishop of Durham, who had governed the northern borders of the English realm after William the Conquerer. Thus, Baltimore could grant lands, establish manors and courts, and collect any rents, taxes, and fees he decided to impose. He could wage war and incorporate towns and boroughs. In return, he was obligated only to pay a symbolic annual tribute of two Indian arrows to the king. There were, however, limitations both in theory and practice to this enormous power. The charter guaranteed all settlers the rights of native-born Englishmen, specified that laws could be passed only with the consent of freemen, and required that all churches be consecrated and dedicated to English law—a stipulation designed to prevent the Catholic church from becoming the established church of the colony. Ironically, Calvert received little money from the Catholic gentry, few of whom were actually interested in migrating; Baltimore family money largely financed the venture.

Two ships, the *Ark* and the *Dove,* set sail from England on November 22, 1633, with Cecilius's younger brother, Leonard, as governor and 138 passengers, including two Jesuit priests and seventeen gentlemen, mostly Catholic. The majority of the future settlers were Protestant servants, laborers, yeomen, and craftsmen of various sorts and descriptions. The sea voyage was typically stressful; the two ships were separated during a severe storm, and the passengers suffered the usual duress under adverse weather conditions and lack of fresh food and water. Twelve people died. After a brief stopover in Barbados, first landfall was made on February 24 at Point Comfort, Virginia. On March 25, Father Andrew White celebrated the first mass at Blakiston Island at the mouth of the Potomac River. The group settled on St. George's River, later renamed St. Mary's River. Father White's comment that "this baye is the most delightfull water I ever saw"[17] reflected once again the utopian vision of the New World landscape that was so common in the southern colonies.

Maryland settlers wrote of the open, parklike lands (the abundance of strawberries, raspberries, deer, tur[herons, and geese.

Calvert had read John Smith's account of the ear[instructions reflected an awareness of that colony's e> thus warned the settlers not to disperse into the wildern(ing homes within a town, and to plant sufficient amounts avoid starvation. Calvert intended to create a social structu proprietary interest. He granted outright about sixty large thousand acres or more. Those who brought five or mo ...er ten, then twenty) to the colony received two thousand acres and had to pay only a small annual quitrent. Smaller grants to individuals were more popular in the long run and certainly more numerous. Settlers received one hundred acres for transporting themselves to the colony, one hundred for their wives and each servant, and fifty for each child. After the first decade, though, the total was reduced to fifty acres altogether, and in 1683, the "headright" was completely abolished.

As they did in all English colonies, the settlers soon expressed a desire for a certain degree of self-determination, and Baltimore's charter guaranteed that. The assembly first met in February 1635, but Baltimore refused to approve its limited legislative program. It next convened in 1638, rejecting a series of laws sent over by the proprietor. The freemen claimed the right to initiate legislation and passed four-teen bills of their own, all of which Baltimore vetoed. But Calvert finally gave in, and from 1639 on, the Maryland legislature, with two representatives from each dis-trict, met regularly. During the early years, Catholics predominated, but all freemen retained the right to vote. And as society grew more complex later in the century, the county courts played an increasingly central role in civil life, their powers and responsibilities similar to those of the Virginia courts.

Non-Catholics always outnumbered Catholics in the colony, and Baltimore made every effort to ensure religious harmony and to ease fears of Catholic domi-nation. He reacted angrily to early Jesuit attempts to enlarge their powers and sub-sequently revised the conditions of their land grants. After a period of civil turmoil, he appointed the Protestant William Stone as governor in 1648. Stone permitted a group of Puritans to establish a small community named Providence at the mouth of the Severn River, and in 1649, the assembly passed an "act concerning Religion" that formalized toleration and guaranteed the "free exercise" of religion. Still, there were limitations. Anyone who denied the divinity of the trinity could be put to death, and those who blasphemed against the Virgin Mary or the saints could be punished by fine or whipping. But the punitive measures were rarely implemented. Even the occasional blasphemy prosecutions that took place later in the century were not tried as capital offenses, and Quakers and other minority sects eventually found a refuge in Maryland.

Conflict did arise elsewhere. The first serious crisis the young colony faced involved William Clairborne, a Virginia councillor. Clairborne had set up a trading post on Kent Island in the upper Chesapeake region before the Marylanders arrived. The island was ideally located for trade with the Indians, and in 1631, Clairborne built a stockade, church, and store, convincing a number of fellow Virginians to settle on the island and share the benefits of his profitable trade with the Susquehannocks. He refused to recognize Maryland's jurisdiction, arguing (with some justification) that the new grant did not include areas already settled. In the spring of 1635, Clairborne and the Marylanders squared off in armed conflict, leav-ing four dead. Maryland eventually subdued the interlopers, and the Crown affirmed the colony's ownership of the island. During the 1640s, amidst the difficul-

accompanying the English Civil War, Clairborne made a final abortive attempt to reclaim his land. At the same time, the colony was forced to deal with the intrusion of a Cromwell sympathizer named Richard Ingle. In 1645, Ingle actually took control of the colony (Gov. Leonard Calvert was in England at the time) and demanded that the settlers declare allegiance to the Puritan Parliament. Ingle and his men terrorized those who resisted and destroyed their property. Only in late 1646 did the governor return with an expedition, forcing both Ingle and Clairborne to surrender.

Meanwhile, though, Calvert's enemies in London were growing, and Clairborne was waiting for the opportunity to gain revenge. While Gov. Stone was away in 1649, the deputy-governor, Thomas Greene, proclaimed Charles the rightful king of England. Stone quickly retracted the motion, but Baltimore's enemies now had cause to take action against the colony. On March 12, 1652, Clairborne and William Bennett appeared in Maryland as parliamentary commissioners with a Commonwealth fleet. Two years later, Parliament placed the colony under Puritan rule. The new government forbade Catholics practicing their faith and no longer required settlers to take an oath of loyalty to the proprietor in order to receive land grants. The Puritan William Fuller headed a new commission government.

Baltimore did not suffer defeat lightly. He appealed successfully to Cromwell to restore his rights, and Gov. Stone assembled a small force of one hundred or so men on the Severn River in March 1655. The Puritans countered with a larger and stronger force. Stone lost almost half his men in the battle and was forced to surrender. The Puritans executed four of their prisoners and held Stone and his council captive for more than a month. The crisis ended only in 1657, when Bennett and Clairborne reached an agreement with Baltimore that restored religious toleration and recognized his proprietorship. Clairborne, at long last, relinquished his claims to Maryland territory.

Though early Marylanders found themselves engulfed by military and political conflict, they did not have to deal with organized resistance from the indigenous population. Maryland Indians were Algonquians who were dispersed in many small villages. On the western shore of the Potomac, the Piscataways dominated a confederacy of lesser tribes, and on the eastern shore, the Nianticoks held a similar position. Both groups were peaceful, and in the long run, they either moved away or were decimated by disease. Only the Susquehannocks on the northern bay, members of the Iroquois family, created some problems in the 1640s, goaded and armed by the Dutch and Swedes. Even they eventually lost their power and influence.

When Father White first saw the Indians, he emphasized the bright reds and blues they painted on their faces and the shells, teeth, beads, and feathers with which they decorated their bodies. He praised their skill with bow and arrow and their "loveing and kinde nature."[18] The Yaocomaco Indians shared food and their already cleared land with the settlers and helped them avoid the suffering of the early Virginians. In return, the English provided them with hoes, hatchets, and other tools and promised they would protect them from the powerful Susquehannocks.

But while white-Indian relations were more peaceful in Maryland than in Virginia, the end result was the same. Farmers let their livestock roam freely, destroying Indian crops; the Indian saw these foraging animals as fair game for hunting. Different conceptions of property rights created the same problems they did everywhere in the New World. Englishmen plied Indians with alcohol, and settlement expansion soon threatened Indian land. It seemed that even initially friendly relations between Europeans and Indians could not forestall the inevitable process of white conquest.

   Misled by the example of Spain and by unrealistic expectations, England's initial colonial venture got off to a rough start. But Chesapeake settlers eliminated Indian resistance within a few decades, and they discovered their longed-for source of wealth in tobacco. As military and civil conflict receded in Virginia and Maryland, political and social stability began to take shape. Unfortunately, the thirst for riches remained the dominant factor in Chesapeake life, and prosperity would ultimately rest on the oppressed backs of indentured servants and African slaves.

❧ *Chapter Four* ❧

The Settlement
of New England

Families huddled together abroad a small ship, seeking refuge and religious liberty in the wilderness of an uncharted land: this is the image of the Puritan migration often portrayed in popular literature. It is as much myth as history, though, and like most such myths, it contains some truth and a good deal of distortion. The flight from England cannot be attributed to a single cause. Religion was certainly the most obvious motive, but economic, political, and social factors were also significant concerns. The particular meld depended upon the character of the local English experience and the expectations migrants had of the New World. While this "Great Migration" drew about twenty-one thousand English people to Massachusetts alone by 1642, this total represented less than one-half of 1 percent of the population of England, and migrants to the Caribbean and Chesapeake areas outnumbered those who went to New England. Of the 377,000 who left England for the New World between 1630 and 1700, only thirty-nine thousand went to New England. The issue is not just why people left England, but why they chose New England as their destination.

Once here, New England settlers—including the Pilgrims at Plymouth and the Puritans at Massachusetts Bay—dealt more successfully with their environment than their southern counterparts had. They resolved a series of complex and bitter religious disputes, quickly established a smoothly functioning government, established a reasonably healthy economy, and expanded settlement to the west, south, and north. Like all other Europeans who migrated to the New World, New Englanders developed a culture both constrained by their Old World cultures and molded by the New World environment. Here more than anywhere else in English America, settlers succeeded, for a time at least, in forming the traditional society of their dreams.

Significant Dates

1605	George Weymouth explores New England coast
1606	Plymouth Company chartered
1607	Settlement and demise of Sagadahoc
1608	Separatists leave England for Holland
1620	Plymouth Colony settled
	Council for New England receives charter
1622	Merrymount settled
1623	Dorchester Company settlement at Cape Ann
1626	Naumkeag (Salem) founded
1628	New England Company established
1629	Massachusetts Bay Company established
1630	Boston settled
1632	Watertown protest
1635	Roger Williams founds Providence, Rhode Island
1634–36	First Connecticut settlements
1636	Roger Williams banished from Massachusetts Bay
	Williams founds Rhode Island
1636–37	Pequot War
1637	New Haven founded
1637	Anne Hutchinson banished from Massachusetts
1639	Connecticut's Fundamental Orders
1644	General Court agrees to sit as two separate houses
1645	Hingham milita case
1648	*Books of the General Law and Liberties*

Presettlement Contacts

The English knew something of this region long before they settled here. In 1524, Giovanni da Verrazzano landed both in the future Newport Harbor and on the coast of Maine. In 1525, Estavan Gomez entered the Penobscot River estuary in his search for the Northwest Passage, and he was likely followed over the years by many wandering seamen, fishermen, and fur traders. But for a long time, the area remained known largely through shadowy legends and suggestions of great treasure.

Contact increased dramatically in the early seventeenth century. In 1602, Matthew Gosnold explored the New England coast, establishing relations on the southern Maine coast with natives who wore European clothing and spoke a few words of English. Gosnold landed and fished at Cape Cod and went on to Buzzards Bay and Cuttyhunk, but an attempt at settlement failed when the chosen crew members refused to stay. Martin Pring toured the area in a 1603 voyage. His account glowingly described the wealth of harbors, fish, and furs of the region, noting in particular the abundance of fertile land. The forests, Pring observed, would yield sassafras and timber, and the natives were docile and cooperative. Increasingly, promotional literature depicted New England as something of an earthly paradise, graced with abundant natural resources and perfectly suited to colonization. But like American settlers everywhere, these explorers remained blind to the particulars of Indian culture.

Early Settlement Attempts

George Popham and Sir Ferdinand Gorges headed the group of merchants who sponsored the exploratory voyages by Gosnold, Pring, and George Weymouth; the Crown granted this group the Plymouth Company charter in 1606. Gorges became president and quickly moved to further explore the territory and to establish a base to collect goods that could be exported to England. Two vessels left England in August 1607, anchoring several weeks later at the mouth of the Kennebec River in Maine. Poor leadership doomed the settlement, known as Sagadahoc, and the colonists abandoned the site in the spring of 1608. In 1614, John Smith spent three months exploring New England and actively promoted the area. He described the Massachusetts coast as "the Paradise of all those parts,"[1] with a large population, excellent harbors, and cultivated fields. Only the lack of an industrious people, he believed, kept the area from achieving its potential. Gorges continued to send expeditions to acquire furs and fish in the area south of Casco Bay, Maine, and one of his agents wintered there in 1616–1617 in hopes of proving the area to be habitable. But there was still no permanent colony in 1620, when the Crown granted Gorges a new charter for a group called the Council for New England.

Plymouth Colony

The first permanent settlement, at Plymouth, appeared in the same year as Gorges's new patent. The Pilgrims were Separatists, members of a variant of English Protestantism that found its roots in the writings of such ministers as Robert Browne during the 1580s. On most points of theology and polity, the Separatists agreed with their Puritan counterparts, but unlike the Puritans, they believed the English church was too corrupted by popish beliefs to be saved from within. The only solution, they thought, lay in complete separation.

The English government persecuted the Separatists throughout the 1590s and executed several of the sect's leaders. But the Crown also allowed Separatist minister Francis Johnson to plan a North American colony after his release from prison. Johnson's attempted settlement at the mouth of the St. Lawrence River failed, and he eventually became pastor of a Separatist congregation in Amsterdam. This parish became the model for a congregation organized in Nottinghamshire in 1606, which itself subsequently split into the Gainsborough and Scrooby churches. When the government resumed persecution shortly thereafter, the entire Scrooby congregation attempted to flee the country, an act that required government permission. They were caught and jailed for thirty days. The Crown ultimately granted them permission to migrate to Leiden, Holland. They settled there in 1608, finding employment as weavers, carders, and bakers. The Gainsborough group followed, but they remained distinct and did not play a role in American settlement.

Under the leadership of John Robinson, the Scrooby group lived peacefully for over a decade in Holland. The government would not allow them to join the guilds, however, and they were uncomfortable with Dutch culture. They were particularly dismayed by the Dutch failure to observe the Sabbath, and they feared that their children would lose both their religion and their nationality. Rumors of Spanish plans to reconquer Holland convinced them to move again. William Brewster, the original organizer of the Scrooby congregation, successfully approached Sir Edwin Sandys for permission to settle within the boundaries of the Virginia Company's charter, and James I gave his approval. The penniless congregation accepted an offer from the London ironmonger Thomas Weston to form a joint-stock company with himself and a group of investors. Three groups of associates resulted: merchant-adventurers (investors who would remain in England), merchant-planters (investors who would settle in the colony), and planters (whose only investment was their own labor). All property would be owned in common for seven years, after which the assets would be divided—though the merchants would retain half ownership of all land and houses. All laborers would work only for the company. Thus, there were no private homes or gardens, a condition the settlers accepted only reluctantly.

The Pilgrims purchased the *Speedwell* for the first stage of their journey, from Holland to Plymouth, England. The ship proved unseaworthy, though, and the 102 passengers had to crowd onto Weston's chartered ship, the *Mayflower,* a small vessel of only 180 tons. They sailed from Plymouth on September 6, 1620. Only thirty-five of these travelers were from the Leiden congregation of 238 Separatists, though many others were friends and relatives. Traveling with them were several "strangers" (non-Separatists) to provide needed skills, including Miles Standish, recruited for his military prowess, and John Alden, a cooper. Their destination was the northern reaches of the Virginia Company grant, but after a voyage of over two months, they landed, perhaps intentionally, at Cape Cod, far to the north of their announced destination. One child was born on the voyage and only one passenger died, but the lack of provisions and subsequent suffering weakened the colonists and took its toll during the coming winter. Because they were beyond the boundaries of the Virginia Company charter, the colonists were forced to create some form of legal basis for their colony. Hence, forty-one adults signed the Mayflower Compact, in which they consented to "covenant & combine our selves togeather into a civill body politick, for our better ordering & preservation"[2] and agreed to pass such laws as would be necessary for the good of the colony. Legally groundless, the compact at least created a government of mutual consent. More important, it reflected the New World colonists' persistent concern with order, one of the most significant of English values. William Bradford later noted that the compact was "occasioned partly by the discontented & mutinous speeches that some of the strangers amongst them had let fall from them in the ship—That when they came a shore they would use their owne libertie; for none had the power to command them."[3]

The colonists explored Cape Cod for several weeks before settling in at Plymouth on Christmas Day. The site fulfilled the most important criteria they had established: available fresh water, a deep harbor, an abundance of timber, and good soil. They arrived too late in the year, though, to prepare adequately for a New England winter, and most suffered through the next few months on board the ship. In January, the common storehouse burned, destroying some supplies, and by March, almost half of the settlers had died. Spring brought relief. The weakened but thankful settlers constructed a fort, planted crops, and caught food in waters teeming with fish. Most crucial was the assistance the colonists received from the local Wampanoag tribe, particularly through the intervention of Samoset and Squanto; the former had learned English from fishermen on the coast of Maine. The sachem

Massasoit negotiated a treaty with the whites, and by the fall of 1621, conditions had improved sufficiently to warrant the celebration of the first Thanksgiving. The colonists invited Massasoit and ninety of his warriors to join them in the feast.

Pilgrim-Indian relations were typical of the future course of events in New England. Europeans proved completely ignorant of the topography of the area, overlooking abundant evidence of recent human occupation—burial sites, abandoned fields—and showing little understanding that the Indians had recently been devastated by disease. Indeed, they believed that God had cleared the land in preparation for them. Yet the tragic interaction of cultures had already begun even before the landing at Plymouth; Squanto's own experiences provide insight into how such early contacts affected both European and Indian societies in the New World.

Squanto was a member of an Algonquian tribe known as the Patuxet. In 1615, these people numbered about two thousand in the Plymouth Bay area, a small proportion of the nearly twenty-five thousand Indians cultivating the land between Massachusetts and Plymouth bays at that time. Almost every early English expedition to these areas generated some hostility; most of them, in fact, took captives to England for promotional purposes. Squanto suffered such a fate in 1614. He was apparently sold into slavery in Spain, but by 1617, he ended up living in the London home of the treasurer of the Newfoundland Company. He eventually met the company's director, Gorges, and returned to New England in early 1619 under his sponsorship. He found most of his tribe dead from the smallpox epidemic that ravaged eastern New England tribes in 1616.

Squanto remained in the area and served as a diplomatic intermediary between the English and the Indians. He helped negotiate an alliance, for instance, between the settlers and the local Pokanoket Indians against the Pokanokets' traditional rivals, the Narragansetts. The local tribe had lost many of its people to smallpox, while the Narragansetts had escaped the disease; the Pokanokets thus saw the treaty as an opportunity to safeguard their homeland and maintain their independence. As Europeans generally did, the colonists took their agreement to signify the Indians' voluntary submission to English domination. They rewarded Squanto for his services by allowing him to return to his home at Patuxet, and he became the Plymouth Colony's guide and liaison to the Indians. Before his death in 1622, he made a final attempt to restore the Patuxets to power under his leadership by setting the Pokanokets against the English. Yet so indispensable had he become, even this act did not deter the English from continuing to rely upon his diplomatic skills.

Clearly the Indians had their own agendas in dealing with the invaders. Large-scale violence between Indians and whites at Plymouth came only after the Pilgrims discovered the Indians' underground cold-storage cellars and stole their corn. The Indians' first response to this theft was to minimize contact with the Europeans, in the hope that they could still use the English against the Narragansetts. But in 1622, sixty non-Pilgrims who settled north of Plymouth at Wessagusett stole corn from the Massachusetts and threatened attacks when the Indians refused to trade. Miles Standish then proved his value to the colony by leading a raid on the reluctant Indians, killing eight and impaling the sachem Wituwamet's head on the fort's palisades. Rev. John Robinson, still in Holland, wrote to the colony in shock, asking if they were beginning to act like savages themselves. From that day on, the Indians referred to the English as "wotowquenange," or cutthroats.

While settling their relations with the region's Indians, the Pilgrims were also finalizing their affairs with Weston and his group. Weston had continued to take advantage of the settlers, expecting them to feed and house the fishing expeditions he sent over. Through his actions and those of his successors, the Pilgrims found themselves sinking deeper and deeper into debt. The enforced communalism was a further irritant, since the investors made them ship any accumulated surpluses back to England even while allowing the new colonists they sent over to farm their own land and keep the profits. In 1623, Bradford modified the communal system by assigning land for their own use to each family based on family size, though the company retained ownership. He made these garden allotments permanent in 1624, and in 1632, the government distributed pasture and meadow lots on the edge of town to the settlers. The Pilgrims bought out the remaining London investors in 1627 at the cost of a twenty-four hundred pound debt. And despite repeated attempts by Bradford and a solicitous, respectful attitude toward the Crown, the colony never succeeded in gaining a royal charter.

Plymouth grew slowly. It had only 124 inhabitants in 1624, three hundred in 1630, and a paltry three thousand as late as 1660. While migrants came from both rural and urban backgrounds, most were simple agricultural folk. Brewster was the only original settler with any financial experience, and only he, John Carver, and Edward Winslow were classified as "gentlemen." Few had any substantial education, and during the history of the colony, only three settlers with university degrees, all ministers, became permanent residents.

Most of the settlers came to Plymouth to improve themselves materially as well as spiritually, and they moved often in the early years in search of land and the right setting. New towns sprang up quickly—Duxbury in 1630, Scituate in 1636, and eight other towns by 1640. The leaders of the tiny colony voiced concern over this fragmentation of the community, but for the first part of the century, the colony remained a traditional society where wealth was judged solely in terms of land, families formed the colony's social core, and social and economic divisions were limited.

The settlers proved fecund and healthy in an environment free of European disease. The average family produced seven or eight children who reached maturity, and life expectancy remained high throughout the century. Economic growth, on the other hand, was distinctly limited. The fur trade was the most profitable enterprise, and the colony established trading posts in 1627 on the southwest coast of Cape Cod, in 1629 on the Kennebec River in Maine, and in 1633 at Windsor on the Connecticut River. By the 1640s, though, fur-bearing animals were becoming scarce throughout New England, and despite modest shipbuilding efforts and a small ironworks, the colony was unable to sustain any increase in the standard of living after mid-century.

The colony's political structure was similar to that of its more populous neighbor, Massachusetts Bay. For most of the century, the majority of adult males were freemen, and until 1638, all freemen gathered in Plymouth four times a year for General Court meetings, electing the governor and seven assistants annually. These eight individuals comprised the highest judicial body in the colony and exercised considerable authority over day-to-day administrative affairs. After 1638, adult males of "good character," a requirement later transformed into church membership and twenty pounds worth of property, could be elected representatives from each town. Town meetings of all resident householders regulated local affairs, and officials such as fence-viewers and constables, positions drawn from the settlers' English experiences, dealt with particular administrative needs.

Religion, of course, was the basis of the colony's existence; while its cohesive power lessened with time, it remained a powerful determinant of the Pilgrims' world view. Like Puritanism, Separatism's emphasis on exemplary personal behavior reflected its constant concern with God's presence in the community. The colony's leaders tended to see misconduct everywhere. For a while, at least, this

❧ *Documents* ❧
Fleeing the Old World

The following selections by William Bradford and John Winthrop are representative statements of the pressures pushing Separatists and Puritans to leave their homelands. Bradford offered several "sundrie and solid reasons . . .," the most pressing of which is excerpted here. Winthrop's concise, powerful summary provides insight into the combination of secular and religious motives that impelled Puritans to flee England in haste.

> For many of their children . . . were, often times, so oppressed with their hevie labours, that though their minds were free and wiling, yet their bodies bowed under the weight of the same, and became decreped in their early youth; the vigor of nature being consumed in the very budd as it were. But that which was more lamentable, and of all sorowes most heavie to be borne, was that many of their children, by these occasions, and the great licentiousness of youth in that countrie, and the manifold temptations of the place, were drawne away by evill examples into extravagante & dangerous courses, getting the raines off their neks, & departing from their parents. Some became souldiers, others tooke upon them farr viages by sea, and other some worse courses, tending to dissolutnes & the danger of their soules, to the great greefe of their parents and dishonour of God. So that they saw their posteritie would be in danger to degenerate & be corrupted.

William Bradford, *Of Plymouth Plantation,* Harvey Wish, ed. (New York: Capricorn Books, 1962), 39–40.

was a society of close personal and moral observation, one that did not hesitate to punish transgressors—even when they were not Separatists.

The best known of these individuals was Thomas Morton. Thomas Weston had unsuccessfully attempted to establish an offshoot settlement at Mount Wollaston (Wessagusett) in 1622, and Morton settled on the abandoned site, changing its name to Merrymount. That, at least, was the name the Pilgrims preferred. Morton himself also referred to the settlement as Marry-Mount, Mary-mount, and Mare-mount, all suggestive of erotic and disorderly behavior. He attempted to revive pagan May Day revels, with Indians and whites dancing and drinking around a maypole and apparently expressing their sexual desires. The Pilgrim authorities responded quickly and sent Miles Standish to disperse the settlement and end the scandalous behavior. Morton's real crime, though, may have been his popularity with the Indians. They preferred to trade with him rather than the colony's leaders, and there were rumors that he was selling them firearms. In his published account of the incident, *The New English Canaan* (1637), Morton portrayed the Indians as

3. This land growes weary of her Inhabitants, soe as man whoe is ye most pretious of all creatures is heer more vile & base than the Earth we Treat uppon, & of lesse price among us, then a horse or a sheep. . . . All Townes complaine of the burthen of their poore though we have taken up many unnecessary, yea unlawful trades to mainteine them. . . . & thus it is come to passe that children, servants & neighbors (especially if they be poore) are counted the greatest burthen which if things were right it would be the cheifest earthly blessinge.

4. The whole earth is the lords Garden & he hath given it to the sonnes of men, with a generall condition, Gen. 1. 28. Increase & multiply, replenish the earth & subdue it . . . , why then should we stand hear striveing for places of habitation, (many men spending as much labor & cost to recover or keep somtymes a Acre or two of land as would procure them many hundred as good or better in an other country) and in ye mean tyme suffer a whole Continent, as fruitfull & convenient for the use of man to lie waste without any improvement.

John Winthrop, "Reasons to Be Considered for Justifying the Undertakers of the Intended Plantation in New England," reprinted in Jack P. Greene, ed., *Settlements to Society, 1607–1763: A Documentary History of Colonial America* (New York: W. W. Norton and Company, 1975), 62–3.

primitive innocents, wise, honest, generous, and open in their sexual expression. He pictured the Pilgrims as hypocritical bigots seeking only gain; Standish was referred to as Captain Shrimpe. Morton's joyful embrace of pagan and Indian values threatened the Plymouth settlers' desire to solidify their own more restrained, Christian English identities.

Considering the primacy of religion in the colony's ethos, it is ironic that its institutional religious life remained unsettled for so long. Indeed, since John Robinson had not migrated with his congregation, the colony had to make do for some time without a pastor. William Brewster preached but could not administer sacraments. The majority of the colonists were not Separatists, moreover, and since Separatists admitted only their own to their services, most of the residents were left without a church. The merchant-adventurers sent John Lyford, an Anglican minister, but he proceeded to baptize, serve communion, and conduct services in accordance with the Anglican *Book of Common Prayer* and was soon ordered to leave the colony. The small congregation finally ordained Ralph Smith as minister in

1629, and he administered the sacraments to the colony's faithful for the first time. But after 1654, the church went without a pastor for almost fifteen years, frequently resorting to the use of lay preachers. The colony's continuing poverty and isolation undoubtedly made it an unattractive opportunity for the few available Separatist ministers. Finally, in 1668, the congregation ordained John Cotton the younger.

Despite these difficulties, Plymouth remained a colony focused primarily on the spiritual world. Its inhabitants were economically ambitious, certainly, but such activity was not incompatible with their essentially religious conception of history. Their faith in God's purpose guided their every action. Doctrinally, church membership at first depended solely upon good behavior, but by the late 1640s—sometime after Massachusetts took a similar step—the colony began to require a confession of faith and a declaration of the working of grace in the individual's soul for church membership. Each town contained at least one congregation, and in true Separatist fashion, each congregation controlled its own affairs, resisting any larger institutional structure. Religious pluralism consequently was the single most visible characteristic of Plymouth.

Small, poor, uninvolved in larger economic networks, and held together largely by traditional family ties, Plymouth nonetheless reflected a high degree of individualistic behavior and weak community ties. As elsewhere, the reality of New World conditions overwhelmed plans for recreating old World society.

ᴥ *Documents* ᴥ
Entering the New World

Both Pilgrims and Puritans had cause to reflect on their future as they stood on the brink of a new life, and both of the following statements provide insight into their reasons for leaving the Old World and their expectations and hopes for the New. The first excerpt is from the "Mayflower Compact," the second from John Winthrop's lay sermon on the *Arbella*.

> In the name of God, Amen. We whose names are underwritten, the loyall subjects of our dread soveraigne lord, King James . . . , haveing undertaken, for the glorie of God, and advancemente of the Christian faith, and honour of our king & countrie, a voyage to plant the first colonie in the Northerne parts of Virginia, doe by these presents solemnly & mutualy in the presence of God, and one of another, covenant & combine our selves togeather into a civill body politick, for our better ordering & preservation and furtherance of the ends aforesaid; and by vertue hearof to enacte, constitute, and frame such just & equal lawes, ordinances, acts, constitutions, & offices, from time to time, as shall be thought most meete & convenient for the generall good of the Colonie, unto which we promise all due submission and obedience.

William Bradford, *Of Plymouth Plantation,* Harvey Wish, ed. (New York: Capricorn Books, 1962), 69–70.

Massachusetts Bay

Massachusetts was yet another offspring of the disruptive social change besetting English society. By 1600, large landowners dominated most English parishes, agriculture was becoming increasingly profit-oriented, and ordinary English men and women found it increasingly difficult to eke out a living. Chaos and immorality seemed to threaten the traditional order of English society everywhere. Hordes of people roamed the countryside seeking jobs or simply escaping unbearable conditions, while the endless search for opportunity brought dizzying rides both up and down the social ladder. Many of the first migrants to New England came to escape this upheaval.

Though fewer than 10 percent of the early settlers came from London, the first decade of migration to New England was heavily urban. One-third of the settlers came from small market towns and another third from large towns. The majority came from the east of England—the geographic center of the migration was the market town of Haverhill, where the counties of Suffolk, Essex, and Cambridge meet. Most New England families came from within a sixty-mile radius of Haverhill. The West Country was an important secondary source, though most of the families from this area tended to move to Connecticut or Maine.

Now the onely way to avoyde this shipwracke [the revenge of the Lord], and to provide for our posterity, is to followe the counsell of Micah, *to do justly, to love mercy, to walk humbly with our God*. For this end, wee must be knitt together, in this worke, as one man. Wee must entertaine each other in brotherly affection. Wee must be willing to abridge ourselves of our superfluities, for the suppl of other's necessities. Wee must uphold a familiar commerce together in all meekeness, gentlenes, patience and liberality. Wee must delight in each other; make other's conditions our oune; rejoice together, mourne together, labour and suffer together, allwayes haueving before our eyes and our commission and community in the worke, as members of the same body. The Lord will be our God, and delight to dwell among us, as his oune people, and will command a blessing upon us in all our wayes. . . . For wee must consider that wee shall be as a citty upon a hill. The eies of all people are uppon us.

John Winthrop, "A Modell of Christian Charity," from *Collections of the Massachusetts Historical Society*, 3d ser., vol. 7 (1838), 48.

❧

Farming was more advanced in the east of England and more completely tied to the urban food markets and the wool markets. As the most highly urbanized section of England, the region was home to many artisans and skilled craftspeople. It also had a long history of rebellion against arbitrary power and would be the greatest source of strength for Parliament in the early years of the English Civil War. Finally, it was well known as a hotbed of religious radicalism. Most of the Marian martyrs had come from East Anglia, and Puritanism was especially strong in the region's smaller towns.

These people were thoroughly familiar with conditions in New England by 1630. In addition to the sources we have already discussed, they were particularly influenced by Francis Higginson's *A True Relation of the Last Voyage to New England.* Higginson and others presented a strongly favorable picture of the region, portraying it as an attractive option for people disenchanted with life in England. And there were many such people throughout East Anglia. Inhabitants of Rowley in Yorkshire, for instance, lived in an area of heavy Puritan influence and were subject to a good deal of religious persecution; the appearance of the plague only served to heighten their insecurities. Residents of Norfolk County's Hingham suffered from persecution, failing harvests, and a depression in the cloth trade. Puritans in Watertown complained of food shortages, malnutrition, and a growing number of beggars and vagabonds.

The majority of the migrants came to America to live as they had—or thought they had—before encountering difficulties in their homeland. They wanted to live where they could enjoy a life centered on land, family, and village amidst friends and relatives of moral, godly character. Rural or urban, these were sober, middle-class folk. It was religion, though, that proved to be the most common unifying factor in migrants' decisions to leave their homeland. Puritans fled persecution and complained of the continued prevalence of Catholic-like ritual and structure in the English church, but they were moved most of all by a pervasive sense of impending doom, a fear that England had betrayed its role in God's millennial plans and that the day of judgment was imminent. Far from being protectors of Protestantism, England's monarchs seemed only to make matters worse. James I had lavished money on a corrupt court and appeased the Catholic nations of Europe. Charles I appointed William Laud bishop of London in 1628 and archbishop of Canterbury in 1633. Laud supported ceremony and ritual in the Anglican church and forced Puritan ministers to either conform or lose their preaching licenses. Charles lived extravagantly, and his constant search for income alienated many of the local gentry. Tired of Parliament's refusal of his requests, he ruled without it after 1629.

The leaders of the Puritan group that made the initial decision to migrate—John Winthrop, Thomas Dudley, and others—also sought out those who would bring some resources to the colony; they did not want the poor. Winthrop in particular spent much of the winter of 1629–1630 actively recruiting prospective settlers, exploiting family connections and professional associations. Family and neighborhood connections seem to have been the most decisive factor in influencing many to make the move. Even for committed Puritans, this was not an easy step, and most needed the support of those closest to them. Unlike the Chesapeake, New England was intended to be a social experiment from the beginning. What society could succeed without a core of supportive friends and family members? The Hingham minister Peter Hobart led his family and many fellow congregants in a group exodus to the New World; countless others shared a similar experience.

Only a few of the migrants were gentlemen, and even these came from minor gentry families and generally assumed leadership positions. Yeomen, who comprised up to 15 percent of English households, constituted only 2 percent of the

John Winthrop. 🙠

migrants to New England. Laborers, the poor, and the illiterate, all common in England, were less so in New England; they comprised no more than 25 percent of the migrants. About 20 percent of the colonists had worked in the textile industry, usually at the low end of things; about 10 percent were woodworkers; and more than half were artisans or had practiced some sort of craft. Most, of course, would have to become farmers and jacks-of-all-trades in the New World, and that seems to be exactly what was expected.

Winthrop himself provides a clear example of the agonizing personal decisions migrants had to make in leaving their homes, jobs, and extended families, embarking on a highly dangerous ocean voyage, and settling anew in what they saw as wilderness. Born in 1588, John Winthrop matured admist the dramatic social and economic changes altering forever the face of England. Groton Manor, his family homestead, contributed to the growing market economy of East Anglia, but only in a small way. The family made most of the products they used. An intense, religious youth, Winthrop was drawn to the emotional reassurances provided by Puritanism. He walked miles to hear a good sermon and often sang psalms and read religious tracts. The changes he saw transforming the world of his parents only heightened his religious commitment—families ruined by economic mischance, epidemics killing hundreds, and poverty and violence becoming facts of life in the country-side. Winthrop received a legal education at Cambridge and was appointed to a governmental judicial post, but by the end of the 1620s his fortunes were in decline. He held no office, was in debt, was concerned over his ability to provide for his sons' futures, and was increasingly convinced of England's impending doom. Like others, he was particularly struck by Charles I's growing ties with Spain and the king's failure to defend the Protestant cause in the Netherlands. When Laud stepped up the attack on Puritan clerics after 1628 and forced leading ministers like William Ames into exile, it seemed that God had finally declared the moment of vengeance at hand.

The life of John Dane, born about 1612 to a tailor, provides similar insight into the motives of more ordinary Englishmen. From age eight on, Dane was continually beset by guilt over his disobedience to his parents; he apparently often ran out to play without first asking his father's permission, for which "sin" he was beaten. At eighteen, he took up dancing, and when his father beat him for pursuing such a profane activity, Dane left home—"to seek my fortune," as he said. For a while, he seems to have been a sort of virtuous Tom Jones, defending his character against the advances and temptations of unvirtuous maids. On one occasion, while staying at an inn at Hertford, he returned late one night to find the inn's door locked. When he knocked and was admitted, "the hostess sat in a chair by the fire in her naked shift, holding her breasts open. She said to me . . . 'come, let us drink a pot,' and several times reiterated her words. I said I was so sleepy that I could not stay with her now, but I would drink a cup with her in the morning, and so I hastened away to my chamber." From the perspective of old age (Dane was over sixty when he wrote this account), the tailor was a bit hard on himself. "Here I took no notice of the goodness of God in restraining me," he remembered, "but rather ascribed it to myself. . . ." He continued to wander the English countryside, preserving his honor against such temptations until he finally received the word of God. He migrated to New England, "thinking that I should be more free here than there from temptations . . .,"[4] but he found the devil in the New World as well. So, too, would many Puritans suffer future disillusionment in their search for spiritual and secular peace.

Not everyone came to New England in flight from the devil. The London authorities were rumored to want Robert Wright, a linen draper and brewer, "for clipping the king's coin." Christopher Gardiner, a London adventurer, abandoned two wives in London to live with Mary Groves, "a known harlot," in Boston. William Schooler wounded a man in a duel in England and abandoned his wife there to come to the New World, where the Massachusetts government eventually hanged him for raping and killing a female servant. The Puritans may have believed New England to be a brave new world, but they could not completely escape the vagaries of human nature.

Settlement

The Massachusetts Bay area was the focus of growing English interest throughout the 1620s. In 1623, the Council for New England sponsored a settlement attempt led by Sir Ferdinando Gorges's son Robert. Wintering at the abandoned Weston site at Wessagusett, the group of gentlemen, mechanics, farmers, traders, and clergymen suffered through a dispiriting season, and Gorges returned to England in the spring. The remainder drifted in small groups to the north shore area and established fishing stations. Their failure reflected Sir Ferdinando's continuing and unrealistic desires to establish a manorial system in the New World. His schemes sought income from land ownership rather than from trade, fishing, or agriculture. The council could not even control settlement under its own grant as small, independent settlements began to appear in the area. Plymouth was one such site, and small fishing stations sprang up in the region north of Cape Ann; the most significant were Monhegan and the Isle of Shoals, island stations that remained important until the 1640s.

In 1623, the Dorchester Company, under the council's auspices, organized a permanent colony at Cape Ann. The colony was too far from the fishing banks to prosper, but Roger Conant did establish a small settlement on the nearby Naumkeag Peninsula in 1626. Meanwhile, the Reverend John White, a key member of the Dorchester group, began to encourage the London Puritan community to consider the area as a possible refuge for persecuted Puritans. In 1628, the council granted the London group the Dorchester Company's old patent, under the title of the New England Company. The grant encompassed an area that extended from three miles north of the Merrimack River to three miles south of the Charles River, from sea to sea. Company leaders chose John Endecott to lead a group of forty settlers to Naumkeag, now renamed Salem (Hebrew for peace). In March 1629, they received a royal charter and became known as the Massachusetts Bay Company. Endecott and later immigrants established a settlement along the South River, on the opposite side of the peninsula from the Conant group. They built houses and planted crops, turned to fishing, grazing, and harvesting grasses from the marshes for food and export products, and even started a shipbuilding industry. The area soon became crowded, and settlers dispersed to other sites along the north and south coasts.

Meanwhile, back in England, the Massachusetts Bay Company was busily working out the details of a governing structure. The charter formed twenty-six investors into a corporation that had all property and administrative powers. A governor, deputy-governor, and eighteen assistants who would wield these powers were to be elected annually by the company's membership. The entire membership would meet quarterly in a General Court that could pass all laws necessary, provided "such laws and ordinances be not contrary or repugnant to the laws and statutes . . . of England."[5] In all, the company had about one hundred investors, mostly moderate Puritans who remained outwardly conforming members of the Church of England.

Joint-stock companies normally kept their headquarters in England, allowing the Crown to oversee their activities and making it possible for anyone to purchase shares. The Puritans wanted both to avoid royal interference and to restrict membership in the company. Their original charter, for some unknown reason, did not stipulate that the company had to have its headquarters in England. Thus, in late August 1629, Winthrop, Dudley, and ten other Puritan leaders met secretly in Cambridge and pledged to move to the new colony if the company would surrender to them all legal authority and the charter itself. Agreement was quickly reached, committing the group to erecting a separate, self-governing colony. On March 29, 1630, seven ships (including the *Arbella,* with Winthrop on board) and almost a thousand settlers left Southampton. Seven more ships left England at the end of April; seventeen vessels in all made the voyage during that year.

Landing at Salem, the leaders immediately expressed their dissatisfaction with the location, undoubtedly due to the small colony's inability to handle their substantial needs. An exploration party led by Winthrop concluded that the entire company should settle along the Mystic River (Medford), but Dudley offered an alternative site along the Charles River. They agreed on a compromise site at Charlestown, at the mouth of the Charles, settling there in June 1630. But the colonists began to disperse almost immediately, and new settlements quickly appeared at Watertown, Roxbury, and Medford, while the principal group, including Winthrop, finally decided to move to the Shawmut peninsula, now renamed Boston, which rapidly became the colony's largest community. By December 1630, there were seven settlements: Salem, Dorchester, Boston, Medford, Charlestown, Watertown, and Roxbury.

These first immigrants all saw the voyage as a rite of passage of great import. Their decision to migrate, as we have seen, was a difficult one, and small husbandmen with families had to come up with about twenty-five pounds to pay for their passage and accumulate supplies to see them through—equal to the annual rent for a family farm in England. The crossing took eight to ten weeks and offered all the sufferings of ocean travel at the time; seasickness was particularly painful for these farmers for the first week or two. But they adjusted, passing the time with tales of sea serpents and prayer. The Cooper family of Brampton, Suffolk, was like many others that migrated. The group included Benjamin; his wife, Elizabeth; their four children; a son-in-law; Benjamin's sister; and two servants. Benjamin died on the voyage (death rates were actually rather low among the Puritan migrants), and as a result, we have a detailed accounting of his estate. The Coopers brought a good deal of food and clothing, along with cloth, two carpets, twenty-eight pairs of sheets, table linens, napkins, blankets, curtains, seven feather beds and three flock beds, a variety of weapons and agricultural tools, and cooking and eating utensils. They did not bring any vehicles or materials to construct a house; most of the migrants knew they would have to rely on local artisans. In their later letters home to friends and relatives, they encouraged artisans, particularly carpenters, to migrate and offered advice about what they should and should not bring with them. Most of the early colonists arrived in the summer and spent several weeks in Boston seeking information about various communities. Though many families moved about a good deal, most settled permanently within five years, many within a year.

The Puritans' first winter in the New World was no different from that experienced by most North American settlers during the early decades of the century. More than two hundred died, many from fever and scurvy, and another hundred returned to England. But by the end of 1631, reverse migration had slowed, and more than two thousand new settlers had arrived, bringing with them much needed supplies. Winthrop's leadership was critical during this period. He gave of his own resources, sent men to buy corn from the Indians, and established a successful farm on the Mystic River to set a positive example for the rest of the settlers. The leaders of the nascent colony also recognized the need to establish some form of governmental control immediately and held three meetings in August and September 1630. They passed a variety of measures, transferring certain practices from the Old World and establishing new ones to deal with the unique circumstances of the New. They set minimum wages for carpenters, sawyers, and other laborers and fixed commodity prices. They embargoed corn exports to preserve the precarious food supply and prohibited the sale of firearms to Indians to maintain the settlers' technological superiority.

The fledgling communities benefited most from the relative absence of Indians in the area. The Massachusett and Pawtucket tribes had been gravely weakened by epidemics and raids by neighboring tribes and actually hoped that the colonists could provide them with some protection against their Indian enemies. Thus, the first towns were settled with Indian consent, but with no acknowledgement of native ownership of the land. For their part, the English believed it was God's will that they occupy and cultivate the earth. They embraced the concept of *vacuum domicilium,* the notion that lands that were not in productive use were not in fact owned by their inhabitants. Few English settlers recognized the systematic ways in which Indians used their land. Colonists simply assumed that they had sovereignty over the land and its inhabitants. It was several years before they began to purchase land from sachems, and only when problems emerged over possible Indian inheritance claims to white-occupied land.

Religion

Historians agree that Puritanism played a major part in this migration, but there is little consensus about what made New England Puritanism unique and distinctive.

Puritansim is not definable as a particular set of social, economic, or political attitudes. The bulk of the colonists' "cultural baggage" in these areas was carried over
substantially from their English experiences. Though English Puritans established
the general parameters of belief and practice, Puritanism itself underwent crucial
changes in doctrine and structure as a result of this passage to the New World.
Ministers and laity alike, finally free from persecution, were now forced to be more
precise in defining their religious tenets to bring some order to the often perplexing
diversity of beliefs that existed under the rubric of Puritansim.

Their first task was to establish churches. A congregation generally started with
a small group of pious candidates who examined each other to assure themselves
of their own religious purity. They were then similarly questioned by other members of the community. In Dedham (founded in 1636), the eight candidates asked
the town's inhabitants "if they had any offences or grievances in their spirits from
any of us and knew any just cause which might move us to leave out any, that now
they would faithfully and plainly deal with such a one." The leaders who emerged
unscathed from this process were known as the "pillars of the church," and they
signed a covenant in which they promised "to live together . . . according to the
rule of love in . . . faithful mutual helpfulness in the ways of God for the spiritual
and temporal good and comfort of one another. . . ."[6] These individuals then examined all those who wished to be admitted to the congregation. All members chose
the congregation's officers and then selected and ordained the pastor. If the congregation was large enough, a second minister, a teacher, was also appointed. The
pastor was responsible for preaching and administering the sacraments. Ruling
elders and deacons shared other duties.

The early migrants generally represented the moderate center of Puritan doctrine. Yet even they often disagreed on major issues of belief and polity, and the
dialogue and disputes between these various groups were instrumental in defining
New England Puritanism. Puritanism may have been a monopoly religion in early
Massachusetts, but it was not a monolith; considerable institutional and theological
diversity existed from the beginning. There was ambiguity and often bitter disagreement over such essential matters as covenant theology and the process of conversion. Inevitably, however, a unified, clearly identifiable religious experience that
can be confidently called Puritanism emerged.

The essential Puritan beliefs included the following: God's essence was hidden
and unknowable, he possessed absolute divine sovereignty, and he was benevolent
and caring. Puritans believed that humans, on the other hand, had been corrupted
by original sin and that their faculties, or intellectual and moral abilities, were subsequently disordered. With the fall of Adam, the human will had lost its inclination
for good and could not be saved without God's intervention. Predestination alone
determined man's fate, and nothing a person could do on this earth could change
the certainty of his or her destiny. Puritans were further distinguished by their
unyielding belief in the Bible as the sole source of the Word of God, and by their
emphasis on the sermon as the center or worship. They believed that the church
had been imperfectly reformed and that it contained far too many elements of formalism and ritual; the sacraments and the legalistic trappings of worship that characterized the Anglican church were meaningless to them. The Puritan conception of
a church gradually evolved into a conviction of the relative equality of minister and
parishioners; a true church consisted of a group of believers who chose a pastor to
serve them. Thus, Puritans sought to complete the Reformation by returning to the
original simplicity of the primitive church. Anglicans, on the other hand, increasingly emphasized free will and the ability of humans to effect their own salvation.

Puritans were thus differentiated not so much by the specific tenets they
espoused but by the tenacity of their commitment and the fervor of their belief.

Puritanism spoke to the need for direction and assurance, for conviction and psychological certitude. Faith explained the external world. The divine scheme justified (or damned) the pursuits of men; self-discipline helped individuals adapt to (or fight against) the evils of the secular world. Preachers brought to their congregations quickened religiosity and an emphasis on the emotional, experiential aspects of conversion with the resultant strengthening of community ties. Puritanism was most traditional, finally, in its emphasis on the centrality of the sacred and the relative unimportance of this life. At the same time, by emphasizing the imminence of God's final judgment and the uncertainty of individual salvation, Puritanism promoted a powerful sense of loss, confusion, and anxiety. The tortuous complexity of Puritan theology heightened this sense of uncertainty. Ministers and laity alike walked a doctrinal tightrope.

The covenant was at the heart of Puritan theology. It defined the relationship between God and humans and laid out the rules and responsibilities of each; it identified the Puritans as God's chosen people and gave them a collective identity. Covenantal thought, of course, was not unique to Puritans but present in a wide variety of reformed religions. It was the precise form of the Puritan covenant that was unique. Puritans believed that in the original covenant of works, God promised Adam and his descendants eternal happiness if they would obey his will without question. Original sin destroyed this covenant, and humans became subject to physical suffering and death, their spiritual facilities became disoriented, their souls corrupted, and their wills man-centered rather than God-centered. Instead of recognizing the need for a proper relationship with God, humans now sought gratification of the senses; passion ruled over reason. After the Fall, then, men and women were by nature sinful, dead to the voice of God. They deserved only external damnation.

God still required obedience, but it alone could no longer earn salvation. In his infinite mercy, God decided to limit his own power and to rescue a select few from eternal damnation. He did this through the covenant of redemption, whereby his son Jesus Christ saved these men and women through his sacrifice on the cross. Through Christ's death and his voluntary atonement for the sins of humans, God also created a covenant of grace that allowed the chosen few to realize their sinfulness and to receive saving grace through the irresistable action of the Divine Spirit. The covenant of grace involved a true conversion, a change in the nature and behavior of the saved.

The complexity of this process gave rise to a number of doctrinal debates among New England Puritans. The nature of predestination itself, for example, created a paradox that neither ministers nor laity was ever able to solve. If one was saved, why bother to lead a holy life? Why not simply enjoy oneself, since God had already foreordained one's fate? If one was damned, the same logic could readily apply. Ministers explored a variety of answers to such questions, but there were some universal beliefs. Puritans believed, for instance, that no one could ever be sure of salvation. This was essentially a religion of anxiety, and its promises stopped short of complete assurance. Uncertainty and doubt concerning their salvation constantly wracked even such eminent Puritan ministers as Thomas Shepard.

Puritanism found itself most torn over the nature of the covenant of grace. At one extreme were those who believed that God's divine presence came suddenly and without warning, unsought by human intention; others argued that humans had to prepare thoroughly and carefully for the presence of God in their soul and that these very actions could ensure salvation. To chart a course between these poles, Puritan ministers developed a detailed description of the process of conversion, designed both to alleviate the laity's concerns and to guard against doctrinal heresy. But the ministers themselves could not agree on the nature of the process.

❧ *Documents* ❧
The Struggle for Salvation

The first selection below, from a diary kept by Elizabeth White and discovered only after death in 1669, suggests the intense anxiety over salvation that plagued many of the laity. The second selection, from the diary of the Reverend Michael Wigglesworth, reveals that ministers, too, suffered such doubts.

> O how loath was I to acquaint him (her minister) with my sad State! I was ashamed to tell him that I was yet a Stranger to God and all Goodness, till it was forced from me. . . . then there came many Sins to my Remembrance, which I had taken no notice of before, counting them small Sins; . . . and I thought that there was no Mercy for me, but he perswaded me there was hope of Mercy for such as I, and that the Lord waited to be gracious to poor Sinners, and then I was a little satisfied for the present; but then I was troubled with Blasphemous Thoughts, which were very grievous to me: I thought I had a Heart worse than the Devil, and wondered that I was not consumed in some strange Manner. When I have seen a Spider, which of all Things is most loathsome to me, I have been ready to wish my self such a one, esteeming of it to be in a far happier Condition than I was; I was afraid to be in the Dark, lest I should meet the Devil. . . .

The Experiences of God's gracious Dealing with Mrs. Elizabeth White. As they were written under her own Hand, and found in her Closet, after her Decease, December 5, 1669 (Boston: 1741), 5–6.

> I feel such distractions in holy duties, such deadness of heart at lecture, such pride in divine assistance and in my own notions, even then when I have been taught to have no confidence in the flesh, a pang of worldly desires amidst hearing the word, that I am ashamed to lift up my face to heaven. . . .
>
> But above all, my vileness breaks forth again while I am hearing the word. An atheistic irreverrent frame seizes upon me; and while God is bidding me see His glory I cannot see it; vile and unworthy conceptions concerning God come into my mind. . . . Blind mind! Carnal heart! I am afraid, ashamed, heavy laden under such cursed frames of heart as ever and anon beset me. My soul groans, my body faints, Lord, while I pray and cry for pardon and redemption.

Edward S. Morgan, ed., *The Diary of Michael Wigglesworth, 1653–1657* (New York: Harper & Row, 1965 [c. 1946]), 55.

Some stressed the careful, rational preparation of the soul for the reception of grace. Such "preparationists" (or intellectuals) as Thomas Hooker of Connecticut believed that true contrition could signal grace even before it came. Most ministers shied away from this extreme position, since it seemed to put too much power in the hands of humans and too little in those of God. Others believed that even the elect could do little to prepare themselves for God's presence, that the spirit came when and how it wished. These "voluntarists" comprised an important element of the migration to New England during the second half of the 1630s.

The disagreements heightened rather than assuaged anxiety and doubt among the brethren, and the laity sought answers elsewhere. They turned to Foxe's *Book of Martyrs* for models, avidly searched Scripture for assurances, examined their own souls for signs of salvation, and learned as much from each other as they did from the ministry. In time, they were able to impose their own meaning on the nature of conversion.

During the early years of settlement, accommodating such differences of belief and polity seemed relatively easy. The establishment of new standards for church admission, for instance, came with minimal conflict. John Cotton's arrival in Massachusetts in 1633 was a key turning point here. Cotton was perhaps the most renowned Puritan minister in both New and Old England. His migration involved considerable soul-searching because he often felt that he was abandoning the cause by leaving England. Immediately upon his arrival, he assumed the post of teacher in the Boston church, and his preaching soon stimulated a revival. The new converts, drawing upon the practice of lay sermonizing then current, related to the congregation how they had come to believe in their election. Quickly, this relation became an essential step in the conversion process, and new members soon faced the requirement of making a profession of faith and an explication of the workings of the grace God had wrought within them. In 1636, a new Dorchester church was prevented from forming because its members could not so describe their experiences. By 1640, the requirement was widespread in Massachusetts and New Haven, somewhat less so in Connecticut. It was not always easy. In Dedham, the minister allowed Robert Hinsdell's wife to make her profession privately, since she proved to be "fearful and not able to speak in public, . . . fainting away there. . . ."[7] In time, the conversion relation was further reduced to a formula—a clearly outlined prescription of how the individual's faith had been attained, together with various preparatory rules. In seeking to define who was truly saved, Puritans thus ran the risk of relying upon the very sort of ritual they had rejected in the Anglican church.

Roger Williams   The conversion narratives were a way in which Puritans addressed one of their most vexing theological questions: if only God knew who was truly saved, how were humans to judge the validity of their churches? Individuals such as Roger Williams came to feel that no solution to this problem was within human reach. Williams arrived in Massachusetts Bay in February 1631. Possessed of a brilliant intellect and strong Separatist learnings, he refused to accept an appointment as a teacher in the Boston church unless the church fully repudiate its ties to the Church of England. He moved to Salem, but the General Court questioned his suitability to become a teacher there. He and his wife then moved to Plymouth, but he eventually concluded that even its church was insufficiently Separatist for him. Returning to Salem in 1633, he became an unofficial assistant to the Reverend Samuel Skelton. There, he questioned the growing tendency of Massachusetts ministers to consult with each other, accusing them of drifting toward Presbyterianism and abandoning the most basic tenet of congregational polity, the independence of each church. Williams upset the authorities still further by arguing that the king had no right to grant land to the Puritans since it belonged to the Indians. In late 1633, the court censured him, and he was penitent. But problems arose again the following spring when Skelton died and the church called Williams to become its pastor.

⮞ *Documents* ⮜
Justifying a
Conversion Narrative

At mid-century, Puritan ministers gathered to codify their principal beliefs. The result, the Cambridge Platform (1648), reflects an attempt to find a middle road among competing elements in the church. The excerpt below justifies the introduction of a conversion narrative.

> The Doors of the Churches of Christ upon Earth do not by God's appointment stand so wide open, that all sorts of people, good or bad, may freely enter therein at their pleasure, but such as are admitted thereto, as members, ought to be examined and tried first, whether they be fit and meet to be received into church society, or not. The officers are charged with the keeping of the Doors of the Church. Twelve angels are set at the Gates of the Temple, lest such as were ceremonially unclean should enter thereinto. . . .
>
> The weakest measure of faith is to be accepted in those that desire to be admitted into the Church, because weak Christians, if sincere, have the substance of that faith, repentance, and holiness which is required in church members; and such have most need of the ordinances for their confirmation and growth in grace.

"The Cambridge Platform," H. Shelton Smith, Robert T. Handy, and Lefferts A. Loetshcen, eds., *American Christianity,* 2 vols. (New York: Scribner's, 1960), 1:129–30.

Within a year, Williams informed Salem that he could not in conscience communicate with other churches nor even maintain communion with the Salem church unless it joined him in denouncing such ties between churches. Threatened by the General Court, Salem began to back away from its ties with Williams. The court called Williams twice more before it, and the second time he refused to recant his views. In October 1635, the court ordered him banished from the colony. His poor health brought temporary respite, but in January 1636, because the unrepentant Williams continued his agitation, the court issued a warrant for his immediate removal to England. Warned by Winthrop, with whom he maintained a warm relationship, Williams escaped to found Providence, Rhode Island.

Though his beliefs threatened both the legal and spiritual validity of Massachusett's existence, Williams was in many ways a logical extension, albeit a radical one, of essential Puritan beliefs. He believed that the apostolic succession had been cut in the fourth century when the Roman emperor Theodosius made Christianity the state religion and that no true church had existed since then. Since church and state, moreover, were based on different and incompatible principles, the two must be separate. Williams argued that the state was based on force, the church on love; if the state intervened in church affairs, not only would it be promoting a false church, it would be perverting and corrupting the church. Finally, Williams became increasingly concerned about purity of worship. He came to believe that the elect could not worship with the unregenerate, even if they were part of the same family. He withdrew even from the church he founded in Providence, and he found religious peace only after a long pilgrimage.

Anne Hutchinson   The case of Anne Hutchinson proved more disruptive to the Puritan sense of religious unity. Hutchinson arrived with her husband, William, in Boston in 1634. Her father had been imprisoned twice for religious unorthodoxy in England, and she had come to New England in part to follow John Cotton, whose sermons and teachings she had admired. During the summer of 1635, she began weekly meetings in her home, where she gave oral summaries of the Sabbath sermon for women who had been unable to attend the service. At the time, such meetings were not unusual; rigid preparationism was still in its infancy, and ministers encouraged the laity to seek the word on their own. Winthrop himself had preached on occasion. But John Wilson's preaching at the Boston church began to disturb Hutchinson. A preparationist, Wilson typified the growing drift among some ministers toward an emphasis on human action delineated by clear, ritualistic boundaries. Cotton explicitly opposed this tendency, arguing that the laity was being lulled into a false sense of security by an undue emphasis on good works. At the same time, some of the laity had begun to believe that once assured of salvation, a person was freed from the manmade laws of church and state and took his or her commands only from God. This group, known as Antinomians ("against the law"), elected a sympathizer, Henry Vane, as governor in 1636.

By the summer of 1636, Hutchinson's meetings began to attract a different sort of person—merchants who resented ministers and magistrates judging their business practices. If they could draw assurance directly from God, they felt, they would not need to listen to the colony's civil or religious authorities. Hutchinson began to argue that the Massachusetts clergy, with the sole exceptions of Cotton and John Wheelwright, her brother-in-law, preached a covenant of works rather than of grace. She moved toward a more mystical conception of grace, stressing an individual's sense of inner conviction that he or she had been saved. In this conception, the spirit operated independently of sermon and Bible alike and had no relationship to outward conduct or the performance of good works. Supported by a majority of her congregation, Hutchinson even made an abortive attempt to establish a new church headed by Wheelwright.

Such teachings could not be tolerated by clergy and political leaders who were struggling to define a theology that was threatening to become more diverse by the day. Hutchinson's beliefs were at the outer limits of acceptable practice and a clear threat to clerical authority. Thus, when she and her followers walked out of the meeting house when Wilson rose to preach, the colony's leaders felt they had to take some action. A majority of the church, however, protected her from censure, and Gov. Vane's support kept her from being prosecuted. When Winthrop won the gubernatorial election of 1637, however, the dissidents faced prosecution. A synod, or conference of ministers, was called to discuss a list of eighty-two errors that threatened Puritan orthodoxy. The synod condemned private religious meetings in homes and forbade critical questioning of the clergy. The General Court then banished Wheelwright and several others and placed Hutchinson on trial. As it had with Williams, the colony leadership sought to deal with dissent and religious difference of opinion through expulsion, narrowing the span of permissible discourse in the Bay Colony.

The members of the court revealed their true concerns in their interrogation of Hutchinson. They often heaped scorn upon her simply because she was a woman.

To hold meetings in her house, Winthrop declared, was "not tolerable nor comely in the sight of God nor fitting for your sex." The governor believed that women should be submissive and supportive and described Hutchinson as "woman of haughty and fierce carriage, nimble wit and active spirit and a very voluble tongue. . . ." Most damning, though, were "her speeches in derogation of the ministers among us, and the weakening of the hands and hearts of the people toward us." Her threat to social peace and her refusal to defer to male leadership were unacceptable transgressions. For her part, Hutchinson matched her accusers' scriptural evidence passage for passage. But when asked how she knew one of her assertions to be true, she replied that God had so instructed her "by the voice of his own Spirit to my soul."[8] In the end, Hutchinson marked herself as unwilling to accept the institutional structure of the church or to bow to male religious and social domination. The General Court banished her.

Williams and Hutchinson were only the most visible of the many who remained outside the Puritan religious mainstream. The paradoxes of Puritanism invited a bewildering variety of solutions. While the most extreme of these— England's Levellers, Ranters, and others who appeared during the civil war—did not invade New England's shores, the heterogeneity of religious persuasion remains impressive. Yet most dissenters had little political or religious impact, since they remained isolated in small groups within orthodox Puritan congregations; magistrates prosecuted them only if they tried to proselytize. Most lost whatever influence they might have hoped to exert as ministers co-opted their platforms, altering official doctrine and practice to include as many of the faithful as possible or condemning certain beliefs as unacceptable. In this sense, the New England Puritanism that ultimately prevailed was a result of conflict and dialogue between dissenters and establishment ministers, as well as between ministers and laity. Those who could not accept the result moved, willingly or otherwise. Even John Cotton, one of the most highly regarded ministers of his generation, retreated from his earlier position and lost some of his power in New England ministerial circles.

One of the key divides in this process came in the mid- to late 1630s. Winthrop and his cohort of migrants had fled God's judgment on England, but they always retained the belief that only a few wicked men had subverted the Almighty's purpose. Those who fled the later Laudian persecutions embraced a far more bitter, disillusioned, and militant vision. Dissidents of sharply sectarian views, including many Separatists, arrived in significant numbers. The General Court began to intervene more actively in church affairs after this influx, seeking to control a threatening diversity—and popularization—of church polity. In 1648, New England ministers met in a synod, hoping to agree on a statement of common doctrine and practice. The result, the Cambridge Platform, was accepted by Massachusetts, Plymouth, Connecticut, and New Haven churches. Magistrates and clergy agreed to work together to enforce the platform, with mixed results. In the early 1650s, the court twice stopped Boston's Third Church from ordaining Gabriel Powell, a candidate who had no formal education, and the magistrates openly expressed their concern over the proliferation of radical sects in England during the civil war. But they had little success in their efforts to eliminate lay preaching. And Baptists, Quakers, and other dissenting groups were about to strike a major blow at Puritan hegemony.

Government

The Massachusetts Bay charter gave power to the freemen or company shareholders, who were required to meet four times a year as a General Court. But only a dozen or so members of the company actually migrated to the colony, and the eight qualified freemen who attended the first meeting in October 1630 voted to transfer all legislative and appointive power to the Court of Assistants—themselves. And while the Court of Assistants voted to open freemanship to any adult male who wished to apply, it also ruled that freemen could vote only to elect assistants, who in turn would choose the governor and deputy-governor from among themselves.

The assistants now proceeded to grant lands and set town boundaries, vote taxes and appoint officers, and banish those they viewed as unfit to remain in the colony. Acting in their judicial guise, they also issued judgments in cases of drunkenness, manslaughter, and the use of tobacco, dice, and cards. By the next General Court meeting in May 1631, they had admitted 118 settlers to freemanship. At this meeting, the assistants took a step that proved decisive to the political future of the colony, ruling that henceforth only church members could be admitted to freemanship. During the early decades, this provision actually expanded the franchise greatly beyond that which would have applied in England since most males did, indeed, belong to the early churches. While the Puritans continued to believe in deferential rule by a small social elite, the extension of freemanship established a new standard of community membership that drastically altered English precedent.

The leaders continued to modify the colony's governmental structure over the next two decades in response to internal and external pressures. Early in 1632, for instance, critics of the New England polity pressured the Privy Council to launch an investigation of the colony's practices. The assistants responded by taxing the towns in order to erect fortifications against possible interference from London. But some refused to pay; as the town of Watertown noted, freemen had a right to be involved in such decisions. Winthrop stood his ground, but he did allow the towns to appoint a committee of representatives to advise the assistants on taxation issues. The towns answered by demanding to see the charter, and the freemen discovered that they had been denied their legislative rights from the beginning. In May 1632, the entire General Court won the power to select the governor and the deputy-governor, though they could choose them only from among the assistants (eventually all freemen could vote for the officials). Each town was now allowed to elect two or three representatives to the General Court, which in its entirely claimed the power to levy taxes, grant lands, and make laws, as the original charter had stipulated. In 1636, the General Court established a court system, and in 1641, it further restricted the discretionary power of the magistrates by codifying the colony's laws in *The Body of Liberties,* a process extended with the 1648 publication of the *Book of the General Laws and Liberties*.

The most dramatic change in governmental structure came in 1644. Until this time, both legislative bodies, the assistants and the deputies, sat as one group, and the assistants retained the power to veto the votes of the deputies. Now, the widow Goodwife Sherman issued a complaint that the merchant Robert Keayne had stolen and butchered her prize pig; Keayne maintained his innocence, and the matter eventually came before the General Court. The majority of the deputies found for the widow, but the assistants favored Keayne and vetoed the decision. Winthrop attacked the deputies for not agreeing with the assistants and accused them of trying to establish a democracy by insisting on e same political powers as their social superiors. The deputies held their ground. The two sides finally worked out a compromise; the deputies would sit as a separate house, and the assistants would serve as the upper house of the legislature.

Though the deputies had considerable popular support from the beginning, this was not a democracy. Most people in the early seventeenth century continued to believe in a world of order and social hierarchy. Deference prevailed in political life, as voters usually accepted the claims of male, propertied officeholders, including the deputies, to superior wisdom and skill in government. Winthrop best expressed these beliefs in his commentary on the 1645 Hingham militia case. This complex situation developed when a minority faction of Hingham's inhabitants succeeded in electing their candidate, Anthony Eames, to the captaincy of the town's militia. The majority, led by pastor Peter Hobart, chose a rival captain and refused to obey Eames's orders. The assistants heard the rancorous case and decided in favor of Eames. Winthrop then lectured the deputies and freemen on the principles of deferential government, reminding them that once a leader had been elected by his people, the voters were bound to follow his rule; they would have their chance to register their discontent at the next election.

Consensus was far more important than majority rule in this society, and throughout the century, the General Court made adjustments to allow as many people as possible to participate politically. Nonfreemen who took the oath of allegiance could vote for minor militia offices and hold the offices themselves, and in 1647, the General Court ruled that males twenty-four years of age and older who took the oath could serve on juries and vote for selectmen. By 1664, the franchise was opened to all who possessed ten pounds of ratable property and were orthodox in religion. Town officials often ignored legal restrictions in their desire to make sure that everyone with a stake in the society was represented. Thus, a father would speak for his children, wife, and servants. At mid-century, about half of the adult males were freemen, but Massachusetts's political society embraced the majority of its inhabitants in one way or another, and most supported the government. Ironically, many who were eligible decided not to seek the franchise, apparently wishing to avoid the often burdensome duties attached to it.

New England Towns

Town meetings are the stuff of New England political myth, and with good reason. For many years, the General Court allowed local government to follow its own paths with little coercive pressure from the top. A town began when a group petitioned the court to establish a new settlement. In 1642, for instance, a group of settlers who had petitioned the court for a land grant were granted an area of four square miles with the power to divide the land as they saw fit, provided they occupied the tract within two years. As other towns did, the group then laid out a tract and appointed a committee of proprietors to select settlers, choose sites for home lots, deal with the specifics of land distribution, and resolve a host of other concerns. The covenant sworn by all members of the new town was particularly significant. These early settlers faced a strange country and a strange people, suffered a profound fear of the wilderness, and lived with a gnawing loneliness and sense of loss. Thus, their need for unity and a protective identity was intensified, and these desires were most clearly expressed in the early town covenants. In these communal rituals, inhabitants pledged to live together in love, peace, and brotherhood, forgoing personal gain for the benefit of all. The covenants clearly represented the ideals of the traditional society that the early settlers sought to recreate.

The court required each town to support a minister and a church and, if it had a population of more than forty, to send a representative to the General Court. In part, proprietors allotted land according to wealth and status. Hence, status in England, to a degree, determined status in America. Family size and service to the community, however, were equally important considerations, and the gap between the wealthiest and poorest settlers was much narrower than in similar English towns; most farms ranged from fifty to 150 acres in size. In Billerica, the median

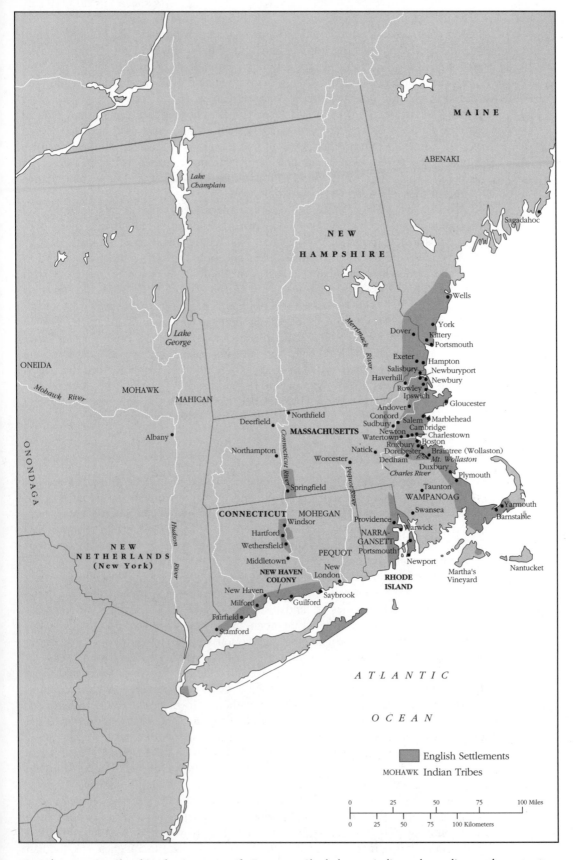

MAP 4.1: New England in the Seventeenth Century Shaded areas indicate the earliest settlements.

grant to 115 men in 1651 was sixty acres, the mean ninety-six acres. The original settlers of Rowley received house lots on only one and a half to two acres in size, and either four and a half or eight acres in the first division of arable land. Since original settlers became town proprietors and were able to control the division of additional common lands in the future, their holdings could increase considerably over time, a necessity if they were to provide for their children. The only common element in the division of land across the colony was its variability—no two towns were alike in their methods of dividing the bounty of the New World.

Land allotment patterns depended on the particular mix and experience of the new town's leaders and settlers, and the tracts and towns themselves varied widely in size and shape. The mix of types of land also varied, with meadows, ponds, marshes, timber, rocky uplands, and sometimes areas cleared by Indian burning practices. House lots, averaging four to six acres, centered around a meetinghouse and were frequently laid out on each side of a central street. The proprietors allocated unallotted land outside the center of town in a series of later divisions and made a conscious attempt to provide each family with a mixture of meadows, fields, and upland timber tracts. Edmund Rice, a leading citizen of Sudbury, had a four-acre house lot, thirty-three acres of river meadow, fifty-four acres across the river, and a share in the town's open fields.

No matter what kind of town they lived in, few settlers were happy with plots scattered willy-nilly across the landscape, and in most towns they quickly worked to consolidate their various holdings and move closer to their fields. The General Court, disturbed by such dispersal away from the town centers, passed laws requiring all houses to be within a certain distance of the meetinghouse, but people continued to pursue their own goals. New nodes of population quickly emerged and sometimes houses were even dispersed along paths or roads, widely separated from each other. Only a few towns were like early Andover, a classic nucleated village, inhabitants living around the meetinghouse and working together in a traditional open field system. By the 1640s, the Dedham town meeting allowed farmers to fence in their lots, and an active land market enabled individuals to consolidate their holdings.

The common field system was little more than a memory by mid-century in Dedham, and towns like Andover followed suit. The first allocation of land in Andover dispensed house lots within a narrow range of size—four to twenty acres. The first open field division of 160 acres divided the land between twenty-one lot holders at the rate of one acre per acre of house lot, and the second division followed the same pattern. But the third division indicated a shift, allocating four acres for each acre of house lot, with land not from a single field but widely dispersed throughout the town. At the same time, the selectmen granted newcomers land in a single piece, rather that in house lots and small portions scattered around the town. The village center remained, but by the early 1660s, many of the town's early residents were moving away from the center and consolidating their holdings, which was made possible by the generous size of the third allotment. Within twenty years, half of the town's inhabitants lived in the south end. The final blow to the open-field system came with the fourth division in 1662, which allowed each resident to take up at least eighty acres anywhere within four miles of the meetinghouse. In a few years, residents were selling plots to anyone who wished to settle there. Not all towns changed so rapidly, of course. People in towns such as Rowley seemed reluctant to consolidate their holdings, and even in Dedham, only a few farmers had consolidated all of their land and moved their homes away from the village. As many different patterns existed as there were towns. All, though, were moving in the same direction.

Town government also followed English precedent, continuing the intense ties with the past. The General Court gave the town meeting the power to regulate local concerns and to make local bylaws and ordinances; to elect local officers, such as constables and highway surveyors; and to deal with such concerns as the care of the poor and the regulation of local schools. Selectmen replaced the familiar vestry, but their duties were essentially the same. The meeting itself derived from a strong English tradition. East Anglian local government had been run by town meetings and selectmen for centuries. As in England, the specific powers and frequency of the meetings varied from town to town. The town meeting dominated political activity in villages such as Rowley. Here, too, inhabitants shared political duties equally and rotated through the local offices regularly; everyone shared in the daily burdens of ensuring adherence to the drainage, fencing, and livestock regulations so critical to life in small, open-field villages. Normally, the turnout for meetings in such towns was rather low—perhaps 10 percent to 30 percent of the adult male population But when a controversial issue was on the docket, close to 100 percent of the adult males could be counted on to attend, reflecting the town's desire to reach consensus on major decisions.

On the other hand, in Dedham, the selectmen made the crucial decisions, judging guilt or innocence when someone's cattle escaped to trample a neighbor's field or allowing farmers to take hay and firewood from the town commons. These seven officials met formally ten times a year and much more often informally, in smaller groups of four or five. John Gay's petition to build a new barn provides insight into how these men dealt with the daily problems of life in small, agricultural villages. Gay wanted to build the structure on public land closer to his fields. Two of the selectmen, Daniel Fisher and Thomas Fuller, went out to physically examine the site. Since Gay had no more public land coming to him, they worked out a deal. Gay agreed to allow the town to run a road across his house lot, and the town gave Gay the two acres of land he wanted for his barn, together with four acres of swampland leading from his fields to the Charles River. The entire process took only two weeks.

Not all New England towns were models of harmony and peace. Even those that embraced traditional social values found themselves constantly rent by internal conflict and bickering. Some, such as Ipswich, did not hesitate to bring suit against their own residents over such transgressions as the failure to pay taxes. It seems, though, that at least some towns and individuals had different goals from the very beginning. Newbury, settled by colonists from varied English backgrounds, began with a rigid social structure and marked inequalities in wealth. The town maintained an active land market and even sold proprietary rights. William Ilsly, typical of the wealthier inhabitants, raised cattle, sheep and hogs, engaged in dairying and cloth making, and even invested in an ocean-going vessel. Unlike in other New England towns, here there were no social or economic restrictions on the free market.

More spectacular exceptions can be found in the urban centers of early New England—Boston, Salem, and Springfield. But for the first few decades of the colony's life, these towns seemed more anomalous than typical. They served as magnets for those migrants who had more enterpreneurial ambitions. But most of the early settlers came here for more traditional reasons. The New World offered these people a degree of landed wealth they could only have dreamed of in England. Ownership of land brought control and mastery of life; it made the owner a full member of the community. But a farm offered more than just support for its immediate inhabitants. New Englanders worked both for themselves and for their descendants, to create a patrimony that would guarantee their children the same sort of lives they enjoyed. Most early towns, however they handled its distribution, had more than enough land to fulfill this traditional goal for some years. Even the many servants who came with the first settlers (almost 20 percent of the total emigrants) found opportunity unlike anything they had hoped for in England. Within a few years, most of them were free and owned their own farms; a few even became town proprietors and surpassed their former masters in accumulated wealth.

Society and the Economy

Early New Englanders pursued economic goals in ways and with attitudes that were profoundly traditional. They had left England, after all, in part to escape the growing incursion of modern economic forces into their daily lives. Thus, the early settlers were primarily farmers, exchanging goods and services within their own and neighboring communities. Even merchants and artisans generally pursued these careers only part-time. This was a barter economy. Farmers transported local surpluses to market only after they had seen to their immediate familial and community needs. Storekeepers kept informal accounts that might reach indefinitely into the future and routinely accepted produce or labor in payment. The colony expected even merchants who engaged in transatlantic trade to put community needs first. Both ministers and the General Court condemned usury and required that interest rates be reasonable. They expected lenders to forgive the poor if they defaulted on their debts. The merchant was to be more of a steward than a capitalist.

The incident that best illustrates these beliefs involves, again, Robert Keayne. Keayne had been a rich merchant-tailor in London. He married into the ministerial elite in Boston, was a church member, and owned a thriving import business. In 1639, some of his customers complained of being overcharged for a bridle and a bag of nails. The General Court subsequently charged him with making excessive profits and fined him one hundred pounds (the deputies thought this too light and voted a two-hundred pound fine). His church also found him guilty, and John Cotton denounced him and threatened him with excommunication. Keayne was never the same man after this; he tried to clear his name by giving away large sums of money and turned to drink in an apparent effort to salve his conscience. Cotton took advantage of the incident to lay out the economic principles of a truly just community, principles that further support the image of early New England as a profoundly traditional society.

The rising and setting of the sun and the changing of the seasons governed daily economic activity. But while most of the early settlers willingly—even eagerly—became farmers, the results of their efforts were hardly all that they hoped for. The rocky New England soils and harsh winters made farming an increasingly demanding and often unrewarding activity. The hardest tasks were plowing, sowing, haying, and harvesting, which together took up about seventy or eighty days a year. In the fall, farmers picked fruit, drying or distilling it into cider, and butchered meat for the winter. Families filled the cold, dark days of winter with a variety of tasks, repairing farm implements and making clothes. For the first few decades, these activities ensured a reasonable degree of prosperity.

Indeed, the average New England farmer enjoyed a quietly prosperous standard of living. When John Pers of Watertown, also a part-time weaver, died in 1661 at the age of seventy-three, he left an estate valued at 285 pounds, about average among Massachusetts farmers, with about half of the value in his house and land. He owned two oxen, five head of cattle, one horse, two sheep, and six pigs. His two-story house had five rooms and a lean-to and contained a variety of tools and kitchen implements, sheets, blankets and pillows, several beds (he fathered seven children), two tables and chairs, a cupboard, a trunk, and a chest, and one bit of

❧ Documents ❧
False Profits

In part, Puritans fled England to avoid the competitive ethos of an emerging capitalistic economy. Nowhere is this more obvious than in the case involving Robert Keayne and the reactions to it. The first excerpt offers Keayne's defense of his actions and his somewhat bitter observation that what for him had been a sin had since become commonplace behavior. The second, John Cotton's statement of a just price, indicates just how serious early New Englanders were in their rejection of economic self-interest.

> The oppression lay justly and truly on the buyer's hand rather than on the seller; but then the country was all buyers and few sellers, though it would not be seen on that side then. . . . But now the country hath got better experience in merchandise, and they have soundly paid for their experience since, so that it is now and was many years ago become a common proverb amongst most buyers that knew those times that my goods and prices were cheap pennyworths in comparison of what hath been taken since and especially [in comparison with] the prices of these times. Yet I have borne this patiently and without disturbance or troubling the Court with any petitions for remission or abatement of the fine. . . . But I have not been persuaded to it because the more innocently that I suffer, the more patiently have I borne it, leaving my cause therein to the Lord.
>
> Yet I dare not subscribe to the justness of that time's proceedings against me, nor did my conscience to the best of my remembrance ever yet convince me that censure was either equal or deserved by me.

Bernard Bailyn, ed., *The Apologia of Robert Keayne: The Self-Portrait of a Puritan Merchant* (New York: Harper & Row, 1965), 48–9.

luxury—a looking glass! He also owned a barn with the typical run of agricultural implements and a small shop with a loom. For at least the first two generations, almost every New England farmer possessed far more land and wealth than he could have ever hoped to acquire in England.

Land allotment usually contained forest and other areas unsuited for farming, but New Englanders put this acreage to good use, gathering wood or harvesting hay for market. Kitchen gardens were universal, producing beans, cabbage, and vegetables for the family, much of which was stored in a root cellar for winter consumption. Fruit trees were common, and even in the early years, livestock and poultry pens were everywhere. Indian corn, wheat, and rye were the most popular crops, along with peas, beans, oats, barley, and other grains. Production averaged about eighteen bushels per acre for corn and eight for wheat. Most farmers had

Some false principles were these:

1. That a man might sell as dear as he can, and buy as cheap as he can.
2. If a man lose by casualty of sea, etc., in some of his commodities, he may raise the price of the rest.
3. That he may sell as he bought, though he paid too dear, etc., and though the commodity be fallen, etc.
4. That, as a man may take advantage of his own skill or ability, so he may of another's ignorance or necessity.
5. Where one gives time for payment, he is to take like recompense of one as another.

The rules for trading were these:

1. A man may not sell above the current price, i.e., such a price as is usual in the time and place. . . .
2. When a man loseth in his commodity for want of skill, etc., he must look at it as his own fault or cross, and therefore must not lay it upon another.
3. When a man loseth by casualty of sea, or, etc., it is a loss cast upon himself by providence, and he may not ease himself of it by casting it upon another . . . ; but where there is a scarcity of the commodity, there men may raise their price; for now it is a hand of God upon the commodity, and not the person.

John Cotton, "On the Just Price," from James Kendall Hosmer, ed., *Winthrop's Journal: "History of New England," 1630–1649* , 2 vols. (New York: Scribner's, 1908), 1:317–8.

some combination of cattle, oxen, sheep, chicken, ducks and goats. But they clung to stubbornly traditional farming techniques, ignored crop rotation, and made only minimal use of fertilizers. This intensive use of fenced-in, stable fields, rapidly exhausted the soil and weakened an already precarious productivity ratio.

Farmers gradually expanded their economic activity. Grazing cattle for market was a significant part of the economy almost from the beginning. The animals roamed free for much of the year, until the towns hired herdsmen to transport them to market. By 1650, Boston was the marketing center for herds from several Massachusetts, Connecticut Valley, and Rhode Island towns. In 1648, in fact, Boston petitioned the General Court for permission to hold two fairs a year, one solely for cattle. Pigs, chickens, and goats were also important. Rhode Island became the largest producer of sheep in New England, and horses were central to the West Indian trade.

For much of the first decade, New England depended heavily on the substantial wealth early migrants brought with them, including lumber, grain, and cattle. The end of the Great Migration was economically devastating. By the early 1640s, it was painfully obvious how underdeveloped the New England economy was, lacking a major staple export or any sort of manufacturing. The region was having difficulty even feeding itself, and England shut out certain exports, such as fish, that competed with its own products. In the face of growing scarcities and rising labor costs, the General Court sought to reassert traditional economic values. It passed laws to control rising prices and to deter the colonists from pursuing excessive profits. At the same time, England's self-absorption with its civil war during the 1640s allowed the colonies, particularly Massachusetts, to boldly extend their economic reach into the wider world.

New England's first involvement in the Atlantic marketplace began with the fur trade. For over a decade, the fur trade helped New Englanders deal with the most crucial flaws in their economy—a lack of currency and a constant imbalance of trade. The region simply did not have either the exports or the currency to pay for the rising volume of imports from England. First Plymouth, then Massachusetts, turned to furs as a means of answering this need. Plymouth profited from the trade until 1641, when the Bay colony began to intrude into its territory. Massachusetts established its own trading fort on the Kennebec River in Maine, then pressed further into the interior of New Hampshire and up the Connecticut River Valley. William Pynchon set up several trading posts around Springfield, and most frontier towns traded in furs. For a short time, the European demand provided ample benefits to the traders. Unfortunately, by the 1660s, New Englanders had destroyed the population of beaver and other fur-bearing animals throughout the area and even far into the hinterland.

Fishing was a second major industry. English fishermen had long reaped the harvest of the offshore banks and even wintered on the mainland, and, as we have seen, the first New England settlements were small fishing villages on the coast. Initially, the colonists plied their trade fairly close to shore, working a series of smaller banks within the Gulf of Maine and catching healthy supplies of cod, haddock, hake, and mackerel. The onset of the English Civil War disrupted the West Country monopoly on the larger banks, and after 1641, New Englanders switched from their small thirty-foot shallops to larger ketches and moved out onto the Grand Banks to the east of Newfoundland. But by the time of the Restoration, the region completely controlled its own fisheries. Merchants traded the fish to Spain, Portugal, and various Atlantic islands, as well as the West Indies. Permanent towns replaced small fishing villages, and fishermen in such places as Marblehead had little concern for religion and the sort of life that the region's leaders liked to encourage. Fishing also created substantial demand for new ships, laying the basis for an industry crucial to New England's economic future.

The timber industry, finally, remained an important component of the New England economy throughout the seventeenth century. The English faced constant shortages of wood. When the colonists landed in New England, they were overwhelmed by the abundance of the forests and used every possible method to rapidly cut all accessible timber. They only used the best wood, even for such mundane purposes as fencing, and left much of the rest to rot. The town sawmill quickly became an important community enterprise, turning out clapboards, staves, shingles, and other products. Merchants seeking investments continually looked to virgin forest areas. White pines from northern forests became a staple of the English mast trade, and timber products comprised a major component of the West Indian trade.

None of these efforts was sufficient to establish true economic independence, and during the 1640s and 1650s, the Massachusetts government tried to expand trade and economic activity. The General Court sought to encourage exports and discourage imports through a systematic program of domestic manufacturing and a search for new markets. It attempted to stimulate the domestic production of clothing, shoes and boots, glass, and ironware through grants of land and money, bounties, and local monopolies. But these efforts largely failed due to the high cost of labor, continued capital shortages, a lack of entrepreneurial skills, and the small local market. What capital there was tended to move into the more profitable cattle and corn markets. Early efforts at iron production were more elaborate but equally unsuccessful; again, a scarcity of capital prevented investors from exploiting ore deposits around Saugus and Braintree. In 1643, John Winthrop, Jr. traveled to London and succeeded in getting both financial backing and skilled ironworkers, and by 1648, a furnace and refinery at Saugus was producing a ton a day. Profits lagged, though, and the works declared bankruptcy in 1652 and folded completely in 1676.

Nonetheless, it was trade that brought New England its economic salvation, precarious though it was. By 1640, shipbuilding and oceangoing trade were already the leading enterprises in Boston, Charlestown, and Salem, establishing a solid foundation for further growth and a fundamental reorientation of the colony's economic life. Boston became the principal entrepôt for a trade that stretched to all corners of the Atlantic world, as New England merchants, using their London friends and relatives as sources for capital and marketing arrangements, proved the equal of anyone in seeking profitable markets. Cotton, sugar, and indigo came from the West Indies; wine from the Canaries and Madeira; oil, soap, wines, raisins, lemons, fruits, and salt from France, Spain, and Portugal; and clothing and household goods from England. In exchange, New Englanders sent fish, and foodstuffs to Spain, Madeira, and the Canaries; fish, provisions, lumber, barrel staves, shingles, horses, and other wood products to the West Indies; and foodstuffs to Newfoundland. By the 1650s, New England captains were also extensively involved in the coastal trade, often stopping in the Chesapeake. New England was in particular need of specie for pay for goods imported from England. Bills of exchange were sometimes used for payment, but cash and barter were the norm—Spanish, Portuguese, French, and Dutch coins were all common. In 1652, the colony even established its own mint, a short-lived enterprise, and passed a law limiting legal money to its own coins.

The vast bulk of this trade was conducted out of Massachusetts ports. Plymouth, particularly after the decline of its fur trade, had no overseas trade to speak of, and Connecticut exported its produce through Boston. New Haven had perhaps the most ambitious of the New England merchants. The colony sponsored trading settlements on Long Island and the Delaware River, but these efforts proved unproductive in the long run. Rhode Island, finally, was inhabited mostly by subsistence farmers throughout the seventeenth century, even after Newport became involved in the West Indian trade during the 1650s.

Connecticut And New Haven

New England grew steadily from its initial seedlings in Massachusetts Bay and Plymouth as religious dissension and an increasing demand for land overpowered the initial desire for close settlement. The first offshoot appeared along the Connecticut River. This area was largely unknown before 1632. Dense forests and travel difficulties had kept most Europeans from exploring what they perceived as a wilderness. The settlement process was complicated when the Council for New England granted the region to the Earl of Warwick in 1630.

Edward Winslow from Plymouth Colony established the first trading post at the future site of Windsor, Connecticut, in 1632. The following year, the Dutch, eager to defend their own fur-trading activities and territorial claims, established an outpost at Hartford. In June 1635, the first group of permanent colonists left Dorchester, Massachusetts, and settled around the Windsor site. In the meantime, Warwick had transferred title for his grant to the Puritan-dominated Providence Company, which now authorized John Winthrop, Jr. to lay out a settlement at the mouth of the Connecticut River at Saybrook. Liberally supplied, Winthrop demanded that all Connecticut settlers recognize him as the colony's leader or leave, arguing that the region lay beyond Massachusetts jurisdiction and could be legally settled only with the consent of the Warwick grantees. The situation was further complicated when Rev. Thomas Hooker and his parishioners from Newtown, Massachusetts, settled in the Hartford area in late 1635. Ultimately, the dispute was settled peaceably. All agreed to establish an eight-man commission to govern the new settlements for a year until the confusion could be sorted out. Settlers continued to arrive in the interim, so that the colony had a population of about eight hundred by the end of 1636. The complexity and rivalry that dominated relations between Indians and white traders and between Indians themselves meant that whites met little native resistance before the onset of the war with the Pequot Indians in 1636.

People moved to Connecticut for many reasons. Hooker's group, for instance, came in search of suitable land, while Hooker had grown disillusioned with political and religious events in the Bay Colony. He had no patience with dissidents, such as Roger Williams and Anne Hutchinson, but he was disturbed by the growing strictness on admission to church membership there. He believed that there were no viable means of discovering who was truly regenerate in spirit. Consequently, throughout the seventeenth century, Connecticut churches were far more inclusive in membership than their counterparts in Massachusetts. Politically, Hooker believed the power of the government rested with the people. But this was not a democracy. Most male adults could vote, but elected leaders ruled relatively free of restraint and expected deferential respect and obedience from the citizens.

The 1639 Fundamental Orders codified the existing system of government. These consisted of a preamble and eleven orders or laws. The preamble was a covenant binding the three river towns; it simply confirmed what had existed since

English Fowling piece brought to Connecticut in 1640. Firearms were an essential part of life on the New England frontier. ❧

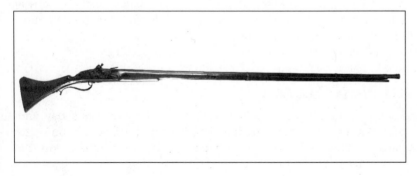

Table 2 ❧ New England population growth

	Massachusetts	Plymouth	Connecticut	Rhode Island	New Hampshire	Maine
1630	1,000	400			500	400
1640	9,000	1,000	1,500	300	1,000	4,000
1650	14,000	1,500	4,000	800	1,000	1,000

U.S. Bureau of the Census. *Historical Statistics of the United States, Colonial Times to 1970,* 2 vols. (Washington, DC: Government Printing Office, 1975), 2:1168.

1636. The laws established a governmental structure based on the Massachusetts model and gave the General Court supreme authority within the colony. Connecticut remained a small, agricultural colony for the first half of the century, beginning significant growth only in 1663, when it received a royal charter and absorbed the colony of New Haven.

William Pynchon, who had founded a private empire in the Springfield area during the early seventeenth century, also figures in the Connecticut story. Pynchon was among the first settlers of the Connecticut River Valley, establishing a fur-trading house at Agawam (Springfield). The area was initially under Connecticut jurisdiction. During the Pequot War, however, Pynchon became embroiled in a controversy with the government over the lack of defense provided for his post and his alleged failure to supply the colony with corn. As a result, he removed the post from Connecticut control in 1639, intending to join Massachusetts. Massachusetts appointed him chief judge and magistrate in 1641 and allowed the settlers to appeal his decisions to the General Court, but not until 1649 did the town become a full member of the Bay Colony.

The northern shoreline of Long Island Sound, meanwhile, became an attractive colonization site after the Pequots' defeat in 1637. Only small tribes, such as the Nehantics, Quinnipiacs, Hammonasetts, and Paugassets, then inhabited the region, and they offered little resistance to the white invaders. The origins of the New Haven settlement lay in the growing pace of persecution in England by 1635 under the Laud Commission. Rev. John Davenport, pastor of St. Stephen's Church in a mercantile section of London, was at the core of a small group increasingly alarmed by Laud's actions. Davenport had been part of the planning group for the Bay Colony and was a close friend of John Cotton and Thomas Hooker. He eventually made up his mind to leave England, traveling in disguise through the English countryside to recruit settlers, including his boyhood friend and merchant, Theophilus Eaton. Despite offers to settle in Massachusetts, the group was not happy with prospects in Boston. Economically ambitious and mercantile in orientation, they desired a harbor of their own. Thus, in March 1638, they left Boston for New Haven (then Quinnipiac), having sent ahead a small exploratory group.

Davenport and Eaton purchased land from the Indians, but despite years of trying, they were never able to acquire a royal charter. The colony grew to include several other settlements, most notably Milford, Guilford, and Stamford along Long Island Sound. Eaton ruled dictatorially as governor until his death in 1658, even after the four towns drew up a "fundamental agreement" in 1643 that provided for a General Court that consisted of two deputies from each of the four principal towns.

Disputes with its neighbors plagued the colony from the beginning, because of its awkward and intrusive geographical nature and its threat on Connecticut and Dutch territorial claims and commercial ambitions. In 1640, Davenport formed the Delaware Company to explore trade possibilities in the Delaware River basin. The Swedes, who controlled the area, gave the small expedition permission to settle on the east side of the river, but the settlers went beyond this grant and purchased land from the Indians on the west bank. The Dutch intervened and destroyed the trading post, and eventually the Swedes arrested the leaders when they continued to trade with the local Indians without permission. An eventual compromise allowed the New Haven settlers to stay, but they continued to push for more concessions. In the end, however, the outpost simply faded away.

These various expansionistic and trading efforts severely drained New Haven's capital resources, and the colony remained a loose collection of agrarian communities. The General Court and church, though, maintained close supervision over settlers' personal lives and punished drunkenness, sexual offenses, and even card playing, dancing, and singing with a single-mindedness unknown elsewhere in the New World. Still, by 1660, New Haven was precariously situated, and it was no surprise that Connecticut was able to absorb it when it received its new charter in 1663.

The Eastern Frontier

In 1622, the Council for New England granted Sir Ferdinando Gorges and Capt. John Mason all the land between the Merrimac and Kennebec rivers. Settlement dragged over the next several years, and the two divided their holdings in 1629, Mason receiving the territory south of the Piscataqua River. This region was to become known as New Hampshire. After Mason's death in 1635, Massachusetts gradually extended its control over the area, annexing it in 1643 and holding it until the Crown intervened in 1677. Strawberry Bank (Portsmouth) was the principal early settlement, followed by several others, including John Wheelwright's at Exeter. The northern sector, meanwhile, was relegated to secondary status while Gorges schemed to gain control of all of New England under Laudian auspices. He finally received a royal charter in 1639 for his lands, which were henceforth to be known as the Province of Maine. Several small villages had already emerged, including Saco, Kittery, York, and Pemaquid. Gorges's death and the confusion that accompanied the English Civil War allowed Massachusetts to reinterpret its charter in 1652 to claim the entire Maine region, which it controlled until 1820.

Rhode Island

After his banishment from Massachusetts, Roger Williams had gone to Seekonk, but Gov. Edward Winslow had warned him that he was trespassing on Plymouth Colony territory. His small group then moved to the Great Salt River, an estuary of Narragansett Bay, and settled on the eastern side of the river, founding Providence. Williams had become a friend of the Narragansetts during his stay at Plymouth, and he now purchased land from the Indians out of his own resources. He and his fellow colonists constructed simple shelters, and every head of family received a five-acre lot and a six-acre field.

Rhode Island had a very dense Indian population in the early seventeenth-century, and Williams's friendship with the Indians and respect for their rights served the young colony well. But here as elsewhere, Indians had their own agendas. The Narragansetts hoped to use Williams as in intermediary with the Puritan settlements to the north and to establish a barrier against the Wampanoags and their ally, Plymouth Colony. The Wampanoags let Williams occupy the land he did because it was their frontier against the rival Narragansetts. They also slyly granted him additional land that they claimed but no longer controlled.

The new colony was economically underdeveloped and primarily agricultural throughout its early decades. In 1641, its main crops were corn, tobacco, and swine. In the long run, sheep and tobacco became staples, but there was no grist-mill in the colony until 1646. Williams's concerns were not primarily economic. He specified that every man should have an equal share of land and that the colony was for those who were destitute, especially for conscience's sake. From its beginning, then, Rhode Island became a refuge for those persecuted for religious and civil beliefs.

Anne Hutchinson and her husband, her follower William Coddington, and others soon joined Williams in their flight from religious persecution. Coddington and the Hutchinsons purchased the island of Aquidneck from the Narragansetts and established the settlement of Pocasset (Portsmouth) on the north end. With Coddington as chief magistrate, the group attempted to establish a Bible common-wealth—a colony that would be governed according to the Bible. Coddington fled the resultant political and religious disorder, though, and founded Newport on the southern end of the island in 1639. The Pocasset settlers proclaimed full religious liberty in 1641. The towns soon united and then split again, and Coddington continued to pursue his own economic ambitions. The colony finally achieved a degree of unity in 1644, when Williams traveled to England and obtained a patent that specifically covered Providence, Portsmouth, and Newport and granted the towns sufficient civil authority for self-rule. Still, as late as 1650, Coddington succeeded in convincing English officials to appoint him governor of Aquidneck for life, abrogating the 1644 patent. It took yet another trip to England by Williams in late 1652 to get this grant annulled.

In May 1647, freemen from Providence, Portsmouth, Newport, and Warwick met at Portsmouth as a General Assembly to organize the government and draw up a body of laws. The assembly established a federal system, under which the towns became part of a larger community but retained their corporate rights. In the first year, the assembly consisted of all freemen who could attend, with a quorum of ten from each town empowered to act with full authority. Since land was so readily available, most of the colony's inhabitants were freemen. Voting on issues concerning the central government was by towns, and towns could also initiate legislation. The assembly met four times a year at a location rotating among the four towns. In 1654, Williams was elected president, which finally and permanently solidified centralized political control.

Colonial Rhode Island is most interesting for the variety of its religious beliefs. Williams stressed liberty of conscience and the separation of church and state. He conceded civil powers to magistrates but contended that their authority was limited to such matters—just as the church authority was limited to spiritual matters. His completely secular view of the state was unique for his time. In religious polity, Williams argued that only those with a reasonable hope of salvation should be included in his church and that there should be no compulsory attendance or state support. The original church, in fact, soon adopted a policy of adult baptism, moving in a direction sharply different from that being taken in Massachusetts. Williams continued to follow the logical dictates of his conscience and religious principles in his search for religious purity. At one point, his quest for purity of worship forced him to conclude that he could take Communion only with his wife. Having departed from all organized churches, he now preached to anyone who would come to his trading post. He finally became a Seeker, one who sought to live a humble, pious life while waiting for God to reveal a fresh start for the Christian church.

Anne Hutchinson, meanwhile, proved to be a weak religious leader, and much of her thunder was stolen by Samuel Gorton, one of the most fascinating religious figures of early America. Little is known of Gorton's background or personal life, but he appears to have been a hot-tempered and pugnacious person also capable of great tenderness; he inspired great devotion among his followers and violent antagonism from his opponents. After his arrival in Boston in 1637, he moved to Plymouth and then Portsmouth seeking liberty of conscience. He immediately denied the jurisdiction of Rhode Island courts, arguing that without a Crown charter, they had no authority. Driven from Portsmouth, Providence, and Pawtuxet, he eventually founded Shawomet, later renamed Warwick. Hostile neighbors in a land dispute called in the Massachusetts authorities, who were delighted to intervene in Rhode Island affairs. They seized Gorton and threw him in jail. But his supporters eventually forced his release, and he fled to England, successfully obtaining a land grant from the duke of Warwick. This prevented further harassment from the Bay Colony.

Gorton disavowed all theological systems, agreeing with Hutchinson in her doctrine of grace but disagreeing over other matters, such as the nature of the Trinity. He censured all ministers and embraced his own peculiar brand of mysticism, teaching that Christ had been incarnated in Adam, making all humans divine. Christ's later resurrection, he contended, began a process of regeneration that would restore the image of God in all humankind. After Gorton's death, most of his followers became Baptists or Quakers. In 1771, the last Gortonite, John Angell of Providence, showed a visitor three books that he claimed Gorton had written in heaven, saying that no one could understand them unless they, too, were their.

Quakers and Baptists also prospered in Rhode Island, the former attracting those drawn to mysticism, the latter those seeking communal purity in the church. In the end, two broad strains characterized religious experience in the colony. The biblicist strain, headed by Williams and typified by the Baptists, sought to purify the church as much as possible, to admit only those whose beliefs and actions gave some assurance of their salvation. The second, more mystical vein began with Hutchinson and continued to embrace all those who believed in the inspiration of the Holy Spirit, most obviously the Quakers. Both strains rejected ceremony, learning, and hierarchy. They generally met in private houses or even fields. At the end of the century, only a few meeting houses had been erected. All congregations allowed women to participate in church affairs to an unparalleled extent—Baptists let both sexes vote in church meetings, Gortonites saw no distinction between sexes, and Quakers even welcomed some women as ministers and all as full members of meetings, though they later set up separate meetings for women. While Rhode Island churches may have been unique in their openness to women's religious role and in their religious toleration, they maintained strict discipline among their members. Nonetheless, it is clear that Roger Williams had, indeed, established a more tolerant alternative to Massachusetts Puritanism.

Indian-White Conflict

Williams and Hutchinson represented threats to Puritan unity from within; equally significant challenges came from without. Both the Pilgrims and the Puritans had the good fortune to land on coasts where disease had sharply reduced the Indian population. Entire villages disappeared during the 1616 smallpox epidemic. This fact alone may have accounted for much of the success of the early New England settlements. Not only did colonists receive valuable help by way of food and supplies from the natives, but they also escaped the need to deal with a large, resistive population when their methods and intentions finally became clear to Indians. As in Virginia, moreover, early white attitudes in New England were not completely negative, and the Massachusetts charter seemed to offer some purer motivation by trumpeting its intention to convert the natives. The Bay Colony seal consisted of the picture of an Indian calling out, "Come over and help us."

More than religious brotherhood, though, dominated the colonists' reactions to their neighbors. Indians seemed uncivilized, following a "scattered and wild course of life." As the minister and missionary John Eliot noted, "we labour and work in building, planting, clothing our selves &c. and they doe not."[9] From the first, settlers refused to allow Indians to enter towns, and any colonists caught selling arms to them would be deported to England. Good intentions notwithstanding, a garrison mentality predominated, and no missionary activity took place for more than a decade. Sachems had made overtures of friendship during the first year of Massachusetts settlement and had freely given corn and sought trade. But in 1633 and 1634, when smallpox ravaged the New England coastal tribes and again killed thousands, the Puritans saw in the tragedy a sign of God's intervention on their behalf at a time when they needed more land. As the Charlestown records note triumphantly, "[W]ithout this remarkable and terrible stroke of God upon the natives, we would with much more difficulty have found room, and at far greater charge have obtained and purchased land."[10] Whites built upon this advantage by moving beyond their initial rationales for occupation, purchasing questionable claims by rival Indians, for instance, and then turning to the courts to resolve the "conflict." With uncertain frequency, they also resorted to less subtle stratagems: letting livestock loose in fields, plying Indians with alcohol, and fining natives for such offenses as walking on the Sabbath or illegally entering a town. The Indians, of course, were far from passive. They retaliated when whites stole from or cheated them. The first climactic confrontation in New England came when both sides found themselves immersed in a complex web of tribal conflicts, land hunger, and trade expansion. The result was the Pequot War of 1636–1637.

The ostensible cause of this conflict was the murder of two white ship captains and their crews. One, John Stone, killed in 1634, was an outlaw already; the other, John Oldham, was found dead off Block Island in 1636. The real causes, however, lay in Puritan hostility to the Indians, trade rivalry with the Dutch, and intertribal disputes. The Dutch controlled trade with the New England Indians in the early 1630s through the Pequot and Narragansett tribes. In 1632, they purchased land on the present site of Hartford from the Pequot grand sachem, intending to build a trading post to defend against English incursion. Some tribes were already shifting their trading allegiances to the English. Most notable among these were the Mohegans, who were expanding their own territorial claims and contesting Pequot authority over them—apparently with the support of the Narragansetts. The Mohegans put pressure on the Dutch to occupy the Hartford area to help them protect their claims. The Pequots, an aggressive people (the name means "destroyer") who had invaded the region from the upper Hudson River valley in the 1590s, were anxious to maintain their hegemony and killed some Narragansetts trading at the new fort. In reaction, the Dutch killed the Pequots' grand sachem and closed the fort to them, and the Narragansetts mobilized for war.

At this point, the Stone incident occurred. The Western Niantics killed Stone after he kidnapped some Indians for ransom, and his personal background was sufficiently notorious so that few likely mourned him. Indeed, it was two years before war broke out, indicating that other causes were the source of conflict. By 1634, Pequot attempts to regain their trade monopoly resulted in skirmishes with the Dutch in which the Pequot sachem Tatohem was killed. By now, the tribe was at war with the Dutch, the Narragansetts, and the Mohegans, and they sought to defend their position by seeking aid from Massachusetts. They invited the colony to settle the Connecticut River valley and establish a trading relationship. But colony officials apparently decided to up the price, making the deal seem more like tribute than a "present" and thus implying subordination in the Pequots' eyes. As in all such cases, the Pequots felt the treaty was a pact between equals, while the Puritans saw themselves in a decidedly superior position. They insisted, in fact, that the Pequots become their police force among the Pequot tributary tribes, a function decidedly contrary to the obligations of superior tribes. In the end, the Pequots refused to subject themselves to Massachusetts control, but they did allow the Connecticut settlement to go unmolested. The treaty also established peace between the Pequots and the Narragansetts, a major goal for the Pequots.

Almost two years later, amidst rumors of a planned uprising stirred up by the Mohegan sachem Uncas, the Puritans called the Pequots to another council and pushed their earlier demands that the Pequots deliver Stone's killers. The Pequots refused, but they also kept the peace until the English attacked. Within a few days of the meeting, Block Island Narragansetts killed Oldham. The reason for his death is unclear, but he was an important figure in high Massachusetts circles. Predictably, the colony blamed the Pequots for his death.

The Narragansetts killed those responsible for Oldham's death, but that was not enough. In late August, the Puritans sent out their own forces against both the Narragansetts and the Pequots on the island. The expedition was a disaster, as was a second foray into Pequot territory on the mainland. Understandably, the Pequots regarded themselves as wronged and acted to defend themselves. The launched a seige of Fort Saybrook that lasted nine months, and they sought to establish an alliance with the Narragansetts, proposing a joint struggle against the aggressive English encroachments. But the quick actions of Roger Williams, together with the Narragansetts' perception of their own self-interest, led instead to a formal English-Narragansett treaty. Connecticut finally declared war after a group of local Indians, driven from their homes near Wethersfield by the English despite a prior guarantee, sought assistance from the Pequots, who staged a retaliatory raid. The colony sent a ninety-man expedition together with about seventy Mohegans under Uncas to relieve the Saybrook siege in April 1637. Gaining further assistance from the Narragansetts, the force then massacred the inhabitants of a secondary Pequot village on the Mystic River, mostly women and children. The expedition's intent was to rid itself of all Indians, so it set the village afire and drew a tight ring around it to prevent escape. The Narragansetts were appalled at the plan and withdrew before the attack. New expeditions from Connecticut and Massachusetts were sent out to hunt down the remaining Indians, while Mohegans and Narragansetts pursued others, sparing most only to have a company of Massachusetts troops take charge of the captives. This group and all other captured Pequots were then scattered throughout the empire, many sold into slavery in New England or the West Indies. Those who escaped the English hid among the Mohegans or Eastern Niantics, but the Pequots ceased to exist as a tribe. No one ever bothered to bring to justice Captain Stone's killer, who never tried to hide his identity or deed.

The English had broken the resistance of the strongest most dangerous Indian opponent in southern New England, establishing their military superiority and opening the interior to white settlement. Uncas and the Mohegans ceded their lands to Connecticut and became the colony's tributary tribe. Seeking greater power, the sachem lost any true independence. But it would be over a century before the colonists were finally able to extirpate the last vestiges of Indian resistance.

The unexpected brutality of the whites shocked the Indians. In describing the burning of the Pequot fort, Gov. William Bradford of Plymouth noted, "It was a fearfull sight to see them thus fryer in the fire . . . , but the victory seemed a sweete sacrifice, and they gave the prays thereof to God, who had wrought so wonderfelly for them, thus to enclose the enimise in their hands, & give them so speedy a victory over so proud and insulting an enimie."[11] Bradford's comments point to a deeper, psychological explanation for the timing of the war and for its ultimate meaning. The Indians served as a counterimage of English civilization; colonists portrayed them as lacking in piety, purposefulness, and a work ethic. In the face of growing internal discord in New England, moreover, especially the recent disruption caused by Anne Hutchinson and Roger Williams (the Saybrook siege took place at the same time as the Antinomian crisis), the Puritans sought to bring a stronger sense of order and control to their external environment. The Pequots in particular, and Indians in general, came to stand for everything the Puritans feared in themselves. Threatened by religious diversity, social pluralism, and nagging self-doubt, they struck out at those who represented the most visible threat to their self-contained, idealistic hopes.

When John Winthrop stepped upon the shores of Massachusetts Bay in 1630, he saw before him a forested wasteland populated with "savages." Winthrop intended to transform this land into a tribute to his God, into vibrant proof of the righteousness of God's ways. It was to be, in the oft-repeated words of Winthrop himself, "a citty upon a hill." In seeking this goal, Winthrop and his fellow New Englanders transformed their inherited English traditions into a culture of their own, a society steeped in social and religious traditionalism.

Yet there were those who dissented from this view from the very beginning, and the very success of the New England vision would sow the seeds of still greater division. Prosperity encouraged the pursuit of profit and self-interest. Healthy, fecund families created population pressures. Ministers and laity alike were unable to maintain the original level of spiritual intensity. Indians chafed under New England's cultural and territorial expansion. And England could no longer ignore its prosperous offshoots in the New World. The last decades of the century would bring far-reaching change and social discord. For many, the "citty upon the hill" was about to become Babylon.

❧ *Chapter Five* ❧

England Pursues An Empire

The seventeenth century was a time of crisis for all of Europe. Political theorists, such as Thomas Hobbes and John Locke, presaged profound transformations in attitudes toward government. Religion became a divisive rather than a unifying social force. European economies began to move decisively toward a capitalistic framework. The struggle between king and Parliament in England reflected such larger forces. Culminating in the English Civil War, this conflict also shaped the structure of the first British empire and influenced Britain's efforts to establish a rational system of political and economic regulation for its geographically far-flung colonies. With the restoration of the Stuart dynasty to the throne in 1660, the Crown pursued its efforts to bring order to the empire. It also encouraged the economic development of its Caribbean colonies and oversaw the establishment of several new settlements on the mainland. The lack of any overriding rational principle, though, together with political unrest within England and political and social upheaval in America, stymied the London's attempts to bring order to this growing empire. And despite closer oversight, the Crown failed to even slow the growing rift between British and American interests.

The English Civil War

The battle between king and Parliament in England was, at its most obvious level, a political conflict over sovereignty. The Stuart monarchs claimed to rule by divine right, while Parliament intended to establish control over the government's purse strings and thus over the basic policy decisions of the empire. This political struggle embraced a larger conflict between the traditional landed wealth of England and the rising economic power of merchants and market-oriented farmers.

Significant Dates

1603	James I becomes king of England
1609, 11	Henry Hudson explores the Hudson River region
1624	Dutch West India Company establishes New Netherland
1625	Charles succeeds James to the throne
1626	Dutch purchase Manhattan for sixty guilders
1624–32	British settle Caribbean islands
1638	Swedish colonists settled on the Delaware River
	Willem Kieft becomes governor of New Amsterdam
1642	English civil war begins
1643–45	Dutch-Indian War
1646	Peter Stuyvesant becomes governor of New Amsterdam
1649	Charles I beheaded
1649–60	Interregnum
1652–54	First Anglo-Dutch War
1655	Dutch take control of New Sweden
	Peach War
1658	Oliver Cromwell dies
1660	Restoration of the Stuarts (Charles II) to English throne
	First Navigation Act
1662	Crown establishes Council on Trade and Plantations
1663	Second Navigation Act (Staple Act)
	Proprietary grant issued for Carolinas
1664	English capture New Amsterdam in Second Anglo-Dutch War (1664–1667)
	Commission appointed to tour and inspect the colonies
1665	Duke's Laws issued in New York
	Concessions and Agreements of New Jersey
	Concessions and Agreements of Carolina
1669	Fundamental Constitutions issued for the Carolinas
1670	Charles Town founded
1672–74	Third Anglo-Dutch War
1673	Third Navigation Act (Plantation Duty Act)
1676	Quintipartite Deed
1677	Culpepper's Rebellion
1680	Charleston moved to Cooper and Ashley rivers
1681	William Penn receives the charter for Pennsylvania
1682	Pennsylvania Frame of Government and the Forty-Two Laws
1683	Charter of Liberties issued in New York
1696	Board of Trade established
1701	Pennsylvania Frame of Government
	Delaware receives a separate charter

Puritanism proved to be a decisive catalyst for revolution, as radical English Protestants sought to carry the English Reformation to its logical conclusion.

Henry VIII and Elizabeth I were able to work through Parliament to achieve their political and religious goals. Under Elizabeth, though, the House of Commons grew increasingly restless, serving as an important vehicle for radical Puritan protest. Elizabeth's death in 1603 marked the end of the Tudor dynasty, and King James VI of Scotland, the son of Mary Queen of Scots, ascended the throne as the nearest blood heir, establishing the reign of the Stuarts as James I (1603–1625). James understood little of England's political or religious heritage. He fully embraced the idea of the divine right of kings, believing that his power to govern came directly from God and that he was thus responsible to no other earthly being.

James's principal claim to fame, like that of his son and successor Charles I, is that he managed to alienate some of the most powerful groups in England. Inflation and the increasing costs of government (including those stemming from his own lavish court) forced James to seek more money from Parliament, which rejected his requests. His Catholic family background made many Englishmen uncomfortable, and anti-Catholic feeling intensified with the discovery of the Gunpowder Plot (1605), an attempt by Catholic extremists to blow up Parliament.

The most significant opposition came from the Puritans. Puritan leaders met with Charles in 1604, hopeful that his experience with Presbyterian church government in Scotland would favorably dispose him toward similar changes in the Anglican church. They asked him to abolish the rule of bishops in the English church, but he reacted angrily—bishops were appointed by the Crown, after all, and provided a major source of support for the monarchy. James thus alienated the growing number of Puritans who had become members of the gentry, served in Parliament, and held critical local positions as justices of the peace and sheriffs.

While James may have been simply unlucky or unwise in his pronouncements and in the timing of his actions, his son Charles I (1625–1649) was foolish. James had begun a war with Spain, and Charles demanded money from Parliament to continue the conflict. They in turn insisted on constitutional reforms before granting him the funds. In 1628, the House of Commons passed the Petition of Right, which prohibited taxation without parliamentary consent. By 1629, Charles had had enough, and he embarked on an eleven-year period of personal rule, during which he refused to call Parliament. He developed a variety of stratagems by which to raise money, including the extension of the collection of Ship Money—a tax on coastal towns to provide for defense—to interior towns and counties. Such measures only served to further alienate both the landed gentry and the merchants who suffered the most from these new levies. His interference with local rights, as we have seen, motivated many Puritans to flee to the New World.

Charles also pursued a disastrous religious policy. He married Henrietta Maria, the Catholic sister of Louis XIII of France, and enforced a policy of high Anglicanism under William Laud, the archbishop of Canterbury, that struck particularly hard at Puritans. Finally, he attempted to impose the Anglican *Book of Common Prayer* on the Presbyterian Scots, prompting rebellion in England's northern province. Desperate for money to put down the revolt, Charles called Parliament in 1640. This "Long" Parliament (which met in various guises until 1660) abolished the hated arbitrary court of Star Chamber, prohibited the collection of taxes without parliamentary consent, and passed the Triennial Act, which required that Parliament meet at least once every three years. But the Puritan radicals wanted to go further. When Charles tried to arrest them, civil war began.

The Royalists, or Cavaliers, consisted of the higher nobility, some members of the gentry, the Anglican clergy, and many peasants, while the parliamentary forces, or Roundheads, included some powerful nobles, the remaining landed gentry, middle-class merchants, and the Puritans. Various local and regional forces were also critical in determining individual loyalties. In the end, though, religion was the clearest point of division. English Puritans saw the war as an opportunity to establish God's kingdom on earth.

Cromwell established the New Model Army, a strikingly religious-oriented force, and captured Charles I in 1646. The Roundheads themselves now split. The radicals, led by Cromwell, favored a broad policy of religious toleration and opposed a Presbyterian church structure. They opened negotiations with the king, but Charles undermined his own position by fleeing and seeking military assistance from the Scots. Cromwell and the parliamentary forces again defeated the monarch, and this time they decided to permanently solve the problem of divine-right monarchy—on January 30, 1649, they beheaded the king.

Cromwell now ruled England as a commonwealth (1649–1653). He faced a legion of military and political problems, including rebellion in Ireland and an explosion of radical religious and social feeling at home. By enlisting in Cromwell's New Model Army in the struggle between king and Parliament, many commoners for the first time played a political role in English life. Cromwell now confronted the consequences of his policies of religious toleration and expanded political participation. Ordinary English men and women joined such religious groups as the Levellers, the Ranters, the Differs, and the Seekers and began to question the power of the established church, to pursue political rights (including the right to vote), and to attack enclosure, and even to question the right of private property. A true member of the landed gentry, Cromwell was revolted by such radical notions. He introduced England's only written constitution, the Instrument of Government, in 1653 but quickly abandoned this path and in 1655 divided the country into eleven districts, each ruled by a major general. The Puritan Revolution, as some have termed it, had collapsed into tyrannical military rule. Cromwell died in 1658 and was succeeded for a brief period by his son Richard. The people of England, however, were tired of war and division. In 1660, Charles II (1660–1685), the son of Charles I, was restored to the throne.

The English Civil War was profoundly significant for the American colonies in a number of ways. Religiously, it caused New Englanders to reevaluate their own mission and their place in God's sacred plan. Many in the New World began to fear that God had not abandoned England but rather had been testing his people. By fleeing England, it now seemed, they had failed the test and were left on the outside looking in at God's deliverance of the English people. Politically, the war furthered the cause of constitutional, parliamentary government, a process that culminated in the Glorious Revolution of 1688. Economically, it marked a decisive turning point in the evolution of English capitalism, empowering the burgeoning mercantile forces of the realm. Finally, by giving voice to merchants and politicians who had an economic stake in England's growing overseas empire, it forced London to confront the larger implications of the nation's expansion.

A New Imperial Policy Takes Shape

The emergence of new sources of raw materials and potentially crucial markets for finished goods in the American colonies raised the stakes of national rivalry. European countries increasingly sought economic domination rather than self-sufficiency or the mere accumulation of bullion. Colonies became more important than ever, and England looked with envy on the French and Spanish empires.

Charles I took the first steps toward a more coherent colonial policy when he created the Commission on Foreign Plantations in 1634, hoping to curb New England independence. Before he could act, Parliament rose against him. Initially, radical Puritans in Parliament successfully implemented a more tolerant attitude toward the American colonies, but supporters of this policy lost their influence after Charles was executed. A group of powerful merchants who were more concerned with England's commercial future replaced them. Their principal enemy was no longer Spain but Holland, which dominated world trade during the mid-seventeenth century.

Holland owned sixteen thousand of the twenty thousand or so ships engaged in European trade during the first half of the seventeenth century, dominating the world's commerce from Brazil to Formosa. The Dutch traders' ships were of superior design and unsurpassed seaworthiness, and colonial merchants preferred their varied merchandise, excellent credit terms, and the high prices they offered for colonial goods. The economic disruption the civil war brought to England increased Holland's advantage in the American colonies, as Englishmen preyed on each other's shipping. Once the war ended, however, English merchants began to pressure their government to break Dutch control of the North American trade. Parliament's first response to these pressures was the Navigation Act of 1651. The act contained three principal provisions: all goods from Asia, Africa, and America sent to England or its colonies had to be transported in ships with an English master and a majority of English seamen; goods sent from Europe to England or its colonies had to be carried in similar ships or in the vessels of the countries where they originated; and other foreign goods could be imported into England only from the place of production or the ports from which they were first shipped.

The British found the measure difficult to enforce, and colonial trade with Amsterdam continued almost unabated. Cromwell had been somewhat reluctant to put pressure on the Dutch anyway. He regarded Catholic Spain as England's true enemy and felt something of a kindred Protestant spirit with the Dutch. Despite his feelings, England entered into the first Anglo-Dutch War (1652–1654). Cromwell showed little enthusiasm for the conflict and the peace settled none of the outstanding issues, but he was now free to pursue his traditional enemy, Spain. He wanted revenge for the Spanish seizure of the English island of Tortuga in 1635 and of Providence Island (off Nicaragua) in 1641. In dire need of money, he also hoped Spanish wealth would provide an inflow of bullion. In 1654, he sent a fleet under Robert Venable and William Penn, Sr. to the West Indies. The eight-thousand man force failed to capture Hispaniola, but it did take Jamaica. Though this island would soon become the center of English trade with the Spanish colonies, Cromwell died before he saw his larger ambitions fulfilled. He also failed in his tentative efforts to bring a coherent system of rule to the North American colonies. He established the Committee for Foreign Plantations in 1655 and the Committee for America in 1656, but both were disbanded after his death.

The next, and more crucial, step in the emergence of a new imperial policy came with the restoration of Charles II to the throne in 1660. During the reigns of Charles and his brother James II, England moved to consolidate its North American colonies, to control and regulate trade, and to centralize and improve the administration of this vast empire. At least some of the support for the emerging policy came from the particular interest groups that increasingly dominated London politics and the growing empire. Each of these groups saw in expanded colonial trade an opportunity to solve their own problems. The king needed an income independent of parliamentary control. Merchants sought to exclude the Dutch completely from English trade. The landed gentry sought to strengthen the British navy and to reap the profits from a stronger and wealthier shipbuilding industry. It was the policy of mercantilism, however, that provided a degree of unity among these competing interests.

The term *mercantilist system* was actually coined in the eighteenth century by Adam Smith, and English policy one hundred years earlier was far from the rational, unified system the phrase implied. No one had worked out the laws of the empire, and mercantilism had come to mean different things to different people. Still, there are certain definable trends, and London made a concerted effort to amend and reshape its colonial policy to accommodate mercantilist goals during the half-century following the Restoration. As Charles II sought to increase Crown revenues, he turned to the expansion of foreign and colonial trade and the allure of increased customs duties. James, Duke of York was a particularly strong supporter of attacks on Dutch mercantile power. He backed the creation of the Royal African Company to break the Dutch monopoly on the African slave trade and in general was the leader of a group of important figures who evinced a growing interest in colonial affairs.

Thomas Mun laid out the basic principles that guided English commercial policies during these years in *England's Treasure by Foreign Trade* (1664). Mun argued that England should reinvest its specie, since idle money would cause inflation and thus reduce exports. The proper investment of natural resources would build up artificial resources, which in turn would bring greater profits. In particular, the government should steer resources toward the cloth industry and the fisheries, breaking the country of its dependence on Baltic and Dutch supplies. The hero in this scheme was the merchant. While national interest remained the goal, commerce now provided the means to achieve it. Colonial settlements after 1660 were part of an overall economic expansion and reflected the growing awareness that trade with overseas colonies was essential to Britain's economic well-being. Regulation of this trade was both logical and necessary.

Parliament moved to achieve this goal by passing various measures known collectively as the Navigation Acts. The act passed in 1660 was designed to replace Cromwell's 1651 measure. Titled "An Act for the Encouraging and Increasing of Shipping and Navigation," it contained two main provisions. First, no goods would be allowed into or out of the colonies except in English-built and -owned ships with the master and three-quarters of the crew English. Second, certain specified, or enumerated, goods that were particularly profitable or desirable could be exported directly from the colonies to England, Ireland, or other English colonies only, and the colonists were required to pay customs fees on them. English merchants could then reexport the goods to other European nations. The first goods so listed were sugar, tobacco, raw cotton, ginger, indigo and dyewoods. The Crown added rice and molasses in 1704 and wood rosins, tars, and turpentines, vital to shipbuilding, in 1705. Other products were added later in the century.

Parliament passed the next Navigation Act in 1663. Titled "An Act for the Encouragement of Trade," it was more commonly known as the Staple Act. The measure required that any commodity going from Europe to the colonies had first to pass through England, where it would be loaded onto English ships and thence shipped to the colonies. It also stipulated that colonists post bonds on their cargoes when carrying enumerated goods from one colony to another—an effort to control colonial evasion of the 1660 act. The act gave the commissioners of customs in London the power to appoint collectors in the colonies, and the Crown immediately named five for Massachusetts, New York, Virginia, Maryland, and the Carolinas.

Economic control necessitated greater administrative control. Thus, in 1662, the Crown established the joint Council on Trade and Plantations, or the Lords of

❧ *Documents* ❧
England Seeks to
Control Colonial Trade

The following excerpts are taken from the Navigation Acts of 1660 and 1663. In each case, the reasoning and specific regulations offer insights into the nature of mercantilist policies. The first document also reminds us that the British empire and British trading concerns extended farther afield than North America.

> For *the increase of shipping and encouragement of the navigation of this nation, wherein, under the good providence and protection of God, the wealth, safety and strength of this kingdom is so much concerned.* . . . That. . . . no goods or commodities whatsoever shall be imported into or exported out of any lands, islands, plantations or territories to his Majesty belonging or in his possession, or which may hereafter belong unto or be in the possession of his Majesty, his heirs and successors, in *Asia, Africa* or *America,* in any other ship or ships, vessel or vessels whatsoever, but in such ships or vessels as do truly and without fraud belong only to the people of *England* or *Ireland* . . . , or are plantations or territories, as the proprietors and right owners thereof, and whereof the matter and three fourths of the mariners at least are *English.* . . .

The Navigation Act of 1660, in Danby Pickering, ed., *The Statutes at Large,* 46 vols. (Cambridge, England: J. Bentham, 1762–1807), 7:452.

> . . . . *in regard his Majesty's beyond the seas as inhabited and peopled by his subjects of this kingdom of* England; *for the maintaining a greater correspondence and kindness between them, and keeping them in a firmer dependence upon it, and rendring them yet more beneficial and advantagious unto it in the further improvement and increase of* English *shipping and seamen, vent of* English *woolen and other manufacturers and commodities, rendring the navigation to and from the same commodities of those plantations, but also of the commodities of other countries and places, for the supplying of them; and it being the usage of other nations to keep their plantations trade to themselves.*

The Staple Act of 1663, from Danby Pickering, ed., *The Statutes at Large,* 46 vols. (Cambridge, England: J. Bentham, 1762–1807), 8:161.

Trade, as a standing committee of the Privy Council staffed with several of the government's most powerful ministers. The Crown appointed the Earl of Shaftesbury as president and John Locke as clerk. Shaftesbury was personally involved in the Iron and Steel Corporation, the Royal African Company, the Whalebone Company, and the establishment of colonies in the Carolinas, Bahamas, New Providence Island, Barbados, and Hudson Bay. He understood from personal experience how important it was for the success of the government's policy that it cultivate the interests of merchants and manufacturers. By 1675, he succeeded in centralizing colonial administration in the Lords of Trade and in convincing the Crown to establish further restrictions on the colonies' ability to act independently.

But the colonies were not cooperating. New England vessels often loaded tobacco in the Chesapeake, carried it to Boston, and then took it directly to Europe, avoiding customs duties and violating the act of 1660. The colonies claimed the route technically satisfied English shipping laws, but Parliament disagreed. To eliminate this "broken voyage," Parliament passed the Plantation Duty Act of 1673, which required that customs commissioners be appointed for the Caribbean islands, the southern colonies, and New England. But confusion over the details of enforcement continued, as the colonies believed that once they had paid the duties, they could take their cargoes anywhere they wanted. As a result, three years later, the British began to require masters to post bonds ensuring that they would land enumerated cargoes only in another colony or in England.

In 1675, the Lords of Trade sent a proclamation to the colonies demanding adherence to the trade acts and requiring that governors and all royal officials provide assistance to the customs officers in enforcing the laws. They also sent circular letters to the governors outlining the proper procedures and requiring them to take an oath to execute the acts. Over the next few years, the Lords demanded more and more information from the governors, to little effect. A typical result of such inquiries can be found in the Lords' request in 1680 that the customs commissioners provide quarterly reports for colonial exports and imports. The commissioners took a full year to produce a thirteen-hundred-page report—which covered only one year of trade passing through London alone, was poorly organized, and required much further analysis.

But the demand for information remained urgent. The Lords were reacting to growing evidence that New England trade in particular was open to all of Europe and that the colonies were directly importing European goods at a discount of up to 20 percent below British prices. Edward Randolph, whom the Lords appointed collector, surveyor, and searcher of customs in New England in 1678, made it his life's work to correct this situation. He first visited Boston in June 1676, ostensibly on proprietary business for the New Hampshire colony but in reality as a spy to investigate Massachusetts's evasion of the trade acts. His reports were crucial in pushing the Crown to take action against the obstreperous colony. Randolph considered the Bay Colony's leaders "inconsiderable Mechanichs" and Puritan ministers "generally inclined to sedition, being Proud, Ignorant, and Imperious."[1] He noted that French ships frequented the colony and landed many illegal goods, that the colony did not require oaths of allegiance to the king, and that it had annexed Maine and New Hampshire with no authority and against the wishes of the inhabitants. When he returned to the colony as collector of the customs in 1679, he conscientiously enforced the provisions of the Navigation Acts but found himself thwarted at every step by uncooperative colonial courts. His experiences and recommendations eventually led the British Court of Chancery to recommend in 1684 that the Crown revoke the Massachusetts charter.

Interrupted by the imperial upheavals of the 1680s, the Crown completed its new economic regulatory structure with the passage of the Navigation Act of 1696, formally titled "An Act for Preventing Frauds and Regulating Abuses in the Plantation Trade." The act strengthened the customs service and enlarged the search powers of revenue officers, tightened the enforcement obligations of the governors, and established a system of vice-admiralty courts to try crimes related to the Navigation Acts. The colonists particularly resented these courts, since they consisted only of a judge, register, and marshall and did not have a jury. In the same year, William III replaced the Lords of Trade with the Board of Trade. Though still subordinate to the Privy Council, the board was responsible for the general supervision of trade in the colonies, a task that now encompassed a wide range of bureaucratic functionaries appointed to administer and enforce the trade acts. It was also empowered to examine colonial laws and governors' reports before forwarding them to the Privy Council for approval and action.

The colonists responded to the Navigation Acts with ambivalence at best. Virginians actively protested the new customs duties. The exclusion of the Dutch from American trade created artificially low prices on many crops and hurt small planters in particular. As early as 1670, total import duties on tobacco alone were almost one hundred thousand pounds. New Englanders ignored or circumvented the laws as much as possible, often picking up enumerated goods and sailing to another colonial port, thence to Holland or France without paying any customs duty. The 1673 act stopped only some of this activity.

Still, the Navigation Acts seemed to work fairly well overall, and by 1700, American goods moving through English ports accounted for one-quarter of all English exports. During the eighteenth century, smuggling from Europe to America declined, and the colonists became accustomed to importing English goods, with the wealthier merchants developing ties to London merchants and mercantile houses. English merchants also invested a growing proportion of their capital in colonial ventures. Sugar plantations were particularly profitable, but other avenues, such as shipping and financial services provided to the colonists, also proved lucrative. From 1670 to 1730, net returns on capital investment in the shipping industry alone were 5 percent to 10 percent a year, and colonial products generated much new business in England in such areas as sugar refining and tobacco processing. The colonists also gained unique advantages from being part of this system. They profited from war contracts and guaranteed markets, and they benefited in particular from British naval protection against pirates, Dutch predators, and the growing threat from the French presence to the north. Finally, the requirement that goods be transported in English ships stimulated the colonists' own shipbuilding industries.

The British Empire In The Caribbean

The beginning of England's colonization in the Caribbean added urgency to its plans to regulate colonial trade. After the defeat of the Spanish Armada, the Caribbean became more than ever a staging ground for English privateers who traded with Spanish settlers, sacked Spanish towns, and plundered Spanish silver ships. Spain was growing weaker by the year, and the Dutch, French, and English all moved to take advantage of its decline. The Dutch captured much of the Spanish New World trade, while the French and English established their own island colonies.

England built frontier outposts on St. Kitts (1624), Barbados (1627), Nevis (1628), Montserrat (1632), and Antigua (1632). Adventurous English youth settled these islands, and they seemed to have spent most of their time drinking and cultivating a decidedly uncompetitive strain of tobacco on small farms—until sugar transformed the Caribbean. During the 1640s, English settlers on Barbados learned from the Dutch how to process sugar cane. With the Dutch supplying slave labor and marketing the crop in the Netherlands, French and British colonies quickly established sugar plantations.

Spain and Portugal had already established such enterprises on the Canary and Madeira islands, but the Caribbean quickly surpassed their production. England made more money from the sweet drug than from all its other American products combined. The reason for this spectacular profitability lay in sugar's impact on European diets. Medieval villagers had subsisted on bread, beans, peas, and a little milk, butter, and cheese, with a rare treat of pork, rabbit, or fish. As African slave labor made sugar plantations more profitable for the Spanish and Portuguese, production skyrocketed and brought upper-class eating habits within reach of the merchant and middle classes, who devoured sweetened pastries and puddings. By mid-eighteenth century, even the poorest Europeans addictively sought sugared products, particularly a heavily sweetened Indian tea. After 1700, sugar became so profitable that it spurred military and diplomatic rivalries between nations.

Colonies Established

The British Caribbean empire began when the Bermuda Company (a subsidiary of the Virginia Company) settled Bermuda in 1612. The colony was initially shaped by Puritan church polity and moral discipline. Its relatively healthy climate also encouraged the early settlers to form villages not unlike those of the early New England settlers. The pressure to find a profitable staple, though, gradually transformed this society. The colonists began in 1616 to import African slaves, who labored at tobacco production for the next several decades. Caribbean tobacco was never as profitable as its mainland counterpart, however, and over time, the settlers turned to livestock and foodstuffs. Royalist elements drove the Puritan government out of power in 1644, and the colony subsequently lost most of its similarities to New England. Mid-century Bermuda was fairly stable, with a total population, white and black, of about three thousand. But the colony ran into bad luck after the Restoration. Power was increasingly concentrated in a few hands, the General Assembly lost what little influence it had, and in 1684 the Crown dissolved the Company and took control. Here, at least, most people benefited from centralization. Under company rule, the population had consisted largely of tenants and shareholders victimized by the powerful plantation owners.

The voracious search for wealth and the victimization of laborers early became the dominant themes of British Caribbean settlement. One historian has characterized the early English settlers as Protestant *conquistadores* seeking their own El Dorado—at first in mines and in looting Spanish ships and colonies, then in the soil. In these more than in other British colonies, native inhabitants were able to delay English settlement and to continually harass planters. Caribs were as important in hindering settlement of the Leeward Islands as were attacks by the Spanish; fierce maroons controlled the interior of Jamaica until the 1740s. The sea became a lifeline for these early colonies and the militia a critical component of daily life.

Barbados was easily the most valued of the English Caribbean colonies, serving as a prototype for the others. It was first settled in 1627, and as in Bermuda, its economic activity initially focused on tobacco production, with some cotton and indigo added in the 1630s. But Barbados proved much more successful in producing desirable English staples than did Bermuda, creating a rush of settlement there and on the other Leeward Islands (Antigua, Montserrat, Nevis, and St. Kitts). The island's profitability shaped its social structure; most migrants were single males, and indentured servants provided most of the labor. Barbados quickly became as competitive and exploitative as the Chesapeake, with a sharply hierarchical social structure and a life-style that, along with an unhealthy climate and the presence of a variety of debilitating diseases, hampered the development of stable families. The introduction of sugar during the 1640s cast this society in stone. By 1700, a few hundred families controlled the island's land, wealth, and politics, revelled in a luxurious,

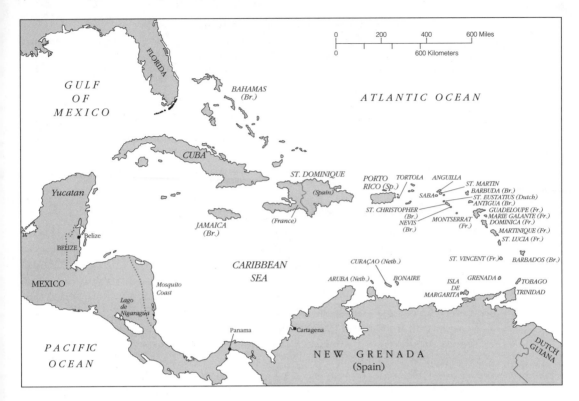

MAP 5.1: The West Indies ◆

unbridled life-style, and established a system of black slave labor that quickly became the cruelest, most exploitative in the Western world.

A 1680 census of the island's population offers a unique view of the Barbadian social structure. The island's 175 largest planters, representing only 7 percent of the property holders, controlled more than half of the wealth; their estates averaged 210 acres in size and had about 115 slaves each. Samuel Newton, one of the larger planters, owned 581 acres, fifteen white indentured servants, and 260 slaves. These same men controlled the colony's political and military offices—the assembly, the council, the courts, the justices of the peace, and the parish vestries. They lived in two- or three-story wooden houses furnished with four-poster beds, framed pictures, and plentiful supplies of pewter. At the same time, thousands of others held less than ten acres of land and owned no slaves. Few of these men could establish any sort of family life, and most lived in shacks that barely sheltered them from the elements. Among the 2,639 property holders listed in the census, the median size of a farm was only ten acres.

The men and women who lived on Barbados and the other islands were unique among British colonials in their wealth and power. James Drax was perhaps typical. Drax came to Barbados in 1627 from an obscure (likely yeoman) background in England, with only three hundred pounds of company stock. Over the next decade, he became a highly successful tobacco and cotton planter, acquiring more than forty white indentured servants. He became one of the first Barbadians to move into sugar after 1640 and immediately established valuable trading links with the Dutch. After 1664, he began importing large numbers of African slaves. One of the richest men on the island, he identified with the parliamentary cause during the English Civil War and was knighted by Cromwell during a 1658 visit to

England. His Puritanism, though, did not extend to his life style. His plantation home, Drax Hall, was worthy of the English nobility. In later life, like many others, he divided his time between London and Barbados.

Society and Economy in the Islands

Sugar production was both costly and labor-intensive. Cane had to be turned into molasses or rum, requiring substantial investment in processing equipment—a mill, large boiling pots, and sometimes a distillery. The process required a few skilled workers to run and maintain the machinery and a much larger unskilled labor force to work in the fields. Yellow fever and other tropical diseases took a heavy toll on the white planters, however, and the drive to produce more and more sugar left the islands precariously dependent on imports for food. Between 1640 and 1700, the English imported more than 250,000 black slaves to the Caribbean islands—134,000 to Barbados alone. As the century progressed, white and black laborers alike frequently united against their masters, and servant mutinies and slave rebellions became commonplace. Planters meted out severe punishments for the smallest of "crimes" and often noted their fears and their sense of living in a constant state of siege. The white population declined precipitously; on Barbados, it fell from thirty thousand in 1650 to about 15,500 in 1700. By 1750, the black-white ratio was seven to one on the Leeward Islands and ten to one on Jamaica. Increasingly, this was a world of absentee landlords and exploitative labor systems, with little account given even to the survival of the workers, who could readily be replaced by new slave imports. This pattern was repeated in other Leeward Islands and, somewhat later, in Jamaica—though there, privateering and the fortunes gathered by buccaneers provided an early abundance of wealth.

Barbados was England's first slave society. Here as elsewhere, Africans labored amidst a deadly disease environment. They brought hookworm, leprosy, elephantiasis, and encephalitis with them, while whites contributed tuberculosis and venereal

Sugar production in West Indies (courtesy of The Library Company of Philadelphia). ❧

disease; the environment itself bred yellow fever and other tropical diseases. Sugar plantations required year-round work, subjecting Africans to extreme physical stress as well. Plantation owners easily justified this situation. Blacks were, the Barbadian slave code averred, "an heathenish, brutish, and an uncertain, dangerous kinde of people."[2] Whites believed that only fear would keep them under control. Hence, black criminals were burned alive, beheaded, or starved to death. When the authorities discovered a slave conspiracy on Barbados in 1692, they hired a woman named Alice Mills to castrate forty-two blacks—"which says," according to historian Winthrop Jordan, "a good deal about Barbados and something about Alice Mills."[3] Jamaica was cursed with the most brutal race relations of all, since blacks outnumbered whites there by such a large margin. The island had no provision for due process at all, and planters commonly punished blacks by branding their faces, rubbing salt and urine into their wounds, and tying cart chains around their necks. Thomas Thistlewood, an overseer and small planter, developed something called "Derby's dose," "whereby the slave Derby would defecate into a culprit's mouth, which would then be gagged shut for hours."[4] Some slaves did succeed in becoming skilled artisans, and others worked in service occupations in the towns. Domestic house slaves often bought and sold goods in the colony's market. But on the whole, it is hardly surprising that Caribbean slavery has been characterized by historians as the cruelest and most inhumane of American slave systems.

Men like Samuel Newton quickly developed a division of labor for their slaves. There were usually three or four work gangs. Men and women at the peak of their physical strength comprised the first gang, performing the plantation's most demanding labor from January to May—cutting the cane, carrying it to the mills, and processing it into sugar. At other times, they planted cane and food crops and tilled the fields. Adolescents comprised the second gang, planting such food crops as corn, weeding the fields, and tending the livestock. Blacks from both of these gangs also carried out the various specialized tasks of processing the cane. Women also served as "sick nurses" and took care of small children.

Children from five to twelve years old made up the third gang, collecting grass and fodder for the livestock, weeding fields, and tending the smaller livestock and fowl. The smallest children, finally, sometimes worked in a fourth gang, collecting vines and insects to feed the animals their older siblings tended. About one-quarter of the slaves on the average plantation were disabled, pregnant, or too old or young to be employable. The planters regarded various skilled positions as particularly valuable—the black drivers who oversaw the gangs, the "ranger" who supervised all of the gangs and reported directly to the plantation manager, and the skilled craftsmen and tradesmen, such as masons, carpenters, coopers, and blacksmiths. These individuals enjoyed certain privileges denied the field hands—more clothing and better food, larger houses, and even monetary payments. Undoubtedly, these small rewards did little to lessen the misery of being a slave on these islands of death.

New British Colonies On The Mainland

The British also established several colonies on the mainland in the quarter century after the Restoration: New York, New Jersey, Pennsylvania, North Carolina and South Carolina. Settlers in each of these colonies experienced many of the same adjustment problems of earlier migrants, as they confronted the disconcerting reality of the New World environment, suppressed the native population (except in Pennsylvania), and sought to mold Old World institutions to a new way of life. In

New York, the presence of an entrenched Dutch culture made the adaptive process still more complex.

The Dutch in Colonial North America

The Dutch were the first Europeans to occupy the area we know today as New York. Holland freed itself from Spanish control in the early seventeenth century, negotiating a truce in 1609 that ended forty years of warfare. The Dutch then moved to combat Spanish religious and secular power and to expand their own commercial involvement throughout the world. Bolstered by a strong materialistic, bourgeois tradition among its merchants, Holland was the world's greatest trading nation by 1648. Its trading outposts ranged from Archangel in Russia to Recife in Brazil, where they temporarily wrested control of that colony from the Portuguese, and from Nagasaki, India, and the East Indies to New Amsterdam, which was perhaps the least important of the Dutch colonies. This empire had no interest in establishing permanent communities. Its citizens enjoyed prosperity and religious freedom in their homeland and had little motivation to migrate to forbidding foreign lands.

The Dutch formed the Dutch East India Company in 1602. One of the company's first important ventures was an expedition to North America in search of the elusive Northwest Passage, and Dutch traders were already familiar with the lower reaches of the Hudson River by 1600. Thus, when Henry Hudson entered its mouth and sailed northward in *De Halve Maen (The Half Moon)* in 1609, he encountered over and over again canoes filled with Indians eager to trade. Hudson's ship was hardly suitable for a major exploratory voyage; it was only sixty-three feet long and eighty tons in weight, with a hold depth of six feet or so and a crew of eighteen. He left Amsterdan on April 6, sailed from Newfoundland south to Cape Cod and then Virginia, then turned northward again before entering the Hudson. He explored the river as far as present-day Albany, and was finally convinced that this was not the Northwest Passage. He returned to England, where his mixed English and Dutch crew refused to continue on to Holland. He put in for the winter and embarked on another search for the passage in 1611. His luck was even worse this time. His desperate crew mutinied over his determined search in the face of deteriorating conditions and set him adrift in the frigid waters of Hudson Bay.

As a result of his voyages and that of Adrian Block, who circumnavigated Long Island in 1614, the Dutch government granted a charter to thirteen merchants that guaranteed them a trade monopoly for four voyages over a three-year period. This company made a good profit on the fur trade, but pressure from other groups to share the bounties kept it from receiving a charter renewal. Instead, the government chartered the Dutch West India Company on June 3, 1621. The founding of this joint-stock company, with exclusive rights to trade in the New World and in parts of Africa and Australia, highlighted the Dutch goal of creating a colonial trading empire. In May 1624, the company sent out thirty families (mostly Waloons, French-speaking refugees from southern Netherlands) that reestablished an earlier trading post at Fort Orange (Albany) and several other locations. Gov. Peter Minuit led a later contingent of colonists who arrived in the colony with horses, cattle, hogs, sheep, seeds, and plows. Minuit's successor as governor, Willem Verhulst, purchased Manhattan from the Indians for sixty florins worth of merchandise, and Minuit acquired Staten Island. The Dutch relocated the colony on Manhattan in 1626, since the island was sheltered, easily defended, and centrally located between the Albany and Delaware River trading posts.

The company's Amsterdam commissioners envisioned a trading outpost, with the settlers all employed by the company at low salaries. Dependence on the fur

NIEUW AMSTERDAM
of t'dpas Amstotams.

New Amsterdam, about 1640. ❧

trade required good relations with the Indians, and the company intended that the settlement grow enough food to become self-sufficient. In fact, the commissioners felt so strongly about this that they sent little aid over between 1626 and 1628, putting their investments into more lucrative areas of their empire and hoping that individual initiative would get the New World outpost off the ground.

Profits proved disappointing, and in 1630, there were still only three hundred people living in the colony. In an attempt to encourage settlement, the company established a class of entrepreneurs known as patroons. It accorded this status to those who brought over at least fifty people to the colony; in return, they received land either eighteen miles along one bank of the Hudson or nine miles along both sides. The company also gave a patroon judicial and administrative powers and the right to engage in trade from Newfoundland to Florida, provided he paid a 5 percent commission to the company. Only one of these patroonships, that of Killiaen van Rensselaer, achieved even minimal success, and in 1629, the company issued a new charter providing for smaller grants to less wealthy individuals. The Dutch middle class was so well off, however, and the terms of settlement so relatively ungenerous that few took up the offer.

The company made a final effort to stimulate immigration in 1640, when it issued the Charter of Freedoms and Exemptions. This document offered two hundred acres of land to anyone who brought five adult immigrants to the colony, and it gave the colony greater powers of self-government. Population doubled between 1638 and 1643, from less than a thousand to almost two thousand, but many of the new arrivals were transients, and the increased pressure on available land worsened relations with the Indians. When the Dutch first landed, they purchased land from the several small tribes that inhabited Manhattan. The Indians assumed they had the right to continue to use the land until the Dutch decided to farm on it, and Indian and white fields often abutted each other. Indian dogs attacked Dutch cattle, and Dutch cattle trampled Indian fields.

Conflict intensified with the arrival of Gov. Willem Kieft (1638-1647). Kieft assumed that he held political jurisdiction over the tribes and tried to collect taxes from them. One Indian commented that Kieft "must be a very mean fellow to come to live in this country without being invited. . . and now wish to compel them to give him their corn for nothing."[5] Angry warriors began to raid the outlying settlements in the summer of 1641, beginning four years of intermittent warfare. In 1642, a band of Hackensacks murdered two Dutch farmers whose cattle had trampled their corn and who had swindled them in trade. The Indians offered to pay his widow "to wipe away her tears,"[6] in their traditional fashion, but they would not give up the accused murderers. A year later, the Dutch retaliated, attacking two encampments of Wecquaesgeeks they had earlier granted refuge to and butchering the women and children. In February 1643, Dutch soldiers surrounded an Indian village and massacred the inhabitants, leading to open warfare. Kieft continued a policy of intimidation and killed almost one thousand Indians. Peace came only two years later. Kieft also confronted serious internal problems. The New Amsterdam settlers were a highly litigious lot, turning to the courts at every opportunity. They engaged in extensive smuggling and routinely embezzled funds from the fur trade. In 1644, the company recalled the governor and demanded an accounting of his administration.

Complaints from the colony's settlers were partly responsible for Kieft's recall and led to a partial reorganization of the government. The company appointed a director-general, a deputy, and a financial officer to sit as a council and rule the colony autocratically, subject only to occasional consultation with representatives from the settlements. Peter Stuyvesant arrived as Kieft's replacement in 1647 to implement the new government. He was not encouraged by what he saw. New Amsterdam had one thousand people, an unfinished church, and stinking, muddy streets; only its thirty-five taverns distinguished it in any way. It was Stuyvesant's own willpower that salvaged respectability for the colony. Known in history for his peg leg (embroidered with silver bands), the new governor's earlier career as a ministry student in the Dutch Reformed Church was cut short when he was expelled for pursing extracurricular activities with his landlord's daughter. He became a clerk for the Dutch East India Company and headed its post at Curacao; in 1644, he lost his right leg leading a siege against a Spanish garrison on St. Martin's Island. His personality was a mixture of stubbornness, piety, culture, courage, and diplomacy, and he found himself constantly embroiled in controversy with the colony's settlers.

Peter Stuyvesant. ❧

Stuyvesant began his administration by banishing Quakers from the colony, denying citizenship to Jews, and refusing non-Calvinists voting rights. He fought with the colonists over taxes, morality, and land purchases from the Indians and with the company over religious toleration and the control of the fur trade. He levied a 30 percent customs duty on trade to raise revenue and succeeded only in driving away trade from the Chesapeake and New England colonies. The colonists accused him of tyrannical conduct and of controlling the Indian trade for his own benefit.

The principal theme of the governor's administration was the conflict between local government and provincial authority. Towns sought greater autonomy and looked to the company as their protector, patterning their demands after the New England townships on Long Island. At first, two traditional Dutch officials (schouts and schupens) attended to governmental and judicial affairs in Dutch towns. But town charters did not provide for popular participation in government, and the company allowed only those who owned land to vote. In 1649, a group of inhabitants petitioned the company for "suitable municipal government," and in 1652, the company ordered Stuyvesant to establish a government based on the Amsterdam model, including two mayors, five aldermen, and a sheriff. Stuyvesant, however, stubbornly resisted the spirit of his instructions and appointed the officials rather than allowing them to be elected.

Autocratic he certainly was, but Stuyvesant was also efficient. He managed the colony's economy, enforced laws against the sale of liquor to Indians, introduced provisions to control fire, cracked down on smuggling and embezzlement, and required everyone to attend Sunday services. He even dared to partially extend the colony's judicial system into the Rennselaerswyck patroonship. Many of his actions stemmed from his fear of instability in such a diverse settlement. His first reform in 1647 was an order for all bars to close at 9 P.M., with penalties for drinking on Sundays and knife fighting. Disorderly sailors, sexual promiscuity, reckless wagon driving, and tavern brawls were apparently common problems, and Stuyvesant eventually established, in 1658, the "Rattle Watch," a group of nine men who patrolled the town keeping an eye out for pirates, vagabonds, and robbers. They carried a wooden hinged clapper, or "rattle," to sound the alarm.

He had little success, though, in imposing order—ethical or not—on Dutch-Indian relations. When Stuyvesant left the colony briefly, the Mahican, Pachamis, Esopus, and Hackensack tribes launched a surprise attack on Manhattan Island, destroying much of the settlers' personal property while sparing their lives. The Indians attacked and burned other settlements as well, killing fifty colonists in all. Stuyvesant subsequently strengthened the colony's defenses, forbade new farms in isolated areas, prohibited Indians from staying overnight in the town and from bringing arms in, and imprisoned drunken Indians until they told him who had sold them the alcohol. With the fur trade depleted, the Indians no longer offered any benefits to the whites and had become obstacles to the colonists' growing need for land. Dutch-Indian relations at Albany, however, continued to be positive for some time, as the fur trade there remained highly profitable. The Dutch even gave the Mohawks firearms to use against the Huron, French allies who threatened Dutch control of the region's trade.

The inhabitants of New Amsterdam lived in perhaps the most polyglot of any seventeenth-century North American colony. By the end of Dutch settlement, with a population of less than nine thousand, the colony contained Dutch, Belgian, French, English, Portuguese, Swedish, Finnish, and African settlers. A visitor might hear any of at least eighteen different languages and worship with religious groups that included Lutherans, Congregationalists, Quakers, Catholics, and Jews, who were forced to live in a ghetto in New Amsterdam. Though most people lived in or around New Amsterdam, settlements also existed at Fort Orange, a short-lived trading fort in Hartford, Connecticut, and in farming villages at the west end of Long Island, on upper Manhattan, on Staten Island, and along the Lower Hudson valley. The company was also the first to import slaves into North America—so many that by 1664, almost one-fifth of the fifteen hundred inhabitants of Manhattan were black.

The close proximity of the colony of New Sweden added to the ethnic diversity of this region. Sweden established the West India Company in 1638 and sent fifty colonists to settle on the Delaware River—led, ironically, by Peter Minuit. The group built Fort Christina near present-day Wilmington, Delaware, and established several other tiny outposts. At first, the Dutch did not object, since Sweden was their ally during the Thirty Years' War (1618–1648). Then in 1641, a group of Puritans from New Haven arrived, intending to profit from the fur trade. The Dutch ousted this group, but another came in 1643. The Swedish settlement's governor was Johann Printz, who was called "Big Tub" by the Indians because he weighed more than four hundred pounds. Printz struck an accommodation with the Puritans, and the two groups coexisted for several years. His more ambitious successor, Johann Rising, decided to rid the area of the Dutch and captured one of their forts in 1654. Stuyvesant responded with an expedition against the Swedes in 1655 and took control of the colony.

The demands of New England migrants on Long Island presented the Dutch with one of their most intractable problems. In June 1640, a group from Lynn, Massachusetts, founded Southampton, bringing with them their own churches, town meetings, and communal land systems. Connecticut established claims over several other towns on the island. In December 1653, delegates from these towns convened to protest the autocratic rule of Stuyvesant and to petition for the rights of free citizens, including the right to participate in making their own laws. Stuyvesant dissolved the meeting, asserting that authority came only from God and the company, "not from a few ignorant subjects."[7] The dissidents continued their protests led by John Scott, an ex-indentured servant and buccaneer. In 1663, Scott took the title of "President" for himself and organized the six towns into a short-lived independent "combination," separate from both New Netherland and Connecticut. The controversy ended the following year, when Connecticut ceded its claims to New York in exchange for a more favorable western boundary.

As mid-century approached, the Dutch faced a more serious threat to their hegemony over New Amsterdam—the English. As the Dutch had done to the Spanish before them, the English now sought to replace Holland as the world's great imperial power. They succeeded in a series of three conflicts, beginning with the First Anglo-Dutch War (1652–1654). It was the Second Anglo-Dutch War (1664–1667), though, that was most relevant to affairs in the New World. In 1664, Charles II granted his brother James a charter for an unequaled expanse of land in the New World. New York, as James renamed the territory, included all of what was to become New Jersey, a stretch of land on the western side of the Delaware River, the western half of Connecticut, eastern Maine north to the St. Lawrence River, and all of the islands (except Block Island) from Cape Cod to Cape May. James in turn granted the area known as New Jersey to Sir John Berkeley and Sir Philip Carteret in 1665, as payment for an outstanding debt. In 1667, the Nicolls Commission gave the western half of Connecticut to the Connecticut colony. Even without this additional territory, James now possessed a grant that promised to make him one of the wealthiest and most powerful of the new proprietors. Only one barrier stood in his way—the Dutch.

In 1664, James sent a fleet, known as the Commission of 1664 and headed by Sir Richard Nicolls, to conquer the Dutch colony and investigate conditions in the other mainland colonies. The Dutch surrendered immediately. To his credit, Nicolls made the transition to English rule as painless as possible. He renamed New Amsterdam New York City and offered generous terms: the Dutch could leave with their belongings or stay in the colony with their land titles confirmed. The terms also required those who stayed to swear an oath of allegiance to Charles, though they would not have to fight for the English in the event of war. Finally, the treaty allowed the Dutch settlers to trade directly with their homeland, granted the Dutch Reformed Church complete freedom of worship, and made English law applicable only where the English outnumbered the Dutch.

New York

As governor of the New York colony, meanwhile, Richard Nicolls introduced a body of legislation known as the Duke's Laws, initially designed to apply only to Long Island and Westchester County. A special meeting of thirty-four delegates from seventeen towns (thirteen English, four Dutch) approved the laws in March 1665. Though they provided for elected town governments and boards of aldermen, the laws did not allow an elected assembly, town meetings, public schools, or widespread freemanship. They required that residents surrender all old land deeds and patents, necessitating new surveys and fees to pay for the new patents—a stipulation that caused considerable discontent. Long Islanders, particularly the many settlers from New England, severely criticized the laws. Nicolls soon tired of the colony's disputes and resigned his post, succeeded by Col. Francis Lovelace (1667–1673).

Lovelace was a cautious but autocratic governor, ruling through his councillors or by special commissions. He successfully dealt with growing problems in Indian relations, boundary disputes, and a rebellion in New Jersey. He also improved communications and transportation within the colony and worked hard to expand trade and promote shipbuilding. In 1676, James ordered the Duke's Laws applied to the entire colony, though he also reaffirmed Dutch land titles and continued religious toleration. The most momentous event of Lovelace's administration, though, was the Dutch recapture of the colony in 1672 during the Third Anglo-Dutch War. Lovelace was away when Dutch warships appeared in New York harbor. When the British captain temporarily in charge asked the Dutch what they wanted, the fleet admiral responded that they had come to take what was theirs. The captain then asked for his commission; the admiral answered "that it was in the barrel of his cannon and that the English would see it soon enough if they did not surrender the fort."[8] The Dutch retook the town on June 30, 1673, after one day of fighting. Their victory was short-lived, because the English won the colony back in October.

Edmund Andros (1674–1682) and then Thomas Dongan (1682–1687) succeeded Lovelace and guided the colony toward institutional maturity. The population increased from six thousand in 1673 to fifteen thousand by 1685. The Dutch maintained their economic and cultural stronghold in Albany, but English culture gradually began to assert itself elsewhere. The Crown ordered a representative assembly established, and on October 17, 1683, Dongan presided over its first meeting and presented the Charter of Liberties and Privileges, a new frame of government. The charter affirmed the colony's right to an elected assembly, provided for representation by county (there were twelve), and recognized the assembly as the "Supreame and only Legislative power under his Royall Highnesse." It also stated that bills passed by the assembly would be law until repealed or vetoed by the duke, gave the legislature the power to control its own sessions and set its own qualifications for membership, and granted the franchise to any who could qualify under English law. The document was particularly protective of individual liberties, quoting directly from the Magna Charta regarding liberty of the person, affirming the principle of no taxation without representation, and guaranteeing liberty of conscience for all Christians. New York had taken its first significant step toward establishing an English cultural identity.

New Jersey

The Dutch were the first to try to establish settlements in the New Jersey area in the 1630s, 1640s, and 1650s, but they failed to maintain a permanent presence. The first English attempt came in 1634, when Charles I gave the New Jersey-Delaware region to Sir Edmund Plowden and several partners, but the group was unable to launch an expedition. By mid-century, only small groups of settlers from New Amsterdam, Long Island, and New Sweden populated the region. After the British conquest of New Amsterdam in 1664, Sir Richard Nicolls began to promote settlement in the New Jersey area to Rhode Island Baptists and Long Island Quakers, unaware of the fact that James had granted rights to the region to Sir George Carteret and Sir John Berkeley. Their deed (not really a charter) included an area of 5 million acres, with the power to grant headrights of sixty to 150 acres per person over a three-year period. The following year, the proprietors issued Concessions and Agreements that granted liberty of conscience, freedom of trade, and the right of self-government by an elected assembly of two delegates from each town. Generous offers of land were made to settlers and to servants at the end of their term of indenture.

The conflicting grants made by Nicolls on the one hand and Carteret and Berkeley on the other sowed the seeds for bitter disputes over land rights, and the situation became still more muddled in 1674, when Berkely sold his share to John Fenwick, who was buying the land for a small group of Quakers headed by Edward Byllynge and including William Penn. In 1676, Carteret and the Quakers signed the Quintipartite Deed, formally dividing the territory into East (Carteret) and West (Quakers) New Jersey. In the next few years, more than fourteen hundred Quakers migrated to West Jersey under a set of Concessions and Agreements that guaranteed annual elections, secret ballots, universal male franchise, and a powerful legislature. When Carteret died in 1682, East New Jersey was auctioned off to Penn and his associates.

This quixotic train of sales and purchases paralleled the tumultuous history of the early years of both colonies. English colonists staged ongoing protests against proprietary rule in East Jersey. Beyond the guarantees provided by the Concessions, the settlers sought release from quitrent payments and established greater control over local government through town meetings and local remonstrances and resolution. In 1672, an illegal convention all but deposed Gov. Carteret, who sailed to England in despair. Land speculation was rampant, and a variety of factions competed for political power. West Jersey experienced similar factionalism, though the real crisis here began in 1692, when the colony was purchased by the West New Jersey Society, an Anglican group that sent settlers over in large numbers and generated considerable opposition from the Quaker settlers.

Political and social conflict generated fatigue more than anything else, and many elements in both colonies gradually came to favor a transition to royal government. East and West New Jersey were reunited in 1702 under Crown rule. The new government did not, however, end factionalism. Proprietors kept their land rights and sought to maintain their influence while squabbling even among themselves, and landlord-tenant disputes continued to escalate over such issues as rents and leases. These disagreements plagued life in New Jersey throughout the eighteenth century.

Pennsylvania

The story of Pennsylvania begins with George Fox, who founded Quakerism in England in 1647. Fox established a religion that drew its inspiration and strength from "a God of Love and Light whose benevolent spirit harmonized the universe."[9] The Quaker doctrine of the inner light sprang from the belief that every soul contained divine goodness and virtue as a gift from God, so that all individuals could experience salvation if they accepted the existence of this perfection within themselves. Men and women thus became their own priests, and Quakers repudiated sacraments, ceremonies, oaths, tithes, and a paid, professional clergy. They denied original sin and predestination, used *thee* and *thou* in conversation instead of the more deferential *you*, and refused to doff their hats to their social superiors. The English government regarded them as dangerously subversive, and from 1661 to 1685 imprisoned almost fifteen thousand of them, executing 450. William Penn was jailed four times. Yet during these same years, membership in the sect doubled, and as the initial stage of zealous advocacy waned, the Quakers began to develop a solid institutional structure to support their members and extend their proselytizing overseas.

Fox emerged from prison in 1666 to lead a four-year campaign to construct a system of group discipline. He established a structure of meetings—men's and women's meetings, meetings for worship and for business, and monthly, quarterly, and yearly meetings. Elders provided what hierarchical leadership there was, and overseers counseled members and offered personal and religious support. Lay missionaries and preachers helped spread the word. The meetings oversaw marriage, sex, business, personal habits, and involvement in politics and the law.

Despite this shift to a more moderate, institutional emphasis, Quakers remained unshaken in their essential beliefs. They maintained their faith in religious freedom and social pluralism, the sanctity of property, a strong work ethic, sexual prudery, the importance of the family, and simple tastes in their daily lives. Quakers pursued "the Lamb's War," a crusade of the meek. They dressed in plain black cloth and adopted policies of pacifism and civil disobedience. Most unusual for their times, Quaker women had far greater equality than did most other western European groups. Spiritual equality was unquestioned. Margaret Fell, Fox's wife, was just as critical to the group's success as he was, and she labored to establish women's right to participate in church services on an equal (if separate) basis, to preach, and to establish their own meetings.

As with all English immigrants, New World Quakers were formed by the Old World environment they came from. More family-oriented than Virginians, less so than New Englanders, Quaker men and women came from the middling ranks of English society. Most were farmers, craftspeople, laborers, and servants, while few were members of the nobility. Geographically, the movement drew its heaviest membership from the North Midlands, especially the counties of Cheshire, Lancashire, Yorkshire, Derbyshire, and Nottinghamshire. These were among England's poorest regions, with many desperate farmers struggling to produce a surplus to bring to market, making barely enough to get by even in good years. Much of the area was still wooded and remote, and even in the seventeenth century, wolves and wild boars could surprise the solitary walker. Religious differences split the region's inhabitants. The ruling elite tended to emphasize its Norman-

French, Catholic background, while the shepherds and farmers were largely Protestant and evangelical. Radical sects flourished here, and the Quakers were most numerous in the poorer regions.

William Penn, Sr. had commanded a fleet under Oliver Cromwell and captured Jamaica in 1655, but he later aided Charles II in his successful attempt to regain the Crown. Charles gratefully knighted him and made him lord high admiral, giving him an estate in Ireland, where William Penn, Jr. spent his boyhood. As an adolescent, the younger Penn experienced mystic visions. His father sent him to Christ Church at Oxford to calm him down, but the reverse happened. He was shocked by the "hellish darkness and debauchery"[10] of Oxford and refused to attend chapel, and he was expelled for nonconformity. He returned to Ireland, where his father assigned him the task of managing the family estates, undoubtedly hoping that business affairs would take his son's mind off religious fanaticism. But the younger Penn heard the Quaker Thomas Loe preach and was immediately converted. Appalled, his father tried beating the apostasy out of his son; failing this, he sent him on the European grand tour. While in France, Penn went to the Huguenot town of Saumur, a center of Protestantism in the southwest region, where he studied with the liberal theologican Moses Amyraut and became more confirmed than ever in his views.

On his return to England, Penn gradually became one of the Quaker's leading lights, second only in fame and influence to Fox. The government locked him in the Tower of London in 1668 for writing a Quaker book, and there he wrote *No Cross, No Crown,* perhaps his greatest work. He was arrested again in 1670 for preaching outside a locked meetinghouse in London. He argued his case so well that the jurors refused to convict him on the charge of inciting to riot and found him guilty only of speaking in the streets, even though they were threatened with imprisonment themselves. The case marked an important turning point in British legal history, establishing the inviolability of the jury deliberation process. He was arrested yet again in 1671 and sent to Newgate prison, where he refused the comforts his rank entitled him to and wrote *The Great Case of Liberty of Conscience.* He subsequently traveled throughout Europe, meeting with a number of influential German pietists. Penn also became a trustee of West Jersey and drew up its Fundamental Laws, and he became active in British Whig politics. He believed that restrictions should be placed on the growing court influence in England through frequent Parliaments that could establish checks on tyrants and "arbitrary ministers."

America appealed to Penn as a place where he could plant a model colony, an example for all Christians in its preservation of liberty of conscience (excluding, of course, atheists and nonbelievers). He petitioned Charles II for a grant of land in lieu of payment of a debt of sixteen thousand pounds the Crown owed his father. On March 4, 1681, Charles granted Penn a charter that gave him a stretch of land from forty degrees to forty-three degrees latitude north and five degrees longitude west of the Delaware River, an area of about six hundred thousand square miles, or six times the size of England itself. The charter empowered Penn to receive quitrents from all settlers, obligated him only to pay the king two beaver skins a year and one-fifth of all gold and silver discovered in the colony, and gave him the power to appoint all officials and to veto all laws passed by the freemen. As a concession to the increasingly serious British efforts to regulate the empire, the charter also contained a clause explicitly requiring enforcement of the Navigation Acts. In 1682, the duke of York granted Penn the eastern part of the peninsula between Chesapeake and Delaware bays, giving the province direct water access.

Penn promoted the colony widely, publishing tracts in several languages, visiting the Rhineland and Holland twice, and drawing heavily on his friendships with

William Penn at age fifty-two. ❧

German pietists. He even wrote a pamphlet, The Benefit of Plantations. . . ," in which he touted the mercantilist benefits of the new colony. There were already fourteen hundred Quakers in West Jersey by 1681, and in 1682, twenty-three ships arrived in Delaware Bay with more than two thousand Quaker settlers. In the next three years, ninety more shiploads came to Pennsylvania.

The Land and the Indians   These first settlers described the land with the same awe we find in almost all early European accounts. The area offered them substantial economic opportunity; the Delaware River valley was laced with creeks and small rivers surrounded by abundant deposits of building stone, coal, copper, iron ore, and oak, walnut, and chestnut trees. The soil was rich and fertile, the climate temperate. A 1681 promotional piece, "Some Account of the Province of Pennsylvania," described a land full of fish and fowl, deer and timber, one that was "600 miles nearer the Sun than England. . . "[11] and was best for the industrious, ingenious, and genteel of England who had found themselves, through no fault of their own, disinherited. Indians were not a serious obstacle. A tribe known as the Lenni Lenapes (Delaware) lived in this region of the coast, and they gave the English a friendly welcome. The Iroquois had earlier dispersed the most threatening tribes of the region, the Susquehannocks, and the valley was only sparsely inhabited when the colonists landed.

Penn's respectful treatment of the area's Indians was even more important in insuring peaceful relations. His attitude was a combination of kindness and paternalism. Penn thought the Indians were descended from the Old Testament Jews and that their religion resembled primitive Christianity; he did not really grasp Indian attitudes toward land and wealth. But his basic motives of love, equity, and justice were almost unique in the English settlements. He accepted Indian statements of friendship at face value and treated them with the same equanimity he showed to Europeans.

Penn purchased land from the Indians and only then resold it to settlers; he believed the Indians were the rightful owners and gave them lavish trade goods in exchange. He prohibited the sale of alcohol to Indians, regulated the fur trade, and learned their language. By the end of the century, tribes from Maryland, Virginia, and

North Carolina were moving to Pennsylvania, and even the Shawnees and Miamis were moving east from the Ohio valley. Later, of course, the Scotch-Irish, Palantine Germans, and Swiss settlers who dominated eighteenth-century migration would show little such respect for the Indians or their land claims. But while he lived in the colony, Penn was able to enforce the policy he expressed to the Delaware chiefs: "The king of the Country where I live, hath given me a great Province; but I desire to enjoy it with your Love and Consent, that we may always live together as Neighbors and friends."[12]

Settlement Proceeds   Penn's initial plans for settlement envisioned neighborhoods of five to ten houses close together on ten-acre lots, surrounded by fields with 450 acres of land per family. He expected each such township to cover about five thousand acres and have only about fifty people. Though by 1685 about fifty townships had been established, settlement patterns rarely conformed to Penn's plans.

By 1700, Pennsylvania had twenty-one thousand settlers; about half had come as indentured servants, the rest as free farmers or artisans. Most were English, Irish, or Welsh Quakers, but there were also Catholics, Lutherans, Baptists, Anglicans, Calvinists, and Quakers from Germany and Holland. They built their homesteads west along the Schuylkill River and then along the Susquehanna, living on dispersed farms that were larger than their counterparts in New England. At first, people settled with their European brethren, but gradually intermarriage and geographical mobility created an ethnic and religious mosaic. Only the Quakers showed restraint, forbidding intermarriage with members of other faiths and limiting the size of their families to ensure enough land for their children. Even they constantly moved short distances, in patterns that closely resembled those of the English North Midlands.

But Quaker families were never isolated. They built their homes in clusters that resembled the rural neighborhoods of northern England. Though the communal pastures and meadows of Penn's idealized vision never existed in these settlements, the Quaker concept of the "loving neighborhood" helped counter the potential disruptiveness of dispersed settlement. Quakers valued a Christian reputation for doing good

Plan for the City of Philadelphia, from a Dutch translation of one of Penn's promotional tracts, *Missive van William Penn* (Amsterdam, 1684). Penn's desire for ordered settlement was reflected in his planned design for Philadelphia. ❧

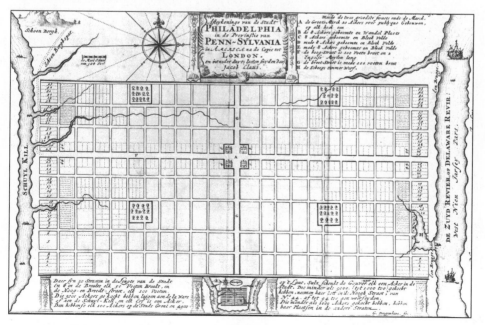

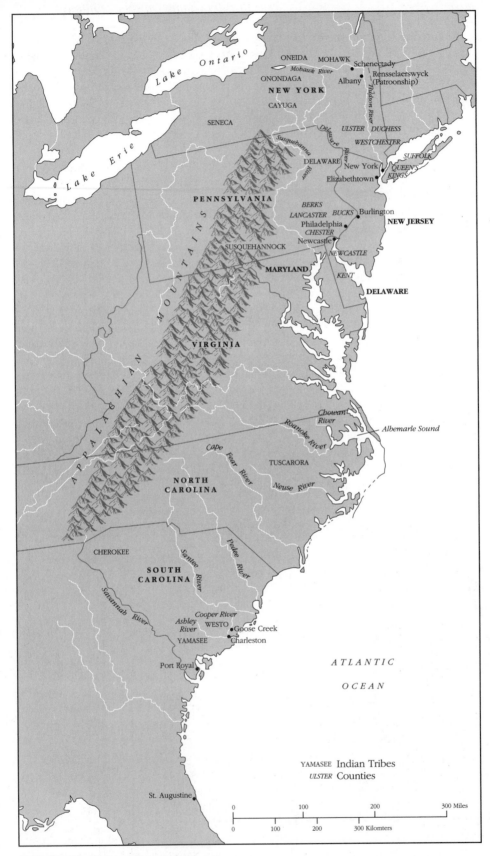

Lake Ontario

ONEIDA MOHAWK
Schenectady
Mohawk River Albany Rensselaerswyck
ONONDAGA (Patroonship)

NEW YORK
Hudson River

CAYUGA

SENECA

ULSTER DUCHESS
WESTCHESTER

Susquehanna River *Delaware River* *SUFFOLK*

DELAWARE New York *QUEEN'S*
KINGS

Elizabethtown

M *BERKS*
O *LANCASTER BUCKS* Burlington
U **PENNSYLVANIA** Philadelphia **NEW JERSEY**
N *CHESTER*
T Newcastle
A SUSQUEHANNOCK *NEWCASTLE*
I
N **MARYLAND** *KENT*
S
DELAWARE

VIRGINIA

A
P
P *Chowan River*
A
L *Roanoke River* Albemarle Sound
A
C *Cape*
H *Fear River* TUSCARORA
I
A *Neuse River*
N **NORTH CAROLINA**

CHEROKEE *Santee River* *Pedee River*

SOUTH CAROLINA

Savannah River *Cooper River*
Ashley River WESTO • Goose Creek
YAMASEE Charleston

Port Royal

ATLANTIC

OCEAN

St. Augustine

YAMASEE Indian Tribes
ULSTER Counties

0   100   200   300 Miles

0   100   200   300 Kilomters

MAP 5.2: The Restoration Colonies

above all. Those who lost their honor were required to stand before the community and shame themselves or face expulsion from the association. Neither democrats nor social levelers, Quakers nonetheless pursued a form of social equality that held rich and poor alike to the same standards of spiritual accountability.

Penn's terms of settlement reflected similar sentiments, since they were among the most generous of all in the British colonies. Any settler could purchase one hundred acres for five pounds and was required only to pay a nominal quitrent of one shilling per acre per year. Indentured servants who completed their terms would receive a headright of fifty acres. Still, Penn never believed in economic equality, and the terms for the wealthy were even more generous. Those with sufficient capital could purchase five thousand acres for only one hundred pounds and receive a bonus of five acres in Philadelphia. Those who purchased more than five thousand acres were allowed to form their own townships; forty-one individuals acquired parcels of five thousand to ten thousand acres. As proprietor, Penn also kept one-tenth of the land for his own use. Indeed, Penn enjoyed being a proprietor and actively used the proceeds from lands sales and the fur trade to accumulate capital and to pay off his burdensome debts.

He also encouraged merchants to migrate to the colony by supporting the Free Society of Traders in Pennsylvania, a London group that invested in Pennsylvania real estate. One member, Samuel Carpenter, arrived in Philadelphia from Barbados in 1683 and built the first wharf in Philadelphia. He had extensive interests in grain mills and timber lands, engaged extensively in land speculation, and maintained a profitable West Indian trade. Members of the society also figured prominently in Pennsylvania's early power structure. Nicholas More was the society's president and became the provincial secretary, clerk of the Provincial Council, and chief justice of the Provincial Court. Others in the close-knit group held a similar range of offices, and their children generally married into other leading families of the colony. Quakers carefully guarded their power well into the next century. German immigrants, for instance, dominated the population of Lancaster County after 1720, but members of the one hundred or so Quaker families who lived there controlled the government. Similar patterns persisted in Bucks County, Chester County, the Welsh Tract, and Philadelphia itself.

Government   While Penn's social vision was traditional in its allocation of power to the wealthy, Pennsylvania was truly a "holy experiment" in its religious toleration and in its introduction of Whiggish republican ideas into the government. The Frame of Government of 1682, accompanied by another document called the Forty Two Laws, established the basic structures of the colony's government. The proprietor or his deputy served as governor. The Provincial Council consisted of seventy-two members, one-third elected annually for three-year terms. The council initiated legislation, which a two-hundred member Assembly accepted or rejected. The laws granted freemanship and the right to hold office to any white male who bought one hundred acres of land or received fifty acres after completing a term of servitude or who paid a personal tax. About 50 percent of Pennsylvania's adult males qualified under these terms. Wealthy Quaker merchants came to dominate the council, much as Penn intended, while the assembly included members from the more rural areas and the lower counties. The governor and the council controlled the treasury and courts and chose the judges, while the governor selected various local officials, such as the sheriffs, from lists submitted by the freemen. The Forty-Two Laws reflected English liberal economic ideas, particularly the inviolability of contract and private property. They required that children be taught trades, that prisons serve as workhouses, and that debts be paid or the debtor forfeit an appropriate amount of his own goods in payment.

Though he carefully rationed power to the political and economic elite, Penn's plan for provincial government called for frequent elections and extensive popular

♣ *Documents* ♣
The Promise of Pennsylvania

Pennsylvania was prosperous from the beginning, a condition that heightened its appeal to those who sought better opportunity than England offered.

> Corn and Flesh, and what else serves Man for Drink, Food and Rayment, is much cheaper here than in England, or elsewhere; but the chief reason why Wages of Servants of all sorts is much higher here than there, arises from the great Fertility and Produce of the Place; besides, if these large Stipends were refused them, they would quickly set up for themselves, for they can have Provision very cheap, and Land for a very small matter, or next to nothing in comparison of the Purchase of Lands in England; and the Farmers there, can afford to give that great Wages than the Farmers in England can, for several Reasons very obvious. . . . Here are no Beggars to be seen (it is a Shame and Disgrace to the State that there are so many in England) nor indeed have any here the least Occasion or Temptation to take up that Scandalous Lazy Life.

"Colonist Gabriel Thomas on High Wages and Great Opportunities in Pennsylvania, 1698," reprinted in Karen Ordahl Kupperman, ed., *Major Problems in American Colonial History* (Lexington, MA: D. C. Heath and Company, 1993), 292–3.

participation, while his ideas on local government reflected Quaker notions of mediation and consensus. Sheriffs served as social referees who kept peace between the groups. The proprietor appointed county justices, and officials called peace makers assisted the justices and arbitrated civil disputes; defiance of their judgments was severely punished. Quaker meetings arbitrated disputes between Quakers, forbidding members to "go to law" against each other. Quakers dealt most severely with crimes that violated the private rights of others, intruded into the peace of another, or involved violence against a woman, though even here they stressed rehabilitation rather than vengeance or humiliation.

Religion   Politically, Penn sought to perpetuate a deferential government that also ensured popular participation and the preservation of social peace. Economically, he envisioned a liberal, prosperous society with a proper balance of trade, industry, and farming. Socially, he embraced a vision of community where people of different beliefs could live together in peace and harmony, a society that, paradoxically, rejected the materialistic impulses of the modern world. But religion remained central to the colony's basic ethos. Like the Puritans, Quakers sought to recreate the primitive church—but with crucial differences. Quakerism centered around the notion of the inner light, a belief with profound democratic implications. Quakers gathered for meetings at least once a week. Members arrived quietly, with no frivolous conversation or laughter. Men and women entered through different doors and were seated by order of arrival—not by rank, except for the elders. Once all were present, a time of silence ensued, during which everyone was expected to engage in "turning the mind to the light."[13] People rose and spoke spontaneously, as the spirit moved them, including children, women, and even strangers. A second period of silent contemplation ensued when there seemed to be no more messages, and the meeting ended when those present seemed to feel it was over, a consensus formalized when the elders rose and shook hands with one

⁖ *Documents* ⁖
Turning to the Light

Quakers were noted for their belief in loving, gentle behavior and their unique style of worship. The following documents illustrate these. The first is a poem by an ordinary American Quaker; the second is a description of the second stage of a Quaker meeting, the time of "turning the mind to the light"; the third is a statement by George Fox describing his belief in pacifism.

> For love in all things doth Oneness call,
> Thinking no evil, but pure good to all,
> Yea, love is God, and God is love and light.
> Fullness of pleasure, joy and great delight.

Caleb Raper, Commonplace Book, 1711, reprinted in David Hackett Fischer, *Albion's Seed: Four British Folkways in America* (New York: Oxford University Press, 1989), 426.

> So Friends, when you come together to wait upon God, come orderly in the fear of God; the first that enters into the place of your meeting, be not careless, nor wander up and down, either in body or mind; but innocently sit down in some place, and turn in thy mind to the light, and wait upon God singly, as if none were present but the Lord. . . . Then the next comes in, let them in simplicity of heart, sit down and turn in the same light, and wait in the Spirit; and so all the rest coming in, in the fear of the Lord, sit down in the pure stillness and silence of all flesh, and wait in the light.

The English Quaker Alexander Parker, 1660, quoted in David Hackett Fischer, *Albion's Seed: Four British Folkways in America* (New York: Oxford University Press, 1989), 523.

> Ye are called to peace, therefore follow it. . . seek the peace of all men, and no man's hurt. . . keep out of plots and bustling and the arm of the flesh, for all these are amongst Adam's sons in the Fall, where they are destroying men's lives like dogs and beasts and swine, goring, rending and biting one another and destroying one another, and wrestling with flesh and blood. From whence arise these wars and killing but from the lusts?

George Fox, *Journal*, John L. Nickalls, ed. (Cambridge, England: Cambridge University Press, 1952), 357.

another. Quakers were pacifists. In 1651, George Fox was locked in a dungeon for refusing to fight at the Battle of Worcester, and his experience made the "testimony of peace" central to Quaker beliefs from that point on.

The meetinghouses were simple buildings, patterned after those in England. Most were rectangular with stone walls and double doors for both men and women, intensely lit within, and with numerous large windows set high in the walls. The interior walls were often whitened to heighten the effect of spiritual intensity. There were no pulpits or altars. This quiet, simple religiosity was punctured a bit by the more extremist elements of Quakerism that sometimes emerged—beliefs in witchcraft (though no Quaker court ever condemned an accused witch, mobs did occasionally hang or stone suspects to death), prophecies, divination, reincarnation, the resurrection of the dead, and the healing power of the Holy Spirit. In this, at least, Quakers were one with other English migrants, continuing to embrace a more traditional magical popular culture that often conflicted with the literate culture of learned clergy.

The final years of the century witnessed escalating political conflict and brought little rest for Penn. The Crown harassed the proprietor constantly, suspecting him of being involved in Jacobite plots against the government. War brought depression to the family's Irish estates, and Penn's secretary, Philip Ford, began to press Penn for payment of the huge sums he claimed to be owed. Finally, Lord Baltimore pursued counterclaims against Penn's grant. Penn left the colony and returned to London in 1684 to defend himself and his charter. He was able to return only in 1699, leaving for England again in 1701. In Pennsylvania, much of the discord centered on the Quaker Assembly's battle to enlarge its own power. In 1695, Penn gave it the right to initiate legislation, but the real breakthrough came in 1701, when Penn gave up the struggle and issued the Charter of Privileges. This document established a unicameral legislature, unique in the British colonies. The proprietor retained only the power to appoint the governor and council members, who now served only in an advisory capacity, and to veto laws. Penn granted the three lower counties (later to become Delaware) a separate assembly.

The intense factionalism that seemed to pervade Quaker political society continued to discourage and disillusion Penn. As one of the proprietor's governors noted, it seemed that a Quaker "*prays* for his neighbor on First Days and then *preys* on him for the other six."[14] After one lengthy battle to defend his charter against rival claims from the descendants of Lord Baltimore, Penn found himself defrauded by colonial agents and spent time in a debtor's prison. He died in 1718.

The Carolinas

Spanish explorers were the first Europeans to view the Carolina region. Lucas Vasquez de Ayllon first landed in the area while on a slaving voyage in 1520. He subsequently attempted to establish a settlement in 1526, but fever, mutiny, and attacks by the local Indians left 350 of the five hundred settlers dead, and the survivors returned to Spain. De Soto, as we have seen, moved through the area in 1540, and Pedro Menéndez de Aviles stationed a garrison on the coast in the 1560s. French visits to the region dated back to Verrazzano's voyage in 1524 and to Jean Ribault's abortive attempt to establish a base at Port Royal in 1562.

English interest in the area was much slower to develop. Early promotional pamphlets described the climate and topography in glowing if naive terms, and indeed the semitropical coastline led some of the first settlers to experiment with growing oranges. English explorers were awed by the variety of plant and animal life, particularly the large numbers of alligators. The underlying reality was substantially different from the honey-coated ideal. The low-lying, swampy coastline offered an ideal breeding ground for malarial mosquitoes. The drier and higher ground inland, particularly in the western mountains, was cooler in the summer but could be bitterly cold in winter. Malaria, dysentery, and yellow fever were constant companions of the early settlers, and even in the eighteenth century, more than half of the Anglican missionaries who braved the colony were dead or seriously ill within a decade of their arrival.

Charles I made the first English grant in the Carolinas, giving Sir Robert Heath a parcel of land between thirty-one degrees and thirty-six degrees latitude, sea to sea, in October 1629. Heath's plans to establish a colony of Huguenots never materialized. New England Puritans settled in the region briefly in 1662 and 1663, and a 1664 attempt by a group of Barbadians failed within three years. In the meantime, Virginians were constantly moving southward into the Albermarle Sound region (later to become North Carolina). While these settlement attempts were sputtering along, the seeds of a more permanent effort were being sown in England. Sir John Colleton, a friend of Charles I, went into exile in the Caribbean during the civil war. After the Restoration, Colleton, Sir William Berkeley, and six others petitioned Charles II for a patent for the area south of Virginia. Berkeley was actually of little importance in this group, which included Edward Hyde, lord high chancellor and father-in-law of the duke of York; Gen. George Monck; George Carteret, the richest man in England; and the earl of Clarendon, Charles's chief minister. All of these men also served on the various committees and councils that directed the colonies and the empire's trade and were involved in other commercial enterprises, such as the Royal African Company.

In March 1663, Charles granted the eight petitioners a charter for Carolina, displacing the Heath patent. The boundaries of the colony stretched from thirty-one degrees and thirty-six degrees latitude (extended to twenty-nine degrees in 1665). The grant guaranteed the king a nominal annual payment and one-quarter of all gold and silver discovered in the colony. It included a bishop of Durham clause with full feudal powers, but it also guaranteed freedom of worship and required that all laws receive the advice and consent of the freemen. Charles hoped to achieve several aims: to accommodate the population surplus drifting down the Virginia coast, to provide an outlet for Barbadians facing a growing scarcity of land, and especially to put pressure on the Spanish to accept English claims to the area. Shortly after, the Spanish agreed to the

Table 3 ❧ Population growth in the middle colonies

		New York	New Jersey	Pennsylvania	Delaware	North Carolina	South Carolina
1660	White	4,336			510	980	
	Black	600			30	20	
1670	White	5,064	940		660	3,700	170
	Black	690	60		40	150	30
1680	White	8,630	3,200	655	950	5,220	1,000
	Black	1,200	200	25	55	210	200
1690	White	12,239	7,550	11,180	1,400	7,300	2,400
	Black	1,670	450	270	82	300	1,500
1700	White	16,851	13,170	17,520	2,335	10,305	3,260
	Black	2,256	840	430	135	415	2,444

U.S. Bureau of the Census, *Historical Statistics of the United States, Colonial Times to 1970*, 2 vols. (Washington, DC: Government Printing Office, 1975), 2:1168.

Treaty of Madrid, recognizing English occupation of the coast south to modern Charleston.

Plans for settlement reached fruition with the 1665 Concessions and Agreements. This document reserved for the proprietors the right to veto all legislation passed in the colony, and it allowed them to collect quitrents of a halfpenny per acre per year. Beyond these restrictions, it was one of the more liberal of British colonial charters. It promised almost complete self-government, gave the elected assembly the power of taxation, and guaranteed freedom of conscience. It established a headright system that promised 150 acres of land to each new arrival and each of their dependents. Finally, it guaranteed male servants ten acres of land and females six acres at the end of their terms of indenture.

Three separate attempts at settlement came to naught. A group of Barbadians hoped to establish a colony at Port Royal, the site of the earlier French effort, but the largest of their three ships sank, taking most of their supplies to the bottom. Another attempted settlement at Cape Fear lasted only briefly. A few settlers remained around Albermarle Sound under Berkeley's general supervision. Their tiny outpost offered little promise for the future.

In 1669, Anthony Ashley Cooper, the later earl of Shaftesbury, galvanized the proprietors into action. Cooper had long been interested in colonial affairs. He had owned a Barbadian plantation, participated in the slave trade, and served on the Council for Foreign Relations. He seems to have gained a new energy and commitment in 1668, when he was almost killed by a liver abscess. The surgeon who saved him was John Locke. Cooper lived the rest of his life with a drain in his stomach, and Locke became a friend, servant, and permanent member of his household as well as secretary for the proprietors. The two likely collaborated on one of the most interesting documents of early American history, the 1669 Fundamental Constitutions. This unusual plan of government guaranteed both religious toleration and state support of the Anglican church, and it explicitly gave masters absolute power over their slaves. More exceptional, however, were those provisions dealing with land grants and political and social power.

Shaftesbury envisioned several counties, each with forty squares of twelve thousand acres each. In each county, eight squares were reserved for the proprietors and twenty-four for the freeholders. But each county would also contain other noble figures who received equally impressive grants of land. At the top of this hierarchy sat the chief proprietor, known as the palatine; the rest of the proprietors were referred to as seigneurs. Below them came two caciques who would receive twenty-four thousand acres and four landgraves who would get twelve thousand acres. Last came the lords of the manor, from three thousand to twelve thousand acres each. The remainder of the free population would be known as leet-men, and they would live and work on the nobels' estates. Though their status was more serf-like than anything, they undoubtedly found the guarantee of ten acres upon their marriage, together with the sense of security the manor system promised them, preferable to a life of poverty in England. Rather than a popularly elected assembly, the Fundamental Constitutions created the Council of Nobles, which would administer justice and initiate legislation in the colony. Small landowners elected representatives to a parliament that could accept or reject proposed bills but not initiate legislation. Finally, eight administrative courts, each headed by a proprietor, oversaw the entire government.

From our perspective, the Fundamental Constitutions seem to portray a fantasy world, but we must remember that Shaftesbury designed this society to reflect the prevalent Whiggish belief that republics degenerated over time. He rooted this government system in the widespread ownership of land and in a carefully designed balance of power that was designed to forestall political and social corruption. It was, to be sure, far less equitable than many other such designs. But English noblemen and women were not egalitarians. Their main concerns were stability and order, and they allocated power to their social underlings only when it furthered those primary goals.

Like all other such schemes in the New World, of course, this paper utopia never made the transition to reality. The Council of Nobles never actually existed, and very few individuals purchased manors. Migrants ignored the requirements for settling in compact, rectangular patterns and developed instead a mixture of small farms and large plantations. The government became bicameral in 1693, erasing the last vestige of political dominance by proprietors and nobles.

Despite the restrictive nature of settlement designs, the colony began to emerge as a recognizable entity in 1669. Berkeley had already taken charge of settlement in the Albermarle Sound area, appointing William Drummond as the first governor and directing the sale of land grants. Early immigrants to the northern region came mostly from Virginia and Bermuda, and Albermarle long remained dependent on Virginia for its trade and economic well-being. In August 1669, Capt. Joseph West sailed from England with three ships and more than one hundred settlers. Problems beset the group from the beginning. Sir John Yeamans, the ostensible leader of the expedition, decided to remain in Barbados, and he appointed the eighty-year-old William Sayle to take his place. Further delayed by storms, the small fleet finally anchored just north of modern Charleston on March 15, 1670. The settlers moved south to Port Royal, but the area proved uncomfortably close to the Spanish and the swampy environment a danger to health, so they moved north again to the Ashley River. There, at the mouth of the Ashley and Cooper rivers, they founded Charles Town with some from Barbados and a few Huguenots. In 1680, they permanently relocated the town on the neck of land between the two rivers where they flowed into the harbor.

Political division and bitter factionalism plagued the colony from the beginning. A council consisting of the governor and deputies took control, and the first parliament did not meet until the summer 1671, since there were not yet enough freemen in the colony to serve in office. At the first assembly meeting, the representative refused to accept the Fundamental Constitutions and ignored the orders of the London government. Instead, they adapted the system of local government from their earlier Barbadian experience. West succeeded Sayle as governor after the latter died in March 1671. Yeamans forced out West, whom the proprietors in turn restored to power. Yeamans was an excellent representative of the early Barbadian settlers, putting self-interest and his drive for fortune above all else—he sold his produce to the Barbadians at handsome profits, even while the Carolina colony was still seriously short of food.

Hoping to increase the population, the proprietors initiated a recruiting drive aimed at Huguenots and English dissenters. They installed a dissenter, Joseph Morton, as governor, appointed several other dissenters to office, and revised the Fundamental Constitutions to increase the colony's appeal to non-Anglicans. They also established three counties to serve as election districts: Berkeley and Craven counties would jointly send ten members, while Colleton County would have ten of its own. Berkeley was much more populous than Colleton, but the latter was inhabited mainly by dissenters, who would therefore have disproportionate strength in the Assembly. The Anglican Goose Creek men of Berkeley County were alarmed at this development and initiated thirty years of fierce political infighting, promoting themselves as protectors of liberty against destructive innovations in the Fundamental Constitutions. And in the end, they broke the proprietors' power.

White-Indian Relations   A number of large Indian tribes inhabited the Carolina region, including the Yamasees, Apalachees, Tuskegees, Westos, and Creeks. While Indians in Spanish Florida likely viewed English arrival as a threat, Carolina's coastal Indians may have perceived the whites as potential allies against their western neighbors, who had been attacking them for years. Even inland tribes, such as the Creeks and Westos, saw ways of fitting the newcomers into their own agendas. The Creeks, for instance, may have recognized the possibility of building an alliance with the whites to extend their control of the interior. The settlers immediately recognized the trade potential in pursuing such relationships. They established friendships with the coastal tribes soon after settling and shortly after formed a military alliance with the Creeks.

Hoping to avoid a repetition of Virginia's disastrous experience with the Indians, the proprietors planned to regulate Indian trade through their own agents. But settlers ignored this policy from the start. Barbados planters were, in fact, originally attracted to the colony in part by the prospects of trade with the Cherokees, Creeks, and Choctaws. They were particularly drawn to deerskins, used for warm and durable clothing in Europe. So when the proprietors established a monopolistic trading agreement with the Westo Indians, the resentful planters decided to eliminate the innocent Indians. They armed a group of Shawnees who had migrated eastward from the other side of the Appalachians and hired them to start a war with the Westos. Within three years, only fifty Westos survived.

Carolina Society   Many of the first settlers viewed Carolina as a country "so delicious, pleasant, and fruitful that were it cultivated doubtless it would prove a second Paradise."[15] But political conflict, deteriorating Indian relations, economic development,

---

❧ *Documents* ❧
Fortunes and Surprises
in the Carolinas

By the time the Carolinas were settled, economic conditions in England were beginning to improve, and settlers were familiar with the New World landscape. As the first of these documents indicates, though, a settlement such as Carolina, with its enticements to English nobility, could still attract considerable interest—though few seemed eager at first to take advantage of the opportunities described here. The second selection shows that surprises still lay in wait for colonists who explored the unsettled backcountry regions.

> Is there therefore any younger Brother who is born of Gentile blood, and whose Spirit is elevated above the common sort, and yet the hard usage of our Country hath not allowed suitable fortune; he will not surely be afraid to leave his Native Soil to advance his Fortunes equal to his Blood and Spirit, and so he will avoid those unlawful ways too many of our young Gentlemen take to maintain themselves according to their high education, having but small Estates; here, with a few Servants and a small Stock a great Estate may be raised, although his Birth have not entitled him to any of the Land of his Ancestors, yet his Industry may supply him so, as to make him the head of as famous a family.

and the growing diversity of inhabitants soon produced a land marked more by disease and destructive ambition than the blessings of paradise. The first few decades brought immigrants from Barbados, Switzerland, Scotland, Ireland, France, England, and the colonies of New England, New York, and New Jersey; these groups lived in constant and fierce competition with each other.

Economically, north and south followed different patterns from the beginning. Pine barrens dotted the northern regions, and small tobacco farmers from Virginia were the first successful settlers. A mixed economy blended livestock grazing, tobacco and food production, and naval stores—turpentine, resin, pitch, tar, and lumber. In 1720, North Carolina was still 85 percent white, with a healthier climate and more extensive family settlement than its neighbor to the south. In South Carolina, beef, furs, lumber, and naval stores were the most successful products at first, and by the 1680s, large herds of cattle (up to eight hundred) roamed the open range in the less settled areas. The settlers sent these, other products, and Indian slaves to the West Indies in exchange for sugar products and, increasingly, black slaves. Even while this trade was developing, planters began to move up the rivers and experiment with sugar, indigo, tropical fruits, and tobacco before settling on rice as the most profitable staple. The demands of rice cultivation and the malarial climate were to produce by 1720 a population of eighteen thousand, of which more than half were blacks. Both regions, though, still lacked a clear

"A Brief Description of the Province of Carolina on the coasts of Florda" (1666), in B. R. Carroll, ed., *Historical Collections of South Carolina*, 2 vols. (New York: Harper and Brothers, 1836), 2:16.

> Viewing the Land here, we found an extraordinary rich, black Mould, and some of a Copper-colour, both Sorts very good; the Land in some Places is much burthen'd with Iron, Stone, here being great Store of it, seemingly very good:. . . When we were all asleep, in the Beginning of the Night, we were awaken'd with the dismall'st and most hideous Noise that ever pierc'd my Ears: This sudden Surprizal incapacitated us of guessing what this threatening Noise might proceed from; but our *Indian* Pilot (who knew these Parts very well) acquainted us, that it was customary to hear such Musick along that Swamp-side, there being endless Numbers of Panthers, Tygers, Wolves, and other Beasts of Prey. . . .

John Lawson, *A New Voyage to Carolina (1709),* Hugh Talmage Lefler, ed. (Chapel Hill: University of North Carolina Press, 1967), 32–3.

identity at the turn of the century, reflecting a diversity of settlement and a lack of shared assumptions and goals.

South Carolinians also proved themselves as eager as any Americans to push westward in their search for land, Indian captives, and mineral and animal wealth. Here, though, they met considerable resistance from the strong Creek and Choctaw tribes, a persistent Spanish presence, and growing French penetration. For thirty years, Carolina settlements were armed villages and concentrated around Charleston. One "benefit" the planters reaped from this situation was expansion of the Indian slave trade, which was a major factor in the colony's economy for its first several decades. The planters often encouraged Indian warfare so they could accumulate Indian captives, and they gave bounties to tribes to supply them with captives from other tribes. They kept some but sent most to New England, Virginia, or the West Indies. By 1710, the colony had exported twelve thousand Indians. The 1708 census counted fifty-three hundred whites, twenty-nine hundred black slaves, and fourteen hundred Indian slaves.

This was an expansionist, exploitative society, and violent uprisings and bitter political disputes marked the colony's first four decades. In 1677, John Culpepper led a rebellion in North Carolina against the payment of customs duties on tobacco. For the next two years, settlers sporadically protested against British attempts to enforce the Navigation Acts. In 1685, the proprietors ruled that all members of the assembly had to take an oath to support the Fundamental Constitutions before taking office. The legislature objected, and the proprietors dissolved it twice before declaring martial law. In 1689, the colony participated in its own small way in the Glorious Revolution when it threw out the proprietary agents and proclaimed William of Orange King of England. Even governors were not safe from the planters' ire. They forced James Colleton out of office in South Carolina in 1690, while Seth Sothel bears the dubious distinction of having been forced out of both North Carolina (1689) and South Carolina (1691). In 1691, the proprietors finally abrogated the Fundamental Constitutions, and in 1693, the legislature won the right to initiate legislation.

The proprietors also tried to deal with these difficulties by splitting governmental responsibility. A deputy-governor ruled North Carolina after 1689, a full governor after 1712. Nothing seemed to help. After 1700, the antiproprietary party gained strength and complained to the Crown that the proprietors had failed to protect them from pirates and the Spanish, had failed to send aid during the Yamasee War in 1715, had taken colony land for themselves, and had often repealed the assembly's laws. In 1719, the colony staged a so-called revolution when a convention delegated by the "people" proclaimed Col. James Moore governor. Eventually, the proprietors grew weary of trying to control such seemingly obdurate settlers, and they began to negotiate with the Crown for a transfer of ownership. South Carolina became a royal colony in 1721, North Carolina in 1729. Only then were clear lines of authority fully established.

The Crown's plans to establish a uniform administrative structure for the empire were both necessary and ambitious, but political developments in England and the divergent, independent growth of both old and new colonies in America stymied British hopes. The Caribbean islands moved rapidly toward an exploitative, staple economy. New York meandered with no clear sense of direction in the years after its takeover from the Dutch. Pennsylvania prospered from the beginning, and for a time, its idealistic Quaker vision co-existed peacefully with the more ambitious economic goals of its wealthier immigrants. The Carolinas foundered for several decades before finding political and economic stability. In the early 1680s, London finally resolved to consolidate political control over its North American possessions. But it was too late. Disruptive developments within the colonies themselves, the sudden end of the Stuart dynasty, and the beginning of England's epic struggle with France combined to make the end of the century a volatile, uncertain time for English men and women on both sides of the Atlantic.

❧ *Chapter Six* ❧

Colonies in Crisis,
1660 to 1692

A critical series of conflicts tore through the social fabric of the older American colonies during the last decades of the seventeenth century. In both the Chesapeake and New England, settlers sought to resolve problems generated by economic growth, physical expansion, and social complexity. While unrest continued to plague the Chesapeake, the trend was toward greater stability, particularly after the planters found a more reliable labor supply in slavery. In New England, instability in religion and in village and town structures began to threaten the fragile cohesion achieved during the earlier decades. In both regions, expansion brought bitter and destructive conflict with Indians, who sought to resist further white encroachments. Finally, England attempted to impose tighter control over its American colonies, which ignited rebellion in several colonies during the late 1680s. Before either England or the colonies had the chance to contemplate the meaning of these events, the first of the great wars for empire between England and France scourged the northern colonies. The cumulative impact of these upheavals permanently transformed the political and social topography of early America.

The Chesapeake

High death rates, weak social institutions, and political strife continued to characterize much of Virginia life at mid-century. Only by 1700 did a strong nuclear family structure and a clear pattern of social authority emerge; blacks and the poor, however, failed to benefit much from these changes. But in many ways, society

Significant Dates

1643	Counties and quarter courts established in Massachusetts
1645	William Berkeley becomes governor of Virginia
	Thomas Mayhew, Jr. begins Martha's Vineyard mission
1646	Child protest
	John Eliot first preaches to Indians
1651–74	Massachusetts Indian praying towns established
1656	First Quakers arrive in Massachusetts
1660	Execution of Mary Dyer
	Berkeley restored as Virginia governor
1662	Half-way covenant adopted
1666	Viceroy de Tracy attacks Mohawks
1670s	"Covenant Chain" established between English and Iroquois
1675	King Philip's War
1675–76	Bacon's Rebellion
1679	General Court calls the Reforming Synod
1680	New Hampshire becomes a royal colony
1683	Crown institutes *quo warranto* proceedings against Massachusetts charter
1685	James II accedes to English throne
	Dominion of New England created
1686	Sir Edmund Andros arrives in Boston as dominion governor
1688	Glorious Revolution; William III invades England
1689	Revolts in Massachusetts, New York, Maryland
	War of League of Augsburg begins
1690	Attack on Schenectady
	Gov. William Phips attempts to invade Canada
1692	Salem witchcraft trials
1697	Peace of Ryswick
1701	Grand Settlement between Iroquois and French
	Iroquois-English agreement signed at Albany
1705	Virginia slave code

had become much more coherent by the 1660s. Gov. William Berkeley was a key figure in this achievement. Like many others before and after him, Berkeley viewed his appointment as an opportunity for significant career advancement. Unlike most others, his personal tact and administrative skills helped heal the factionalism of an immature society. He presided over the Virginia assembly's rise to power, decentralized political and social control to allow the gentry a greater measure of local rule, and for a time at least, gained the loyalty of colonials to a degree almost unparalleled in the seventeenth-century royal colonies.

Berkeley's Virginia

Berkeley's first success came in 1644, when Opechancanough made one last attempt to drive the English from his territory. His failure allowed Berkeley to formulate an Indian policy that protected the natives on reservation land in the western portion of the colony and prevented future clashes into the 1670s. The colony walked a still more dangerous tightrope during the English Civil War. Virginia successfully maintained neutrality during the 1640s, but the Puritan victory emboldened Parliament to extend its control over the American empire. In October 1650, it forbade ships from trading in Virginia without a license, and when the colonists continued to encourage the Dutch trade, Parliament appointed a four-man commission to restore order and loyalty. Threatened with military attack, Berkeley surrendered power. London designated the House of Burgesses as the ruling authority and gave residents a year to adhere to the religious and political dictates of Parliament or to leave the colony. In practice, only staunch royalists found themselves on the outs; otherwise, little changed. Berkeley had worked closely with the assembly to create a tightly-knit ruling oligarchy during the 1640s. Through the burgesses, this group controlled its internal affairs, successfully claimed the power to raise public revenues, and established a county government system. The colony thus retained considerable political independence despite British interference. Charles II restored Berkeley to the governorship in 1660.

Even in exile, Berkeley pursued his vision of a stable, hierarchical Virginia society. He actively recruited Virginia's elite from among English royalists taking refuge from the Puritan government; the vast majority of the colony's leading families arrived between 1640 and 1669, with most from 1647 to 1660. These men were primarily younger sons of prominent English families; two-thirds were from the south and west of England, and a substantial number came from London. As a group, they consciously sought to recreate a part of England that was dotted with large manors, ruled by a small landholding class, and less densely settled and more heavily wooded than the rest of England.

This ruling elite presided over a Virginia society of growing complexity. As migration increased and living conditions improved, the population rose. In 1644, there were only about eight thousand inhabitants spread across Virginia's vast territory; by 1675, thirty-two thousand men and women had settled all of the land east of the fall line. Berkeley understood the implications of such growth, and with the Restoration, he devised an ambitious scheme to overhaul Virginia's basic economic structure. He proposed to construct a series of towns to provide for better defense against the Indians and foreign enemies and to encourage the development of the arts and skills that were essential to a truly civilized society. He envisioned new industries for the colony, including shipbuilding, iron smelting and forging, and cloth production. Farmers, finally, would diversify into corn and wheat for export to the West Indies sugar islands.

Berkeley traveled to London in 1661 and presented his plan to the king. Charles favored the proposals, since they would fit well within England's own rapidly expanding economy. But for all the verbal encouragement he received, Berkeley got precious little financial support. British capital continued to flow into British, rather than colonial, industries; the outlawing of the Dutch trade by the Navigation Acts, together with the continued depression in tobacco prices, meant that there was little spare capital in the colony. The governor did try to move ahead with his plans for building new towns, proposing that he and members of the Virginia Council (upper house) build homes at all of the recommended locations to encourage the production of silk and naval stores in those places, but the council was not interested.

The burgesses were more cooperative. Besides voting to build a "real" house in Jamestown, made of bricks with a slate or tile roof, they approved the payment of bounties for ships, cloth, and silk and ordered the establishment of a loom in every county, at public expense. Of course, all of this was expensive; the colony's poll tax provided some support, and Berkeley put a good deal of his own money into the effort. But little came of it all. The governor complained that even the largest of Virginia planters hoped to make their fortune from their holdings here and then return to England. Corn production did increase, and Berkeley sent three hundred pounds of silk to the king in 1668 to show him what the colony could produce even without the skilled workers he had pleaded for. But even his attempt to boost tobacco prices by halting production for a year fell by the wayside, as Maryland refused to cooperate. Lord Baltimore was fearful that the smaller planters would revolt against such restrictions and that the whole thing would cost the colony more money than it was worth. Tobacco prices remained low as expansion to the frontier continued to glut the market.

In the face of this depressed economy, personal involvement in government proved critical if Virginians were to establish their fortunes. Berkeley himself made a fortune from gifts assigned to him by the burgesses: annual tributes in beaver from the Indians, numerous fees—two hundred pounds of tobacco, for instance, for every marriage license granted in the colony—and 350 pounds annually from every tavern. The colony's secretary received fees for every official document produced in the colony, including eighty pounds of tobacco for every land patent and forty for every marriage license. Council members were eligible for a variety of positions, such as secretary, and every colony office—sheriff, auditor, and the others—carried with it substantial revenues in fees. Multiple office holding became the lucrative rule for the Virginia gentry. Finally, they all engaged in land speculation, incorporating land on the frontier for their own or their sons' use or simply to sell off in the future at handsome profits.

Despite Berkeley's complaints about the instability of the gentry, these wealthy individuals headed a new and clearly defined Virginia social structure. Here, Berkeley's recruitment efforts had paid some dividends. Only about 375 planters dominated Virginia life between 1660 and 1676, most of them Berkeley's recruits. Col. Richard Lee was typical of this group, though he migrated to Virginia relatively early (1640). By 1663, Lee was Berkeley's chief lieutenant and owned at least seven plantations. He was proud of his Saxon heritage and paraded his English connections openly—he had his silverplate, for instance, marked with his coat of arms, which also hung above his front door. Lee and the other members of the Virginia aristocracy each held an average of forty-two hundred acres and served as the chief sources of credit in their communities. They commonly intermarried; in 1724, all twelve council members were related by blood or marriage to one another. They also served as justices of the peace, sheriffs, burgesses, and members of the governor's council.

The gentry succeeded because their initial advantages gave them the edge in Virginia's raw, competitive economic environment. When Ralph Wormeley died in 1701, his estate was worth more than three thousand pounds and included sixty-four hundred acres of land on ten separate farms, each with black slaves and white servants. Though men such as Wormeley achieved gentility, it would be some time before they attained the level of leisure most English men and women associated with a true ruling class.

The majority of Virginia planters were not part of this tiny elite, though mid-rank planters did achieve some upward mobility. Most paid their own passage to Virginia, and many even brought a few servants with them. They cultivated tobacco on several hundred acres and pursued a variety of other economic activities—working as factors, for instance, for English or Dutch merchants. They also served as constables, undersheriffs, deputy clerks, churchwardens, grand jurymen, and surveyors of highways—they were the backbone of daily political life. We can make only the most tentative generalizations about the small planters. Some were recent immigrants of marginal wealth, others were artisans and craftsmen pursuing wider opportunities. For a while, many were former servants. These planters generally held between fifty and two hundred acres of land and occasionally served in minor county government positions but otherwise achieved little political power and minimal economic success.

Next down the ladder came the new freedmen, those who had worked off their indentures and now hoped to become planters themselves. This group faced more and greater difficulties after mid-century. Large planters feared competition in an already depressed tobacco market and deliberately sought to limit the opportunities available to the freedmen. During the early decades, a person who completed his indenture might hope, if he was lucky, to become a middling planter. As time passed, even this likelihood became remote, as the planter elite and land speculators amassed huge tracts both in the tidewater and on the near frontier. They also began to complain of the upsurge of footloose, drifting young men wandering the Virginia landscape—a sight that reminded them too much of the England they had left behind. Many young freedmen had little choice but to move to the frontier, where they attempted to drive the Indians off their land. Some turned to crime, and few retained any feeling of loyalty to a ruling class that had so callously exploited them.

Henry Davis was a Middlesex County servant who had gained his freedom by 1678. He rented land for a year and in 1679 purchased one hundred acres and married Ann West. But by 1683, the couple was deeply in debt, to the amount of fifteen hundred pounds of sweet-scented tobacco. Two years later, Davis sold his

Table 4 ❧ Population of New England, 1660–1700

	Massachusetts	Plymouth	Connecticut	Rhode Island	New Hampshire
1660	20,000	2,000	8,000	1,500	1,500
1670	30,000	5,000	13,000	2,000	2,000
1680	40,000	6,000	17,000	3,000	2,000
1690	50,000	7,000	22,000	4,000	4,000
1700	56,000	*	26,000	6,000	5,000

U.S. Bureau of the Census, *Historical Statistics of the United States, Colonial Times to 1970*, 2 vols. (Washington, DC: Government Printing Office, 1975), 2:1168.

land, and the next year, he became a renter again. During this time, the Davis's two children died in infancy. They spent the next few years moving from one rental to another, the county providing them poor relief for part of that time. The combined strains of financial and personal loss seemed too much to bear. The county court charged Ann with beating a servant, Sarah Gambell, "with an Iron about fourteene Inches Long"[1] and beating her again a few days later, causing her death. She was convicted and hanged.

Fearful of the threat such people presented to a stable, orderly Virginia, the burgesses in 1670 introduced a new franchise requirement of fifty acres owned or leased, essentially depriving many young Virginia males of the right to vote. They also did all they could to prolong servitude, adding months and years of service to indentures for even the smallest transgressions.

Indentured servants were even closer to the bottom of this society. They constituted as much as half of the population at any point in time before 1700. As we have seen, early Chesapeake planters relied heavily on their labor in the tobacco fields. Between 1550 and 1650, the working conditions of the English laboring poor had worsened, and population increases had created a labor surplus among agricultural and textile wage workers and domestic servants. The price revolution had also reduced by half the real wages of those who did have jobs. Many servants, representing a cross-section of ordinary working men and women, decided to emigrate to America. A few were skilled, many were yeomen, husbandmen, or artisans, and about one-half had no stated occupation. They were desperate for work and came because they had few other options. By the 1680s and 1690s, these same groups were finding jobs in England. Population growth had slowed, real wages were increasing again, and a series of good harvests had brought general prosperity to the English countryside. Even earlier, word had begun to filter back to England of the terrible working conditions to be found in the Chesapeake, making the area increasingly less appealing. As soon as most English laborers had a choice, they chose to remain in their homeland.

The search for a new supply of labor, then, was inevitable. In 1619, Dutch merchants sold a few Africans to Virginia planters, but the status of these early captives remains unclear. Though lifelong slavery clearly existed in the Chesapeake by the 1640s, there were fewer than five hundred slaves in Virginia in 1650, less than 3 percent of the population. Slaves still cost more than indentured servants, and their life expectancy remained short. Black slaves were simply a bad investment. After 1650, people began to live longer due to improvements in diet and environment, and by 1700, there were sixteen thousand blacks in Virginia (28 percent of the population) and thirty-two hundred in Maryland (11 percent). As the supply of white labor from England dried up, it made more economic sense to purchase Africans who, though initially expensive, would work for a lifetime, provide offspring who would do the same, and be more readily identified and controlled if they sought to rebel.

The ethnocentrism and racial attitudes of the seventeenth-century English provided important emotional and psychological support for this economic decision. American colonists assumed that blacks were culturally and intellectually inferior, and English culture was suffused with negative preconceptions about blacks. Colonial whites systematically expanded the scope of discriminatory laws to openly and explicitly dehumanize blacks while salving their guilt over slavery. By the 1640s, laws prohibited blacks from using firearms; by the 1660s, marriages between white women and black slaves were described as "shameful Matches."[2] A 1662 law bound black children to their mothers' status, and a 1667 statute stipulated that conversion to Christianity did not confer physical freedom on slaves. The emerging "black codes" of Virginia law severely punished interracial sex and banned interracial marriage. Toward the end of the century, blacks lost the right to testify in court, to engage in any commercial activity, to hold property or participate in politics, to travel without permission, to assemble in numbers of greater than two or three in public places, and to legally marry. By the time the burgesses published the first consolidated slave code in 1705, even voluntary manumission was all but legally impossible. Chesapeake law clearly defined black slaves as less than human. Whites could rest assured that they were committing no sin in enslaving them.

Bacon's Rebellion

As the year 1675 dawned, Berkeley's idealized Virginia, the planters' vision of limitless economic gain and political power, and the servants' and ex-servants' hopes for a better life all faced powerful threats. Berkeley's grandiose plans had come to naught. In 1667, rain had destroyed fully half of the colony's tobacco crop—not enough to permanently raise the price but more than enough to seriously hurt the small planters. In 1673, Dutch war ships scored one of their few victories in the Third Anglo-Dutch War, destroying nine tobacco ships in the James River, and planters had to pay substantial sums to construct forts and provide for the colony's defense. A 1663 plot by a group of servants to seize arms from their masters and march on the capital to demand their freedom added to the uneasiness among the upper classes. Indians, and white attitudes toward them, provided the final ingredient necessary to spark a violent response to an increasingly unstable situation.

In July 1675, a group of Doeg Indians tried to steal some hogs from a plantation in Stafford County in response to the owner's failure to pay for goods purchased from them. Further upriver, Indians killed a white man under unclear circumstances. The militia retaliated, chasing the Doegs into Maryland and killing several of them, along with some innocent Susquehannocks. Berkeley's response was too tepid for both Virginians and Marylanders, and a joint force of planters cornered a Susquehannock band in September and massacred five of their chiefs who had been sent out to parley. The result was an onslaught of attacks by the Susquehannocks, including the massacre of thirty-six colonists in January 1676. Other tribes took advantage of the situation to seek revenge for their own perceived wrongs, and the frontier was quickly afire.

The slaughter of the innocent Susquehannocks outraged Berkeley, but the Indians indicated that they were satisfied with their revenge and would willingly accept peace. The governor accepted their proposal, and the frontier was quiet that spring; Berkeley constructed a series of defensive forts, financed by still more taxes. But land hunger, taxes, and the monopoly Berkeley and his allies (the Green Springs Faction) maintained over the fur trade continued to fuel discontent among the Virginia gentry, and by April, the planters of Charles City County had had enough. They began to arm, and they found a leader in Nathaniel Bacon.

We know relatively little of Bacon's background and personality, except that he had been an ambitious young member of the English country gentry when his family apparently sent him to Virginia to keep him out of trouble and allow him a fresh start. Bacon hoped to turn his personal connections to advantage—his cousin, Nathaniel Bacon, Sr. was the auditor-general for the colony and a councillor. Bacon and his wife, Elizabeth, arrived in 1674 and quickly settled on a plantation in Henrico County. Within six months, the governor appointed him to the council, an astonishingly rapid rise to power. He also began to gather a following of influential men who shared a hatred of Indians and a desire to profit from the trade monopolized by Berkeley's group of insiders. After the Charles City gentry approached him,

✤ *Documents* ✤
Bacon's Rebellion

Bacon's rebellion threatened the fragile stability Virginia had finally achieved after the chaos of its early years. The rebels did not question the essential framework of Virginia society, though; for the most part, they simply sought to force a wider sharing of the wealth, if at the expense of the region's Indians. The first document represents Bacon's attempt to portray the Green Springs Faction as self-seeking opportunists. Gov. Berkeley, of course, saw things a bit differently, as the second document makes clear. He issued his remonstrance in late May, 1676, shortly after he had declared Bacon a rebel.

> Wee appeale to the Country itselfe what and of what nature their Oppressions have bin or by what Caball and mystery the designes of many of those whom wee call great men have bin transacted and caryed on . . . , and see what spounges have suckt up the Publique Treasure and wither it hath not bin privately contrived away by unworthy Favourites and juggling Parasites whose tottering Fortunes have bin repaired and supported at the Publique chardg. . . .

> Judge therefore all wise and unprejudiced men who may or can faithfully or truely with an honest heart attempt the country's good, their vindication and libertie without the aspersion of Traitor and Rebell . . . , may all the world know that we doe unanimously desire to represent our sad and heavy grievances to his most sacred Majesty as our Refuge and Sanctuary, where wee doe well know

Bacon quickly began to make military preparations and wrote the governor for a commission to lead his small army. Berkeley reacted angrily and sent out his own force to head off Bacon, who left before the governor's troops arrived. On May 10, Berkeley proclaimed him a rebel and removed him from the council. The governor also dissolved the assembly and called for new elections, the first in fourteen years.

Bacon, meanwhile, was busy seeking revenge against the Indians. With assistance from some friendly Occaneechees, he successfully assaulted a band of Susquehannocks. Then he quarreled with the Occaneechees and attacked them as well. His successes broadened his popularity, and he was elected a burgess from Henrico County. Bacon supporters, in fact, packed the new House of Burgesses. The rebellious Bacon cautiously approached Jamestown by boat with an armed escort, but Berkeley easily captured him. To the surprise of everyone, the governor pardoned the young rebel and promised him a military commission, probably playing for time in hopes of increasing his own power.

Bacon soon reappeared at Jamestown at the head of an army of four hundred men. In a dramatic confrontation, Berkeley refused Bacon his commission. Bacon responded with an oath: "God Damn my blood! I'll kill governor, council, assembly and all, and then I'll sheath my sword in my own heart's blood!"[3] Frightened by

that all our Causes will be impartially heard and Equall Justice administred to all men.

Bacon's "Manifesto," *Virginia Magazine of History and Biography,* 1 (1893), 55–58; reprinted in Warren Billings, ed., *The Old Dominion in the Seventeenth Century: A Documentary History of Virginia, 1606–1689* (Chapel Hill, NC: IEAHC, University of North Carolina Press, 1975), 278–9.

Now my friends I have liv'd amongst you fower and thirty years as uncorrupt and diligent as ever governor was: Bacon is a man of two years amongst you his person and qualities unknow to most of you and to all men Its by any vertuous action that ever I heard of, and this very action wherein he so much boasted was fully foolishly and as I am informed Treacherously carried to the dishonor of the English nation. Yet in it he lost more men that I did in three wars and by the Grace of god wil put myselfe to the same dangers and troubles again when I have brought Bacon to acknowledge the lawes are above him and I doubt not by the assistance of god to have better successe than Mr. Bacon has had the reason of my hopes are that I wil take councel of wiser men then my selfe But Mr. Bacon has none aboute him but the lowest of the people.

Berkeley's "Demonstration and Remonstrance," reprinted in Warren Billings, ed., *The Old Dominion in the Seventeenth Century: A Documentary History of Virginia, 1606–1689* (Chapel Hill, NC: IEAHC, University of North Carolina Press, 1975), 271.

Bacon's anger and his show of force, the burgesses surrendered and gave the rebel his desired commission. Berkeley had lost the confrontation. The burgesses sought to address some of the colony's grievances with the passage of what historians have called Bacon's Laws, though Bacon himself had little to do with them. These laws opened local offices to more individuals by limiting their terms, lengthened the time allowed for debt payments, and in general sought to remedy many grievances of the closed-out newer gentry. Though most of this legislation was later repealed, it was eventually reenacted.

As Bacon continued to seek out his Indian victims, Berkeley again declared him a rebel. Bacon now determined to rid himself of the governor once and for all. He arrived at Middle Plantation on July 29 and issued the "Manifesto and Declaration of the People," indicting Berkeley and his Indian and trade policies, portraying the governor and his supporters as "gentlemen" and "grandees," and defending his own forces as the "poorer sort" and "the people."[4] But Bacon was not preaching democracy; the revolt was a much more complex affair. His cause was a magnet for planters frozen out of the more remunerative areas of power controlled by Berkeley and his inner circle. He also attracted a large number of ex-indentured servants who faced lives of poverty and suffering because of declining

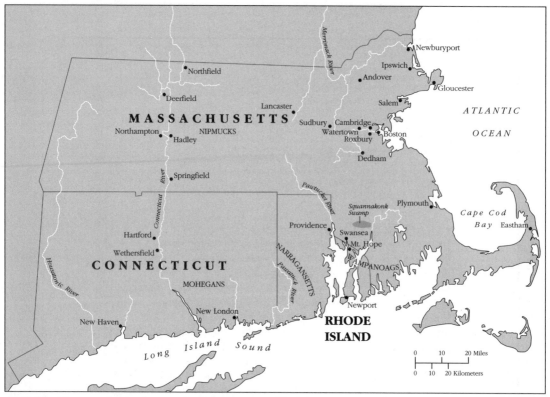

MAP 6.1: Chesapeake Settlement in the Second Half of the Seventeenth Century ⮞

economic opportunity. As the upper classes consolidated their control over Virginia's wealth, they were creating a lower class of whites who visibly and violently threatened their authority. Bacon gave these men a voice, and by increasing the gentry's fear of rebellion by these whites, his revolt provided an additional emotional impetus to the adoption of black slavery.

After he issued the manifesto, Bacon recruited still more planters to his cause and set out in search of another tribe he suspected of involvement in recent raids, the Pamunkeys. While he spent several weeks hunting them in the Dragon Swamp, Berkeley regained his resolve and retook Jamestown. But on September 19, Bacon captured the capital yet again and ordered it burned, an action that cost him some support among the planters. He also began to recruit servants actively, promising them freedom in return, but this too cost him support. All came to a sudden end on October 26, when Bacon died from the "bloody flux" (dysentery).

A bitter Berkeley quickly put an end to the rebellion and hanged twenty-three of the rebels, even though all but Bacon had received royal pardons. British troops arrived in February 1677 to help ensure that disorder would not spring up again and remained in the colony for several years. Two special commissioners arrived with the army to investigate the causes of the uprising. They noted the roles played by high taxes, Indians, and disenchanted servants in creating an incendiary situation that Bacon proved adept at exploiting. The commissioners also put much of the blame on Berkeley and his mode of governing. Their report concluded that the colony in general was far too independent and recommended that the assembly's power be curbed.

The revolt ended Berkeley's career and put the Virginia gentry on notice that they had better pay closer attention both to newcomers seeking power and to the needs of the lower orders of society. It may also have served as final evidence of the need to seek a new, more controllable labor force. The roots of slavery lay in the Chesapeake's economic needs and in the racial attitudes toward blacks. Bacon's Rebellion was the catalyst that convinced Virginia planters of the urgency of adopting this exploitative, forced system of labor.

Adjustment to Empire

Lt. Gov. Sir Herbert Jeffreys succeeded Berkeley. Jeffreys's firm defense of the Crown prerogative forced a realignment of Virginia politics. After 1677, gentry leaders paid considerably more attention to the needs and interests of the lesser planters, but many of them also recognized the need to somehow accommodate England's interests. The result was the emergence of three distinct factions. The "irreconcilables," the core of Berkeley's former ruling clique, continued to oppose royal interference and rallied around Robert Beverley and Philip Ludwell. The "trimmers" saw their future in an alliance with the new royal power. As a group, they had few ties to Berkeley and his cohort. Finally, the "moderates" occupied the middle ground. Their attitude was closer to that of the "irreconcilables," but they also were realistic in their assessment of the political future. Jeffreys had little success in comprehending or dealing with these divisions. Of his successors, only Francis, Lord Howard of Effingham (1684–1688) had any success in comprehending or dealing with these divisions.

Despite a series of heated disagreements, Howard regained some control over the appointment of local magistrates, lessened the local powers of the militia and church vestries, and even succeeded in cutting into the power of the House of Burgesses. The burgesses responded to his measures at one point with an "Address to the King," in which they insisted that they were entitled to the same legal and legislative rights as any Englishmen. Their petition did little to lessen Howard's resolve. His actions reflected London's own attempts to exert more extensive political control over its American colonies.

Maryland

Like Virginia, Maryland experienced considerable turmoil in the years following the Restoration. Charles II restored the Baltimore family to power. Lord Baltimore appointed his brother Philip and then his son Charles as governor, continuing the family's paternalistic rule. The holding of multiple offices by family members and friends remained common; after briefly serving as governor, for instance, Philip became chancellor, chief chancery judge, chief justice of the provincial court, and senior council member. Even the Indian trade was open only to those with the appropriate license. Thus, the ruling class in Maryland remained a closed, largely Roman Catholic group. Assembly members resented this monopoly over power, and in 1669, they issued a statement of grievances that attacked the governor's sovereignty. The proprietor responded by further restricting the franchise to those who possessed fifty acres or a personal estate worth forty pounds and by limiting the number of county representatives allowed to attend the assembly. Like Virginia, the colony faced declining tobacco prices and widespread concerns over the stability of the labor supply, then composed largely of white indentured servants. Fear of a servant uprising heightened the proprietor's sense that those excluded from power were threatening to make common cause with desperate servants seeking greater stability.

Conflict with England added to the growing tension. In 1681, treasury and customs officials charged that Baltimore had obstructed a customs officer. Baltimore and his council had ruled against customs agent Nicholas Badcock in a dispute with a shipmaster over payment of tobacco duties. In retaliation, the Crown threatened to revoke the colony's charter. Then in 1684, George Talbot, Baltimore's nephew, who had been entrusted with the government in 1684 when his uncle left for England, murdered customs collector Nicholas Rousky, further angering the Crown. In 1688, England sought to prohibit the exportation of bulk tobacco from the Chesapeake, hoping to slow the continuing decline in prices. The demand forced the proprietor to call the assembly, which responded to proprietary harangues with a statement of grievances. Proprietary arrogance, economic depression, and planter demands for political power combined to create an explosive atmosphere.

The catalyst was the growing fear of a French-Catholic-Indian conspiracy, touched off when the proprietary government failed to proclaim the new Protestant monarchy after the Glorious Revolution. In July 1689, John Coode, a leading opponent of the proprietor in the assembly during the late 1670s and early 1680s, formed a group of seven hundred to eight hundred men who called themselves the Protestant Association. They captured the state house, the proprietor's plantation, and the governor himself. Coode and the rebellion's other leaders called a convention of four delegates from each county, which set up an interim government, confirmed all officeholders except Catholics, and then dissolved to await instructions from England. But such instructions were not forthcoming, and the next spring, the rebels called another convention to solidify the new government's base. Coode then personally took the group's complaints to England, where he found a sympathetic ear. The Crown annulled the proprietary charter and appointed a royal governor and a new council that was predominantly Protestant and more representative of the economic and social leadership of the colony. The assembly took advantage of the crisis to increase its own power. Baltimore's reluctance to share power with the Protestant majority and the assembly, together with the economic uncertainties of a tobacco-based economy, combined to create fruitful ground for English intervention. The Crown restored the Calvert family to its proprietorship in 1715 but without the feudal powers it had possessed.

New England

The New England colonies faced a series of crises remarkably similar to those that plagued the Chesapeake during these three decades. They confronted growing social diversity, disruptive economic growth, Indian resistance to white expansion, and intrusive attempts by England to integrate the region more fully into a new imperial design. These colonies proved unique, though, in one crucial element. The idealistic social and religious intensity of early Puritan settlement continued to shape and direct New England's response to these events.

Population Growth and Social Change

The most obvious source of domestic disruption in New England was the astonishing rate of population growth throughout the region. Slightly less than twenty-three thousand people lived in New England in 1650; more than ninety-three thousand inhabited the region by 1700. A low death rate was the principal cause of this remarkable growth. New Englanders ate better than their European contemporaries and were free of the diseases and epidemics that took so many European lives. Family size thus became, ironically, a profoundly disruptive element in the evolution of New England society. The average family contained six to eight children, and most of these survived to adulthood. By mid-century, towns founded in the first wave of settlement were rapidly running out of land. As fertile, healthy New Englanders bore more and more children and these children survived in larger numbers to adulthood, it became increasingly difficult for parents to provide enough land for their children.

Most towns kept large amounts of land in reserve (the commons) after the initial division, but these acres generally lasted through only three or four more divisions. After this land was gone, there were few alternatives. New arrivals in such towns could not count on receiving any land in addition to what they could purchase, and third- and fourth-generation sons faced dwindling prospects within town borders. If a farmer began with three hundred acres and had three sons, each could inherit only one hundred acres. If each son had three sons, the remaining land would have to be divided among them. At first, the situation deepened the already strong sense of patriarchy that governed the New England family. The carpenter Henry Ingalls of Andover sought his father's consent before marrying for the first time, even though he was thirty years old! Few fathers divided all of their land among their sons before death; the majority of young New England males had to wait until their fathers' deaths before receiving their inheritance. Richard Barker, Sr. of Andover gave only one of his four sons deed to any of his land before he died in 1692, even though much of the property was wilderness and all but one of the boys eventually built homes on the land. The eldest son, John, built a house on the family land but did not receive a deed until 1683, thirteen years after he married, when he was forty years old. Two other sons waited to marry until they were in their thirties, settling on their father's land but not receiving title until he died. The youngest son remained at home, caring for his parents and inheriting the homestead on the father's death.

Table 5 ❧ Population of the Chesapeake, 1660–1700

		Maryland	Virginia
1660	White	7,668	26,070
	Black	758	950
1670	White	12,036	33,309
	Black	1,190	2,000
1680	White	16,293	40,596
	Black	1,611	3,000
1690	White	21,862	43,701
	Black	2,162	9,345
1700	White	26,377	42,170
	Black	3,227	16,390

U.S. Bureau of the Census, *Historical Statistics of the United States, Colonial Times to 1970,* 2 vols. (Washington, DC: Government Printing Office, 1975), 2:1168.

Farmers also altered the ways in which they passed land on to their children, now preferring deeds of gift to inheritance. This method ensured that sons would get the property without question, but fathers often included restrictive clauses guaranteeing, for instance, the rights of widows. Many sons also began to purchase their inheritances, often at substantial prices and even though they would undoubtedly have inherited the same land in the end. Some parents, finally, simply did not have enough land to divide among all of their sons.

In an attempt to accommodate their families' needs, farmers often purchased property far from the center of town; they consolidated their holdings and moved there or left the distant acres to their sons. New hamlets emerged up to three miles from the town center, and isolated farmhouses began to spring up. As time went on, moving to the frontier, or at least to less-densely settled towns, seemed the most practical response. Those who chose this course won more independence and autonomy from parental control. Thus the communal family settlements of the first generation, idealized from the pulpit and in the minds of later generations, rapidly became an unattainable goal. The New England population once again became highly mobile. Infant mortality gradually increased over the next century, and the average farm size declined. In the 1650s, the average New England farm family owned two or three hundred acres and cultivated 3 percent to 6 percent of their land. In the 1750s, the average was under one hundred acres, with 10 percent to 15 percent under cultivation. The average landholder in Concord, Massachusetts, held 259 acres in 1663; in 1749, the figure had shrunk to fifty-six acres.

Mobility engendered contention. The "outlivers" began to complain of the disadvantages they suffered because of their distance from the town centers, and they began to petition for their own institutions—churches and schools in particular. Many sought to be free of paying taxes for churches they did not attend or highways they did not use. Those remaining in the old town center, of course, resisted such demands. Not only would acceding to them disrupt the desirable communal unity, but it would also increase their own tax burdens, since fewer of them would be left to support the old institutions. Rancorous debate often accompanied the introduction of the petitions, but gradually, many towns were legally split into several precincts, many of which later successfully petitioned to become separate towns. In 1662, for instance, Dedham residents first settled the area that later became Wrentham. They became involved in an exasperating dispute with the rest of the town over public debts and land rights and successfully achieved independent status in 1673. In 1677, Ipswich settlers near the Chebacco River (the area that is now Essex) petitioned the General Court to allow them to build their own meetinghouse. They complained that some of them lived up to seven and a half miles from the existing church, and many of them had to remain there the whole day if they wished to attend the day's second service. The town refused the vote on the petition, but several Chebacco women managed to convince the men to build the new meetinghouse anyway. Aided by a General Court committee, the two sides eventually compromised, and Chebacco became incorporated as a separate parish in 1683.

The degree of independence towns accorded the new districts varied greatly, and precincts often vied for power within the town meeting. In Dedham, one group of outlivers tried to take control of the town meeting by threatening the moderator with muskets. The town solved this particular problem by according equal representation to the various precincts. But whatever form the resolution of these crises took, they permanently destroyed the social unity most of these settlers had originally sought. Those who moved to frontier towns in the hopes of recapturing the early communal experiences merely postponed the inevitable for another generation or two. In Massachusetts alone, proprietors established twenty new towns between 1660 and 1680 and another thirty-seven between 1681 and 1719. The numbers were comparable in neighboring Connecticut. But we must remember that individuals who sought precinct status or to form new towns were not seeking to destroy the local communalism of the New England way of life; rather, they were trying to maintain it, if only for themselves.

Economic Change

While increased geographical mobility introduced instability into the traditional New England way, the accompanying changes in social and economic customs and beliefs were perhaps even more disruptive. Land gradually lost its role as the focus of social experience and individual identity. It no longer served as a symbol of community, as a guarantee of traditional family and social patterns. Instead, it came to represent contention, division, and individual gain. In Watertown, Massachusetts, an active land market attracted speculation by outsiders, and town officials became so frustrated at their inability to control the situation that they turned to the General Court for a solution. In Sudbury, a divisive generational conflict rent the town's communal cohesion, as fathers used their economic control over the land supply to postpone their sons' independence, a strategy commonly employed in older towns.

Colonists caught another disturbing glimpse of their futures in the urban development in Boston and Essex County. From its beginning, Boston had been different, more religiously diverse and more secular. There, merchants set prices and dictated credit terms, and land became largely an investment commodity. Bostonians accepted trade and profit seeking as morally valid and economically necessary.

After 1660, New England merchants began to establish their own firms, often engaging in direct overseas trade with the London market. While such efforts generally relied on traditional familial and personal contacts, they also represented a significant departure from earlier attitudes toward economic activity. Newly arrived merchants were rarely devout communicants of the Puritan churches. They developed their own interests and seemed to have more in common with each other than with ministers and farmers. Wharves and docks quickly circled the Boston town cove, and leading merchants created their own specialized area along Cornhill Street. In 1650, the city's population was almost three thousand, fully one-fifth of all of Massachusetts; by 1700, seven thousand people were crowded into this bustling center of secular activity. Nor was Boston the only such center. Salem, for instance, quickly took on a pivotal economic role in Essex County, becoming a center for a wide variety of mercantile activities and developing a thriving land market.

Port towns in general witnessed an increase in nonfarm occupations, greater disparities in wealth (in Salem, for instance, the upper 10 percent of the population owned 62 percent of the wealth by 1700), more public and frequent litigation in courts, and an open pursuit of wealth and self-interest. They developed more complex relationships with the hinterland towns, regarding them as markets for imported goods and sources of food. Complaints against Boston merchants for high prices and unfair trade practices became common. It was more than just urban growth or wider economic contacts that brought this change; the merchants themselves were different from the guilt-ridden Robert Keaynes of earlier days. Thomas Breedon had little interest in Puritanism; from the time he arrived in Boston in 1648, his interests were solely commercial, and he developed extensive ties with like-minded London merchants. Col. Thomas Temple gained complete control of the Nova Scotia trade. An aristocrat, he too had strong ties with the London political and economic elite. He was related to Lord Say and Sele and cultivated intimate contacts with the government officials who ruled England during the Commonwealth and the Protectorate; he was in Massachusetts to pursue his economic interests only. Richard Wharton remains the best example of the economic entrepreneur with little sympathy for Puritan beliefs or expectations. Shunning church membership, Wharton became the seventeenth-century equivalent of an American tycoon, accumulating extensive wealth through his trade and land speculation interests. He eventually owned half a million acres in Maine and tried to have his territory turned into a manor, over which he would rule as lord. He also tried, unsuccessfully, to win a royal monopoly for a company to develop mines, foundries, and various manufacturing enterprises. He and other members of the council failed in an ambitious effort (the Atherton Company) to gain control over the entire Narragansett territory.

The Pynchon family established monopolistic dominance over the area around Springfield, controlling much of the region's land and trade and all of the sawmills and gristmills. They employed a significant percentage of the adult males in agriculture, processing, or trading. By 1680, at least one-half of Springfield's adult males were tenants, renters, or dependents of the Pynchons, and economic and social stratification in the town was far greater than anywhere but Boston and Salem.

The marketplace, not the community, bonded Springfield society. Most inhabitants had a marketable skill, some in two or three crafts. William Pynchon and later his son John employed forty men full-time in Springfield alone, and at any one time, about half the population was working for a Pynchon, renting land from him, or in debt to him. Many gained success through their ties with the family; Pynchon willingly extended credit to those who enjoyed a patron-client relationship with him and forgave or overlooked long-standing debts. Many more, though, came out on the losing end of this relationship.

William Pynchon. ❧

Isaac Morgan was one of the ordinary renters who survived his relationship with Pynchon. He leased a forty-two acre farm from Pynchon for eleven years late in the century. Pynchon promised to clear five acres of the land, build Morgan a house, and provide him with fertilizer. In turn, Morgan would clear and plow the remaining land, pay taxes on the livestock Pynchon provided him with, and pay a substantial annual rent. Morgan worked hard, both for himself and as a day laborer for Pynchon digging ditches and slaughtering animals. He continued to work for Pynchon even after moving to Enfield in the early 1680s.

Jonathan Taylor was one of those who did not fare so well. He had to give Pynchon his oxen to pay off part of his deepening debt, and later Pynchon even took as payment the five-and-a-half acre parcel of land Taylor owned. Yet Taylor continued to rent his house and land from Pynchon and fell deeper and deeper into his debt. But he was better off than Samuel Marshfield, a man who enjoyed enough status to be elected selectman in Springfield for thirteen years. Marshfield worked as a jack of all trades for Pynchon but was unable to repay his fifty-four pound debt to Pynchon, who seized Marshfield's house and land on the east side of the Connecticut River. Marshfield still owned considerable land on the west side of the river, but two decades later, he owed Pynchon 150 pounds and lost the rest of his land. When he died, his assets totaled sixty-six pounds, but he owed seventy-two pounds.

Pynchon's commercial orientation created a more tolerant and decidedly more secular social atmosphere in Springfield. Artisans in particular found themselves in constant trouble with the law, but because their skills were so essential to Pynchon's economic power, the courts generally overlooked their transgressions or punished them much less severely than would have been the case in an Andover or a Dedham. John Norton was a shoemaker, a valued skill in a frontier community, who was convicted at various times of philandering, drunkenness, and aggravated assault. In 1678, Mary Crowfoote complained of him "taking up her Coates and offering baseness to her. . . ."[5] Norton pleaded drunkenness as an excuse and received only a two pound fine. Profit, not social or moral cohesion, guided the severity of punishment in Springfield.

Economic growth brought social dislocation. From 1650 to 1710, Massachusetts experienced a 295 percent growth in real aggregate economic output. As early as 1666, its residents owned thirty ships of more than one hundred tons and seven hundred smaller ones. Ambitious entrepreneurs built a number of ships in New England and sold them to English merchants, taking advantage of the region's lower costs of production. This growing demand for ships and timber, as well as for fish from the Cape Ann area, significantly stimulated the region's economy. But growth in the New England economy was unbalanced and weakened by a lack of specie, low agricultural productivity, and the lack of a profitable export staple.

Merchants pursued solutions to these difficulties in ways that further disrupted the traditional communalism of New England society. Some, like the Atherton Company, turned to large-scale land speculation; others supported the colony's effort to attract foreign coin through overvaluation. In 1686, several merchants formed a loose credit organization called Blackwell's Bank. This effort stirred colonists to debate the very nature of New England society. The leaders of civilized nations, the Bank's supporters argued, should spend their time "studying the necessary advantages of Trade, and forwarding of Manufacture. . . ."[6] An abundance of coin, they believed, would help "to civilize the Ruder Sort of people, & encourages others to follow their example industry & civility."[7] Such rhetoric was a long way from Winthrop's earlier calls for unity and brotherhood.

Robert Keayne had at least tried to adhere to Puritan values in pursuing his vocation as a merchant. And though many wealthy men had been involved in the settlement of early New England, often at considerable profit to themselves, few had questioned the colony's basic ethos. Samuel Shrimpton presaged the values of the future. Shrimpton was the richest man in Boston in 1687. Owner of some of the most valuable land in Boston (including Beacon Hill) and other towns, he built on his inherited fortune by importing manufactured goods and exporting fish and timber. He viewed himself as an English country gentleman and had nothing but disdain for the attempts by the Puritan elite to restrict economic activity. He welcomed the Dominion of New England and its promise of closer ties to England. He was, in short, an eager proponent of the commercial, Atlantic culture that earlier Puritans had fled.

Political and Legal Change

As Massachusetts grew in population, expanded geographically, and faced a bewildering array of disruptive social and economic changes, its legal and political structures grew more complex and more directly involved in daily affairs. In 1643, the General Court divided the colony into counties with quarter courts. While these courts became especially active after 1660, they were significant from the beginning as law enforcement agencies. They had the power to stop any behavior that did not conform to the colony's accepted values, and they sought to regulate trade and economic exchanges according to Puritan standards, assisted by a variety of town and county officials—sheriffs, clerks, treasurers, grand juries, and special courts for outlying districts. While it proved impossible to uniformly enforce anything close to the Puritan ideal of behavior, these courts dealt successfully with the growing number of contentious disputes within and between towns and individuals over precinct and town formation, debts, and disputed land titles. Particularly in the second half of the century, county courts deflected personal animosity by serving as neutral arbiters in seemingly intractable personal and institutional conflicts.

In a similar fashion, the General Court began to dramatically increase its role in regulating the growth and development of the Bay Colony. In the early days of the colony, the court had deliberately granted a good deal of freedom to the towns to conduct their own affairs, a freedom the towns jealously guarded. Even when it did intervene in local disputes, it stressed communal harmony and used the traditional terminology of the English parish system. As early as the 1640s, though, the court began to expand its role by promoting industries, such as fishing and textiles, and by establishing control over the colony's geographical expansion. As intra- and intertown disputes became more common, the court found that neither traditional modes of mediation nor the growing legal system could control the burgeoning disagreements. It thus began to extend its powers in a direction that went far beyond the role of English county governments.

Religious Change

The disintegration of the relatively tenuous edifice of religious uniformity was perhaps the most traumatic experience of these years. There had always been dissent. Puritanism was a religion of broad diversity, and the early Massachusetts ministers struggled mightily to impose a working uniformity upon the most dangerous extremities of belief. But after the start of the English Civil War, change began to come at a pace no one could control. The war itself raised doubts in Puritans' minds about the validity of their mission, because it seemed for some time that God's arrival was certain to come not in Massachusetts but in England. It was, though, the playing out of Puritanism's own natural tendencies that caused the greatest dismay.

Baptists, Quakers, and Presbyterians   Roger Williams founded the first Baptist church in America in Providence in 1638, Dr. John Clarke the next at Newport in 1644. Individual Baptists appeared in Salem, Charlestown, Lynn, Hingham, Scituate, Watertown, and throughout Essex County, Massachusetts, in the late 1630s and early 1640s. Baptists contended that only the true believer could be baptized; they denied that baptism was a sacrament or could be a means of helping men and women prepare for grace. This was a logical, if extreme, conclusion from basic Puritan doctrine and it might have been tolerated or ignored if it had gone no further.

During the early 1640s, however, a number of Baptist pamphlets from England began to circulate in Massachusetts, and the General Court countered with a 1644 law banishing all Baptists. In 1650, a small group established a Baptist church in Seekonk in Plymouth Colony. Then in 1651, John Clarke and two other Baptists arrived in Lynn and led religious services there. They were arrested, tried, found guilty, and fined. One of the three refused to pay, and he was publicly whipped. In 1654, Henry Dunster, president of Harvard University, refused to present his newborn child for baptism. He resigned his position under pressure and moved to Scituate in Plymouth Colony.

After the Restoration, as England put growing pressure on the Bay Colony to allow greater religious freedom, the Baptist movement grew to near-flood proportions—or so the Puritans thought. In May 1665, a Baptist minister baptized nine converts by immersion and established a new church in Charlestown. The General Court disenfranchised the converts and warned them they would be imprisoned if they persisted in their actions. The congregation moved to an island in the harbor, but sympathy for the movement continued to grow. The court later banished three of the group when they refused to leave the colony, but sixty-six orthodox citizens signed a petition stating their belief that the Baptists should be freed and tolerated. Thirteen prominent English congregations also sent the colony a petition pleading for toleration. Eventually, the court freed the imprisoned Baptists, and they showed up once again in Boston. After 1682, no formal indictments were brought against Baptists. It would be another half-century, though, before Baptists were freed of the obligation of paying taxes for both their own churches and the established Congregational parishes.

Quakers presented Massachusetts with an even more disruptive religious and social threat. Quakers, as we have seen, believed in the inner light, the presence of a divine spark in the soul of the converted, and they denied the need for church discipline, an educated, trained ministry, or sermons. Early Quakers were anarchistic and acted without any clear leadership, posing a religious and social threat to Massachusetts order. Puritans argued that Quakers were guilty of pride in their claim that they possessed a unique knowledge of God; rumors spread through the colony that they burned Bibles. When Quakers Mary Fisher and Anne Austin arrived in Boston from Barbados in July 1656, the authorities sent them back. Eight more Quakers soon arrived in the colony and received the same treatment. In October, the General Court passed legislation making shipmasters who brought Quakers to the colony liable to fines and the Quakers subject to whipping, imprisonment, and banishment.

In Rhode Island, meanwhile, a group of Quakers arrived in Newport in 1657, gaining considerable support from former followers of Anne Hutchinson. Puritans seemed to have been particularly fearful of Quaker women. Nine of the first twenty-two Quaker missionaries to New England were women, as were twenty-six of the first fifty-nine sent to America. Puritan attitudes toward women undoubtedly had much to do with this, but the missionaries' behavior certainly did little to calm the near-hysterical ministers. Catherine Chatham paraded through Boston streets in sackcloth and ashes. Lydia Wardel and Deborah Wilson walked naked (symbolizing the spiritual nakedness of non-Quakers) through Boston, protesting against New England pride and brutality against Quakers. Quakers interrupted sermons and walked naked down the aisles of meetinghouses. In June 1658, two Quakers arrived in the colony and were arrested; each had an ear cut off and was threatened with death if they ever returned.

The most famous incident involved Mary Dyer. Dyer and her husband, William, arrived in Boston in 1635. They became church members, but both supported Anne Hutchinson and were subsequently expelled. They moved to Rhode Island, where William became the colony's attorney-general, and converted to Quakerism on a trip to England in the mid-1650s. Returning to Boston in 1656, Mary Dyer was imprisoned by the General Court and freed only when her husband paid a large fine and she promised never to return. She returned in September 1659 with two other Quakers to protest Massachusetts's persecution of the sect. The court arrested the three and ordered them to leave and never return on pain of death. They ignored the order, setting the scene for one of the more dramatic moments in early Massachusetts history. In October, the court sentenced the three to death. While two were hanged, the court reprieved Dyer on the scaffold. She later returned yet again, this time to finally suffer the fate of her colleagues.

Such actions brought a quick response from London. King Charles ordered the execution of Quakers stopped. Fearing English interference, the colony had already modified the law, substituting a provision that convicted Quakers be strapped to the back of a cart and whipped from town to town as they were led out of the colony. But they continued to come. In 1674, the Quakers established a Boston meeting, and in the following year, the court passed yet another law prohibiting Quaker presence in the colony. But by this time, there was pressure among the Puritans themselves for greater moderation; even the powerful and respected Reverend Increase Mather urged some indulgence.

Toleration prevailed more generally in the other New England colonies. There was little persecution in Plymouth, and though eight Quakers were expelled from Connecticut from 1656 to 1660, the government proved far more tolerant than its Massachusetts counterpart. Rhode Island was the most accepting of all. Many Quakers held high government positions, and in 1674, Nicholas Eaton became the first of several Quaker governors. Ironically, Roger Williams offered the most important resistance to their worship, opposing their anti-intellectualism and their attacks on the ministry. Williams was a biblicist, a position far removed from that of the Quakers. In 1672, George Fox, the Quaker founder, visited the colony, and Williams challenged him to a debate. The sixty-nine year-old Williams rowed himself from Providence to Newport for the event. Fox did not arrive in the colony in time, but Williams did debate three of his followers and found himself heckled by the audience.

One other strain of religious dissent deserves mention—Presbyterianism. In May 1646, Robert Child and several others petitioned the Massachusetts General Court to nullify the charter and make the colony dependent upon the then-sitting Presbyterian Parliament in England. Child was a Presbyterian and an influential man in Boston, and the six other signers were well-known in the community. Arguing that the people of the colony were disenchanted, they threatened to appeal to Parliament if a Presbyterian system was not established. The court viewed the petitioners as conspirators seeking to overthrow the government. It fined them and had their ship searched when they attempted to leave for England; a petition was discovered that demanded liberty of conscience, a Presbyterian system of church governance, and the appointment of a governor-general for the colony.

The English decided to stay out of the controversy and not to encourage appeals from the colony, but the Child incident and the violent reactions to Quakers and Baptists were only part of larger Puritan concerns. Faced with uncertainty in their religious lives and fearful that events in England signaled God's decision to bypass them in favor of their old homeland, Puritans struck out at those who seemed to present the gravest threat to traditional, religious communalism. They sought to narrow the boundaries of religious dissent while clarifying their own theological position, codifying basic Puritan beliefs in the "Cambridge Platform." For a while at least, some seemed to feel they had succeeded in repelling the threat. Edward Johnson, in his *Wonder-Working Providences,* argued that New Englanders had passed God's test; when the Devil was more active, he claimed, it was the surest sign that Armageddon was near. But his contention, and others like it, rings false; too many other settlements and events reflect a more powerful fear of loss and decline. The "half-way covenant" controversy, moreover, proved that Puritanism could not maintain its balance on the tightrope of doctrinal compromise.

The Half-Way Covenant   Children were always central to the Puritan vision. Adults feared for the souls of young people and worked their fingers to the bone to provide for their future well-being. They worried over the effect Quakers, Baptists, and others might have on impressionable young minds. The General Court complained of the influence exerted by "divers loose, vaine, and corrupt persons, both such as come from forraigne parts, as also some others heere inhabiting or residing, which insinuate themselves into the fellowship of the younge people of this countrie, drawing them, both by night and by day, from their callings, studies, honest occupations, and lodging places, to the great dishonour of God, greife of their parents, masters, teachers. . . ."[8]

Such concerns were well-founded. During the early years of the colony, the church had been able to claim a majority of the population as full members, and most others seemed to have at least sympathized with the Puritan cause. In Dedham, 70 percent of the men belonged to the church in the 1650s, and 80 percent of their children were baptized before 1660; in Watertown at mid-century, 250 adults from 160 families were members. Lay adherence was far above that in England at the same time, and piety matched physical attendance—sermons lasted up to two hours, and many summarized them in notebooks to study later in the week. Gradually, though, membership levels began to fall, and those in full communion faced the prospect of becoming a minority in the population. Lacking the emotional experience of their elders and reluctant or unable to make full and open confessions of faith, many second-generation New Englanders failed to progress from baptism to full communion. Without persecution, an ocean voyage, and the drama of establishing new settlements, a sense of spiritual urgency proved difficult to duplicate. Their parents also may simply have been impatient, expecting them to experience conversion at a much younger age than they themselves had.

The issue came to a head after 1660. To deny the third-generation children baptism would dictate the inevitable death of the Puritan movement, but first-generation settlers would not see the purity of their mission compromised. Church doctrine allowed only the children of full church members to be baptized upon birth; men and women of the second generation, however, had become full members in shockingly small numbers. Hence, their children, or the grandchildren of the first generation, could not be baptized. The Cambridge Synod of 1648 decided to continue to limit baptism to children of full church members, but a meeting of ministers from Massachusetts and Connecticut took up the issue again in 1657. This group recommended that all mature, baptized adults whose parents were full church members and who would testify to their own faith and promise to obey church rules should be allowed to have their children baptized. In most congregations, though, first-generation settlers continued to block the implementation of this agreement. The ministers called yet another synod in 1662, attended by more than eighty lay and ministerial representatives. This group forwarded a favorable report to the Massachusetts General Court, which in turn recommended that all New England churches adopt the compromise. The term "half-way covenant," coined by historians much later, refers to this agreement made by the parents and to their status as "half-way" members, or members who had not taken communion.

The first generation was still not ready to accept this solution. As late as 1675, more than half of Massachusetts churches refused to accept even the principle of the compromise. Only the trauma of King Philip's War, the intrusion of British government into the Bay Colony, and the general despair over God's apparent abandonment of his colony convinced Massachusetts churches to accept the covenant. Many churches did so only after the death of the first-generation patriarchs allowed church and community control to pass on to the second generation. The Puritans thus successfully brought a majority of the community into the church again. They did so, however, by permanently compromising the purity of their doctrine. From this point on, Puritan churches were generally regional institutions that provided one source of unity for an increasingly diverse population.

The situation was still more complex in Connecticut, where several factions divided congregations. Presbyterialists were the most accommodating, suggesting in 1664 that those who held proper beliefs and led a life of good conduct be allowed to join the church as half-way members, even if their parents had not been baptized. Mainstream Congregationalists were divided, with the strongly conservative New Haven churches particularly resistant to an accommodation. To counter the more radical proposals, the Connecticut assembly announced in 1669 that it would allow any orthodox policy, and Connecticut parishes covered the entire spectrum in their approaches. Wethersfield, for instance, allowed all the outwardly godly to receive communion; the Rev. Gershom Bulkeley brought in 350 new members in four years in a community of fewer than six hundred people. Simon Bradstreet in New London even accepted unbaptized adults from outside the church as half-way members, baptizing them and their children. He did retain the requirement that these converts make a public expression of faith and repentance, but this undoubtedly seemed little to ask in the face of such open acceptance.

The Puritans had earlier adopted the "narrative of saving grace" as a requirement for full admission out of fear that they would pollute the religious sanctuary by admitting those who had given no outward evidence of being saved. Now, the survival of the Puritan mission itself depended on bringing people back into the church, no matter what the doctrinal cost. At the end of the century, ministers turned to yet another stratagem to achieve this end—the mass covenant renewal, whereby the entire community came together to reaffirm its covenant with God and pledge itself to moral reform. Rev. Solomon Stoddard of Northampton embraced an even more extreme solution, offering communion to everyone whose life was not openly scandalous. He argued that communion could serve as a "converting ordinance," a means of helping people achieve salvation. In this fashion, he hoped he could more effectively spread the control of the church over the growing numbers of unchurched.

Few ministers embraced Stoddard's solution, and covenant renewals had only a temporary impact. Indeed, the crisis over church membership was only one expression of a pervasive and overriding sense of doom that plagued New Englanders during the last few decades of the century. Puritanism in England had disappeared with the Restoration, and the Royal Commission of 1664 had called into doubt the very safety of the New England mission itself. Baptists and Quakers challenged the religious foundations of New England theology and the Puritan's sense of controlled social order and civilized behavior. Disasters seemed to come with every dawn: severe droughts in 1662 and 1666; wheat crops ravaged by mildew and caterpillars in 1664, 1665, and 1668; fires and a smallpox epidemic in 1666; and heavenly lights in 1667 "shaped like a spear and aimed at the heart of New England."[9] Most important, late seventeenth-century Puritans gave their first-generation ancestors a special place in their pantheon of religious heroes. Fleeing persecution and battling against an unforgiving universe, these men and women had succeeded in creating a social and religious utopia—or so the legend went. Inevitably, the descendants of these giants believed that they could not live up to such achievements. In church membership, in the gradual decay of traditional communal villages, and in British interference with colonial government, New England was, in truth, a far different place than it had been thirty years earlier.

The Jeremiad Many among both the ministers and the laity, clinging to those early years as an unattainable ideal, viewed the results as a decline, a fall from grace and from the heights of perfection achieved by their fathers. They could only interpret such change as corruption, a sign that New England was becoming much like the rest of the world. God had singled them out for special attention and for a special mission, as He had done for Israel, and they had failed Him miserably. The jeremiad emerged as New England's fearful recognition of its seemingly inevitable doom.

Like all Puritan sermons, jeremiads began with a quotation from Scripture. In this case, it was generally from Isaiah or Jeremiah, the Old Testament prophets of doom. The minister then followed with a series of condemnations and concluded with a prophetic vision of the future and an explanation of the gap between the ideal to be achieved and the reality of the present. The form actually originated in the sermons of fifteenth- and sixteenth-century England, but there, it had strictly secular implications, threatening worldly disaster. The Puritans carried the jeremiad with them to the New World, where it took on new and more ominous implications. America, after all, was the promised land; the early Puritans fused sacred and secular history and gave their worldly settlement millenial implications. Failure to achieve the ideal thus threatened eternal, not just worldly, disaster. If the Puritans failed to live up to their end of God's covenant, they—and New England—were damned.

Not all New Englanders were mired in such pessimism. Ministers such as William Hubbard rejected the notion that New England had lost sight of its original purpose and had become corrupt and worldly, arguing that the religious and social changes besetting the region were not unique but rather just the latest expressions of the adversity Christians always had to counter when facing the temptations of prosperity. Hubbard supported toleration of dissenters and argued that there were abundant signs of moral regeneration among Puritan youth.

In one sense, then, the jeremiads were expressions of a particular vision of Puritan society, one embraced by Increase Mather, for instance, but not by Hubbard and others like him. Nonetheless, the jeremiads of the 1660s and 1670s, with their tone of near-hysteria, exerted a powerful hold over the faithful. The original Puritan vision was so strong, the guilt of transgression so great, that second- and third-generation settlers were unable to shake themselves loose from its grip. And the first-generation founders were dying off rapidly at the very time the New England

ᴥ *Documents* ᴥ
The Decline of Piety

New England's problems were of a different sort than those of the Chesapeake. Puritan ministers bemoaned the decline of piety among the laity, while the laity seemed unable or reluctant to follow the religious paths laid down by their parents. The first two documents below are typical statements of near-hysterical concern by ministers. The most serious blow to New England's self-image, though, came with King Philip's War, as the final document suggests.

> God will tell you one day you had your *Cotton* and your *Norton,* and your *Hooker,* and your *Sherpherd,* and your *Rogers* . . . you had my Ministers, and there is never a Minister that God hath sent, but the time will come, when as, if you have heard them, and obeyed them, I what a sweet meeting that will be, and then may they say, Lord, here we are, and the Children thou hast given us. But otherwise God will say, Why did you not receive them? Whence they come to despise the Prophets . . . the wrath of the Lord rose against his people, so that there was no remedy.

John Wilson, *A Seasonable Watchword* (Cambridge, MA: 1677), 6–7.

> Whence cometh it, that Pride, and Luxurie
>   Debate, Deceit, Contention, and Strife,
> False-dealing, Covetousness, Hypocrisie
>   (With such like Crimes) amongst them are so rife,
> That one of them doth over-reach another?
>   And that an honest man can hardly trust his Brother?
>
> How is it, that Security, and Sloth,
>   Amongst the best are Common to be found?
> That grosser sings, in stead of Graces growth,
>   Amongst the many more and more abound?
> I hate dissembling shews of Holiness.
>   Or practise as you talk, or never more profess.
>   . . . .

way of life seemed in such dire straits. To a minister such as Samuel Willard, the problem seemed obvious: "When great and good men die thick and fast, it portends declension."[10] In 1679, the Massachusetts General Court called a Reforming Synod, which listed in painful detail the shortcomings of the New England people: the neglect of religion in church and family, intemperance, worldliness, and the lack of a public spirit. The synod recommended church covenant renewals, stronger church discipline, and proper religious education for the region's children. All of these approaches were tried, and all were found wanting. Ministers contrasted their own situation with that of their fathers, and the results bred a profound

Ah dear New England! dearest land to me;
  Which unto god hast hitherto been dear,
And mayst be still more dear than formerlie,
  If to his voice thou wilt incline thine ear.

Consider wel & wisely what the rod,
  Wherewith thou art from yeer to yeer chastized,
Instructeth thee. Repent, & turn to God,
  Who wil not have hus nurture be despized.

Michael Wigglesworth, "God's Controversy with New-England," *Proceedings of the Massachusetts Historical Society,* ser. 1, vol. 12 (1873), 86–91, 93.

That the Heathen People amongst whom we live, and whose Land the Lord God of our Fathers hath given to us for a rightfull Possession, have at sundry times been plotting mischievous devices against that part of the English Israel which is seated in these goings down of the Sun, no man that is an Inhabitants of any considerable standing, can be ignorant. . . . And whereas they have been quiet untill the last year, that must be ascribed to the wonderfull Providence of God, who did . . . lay the fear of the *English,* and the dread of them upon all the *Indians.* . . . Nor indeed had they such advantages in former years as now they have, in respect of Arms and Ammunition, their bows and arrows not being comparably such weapons of death and destruction, as our guns ans swords are, with which they have unhappily been furnished. Nor where our sins ripe for so dreadfull a judgment, untill the *Body of the first Generation* was removed, and another Generation risen up which hath not so pursued, as ought to have been, the blessed design of their Fathers, in following the Lord into this Wilderness, whilst it was a land not sown.

Increase Mather, *A Brief History of the War with the Indians in New England* . . . (Boston: 1676), 1.

sense of loss and guilt: "The days wherein you live are backsliding times *evil dayes,* times of great degeneracy and apostacy."[11] Many felt they could no longer avoid the inevitable question: had New England lost its way?

White-Indian Relations

After a decade or two of initial prosperity and harmony, both secular and spiritual conflict beset the New England experiment. The decreasing availability of land and the fragmentation of a tenuous religious unity raised frightening concerns for the future. Amidst growing uncertainty over their own identity, New Englanders began to view Indians as disturbing reminders of the barbaric, uncivilized threat the "wilderness" that was the New World seemed to present. They sought to resolve these fears—at least partially—by energetically pursuing a program to transform these "savages" into civilized beings.

Making Red Men White   After defeating the Pequots, the New England colonies turned to a variety of stratagems to control the Indians—to turn them into farmers or artisans, for instance. The Indians were not eager to accommodate white demands. They retained their traditional farming methods, using no plows, fencing, or fertilizers as the English did, and women continued to be responsible for cultivating crops. Indians learned only those trades that helped them maintain their independence—broom making and basket weaving—and they willingly kept livestock, an occupation that also provided them with a source of meat. In the face of such persistent cultural resistance, the English settlers turned to their most powerful weapon—religion. As early as 1643, an Indian by the name of Hiacoomes approached Thomas Mayhew, Jr., a Puritan minister on Martha's Vineyard, to request instruction in Christianity. Mayhew responded positively, and the Vineyard proved to be the site of one of New England's most successful missionary experiments. It was a completely voluntaristic mission on both sides, and Mayhew respected Indian cultural independence.

The Reverend John Eliot's efforts to convert the Indians were more typical. Eliot was a complex figure. In 1634, he had opposed the Massachusetts friendship treaty with the Pequots, and the reasons for his changed attitude toward Indians remain something of a mystery. He apparently came to believe that the New England Indians were remnants of the ancient Jews and that their conversion would signal arrival of the Millennium. His motivation may be unclear, but his commitment was not. Indians heckled him during his first sermon to them at Dorchester Mill in 1646, but he refused to abandon his new ministry. In response to this incident, the General Court reorganized the colony's system of governance over the Indians, passing laws suppressing native religion and laying the basis for what were known as the praying Indian towns. From 1651 to 1674, the court established fourteen such towns, the first and by far the most successful at Natick. But at their height, the towns contained only about eleven hundred Indians, and only about 10 percent of these were ever baptized. In 1674, the largest of these towns had only twenty-five to thirty adult men, and during King Philip's War, most of the converts and inhabitants left to rejoin their Indian comrades. The towns did recover somewhat after the war; in 1698, there were thirty congregations of praying Indians, served by thirty-seven full-time Indian preachers, teachers, and catechists.

Streets and lots in the villages deliberately reproduced the English sense of space. Men ploughed the fields, and English cows and goats grazed the meadows and hogs rooted in pens. Laws imposed strict Sabbath observance (contrary to the more leisurely Indian notion of time) and fines for idleness, drunkenness, body greasing, excessively long hair (males) or naked breasts (females), gambling, and powwowing—that is, resorting to Indian rituals for curing illness. In sum, the General Court adopted physical and legal structures that were explicitly designed to break down Indian custom. Puritan ministers expected converts to become English, to abandon their own culture and its values. They were to live and work in the English way.

Eliot also instituted an educational program that was primarily religiously oriented. Eliot had pointed the way with an early Algonquin translation of the Bible, and by 1672, a small library of books was available. Religious education began with

John Eliot (1659 portrait). ✒

the Bible and stressed the god of evil rather than of good, since that seemed to be the one Indians responded to most readily. The message white missionaries brought to the Indians was clear: all Indians lived in a state of sin, and repentance was necessary for salvation. The missionaries stressed an inward, passive piety, more appropriate to the political and social goals of the missions. The sermon was central to the service, and Indian confessions resembled the English in style and structure, though they were distinctly more emotional in content.

For more secular instruction, Indian children were at first admitted to the colony's elementary schools for free and later to one of three special grammar schools to study English, Latin, and Greek. But they could not cope with the drastic changes the regimen of study imposed on their lives, and several died trying. Schools were then established in the praying villages with Indian teachers—thirteen of them by 1662. But Eliot found that Indians could not learn a new language and a new religion at the same time. Indian Superintendent Daniel Gookin established a free school in Marlborough in the late 1670s. But neither this nor later attempts at Stockbridge, Massachusetts, and Lebanon, New Hampshire, enjoyed any real success. Harvard built an Indian college in the 1650s, but only a few Indians attended and only one completed the four-year curriculum.

Indians clearly grasped the intellectual content of Christian theology and asked particularly difficult questions of their instructors regarding death, evil, and hell. Why, they wondered, would God punish even the repentant for all eternity? Or why would He not interfere to aid the blessed in this life? Indians participated actively in their instruction, and converts scrupulously observed their religious duties. When alone, however, they often returned to their own beliefs and practices. They were caught between two worlds. Those who resisted conversion were from tribes with strong sachems. Those who converted often did so for reasons that were entirely logical from their perspective: given the English superiority in scientific and military technology, the English god seemed more powerful than their own.

King Philip's War   The Puritan attempt to control the Indians through religious conversion was a failure, and for many settlers, it did not seem to deal forcefully enough with issues of defense or land hunger. In New England, as in most other English colonies, coercion provided a more satisfactory solution. The New England Confederation, a united organization of the New England colonies (except Rhode Island), sought to guarantee military preparedness in the case of another Indian outbreak. In 1643, when the Narragansett sachem Miantonomo sold a large tract of land to the hated Samuel Gorton, the confederation arranged for Miantonomo's murder by his Mohegan enemies. The sachem had earlier earned white enmity by unsuccessfully attempting to create a pan-Indian alliance to drive the settlers from his territory. In 1645, the confederation threatened war against the Narragansetts to force cession of a large area of land.

After 1660, New England Indian policy took a dramatic turn toward violence. The arrival of the 1664 Royal Commission and the movement to recall the New England charters made the tenuous nature of these documents clearer than ever. The individual colonies had already resorted to a legal stratagem to solidify their status: by gaining the loyalty or control of tribes and establishing a "protectorate" over them, the colonies established legal control over the land. Prior to 1660, the settlers used this policy primarily to gain a monopoly over the right to purchase lands from the tribes; now the stakes were higher than ever. Plymouth in particular relied heavily on its "protectorate" over the Wampanoags, thus making attempts by Rhode Island and Massachusetts to purchase Wampanoag lands serious threats to the small colony's legal status. Rhode Island depended on its control of the Narragansett tribe; thus, it reacted strongly when Massachusetts and Connecticut tried to coerce the Narragansetts into accepting their own expansion into the tribe's territory.

The focal points of the land disputes in southern New England were Rhode Island's borders with its neighbors—Plymouth, Connecticut, and Massachusetts—all of whom claimed substantial parts of the tiny colony, particularly the Narragansett territory. In theory, the Indians could bargain among the three contenders, but in practice, this meant little more than a choice of which colony would preside over their disintegration. Ironically, the 1664 commission became an important potential ally for the Indians, who welcomed the commission's argument that no colony could dispose of conquered land unless the cause was just and the land lay within its charter boundaries. The commission designated Metacom of the Wampanoags (called Philip by the whites) a "free sachem," whose oath of obedience was to the king and not to a particular colony. In fact, his sale of land to both Plymouth and Rhode Island was a conscious and aggressive act of independence and a clear statement

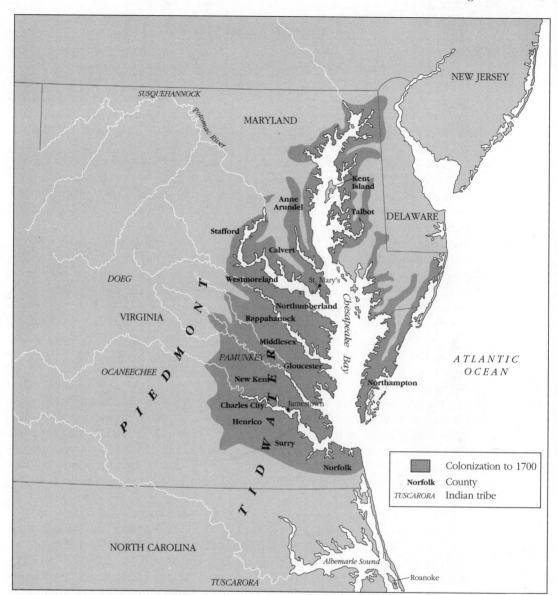

MAP 6.2: Southern New England at the time of King Philip's War &.

that he, not the colonists, possessed legal ownership to his people's territory. The New England colonies could not accept this re-definition of white-Indian relations.

In 1664, Edward Winslow of Plymouth arrested Wamsetta, Metacom's brother, in a bald-faced attempt to force him to sell his land to Plymouth colony. Wamsetta died while in custody, and the Indians charged that he was poisoned. Colony officials then summoned Metacom to Plymouth and accused him of plotting retaliation. He denied the accusation and promised (under coercion) that he would sell none of his lands without the consent of the Plymouth government. Plymouth next established a new town, Swansea, at the neck of Mount Hope Peninsula, the location of Metacom's village. When the Indians objected, the English fined Metacom and forced him to declare that his people were already subject to both Plymouth and the king. Metacom appealed in vain to the Massachusetts authorities to intervene.

At this point, it seems that Metacom had already begun to covertly stir up Indian discontent. His plans were hastened by the trial of three Wampanoags for the tribal revenge murder of a christianized, Harvard-educated Indian, John Sassamon, who had previously been Metacom's assistant. Sassamom was caught between two cultures. Though he fled white society in the end, he also informed the Plymouth government in 1675 that the Wampanoags were planning an attack. In June, the English hanged his three killers. Haphazard looting and burning followed this execution, indicating perhaps that Metacom was trying to restrain the younger, more aggressive Indians.

The English drew first blood, shooting several Indians they discovered taking items from a house that the English had abandoned. Then on June 20, 1675, Metacom attacked Swansea. On June 30, troops from Massachusetts, Plymouth, and Rhode Island attempted to sweep the Mount Hope Peninsula, but they succeeded only in driving the Wampanoag leader into closer contact with the neighboring Pocassets. Meanwhile, the English were attempting to establish an alliance with the Narragansetts and Nipmucks or at least to convince them to remain neutral. The Nipmucks in particular had long been friendly to the settlers and had supplied a large proportion of the inhabitants of the praying villages. The Narragansetts decided to declare neutrality, but the Nipmucks joined Metacom. By mid-August, hostilities had moved into Nipmuck country and to the upper Connecticut River valley. The Indians launched raids on Lancaster, Hadley, and Northfield, Massachusetts, during the last two weeks of August and the first week of September. Finally, on September 9, the New England Confederation declared war and assembled a one thousand-man army.

Fighting continued to spread throughout the New England frontier, and Massachusetts abandoned Northfield on September 2 and Deerfield soon after. After peace negotiations with the Narragansetts broke down, an English force invaded the main Narragansett village in December. The so-called Swamp Fight ensued. The English killed six hundred Indians, mostly women, chilren, and wounded men, losing eighty men of their own. The Narragansett survivors took refuge with the Nipmucks.

During the winter of 1675–1676, Metacom sought assistance from the Mohawks, but at the urging of New York Gov. Edmund Andros, the Iroquois tribe refused and instead attacked several of Metacom's camps. The Western Abenaki territory in Vermont became a center of operations for a while, and the Narragansetts sought refuge there after the Swamp Fight. But they soon returned to the east to seek their revenge. Led by the warrior Canonchet, they attacked Lancaster, Massachusetts, on February 20, taking the famed Mary Rowlandson captive. On March 26, they ambushed a company of sixty-five Plymouth soldiers and twenty Indian allies near Central Falls, Rhode Island. The Narragansetts killed fifty-five of the English on the spot and captured and tortured nine of the ten who had fled the battle. Three days later, they attacked and burned Providence, despite the entreaties of Roger Williams. By April, all whites had fled the area in Rhode Island from Point Judith north to Providence. Shortly thereafter, Metacom returned to Massachusetts and launched a massive offensive on Bay Colony and Plymouth towns, striking within ten miles of Boston and attacking the town of Plymouth. In April, an epidemic ravaged the colonies, killing many whites. It seemed that the Indians had a real chance of inflicting a fatal blow on the English settlements, which were increasingly plagued by draft resistance, food scarcities, and profiteering.

The Indians themselves, however, began to suffer from food shortages and disease, and Metacom was having difficulty replacing lost men. His failure to gain supplies from the Mohawks was beginning to have telling effect. Then on May 18, the

English surprised and defeated a large group of Indians at the falls near Deerfield; despite a counterattack in which they killed 150 whites, the Indians suffered dearly. The English now took the offensive with several frontier victories in June and inflicted a decisive defeat on the Narragansetts on July 2. Capt. Benjamin Church, leading the New England forces, harried Metacom from camp to camp and captured his wife and son. In a rage, the Indian leader killed one of his own warriors, whose brother then informed Church where he was. At his own home, Mount Hope Neck, Metacom was killed by an Indian from Church's company. The last large band of Indians surrendered on August 28. War on the northern theater persisted for some time, as the English destroyed crops and disrupted Indian agriculture, trapping, and trading activities. Many Abenaki sought refuge in Canada and in Jesuit mission villages, while others scattered throughout the region, some even appearing in the LaSalle expedition down the Mississippi River in the 1680s. The English sold hundreds of Indians into slavery in the West Indies, including Metacom's wife and son. Hundreds more became tenant farmers, while the English confined the rest to one of the four remaining praying villages.

King Philip's War opened a new chapter in the saga of Puritan attitudes toward the Indians. As the City on the Hill teetered on the brink of failure and as the Puritans failed in their efforts to make Indians into white men, Indians served only to remind whites of the dark barbarism they feared most within themselves. It became necessary to remove them from the landscape. The English also viewed the war as a judgment of God for the sins of New England. As Increase Mather noted, "We may well think that God is greatly offended with the *Heathenisme* of the English People. How many that although they are *Christians* in name, are no better than *Heathens* in heart, and in Conversation? How many Families that live like *profane* Indians without any *Family Prayer?*"[12]

The physical consequences of the war were severe. The casualty rate was unprecedented; the Indians killed six hundred English and wounded many more, while the English killed three thousand Indians. The Indians attacked fifty-two of the ninety New England towns and destroyed twelve of them. They burned more than twelve hundred houses and killed eight thousand head of cattle. English troops completely destroyed several Indian villages. In northern New England, a new multitribal community arose in the upper Hudson River valley. In the decades to come, French and English fought for the loyalty of these Indians, especially the Western Abenaki, while many tribes simply melted away into remote wooded areas, seeking to preserve their individual and communal identities as far away from whites as possible.

Colonial Resistance To British Control

New England

If King Philip's War seemed to embody God's punishment for New England's sins, England's actions during the Restoration raised the equally horrendous specter of royal control. Massachusetts had not endeared itself to England by its actions since the Restoration. It had delayed recognizing Charles II and had claimed the right to determine which English laws were applicable to it. Its reputation for intolerance, resistance to English rule, and evasion of the newly enacted Navigation Acts made it the ideal candidate for testing enforcement of the British desire to tighten control of its North American empire.

Still, Charles II's initial attitude toward the colony seemed surprisingly lenient. Massachusetts sent special agents to London in 1662 with a letter of submission that contained no actual reference to English rule—only an innocuous, very general acknowledgement of allegiance to the king. Charles responded with pleasure at having received the statement of loyalty, confirmed the colony's charter, and asked that Anglicans be allowed freedom of worship and that the franchise be based on property rather than church membership. But Massachusetts failed to take the hint, and Charles grew increasingly troubled by the colony's treatment of Anglicans and dissenters and its persistent evasion of the Navigation Acts. So he took steps to gather the information necessary to legally void the colony's chapter and appointed the Royal Commission of 1664.

Established in part to handle the surrender of New Amsterdam to the British during the Second Anglo-Dutch War, the commission was also charged with discovering if Massachusetts had obeyed the king's orders to stop discriminating against Anglicans and to give the vote to non-Congregationalists. Its membership included Samuel Maverick, a former Massachusetts dissident who had signed the Child petition in 1646. Sir Richard Nicolls, the commission's head, also had secret instructions to persuade the colony's government to accept a supplementary charter that would deprive the colony of much of its independence, including the right to elect its own governor.

When Massachusetts heard that Nicolls was coming, the colony's first fear was that the troops would be used against it. The General Court hid the charter, strengthened the harbor forts, and summoned the militia. It altered the franchise requirements to allow anyone not a church member to become a freeman by a majority vote of the court and a minister's certification that the individual was morally fit, together with a statement from a town selectman that the prospective voter was a freeholder ratable at ten shillings or more. But the colony refused to adopt the oath of allegiance to the king, to extend religious liberty to non-Puritans, or even to allow appeals beyond the General Court to the Crown.

The commissioners were not cowed. They observed that religious persecution continued, that smuggling seemed common and unpunished, and that the colony's franchise requirements had changed little. They filed an extremely negative report that supported revocation of the colony's charter. Charles ordered the Massachusetts government to send representatives to London to answer the charges. They refused, sending two masts as gifts instead. Charles was not amused.

As in other colonies, the threat of greater imperial control split Massachusetts into factions. The commonwealth faction, dominated by agrarian interests and merchants lacking British connections, supported complete independence from royal control, and they generally controlled the lower house. The moderates, merchants with stronger economic ties to England, supported greater cooperation with the Crown and sat on the colonial council. A third group, strongly loyalist in sentiment, consisted of young merchants recently arrived from England. The three groups clashed constantly during these years, their conflicts reflecting the growing economic and social divisions in Massachusetts society and showing clearly how these divisions influenced political loyalties.

The colony gained some breathing room with the onset of the Second Anglo-Dutch War (1665–1667). The earl of Clarendon's political decline in England also eased the pressure, since he was the royal adviser most interested in bringing the colony under political control. But after the successful conclusion of the Third Anglo-Dutch War in 1674, the Crown renewed its drive to centralize imperial control. Edward Randolph's 1676 report to the Lords of Trade proved to be the last straw. The lords concluded that the corporate and proprietary colonies were the main obstacles to greater imperial control, and they convinced the king to invalidate the Massachusetts charter. The colony only made matters worse by arguing that the laws of England were invalid within its boundaries, since the colonies were not represented in Parliament.

In 1682, the Crown ordered Massachusetts to send representatives to London to explain its actions and to discuss revisions in its charter, including the future royal appointment of governors. The General Court rejected all compromise, and in June 1683, the Crown initiated proceedings to have the colony's charter annulled. In October 1684, the Court of King's Bench declared the Massachusetts charter invalid.

Charles now established the Dominion of New England. The dominion's jurisdiction included Massachusetts, New Hampshire, Maine, and the King's Province (Narragansett territory). London appointed a provisional government, headed by the moderate Joseph Dudley, to rule until the new British governor could arrive. In the spring of 1687, the British revoked the Connecticut and Rhode Island charters and incorporated them into the dominion; they added New York and New Jersey a year later. This was the first of two or three such administrative units England planned to establish to govern its North American empire.

While Massachusetts was readying itself for royal rule, Charles died in February 1685. His brother James, Duke of York, succeeded him. James was determined to contain the growth of Parliamentary power and to create a powerful, centralized monarchy sanctioned by divine right. More important, he decided to return England to Catholicism. He allowed Catholics to serve in the army and to hold public office, and he put pressure on the nobility to convert. But even the conservative members of the Tory party resisted the movement to Rome, and the Whigs had already attempted to have James excluded from the succession in 1680 because he was a Catholic. When James's second wife bore a son in the spring of 1688, Tory and Whig leaders decided they had had enough. They invited William of Orange, married to James's daughter Mary, to save England from the perils of Catholicism. By the fall, William and Mary were king and queen of England.

While these events were unfolding in England, the new royal governor of the dominion, Edmund Andros, arrived in Boston in December 1686. His administration was doomed to failure from the start. His instructions called for an appointed council, for instance, but no elected legislature, thus abolishing the long-standing tradition of self-government in the colony. The measures he imposed succeeded only in uniting the colony's political factions. During an economic slump, he raised taxes on horses and cattle, doubled the wine duty, and expanded license requirements for taverns. He strictly enforced the Navigation Acts and refused to yield to the demands of land speculators. Those interested in the Narragansett lands in particular had hoped to gain some advantage by lobbying his government. Most dangerously, Andros forbade town meetings (except for the annual election of officers). Left without a political voice, the disgruntled residents of Essex Country rebelled when the governor tried to collect the higher taxes, arguing that Andros's policies represented "taxation without representation."

Andros negated all private land titles, requiring that future grants be made in the name of the king. The necessity of offering proof of ownership placed many landowners in the hands of avaricious clerks, often Andros's own advisers, who greedily lined their own pockets. In his efforts to regulate trade, the governor issued writs against several leading merchants and removed New Englanders from all important provincial offices. He demanded that Boston provide a meetinghouse for the Anglican church or contribute to building one, but this the Puritans refused to do. On Easter Sunday 1687, he forced his way into the Third Church, and from then on, the congregation had to wait until the Anglican services were over before they could use the building. The final blow came in the summer and fall of 1688, when Indians attacked the northern frontier and Andros called up the militia to defend the area and forbade Boston merchants to continue to sell arms to the Indians. The men resented the winter campaign, particularly since some of the officers appointed by Andros were Catholic. When the governor released all Indian prisoners and promised a general amnesty if the rest would lay down their arms, the colonists despaired. They viewed this as treachery of the basest sort.

Andros thus alienated the entire colony by his autocratic actions. Merchants lost both past privileges and future riches, rising entrepreneurs lost their chances for economic success, and farmers and townsmen lost their rights to self-government and suffered under next taxes which they had not voted for or supported. When news arrived in April 1689 that the Glorious Revolution had deposed James II and that William and Mary had acceded to the throne, the colonists reacted quickly and with unity. A letter instructing officials to remain in their positions apparently never reached Boston, and an armed uprising imprisoned Andros and most of his assistants. The rebels appointed a Council of Safety, with moderate Simon Bradstreet as president. The council issued a proclamation accusing Andros of arbitrary rule and announcing the colony's intention of continuing under the pre-dominion structure until it heard from London. It also took great pains to control the action of the lower classes, who throughout the dominion threatened to take matters into their own hands. While the rebels presented a united front, they struggled to preserve domestic unity.

Perhaps the most successful effort to maintain this unity lay in the cohesive, revolutionary ideology the gentleman leaders invoked to justify their actions. New Englanders explicitly identified Andros with the English "Popish Plot," which had been organized, they argued, to further "the Extinction of the Protestant Religion." Men such as Andros were "intoxicated with a Bigotry inspired into them by the great *Scarlet Whore* [the Catholic church]." England, they feared, was planning to deprive them of the privileges of Englishmen "not to be taxed without their consent. . . ." The colonists felt that Andros and his aides treated them like slaves who deserved none of the rights of the Magna Charta. William and Mary, in contrast, would preserve England and its colonies "from the horrible brinks of Popery and Slavery. . . ."[13]

The new charter that came from London was something less than what the colonists expected. Despite intense lobbying by Increase Mather and others from both the moderate and commonwealth factions, Massachusetts now became a royal colony. The royal charter of 1692 gave England widespread political powers in the colony, including the power to appoint the governor and through him sheriffs, justices of the county courts, and justices of the peace. The General Court lost most of the power it had gained during the seventeenth century. The governor's control over the justices of the peace was particularly important, since many of them were later elected to the General Court; in 1720, for instance, they comprised about 20 percent of the court's membership. Religious toleration was ordered, and the franchise was now based solely on property qualifications. The colony did retain its elected assembly, which was also given the power to elect the upper house (voting with the sitting members of that body), but the overall effect was clearly to shift political power from Boston to London.

The other New England colonies also reacted to the dominion, though none did so with the sense of drama that prevailed in Massachusetts. In Connecticut, which had experienced religious and social changes similar to those in Massachusetts, some disagreement arose between those who sought a renewal of the old charter and those who desired more control from England. The old charter was renewed, and the colony remained self-governing until the Revolution. Plymouth independence had been on thin legal ground from the beginning; the Crown now placed it under Massachusetts jurisdiction. Rhode Island was administered as a county of Massachusetts under the dominion, ruled by Andros from

Boston, but the colony refused to pay the taxes levied by the governor. After hearing of the revolt in Boston, the pre-dominion leaders called a meeting of freemen in Newport. A small group of royalists resisted, but the colony cautiously resumed its old government when William and Mary were proclaimed king and queen. England approved, and like Connecticut, the colony remained semiautonomous until the Revolution.

New Hampshire was the only New England colony to gain uncontested advantage from events during these years. When the Mason family abandoned its claims to the territory before the Restoration, Massachusetts had taken control of the colony until 1679, when the Crown placed it under royal government. It subsequently became part of the dominion. It again became a royal province in 1691, sharing a governor with Massachusetts until 1741. During these decades, it achieved considerable economic independence, and a native-grown elite dominated the colony's politics to their own economic advantage.

New York

The dominion also had a serious impact on political affairs in New York. Gov. Richard Nicolls had attempted to establish order and to conciliate the heterogeneous population that the English had inherited from New Amsterdam. Edmund Andros, who became governor after the colony was recaptured in the Third Anglo-Dutch War, acted more forcefully and began to strip the Dutch of their privileges. While some of the elite accepted the inevitable, most ordinary Dutch citizens in New York proved more recalcitrant. At the same time, New Englanders on Long Island lobbied for the representative assembly that had been refused them. They and others began to refer to British rule of the colony in terms similar to those of Massachusetts, speaking of the Magna Carta and the "known Ancient and Fundamentall Lawes of the realme of England. . . ."[14] The 1683 "Charter of Libertyes and Privileges" offered support for these views, but James became king before the charter could receive final approval. Instead of endorsing the new government, James included the colony in the Dominion of New England.

New Yorkers' discontent with British rule in 1689, then, can be grouped under several categories. First, the Dutch were disaffected by British religious policies, the forced collection of quitrents, and particularly the enforcement of the Navigation Acts, which interfered with their trade with Holland. Second, New Englanders on Long Island objected to quitrents and the lack of a representative assembly. Third, merchants opposed the strict enforcement of the Navigation Acts. Finally, and perhaps most important, considerable discontent existed within the colony over the economic and political control exerted by a small number of mercantile and landowning families, such as the Bayards, Livingstons, and Schuylers. Aided and supported by Gov. Francis Nicholson (1688–1689), these powerful, wealthy families passed laws that introduced controls over grain prices, established a fur trade monopoly for Albany, granted a New York City monopoly in grain milling, and made the city the only official port in the colony. Small farmers and city workers in particular suffered from this legislation. Long Islanders preferred to trade with Connecticut and Massachusetts and resented having to deal exclusively with New York City. Albany resented the New York trade monopoly and favored a looser relationship with the French and the Indians, a policy that would benefit them financially.

By the time Gov. Nicholson received news of the English Glorious Revolution in March 1689, the colony not only faced an internal crisis but was also beset by rumors of an impending French and Indian attack on Albany. Although Nicholson was not Catholic, he had several Catholics on his council. When he did not

⪍ *Documents* ⪍
The Seeds of Rebellion

Though the rebellions in Maryland (Coode's Rebellion), New York, and Massachusetts were motivated by local conditions and grievances, common themes emerged from the rhetoric used to justify these uprisings. The following documents from Massachusetts and New York reflect the particular circumstances residents of each of these colonies faced and the common ways in which they perceived their oppressors.

> But of all our Oppressors, we were chiefly squeez'd by a Crew of abject Persons fetched from New York, to be the Tools of the Adversary standing at our right Hand; by these were extraordinary and intollerable Fees extorted from every one upon all Occasions without any Rules but those of their own insatiable Avarice and Beggary. . . . It was not plainly affirmed . . . that the People in New-England were all Slaves, and the only difference between them and Slaves is their not being bought and sold; and it was a Maxim delivered in open Court unto us by one of the Council that we must not think the Priviledges of english men would follow us to the End of the World. . . .

> Nathaniel Byfield, "An Account of The Late Revolution in New-England, and The Declaration of The Gentlemen, Merchants and Inhabitants of Boston, and The County

immediately proclaim William and Mary monarchs, rumors began to spread of a Catholic plot "to surrender the colony to France," and residents of both Suffolk County on Long Island and Queen's and Westchester counties (Dutch strongholds) removed royal officials from office. The governor proved unable to deal with the popular uprising that soon spread through the colony. On May 30, he even threatened to burn New York City if the people's attitudes did not change. The next day, New York militia companies seized the city fort, and Nicholson fled to England.

The militia captains assumed joint command of the fort. They rotated leadership of the group among themselves and established a council of safety, composed of delegates from the counties. On June 28, they appointed Jacob Leisler captain of the fort, and on August 15 they gave him the title and authority of commander-in-chief. Leisler had arrived in the colony from Germany in 1660. He married a rich widow and became a leading merchant, but his connections were with the older Dutch leaders rather than with the new Anglo-Dutch elite. And he faced opposition from the beginning. Though the Albany traders supported the Glorious Revolution, they distrusted Leisler, fearing that his impetuous behavior would disrupt their fragile relationship with the Iroquois and that they would lose their monopoly over the fur trade. The town recognized Leisler's leadership only after Indians and French raided Schenectady on February 9.

Adjacent. April 18, 1689." in Charles M. Andrews, ed., *Narratives of the Insurrections, 1675–1690* (New York: Barnes & Noble, 1915), 177–8.

> Blessing the great God of heaven and earth who has pleased to make your Majesty so happy an instrument in our deliverance from Tyranny, popery and slavery, and to put it into your Royall breasts to undertake so glorious a work towards the reestablishment and preservation of the true protestant Religion, liberty and property . . . , we having also long groaned under the same oppression, having been governed of late, most part, by papists who had in a most arbitrary way subverted our ancient priviledges making us in effect slaves to their will contrary to the laws of England; and this was chiefly effected by those who are known ennemies to our Religion and liberty. . . .

"Address of the Militia of New-York to William and Mary," in John R. Brodhead, ed., *Documents Relative to The Colonial History of the State of New-York,* 15 vols. (Albany, NY: Weed, Parsons, and Company, 1853–1887), 3:583.

Leisler governed the colony for two years, proclaiming William and Mary, reorganizing the court system, and presiding over a popularly elected legislature that voted to negate the special privileges of the New York City and Albany merchants. Finally, he convened an intercolonial conference at Albany to plan an attack on Canada, the supposed center of the feared popish conspiracy to subvert English liberties in the colonies. In all of this Leisler found support among the older Dutch settlers, small farmers, city workers, and a few wealthy landowning families. The mercantile elite, though, succeeded in convincing the king that Leisler was in fact a rebel, and his own actions lent credence to these accusations. He refused, for instance, to surrender the city fort to royal troops who arrived in January 1691, giving up command only when Gov. Henry Slaughter came in March. By then it was too late. Slaughter had Leisler and nine others tried, and the court ordered both Leisler and his son-in-law Jacob Milbourne executed (Parliament reversed the convictions in 1695).

The legacy of this bitter dispute shaped the course of New York politics for decades to come. Leisler had broken the mercantile monopoly and established a tradition of broad-based, popular political participation. But he was not interested in personal liberties or an egalitarian society. He revived the elective assembly, for instance, simply because he needed money and dared not try to raise it on his own. In the end, the rebellion was motivated largely by a deep economic and religious hostility to the ruling elite. Leisler freed imprisoned debtors, called for the popular election of justices of the peace and militia officers, and sought to increase the role of ordinary people, particularly artisans, in city government. Mobs attacked the property of the wealthiest merchants, and anti-Leislerian propaganda focused on his use of the "rabble" and "drunken crue," as the elite referred to Leisler's supporters.

Much like the revolt in Massachusetts, then, the New York uprising reflected attempts to unite a divided colony torn by economic and social dissent. There were differences, however. The gaps between rulers and ruled were wider in New York, the discontent more intense; the Massachusetts assembly was more powerful and jealousy guarded its privileges. But both colonies (and Maryland as well) found it useful to focus blame for the disorder at least in part on the feared French, Indians, and Catholics. In each case, certain themes emerge clearly: anti-Catholicism, popular discontent against oligarchical and authoritarian rule, and a violent, concerted reaction against centralized imperial control. These themes would emerge again with more profound consequences some seven decades later. For now, they helped establish a new and more participatory tradition of Protestant, popular rule based on English liberties, charters, and the sacred British constitution.

European Conflict Comes To America
British, French, and Iroquois Expansion

The British colonists had more to deal with than internal conflict and upheaval during the last decades of the century. As the British moved to consolidate control over their North American empire, they inevitably came into conflict with the two existing powers in the region—the French and the Indians (particularly the Iroquois). French and British visions of American empire first clashed when both laid claims to Nova Scotia in the early years of the seventeenth century; the English captured the area and returned it to the French three times before 1670. The last exchange came when the English defeated the French-allied Dutch in the Second Anglo-Dutch War, a victory that also removed a buffer between French and English colonies and brought the two nations' fur traders into direct competition.

New York now became the stage where French, British, and Iroquois interests played themselves out. The English directly controlled the Hudson River Indians, but the Iroquois mediated the colony's relations with other tribes, requiring that the Susquehannocks and others to the west and northeast deal with New York only through them. Iroquois warriors even raided the Mohegans in Connecticut and the Piscataways in Maryland to enforce their demands. Gov. Edmund Andros was the key figure in establishing better relations with the Indians. Andros made overtures to the anti-French members of the Iroquois, and in 1675, he formed an alliance with the Mohawks. He helped end Iroquois conflicts with the Mahicans and the Susquehannocks. By the end of the 1670s, Indians and whites were partners in a "Covenant Chain" that had stabilized Indian relations throughout the middle colonies. The Iroquois saw the system as an organization of equals between themselves and the whites, and they won substantial benefits from the arrangement. They achieved secure borders, solidified their position as brokers between other Indians and the English, and gained safe access to Albany traders. The whites may have naively viewed the chain as a means of establishing dominion over the Indians, but the Iroquois viewed the English colonies as part of the chain.

Indeed, the Iroquois brought their own complex agendas to the negotiating table. Iroquois mourning wars, which, as we have seen, assuaged grief and replaced individuals lost to disease, war, or natural death, were dramatically altered by increased contact with Europeans. By the 1640s, the Iroquois had lost almost half their people to epidemics, and these thousands had to be replaced through an institution that had previously dealt with only occasional loss of life. The need for so many adoptees meant that warfare would no longer be a sporadic, brief event but rather a constant search for new Indians to fill the gaps in village and family. The use of firearms raised the stakes still further, replacing ceremonial, bloodless warfare with battles that brought much higher casualties and death. More death brought more mourning wars. Indian involvement in white trading networks dragged the ritualistic mourning wars into the framework of white military conflict. As European goods became essential parts of Indian economies, the Iroquois extended their search for furs into the territories of rival tribes. Beginning in the 1640s, they initiated the Beaver Wars against the St. Lawrence River Algonquians, the Huron, and other tribes to the west and north.

The Iroquois had earlier tried to convince the Hurons to join them. Rebuffed, they all but wiped them out during the 1650s. In the early 1660s, they attacked the New England Abenakis, the sub-artic Algonquians, the upper Mississippi Sioux, and various tribes near Virginia. By the mid-1660s, two-thirds of the people in some Iroquois villages were adoptees. Even so, mourning warfare failed to maintain a stable population. In the 1640s, the Mohawks had seven to eight hundred warriors; in the late 1670s, they had only about three hundred. Warfare had become dysfunctional in this new environment. Raids broke down into murderous violence, Iroquois killing and eating their enemies on the spot or murdering them during the gauntlet ceremony.

All the while, they continued to ambush Indians carrying furs to Montreal, selling the captured goods to the English and the Dutch. In 1666, Viceroy de Tracy decided to attack the Mohawks, the closest Iroquois tribe to Montreal. He had only six hundred troops and local militia who were completely unaccustomed to the American wilderness, and he planned his attack for the depths of the Canadian winter. The men suffered horribly even before they reached the village. Their noses, ears, and fingers were completely frozen, and some had to be carried back, their legs cut by the ice or their arms and hands frostbitten to uselessness. The Iroquois successfully ambushed a second attempt, and the Mohawk village escaped unscathed. De Tracy refused to accept defeat. He lead a force of thirteen hundred French soldiers deeper into Mohawk country and burned four villages. Starving, the Indians sued for peace, and the other Iroquois nations quickly followed suit.

Thus, by the early 1670s, the French were at peace with the Iroquois, and they began to expand their activities in the west. The voyageurs passed beyond the Great Lakes and even the Great Plains, reaching the Rocky Mountains. They built white birch canoes that provided them with the fastest transportation available and the most efficient means of carrying furs eastward. This expansion of trade occurred just as the European demand for furs was increasing, particularly for the more luxurious hides of fox, martin, otter, and ermine. In the cold northern climes, these pelts were heavier and more luxurious than their southern counterparts and thus brought higher prices. A virtual flood of Canadians left the relative comfort of their cabins for the exciting life of the coureurs de bois, trading and even living with tribes far to the west. The government, under the leadership of the Comte de Frontenac, fully supported these activities.

At this juncture, Andros succeeded in establishing the new English relationship with the Iroquois. The French were unable to disrupt the Iroquois-English trade, and they faced even more serious threats in the west. In 1680, an Iroquois force destroyed an Illinois village protected by the French and drove the French forces from their forts on the Ohio River. The Iroquois began to boast that they would drive the French out of New France itself. Governor Frontenac found himself in a delicate situation, since he enjoyed a profitable personal trade with the Iroquois. His indecisiveness convinced the Iroquois that the French were too weak to respond, and the Indians extended their attacks.

It was the English who let the French off the hook, at least temporarily. Until now, New York's governors had been willing to allow the Iroquois to continue their trade with the French. Gov. Thomas Dongan determined to change that policy. He also moved to establish control over the interior and to substitute English influence there for French. He convinced both Albany and the Iroquois to support the policy change, and in the early 1680s, the Five Nations began to attack their western neighbors, the Illinois, Ottawa, and Miami tribes, in support of English goals. Even in these circumstances, the Iroquois continued to play the game, allowing the French governors to call them "their children" and affirming their continued independence. "We are born free . . . ," they asserted, "[w]e neither depend on Yonnondio [the French governor] nor Corlaer [the English governor]. We may go where we please, and carry with us whom we please, and buy and sell what we please."[15] Clearly, though, shifting English priorities had disturbed the area's political equilibrium. The problem worsened when the French invaded Seneca territory in western New York and financial pressures prevented Dongan from aiding his allies. The French ravaged Seneca land and forced them to sign a peace treaty in 1688. Events in Europe soon undermined this brief respite from hostilities.

The War of the League of Augsburg (King William's War) (1689-1697)

William of Orange was no friend of Louis XIV's; he had successfully resisted a French invasion of the United Provinces during the late 1670s. Eager to control his rival's European ambitions, William now joined the League of Augsburg, a coalition of England, Spain, the Holy Roman emperor, and Sweden to counter Louis's invasion of the Holy Roman Empire. The stakes were significant in America as well, as France and England fought for control of the fur trade in the northeast, the western hunting territories, and the Great Lakes trading routes.

The French king decided to concentrate his main efforts against the English and their American colonies, laying plans for a coordinated naval and land assault against both Albany and Manhattan. He reappointed Frontenac (recalled in 1682) governor and military commander. While the French fleet was battling storms in the Atlantic, however, the Iroquois took charge of things. Armed by the English, in July 1689 they attacked the settlement of Lachine, just a few miles from Montreal. They burned homes, killed women and children, and mutilated the bodies. War parties attacked French settlements throughout the summer, surprising inhabitants in their fields and destroying their crops and homes. Their successes forced the French to abandon several of their western posts during 1689.

Frontenac responded ineffectively. He divided his forces and attacked Schenectady, New York, and two villages on the Maine coast. The Schenectady massacre, on February 8, 1690, struck terror in English hearts: "The cruelties committed at said place no pen can write nor tongue express. Ye women big with child, ripped up and yet children alive thrown into ye flames, and their heads dashed in pieces against ye doors and windows."[16] Sixty-two men, women, and children lost their lives there, and another one hundred died in the attack on Fort Royal (Portland, Maine).

In the spring of 1690, the British planned a land and sea assault against the French that was to include substantial troop and supply contributions from the colonies. But only a few volunteers showed up from New York and Connecticut, supplies were short, and the force got only as far as Lake Champlain before turning back. In May 1690, Gov. William Phips of Massachusetts led an expedition that captured Port Royal, Nova Scotia, but a subsequent two thousand-man expedition against Quebec failed, the siege called off because of disease, French reinforcements, and a lack of munitions and supplies. The French retook Port Royal in 1691.

By 1692, the Canadians had also learned how to deal with their Indian foes; instead of waiting for events to come to them, they began to lay ambushes for the Iroquois at river crossings and portages. That year alone, they took more than one hundred Iroquois scalps. In 1693, French troops attacked four Mohawk villages, burning longhouses and food supplies. Shortly after, the Iroquois sued for peace. The Indian confederation's losses had mounted, lessening their ability to resist French attacks. Their English allies did not have enough manpower to help them and could only supply them with arms and ammunition from Albany. Indeed, though they had learned of it in advance, the English had not even warned the Mohawks of the 1693 invasion.

The French-Iroquois truce proved to be brief. The French had seriously weakened their position by attempting to trade directly with the Sioux and Assiniboine tribes of the western plains, thus bypassing and alienating their allies, the Huron and Ottawa middlemen. By 1695, the Iroquois were again attacking Canadian villages. The French responded by sending two thousand troops against the Onondaga, burning villages and crops. The Iroquois again sued for peace, but though both sides were desperate for an end to hostilities, neither trusted the other and negotiations dragged on. The Canadians were on the verge of economic collapse, while between 1689 and 1700, the Iroquois lost at least sixteen hundred people out of a population of about eighty-five hundred. The French, meanwhile, continued to harass English frontier settlements, and in 1696, a French naval expedition captured Fort William Henry at Pemaquid, Maine.

The military struggle finally exhausted combatants in both the Old and the New World. The Peace of Ryswick (1697) established the status quo antebellum and allowed the French to keep Acadia, St. John's in Newfoundland, and partial control of Hudson Bay. They also retained the western trading posts, though here they had to confront certain economic difficulties. The European market had become glutted with furs. Politically, it was impossible to abandon the posts, but economically, things simply could not go on as before. The French eliminated the annual fur trade meetings and sharply cut prices for beaver pelts. For their part, the English colonies, particularly Massachusetts, had suffered traumatically. King Philip's War, the formation of the Dominion of New England, and the Salem witchcraft trials (see chapter 7) had sapped the colony's emotional strength. War brought more death, an influx of refugees from the frontier, and burdensome taxes. The General Court even petitioned London (in vain) for charitable contributions for war victims.

The Iroquois were even bigger losers. Half of their warriors had fallen to battle or disease, and they had to abandon any thought of gaining complete control of the western fur trade. Once again, however, the confederation found a way out of its dilemma. In 1701, it struck a separate peace agreement with the French known as the Grand Settlement. The Iroquois agreed to restrict their hunting to the region east of Detroit (though the French never enforced this), and both sides agreed that the governor of New France would arbitrate future disputes, avoiding armed conflict. Finally, the Iroquois promised to remain neutral in any future wars between the English and the French.

At the same time they were gaining some breathing room in their fight against the French, the Iroquois sent another delegation to Albany. There, they agreed to renew their military alliance with the English, to solidify Iroquois-New York trading relations, and to allow passage of western Indians through their own land to trade at Albany. They also gave the English a "deed" to the same western hunting territories they had granted to the French at Montreal (west from present-day Erie, Pennsylvania, through Detroit to Mackinac, Michigan), with the English agreeing to defend Iroquois hunting rights on those same lands. A third series of negotiations in Philadelphia produced a trade agreement with Pennsylvania in 1704.

While these agreements provided something for both European powers—at the least, a neutral buffer between the two—the Iroquois gained the most. The settlements brought an end to warfare, guaranteed them the right to hunt in the western territories, created potential trade for them with the tribes passing through their territory to Albany, gave them access to markets in both English and French colonies, and maintained their neutrality in future European wars. They turned to the French when it was necessary to arbitrate disagreements with the western Indians, while Iroquois headmen restrained young warriors in their desires to pursue more violent solutions. The confederation came close to becoming involved in European conflicts on only a few occasions over the next several decades. Twice during Queen Anne's War, in 1709 and 1711, the Indians agreed to join English expeditions in retaliation for continued French aggression—but neither of those expeditions actually took place. Even in 1719, when the French built a trading house at Niagara at the invitation of the pro-French Seneca, the Iroquois headmen settled for a similar English fort at Oswego to counter French influence.

In the meantime, Iroquois population stabilized, enlarged in 1713 by the arrival of fifteen hundred Tuscaroras from the Carolinas who were seeking refuge after their defeat by the whites; in 1722, the Iroquois adopted them as the confederacy's sixth nation. The mourning war began to assume its traditional functions again, and the Iroquois vented the aggressive urges of their young warriors against the Catawbas and other tribes of the Virginia and Carolina frontiers. These southern raids provided enough captives to keep the population in balance.

The decades immediately following the English Civil War witnessed profound social and political instability in several of the British mainland colonies. The settlers of the Chesapeake, New England, and New York colonies all found themselves confronting disturbing questions about their own identities, frightened by serious threats from the Indians, embittered by internal factionalism, and challenged by British interference. In each case, the result helped define the social systems and political beliefs that would carry the colonies well into the next century. Finally, the emergence of the colonies as a theater of international warfare was an omen that bode only ill, for Indians as well as whites. As the seventeenth century drew to a close, all North Americans looked guardedly to the future.

❧ *Chapter Seven* ❧

Cultures in Seventeenth-Century America

A society's culture consists of its "normative structure of values, customs, and meanings. . . ."[1] This structure includes material artifacts such as buildings; social mores such as family, gender, and child-rearing practices; and essential beliefs about religion, work, education, wealth, and power. These cultural expressions must be studied as part of two broader problems in seventeenth-century America: the transfer of culture from Europe to the New World and the relationship between this culture-in-transition to the cultural and material conditions already existing in America. Some of these issues have already been addressed in the chapters dealing with New World settlement. In the following pages, we will further explore these themes as they emerge in seven different cultural areas: the centrality of community and order to the early American experience; the relationships between Europeans, Indians, and the land; the rural rhythms of agricultural life; the structure of family and gender beliefs; the significance of magic and witchcraft; the varied expressions of material culture; and the explication of cultural values in education and literature.

Community And Order

At its simplest level, community is a "web of associations"[2] that bind people together within some identifiable territory and help them communicate and share common interests. Such associations also reflect the limitations imposed by social customs, religious beliefs, and economic values. In this sense, historians' traditional portrayal of the early American landscape—community in New England, chaos in the Chesapeake—is seriously misleading. It is more accurate to argue that the two regions simply reflected different expressions of community. Indeed, both were obsessive in their search for order and stability.

New Englanders almost immediately formed clearly identifiable communities, adopting the pattern of life prevalent in East Anglia. Towns and hamlets dominated the early landscape. From the beginning, most of these people pursued order and unity with a shared single-mindedness, and it was the local community—the neighborhood, the town, and the county—that enforced this desired order. In these communities, everything and every person had its proper place, promoting a sense of organic unity and hierarchical balance. Any disruption of this order, any attempt by individuals to move beyond their proper place, threatened the community itself.

The neighborhood served as the first level of enforcement. Disruptive behavior often brought shame upon the individual from those who daily associated with him or her. Neighbors found it easy enough to simply ignore a busybody or to shun the irreligious farmer down the road who persisted in getting drunk on the Sabbath. Often, though, villagers openly confronted someone who disrupted the social peace, and not all targets of such censure took correction calmly. One villager threatened to "set his house on fire and run away by the light" to escape "the hell hounds"[3] who were his neighbors.

If this immediate, personal form of control failed, neighbors most often turned to the "gentle mediation" (arbitration) of personal differences. The disputants chose two or three of their fellow residents (each picked one, and sometimes the county court chose a third) to help them resolve their difficulties and preserve communal harmony and consensus. The mediators might deal with an issue as mundane as assessing the damage done by runaway swine. In more complex cases, they would interview witnesses as well as the contending parties. Everyone realized this saved time and money, since going to court could be a long and expensive process. Rebekah Whipple and John Whipple (relatives) of Providence submitted their dispute to arbitration because "to bring their difference into a Course of law. . . would be greatly troublesome to all partyes. . . and great charge would Ensue upon it. . . and would cause Annimossityes of spirits, and Alination in affection amongst Relations."[4]

If gentle mediation failed, town and church officials became involved in the dispute. Though more formal in their methods, selectmen and ministers still sought to resolve conflict peacefully before it spread beyond the community. The Bay Colony's laws ordered the local constable, for instance, to suppress profanity and debauchery, investigate strangers, "execute warrants, deliver writs, make arrests, and summon town meetings. . . ," and "collect taxes, organize elections, look after lost goods, recover stray animals. . . ."[5] He was expected to visit and inspect all households every three months and call upon town inhabitants to assist him whenever necessary. The grand jury (citizens who brought their own information as observers of neighborhood and community behavior) aided him in performing his duties.

Residents of all the colonies turned to the county courts in more rancorous disputes, such as those involving slander or oral defamation. Eighteenth-century Americans showed an unusual concern for their personal reputations, undoubtedly because gossip and lies about one's character and actions were so difficult to counter and could be so destructive of one's livelihood. Hence, the suits were particularly aimed at restoring the individual's good name and regaining the esteem of his or her neighbors. In 1701, a Pennsylvania couple complained to the court that slander had caused them to suffer "much in their Reputation, and by that means in their Trade."[6] In 1678, the Boston shipmaster Samuel Legg charged that James Flood had unjustly questioned how Legg treated his employees, discouraging several men from seeking work with him. Thomas Chandler sued Job Tyler for calling him "a base, lying, cheating knave. . . [who] had gotten all his estate by cheating, etc."[7] Sometimes, not surprisingly, people sued one another for simple name-calling, such as in the case of the person who called Erasmus James of Massachusetts a "cheating rogue, one-eyed rogue, one-eyed dog."[8]

Personal assaults, theft, and crimes of violence were rare; crimes against order, though, were very common—violations of the Sabbath, disturbing the peace, sexual offenses, idleness, lying, and drunkenness. Even the region's criminal codes were far less violent than those prevalent in England and other European countries. British common law punished hundreds of transgressions with the death penalty, but the 1648 Massachusetts law code punished only thirteen crimes with death. Still, seventeenth-century punishments were certainly excessive by today's standards. Maiming was common, including "the slitting of the nostrils, the amputation of ears, the branding of the face or hands."[9] The General Court ordered Quakers branded on the face and others "burned very deep with a red-hot iron with H. for here-sie."[10] Less threatening offenders found themselves in stocks or pillories with letters on their clothing signifying their particular crime. A dishonest baker was the victim of one of the most imaginative such punishments; he had to stand in the stocks with a lump of dough on his head.

As the population grew and settlements began to move beyond the initial community boundaries, new types of conflict threatened communities throughout New England. After 1660, the decreasing availability of land resulted in a substantial increase in litigation over title claims, a problem exacerbated by the lack of uniform recording procedures. In 1679, Richard Russell of Gloucester petitioned the county court, complaining that the Manchester town meeting had ignored his attempts to determine the boundaries of land he owned there. The growing number of absentee owners and proprietors in urbanized areas, such as Essex County, added to the tension. In 1691, Henry Rhodes of Lynn despaired of settling a boundary dispute with his neighbor James Taylor because Taylor was never there—he lived elsewhere and someone else managed his land. So Rhodes and his son removed a section of fence and led some of their horses onto the disputed land. The county court awarded Taylor damages.

Conflicts over the formation of new precincts and towns often created disagreements too bitter and complex for any local group of citizens to resolve, and ministers and their congregations seemed to show up in court with alarming and increasing frequency. In 1677, for instance, Jonathan Platts brought a complaint against Rev. Samuel Phillips for accusing several townspeople of cheating on the collection of his pay. Increasingly, it seems, residents almost casually turned to the courts as a solution of first recourse. While the earliest settlers viewed litigation as divisive, second- and third-generation New Englanders increasingly turned to court action as a less disruptive and more impersonal way of resolving often bitter personal disputes.

A few of these disputes remain noteworthy mostly for the humorous light they cast on these increasingly contentious settlers. In 1683, the town of Lynn witnessed a confrontation between Benjamin Farr and Josiah Witter over whose land a proposed new road should pass through. The selectmen decided that Witter's property offered the best passage, so they laid out the route. Witter's tenant, apparently at Witter's behest, "went along and pulled up the stakes."[11] The selectmen ordered a second survey and decided that discretion was the better part of improved transportation, because this time they chose Farr's land. The town and Farr sued each other for trespass, and Farr won.

Even the county courts failed to find peaceful solutions to some of these problems, and often the General Court found it necessary to intervene in acrimonious disputes over such issues as the disposition of common fields to later generations and to nonproprietors. When the town of Andover decided in 1675 that just having a house in town was no longer enough to receive land from the commons and that a town meeting would have to determine the division of shares, several residents petitioned the court in protest. Most commonly, the court found itself in the middle of rancorous disagreements over town boundaries and taxes. In 1664, seventeen residents of Marlborough asked the court to appoint a committee to study a long-standing dispute over the payment of taxes. Eighteen others opposed the motion and submitted a counterprotest. It took the court ten years to settle the dispute.

As these few examples remind us, preserving a sense of community was not an easy task for New Englanders. It was all but impossible to establish even a basic sense of community in the early Chesapeake, according to many historians. It was, they argue, a region bereft of community, torn by greed, ambition, and an unbridled pursuit of individual gain, where people settled in patterns far removed from the concentrated town settlements of New England. To some degree, these patterns were likely unplanned—the collection of small market villages, large plantations, and small farms that came to dominate the Chesapeake landscape closely resembled the landscape of the south and west of England, where the majority of these settlers came from. Equally important, tobacco cultivation required much larger and more widely spaced farms and plantations than did the corn and grain culture of the northern colonies.

Recent work has made it clear that a form of community did in fact exist in the Chesapeake, at least in Middlesex County, Virginia, when it was settled at mid-century and on Virginia's Eastern Shore from the earliest years. A "community" in both regions was four to five miles in radius, conforming roughly to the geographical area of a parish. Within this range, settlers participated in everyday economic exchanges and parish duties. Smaller neighborhood units focused on a dozen or two families, clustered within a few miles of each other around creeks, streams, and earlier settlements. These people visited each other in times of illness, helped out during personal crises, and spent their leisure time together. They did all of this despite the considerable obstacles to community that characterized the Chesapeake environment: distance, the scarcity of horses, and poor roads. Planter-merchants had the most extensive contacts with other areas of the Chesapeake, while women, tenant farmers, and small landowners rarely strayed far from home.

Community ties emerged relatively soon after settlement on the Eastern Shore. New landholders had generally lived in the area for several years and had become fully socialized into the mores of the community before they purchased land. Most residents remained in the area, and tenants who stayed long enough had an excellent chance of acquiring their own land. The wealthy dominated high political office, but even the smallest landowners served in local offices.

Settlers first moved into Middlesex County in the early 1650s, and in 1687 more than half the families still had no relatives in the county. But by 1724, more than half were linked by blood to five or more other families; the average head of household had thirty-one relatives living in the county. While these people did not come together as often as their fellow colonists to the north, weddings, court days, and other social occasions provided them with frequent opportunities to celebrate their identity as a community.

As in New England, these extended neighborhoods bore the daily responsibility for enforcing order, and residents often reported cases of servant abuse or births out of wedlock to the justices of the peace. In 1653 on the Eastern Shore, John Williams and John Brown investigated cries of pain they heard coming from their neighbor John Towls's land. They found his servant, Susanna Dowdridge, lying on the ground, her clothes torn and her body covered with blood and mud; she presumably had been beaten by Towls. They took care of her when he refused to do so. On another occasion, Benjamin Cowdery's neighbors tired of his constant verbal abuse and took him before the county court, which ordered him to post bond ensuring a more civilized demeanor. Settlers knew whose livestock had trampled their wheat or tobacco, and the neighborhood made sure the offender made good for the damage.

Because of the distances involved, county government was even more critical here than in New England. County officials included justices of the peace, sheriffs, clerks of the court, and such minor figures as constables and tithe takers. Justices took depositions, issued warrants, and disposed of minor disputes, while monthly courts collectively settled petty criminal offenses and civil suits. For more serious disputes, residents turned to the sheriff, an office that rotated among the justices. The sheriff controlled courts and juries, issued writs, and called elections. He also collected the taxes that paid for local administration and services. Finally, he administered the punishments ordered by the courts. Punishments in the Chesapeake depended upon the social status of the individual involved. For serious crimes, the literate could claim the traditional privilege of benefit of the clergy and escape with being branded on the thumb, but the poor and illiterate were hanged. The Chesapeake courts, following English common law, provided the death penalty for hundreds of crimes.

As elsewhere, slander was treated seriously, especially when it involved economic interests. In 1679, George Tyte of Maryland told the court that slanderous assaults on his character would "bring him into trouble vexation scandall and infamy, by which he should be renderd a person not fitt to be imployed or intrusted as aforesaid, not to trade and traffique. . . . "[12] John Lawnes sued Amy Cottell in the Northampton court when she called him a rogue and accused him of falsifying her bill; the court ordered her to apologize and pay him four hundred pounds of tobacco for his expenses. Sexual innuendo of one sort or another was a frequent component of suits for slander. John Gould of Maryland sued Giles Glover for calling his wife a whore—"the greatest infamy that a malitious toung Can Cast upon a woman. . . . "[13] The Northampton County, Virginia, court placed John Remis in the stocks and ordered him to apologize to Goodwife Williams for calling her "a whore and a base whore." Of course, she had first called him "knave and base knave."[14] The servant Mary Jolly brought suit against a fellow servant, Francis Millicent, accusing him of spreading stories that her recent illness was due to pregnancy. Jolly won the suit, and the court ordered Millicent to receive thirty lashes, to pay court costs, and to publicly ask Jolly's forgiveness in church. Finally, the court ordered Mary Rayman to ask forgiveness of Anne Johnson for saying that Johnson was "naught[y]" with her "black shaggy dog."[15] The gentry fashioned many of these laws, of course, to enhance their own position in society, to protect their reputations, and to control the behavior of their social inferiors. They alone were allowed to be drunk in public.

Quaker settlements in the Delaware Valley comprised the third dominant culture in the seventeenth-century British mainland colonies. Here again, community and order were the normative values, and the British cultural heritage was crucial to the formulation of New World mores. Quaker communities enforced order with less coercion and more cooperation than in either New England or the Chesapeake. A Quaker's reputation was based upon love, peace, and neighborliness. Quakers were also far more tolerant of diversity than were other American settlers; they accepted differences and preached "order as mutual forbearance."[16] Even the informal regulation of society, as we have seen, depended relatively little on coercion.

While the Quaker community was even more traditional than that of New England in shunning political and legal forms of mediation, in other ways it was distinctly modern. Quakers tolerated diversity. They may have disapproved of or failed to understand the beliefs and actions of those who differed from their own way of life, but they accepted such differences as reality. Even within their own society, they understood that coercion and avoidance of conflict did little to resolve disagreements.

Europeans, Indians, And The New World
Altering the Indian

Cultural exchange between Europeans and Indians began with the earliest physical contact and the introduction of European disease. Smallpox, measles, influenza, and whooping cough spread to the Indians on European kettles, blankets, beads, and other trading goods. Disease was a key factor in Indian-white contact throughout North America. Hernando de Soto, exploring the Carolina chiefdom of Cofitachequi in 1540, discovered that two villages had been recently decimated by smallpox. About ten thousand Indians inhabited the coastal Carolinas in 1685; by 1700, there were only six hundred left. The Catawbas, further inland, saw their numbers shrink from five thousand to five hundred by 1759. Even the Cherokees, relatively isolated at first from white contact, fell from thirty-two thousand strong to sixteen thousand by the 1690s and to only seven thousand by 1763. The Creeks were somewhat more successful in protecting themselves from the impact of disease but only because their location farther inland allowed them to limit their contacts with Europeans in time to prevent the introduction of deadly diseases. In New England, the ravages of smallpox decimated the Indian population even before whites settled those shores permanently. About 1 million Indians were living east of the Mississippi in 1600. In 1763, only 150,000 were left.

The impact of disease extended beyond the tragic loss of life. As village populations were decimated and the survivors weakened, Indians missed key phases of their subsistence cycles. Times of scarcity that previously produced hunger now brought death. Epidemics disrupted kinship and authority networks, and the religious basis of Indian culture was called into question when shamans' powers proved useless against the new diseases. Indians often turned to traditional cures with disastrous results. The sweat lodge, the early equivalent of today's sauna and a site of spiritual purification for Indians, proved to be the worst possible treatment for smallpox. Many smallpox victims, particularly in the south, committed suicide. In the end, European disease paved the way for settlement by clearing the land of large numbers of potentially resistive Indians and by weakening, perhaps fatally, the cultural backbone of those who survived.

Indian culture also suffered from the growing dominance of European languages. The English believed that their language would help them civilize the Indians, because "changing of the language of a barbarous people, into the speech of a more civil and potent nation" was one method "to reduce such a people unto the civility and religion of the prevailing nation."[17] The settlers gradually introduced their own symbols into their dealings with the weakened Indians. Virginia issued medals to friendly Indians, so that the settlers would not have to decipher tribal markings and other symbols to distinguish friend from foe. New York used red ribbons for the same purpose. Both white and Indian symbols continued to be used simultaneously for some time, with Indians delivering symbolic belts of wampum and giving speeches simultaneously. At first, the Indians succeeded in controlling these diplomatic exchanges, coming to conferences when they pleased, performing their preliminary rituals, and giving long speeches filled with metaphors "that invested kinship terms and everyday objects with deeper meaning."[18] Whites sat impatiently through these ceremonies. As soon as the colonists gained control of the situation, they forced the Indians to abandon such time-consuming rituals. Indians then came to meetings when they were told to, and the exchange of gifts came to signify submission rather than communication. In the end, the English language and symbolism triumphed. Most Indians remained illiterate, and colonists readily imposed their control on Indians in legal documents and exchanges of all sorts.

Whites also succeeded in imposing a European legal system on Indians. While they remained physically distant from the settlers, Indians could essentially ignore the white legal system, and at first, settlers had to treat the Indians with some semblance of fairness, since retaliation remained a possibility. The New England colonies established Indian courts. Indians sat on juries, served as constables, and gave court testimony in cases involving their people. The courts even occasionally punished colonists for unfair treatment of Indians. As whites gained the ascendancy in numbers and military might, the relationship changed. After the trauma of King Philip's War, Massachusetts replaced Indian courts with individual white guardians, giving these men extensive personal powers over the Indians. The government established curfews and restrictions on travel and assembly. The Indians themselves provided another reason for whites to hasten their legal control: some learned English law only too well, registering their land and writing wills to pass it on to the next generation, even suing whites in court for trespassing and uncollected debts. But the colony moved quickly to close off such recourse, and by 1700, courts were imposing blatantly unequal sentences for similar crimes. Few whites were ever again convicted of crimes against Indians.

Altering the Land

The two cultures clashed most dramatically in their attitudes toward wealth. Indians embraced a communal notion of land and wealth; their sense of personal ownership extended only to items they could carry with them as they moved. By contrast, even in the relatively traditional society of New England, whites embraced a notion of wealth that was based on accumulation and personal ownership. They regarded the land as the source of their well-being and as an investment for the future—if only for the future of their own children. They sought to shape and pattern the land, building fences, carefully bounding their fields, and consciously manipulating the environment to give the landscape a productive purpose. Land was capital. It required care and attention to produce an investment. For Puritans, the desired return was communal and religious prosperity that would guarantee continued security for their children and their children's children. For Virginians, it was a hierarchical, exploitative community that allowed the select few to accumulate vast wealth and power. For Quakers, it was both material prosperity and a communally based love ideal that would allow them to prosper in communion with their god and without harming their fellow humans.

Europeans brought with them ideological, cultural, and biological baggage that permanently transformed the American landscape. Early explorers and settlers ecstatically described the abundance of trees and the variety of species they saw when they landed; in contrast to the shrinking forests of England, vast stands of hemlocks, hickories, oaks, and pines graced the land. The colonists responded by using the trees freely and indiscriminately—they made tables, for instance, two and a half feet wide from a single board! Wood fires warmed colonial hearths; the typical New England home used thirty to forty cords a year. Wood fueled such business enterprises as barrel and shingle production. Craftsmen used only the best quality woods to produce furniture that today remains a marvel of quality construction; farmers used less desirable lumber to fence their lands. Whatever failed to meet the colonists' critical standards was left to rot. In this way, early New Englanders depleted whole stands of white pines, hickories, and cedar; large white oak trees all but vanished.

As New Englanders cleared their fields and plundered the forests, they inadvertently changed the climate. With fewer trees, the sun warmed and dried the soil. The lack of a protective forest canopy to moderate temperatures and reduce wind speed meant that the surface of the land became hotter in summer and colder in winter. And as winter neared its end, the sun melted snow more quickly, leaving still-frozen ground exposed. The spring runoff became a torrent without soft soil to absorb its excess, increasing erosion and flooding.

European animals also altered the land. Hogs, previously unknown in America, compacted the soil and reduced its oxygen content. Cattle drives stamped down the land, and cattle and sheep grazing cleared the land for European species of grasses and weeds; most of the weeds that drive twentieth-century gardeners crazy came from Europe—dandelions, chickweeds, nightshades, and stinging nettles. English cattle grazed more closely and densely than native animals, encouraging the growth of woody, thorny plants that proved difficult to remove and could overrun an entire pasture in relatively short order.

European insects and plant diseases also accompanied humans on their transatlantic migration. The Hessian fly ultimately destroyed wheat cultivation in Connecticut, and other crop diseases, such as the oft-bemoaned "blast" (black stem rust), could decimate a wheat crop in any given year. Among many other pests, colonists brought the black fly (the bane of Maine fishers and campers to this day), cockroaches, and the gray rat to these shores.

New England agricultural techniques combined traditional European methods with others borrowed from the Indians. Settlers adopted maize, potatoes, tobacco, peanuts, pumpkins, squashes, tomatoes, and watermelons from the Indians. Corn proved to have more diverse uses than European grains. It was easier to grow, provided a higher yield per acre, ripened earlier, and required less soil preparation. At first, farmers also adopted the Indian method of planting corn in small hills two to four feet apart, with other crops in between. They soon abandoned this practice, though, perhaps because of the seemingly disordered, irregular picture it produced in the fields. Instead, they cross-plowed their fields and planted corn at the intersections of the furrows, in the traditional European pattern.

Colonists followed the rhythms of the sun and the seasons in their work, performing the same tasks day in and day out. Farmers began plowing in late March, then harrowed the fields to further crumble the earth and prepare it for seeding. After sowing, they repaired farm buildings and harvested the winter wheat crop. During the summer months, they weeded the crops, cut and dried the hay and carted it to the barn. Harvest came in September and October, and in late fall, they slaughtered animals to provide meat for the coming winter. December and January were relatively quiet months, but farmers were busy in February with calving and foaling.

These patterns contrasted sharply with the seasonal lives of Indians. Europeans lived their more ordered and regular lives in one place, farming the land with a careful eye to accumulation—if not for the market, then certainly for their own use and local exchange. To Europeans, Indians seemed impoverished, pursuing a "scattered and wild course of life."[19] They believed that a people who did so little and moved so much simply did not deserve the land. Ironically, the life Indians led was exactly the sort of life the Europeans had fantasized for themselves when they first began to explore the New World—a life of leisure, in which work would not be necessary and in which the blessed land would support them.

Trade and Culture

Disease destroyed Indian communities abruptly and directly. Trade was more subtle in its corrosive impact. Indians initially viewed this trade as part of their own traditional practice of gift-giving, as ritual that cemented the bonds between people. Whites viewed it within the framework of commodity exchange and profit. At first, the European traders and settlers were able to take open advantage of this situation, since Indians cared little about prices and gave what the colonists said was fair. By 1643, though, Roger Williams commented that the Indians were "marvellous subtle in their Bargaines." They began to ask for the cloth, clothes, and weapons they most desired, and they demanded fair prices for their own goods. During the early years, trading took place largely within the Indian cultural framework. Indians eagerly sought metal and cloth products that improved their lives, and they incorporated them in ways that often gave them functions unlike those originally intended—the use of brass, for instance, as jewelry. They often substituted European goods for their own traditional items—manufactured cloth for animal skins, metal tools and weapons for items made of stone, bone, or wood. Whites who wanted to succeed in the trade had to provide appropriate gifts and even accept adoption and marriage in the Indian kin network. If the English refused, Indians could readily turn to the French in some places or even to competing English colonies.

It is important to recognize that this was a trade between equals. At first, perhaps, Indians viewed Europeans within a religious framework; in Central America, they sometimes held the Spanish underwater to see if they were immortal. But by 1600, they viewed Europeans as simply different; if anything, many Indians felt the newcomers were rather slow-witted, reflecting the Iroquoian belief "that hairy people were unintelligent."[20] From this point on, Indians traded only for goods that they valued for exchange or defense purposes, such as hatchets, ironware, needles, and knives—not ornaments or liquor. Their growing dependence on European technology slowly eroded their cultural independence.

In retrospect, this dependence seems to have worked its harm in an almost inevitable and sometimes unacknowledged fashion. The impact of the fur trade on New England Indians provides the best known example. Indians expanded their hunting to acquire the furs that would bring them the desirable European products. In doing so, they rapidly depleted the beaver population throughout New England; they also distorted their own economic rhythms, putting a new and disruptive emphasis on the hunt and altering the seasonal rhythms of pre-European life. When the beaver all but disappeared from the landscape, Indians suddenly found themselves without a commodity to exchange for material goods on which they had become dependent.

The changing role of Indian wampum offers another enlightening example of destructive cultural interaction. Wampum consisted of strings of white and purple beads made by certain southern New England coastal tribes; it was a highly desirable status symbol among New England tribes. Lacking their own currency and seeking an additional commodity attractive to Indians, settlers adopted wampum as a temporary form of money. This demand stimulated production and the previously scarce symbolic item now became a common market commodity. Coastal tribes also used it to buy furs from the more northern hunting tribes, an exchange that exposed both to the notion that even natural commodities had a price in the European scheme of things. As the beaver disappeared by the 1660s and silver coin replaced wampum as the daily currency, the demand for wampum suddenly disappeared. Now, both the Indians who had come to rely on wampum as an exchange commodity and those who relied on the beaver for the same reason increasingly offered their land for trading purposes.

A somewhat similar process occurred in the Carolinas as a result of the high European demand for deerskin, which was supple and durable and could readily be made into superior gloves and bookbindings. For over twenty years, the Yamasees provided the colonists with both deerskins and slaves captured from Spanish mission Indians. As the availability of both began to diminish, the Carolinians continued to supply the Indians with goods, placing them ever more deeply in debt to the colonists. Indian dependency on European goods was a major factor in the 1715 Yamasee War. The deer trade continued even after the war, as whites pushed farther inland in search of the profitable hides. In 1750, Charlestown alone sent 150,000 skins to London.

Historians often portray alcohol as the most devastating of the white man's gifts to the Indians. Indians were at first repulsed by its taste, since they had no experience with fermented beverages. Lacking any tradition of social drinking, they drank for reasons deeply rooted in their own cultures, often to "achieve a dreamlike state of religious possession. . . ."[21] But alcohol had significant destructive effects on Indian life. Indians under the influence made poor bargains in trade and became destructive hunters, and addiction made others still more deeply dependent on European goods. Sachems and other leaders did their best to try and stem the flow of alcohol, with little lasting success.

The firearms trade offers the most dramatic example of the process by which European technology relentlessly destroyed the more traditional, noncompetitive Indian culture. It made sense for Indians to adopt firearms for hunting and warfare, since guns allowed them to kill many more animals than the bow and arrow or knife. But Indians had to depend on the English for repairs to the guns. The sound of the explosion also gave warning to animals and enemies. Most important, the introduction of firearms into a subsistence culture permanently altered the relationship between the Indians and the animals. Previously, Indians hunted only for what they needed. This limitation, together with their respect for animal spirits, meant that human and animal populations were in balance. Now, to acquire the furs that would allow them to purchase the desired European goods, Indians eagerly sought better hunting methods—and guns provided this advantage. Hunters in New England relentlessly pursued the beaver, even breaking into their lodges and killing entire families at once.

Inevitably, these various changes had a profound impact on Indian religious structures. Indian cosmology, we have seen, was based in nature and on a synergistic relationship between Indian and land. As this relationship was disrupted and became increasingly dysfunctional, the core of Indian religion lost its meaning. Even village religious leaders found themselves bereft pf purpose, unable to halt the spread of disease or to counter the growing failure of the hunt. Yet European religion held little appeal for most Indians. Tribes living beyond the frontier line generally ignored the Christian message. Few ministers had any desire to make the long, daunting trek to their territories, and the Indians openly scorned and laughed at those who did. John Eliot and Massachusetts achieved only minimal success in their praying towns, and the Narragansetts and Mohegans defeated in King Philip's War resisted conversion into the eighteenth century. Even the success of the

Mayhew mission in Martha's Vineyard relied on considerable luck—disease spared Christian Indians, and most beneficial of all, "lightening struck a sachem who had mockd a convert. . . ."[22] The Indians here still retained some individuality, integrating old rituals, such as the sharing of tobacco, into Christian services. The Mayhews implicitly understood, as the Jesuits also had, that Indians would not convert if forced to abandon their own identities.

The Eastern Abenaki

The experience of the Eastern Abenaki, the Dawn Land People, provides a concrete example of the impact European values and practices had on Indian culture. Eastern Abenaki territory ranged from the Saco River watershed north to the St. Lawrence River; their myths and belief systems reflected a typical merging of human and animal worlds. Abenakis believed that the woodchuck, their maternal ancestor, taught their own ancestors how to fish, hunt, and build canoes. Like other Indians, they assumed that a life principle existed in every being, both animate and inanimate. Rituals and taboos governing their hunting practices restrained them from exploiting their environment. They believed that a Great Being owned all game animals and that animals also lived in tribes and preyed on each other for food. To be successful in the hunt, the Abenaki tried to think and behave like the animals they sought. They carefully and respectfully disposed of the bodies of animals they killed, since they believed that the bear, deer, and beaver had given up their lives for human sustenance. Indian and animal were equals in a larger fabric of life, enmeshed in an organic relationship with each other that was incompatible with the white view of animals as commodities.

Shamans played a particularly crucial role in this system. Both men and women could become shamans among the Abenaki, and indeed the tribe viewed women as particularly powerful in this role. Abenakis believed shamans had received their powers from an animal helper who had aided them at some critical juncture and that they could transform themselves into this animal. As did other Indians, Abenakis believed shamans controlled the hunt through their ability to communicate with the spiritual world, particularly in times of scarcity. They also greatly valued the shamans' powwowing, or medical ability; shamans often healed by the power of suggestion, of course, but they could also set broken bones and use natural medicines to cure a variety of illnesses. To the English, their incantations were only "diabolical spells, mutterings, exorcisms."[23]

This culture began to experience stress as soon as the Europeans mapped Abenaki territory. Drawing maps and establishing borders differentiated space in a structured, patterned way that was essential to the European use of land, but it imposed artificial boundaries on people who moved to follow the game or as the spirits told them. The Abenaki hastened the process of their own disintegration by their eager adoption of European tools and utensils, putting the material base of their economy beyond their control. They increasingly depended on colonists for these products, and they sought more and more furs to exchange for them. As elsewhere, the supply of fur-bearing animals quickly became depleted.

Disease, though, had the most ravaging impact on Abenaki power and culture. During the first quarter of the century, the Eastern Abenaki population shrank from ten thousand to three thousand, largely due to the spread of smallpox from Massachusetts Bay. Planting cycles were thrown off, hunting groups destroyed, and migration patterns disrupted. When chiefs and shamans died, their helplessness before the new illness undermined the power of their positions and the explanatory force of Abenaki cosmology. A second epidemic in 1638 brought more death, opening up Abenaki lands to Massachusetts colonists migrating north in search of masts and naval stores.

In the wake of these tragic events, the French achieved impressive success in converting the Abenakis to Catholicism. The Jesuits offered a more flexible, less demanding alternative to the rigors of Puritanism. And to the Abenakis as to other Indians in Canada, the French god seemed to possess a power of explanation and spiritual solace that was sorely lacking in the austere, unforgiving Puritan deity. The Abenaki, though, like so many other tribes, remained caught in the middle between French and English imperial rivalries. The French might offer spiritual solace, but the English offered superior food and trading goods at lower prices. Both European powers exerted much effort during the early decades of the eighteenth century soliciting the allegiance of these powerful, strategically located people.

In the end, Europeans succeeded in achieving what became a conscious goal in their relations with Indians, to "multipl[y] their Wants, and put them upon desiring a thousand things, they never dreamt of before."[24] One eighteenth-century Philadelphia commentator put it less subtly: "[T]heir wants will be encreased, while on us they must in a manner wholly depend to have them supplied."[25]

Europeans among Indians

Not only Indians rejected the trappings of Western civilization. A significant number of colonists decided they preferred "barbarous" Indian life to "refined" white culture. Some did so voluntarily. The French coureurs de bois wore Indian breechcloths, leggings, and moccasins, spoke Indian languages, ate Indian food, and married Indian women. Most who adopted Indian culture, though, did so after being captured in raids or battle. Between 1675 and 1763, French and Indian war parties captured about 1,641 New Englanders; two-thirds were male and more than half were children. Indians adopted the captives to replace losses in their own population, but as time went on, such captives became more desirable for their ransom value.

About five hundred of these captives remained in Canada. Most of them were young and female, generally between the ages of seven and fifteen. After enduring a long and arduous journey north, many of them seemed to have been moved by a sense of gratitude to the French for delivering them from the Indians. The Canadian authorities went out of their way to encourage men with desirable skills to remain. Most who chose to stay, though, did so from love—for new spouses, kin, or religion. After instruction in the tenets of Catholicism, they were baptized into the faith and naturalized as French citizens. At least eight of the young girls became nuns.

Others became Indians. Their new families loved the adoptees as their own and often maintained close ties even after their new children returned to the white settlements; Jonathan Hoyt's Indian father visited him constantly at Deerfield after he left. Similarly, the children never forgot their adoptive parents; Elizabeth Gilbert "always retained an affection toward John Huston, her Indian father (as she called him), for she remembered his kindness to her when in captivity."[26] Where did these strong emotions come from? How did the captives overcome the powerful negative images of Indians so pervasive in white society? Undoubtedly, they began to change their minds on the difficult trek northward. Even amidst the harsh conditions, captives found themselves generally well treated; Indians fed them the same food they ate and carried children when they weakened. No female was ever sexually abused—Indians had strong incest taboos, and the males followed the ethic of warrior continence, believing that misfortune or even death would haunt them if they broke the code. Finally, the Indians dressed their prisoners in their own garb

❧ *Documents* ❧
"I Left That Child in the Wilderness"

As some of the accounts in the text make clear, many English captives experienced humane, even loving treatment from the Indians. Others found only sorrow. The selection below, from the "Third Remove" section of Mary Rowlandson's captivity narrative, is a powerful, moving recollection of the death of her infant in captivity.

> I sat much alone with a poor wounded Child in my lap, which moaned night and day, having nothing to revive the body, or cheer the spirits of her, but in stead of that, sometimes one Indian would come and tell me one hour, that your Master will knock your Child in the head, and then a second, and then a third, your Master will quickly knock your Child in the head.

> This was the comfort I had from them. . . . Thus nine dayes I sat upon my knees, with my Babe in my lap, till my flesh was raw again; my Child being even ready to depart this sorrowfull world, they bade me carry it out to another Wigwam (I suppose they would not be troubled with such spectacles) Whither I went with a heavy heart, and down I sat with the picture of death in my lap. About two houres in the night, my sweet Babe like a Lambe departed this life, on Feb. 18, 1675. It being about six yeares, and five months old. It was nine dayes from the first wounding, in this miserable condition, without any refreshing of one nature or other, except a little cold water. . . . There I left that Child in the Wilderness, and must commit it, and my self also in this Wilderness-condition, to him who is above all.

The Narrative of the Captivity and Restoration of Mrs. Mary Rowlandson, in Charles H. Lincoln, ed., *Narratives of the Indian Wars* (New York: Barnes & Noble, 1913), 125–6.

and decorated them, so that, as a twenty-six-year-old English soldier put it, "I began to think I was an Indian."[27]

Once they arrived at the village, Indians forced their captives to run the gauntlet. Even here, though, they frequently showed mercy toward the whites, certainly more than they did to other Indians they captured. Ten-year-old John Bricknell, a Seneca captive, was quickly knocked down, but as he later remembered, "A very big Indian came up, and threw the company off me, and took me by the arm, and led me along through the lines with such rapidity that I scarcely touched the ground, and was not once struck after he took me."[28] After surviving this ritual, captives were washed in the river and dressed in Indian clothes, then welcomed into the tribe with a speech by the adoptive parent. James Smith, adopted by the Mohawks, was introduced to his entire Indian family, each of whom came up "and

shook me by the hand, in token that they considered me to stand in the same relationship to them as the one in whose stead I was placed."[29] Mary Jemison later
remembered, "I was even considered and treated by them as a real sister, the same
as though I had been born of their mother."[30]

Once they earned the Indians' trust, the adoptees became full members of the
tribe. Children adjusted most quickly, learning the language and growing proud
that they were able to withstand the rigors of Indian life; John McCullough, only
eight years old, willingly underwent a daily submerging in frigid water by his adoptive uncle (who broke the ice when it was necessary) so he could grow strong.
English women soon found that their work was less demanding than what they had
been used to back home. All white captives often commented on the strong moral
character of the Indians they lived with; Mary Jemison noted that "the moral character of the Indian was. . . uncontaminated. Their fidelity was perfect, and became
proverbial; they were strictly honest; they despised deception and falsehood; and
chastity was held in high veneration."[31] They excelled, in short, at the very virtues
Puritans sought for themselves. Finally, captives soon came to realize that Indian
life offered them a degree of social equality, mobility, and adventure that they
could never have in white colonial society. As two whites noted, they found in
their new lives "the most perfect freedom, the ease of living, [and] the absence of
those cares and corroding solicitudes which so often prevail with us."[32]

The Colonial Family

English men and women looked to the family to guarantee order and community
and to protect them from a hostile world. They expected family relations to mirror
and support society's own social and political hierarchies. Family harmony was thus
basic to the preservation of social order, and society jealously guarded the right to
intervene in family affairs.

A powerful sense of patriarchy buttressed this desire for peaceful community; it
was strongest in New England, supported by a powerful sense of mutual obligation
at every level—between husbands and wives, parents and children, and masters
and servants. The father was responsible for the spiritual as well as the material
well-being of his wife, children, and servants. At first, selectmen bore the duty of
maintaining this family order. Thereafter, officials called tithingmen took up the
burden, each responsible for overseeing ten to twelve families in their neighborhood. New England laws required all inhabitants to live in family groups. Similar
laws and tithingmen were common in East Anglia, but New Englanders pursued
such oversight with exceptional energy, reflecting their commitment to a communal, relatively traditional social order.

The courts willingly stepped into family affairs when more informal mediation
failed. Authorities intervened in a wide variety of marital issues in the northern
colonies, hearing petitions for annulment, for instance, and seeking to reconcile
estranged partners. In short, they sought to control personal behavior that threatened to disrupt the institution that was most central to public order. It was not an
unusual event when Lawrence Clenton was "severely whipped with twenty stripes
well laid on" for making advances to another woman in 1670 and ordered to support his wife, live with her "as duty binds him, and at least to lodge with her one
night a week."[33] The Boston court ordered William Carpenter in 1672 and Richard
Cowley in 1677 whipped for beating their wives, and courts often required that
husbands post bonds to guarantee their future behavior toward their wives. County
courts in the Chesapeake intervened in similar fashion, though they showed much

more interest in cases of fornication and adultery and were particularly concerned with identifying fathers in bastardy cases, so that the community would not be forced to support the child financially.

New Englanders did not marry at an unusually early age or bear exceptionally large families. After the first few years, New England men married at an average age of twenty-six, women at twenty-three, and these ages even rose later in the century in the face of growing land scarcity and declining economic opportunity. Families averaged seven or eight children (the highest average was the 9.7 children born to the fertile inhabitants of Waltham), but some of these were stillborn and others died from childhood diseases. Cotton Mather fathered fifteen children, but only two outlived him. Births were spaced about two years apart, and most families probably did not have all their children living under the same roof for more than a few years.

Puritans loved their children openly and warmly. They sought to instill a strong sense of obedience to family, minister, and God in them, reminding them regularly and forcefully of their innate sinfulness. Massachusetts, Connecticut, and New Hampshire all had laws stipulating the death penalty for children who chronically abused or beat their parents, though they were never enforced. Parents' concerns and demands reflected a genuine interest in their childrens' spiritual state. Indeed, their diaries and journals show a touching, tender love for children that was all but unmatched in other Western cultures. New Englanders did not coldly arrange economically advantageous marriages for their offspring. Even when land grew scarce and parents struggled to provide a decent patrimony for their sons and daughters, the colonists universally recognized love as a prerequisite to marriage, and few parents withheld their consent from prospective unions.

This concern for familial harmony and the welfare of the young continued as children grew older and parents pursued the traditional practice of "putting out," or sending their children to live with other families. Parents did this for a variety of reasons, and they did so in *all* the colonies, not just New England. They sometimes gave custody to relatives for economic reasons—for apprenticeship or work as a servant. Ray Potter's parents sent him to work as a day laborer for neighboring families off and on from his tenth to his seventeenth birthday. Families sometimes adopted the children of deceased relatives, loving them as their own. Thomas Lothrop of Massachusetts adopted his cousin's orphaned daughter and, as his wife later noted, "She was dearer in his affections than I can express."[34] Apprenticeship was the most formal alternative available; it included both vocational training and poor-law apprenticeship, which simply helped the town support the child at minimal expense.

Family crisis accounted for many instances of putting out. In 1687, Anne Waters of Providence put out her son when her husband was transported as a convicted felon. Authorities often put out illegitimate children as the only practical means of ensuring their proper care. Colonists sometimes abandoned their children, though they did so far less often than their European counterparts. Such a fate befell the young Sarah Rusbie of Warwick, Rhode Island, who eventually was apprenticed to Job Almy for housewifery in 1666. It was most common, though, for parents to put out their children as a way of dealing with economic crisis. Francis Johnson, pressed by creditors, offered them two or three of his children, since he had nothing else to give. It was only children of the poor, in fact, that authorities put out compulsorily. Perhaps least common of all were those cases normally associated with Puritan coldness—putting out children to reform them or because their parents could not control them. Neighbors of the Towsley family in western Massachusetts complained before a magistrate that the children were "[t]heevish pilfering lying. . ."

and that their father was a troublemaker. The court ordered the daughter "wel whipt on the naked body with eight Lashes" and put out to a "suitable family."[35] Authorities in New England, reluctant to impose such extreme solutions, often chastised parents for failing to provide the proper upbringing for their children. But surely this speaks to a widespread concern for the welfare of the young, rather than a cold, emotional distance. In most cases, the community and the courts maintained careful oversight and supervision after they placed children with new families, sometimes bringing charges against masters for cruelty or nonperformance of contractual obligations.

New Englanders showed a similar sense of love and concern in marriage. Husband and wife embraced each other with real affection. Despite their legal superiority, men clearly respected their mates and generally consulted with them on important decisions. Society, they believed, existed to serve God and family to serve both society and God, and earthly concerns paled in the face of these higher goals. But men and women freely expressed their affection for each other. Anne Bradstreet opened her letters to her husband with the phrase "To my Dear and loving Husband."[36] John Winthrop closed his letters to his beloved Margaret with such phrases as "I kiss and love thee with the kindest affection. . . ," "many kisses of Love I sende thee. . . ," and "so with the sweetest kisses, and pure imbracinges of my kindest affection I rest Thine."[37]

Puritans did not reject the pleasures of the flesh; they believed the sexual bond was crucial to the success of marriage and of the family. Winthrop wrote to his wife in openly sensual language, and many among the most pious, such as Samuel Sewall, spoke of their wives with intense affection. Neither were they above cracking a ribald joke or two. The Reverend John Haynes wrote to Fitz-John Winthrop from London in 1660, reporting on his success in shopping for garters for Winthrop's fiancée: "I do not say I am fond of the happyness to kiss her hands, but her feet, having interest in her legs till my Garters be payd, which I adjure you to be carefull of as you would be glad to have a Lady leggs and all."[38] While Puritans punished adultery severely, premarital pregnancy was far from unknown in seventeenth-century New England, particularly in seaport towns. But bastardy was rare. Many cases of sexual dalliance before marriage occurred within the frame of betrothal, which was regarded as a contract almost as binding as marriage itself. Divorce was relatively easy in New England, but it was an unusual event—in Massachusetts, the General Court granted only twenty-seven divorces and thirteen annulments between 1639 and 1692.

As New Englanders passed into old age, their children revered them with a respect appropriate to wise elders. In the early years of settlement in particular, children tended to settle close to their parents and helped provide for them, creating what Philip Greven has called the "modified extended family." Because of New England's longer life expectancies, grandparents were present in a way that had been unthinkable in the Old World. About 6 percent of the population was over sixty years of age, and 90 percent of the children had at least one living grandparent. As economic pressures increased in the late seventeenth and early eighteenth century, the situation would change. But for the time being, New England's elderly were accorded a social status unusual in the early modern world.

Much recent scholarship has portrayed a very different sort of relationship between family and community in the early Chesapeake, and in fact, it took much longer for a patriarchal system to emerge in Virginia and Maryland. High death rates among adults, particularly males, gave the extended family a more crucial role here than it had in New England, forcing the community to provide for orphans, to extend assistance to single parents, and to make allowances for a nuclear family that was often fractured and missing one or more of its essential members. The plight of the Virginia child Agatha Vause was a common one; she lost a father, two stepfathers, a mother, and a guardian uncle before she turned eleven.

Thus, family associations in the first decades of Chesapeake settlement were much more extensive than in New England. Without the supportive networks of a close community, neighborhood and kin relations took on added significance. Many households included step-relatives and wards. There were more servants and fewer children in the typical Chesapeake house than in New England households, because parents died young and had fewer opportunities to bear children. Because of the precarious nature of inheritance, love and children's preferences played a much less decisive role in marriage here than in New England. Parents did not completely discount their childrens' feelings, and orphans retained greater freedom of action in marrying, but complex negotiations over proposed unions were the rule.

Women in particular married at much younger ages here than in New England; those born in Maryland often married before they were seventeen. William Byrd's sister married at sixteen and died in childbirth at seventeen. Young men tended to wait until a more traditional twenty-five or twenty-six, undoubtedly because it took them that long to establish a secure economic position in the community. It was only after 1720 that sex ratios evened out in the region, and throughout the next century, marriage more commonly occurred at twenty-four for men and twenty-two for women.

Even more than New Englanders, Quaker families explicitly and openly embraced a familial ideal of loving, caring relationships. The Delaware Valley was the site of the first openly child-centered family in the Anglo-American world. The Quaker family was much more extended than anywhere else in the colonies, since all Friends embraced each other as "near relations" and regarded grandparents, cousins, uncles, and others as members of the family, even though they did not reside in the nuclear household. And they were all members of the family of God. The Quaker conception of the family was less hierarchical than in other colonies, "a union of individuals who were equal in the sight of God."[39] Spiritual love, rather than authoritarian paternal guidance, held the family together; mates were "help-meets" for each other.

Quakers reared their children with open affection, viewing small children as harmless and innocent, free of the taint of original sin stressed by the Puritans. They were, Quakers believed, incapable of sin until they were at least eleven years old. Even then, parents disciplined their children with reason, using rewards rather than punishment to encourage proper behavior. Love, not coercion, was essential to cultivate "tender plants growing in the Truth."[40] Even Quakers, though, viewed the ages of fourteen to twenty-one (adolescence) as a dangerous time. They enforced strict prohibitions against dancing and other expressions of physical expressiveness during these years.

Indeed, one of the most interesting and unique aspects of Quaker family mores was the unbridled hostility toward the flesh. Quakers viewed lust and sex as sinful, and it was they, not the Puritans, who took the most forceful steps to prevent fornication before marriage. Laws punished sexual crimes severely, particularly those involving the sexual exploitation of servants and other social inferiors, and adultery could bring life imprisonment for the second offense. Single men convicted of sodomy or bestiality could suffer the same fate along with being whipped every three months. One law, disallowed by England, provided that married men convicted of such crimes be divorced and castrated. Many Quakers advocated the restriction of sexual activity within marriage, while a few, such as Mary Dyer of Massachusetts fame, even urged marital asceticism.

❧ *Documents* ❧
Love in the Colonial Family

Early American families were the center of much love, between husbands and wives and between parents and children. Even Puritans, so fearful of damnation and so careful to repress sinful impulses in their children, openly expressed love and affection for each other. The following documents are varied, yet typical, expressions of such devotion. The first is from a prescriptive guide to behavior that is perhaps more reflective of an ideal than of actual behavior. It nonetheless suggests that Puritan patriarchy was often leavened by a loving sense of spiritual and emotional equality. The second is a more profound and graceful expression of conjugal love by the poet Anne Bradstreet. The final selection, from William Penn's advice to his children, reflects the Quaker emphasis on love, brotherhood, and the preservation of the Friends' fellowship.

> The Husband's Government ought to be gentle & easy, and the Wife's Obedience ready & chearful. The Husband is call'd the Head of the Woman. . . . It belongs to the Head to rule and govern.
> . . . Wives are part of the House and Family, and ought to be under the Husband's Government. . . . Yet his government of his Wife should not be with rigour, haughtiness, harshness, severity; but with the greatest love, gentleness, kindness, tenderness that may be. Though he governs her, he must not treat her as a Servant, but as his own flesh; he must love her as himself. . . .

> Those husbands are much to blame who dont carry it lovingly & kindly to their Wives. O man, if thy Wife be not so young, beautiful, healthy, well-temper'd, and qualify'd as you couldst wish; if she brought not so much estate to thee, or cannot do so much for thee, as some other women brought to or have done or their husbands . . . ; yet she is thy Wife, and the Great God Commands you to love her, not be bitter, but kind to her.

Benjamin Wadsworth, *A Well-Ordered Family,* 2nd ed. (Boston: 1719), 35–7.

"To my Dear and loving Husband"
If ever two were one, then surely we.

Quakers took even more extensive steps than their neighbors in New England and the Chesapeake to perpetuate close family ties, spending much of their lives accumulating land to provide for their children. Land here was more fertile and abundant than in New England and more equitably distributed than in the south. Families were also somewhat smaller than in New England, averaging fewer than six children who reached the age of twenty-one. Hence, for several decades,

If ever man were lov'd by wife, then thee;
If ever wife was happy in a man,
Compare with me ye women if you can.
I prize thy love more then whole Mines of gold,
Or all the riches that the East doth hold.
My love is such that Rivers cannot quench,
Nor ought but love from thee, give recompence.
Thy love is such I can no way repay,
The heavens reward thee manifold I pray.
Then while we live, in love lets so persever,
That when we live no more, we may live ever.

Alan Heimert and Andrew DelBanco, eds., *The Puritans in America: A Narrative Anthology* (Cambridge, MA: Harvard University Press, 1985), 146.

Next betake yourselves to some honest, industrious course of life; and that not of sordid covetousness, but for example and to avoid idleness. And if you change your condition and marry, choose with the knowledge and consent of your mother, if living, guardians, or those that have the charge of you. Mind neither beauty nor riches, but the fear of the Lord and a sweet and amiable disposition, such as you can love above all this world and that may make you habitations pleasant and desirable to you. And being married, be tender, affectionate, and patient, and meek. Live in the fear of the Lord, and He will bless you and your offspring. . . .

Finally, my children, love one another with a true and endaered love, and your dear relations on both sides; and take care to preserve tender affection in your children to each other, often marrying within themselves. . . . That so they may not, like the forgetting and unnatural world, grow out of kindred and as cold as strangers. . . .

Jean Soderlund, ed., *William Penn and the Founding of Pennsylvania, 1680–1684: A Documentary History* (Philadelphia: University of Pennsylvania Press, 1983), 168, 170.

Quaker farmers succeeded in leaving their sons two or three hundred acres and more and in granting handsome financial gifts to their daughters. These children married at somewhat older ages than their counterparts in New England (especially among the poorer families), but they also became financially independent upon or soon after marrying. Shortly after Jacob Minshall married Sarah Owen in 1706, his father, Thomas, granted him five hundred acres and a house. When Jacob's brother

Isaac married Rebecca Owen the next year, Thomas granted him 380 acres of land. The Minshalls, to be sure were wealthy. But former servant Ralph Lewis was able to grant three of his sons more than two hundred acres of land for just sixty pounds upon their marriages. This "revolving fund" of payments allowed children to become independent relatively quickly and fathers to finance younger children's starts much sooner than was the case elsewhere in the colonies. This very success, unfortunately, created a crisis in the next century that was not so very different from the one Puritan families were already confronting.

Women In Seventeenth-Century America

Since Europe and America alike were patriarchal societies, women participated only rarely in public affairs. But within the family and in the church and community, women in seventeenth-century America played indispensable roles in everyday life. From the beginning, Puritans viewed women as spiritually equal to men; saved or damned, only God could judge their true worth. The church offered one of the few areas in which women could actively participate. By the end of the century, they dominated church membership as more and more men failed to become full church members.

But while women may have attained spiritual equality, Anne Hutchinson learned that their influence on church affairs was strictly controlled. And while women may have been regarded as consorts by their husbands, their identities were fully recognized only in their roles as wives and mothers. The law offered them protection against physical brutality and guaranteed a certain degree of economic protection, but it did not grant them equality in any sense of the word. Religious and literary images, finally, portrayed women as docile, modest, delicate, frail, and passive, even as their daily lives were filled with hard work and responsibilities.

Women were viewed as both complementary and secondary to their husbands, "simultaneously a housewife, a deputy husband, a consort, a mother, a mistress, a neighbor, and a Christian."[41] Men often failed to view women's duties as "real" work, but it is clear that their chores and responsibilities on the farm and in the home were onerous and demanded well-honed skills. The larger the household, the more food and clothing were needed and the more people there were to be cared for—husband, children, servants, and in the south, slaves. On the frontier, life was even more precarious, as women had less help and fewer close neighbors. They often performed the duties of a "deputy husband." When their husbands were away from home, these women directed employees and servants, dealt with creditors, kept account records, and made other major decisions involving the farm or business. On most farms, women also worked side by side with men for several weeks during the harvest. After the crops were brought in, they continued to milk the cows, feed the pigs, make butter and cheese, and spin wool. Girls began to learn these skills as early as the age of seven, and by twelve, they were performing most of the tasks for which they would later be fully responsible. Most girls also worked for other families, helping out with household chores and perhaps earning a small wage to put aside for a dowry.

Two examples indicate women's range of experiences in seventeenth-century New England. Beatrice Plummer, who died in 1672, lived in Newbury, Massachusetts, as the wife of Francis, a middling farmer. The Plummers' home was typical for a family of their status, with a hall and parlor on the first floor and two storage rooms above; the couple had little furniture. A dairy house held bacon, salt pork, cheese, and butter, with grain stored in one of the upstairs rooms. Beatrice prepared all of the meals: bread, cheese, and leftovers for breakfast; some boiled meat with vegetables for dinner; and bread, cheese, and beer for supper. During the day, she performed the normal range of household chores, including some gardening and gathering of food, and she slaughtered animals and made cider in the fall.

Hannah Grafton's life was both similar and significantly different from Beatrice Plummer's. Grafton lived with her husband, Joshua, and their three children on only one acre of land in urban Salem, Massachusetts. Their home was similar to the Plummers', but the upstairs rooms were used as bedrooms for the children. The house may have been crowded, but its contents also reflected a far greater degree of comfort. The family had silverplate, a silver-headed cane, a pair of gold buttons, and a variety of other luxuries. Though Hannah cooked all the meals, she spent little time making the food itself. She took advantage of Salem's commercial environment, using her credit to buy bread from a bakery and meat from a slaughterhouse. Joshua was a mariner who was often away at sea, and when he was gone, Hannah worked as shopkeeper in the store attached to their house. She owned a spinning wheel and spent a good deal of time making clothes for herself and the family.

Women completely controlled one of the critical professions of early America— that of midwife. Before modern medicine, childbirth brought with it as much fear and anxiety as joy; death was a real possibility for both mother and child. Dorothy Gookin's husband, and later her son, consistently characterized her thirteen deliveries as consisting of "hard travail," "very hard & dangerous travail,"[42] or some variation thereof. During the entire colonial period, between 1 percent and 1.5 percent of all births resulted in the mother's death from exhaustion, dehydration, infection, hemorrhage, or convulsions. Midwives could ease the birth, and most had secret potions of one sort or another that would alleviate the woman's pain. One such mix consisted of a blending of beaver testicles, basil, powdered hair from the head of a virgin, dried ant eggs, and one-quarter pint of milk. In truth, such concoctions likely had little value; alcohol was the only real painkiller available. Puritans viewed the agony of childbirth as a punishment from God for Eve's sin in the garden.

Through the midwife, women asserted their control over the entire birthing experience. New England mothers were segregated during a three-week lying-in period, and only women could visit them during the first two weeks. Men, it seems, found the birth process both fearful and mysterious and did not completely trust midwives. They believed that midwives worked through spirits and occasionally accused them of witchcraft. But midwives' powers did command respect. Communities sometimes offered salaries and houses to attract them, and courts frequently asked them to examine women accused of fornication, premarital sex, and witchcraft.

In New Amsterdam and then in New York, single women enjoyed the same legal rights over property as men. After marriage, they could retain their maiden surnames, buy and sell property, and operate a business without the consent of their husbands. But by and large, women enjoyed few legal rights anywhere in seventeenth-century America. Under the principle of *femme covert,* a woman's personal property became that of her husband's upon marriage. She retained title to any land she inherited from her father, and her husband could not sell this land without her consent. But she could not use its profits, nor could she will it to her children. While her husband was alive, a woman's property rights, in New England at least, were extremely restricted. The law afforded certain minimal protections, however, to widows. All wives possessed dower rights in their husbands' estate. These rights guaranteed the widow permanent ownership of one-third of the estate's personal property and one-third of the landed property for life. In the latter case, this meant the widow retained use, not ownership, of land, since she could not pass it on to her own heirs. Except in the case of extraordinary need, she could sell none of the immovable estate, and she could sell her dower right only by denouncing it publicly, with court approval. If her sons were minors, she controlled all of the property until they came of age, but the courts or her husband's will could dictate final disposition.

Women's economic activities in the northern colonies often extended outside of the home. Single women operated under the legal principle of *femme sole,* which gave them considerable freedom to own property and dispose of it and even to sue in courts. Women worked as teachers and as blacksmiths, silversmiths, shoemakers, tanners, bakers, printers, butchers, tailors, and shipwrights. They operated small stores and even forges. Women innkeepers were common; during the latter part of the century, women ran 5 percent of the inns in New England and 18.9 percent of those in Boston, and those numbers increased during the next century. These women did not hesitate to protect their rights; several petitioned the General Court during the early 1700s to order local justices of the peace to stop discriminating against them in the licensing and operation of their inns and taverns. Wealthier northern women, such as Maria Van Cortlandt Van Rensselaer, exerted considerable economic influence. Van Rensselaer administered her husband's estate of a million acres for fifteen years after he died without a male heir.

Women's legal status in the seventeenth-century Chesapeake was unique, a reflection of the uneven sex ratios and disastrous demographic circumstances of life in early Virginia and Maryland. Maryland women, for instance, enjoyed far more varied and important roles in their society than did their northern counterparts. They exercised significant economic authority, and their husbands' wills explicitly recognized their right and ability to supervise their children. Men throughout the Chesapeake generally made their wives the executors of their estates, though they also often appointed overseers to help the widows and to make sure a future husband would not deprive the children of their inheritances. Margaret Brent, an unmarried Catholic who arrived in Maryland in 1638, oversaw her own economic affairs and those of her brothers and several others. She was the guardian of an Indian princess and executrix of the estate of Gov. Leonard Calvert. Wealthy widows could afford to play the marriage market. Sarah Offley, the daughter of a prosperous London merchant, married Adam Thorougood in 1627. Thorougood died in 1640 at the age of thirty-eight, and within a year, Offley married Capt. John Gookin, who died in 1643 at the age of thirty. In 1647, Offley married Francis Yeardley, son of the former Virginia governor Sir George Yeardley. She carefully arranged that most of the property would remain hers if he died first—and he did just that eight years later. Apparently, he did not resent her economic power, since he once traded seven cattle to buy her a piece of jewelry.

On the other hand, women in this society bore a dual burden. They were expected to be feminine, refined, and virtuous but also to perform farm chores and work in the fields. And unmarried women who gave birth were heavily fined—if a woman could not pay, "she was trussed up like an animal, her dress was ripped open to the waist, and she was publicly whipped in the sight of a shouting mob until the blood flowed in rivulets down her naked back and breasts."[43] Courts ordered women flogged for committing adultery or dragged behind a boat until they were nearly drowned. Economic and social power did not guarantee humane treatment.

A World of Witchcraft And Magic

Magic, Society, and Women

Seventeenth-century Americans lived in a universe alive with spirits and unpredictable danger. They held the ability to understand and perceive those dangers as being essential to the physical and spiritual safety of their communities. By attending to signs, portents, and mysterious phenomena, they hoped to forestall the inevitable process of decay and degeneration that they believed beset all societies and to deflect the unseen hands of evil and fortune that stalked the unfortunate individual.

New England ministers used such portents to telling effect in their sermons. Cotton Mather, for instance, preached of two boys drowning while ice skating on a Sunday to show how God punished Sabbath breakers. The youngsters in the congregation undoubtedly took the warnings to heart. While ministers espoused a more rational culture in print, the laity continued to view the world in openly magical terms. Early New Englanders believed "that unicorns lived in the hills beyond the Hudson, that mermaids swam in waters off Cape Ann, and that tritons played in Casco Bay."[44] Diaries noted sightings of bodies without heads, animals changing shape, trumpets sounding in the night, the birth of monster children, and, of course, ghosts. All Puritans, from the wealthy merchant Samuel Sewall to the lowliest farmer, believed that such occurrences had a divine purpose.

In the Chesapeake, colonists studied the stars and planets for clues to their fortune and fate. In the Delaware Valley, Quakers pursued their own brand of the irrational in their practice of spiritualism, even attempting to communicate with the dead and bring them back to life. Seventeenth-century America was scarcely touched by the scientific revolution. It was a world where the majority of people believed their destinies were preordained and where the true causes of many events in the physical world remained mysteries beyond the individual's influence or understanding. Humans were not agents of change in seventeenth-century America. They were mere instruments, whether in the hands of fortune or of God.

Protestants, Puritans in particular, fully embraced the notion of a predestined future and a natural world manipulated by God. Yet the laity were not so willing to completely give up control over their lives, and magic remained a powerful force in the minds of most American colonists. Seventeenth-century religion assumed the existence of a supernatural authority that determined the course of the universe. Magic, on the other hand, "rests on the assumption that human beings can control occult forces. . . through ritual techniques."[45] It helped ordinary people explain the seemingly inexplicable and predict the future, even heal the sick and protect themselves against possible harm. Puritan ministers did everything they could to wipe out magic, with little success. It simply gave too much solace to people who needed to understand why their cows died suddenly or a child became deathly ill for no apparent reason. In the seventeenth century at least, magic remained the core of a popular culture that resisted the inroads of an elite, more rational view of the world.

"Cunning" and "wise" folk offered their services everywhere in the New World, claiming magical understanding of human and natural events; diviners, such as the accused witch Katherine Harrison, worked as fortune-tellers and offered farmers the brief satisfaction of a glimpse into their future. These people used all sorts of techniques. One involved balancing a sieve on open scissors or shears, then asking the desired question; if the sieve shook or turned upward, the answer to the question was yes. People also used countermagic against perceived wrongs or to correct problems in their lives that they suspected had been caused by a witch or cunning person. In 1656, for instance, Margaret Garrett of Hartford found one side of a cheese she had made full of maggots. She suspected foul play and flung the cheese into the fire, whereupon Elizabeth Seager, who was in the barn, "[c]ryed out exceedingly."[46] Seager came to the house writhing in pain, unaware that she had thereby identified herself as the culprit. On another occasion in Hampton, New

Hampshire, the fifteen-month-old son of John and Mary Godfrey died. They remembered that when the child had become ill, Rachel Fuller had visited and behaved strangely, "standing with her face towards the house, beating herself with her arms, as men do in winter to heat their hands, and this she did three times; and stooping down and gathering something off the ground in the interim between the beating of herself, and then she went home."[47] They accused her of murder by witchcraft.

Ministers did all they could to counter such activities, viewing them as challenges to their own power. They attacked healing magic as an insult to God, arguing that such rituals seemed to imply an automatic cure and that no one could force God to do something. They criticized the belief in astrology that became increasingly widespread during the last two decades of the century with the appearance of the first colonial almanacs. They were most persistent, however, in their vehement, almost hysterical attacks on witchcraft.

Many seventeenth-century New Englanders, like others in the early modern era, accepted witchcraft as a true, ever-present reflection of a hidden supernatural world. The laity widely believed that witches practiced *maleficium*—harming others through supernatural means. Even before the Salem witch trials, 103 New Englanders were accused of being witches, though only fifteen were executed. Overall, between 1620 and 1724, 322 New Englanders were accused of witchcraft, 259 of them women. Thirty-six were executed, of which twenty-nine were women. Ministers, too, accepted the existence of witches, but beyond this, they rejected lay beliefs. The clergy, and most early modern European law, had abandoned the basically medieval conception of witchcraft as an attempt to do practical harm. Instead, they adopted a more theological view and portrayed witchcraft as human collusion with the devil. Again and again in early New England, courts failed to convict witches because the people who brought the accusations presented only physical, not theological, evidence. The laity simply were not concerned about the role of the devil; they just wanted the suspected witch to stop ruining their cow's milk.

The exception seems to be Salem, where forty-three people confessed to practicing diabolical witchcraft (witchcraft in collusion with the devil). But even there, almost all of the evidence supporting the role of the devil came from the afflicted girls or those who confessed to being witches. More important, most of these confessed only under torture or psychological pressure, and many of them later recanted their confessions. The court tied William Proctor and two others "Neck and Heels till the Blood was ready to come out of their Noses and 'tis credibly believed and reported this was the occasion of making them confess."[48]

Throughout the century, most of the accused witches were middle-aged women, and often the accusers were neighbors who had suffered some personal misfortune or had a history of ongoing problems with the accused witch. Some historians have argued that this pattern indicates that New Englanders used witchcraft to deflect social conflict, to project the causes of personal disagreement onto individuals whose personalities or status in the community made them susceptible to such blame. Given a society where social conflict was rapidly increasing and where people perceived a decline from an ideal state of social harmony, such a view makes a good deal of sense. Many people undoubtedly felt a strong sense of guilt over their failure to live up to the earlier standards.

But while social conflict undoubtedly gave rise to particular accusations, we cannot overlook the unique role women played in these events. A very high proportion of accused witches (particularly discounting Salem) lived alone and, along with their daughters, stood to benefit from the substantial acquisition or inheritance of property. The majority of the accused, in fact, were of middling wealth and sta-

❧ *Documents* ❧
Consorting with the Devil

The documents below suggest some of the common beliefs that underlaid the many witchcraft accusations that appeared in seventeenth-century New England. People often resorted to accusations of witchcraft to explain strange and destructive events in their own lives. The first selection, from a New Haven case, reflects these beliefs. The second selection, from the Salem trial of Bridget Bishop, suggests the vivid imagination that fed many of the accusations during the 1692 hysteria.

> June 16, 1653. Goodwife Thorpe complained that Mrs. Godman came to her house and asked to buy some chickens, she said she had none to sell, Mrs. Godman said will you give them all, so she went away, and she thought then that if this woman was naught as folks suspect, maybe she will smite my chickens, and quickly after one chicken died, and she remembered she had heard if they were bewitched they would consume within, and she opened it and it was consumed in the gizzard to water and worms, and divers others of them dropped, and now they are missing and it is likely dead, and she never saw either hen or chicken that was so consumed within with worms.

> John Louder testified, that upon some little controversy with Bishop about her fowls, going well to bed, he did awake in the night by moonlight, and did see clearly the likeness of this woman grievously oppressing him; in which miserable condition she held him unable to help himself, til near day. He told Bishop of this; but she denied it, and threatened him, very much. Quickly after this, being at home on a Lord's day, with the doors shut about him, he saw a black pig approach him; at which he going to kick, it vanished away. Immediately after, sitting down, he saw a black thing jump in at the window, and come and stand before him. The body, was like that of a monkey, the feet like a cock's, but the face much like a man's.

David Hall, ed., *Witch-Hunting in Seventeenth-Century New England: A Documentary History, 1638–1692* (Boston: Northeastern University Press, 1991), 68, 299. Copyright 1991 by David D. Hall. Reprinted with the permission of Northeastern University Press, Boston.

tus. These women were often daughters of parents who had no sons or sons who had died without children of their own. Many of them were involved in extensive commercial activities—spinning, bee keeping, beer making (all designed to make a profit)—while others were quite vocal in expressing discontent with their lives. Sexual themes also emerge from the court records. Men often told of being forced to have sex with accused witches who seemed possessed of uncontrolled carnal appetites. In the early decades, there were stories of such women having sexual relations with the devil. Witches were believed to derive their powers from a covenant with the devil, and courts often examined the accused for the so-called "Devil's mark" or "witches' teat." Men generally viewed women as carnal objects, as lustful creatures somehow innately evil and threatening. Wives and single women who refused to accept their limited social roles only increased these fears and heightened the Puritan dread of social disorder.

Two examples of pre-Salem accusations illustrate these themes. Eunice Cole of Hampton, Massachusetts, (now New Hampshire) had no children, and before his death, her husband had signed a "deed of gift" transferring all of his estate to her. Cole had been charged with lesser crimes on several earlier occasions, including "slanderous speech," and in 1656, she was brought to trial for witchcraft in Boston. Thomas Philbrick accused her of being responsible for the death of two of his calves, since she had told him that if his animals ate "any of hir grass she wished it might poyson them or choke them." A constable who had whipped Cole as punishment for a earlier crime testified that when he stripped her to administer the punishment, he saw "under one of hir brests. . . a bleu thing like unto a teate hanging downeward about thre quarters of an inche longe. . . [with] someblood with other moystness [which she said] was a sore." Cole was convicted and sentenced to imprisonment for life or "the pleasure of the court."[49] Though eventually released, she spent the rest of her life in and out of jails and being accused of witchcraft.

Katherine Harrison of Weathersfield, Connecticut was married to John Harrison, a wealthy landowner. John died in 1666, leaving Catherine one of the wealthiest women in the town. She did not remarry and managed her own economic affairs. Over the next few years, neighbors repeatedly vandalized her property, destroyed her crops, and killed her farm animals. She had a reputation of being "a great or notorious liar, a Sabbath breaker and one that told fortunes,"[50] and in the fall of 1668, she had been fined a considerable sum for slandering two of her neighbors. She was tried for witchcraft in 1669, but the court could not reach a verdict; she may also have been tried and acquitted the year before. The county court found her guilty of witchcraft in the fall of 1670 and ordered her to leave town. She moved to New York but was harassed even there. She escaped suspicion and persecution only when her daughter married one of her New York accusers, who then became her protector. Harrison was also a healer, whose success at curing illness apparently aroused further suspicions. Both Harrison and Cole struck at the core of Puritan patriarchy, refusing to behave in the humble, supplicatory fashion expected of them and controlling large amounts of land and property.

Hysteria at Salem

Salem presents a somewhat different picture both because of the number of accusations involved and because this case of mass hysteria represents the clearest connection between witchcraft accusations and community conflict. Though of smaller scale, this episode more closely resembled the European witch crazes than it did other accusations of witchcraft in New England earlier in the century.

The Salem outbreak began in early February 1692 with episodes of fortune-telling among young girls. Books exploring the subject had recently appeared in New England, and Puritan daughters in the pangs of early adolescence began to experiment with such diversions as casting spells. In Salem Village, a small group gathered at the house of Rev. Samuel Parris that included his nine-year-old daughter, Betty, his niece Abigail Williams, and two of their friends. But things began to get out of hand, and the girls became frightened and upset. They began to crawl into holes, creep under chairs and stools, sit or stand in odd positions, and engage in upsetting antics. They would fall to the floor on their hands and knees and make choking sounds or simply fall and begin screaming. Concerned about the girls' behavior, Parris turned to the local physician, who immediately pronounced them in the hold of the "Evil Hand." One woman proposed that "witch cake," rye meal mixed with urine from the afflicted girls, be fed to a dog. If the girls were, indeed, bewitched, the dog would display physical symptoms similar to their own.

By early 1692, the affliction was beginning to spread. Seven or eight more girls between the ages of twelve and nineteen were affected, including three from the house of Thomas Putnam. The girls apparently welcomed the attention that their screaming and moaning attracted. Under intense questioning, the girls named their afflicters: Sarah Good, Sarah Osborne, and Tituba, a slave and cook in Parris's house. The first was married to an oft-unemployed laborer, and she herself smoked a pipe and often begged from door to door in the village—hardly the Puritan stereotype of a goodly woman. Sarah Osborne, though prosperous, no longer attended church and lived openly in sin with an overseer on her farm after the death of her husband. Tituba was immediately suspect as a slave. She had come from the West Indies and had often shown the girls magic tricks. On March 1, Tituba confessed, apparently hoping she could save herself by claiming she had stopped working with the Devil and naming others who continued to do so. She accused both Sarahs and identified a "tall man from Boston" as the ringleader. She spun a tale of rats, yellow birds, dogs, and something "Hairy" that "goes upright like a man."[51] Since the three women were in jail the populace almost felt safe— except for the tall man from Boston and the fact that the girls continued to be tormented.

Things took a turn for the worse the following March. Two of the three accused in that month were church members and married to prosperous freeholders. By the end of April, the accused included a Harvard minister, by May two selectmen, and later some of the most prominent individuals in the colony. The girls identified the man in black as the influential John Alden, the son of John and Priscilla Alden of Plymouth, but he was able to escape and hide with friends. None of these people was ever brought to trial, but only their social influence held the accusers at bay until the hysteria subsided. In mid-April, the first signs of a break in the girls' accusations appeared, as the young Mary Warren, who apparently had a crush on one of the accused farmers, John Proctor, admitted the whole thing to be a hoax. The resultant pressure proved too much for her, though, and she retracted her confession and accused many others of witchcraft.

In May, the new royal governor, Sir William Phips, arrived in Boston. Phips believed in witchcraft, but he was determined to get to the bottom of these unsettling events. He appointed a special court of seven judges with Deputy Gov. William Stoughton as chief justice. By now, almost fifty people had been jailed, and they placed all their hopes in this court. Unfortunately, the judges did not seem disposed to settle things in favor of the accused. They quickly decided to accept two kinds of evidence: descriptions of the girls' behavior and descriptions of the spirit shapes they saw (spectral evidence). They also ruled that those who confessed would not be punished (though they would have their property confiscated) since a confession would indicate that they had broken the hold of the Devil.

The accusations continued during the trials, and spectral evidence became all important. Bridget Bishop was the first convicted and hanged, followed by Rebecca Nurse and Sarah Good. Giles Cory, the husband of the accused Martha Cory, had heavy stones piled on his chest in an attempt to force him to enter a plea. He did not and was crushed to death. The court executed twenty in all, and several more died in prison. Then, on September 22, the panic suddenly ended. The General Court, finally realizing its errors, dismissed the trial court and established a new one with new rules, and Phips began releasing prisoners on bond. The new court did sentence five more confessed "witches" to be hanged, but Phips overruled the convictions. The court insisted that the released prisoners pay for the costs of room and board incurred during their imprisonment, though, and kept several in jail for months until their bills were settled.

More than a decade later, Anne Putnam, one of the orginators of the hysteria, applied for membership in the Salem village church. She pleaded for forgiveness for her actions. The church accepted her, but surely there were unsettling feelings among the congregation that day. In 1711, the colony paid the survivors of the executed sums ranging from seven to 150 pounds and reversed the convictions of all but seven of the victims, who had no family alive to speak for them.

Why did this tragedy happen? Essex County was in the midst of rapid social and economic change during these years. Increasingly urbanized and densely populated, it was a place where people did not hesitate to turn to the courts to settle their personal disputes. The gap between rich and poor was growing here, and social contention was common. Women in particular found themselves victimized by many of these changes. Courts frequently released men from child support obligations if they could prove promiscuity on the part of the mother, and they often released men but not women from fines or whipping in fornication cases. Finally, more sons were surviving, and widows suffered accordingly; few now inherited real property.

Salem reflected these changes. The town had split into two distinct sections over the years. The town proper was located on the coast and had long since abandoned its agricultural identity. It was now a burgeoning financial and trade center for the county, embracing values that were anathemas to the original Puritan mission. The village section, in contrast, was inland, cursed by poor land and farms constantly decreasing in size and value. Girls from the village had little realistic hope for prosperous marriages. In 1672, the town finally granted the village limited independence, allowing it to form its own church and hire a minister.

Serious division remained, though, within the village itself. Those furthest from Salem Town most resented its wealth and secularism, while those closest to the border were wealthier and more likely to be involved in modern economic practices and later to be skeptics of the trials. The poorer group, led by the Putnam family, finally succeeded in hiring a minister in 1689—Samuel Parris, a thirty-six-year-old former merchant. So desperate was the church that Parris was able to negotiate a contract that included full personal title to the parsonage and its land. This choice and subsequent events drove a wedge deeper into the community. Parris's opponents refused to attend his services. They held back their tax payments for his 1692 salary, challenged the legality of his grants, and even refused to deliver his firewood that winter. Salem Village was a gloomy, dispirited, and divided place in 1692. And without a charter or a viable government in Boston, there was no countervailing force within the colony to resist the onslaught of events.

The final piece to this tragic puzzle can be found in the women and the girls, the accused and the accusers. Many of the accusing girls had recently lost one or more parents from Indian attacks on the Maine frontier. Most were servants, all were new to the town, and all faced the same bleak marriage prospects. Together, these elements undoubtedly heightened their susceptibility to the normal identity crisis of adolescence. The girls also tended to live in the western part of the village, and several were from the Putnam and Parris families. The accused women, on the other hand, generally lived in the eastern section of the village. Especially early in the hysteria, they also tended to be older women who lived, in one way or another, on the fringes of Puritan respectability. Several were also masters of these servant girls or survivors of the Maine wars themselves.

The brief story of Elizabeth Knapp provides a fitting conclusion to this tale. Knapp was a young servant in the household of Rev. Samuel Willard in Groton, Massachusetts. Orphaned and unable to write, she faced a life of few opportunities. While Willard went out every day into the larger world and made an impressive name for himself, Knapp could only stay in his house and wonder what would happen to her. In the fall of 1672, she experienced a series of fits and "possessions" and confessed to speaking and dealing with the devil. Willard, who kept careful notes of the entire affair, described her behavior as "violent in bodily motions, leapings, strainings, and strange agitations, scarce to be held in bounds by the strength of three or four. . . . " She "barked like a dog, and bleated like a calf" and suffered many other disturbing symptoms. She twice identified Groton women as witches, only to withdraw her accusations. Sometime during the following winter, she recovered; she married in 1674, had six children, and apparently led an unremarkable life until she died early in the next century. Knapp and many others like her, angry, frustrated, and uncertain of their futures, directed their fears and anger inward against themselves and outward onto older women—and later men—who represented everything that they could never hope to achieve. The community itself drew a lesson from this event. As Willard noted, "God hath in His wisdom singled out this poor town, out of all others in this wilderness, to dispense such an amazing providence in. . . . Let us look upon ourselves to be set up as a beacon upon a hil. . . ."[52]

The Story House of Essex, MA, as installed in the Henry Francis du Pont Winterthur Museum. ✦

Material Culture

Despite a widening gap between the rich and the poor, most settlers lived more comfortably in 1700 than people had earlier in the century. Virginia settlers generally began their lives in the New World in one-room cottages, often without doors or windows and frequently with dirt floors and thatched roofs. Log and clay fireplaces or even pit fires in the middle of the room provided the only light and heat for cooking. As soon as possible, they replaced this crude building with a frame house, usually one-and-a-half stories high and rectangular in shape (sixteen by twenty feet), built of rough timbers held together with wooden pegs. These homes had exterior chimneys, shingled roofs, windows, wooden floors and clapboard siding. Family members reached the upper rooms by ladder and used them for sleeping or storage. Despite the improvements, these were still small, dimly lit buildings that provided little privacy. They were sparsely furnished. At mid-century, many houses still lacked tables, chairs, or beds, and families often slept on piles of straw and leaves. Even wealthier planters had only four rooms, two up and two down, and perhaps a porch and a kitchen house. One of the few exceptions was Governor Berkeley's Green Springs mansion, a model for eighteenth-century plantation mansions.

Furniture varied according to the person's place in the social hierarchy. The greater the resident's wealth, the more likely it was that the house was filled with furniture, tables, chairs, and beds. Tools, weapons, and clothing varied in quality and quantity according to social status. The distinctive Chesapeake style, adapted from the architecture of southern England, was still in the future.

New Englanders also began life in the New World in rather humble fashion. The earliest settlers often lived in crude huts, dugouts, wigwams, and daub-and-wattle cabins. After the first decade or so, cottages with clapboard siding and thatched or planked roofs became common. But many continued to live in one-room homes, with an inner loft for sleeping, whose dimensions were typically twenty to twenty-five feet by sixteen to eighteen feet. Even those who were better off spent their early years in two-room, one-story homes, with the ever-present loft for sleeping and storage space.

As conditions improved and families grew, a settler might add a lean-to for a kitchen and two rooms at either end of the house. Ultimately, the typical plan came to closely resemble the homes New Englanders had inhabited in eastern England. A common design consisted of a two-story rectangle with a central chimney and a

A bench from late seventeenth-century Massachusetts. ⟩ᴥ

Wooden tableware. The simplicity of life in early Plymouth (and elsewhere in the colonies) is revealed by the starkly functional nature of furniture and kitchen utensils. ఌ

steeply pitched roof, often with a one-story lean-to added to the back. This was the saltbox, a New England adaptation of a dwelling that commonly graced the landscape of Kent and East Anglia.

A brief look at the William Boardman house, built in Massachusetts around 1687, will give some idea of how New Englanders used these homes. The hall possessed the only continuous fire and was used for cooking, eating, working, and socializing. It might contain a chest or small cupboard, a large table, and chairs, together with the necessary utensils and fireplace equipment. The parlor was furnished with the great bed and perhaps a cupboard with pewter or silver. It was the sleeping room for the parents and accommodated special functions, such as funerals or courting. Wife and daughters performed kitchen chores and dairying tasks in the lean-to. Since the Boardmans were fairly well-off, they also had two sleeping and storage rooms.

Construction of these buildings tells us much about both work and community life in early New England. Siting was important. Houses were ideally situated on a slight rise close to a road, facing south for maximum warmth from the winter sun. Several men would work together to dig the cellar hole and lay the fieldstone walls up the sides from the dirt floor. Next, they laid the oak sills, squared by axe and adze. They then assembled the walls on the ground and raised them into place. They locked the ends into the already-standing corner posts with tree nails, added joists and beams for strength, and completed the frame with the roof rafters, studs, and other finishing pieces. At first, most houses were sided with clapboards—long, narrow boards made from cedar or pine and attached directly to the studs with an inch of overlap. Later, colonists began to use shingles nailed to board sheathing. Shingled roofing also completely replaced the earlier thatched roofing. The chimney, which took up a good deal of the interior space, was constructed of fieldstones bound with clay mortar. Only at the end of the century did the sort of refinements common in England appear in the New World—glass (particularly scarce in the early decades), fancy woodwork, lime plaster walls, and more decorative chairs and tables. Lighting was a problem, the only sources being candles and grease lamps.

The Harlow Old Fort House, Plymouth Colony. ❧

Housing in the Delaware Valley progressed somewhat more speedily toward refinement, since the area was settled late and did not experience the lengthy period of adjustment suffered by other regions. Within the first generation, Quakers abandoned the use of wood for construction and adopted the much more durable gray-brown fieldstone. Both houses and construction methods were similar to those the settlers had left behind in the north of England, though they were forced to use wood for house and window frames and lintels.

Two plans were typical of homes in the Delaware Valley. The Quaker plan house consisted of three rooms on the first floor, a corner staircase, and several fireplaces. A second type was the four-over-four house, with four rooms and central halls on both floors—certainly the most prosperous type of dwelling to be found on the North American continent during the seventeenth century. While Quaker houses were plain, they were also larger and more comfortable than those of other regions. Interiors were bright, clean, and spacious, though austere. Furniture was sparse—a few chairs, a plain board table, a cupboard, a few stools, and a long seat in the parlor. Beds and benches graced the bedrooms. Philadelphia architecture was also distinctive from the very beginning, resembling that found in parts of London and Dublin with brick fronts, raised entries, and simple details. Even here, the emphasis in exterior design and interior furnishing was on use rather than display.

By the end of the century, the early settlers in all the colonies were moving toward bigger houses and greater comfort within them.

Education

All cultures seek to perpetuate themselves and pass their essential beliefs on to the next generation, most obviously through formal education. Nowhere in the early modern world was this desire stronger than in early New England. Puritanism required individual knowledge of the Bible, thus the ability to read was essential if the laity were to understand God's message. The Puritan belief that children were born ignorant and evil also necessitated that young people be taught not only to read but also to understand their proper, ordered place in society. Despite varying rates of compliance with school laws, New England claimed the highest literacy rates in the world at the time. In 1660, about two-thirds of the men and more than one-third of the women in New England could sign their wills, and even higher proportions than this could read.

English colonization took place amidst a widespread boom in English schooling. In the early seventeenth century, English petty schools provided basic literacy skills for two or three years, while grammar schools instructed students in reading, writing, Latin, Greek, and Hebrew over a period of seven years or so. Much instruction also occurred in homes and shops. The people of East Anglia welcomed these improvements, spurred both by Puritanism and by the more mundane demands of a commercialized economy.

Early New Englanders continued the tradition. In 1642, Massachusetts passed a law requiring selectmen to ensure that all inhabitants, including children, could read and understand "the principles of religion and the capital lawes of this country." The intent of the law was clearly religious, since it was the "cheife project of the ould deluder, Satan, to keepe men from the knowledge of the Scriptures."[53] Other New England colonies (except Rhode Island) passed similar laws. Massachusetts followed up with a 1647 law that required all towns with at least fifty households to appoint a teacher who would instruct children in reading and writing in an elementary school and any town with at least one hundred households to establish a grammar school to prepare male youths for the university. Not all towns complied, of course; during the first decade, only about one-third of those towns with fifty households established schools. Those which did not follow the law were subject to a fine of five pounds annually.

New England youth began their education in dame schools, which taught reading and writing to both boys and girls five to seven years of age. Boys then moved on to grammar schools, where they learned Latin, and introduction to Greek, and in some schools, Hebrew. Boston Latin was the first such institution, founded in 1635. The grammar school course involved seven or eight years of study. Later in the century, the curriculum was broadened, and most grammar schools became "general schools," reflecting the shortage of students, masters, and money.

The morning session in grammar schools began at 6 or 7 A.M. and lasted until 11 A.M.; the afternoon began at 1 P.M. and ended at 5 P.M in the summer and 4 P.M in the winter. College graduates awaiting their first ministerial appointments generally taught the classes. Though most of the teachers were likely of average ability and commitment, there were some instructors of genuine distinction. Ezekiel Cheever was educated at Emmanuel College, Cambridge, and made a career of teaching—an unusual choice in the seventeenth century. He migrated to Massachusetts in 1637 and began his career in schools at Ipswich and Charlestown, assuming a post at the Boston Free School for sixty pounds a year (far above the average) in 1671; he taught there until his death in 1709 at the age of ninety-three. Cheever enjoyed an excellent reputation throughout the region, and many of his students went on to Harvard.

A "free school" meant different things in different towns, and during the first decades, most parents paid to send their children to these schools. In Salem, attendance was free to all poor children; in Ipswich, to a limited number only; in Dedham, it was free to all children. It was this last model that ultimately came to prevail, and schools eventually relied on town rates and overall direction from the General Court.

For all of their emphasis on the spirit, Quakers put a great deal of faith in the use of reason, believing it to be an inherent part of the inner light. But they also believed there were limits to what could be learned from books. They were suspicious of a learned clergy and only moderately enthusiastic about encouraging literacy to broaden access to the scriptures; women and the poor, in Quaker society, were often illiterate. Even William Penn argued that too much reading "extinguishes the natural candle. . ."[54] and encouraged his own children not to read too much. Of course, Penn wrote a book to give this advice! Although the Pennsylvania assembly passed a law in 1683 requiring that all children be taught to read and write by the age of twelve, there was little official support for education, and only sectarian schools provided additional opportunities. Quakers established local schools attached to individual meetings and neighborhoods. By 1776, there were about sixty such schools; they charged tuition and generally admitted children of the poor free. The Quakers also encouraged other groups, such as the Germans, to found their own schools.

Literacy rates were much lower in the Chesapeake than in other regions. Only about half of the adult male property owners could write, and most adults in the seventeenth century could not sign their names (roughly the same percentages prevailed in the south and west of England). More than anywhere else in the mainland colonies, Chesapeake society maintained a hierarchical attitude toward learning. There were no public schools here. Some planters sent their children to England to be educated, but most hired private tutors. They provided two or three years of instruction for their daughters in music, dancing, and other skills required of a good gentry wife. There were parish-based schools, but they charged tuition and more closely resembled private academies than public schools. Only two charity schools in Elizabeth City County served the poor. The law required, though, that orphans and bastards receive two years' instruction in reading, writing, and mathematics, and local officials conscientiously enforced this provision.

Though many colonists continued to attend English universities, two colleges were established in the colonies in the seventeenth century: Harvard College in 1636, and the College of William and Mary in 1693 (Yale was founded in 1701). Harvard was founded primarily to train ministers. Henry Dunster became its first president in 1640 (serving until 1654), and at first, he taught all of the courses himself. He modeled the curriculum on that of his own college, Emmanuel College, Cambridge. Most books and all of the instruction were in Latin. Instruction involved a combination of lecture, declamation, and disputation; a moderator introduced a student who argued a position, while others in the class raised objections to the argument. Courses included grammar, logic, and rhetoric (the medieval trivium) for freshmen and sophomores and arithmetic, geometry, astronomy, and music (the medieval quadrivium) for upperclassmen. Students could also pursue studies in ethics, metaphysics, Greek, Latin, Hebrew, and Aramaic, while sciences and higher mathematics became increasingly important after mid-century. During the 1650s, students read and studied Copernicus, Galileo, and Kepler. Students' private libraries included English essays and poetry, Spanish literature, and books on medicine and science. Most of the students were from wealthy families or were sons of ministers; only a few were sons of artisans or tradesmen. John Wise, for instance, who was a member of the class of 1673 and became best known for his resistance to Edmund Andros in 1687, was the first son of an indentured servant to graduate from the college. William and Mary offered similar opportunities to Chesapeake gentry families who could now educate their sons in Virginia rather than England, thus strengthening their social identity as a privileged American ruling group.

Reading And Literature

Family, church, and literature were equally critical vessels of cultural transmission. But considerable disagreement existed over what cultural values should be passed along. The controversy over the half-way covenant is only the most obvious example of generational and doctrinal differences over central cultural values. New Englanders divided over one of the most critical cultural issues of the early modern world: the struggle between the oral folk culture of the common people and the more literate, elite culture of the ministers and university-trained leaders. Folk culture included interest in magic and the occult, but it was also a face-to-face, oral culture that hinged on the ritual affirmation of community and traditional values. In seeking to expand the hegemony of their own literate culture, ministers had to accommodate these popular beliefs if they were to retain and enlarge their special status within the community. The centrality of the Bible to Puritan religious beliefs aided them in this struggle. For Puritans, Scripture was more than just a "how-to" guide to religious practice; it was a direct message from God and a sacred time. The first step in gaining access to this truth was learning how to read. The laity treated even sermons as books, studying printed versions intensely.

Ordinary New Englanders owned a Bible and little else in the way of reading material during the early decades. But while the first newspaper did not appear until 1704, the commercial book trade began to grow after 1660, and New England printers were successful enough to boast of a number of best-sellers during the final decades of the century. This new market presented a threat to the delicately balanced religiosity of laity and ministry alike. Booksellers and printers refused to accept any form of control or censorship. New types of publications emerged to compete with the moralistic writings of the ministry. Books that contained life histories of ordinary people that showed they "were actors in the greatest drama of them all,"[55] became particularly popular. Devotional works sold well throughout the colonies, as the laity embraced them eagerly as handbooks of piety. Three of the most popular were Lewis Bayly's *The Practise of Pietie*, Richard Allestree's *The Whole Duty of Man*, and Richard Baxer's *The Poor Man's Family Book*. Bayly's work was typical. It instructed families how to read the Bible, how to perform good works, and how to behave in church. Anxious church members read such books to learn how to live as good Christians.

Not all popular literature addressed religious concerns, even in the seventeenth century. Many avidly purchased books that sought to nurture civility as well as proper religious behavior, such as books by Plato, Aristotle, Thomas More, and Machiavelli and even Castiglione's *The Courtier*. New Englanders and others read Henry Peacham's *The Compleat Gentleman* (1622) and Richard Brathwaite's *The English Gentleman* (1630). The first resembled Castiglione's book in its emphasis on upper-class manners, but the second argued that virtue would be found as much in personal goodness. Brathwaite's was a manual of piety and civility both, inaugurating a tradition that would persist among the American gentry.

New England also produced works of real literary merit, such as John Winthrop's *Journal* and William Bradford's *Of Plymouth Plantation*. Both of these works reflect the authors' concern to discover true, or sacred, history beneath the misleading veneer of human events. Winthrop and Bradford searched daily happenings for signs or portents of God's true intentions. In 1646, for instance, a snake crawled into the Cambridge, Massachusetts, meetinghouse in the midst of an important meeting of ministers and magistrates. Such an event hardly seems surprising in a settlement located in a forest. To Winthrop, however, "[t]he serpent is the devil; the synod, the representative of the churches of Christ in New England. The devil had formerly and lately attempted to their disturbance and dissolution; but their faith in the seed of woman overcame him and crushed his head."[56] The snake thus symbolized the devil's dismay at the ministers of God coming together in harmony to promote the true interests of the church.

Bradford interpreted the flight of the Pilgrims from England in the same vein—a struggle between light and dark, good and evil, with God's chosen people successfully crossing the vast Atlantic to further his glory: "What could now sustaine them but the spirite of God and his grace? May not & ought not the children of these fathers rightly say: *Our fathers were Englishmen which came over this great ocean, and were ready to perish in this wilderness; but they cried unto the Lord, and he heard their voice, and looked on their adversity. . . .* "[57] Plymouth thus took on special meaning, like Massachusetts Bay, as the light of God in the wilderness, the precursor of His triumph on earth.

Edward Johnson's *Wonder-Working Providence of Sion's Saviour in New England* reflects similar concerns. Johnson was a ship's carpenter and a Woburn, Massachusetts, militia captain, a man of little formal education. The theme that graced his work was a common one among both New and Old World Puritans—the pilgrim's progress. Johnson's Puritans were soldiers, embarking on "wilderness-work," and New England as a whole was a division in God's army equal to the forces of Cromwell. He published the work in an attempt to stir up a complacent New England, to urge it to recover from what he viewed as its growing materialism: "Yea it may be boldly said that the time is come, and all may see the dawning of the day: you that lo so much for it, come forth and fight: who can aspect a victory without a battel?"[58]

William Wood's *New England's Prospect* (1634), is hardly a great work of literature, but it bears mention as the first popular account of settlement in the Bay Colony. Wood described the region's geography, climate, and plant life; traced the founding of the colony's first towns; and offered a full, detailed account of the Indians and their culture. He also included the first printed map made by a settler of the colony and a list of suggested articles for newcomers to bring with them. The book went through three editions during the 1630s alone. We know little about Wood himself, but his early travel guide has immortalized his name.

Puritan ministers also used a technique known as typology in an even more sophisticated attempt to understand God's larger plan. Typology reflected the belief that Old Testament figures, such as Adam and Moses, foreshadowed the prophecies of Christ and that the historical experiences of Israel prefigured those of the Christian church. These individuals and experiences were known as "types"; Jonah's three days in the belly of the whale prefigured, for instance, Christ's three days in the grave. Ministers often engaged in heated debates over the meanings of such figures and their relevance to the Puritan experiment, since they adopted the controversial position that Israel was a "type" for New England. They interpreted the language of the Bible symbolically, searching every figure and events for its potential relevance and predictive value concerning God's plans for New England.

The ordinary farmer undoubtedly strained to understand the more esoteric theological points the ministers debated among themselves. Lay testimonies and conversion narratives followed set patterns to a significant extent. While they confirm the high level of lay piety, they give no indication of the extent to which the converts understood what they were saying. By examining the literature parents and ministers used to teach their children the essentials of Puritan doctrine, we can gain a more realistic idea of how church members received the complex messages of their ministers. Three works are particularly relevant: John Cotton's catechism, *Spiritual Milk for Babes; The New England Primer;* and James Janeway's *A Token for Children.*

Teachers, ministers, and parents alike used these books to educate New England's youth. Cotton's catechism was first published in England in 1646 and reprinted for more than 150 years. Following a question-and-answer format, it offered children guidelines that would begin their preparation for church membership. Families were responsible for most religious instruction in the seventeenth century, and they used the catechism to give children their first religious instruction. Cotton's guide was only one among many; more than five hundred catechisms were available in this century alone. But Cotton's was the most successful in imparting the sense of hierarchy and order, the preeminence of church and state that were central to Puritan concerns. Obedience and honor were the key principles imparted to toddlers. Thus, "Honor thy Father and thy Mother" became a religious requirement to honor and obey "All our Superiours, whether in Family, School, Church, and Common-wealth."[59]

The *Primer,* also used in church and schools, was a step further along the path to religious knowledge. It taught children the alphabet and beginning reading and contained a syllabarium, a picture alphabet, a catechism, and the story of John

A page from the New England Primer. ❧

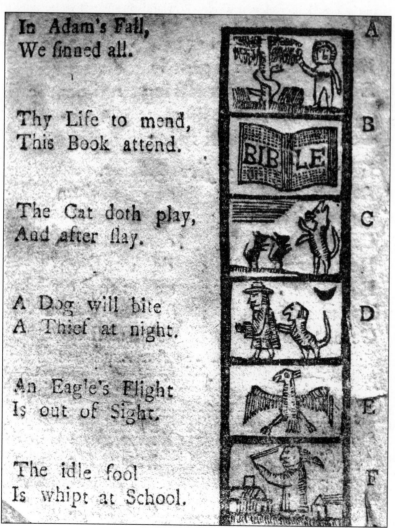

Roger's martyrdom. The rhymes and words were selected to instruct pupils in basic religious tenets, while Roger's martyrdom under Queen Mary served to impress upon young minds the horrors of Catholicism. It remained popular throughout the colonial period and went through many editions after its initial publication in 1683.

Janeway's *Token,* first published in England in 1671, was imported into Massachusetts and published in an American edition in 1700. It provided life histories of model children who loved school and studied their catechism and the Bible. They always respected parents, ministers, and other elders, kept the Sabbath, and were acutely aware of the pains of hell. They also died in childhood or adolescence, and their exemplary lives were portrayed as preparations for death and redemption, happy despite their suffering. Cotton Mather appended an account of seven New England children to the American edition, including one Elizabeth Butcher, whom Mather described as laying in her cradle at the age of two and a half pondering the question "What is my corrupt Nature?"[60]

Captivity narratives were a genre unique to New England. The most famous of these is Mary Rowlandson's *A True History of the Captivity & Restoration of Mrs. Mary Rowlandson* (1682). Indians took Rowlandson and her three children captive in February 1676 during King Philip's War, when they attacked the frontier town of Lancaster. Her youngest child died in captivity, while she and the other children were ransomed and released after eleven weeks. Rowlandson's narrative became a warning to New Englanders who had abandoned the word of God. The surface tale is a true adventure story, but more important to Puritans was the subtext—the story of the inward spiritual journey of a woman who willingly endured the fate God had chosen for her and who returned to civilization more aware of the vanities of material life and the importance of the spiritual journey.

All of this seems far removed from the rarefied achievements of serious European literature. Even the greatest of these works were written primarily for religious purposes. In poetry, though, a few early New Englanders succeeded in mimicking and even approaching the high culture of Europe. The most traditional of Puritan poets was Michael Wigglesworth, a Puritan minister in Malden, Massachusetts. Wigglesworth was preoccupied with sin even more than was usual for a conscientious Puritan, and he was appalled by what he viewed as the "unbridled licentiousness" that seemed to increasingly characterize New Englanders. To chastise his fellow Puritans, he wrote *The Day of Doom* in 1662, an early best-seller. Surely the most damning, and depressing, poem ever published on this side of the ocean, it was hardly a model of literary style. But like all early Puritan literature, that was not its goal. The poem opens with the coming of Judgment Day and concludes with a frightening picture of the agony of the damned; its postscript warns readers that they are closer to the fires of hell than they think. What fears darkened young minds as children heard these lines?

Two other early New England poets moved beyond the didactic in their work. Anne Bradstreet remains the most recognized and accomplished of seventeenth-century American literary figures. Her early poems focused on Europe and were conservative in content and style; they were public declamations, imitating Renaissance models, for instance, in praising Elizabeth and finding the Stuarts wanting in comparison. Her first work, *The Tenth Muse, Lately Sprung up in America,* was published in London in 1650. She later disclaimed this early material as derivative. Her mature poems reflect both her adherence to Puritan doctrine and "her savoring of earthly faces, sights, touch. . . . "[61] While she viewed herself as a pilgrim, here on earth only in preparation for salvation and life in heaven, her subjects grew out of daily life—a child's sickness, pregnancy, her house burning down. These were works of love and sorrow, celebrating marriage or grieving the death of a child.

The other major American poet from this century was Edward Taylor. Taylor served as minister to the Westfield, Massachusetts, congregation from 1671 to 1729. His most important work was not discovered until 1937—*Preparatory Meditations before my approach to the Lord's Supper,* a series of private meditations on Scripture. His beliefs were orthodox, and he championed the anti-Stoddard position in the Connecticut Valley debate over communion. He used typology extensively, and like Bradstreet's, his poetry was religiously inspired and written in response to specific events and for specific ends. He used his poetry to further his understanding of the needs of his flock. But Taylor's work also reveals an intriguing tension between the spiritual demands of Puritanism and the seductive appeals of language. His themes stress both self-loathing and the glorification of and desire for God—typical Puritan concerns. His work also evokes, however, a powerful sense of wonder, a delight in the sensuality of Old Testament language, and a joy in the use of vivid, physical imagery, characteristics reflecting the metaphysical tradition. In this, he most closely resembles Jonathan Edwards, who embraced John Locke's modern explanations of perception only to employ them as a means of furthering human understanding and love of God.

At the end of the century, New England stood almost alone in the diversity and breadth of its cultural development. But its literary accomplishments remained focused largely on religion. Still, there were clear signs pointing toward the future, signs most visible, in all their contradictions and inconsistencies, in the life of Cotton Mather (1663–1728). Mather's most productive work came after 1700, but his education and interests were shaped earlier, influenced by his father, Increase, and the burdensome weight of the myth of the Puritan Founding Fathers. Mather's piety cannot be questioned. He spent six hours a day in prayer and meditation, embraced millennial beliefs throughout his life, and became increasingly mystical in his efforts to discover the exact time of Christ's coming. He read Thomas a Kempis (the medieval Christian mystic) and corresponded extensively with German pietists. The intensity of his religious commitment is certainly understandable. In addition to the influence of his religion and his family, his life was filled with tragedy. Two of his wives died before him, and a third went insane. He outlived all but two of his children, and his namesake son's profligate, dissolute behavior proved an intense embarrassment to him. Mather was voracious in his intellectual appetite, reading everything he could get his hands on, writing hundreds of sermons and pamphlets, and showing particular interest in science. In 1720, he advocated inoculation for the smallpox epidemic sweeping Boston, a brave position in the face of stiff resistance from clergy and so-called physicians alike. He sought to adapt even his piety to a changing world, establishing "do-good" societies to encourage proper behavior among his parishioners in a society that was growing more secular by the day. Mather is often more remembered for his arrogance and difficult temperament; he deserves to be seem as a seventeenth-century Puritan who tried his best to make sense of his colony's entry into the modern world.

John Smith, one of the earliest—and most secular—Englishmen to write about the New World, provides an apt coda to these comments. An adventurer first and foremost, Smith remains the most important seventeenth-century American literary figure outside of New England. In *A Description of New England* (1616), Smith wrote that an heroic mission awaited those who would settle in that glorious land. In *A True Relation of. . . Virginia* (1608), he spoke of chivalry, adventure, and American abundance, along with the need for practicality and discipline in dealing with the demanding environment. And in his *Generall Historie of Virginia, New-England, and the Summer Isles* (1624), he spun a romantic tale of Englishmen and noble savages. But Smith never lost sight of the source of his vision, a source that would linger and haunt the American mind for decades to come: "What so truely suits with honour and honesty as the discovering things unknown: erecting towns, peopling countries, informing the ignorant, reforming things unjust, teaching virtue; and gain to our native mother country a kingdom to attend her."[62] In every way, seventeenth-century American culture represented a dialogue between colonists, Indians, and the land on the one hand and European culture on the other. In 1700, American colonists remained English men and women, but their identities were in flux. Old World habits and beliefs struggled to find accommodation with New World conditions. The very process of "erecting towns, peopling countries, informing the ignorant, reforming things unjust," and "teaching virtue" made the colonies much more than mere attendants to the mother country. The colonies' very existence as a "new world" gave these activities an alluring religious and secular idealism that was all but unattainable.

ᐇᴥ *Chapter Eight* ᴥᐂ

The Peopling of Eighteenth-Century America

As late as 1700, the vast majority of settlers in the British mainland colonies came from England. The Dutch, meanwhile, remained a significant element in the New York population, and from the beginning, Pennsylvania attracted a greater diversity of settlers than any other colony. The English had already begun to transform the labor force in the southern colonies by importing large numbers of Africans as enslaved labor. It was waves of European and African immigration in the eighteenth century, though, together with unprecedented natural growth, that dramatically increased the population and changed forever the cultural dynamics of the British colonies.

Population Growth

About forty thousand whites inhabited the mainland colonies in 1650; their numbers had grown to 235,000 by 1700 and 2.1 million by 1775. By that year, there were also about 540,000 blacks and fifty thousand Indians. This growth represented an annual increase of slightly more than 3 percent. The economic impact of such rapid population growth was profound, if only in its expansion of the demand for necessities and ordinary economic goods. Population growth alone, for instance, was responsible for more than 75 percent of the increase in aggregate economic output during the eighteenth century, while per capita output increased little. As a result, the English colonists possessed the highest per capita standard of living in the Western world at the time. As Benjamin Franklin observed in his influential pamphlet *Observations Concerning the Increase of Mankind,* this rate of growth also had important ideological ramifications.

Significant Dates

1450	Portuguese begin to export slaves to Europe and eastern Atlantic sugar islands
1510	Spain legalizes sale of Africans to the New World
1619	First Africans arrive in Virginia
1662	Virginia law declares children inherit the status (free or slave) of their mother
1680–20	Transformation of Chesapeake labor force
1683	German pietists settle Germantown, Pennsylvania
1685	Revocation of the Edict of Nantes
1705	Virginia slave code
1707	Act of Union
1709	Swiss Mennonites arrive in Pennsylvania
1710	Palatine Germans settle in New York
1712	New York slave rebellion
1717	Scotch-Irish arrive in Delaware and Boston
1720	Lutheran and German Reformed migration into Pennsylvania begins
1730	First settlements in the Shenandoah Valley
1735	First Moravian settlement in Pennsylvania
1739	Stono Rebellion
1740	Great Charleston fire
1741	New York slave conspiracy
1750	Benjamin Franklin publishes *Observations Concerning the Increase of Mankind*
1758	First African Baptist Congregation established in Lunenberg, Virginia

Franklin wrote this essay in 1751 to attack proposed parliamentary restrictions on the colonial iron industry. He calculated (accurately) that the American population was doubling about every twenty-five years and argued that these growing numbers would provide an immense market for British manufactures. He also contended that within a century, there would be more British citizens in America than in England—and that ultimately, the seat of the empire would be on this side of the Atlantic.

Much of this increase, as Franklin noted, was due to the abundance of land in the New World. Economic independence was now possible at a much earlier age than in Europe. Colonial men typically married in their middle twenties and women even earlier, both about two to three years earlier than their European counterparts. More land meant abundant harvests, lower population density, and plentiful supplies of wood for fuel. With a healthier, less concentrated population, epidemic diseases had much less impact here than in the Old World. While Europe averaged about forty deaths per thousand a year, the thirteen mainland colonies had only fifteen to twenty-five. The advantages were cumulative; more women survived to bear children, and more of those children survived. The importance of diet can be further illustrated by the different experiences of black slave children. The youngest were severely deprived nutritionally; more than half died before they reached their fifth birthdays. Owners apparently thought it was not worthwhile to feed youngsters who were not contributing to their wealth through direct labor. Between the ages of eleven to fourteen, however, when boys and girls could begin working, they received much more nutritious diets, and their death rates approached those of whites. And compared with Latin American slaves, English slaves lived in a better climate and had lower rates of disease, more even sex ratios, less arduous labor requirements, and a significantly longer life expectancy. By the 1770s, native-born black women in the mainland colonies bore seven to nine children. As the colonial period came to a close, black and white Americans alike were reproducing at a rate unmatched anywhere else in the world.

Immigration

Natural increase provided most of the population growth in the mainland colonies, but immigration remained substantial and added significantly to the area's ethnic and cultural diversity. First, a substantial migration from Europe occurred between 1760 and 1775, one that has only recently been studied in full. Some 220,000 people came to the mainland colonies during these years. Second, about fifty thousand convicted felons were transported from England to the colonies during the eighteenth century, about two-thirds of them to the Chesapeake. They were generally put under the charge of local British merchant-contractors, who received five pounds per convict. The contractors then sold them under terms much like those accorded indentured servants—except their terms were longer, and they received no freedom dues. Still, they were not popular in most colonies, and several governments took measures to limit their importation. Maryland, Pennsylvania, and New Jersey attempted to place prohibitive duties on their importation (England disallowed the latter two laws), while in 1736, Virginia passed legislation that required the payment of freedom dues in order to make convicts a less attractive investment.

Third, Europeans brought black Africans here against their wills in the largest migration of the century. Finally, a bewildering variety of Europeans fled their homelands in the first decades of the eighteenth century to seek greater opportunities in the British colonies. These included Germans, Scotch-Irish, Scots, Huguenots, Welsh, Swiss, Italians, and Jews. The majority of these people entered the colonies as indentured servants or redemptioners. Indentured servitude functioned in much the same way as it had in the Chesapeake during the seventeenth century, though it provided significantly more reliable opportunities for the new arrivals. Eighteenth-century servants came from a wide spectrum of English and European society; they ranged from farmers and artisans to unskilled laborers and domestic servants, though few had any prospects of becoming landowners in their homeland. Even those who started at the bottom in America had living standards comparable to what they had left behind, and their long-term prospects were much better. Those with skills could negotiate with merchant-contractors for shorter terms and higher freedom dues, giving them an even more favorable start.

Redemption was a variation on indentured servitude, particularly common among Germans. Under this system, migrants agreed to pay the costs of transportation to the New World within a week or two of arrival. They signed no contract in Europe; rather, captains or merchants paid for their passage. If the migrants could not repay the costs on arrival and no relative or friend came to their aid, the captains sold them as workers for a specified length of time; five years was the most common. Redemptioners came both as families and as members of a larger group; from 1727 to 1776, about two-thirds of the sixty-five thousand to seventy-five thousand Germans who entered Philadelphia were redemptioners.

German Migrants

Germans were the largest single non-English European group to make their way to these shores. From 1683 to 1783, about half a million Germans left their homeland, moving to Hungary, Russia, Spain, and the French colonies; of these, about 125,000 came to British North America. Before 1688, migrants came primarily from northern Germany and Hansa cities, fleeing religious persecution. After the War of the League of Augsburg (1689–1697) and the War of Spanish Succession (1702–1713) devastated the Rhineland, more people left the German southwest. Peasants also left to escape their servile, feudalistic relationship with their lords. William Penn sponsored the first group of Germans to arrive in America, pietists from Frankfurt-on-the-Main led by Francis Daniel Pastorius and Johannes Keplius. They settled at the future site of Germantown in 1683.

These and later groups viewed America as a land of high wages and low taxes and a way to escape the mandatory military service of their homelands. To them, Pennsylvania did indeed seem like the promised land, a place with no beggars and servant women who dressed as well as the German nobility; songs circulating in German villages perpetuated stories about the fabled lands to the west. The first large group to land in the eighteenth century arrived almost accidentally. The British gave asylum to about thirteen thousand Palatine refugees during the War of Spanish Succession, then decided they could not provide for them in England. The government sent about 650 of them to North Carolina to join earlier Swiss settlements and settled more than twenty-three hundred in New York under contract to make tar and pitch, mostly on the Livingston estate. There, the Palatines found only exploitation and continued poverty; they protested so much that their colonial employers moved them to Pennsylvania and northern New Jersey. The experience in New York steered other Germans away from New York for much of the remaining colonial period.

The first large German migration arrived in Philadelphia in 1717; about two thousand were to disembark here annually for the next fifty years. Before 1727, the migration included mystics and spiritualists—Schwenkfelder communities, Rosicrucians, Protestant monastics, and radical pietists—who settled north of Lancaster. After that, when the largest number came, the migrants were primarily Lutheran, German Reformed, and Moravian. By the 1770s, Lutherans alone made up more than half the Germans in North America, and by 1775, almost 10 percent of the population in the British mainland colonies was German-speaking.

Despite their clear religious identifications, these groups left Germany primarily for secular reasons. Most came in family groups, attracted by the avalanche of promotional literature churned out by ship captains, merchants, and land companies that sent agents to Germany to encourage the peasants' utopian fantasies of North America. A dozen or so English and Dutch firms worked in Rotterdam and Amsterdam to attract prospective settlers to the Netherlands. Representatives met the migrants at the border and transported them to Dutch ports, where recruiting agents known as *neulanders* (newlanders) competed to draw passengers to their masters' ships. These entrepreneurial shipowners found future buyers for the migrants in North America, wrote the redemption contracts, and attended to all the details of the crossing. The neulanders soon expanded their roles, moving into the countryside and even Germany and Switzerland, often passing themselves off as wealthy returned emigrants who wanted to aid their compatriots in seeking their fortunes in America.

The migrants often sold all they had to raise the money for the passage. The voyage itself was a horrific experience for these families. Gottlieb Mittelberger was an organist and music teacher from the Duchy of Wurttenberger who was commissioned in 1750 to bring an organ to the New World. His account of the crossing remains memorable. Mittelberger spent several weeks traveling down the Rhine and waiting in port for a ship, using up most of his money in the process. On board, passengers were packed into spaces measuring two by six feet. They were assaulted by repulsive smells, rotten food, sea sickness, and disease—smallpox, typhus, dysentery, scurvy. Lice were everywhere. The food was bad, the water "thick with dirt, and full of worms. . . ."[1] Ocean storms were terrifying. Mittelberger's ship sailed through one for three days and nights, which convinced the passengers that they were surely lost. Children under seven rarely survived, and one woman who could not give birth under the horrible conditions and died "was pushed through one of the portholes into the sea because her corpse was far back in the stern and could not be brought to the deck."[2] Overall, about 5 percent of the passengers died during the crossing and another 5 percent soon after arriving.

Once here, Germans proved to be among the most mobile of early Americans, following valleys and rivers to Maryland, Virginia, the Carolinas, and Georgia. The Palatines and Swiss founded New Bern, North Carolina, in 1710, and Lutherans established a community at Ebenezer, Georgia, in 1736. In Pennsylvania, they settled along the Schuylkill river and spread east and west into Lancaster, Berks, and Northampton counties. Another group settled in western Maryland, where they became successful grain and cattle farmers. Massive barns were a unique feature of this community, built on masonry foundations and often larger than the neighboring houses, with Old World-style hex signs on the gabled ends to ward off evil spirits.

Unlike many other groups, Germans maintained close ties with their home communities, establishing support networks within the colonies and back to Germany. By the 1720s, the Halle missionary group had become the most extensive of these networks. This German group supported religious, linguistic, and scientific expeditions throughout the world, and they were particularly generous in their efforts to establish connections with the British colonies. They supplied German communities with printed materials and supported orphanages and educational efforts in America. Other support systems did not come close to matching the Halle group's success. German Reformed groups relied on Amsterdam and Switzerland for money and ministers, and little of either came. These Germans thus became anglicized much more rapidly than others, and only continuous migration and strong leadership from merchants and clergy helped them preserve anything of their Old World identity.

Philadelphia became the center for New World Germans by the 1750s and played a critical role in preserving Old World, German identity amidst the transformative New World environment. Its influence extended as far south as the Shenandoah Valley in Virginia. A decade later, Charleston began to play a similar role in the southern region. There, leading Lutheran families provided stability for parish affairs, and a group of prosperous German artisans became a vital part of the city's economy, some even acquiring low-country plantations. But even they received most of their news and material from Philadelphia.

❧ *Documents* ❧
Good Land and Painful Contempt

The earliest Scotch-Irish immigrants, as Robert Parke's letter shows, were lucky to find good land relatively near the coast, and they urged their friends and families to follow. Once here, though, they often suffered painful opprobrium. In the second selection, Benjamin Franklin shows a similar disdain of the Germans.

> Dear sister, I desire thee may tell my old friend Samuel Thornton that he could give so much credit to my words and find no "ifs" nor "ands" in my letter, that in plain terms he could not do better than to come here, for both his and his wife's trade are very good here. The best way for him to do is to pay what money he can conveniently spare at that side and engage himself to pay the rest at this side, and when he comes here, if he can get no friend to lay down the money for him, when it comes to the worst, he may hire out two or three children. And I would have him clothe his family as well as his small ability will allow. . . . I would have him procure three or four lusty servants and agree to pay their passage at this side. He might sell two and pay the others' passage with the money.

Charles A. Hanna, *The Scotch-Irish in America*, 2 vols. (Baltimore: Geneological Publishing Co.: 1968), 2:67.

Support networks helped American Germans sustain their separate culture far longer than did most other non-English-speaking groups in the New World. Many had made the voyage together in small groups and reestablished their old neighborhoods as soon as they could, maintaining the kinship and social ties of their German villages. German speakers relied on their own clergy, teachers, and merchants to serve as intermediaries with the English world surrounding them. They maintained their own churches, schools, and even taverns to reinforce their culture. They socialized separately, drank coffee rather than the American-favored tea, and even lived in smaller, less specialized homes that were more reflective of their German experiences. Many remained in frequent contact with their homeland, and some even attempted to regain ancestral property they had been promised when they left.

Before the 1750s, these communities ignored English courts and conducted necessary legal matters through their intermediaries. They also retained a medieval, popular religious culture that included German folk songs and witchcraft beliefs. But while Germans continued to use their own language in theology and domestic conversation, they regularly used English in trade, legal, and political matters. After the Seven Years War, American Germans reassessed their position and decided to embrace English public culture. They became increasingly involved in political affairs,

I am perfectly of your mind that measures of great temper are necessary with the Germans; and am not without apprehensions that through their indiscretion or ours, or both, great disorders and inconveniences may one day arise among us. Those who come hither are generally of the most ignorant, stupid sort of their own nation; and as ignorance is often attended with credulity when knavery when mislead it, and with suspicion when honesty would set it right; and as few of the English understand the German language and so cannot address them either from the press or pulpit, 'tis almost impossible to remove any prejudices they once entertain. . . . Nor being used to liberty, they know not how to make a modest use of it.

Benjamin Franklin to Peter Collinson, May 9, 1753; reprinted in David Hawke, ed., *U.S. Colonial History: Readings and Documents* (New York: The Bobbs-Merrill Company, Inc., 1966), 286–7.

recognizing the need for military defense in the backcountry and defending their land grants in the New Jersey title controversy. They were, in short, learning the right of resistance. Even after the Revolution, though, they continued to remain somewhat removed from public life and tied in informal ways to their Old World heritage.

Scotch-Irish

The Scotch-Irish were Lowland Scots whom the English settled in Ulster Province, Ireland, throughout the seventeenth century, though mostly before 1620. Despite their dislocation to Ireland, these settlers maintained strong ties with their homeland, particularly in religious affairs. Their form of Presbyterianism drew heavily from Scottish polity and beliefs, though it was also more tolerant of diversity and more influenced by scripture than by formal ritual. Most of all, it was strongly evangelical, characterized by prayer meetings and community services that often lasted several days and were frequently led by lay members. The migrants would later carry all of these characteristics with them to the New World.

Traditionally, historians have stressed religious persecution as the dominant motive for Scotch-Irish migration. In fact, though they were disestablished by law,

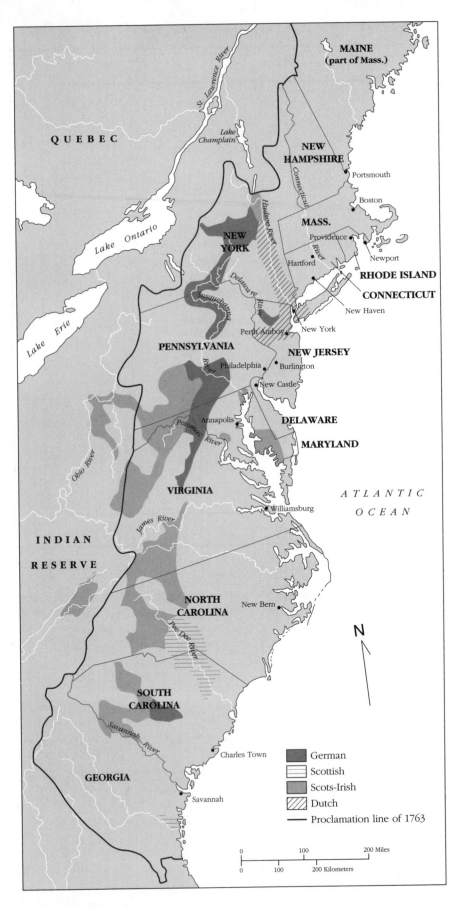

MAP 8.1:
**Concentrations
of Major Non-
English European
Immigrant
Groups in the
Eighteenth-
Century
Colonies**

in practice the Scotch-Irish enjoyed considerable religious freedom in Ulster. It was secular persecution that pushed them to leave. Absentee landlords, high rents, short leases, and bad harvests were the issues migrants complained of. They lived with their cattle in shacks with earthen floors, without windows or chimneys. Like many others, they came in groups and settled together in the New World. Londonderry, New Hampshire; Belfast and Bangor, Maine; Orange and Ulster counties, New York; Tyrone and Donegal, Pennsylvania—these place names come from the Old World. They settled in New England on the Maine coast, in New Hampshire, New Jersey, New York, and in the Allegheny foothills of Pennsylvania. They were particularly drawn to the Delaware River Valley, the more remote parts of the Susquehanna River, and along the Juanita River. By the 1730s, they had moved down the frontier valleys to the backcountry of Maryland, Virginia, and the Carolinas. They were not welcome at first. In Massachusetts, they refused to hold communion with the Congregationalists and denounced their theological errors. In response, the Puritans threw them out of Boston in 1729, and a mob later destroyed one of their churches. Like most American colonists, Bostonians considered them Irish and feared that "these confounded Irish will eat us all up."[3]

Noting their assertive personalities, other colonists regarded them as ideal buffers against Indian attacks on the frontier. Indeed, the English viewed the Scotch-Irish as little more civilized than the Indians themselves. After the 1715 Yamassee and 1756 Cherokee wars, South Carolina offered them inducements to settle in the backcountry. Throughout these years, they often bore the brunt of Indian raids, serving as the main line of defense along many borders during the Seven Years War. They readily moved into Indian country and simply took the land they desired, viewing Indians as mere savages: "It was against the laws of God and nature, that so much land should be idle, while so many Christians wanted it to labor on, and to raise their bread."[4] Such attitudes bespeak a remarkable similarity to even the Puritans who condemned them.

While a few settled in cities as wage laborers after their indentures expired, most of the Scotch-Irish became farmers. For the first time in their lives, they had as much land as they needed and could avoid the labor-intensive practices of manuring and draining that they had been forced to pursue in the Old World. They grew American crops such as tobacco, kept large cattle herds in the southern colonies, and raised hogs, which had been despised in Ireland. But they also maintained certain continuities in their agricultural practices. They preferred, for instance, the well-drained rolling hillsides to the fertile, wet bottomlands and practiced the same grain and livestock subsistence agriculture they had known in Ulster, using the same tools. They continued to grow potatoes and to weave and spin cloth. They also maintained the strong communal orientation that characterized their Ulster settlements. They were industrious and enthusiastically embraced slash-and-burn agriculture, bringing the agricultural techniques of the Delaware Indians to the hillsides of Pennsylvania and the southern backcountry.

As it had with the Germans, the decade before the Revolution proved decisive in Scotch-Irish acculturation to the American colonies. They became more politically aware at the end of the Seven Years War, expressing resentment at the unresponsiveness of Quaker leaders to their exposure on the hostile frontier and advocating the removal of the Indians who blocked their expansion. In the end, their degree of assimilation depended to a large extent on their location. Urban Scotch-Irish were much more likely to adopt American culture than those who inhabited western and central Pennsylvania and the southern backcountry, where they retained a distinctive group identity and strong ties to their Old World culture.

Other European Groups

While the Germans and Scotch-Irish dominated eighteenth-century white migration to the colonies, many other groups lent their own cultural hues to the astonishing mosaic that characterized America by the time of the Revolution. Including Africans, fully one-half of the population of the south was of non-English origin by 1775. Pennsylvania was a true polyglot of nationalities, and the backcountry had a distinctive culture.

Scottish migrants came from a broad social range, including landowners, professionals, merchants, artisans, and tenant farmers. They emigrated in particularly large numbers after the failed Jacobite revolts of 1715 and 1745; after the Battle of Culloden in 1746, in fact, England set out to destroy the clan system that structured Scottish society. Highland Scots came as part of their clans; they were Catholics and often resisted learning English. Lowland Scots migrated individually, settling around the Cape Fear area in North Carolina, the Hudson and Mohawk River valleys, and the New York backcountry.

The Huguenots' (French Protestants) craft skills made them among the most sought-after New World immigrants; colonies were always working on schemes to attract more of them. William Fitzhugh, for example, developed a plan in the 1680s to settle Huguenot tenants on a twenty-one thousand acre tract of land in Virginia, and about eight hundred did move onto an abandoned Indian tract twenty miles or so north of Richmond in the 1690s. Huguenots were fleeing renewed French persecution that had begun with the revocation of the Edict of Nantes in 1685, yet they were often just as unwelcome among colonists who were suspicious of their French cultural heritage. A group of fifty families settled in Frenchtown, Rhode Island, in 1686, only to be forced out by a mob in 1691. Another group moved to Oxford, Massachusetts, in 1687, leaving in 1704. Many took up residence in New York, while about eight hundred settled in Virginia in 1700 and 1701. From New England and New York, they also moved down to the Carolinas; more settled in South Carolina than anywhere else. Huguenots assimilated more rapidly than most other eighteenth-century groups, anglicizing willingly and becoming successful planters, merchants, and craftsmen. Philadelphia Huguenots became important in the development of arts and crafts there. The merchant Andrew Faneuil's son Peter became the wealthiest inhabitant of Boston after John Hancock, and Henry Laurens was a dominant political and economic leader in South Carolina before and during the Revolution.

Many other groups came in much smaller numbers. Welsh Baptists and Quakers settled in the middle colonies and the southern backcountry, while small numbers of Irish Catholics, Italians, and Sephardic Jews lived in scattered groups throughout the colonies, with particular concentrations in Rhode Island and New York. In 1755, the English moved thousands of Acadians from their homeland and unceremoniously dumped them in several Atlantic ports; six thousand were left in Charleston, where they were not welcome. Swiss Mennonites settled in Lancaster County, Pennsylvania, in 1710, fleeing religious persecution in both Switzerland and the Palatinate, to which they had first migrated. A number of pietistic groups left Germany to escape religious persecution and warfare. Of these, the Moravians were the most important. The first Moravians settled in Georgia, but they left that colony in 1739 rather than take up arms against the Spanish. Moving to the backcountry of North Carolina, they established a settlement called Wachovia. Atypically for the frontier, this community isolated itself as much as possible from contact with the outside. A few leaders conducted the community's outside business, and the group received strong support from the Church's American headquarters in Bethlehem, Pennsylvania.

Table 6 ❧ White and black population in British North America, 1700–1760

New England

		New Hampshire	Massachusetts	Rhode Island	Connecticut
1700	White	4,828	55,141	5,594	25,520
	Black	130	800	300	450
1720	White	9,205	88,858	11,137	57,737
	Black	170	2,150	543	1,093
1740	White	22,756	148,578	22,487	86,982
	Black	500	3,035	2,408	2,598
1760	White	38,493	217,734	42,003	138,687
	Black	600	4,866	3,468	3,783

Middle Colonies

		New York	New Jersey	Pennsylvania	Delaware
1700	White	16,851	13,170	17,520	2,335
	Black	2,256	840	430	135
1720	White	31,179	27,433	28,962	4,685
	Black	5,740	2,385	2,000	700
1740	White	54,669	47,007	83,582	18,835
	Black	8,996	4,366	2,055	1,035
1760	White	100,798	87,246	179,294	31,517
	Black	16,340	6,567	4,409	1,733

Southern Colonies

		Maryland	Virginia	North Carolina	South Carolina	Georgia
1700	White	26,377	42,170			
	Black	3,227	16,390			
1720	White	53,634	61,158	18,270	5,048	
	Black	12,499	26,599	3,000	12,000	
1740	White	92,062	120,440	40,760	15,000	2,021
	Black	24,031	60,000	11,000	30,000	
1760	White	113,263	199,156	76,888	36,740	6,000
	Black	49,004	140,570	33,554	57,334	3,578

U.S. Bureau of the Census. *Historical Statistics of the United States from Colonial Times to 1970,* 2 vols. (Washington, DC: Government Printing Office, 1975) 2:1168.

Africans, Slavery, And British America

Black slavery remains the darkest blot on the colonial experience, casting its shadow on the very origins of American society. Slavery, and the people it victimized, has had such a lasting and powerful influence on American history and culture that it should be studied in historical terms, as part of the history of American immigration. Like every other people that formed a part of the American cultural mosaic, Africans brought with them a fully formed culture and made significant changes in adapting that culture to their new environment. Unlike other peoples, they did not leave their homelands voluntarily, and they had to confront a pervasive racism that powerfully shaped American culture.

English Racial Attitudes

More than twenty years ago, Winthrop Jordan argued that the enslaving of blacks was the "unthinking decision" of a people whose beliefs and attitudes were shaped by a prejudice against blacks. Before they even met Africans, the English had negative ideas about blackness in general. Black denoted evil, white purity and virtue. Jordan cited the meaning of *black* before the sixteenth century from the *Oxford English Dictionary:* "Deeply stained with dirt; soiled, dirty, foul. . . . Having dark or deadly purposes, malignant; pertaining to or involving death, deadly; baneful, disastrous, sinister. . . . Foul, iniquitous, atrocious, horrible, wicked. . . . Indicating disgrace, censure, liability to punishment, etc."[5] West Africans were among the darkest people of the continent and had no religion or culture that the ethnocentric English could identify. In this sense, the English evaluated Africans in much the same way they did Indians—as a savage people who lived undisciplined, irreligious, and immoral lives, a people who seemed lazy and of meager, even subhuman intelligence.

But economic need, too, influenced the English decision to enslave Africans. The cultural ethnocentrism that was so characteristic of the English at this time also heavily influenced their perceptions of all peoples, including Africans. But it seems undeniable, given the subsequent developments in the New World, that the English felt somehow differently about Africans, a difference best explained by a preexisting prejudice. Racism may not have caused slavery, but it certainly made the decision to accept and encourage it far easier and helped ease the consciences of whites. Its power stands in particular relief when contrasted with the less racial, though often physically harsher, nature of Spanish and Portuguese slavery in the New World.

African Society

The vast majority of slaves brought to English North America came from the coast or the interior of west-central Africa. About one-quarter came from the hinterland of the "Congo-Angola" coast and another quarter from the coast of southeastern Nigeria, with most of the remainder evenly divided between Senegambia, the Gold Coast, and the coastal region from Sierra Leone to the Ivory Coast. These are among the most livable and geographically varied regions of Africa, including, from south to north, the rain forests of the Guinea Coast and Zaire River basin, the wooded savanna and plains to the north, and the treed grasslands that eventually give way to the southern reaches of the Sahara Desert. The same climactic progression extended from the Guinea rain forests to the southern tip of the continent.

This was a world that bore more than incidental resemblance to contemporary Europe. The African population in 1492 was more than 80 million—roughly the same as Europe. West Africa alone was home to about 11 million people. A number of impressive kingdoms and empires existed in contemporary Africa and dotted its past, particularly in the interior. The kingdom of Ghana was a dominant power between the sixth and tenth centuries A.D., stretching from the Sahara to the Gulf of Guinea and from the Niger River to the Atlantic Ocean. It had numerous urban centers and was famed for its achievements in architecture and art. The empire of Mali replaced that of Ghana, and in the fourteenth century, it was the largest in the world. It is best remembered, perhaps, for the wealthy city of Timbuktu, an Islamic center of learning and culture. A number of lesser kingdoms were renowned for their skilled workers in metal and ceramic, their architecture, large towns, law codes, or well-organized trade structures. Coastal societies were less centralized. Lower Guinea, for instance, was dominated by small kingdoms built upon individual villages, which were in turn structured by kin groups. The kingdom of Benin was a major exception to this pattern. It was the strongest coastal state in Guinea and served as a center of trade for West and North Africa.

West African societies were diverse, with several hundred mutually unintelligible languages and dialects and a range of social customs just as varied. Where the soil was good and the climate hospitable, population increased, and the culture became increasingly sophisticated. But in areas of desert or dense forests, social systems remained relatively undeveloped. Any sort of generalization is thus difficult. Still, we can outline certain elements common to virtually all who suffered the indignities of slavery.

Kin groups shaped black African identity. West Africans tended to be patrilineal, west-central and central Africans matrilineal; in both cases, family and kin groups owned the land communally. Africans did not identify with anything like a tribe but rather owed their allegiances to local ties—the extended family and the village. Clan and national allegiances remained secondary to these bonds. Most Africans were herders or farmers. Herdsmen kept cattle, sheep, and goats in grazing areas where rain was not adequate for crops. Farmers grew everything from rice and maize (brought over by the Portuguese before 1600) in the savannas to yams and bananas in the wooded areas. Slash-and-burn agriculture predominated, and herdsmen and farmers exchanged essential goods with each other. West African cities boasted of active market centers and a thriving export trade of gold, ivory, spices, leather, and iron to North Africa, the Middle East, and even Europe. The

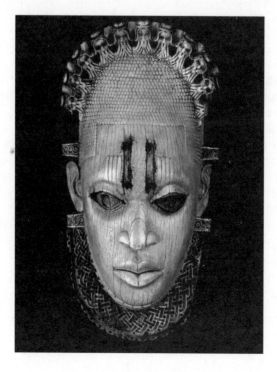

Ivory mask from Benin, reflecting the high degree of artistic achievement of many African societies. ❧

precise economic mix varied according to the region. The people of Upper Guinea, extending from Cape Verde to Cape Palmas, fished and cultivated rice in the coastal swamplands. Those of the Grain Coast, to the south of Cape Palmas, farmed and tended cattle. Still further south, the people of the kingdom of Benin fished and engaged in widespread trade in their dugout canoes.

Religious beliefs were central to African culture, including some that were shared with Europeans—beliefs in spirits, magic, and the effectiveness of amulets, for instance. West Africans believed their personal spirits returned to a greater world after death (in the ground rather than the sky) where they joined those of their ancestors. Their pantheon of gods included a supreme creator and many lesser gods associated with nature—rain, animals, fertility. Spirits inhabited all animate and inanimate objects in the world and could interfere in human affairs. Even ancestors could affect events in this life, since they mediated between the living and the gods. Ritual and magic were essential to controlling the actions of all of these beings, and spirits, gods, and ancestors had to be propitiated regularly. Spirits also made their wills known by speaking through priests. Africans lived in a world, then, where all activities were infused with sacredness.

As in Europe and the Americas, African men and women had specialized social roles. Both men and women headed the cults and secret societies that dominated village spiritual life. Women often (though not always) were responsible for the crops, child care, cooking the food, and making clothing. Men hunted, fished, and tended livestock. Women controlled local trading networks everywhere, directing the flow of goods among families, villages, and even kingdoms. Women also shared political power in West Africa; men governed their own sex, while women directed female affairs. In the Dahomean kingdom, for example, each male official had a female counterpart.

Slavery had been part of African society for centuries, but its function was critically different from the purposes it was to serve in North and South America. Slavery was part of the "domestic mode of production" that was the core of the African economy. The household was the basic work unit; households increased their wealth by producing more, and they produced more by adding workers. Thus, slaves became household dependents, performing the same tasks as other dependents did. But they were always outsiders, "other than kin." This was an occasional trade, designed to provide soldiers, artisans, and servants in personal service only for a limited period of time. The slaves were still regarded as members of society and were protected by law and allowed education and marriage. Their status was not passed on to their children.

African slavery was no different than slavery anywhere else in at least one respect, though—it was accompanied by violence. Slave traders acquired their victims through raids, kidnapping, and warfare. They sometimes trained boys as soldiers and girls as concubines, but they sold most of their captives to merchants eager for the substantial profits that could be earned in selling them off to distant markets. The growth of the Atlantic slave trade caused African kings to extend their raids and warfare with the aid of guns provided by the Europeans. Increasing numbers were also enslaved through the judicial system, as punishment for various crimes.

The Slave Trade

A plantation system existed in the eastern Mediterranean from the thirteenth century on, producing sugar for the European market and using the forced labor of southern Russian Slavs. By the time of Columbus's voyage, the system had expanded into

MAP 8.2: The Atlantic Slave Trade ❧

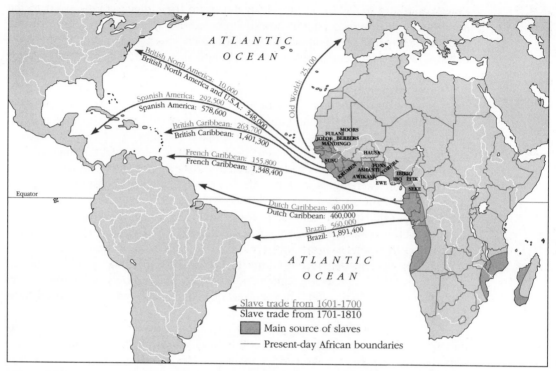

Source of data and routes: Philip D. Curtin, *The Atlantic Slave Trade: A Census* (Madison, WI: The University of Wisconsin Press, 1969), 119–20, 215–6. Reprinted with permission.

the western Mediterranean and to islands in the eastern Atlantic. As European colonization spread throughout the New World and into areas that lacked the more tangible wealth of gold and silver, this earlier plantation system became the logical model for producing a product of almost equal value—sugar. Sugar was a luxury that soon became a necessity for most Europeans, satisfying the desire for exotic sweets among the upper classes and staving off the pangs of hunger among the lower. But sugar cultivation required intensive labor that few would perform voluntarily in an environment unhealthy in the extreme. American Indians refused to adjust to the captive conditions necessary for plantation work and easily escaped to their own people, who lived nearby. White indentured servants were just as susceptible to malarial and tropical fevers as the Indians, and they too could easily fade into the surrounding community before their terms of service expired. As their availability dwindled during the last third of the seventeenth century, Europeans turned to black Africans. Africans had some immunity to smallpox, mumps, and measles, as well as malaria and yellow fever. They lived longer than forced white or Indian workers, and their color made it difficult for them to seek refuge in surrounding communities. European racism made this a decision embraced without serious moral qualms.

No other part of the African diaspora reached the scale of the Atlantic trade, which began in 1450 with the export of slaves to Europe and the eastern Atlantic sugar islands. It received official approbation when a Portuguese captain reached the Benin coast in 1472, and the king of Portugal gave him permission to trade for gold, ivory, and slaves in exchange for guns, iron and copper, brass utensils, and textiles. The trade was transformed when demand began to rise during the early years of the sixteenth century. In 1510, Spain legalized the sale of Africans to the New World, and in 1518, the first slave ship from the Guinea coast landed in the Americas. A clear trading pattern quickly emerged. European ships brought cotton, alcohol, metalwork, and guns to West Africa, then transported slaves to the West Indies and the American mainland and returned to Europe with cargoes of sugar and tobacco.

Europeans forcibly exported more than 11.5 million Africans from the Atlantic coast and brought 10 million of them to the New World. About six of every seven people who crossed the Atlantic to live in the New World were African slaves. Of these, only 5 percent came to the English mainland colonies.

European traders knew they were dealing with a substantial commercial network in which black African traders traveled widely in search of gold, slaves, and other goods in exchange for North African salt, metalware, glassware, figs, and dates. Central Africans had long traded copper, hides, and ivory to the coast in exchange for salt, palm oil, and cloth. Slave traders simply increased the amount of human product in an existing system of exchange. Europeans sought a great variety of products themselves, from gold and ivory to copper and kola nuts, but after 1650, slaves were in demand all along the coast. Africans, too, sought particular goods, including metals, cloth, semiprecious stones, and liquor; even items already available in Africa were often cheaper and of better quality when purchased from the Europeans.

The principal mechanism for transporting slaves to the coast was the slave caravan (or "coffle"); most of these were led by specialized Muslim African merchants with extensive contacts in West African villages. The particular destination of a coffle depended on prices and available goods, but by the mid-seventeenth century, several strong states, such as the Asante, had gained control over the bulk of the trade. These states had European firearms and horses and were able to contain both the Muslim and the European traders within the desired limits. Some areas, such as the Bight of Benin, had inland marketing centers where merchants acquired slaves from chiefs, who had gained them through warfare, kidnapping, tribute, or other means. The merchants then sold the slaves to other traders or marched them directly to the coast. In other areas, such as the Bight of Biafra, the system was more privatized, being controlled by commercial associations. The largest of these by the mid-eighteenth century was the Aro, which provided slaves to coastal associations, which in turn sold them to the Europeans.

Captives were tied together in pairs by the legs and in fours by the neck. They were poorly fed and sheltered and served as porters for the caravan—a six-year-old boy, for instance, had to carry on his head a twenty-five pound stone used to grind the caravan's corn. The trek took as long as two months. For many, changing environments brought exposure to new diseases—those from dry climes often caught malaria or yellow fever in the wet lowlands. The captured African Mungo Park has left us with a vivid description of his own captive ordeal at the end of the eighteenth century. Seventy-three men, women, and children were tied at the neck with leather thongs and marched 550 miles through Gambia. Some ate clay in an attempt to commit suicide, while others died from exhaustion or hunger. The principal historian of the trade, Philip Curtin, has estimated that more slaves died in Africa in this way than at the coast or on the ocean.

Africans consciously protected their roles as middlemen. Whites were only rarely a part of these inland expeditions. They almost always stayed on the coast, where they built outposts or "factories" (also known as barracoons) and collected slaves while waiting for the European ships. The buildings could be stone fortresses or thatched huts, but they were always protected from pirates and other enemies by a military garrison. Death rates at these outposts were shocking, ranging from 250 to 750 per thousand annually. Small African commercial communities developed around the outposts and often contained African-Europeans who served as liaisons between the two peoples.

It was here that most Africans saw their first Europeans. Olaudah Equiano, who left the most complete narrative of an African's experience in captivity, describes his first encounter with whites as an eleven-year-old Ibo boy in 1756, when he saw "white men with horrible looks, red faces, and loose hair."[6] He feared they were cannibals and was astonished at their cruelty when he witnessed one of the ship's sailors being flogged to death. Equiano subsequently experienced much wider exposure to white culture than did most of his fellow Africans, living in Barbados, Virginia, Canada, and England. He eventually purchased his freedom, published his autobiography, and married an English woman. But he never ceased to wonder at the cultural practices of these strange people: "I was astonished at the wisdom of the White people in all things I saw; but was amazed at their not sacrificing; or making any offerings, and eating with unwashed hands, and touching the dead. I likewise could not help remarking the particular slenderness of their women, which I did not at first like; and I thought they were not so modest and shamefaced as the African women."[7] Equiano was not alone in his astonishment. Senegalese women bathed twice a day, and they simply could not believe the filth of the white people who took them captive.

Interior of a Spanish slave ship. ❧

❧ *Documents* ❧
"A World of Bad Spirits"

The slave trade brought indescribable suffering and pain to Africans. In the first selection, Olaudah Equiano describes his first sight of the ship and men who were to carry him across the Atlantic. The men who worked on slave ships labored under horrid conditions themselves, dying in numbers almost as great as the Africans they kept in chains. They and their captains also lived in constant fear of rebellion by the captives, as the second selection, from an account by Capt. Thomas Phillips (of a 1693–1694 voyage) makes clear.

> The first object which saluted my eyes when I arrived on the coast was the sea, and a slave ship which was then riding at anchor and waiting for its cargo. These filled me with astonishment, which was soon converted into terror when I was carried on board. I was immediately handled and tossed up to see if I were sound by some of the crew, and I was now persuaded that I had gotten into a world of bad spirits and that they were going to kill me. Their complexions too differing so much from ours, their long hair and the language they spoke (which was very different from any I had ever heard) united to confirm me in this belief. Indeed such were the horrors of my views and fears at the moment that, if ten thousand worlds had been my own, I would have freely parted with them all to have exchanged my condition with that of the meanest slave in my own country. When I looked round the ship too and saw a large furnace or copper boiling and a multitude of black people of every description chained together, every one of their countenances

Disease threatened the English crews as well, and captains planned voyages accordingly. Ships arrived in the winter and planned to land in the colonies during the most profitable trading season, from April to November. These vessels were of average size, from one hundred to two hundred tons, and carried about two hundred slaves. They required a good deal of equipment, including nets to prevent the captives from escaping when they were near land, and enormous amounts of food for both crew and captives. One slaver, carrying 404 slaves and forty-seven crew members, left Africa with thirteen thousand pounds of food; another with six hundred Africans had thirty-four thousand gallons of water. The ratio of crew to Africans was about one to ten. The crew members were generally from the lower levels of English society or from prisons, received little pay, and worked under terrible conditions. For the slave traders and investors, though, this was a highly profitable business. In 1760, a healthy male adult slave cost 14.10 pounds to purchase and could be sold in Virginia for forty-five pounds. For this reason, traders favored males over the age of ten; more than twice as many men as women made the crossing.

expressing dejection and sorrow, I no longer doubted my fate; and quite overpowered with horror and anguish, I fell motionless on the deck and fainted.

Olaudah Equiano, *The Interesting Narratives of the Life of Olavdah Equiano, or Gustavus Vassa, The African.* Written by Himself. (London, 1789), 70–1.

When our slaves are aboard we shackle the men two and two, while we lie in port, and in sight of their own country, for 'tis then they attempt to make their escape, and mutiny; to prevent which we always keep centinels upon the hatchways, and have a chest full of small arms, ready loaden and prim'd, constantly lying at hand upon the quarter-deck, together with some granada shells; and two of our quarter-deck guns, pointing on the deck thence, and two more out of the steerage, the door of which is always kept shut, and well barr'd; they are fed twice a day, at 10 in the morning, and 4 in the evening, which is the time they are aptest to mutiny, being all upon the deck; therefore all that time, what of our men are not employ'd in distributing their victuals to them, and settling them, stand to their arms; and some with lighted matches at the great guns that yaun upon them, loaden with partridge, till they have done and gone down to their kennels between decks.

Quoted in Daniel P. Mannix and Malcolm Cowley, "Middle Passage," *American Heritage,* 13 (February 1962), 25.

The "middle passage", as the voyage across the Atlantic was called, was truly a frightening experience for Africans, physically and psychologically. Torn from community and kin, the Africans were emotionally alone and isolated. Captives often leaped out of the canoes and drowned themselves even before they were boarded on the ship, and suicide attempts continued at sea; many believed they would be eaten by white savages on the other side of the ocean.

On board ship, few captains loaded their cargo as densely as is often portrayed in the schematic of the slave ship *Brookes*. Still, there was little room below decks, which were generally four or five feet high. Captains kept their captives topside as much as possible, binding them to each other with leg irons fastened to chains running along the decks. Sanitary conditions were primitive, particularly when bad weather forced people below decks for long periods of time. When the wind died, conditions could become deadly. Captains hoped to spend only forty to sixty days at sea; longer voyages meant higher death rates because of contamination of food and water and the ravages of dysentery. Mortality rates averaged about 16 percent, though in most cases, they were lower than this—the occasional epidemics, shipwrecks, or pirate attacks killed more than their share of blacks and whites (crew mortality rates were almost as high as those of the captives). The crew simply threw many of the seriously ill overboard. Conditions improved after the middle of the eighteenth century, as the speed of ships increased and captains began to feed the Africans citrus fruit to prevent scurvy. Still, death on the trek to the coast, in the factories, or during the middle passage meant that only about one in two captured blacks lived to see the New World.

Captains feared shipboard revolts most of all, and many of their punishments and disciplinary actions were undoubtedly designed to instill the proper degree of fear in their charges. Whippings were common. To force resistive blacks to eat, they often applied hot coals to their lips or employed the "speculum oris" (mouth opener), a metal device designed to wrench the jaws apart. John Atkins, a crew member on a 1721 English slaver, recounted the captain's decision to sentence the leaders of one rebellion "to cruel deaths, making them first eat the Heart and Liver of one of them killed. The Woman he hoisted up by the thumbs, whipp'd and slashed her with Knives, before the other Slaves, till she died."[8]

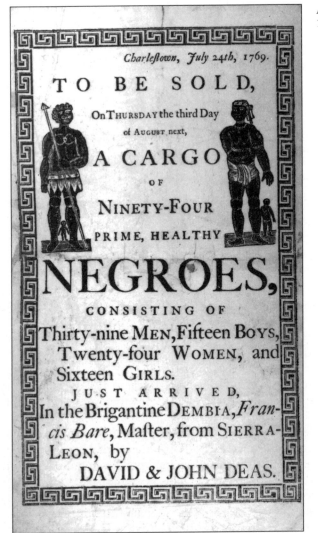

A handbill for a slave sale, 1769. ❧

The New World meant yet another new environment for the blacks, with new diseases, foods, and water. Some ports even required that the new arrivals spend several weeks in quarantine before they could be sold; about 5 percent of the captives died during this time. Either large local planters or merchant firms arranged the auctions; the planters bought most of the Africans for their own use or to resell at a profit. The Chesapeake was the first major North American market, but about a quarter of all blacks imported to the mainland passed through Charleston, the major port of entry. South Carolina began importing blacks directly from Africa after 1700 and quickly became the trade's largest single customer; in the 1730s, the colony imported an average of more than two thousand slaves a year.

English vessels from London, Bristol, and especially Liverpool controlled the trade in the eighteenth century, joined by a growing number of American ships. Rhode Island traders were most heavily involved, though their ships were much smaller than the average; from 1760 to 1775 alone, 271 Rhode Island ships brought thirty-two thousand Africans to the Americas. Blacks imported in the seventeenth century were already "seasoned" in the West Indies, since the mainland market was so small. The ratio changed between 1680 and 1730; by 1720, 80 percent of the slaves arriving in Virginia, Maryland, and the Carolinas came directly from Africa. This shift had major repercussions for the formation of African-American culture.

African-American Culture

The Chesapeake

No group of people can live in the absence of culture, no matter how great their deprivation and suffering, and no people can live in the same space as another without engaging in some form of cultural exchange. Thus, Africans created their own culture in the midst of slavery and prejudice, fashioning folkways and institutions that allowed them to shape their own lives as much as possible. At the same time, African-European cultural exchanges were constant and pervasive, though historians are only beginning to understand how these exchanges shaped colonial American culture.

Some seventeenth-century Chesapeake blacks became free and owned slaves themselves; a few on Virginia's eastern shore even became planters. Anthony Johnson arrived as a slave in 1621; by 1650, he was a freeman with 250 acres of land and a herd of cattle. In 1655, he successfully sued a white planter for detaining one of his own slaves. In Northampton County between 1664 and 1677, ten of the fifty-three black males were free. As their neighboring whites did, these freemen and their children laid out their plantations adjacent to each other and created a strong, supportive network of kin and friends. But their situation soon changed. Despite their skill in using the courts for legal protection, they faced increasingly severe limits on their lives. After Johnson died, a white jury ruled that because he was a "Negroe," the fifty-acre farm he had deeded to his son Richard before he moved north to Maryland should be given instead to a white planter. Johnson's children and grandchildren never equaled his achievements; his sons never became more prosperous than small freeholders. Johnson and the other free blacks of his generation took advantage of the unsettled nature of life in the early Chesapeake to create their own opportunities. Since they arrived there via the Dutch West Indies, they were already partly acculturated to European culture and were able to use the courts effectively; sex ratios were nearly equal, and they established family lives quickly. By 1680, conditions had begun to change.

The transition from a labor system that relied primarily on indentured servants to one of black slavery occurred at different rates even throughout the tidewater. York County tobacco growers were quick to adopt the new labor system, and by the 1680s, more than three-quarters of the bound workers there were black. By 1700, the more northern regions were also well on their way to having a fully black labor force. By 1720, the entire Chesapeake region was dotted by plantations worked predominantly by blacks.

❧ *Documents* ❧
White Fears and
Rationalizations of Slavery

The first selection, by Rev. Hugh Jones, reflects the belief of many English men and women that blacks were actually better off in slavery in Virginia than they had been when free in Africa. The second selection, by William Byrd II, reflects the fears Virginians had that slavery would corrupt whites.

> Their Work (or Chimerical hard Slavery) is not very laborious; their greatest Hardship consisting in that they and their Posterity are not at their Liberty or Disposal, but are the Property of their Owners; and when they are free, they know not how to provide so well for themselves generally; neither did they live so plentifully nor (many of them) so easily in their own Country, where they are made Slaves to one another, or taken Captive by their Enemies.

Hugh Jones, *The Present State of Virginia* . . . (1724), Richard L. Morton, ed. (Chapel Hill, NC: IEAHC, University of North Carolina Press, 1956), 75–6.

> They [slave traders] import so many negro's hither, that I fear this Colony will sometime or other be confounded by the name of New Guinea. I am sensible of many bad consequences of multiplying these Ethiopians amongst us. They blow up the pride, & ruin the Industry of our White People, who Seeing a Rank of poor Creatures below them, detest work for fear it should make them look like Slaves. Then that poverty which will ever attend upon Idleness, disposed them, as much to pilfer as it does the Portuguise, who account it much more like a gentleman to steal, than to dirty their hands with Labour of any kind. Another unhappy Effect of many Negroes is, the necessity of being severe. Numbers make them insolent and then foul Means must do what fair will not. . . . We have already at least 10,000 men of these descendants of Ham, fit to bear Arms, & these numbers increase every day, as well by birth, as by Importation.

William Byrd II to Lord Egremont, 12 July 1736; reprinted in *Virginia Magazine of History and Biography*, 36 (July 1928): 219–28.

Legal codes, as we have seen, now distinguished blacks completely from whites, defining them as not fully human, sharply restricting their movements and activities, and punishing them far more severely than whites for committing the same crimes. The fate suffered by a black named Jacob, in Lancaster County, Virginia, is perhaps representative. Jacob, his white owner Martha Flint, and another white woman stole about six pence worth of goods. The women were whipped, and Jacob, who could have been hanged, received mercy because of the circumstances—he had to stand for an hour with each ear nailed to the pillory. After that, his ears were cut off and he was whipped.

Before 1690, blacks assimilated rather quickly to white norms. They learned English rapidly and generally worked together with whites in the fields. This informal, daily contact led many whites to realize that their slaves did not fit the evil stereotypes English culture had bequeathed them. But the flood of new Africans, which increased rapidly in the years after 1690, disrupted these nascent communities, led to tighter legal restrictions on blacks, and created conflicts among blacks themselves.

The majority of blacks arrived each year between June and August. They were first introduced to the less complex work of weeding the tobacco fields, a job similar to that which many of them had performed in their homelands. Within a couple of months, they began to learn the more difficult tasks involved in harvesting the crop. One in four died during their first year in the Chesapeake, succumbing in large numbers to winter respiratory illnesses. Many attempted to run away almost as soon as they landed. Seven recently arrived blacks belonging to Robert Carter stole a canoe and escaped in July 1727, only to be captured a week later. Others participated in conspiracies, such as those that occurred in three Chesapeake counties in 1710 and in Prince George's County, Maryland, in 1739 and 1740. Most of these blacks were African-born slaves who had not yet established family and community ties in the New World.

It was difficult for blacks to establish any sort of community during this second period, which extended roughly from 1690 to 1740. Planters sent new arrivals, or so-called outlandish slaves, to live and work in small groups on upland plantations, where they were cut off from other blacks and denied access to black women. Even in the tidewater, plantations were still relatively small. About half of the slaves lived in quarters with ten or fewer blacks during this time, and only about one-quarter lived with twenty or more. Most blacks had to find their mates elsewhere, and community life required visiting other quarters. New African arrivals often had to wait several years before they were able to marry, since most African-American women were reluctant to marry African men.

The black population gradually stabilized, and the proportion of native-born blacks (creoles) increased. Imports began to decline after 1740, and plantations throughout the Chesapeake increased in size. More blacks now lived in quarters distant from the master's house, and it became easier for them to establish independent, stable communities. Historians differ as to how difficult this process was and how rapidly it occurred, but it seems likely that by the end of the colonial period, the clear outlines of a separate black community were beginning to emerge.

The nature of this community hinged to some degree on the size of the farm or plantation. Slave ownership was concentrated on three levels in the Chesapeake. Most landowners lived on small family farms; some might own a slave or two at most, and family members still did most of the work. In Maryland, the vast majority of white farmers owned no servants or slaves at all. A middling level of landowners owned a few slaves and ultimately succeeded in becoming big planters themselves or failed completely; their numbers dwindled as the century went on. The largest

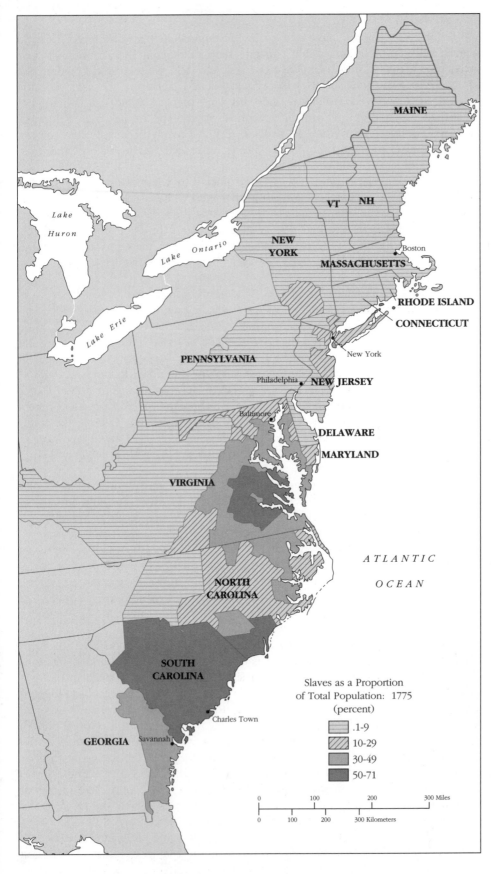

MAP 8.3: Concentration of Slaves in the Colonial Population ❧

Slaves as a Proportion
of Total Population: 1775
(percent)

.1-9
10-29
30-49
50-71

planters were the smallest group numerically in the Chesapeake, but they owned most of the slaves. In Maryland, for instance, only 6 percent of the planters owned two-thirds of all slaves. It was on these larger plantations that slaves found it easiest to shape their own cultural norms. In the evenings, men traveled freely between quarters and socialized with friends and families. Masters themselves contributed to the extended community network by selling slaves to nearby plantations, and kinship lines began to extend across plantations. As quarters rapidly became connected by roads and paths, the networks and interconnections became more and more complex.

Black Families The core of black existence, both as individual and as community member in Africa and America, was the family. Even more than in European society, African families were the institutions of cultural socialization. Young Africans learned their proper social roles and developed their personal and communal identities within the family. Loss of family and kin was perhaps the most devastating experience of the captured blacks. Africans sought to recreate kin networks even aboard ship, looking for relatives and calling friendly adults uncle and aunt. The same pattern of adoptive kinship emerged on larger plantations. Younger blacks accorded their elders respect, for which they received crucial emotional and cultural support.

Almost immediately upon their arrival in the New World, Africans took steps to establish new family structures and kinship ties. Early white attempts to prohibit marriage were useless; blacks accepted common law marriages or devised their own marriage ceremonies, such as "jumping over the broomstick." And despite the early imbalanced sex ratios, most male Africans who survived the first few years eventually found wives. Still, family conditions were far from ideal. Most black women married before the age of twenty, and well into the first few decades of the eighteenth century, they were often forced to rear their children with little help from their husbands, who lived on another plantation. Separations caused further pain and hardship; when white sons received land and slaves from their fathers, they often split black families over still wider distances. But even in these circumstances, blacks quickly reconstituted families and kin relations. And as creoles came to outnumber native Africans, blacks established some degree of stability in their family lives. Widespread kin networks emerged, maintained even in the face of separation and death. Planters made an effort to keep women and small children together and generally sold even men to plantations relatively nearby. The longer families lived in an area, the more extensive its kinship networks became. The strength of these attachments is indicated by the fact that one-third of the runaways identified in Virginia newspaper advertisements ran off to join members of their families who lived nearby.

Ultimately, most slaves in large quarters were related by blood or marriage, and the family came to serve as the organizing focus of most black plantation life. Small domestic groups included blacks who lived opposite each other in the quarter, sharing a yard and eating arrangements. Kinship groups worked together and aided and protected each other. The stability of this family structure may at first seem surprising—a survey of the slaves owned by four large planters, for instance, indicates that nearly half lived in households that included both parents and at least some of the children. The larger the plantation, the more likely this would be; even adolescent children tended to stay with their parents on such estates. But only a few planters had such sizable quarters, and life was probably less stable on the smaller plantations. Still, it is a tribute to the persistence of family traditions among African-Americans that they made some form of family structure their first priority.

Two examples illustrate how blacks remained connected to kin on their own plantations and even across the land to other blacks. Daphne was born on the plantation of Robert Tyler, Sr. in Prince George's County, Maryland, about 1736. She lived with her mother, two brothers, and two sisters until Tyler died in 1738. Tyler's will left three of Daphne's siblings to his granddaughter Ruth, who later married Mordecai Jacob. Daphne stayed on the plantation under six different masters until 1787. She bore ten children and had several grandchildren, all of whom lived with her on the plantation until her fifth master, the grandson of Tyler Sr., died. The grandson left Daphne's younger children to his daughter, who lived several miles away. But Daphne lived until her death with four of her daughters and several of her grandchildren. Over forty-one years, Daphne's family spread across the landscape, remaining close enough to each other to create an interlocking extended family. Similarly, a slave named Old Fanny lived on Charles Carroll's plantation with her five children, nineteen grandchildren, nine great-grandchildren, children-in-law, and grandchildren's spouses, all with ties leading still further afield in the quarter.

On large plantations in particular, blacks lived in square buildings, perhaps twelve feet by twelve feet, generally of wood and relatively impermanent. They acquired more clothing and furnishings the longer they lived in one place, including beds, chairs, kitchen utensils, and other household items. Their diet included meal and some meat (generally pork), and most had small vegetable gardens and raised some poultry. Still, this rather limited sustenance often resulted in nutritional deficiencies that caused bad teeth, eye problems and jaundice, among other problems. The inadequate diet also led to debilitating diseases such as rickets, "dirt eating," hookworm, and pellagra (black-tongue). Material conditions improved after 1740, as houses more commonly contained straw bedding, pots and pans, and tools and as more blacks cultivated their own plots of corn and tobacco. Blacks who lived on smaller plantations or worked as the only slave of a poor planter experienced much worse conditions, sleeping in the same room with their master and enjoying little or no privacy.

Black Religion   African-American folk religion combined elements of traditional African beliefs with selected Christian practices. Loud, celebratory funerals propitiated the spirits of the dead, while providing ritualistic, communal release from the pains of slavery. Black ministers exhorted their congregations to emotional response: singing, dancing, and shouting were all central components of black services, again offering emotional release from the burdens of slavery and cementing the communal relationships of black family and kin networks.

For the first half of the century, Anglicans were the most active white preachers among the slaves. Indeed, for a short time, they actively promoted the Christianization of slaves, arguing that Christianity would make blacks happier and teach them duty and loyalty. But while they tried to convince masters to treat slaves more humanely, these Anglicans rarely questioned the system itself. Thomas Bacon developed the doctrine of "absolute obedience" in Maryland to calm masters' fears that slaves might see baptism as a way toward freedom. Ministers gradually adopted a strongly paternalistic attitude, indistinguishable from that embraced by planters. Bacon praised masters in his sermons before crowds of slaves and owners, reminding the blacks that they had all their cares and needs attended to. Others elaborated on the pictures of African depravity that masters favored, speaking of laziness and lust among immoral slaves.

Poor whites and blacks might join their voices in song and worship on the Chesapeake frontier, but this was a short-lived and unusual situation. Black religious practices threatened to foster both resistance and unity, and Christianity had the potential to make slaves less willing workers. Most important, many slaves understood that baptism was at least a first step toward release from bondage. White missionaries taught the Christian virtues of meekness, humility, and obedience, and blacks received the message of spiritual equality and salvation. Their religious heroes became Moses and Jesus, their religious goal deliverance. In 1730, following a period of extensive missionary activity in the Virginia Chesapeake, several baptized slaves began circulating the message that their admission to Christianity entitled them to physical as well as spiritual freedom. Several hundred slaves gathered in Norfolk and Princess Anne counties to plan rebellion. They were discovered, and their leaders were hanged. Thereafter, whites increasingly resisted the catechization of blacks, arguing that exposure to the message of redemption would make their slaves "proud and saucy."

The Great Awakening initiated a new period of religious activity by white missionaries and a new receptivity to their message among slaves. In Williamsburg alone, nearly a thousand slaves were baptized between 1746 and 1768, recipients of the Baptist message of spiritual equality. Samuel Davies and other Presbyterians also preached actively among southern blacks, and the conservative Anglican minister Jonathan Coucher claimed that he baptized 315 slaves in a single day in 1767.

The revivalists succeeded because their style of preaching was as emotional as the African religious tradition. Through the use of music and the encouragement of body motion and participation by the congregation, they helped blacks forge an uniquely black Christianity, marked by dancing, rhythmic clapping, and singing. Slaves used the experience to channel anger and aggression in ways that would not bring retribution from their masters. They developed songs—black spirituals—that blended African rhythms, Anglo-American melodies, and words that reflected their painful experiences and embraced themes of resistance and rebellion. Most important, blacks embraced the revivalistic message of rebirth as a promise of eternal happiness after death or, often, a rebirth in freedom in this life. More clearly than it did for other Americans, the Great Awakening among blacks pointed the way toward the American Revolution.

Blacks and Work

> I find it almost impossible to make a negro do his work well. No orders can engage it, no encouragement persuade it, nor no Punishment oblige it.[9]

This comment by Virginia planter Landon Carter reflects the inability of white Americans to see past their ethnocentric blinders, to notice even obliquely that the work ethic of black Americans was in fact not very different from their own. In Africa, climate dictated the pace—slow movement and frequent periods of rest and relaxation were the norm. Work presented another opportunity to strengthen the communalism of West African societies, and singing and talking accompanied the daily tasks. Women did much of the heavy labor in these societies, while men protected their villages from attack and managed family and village affairs.

In the colonies, blacks were able to force whites to accept compromises in the daily and seasonal work routines. Masters and overseers could not risk pushing the slaves too hard, since the blacks could respond with feigned illness, broken tools, and sloppy work—or they might retaliate with arson. To some extent, blacks controlled their own work rhythms. Slaves worked longer and more arduously during harvest or when the tobacco needed topping or hoeing. They retained Sundays and evenings for their own activities and claimed a number of holidays, such as "Harvest Home." Both West Africans and English yeomen had traditional celebrations at the completion of the harvest, so there was little cultural resistance to providing slaves with time for these. The women fared less well than the men. Given the traditions of West African cultures, it was not surprising that they labored in the fields along-side the men; very few escaped to the less arduous work of a house servant. They also delivered children under difficult circumstances and assumed the responsibility for household and family chores when they became too old or infirm to work in the fields. Men may have been able to "retire" at such a point in their lives, but women took on child care, weaving, spinning, and other household tasks.

Men also had greater choice in their occupations. Unseasoned new arrivals were almost always assigned to the simplest sort of fieldwork. Creoles, however, had more autonomy, even in fieldwork, and over time learned a variety of skilled trades. On small farms in the north and in urban areas everywhere, the diverse requirements of the economy necessitated that slaves work as blacksmiths, barbers, weavers, or even watchmakers. Well before the middle of the eighteenth century, slaves on large plantations had acquired responsibility for most of the artisanal tasks the economy demanded, so they worked as blacksmiths, butchers, carpenters, cob-blers, and masons. Mulatto Ned trained as a carpenter early in the century in Maryland, and in 1728, Cooper George, on King Carter's plantation, began training his son to follow his trade. Some larger planters even developed a system of slave apprenticeship during the 1770s. Black artisans worked as boatmen throughout the south, carrying goods and supplies to plantations and ports, and as fishermen in South Carolina. In Maryland, slaves were widely employed in the growing iron industry and enjoyed more privileges than almost any other southern slaves, work-ing five-day weeks with considerable freedom of movement. But training was limit-ed to jobs that did not require literacy, and most slaves, despite the educational efforts of the Presbyterian minister Samuel Davies during the 1750s, remained unable to read. Nonetheless, slave artisans enjoyed much greater mobility and inde-pendence than their field counterparts, particularly if they were head artisans or tradesmen who could hire themselves out.

Carolina And The Georgia Low Country

The Carolina proprietors granted extensive lands to the early Barbadian settlers who brought slaves with them, and during the first years, up to one-third of the set-tlers were male black slaves. Still, the overall numbers remained small: in 1708, there were only four thousand blacks in all of South Carolina. Most of them spoke English and acculturated quickly to the European culture. Since the white settlers initially pursued mixed farming and raised livestock, they owned relatively few slaves and worked closely with them.

Blacks used their African skills and traditions to control the grazing business, and they had considerable freedom to travel around the country. On the small farms, they became jacks of all trades. They also raised their own provisions, were legally granted Sunday to themselves, supplemented their diets by hunting and fish-ing, and often produced small surpluses that they traded for needed goods. Whites complained of the freedom their slaves had, but they also recognized that the unique dangers a frontier settlement faced necessitated such allowances. The Spanish presented a constant threat, and the colony offered freedom to any slave who killed an enemy during an invasion. Blacks regularly served in the militia, and though few won their freedom by legal means, more escaped into the backcountry swamps and there established independent settlements or integrated with the Yamasee Indians. A 1706 petition by white planters complained that blacks had even been allowed to vote in a county election. Black culture was fairly uniform during these early years. Leading Charleston planters owned most of the slaves, and the majority of blacks lived near the city and close to each other.

The introduction of a rice-based economy changed all of this. Planters consolidated small farms and created large plantations around swampland to accommodate the requirements of rice cultivation. The hot, humid climate in these areas produced exhausting working conditions and bred debilitating diseases that white workers and owners alike found difficult to overcome. Blacks, though, retained relative immunity to malaria and fevers, a blessing that had originally convinced whites of their suitability for labor in the unhealthy lowland climes where rice was most successfully cultivated. At least some West African blacks were also damned by their own skills and knowledge of rice-growing techniques—the construction of the necessary dikes and the techniques of winnowing and husking the crop.

Blacks soon outnumbered whites by three to one in the plantation areas around Charleston. By 1708, more than half of the population was black, and by 1740, black slaves comprised up to 90 percent of the population in the oldest plantation areas north and south of the city. Rice cultivation began in low-lying freshwater areas, but by mid-century, planters had mastered the regulation of tidal pools along the coastal lowlands. The resulting dramatic increase in acreage under cultivation fueled the need for black labor. Traders now began to import the majority of their slaves directly from Africa. Between 1706 and 1765, ninety-four thousand African slaves entered Charleston harbor.

Slaves now lived in increasingly larger groups and worked in gangs. As tobacco ruled the lives of slaves to the north, rice became the master of slaves in the low country. They labored day after day up to their knees in the mud, under the scorching southern sun. After they harvested the crop, they cleared the canals and repaired the dams necessary to control the flow of the tides. A stable family and community life came only slowly to these blacks. The planters had ready access to slaves in Barbados and Africa and found it easier and cheaper to work blacks to the death, in the West Indies tradition, than to allow them to reproduce. Between 1700 and 1730, deaths outnumbered births among low-country blacks.

Whites ruled their plantations through a chain of command—stewards in the smaller rice ports, overseers, and black drivers on the plantation. Though white planters spent only a few months of the year in Charleston, they were able to live a life of leisure and wealth. To preserve this existence, they constantly expanded their plantations and increased their crop yields. To control the black population, they adopted increasingly harsher slave codes, borrowing from those of Barbados. A "Negro watch" was empowered to stop slaves on sight in Charleston and to confine any found on the streets after 9 P.M. The militia patrolled rural areas with arbitrary powers of control and punishment. Justices of the peace and panels of justices and freemen ruled on more serious offenses. Punishments included castration; nostril-splitting; ear, hand, or toe amputations; branding; and burning at the stake. On the plantation, overseers and masters had essentially unlimited power to enforce their own systems of justice.

As in the Chesapeake, whites in South Carolina also sought to use religion to control black behavior. To be sure, sometimes preachers could not look the other way. Rev. Francis Le Jau was appalled by an 1713 incident in which an overseer encouraged a slave to be baptized, only to punish him later for losing a bundle of rice by enclosing him in a box shaped as a coffin. After a few days, the desperate slave's children slipped him a knife so he could commit suicide. But Le Jau made black candidates for baptism take an oath "that you do not ask for the holy baptism out of any design to free yourself from the Duty and Obedience you owe to your Master while you live."[10] Even the Great Awakening had little permanent impact on white attitudes here. George Whitefield condemned slavery and the white's treatment of blacks when he first visited the colony, blaming slavery for the colony's irreligious behavior and the debilitating addiction to luxury that consumed the planter class. He attracted support from at least one powerful planter family, Jonathan Bryan and his brothers, who worked to convert blacks to Christianity. But South Carolina Assembly members quickly closed ranks. They condemned the Bryans' efforts and forced them to limit their activities to blacks on their own plantations, while Whitefield himself eventually became an apologist for slavery, asking only that blacks be allowed to become Christians. After 1742, evangelicals abandoned their attacks on South Carolina society.

Work in the low country was far different for blacks in Charleston than on a plantation. In the city, blacks worked on the docks and as shipwrights, coopers, gold beaters, silversmiths, and cabinetmakers. Black women controlled much of the marketing process in the smaller ports. Many urban slaves had considerable freedom of movement: they could hire out their own time, open market stalls, work on ships, and even rent houses. The only obligation some had was to pay a portion of their earnings to their owners. So economically successful were some of the creoles that the legislature passed sumptuary laws to prevent them from dressing above their social station, since many were able to buy fine clothing. This success brought with it a certain freedom of action and movement. In 1763, black chimney sweeps raised their prices and refused to work unless customers paid the new rates. In direct violation of the law, many urban blacks patronized taverns and met and socialized in large numbers. The mulatto children of planters also had somewhat higher status in the city; they were occasionally given their freedom and usually held standing as artisans or household servants.

In the rural areas, life was both different and similar. The climate, working conditions, and harsh demands of country life made for short life expectancies for blacks. Still, blacks benefited from working under the task system. Since rice production required individual labor on quarter-acre plots, masters and overseers assigned particular tasks to be completed within the day's time. When the tasks were completed, the individual was then free to pursue his own work and interests. The system began in the rice-producing areas, since unlike tobacco, rice was a hardy plant that did not require constant attention—a few straightforward operations and the essential tasks were completed. The approach proved both successful and easily manageable, and this system of "tasking" soon appeared in a variety of other jobs. Slaves who worked at fencing, for instance, were expected to split about one hundred twelve-foot-long poles each day.

This system enabled blacks to raise their own crops, learn skills, hunt and fish, spend time with their peers, and even sell some of their surplus products at market. The Ball family slaves sold fowls, hogs, and rice to their own masters. Tasking also made it that much easier for low-country blacks to develop a culture free of white influence. Bolstered by the constant arrival of new Africans, West African culture survived here as nowhere else on mainland North America. These blacks retained control over their language and the naming of their children. They even practiced such African traditions as witchcraft and obeah (the use of sorcery to discover and punish personal enemies). Some grew African crops, such as groundnuts and "negroe pepper." Despite laws that attempted to limit their ownership of property, many slaves owned canoes, horses, and cattle and traded throughout the province. Material conditions varied enormously among these people; they lived in homes that ranged from hovels to brick cabins that housed two to four families. But the vast majority of them enjoyed more independence from white cultural control than did blacks anywhere else in the mainland colonies.

Slavery In The North

Slavery in the northern colonies began in 1626, when the Dutch imported blacks to New Amsterdam from Curacao in the Dutch West Indies. The number of blacks increased when Dutch settlement became more permanent and agricultural in the 1640s. They were used to clear land and produce food. But at the same time, the Dutch West India Company gave a sort of half-freedom to its slaves, permitting them to work on their own in exchange for a stipulated amount of labor and a tribute; some blacks attempted, in vain, to have this status become hereditary. Indeed, the legal status of New Amsterdam blacks was quite diverse; in 1664, seventy-five of the 375 who lived in the colony were free. The slaves retained some of these rights after the English took over the colony, and the population remained heterogeneous for some time. In 1698, there were seven hundred blacks in the colony; some were native-born, others were seasoned slaves from the West Indies, and a significant number had only recently arrived from Madagascar. The influx of Africans, which continued into the next century, provided a source of cultural strength for all of the colony's blacks, particularly by reinforcing such rituals as African funeral ceremonies.

By 1770, there were about four hundred thousand blacks in the colonies south of Maryland, compromising about 40 percent of the population. In contrast, there were only about fifty thousand blacks north of that colony, making up only about 4.5 percent of the population. In New York, there were about two thousand slaves in a population of nineteen thousand in 1700 and ten thousand out of a total of seventy-five thousand in 1750. The labor force in some New York counties was over more than 20 percent slave. But northern slavery was always disproportionately urban, and New York City had the greatest concentration of blacks in the colony. In New Jersey, the population of several counties was 5 to 9 percent black. Slavery was already an important part of the economy of the Philadelphia hinterland in the early part of the eighteenth century, and even William Penn preferred using black slaves to white servants on his estate. A number of Philadelphia merchants became important participants in the slave trade with the West Indies.

New England had fewer slaves than any other region. There were only one thousand blacks in New England in 1680, and even in 1775, the entire region housed only fourteen thousand—a bare 2 percent of the overall population. But again they were critical to the local economy in several areas where they were more concentrated. One-third of Massachusetts blacks lived in Boston, half of Rhode Island's in Newport. Blacks made up 20 percent of the population in Newport, 30 percent of South Kingston, and 40 percent of Charlestown.

Most northern blacks worked on small farms that raised provisions and livestock for export to the West Indies. Most masters, urban or rural, owned only a slave or two; work forces of two or three blacks were the norm. The majority of northern blacks lived alone or with only one or two other slaves, often in the same building as their owner. In the cereal-farming regions of New England, Pennsylvania, and New York and in many port towns, owners encouraged blacks to hire themselves out for their masters' profit; economically, they were more status symbols than anything else. Many found jobs as teamsters, wagoners, stockmen, or sailors or in rope walks, shipyards, and sail factories. There were exceptions, of course. The ironmaking industry in Pennsylvania and the tanning industry in New

York depended heavily on slave labor; some iron plantations had as many as thirty to fifty slaves. Blacks commonly worked in the various trades (such as stockmen and dairy workers) and shipyard industries of Rhode Island. Some white farmers in Narragansett Bay had migrated there from the West Indies and sought to reproduce their previous life-style, building large houses, breeding race horses, and owning twenty or more slaves. But without a profitable staple, this was not a true plantation society. Such large concentrations of black workers were unusual in the north.

Slave codes in the north were less rigorous and more laxly enforced than in the south. Puritans viewed slaves as part of the master's family and due all liberties stipulated in the laws of God. In New England, slaves could own, transfer, and inherit property, and whites and blacks were equal before the law. Slave testimony was admitted as evidence against whites, and blacks had access to counsel and were accorded all rights of due process, including the right of appeal. There is also some indication that masters and slaves had closer contact with each other than elsewhere. One visitor to rural Connecticut noted with dismay that slaves ate with the family—"and into the dish goes the black hoof as freely as the white hand."[11] Yet it was also Puritans who seemed to have had the greatest fear of miscegenation, and Massachusetts law banished blacks guilty of sexual relations with whites. The middle colonies' laws were harsher than those of New England, with curfews and prohibitions on the sale of alcohol to blacks. New York experienced slave conspiracies in 1712 and 1741, and its laws were correspondingly more restrictive.

Perhaps surprisingly, the north had about the same proportion of free blacks as did the south. These people lived in more or less the same conditions as did their enslaved counterparts, and whites generally restricted them to menial jobs. While northern slaves could rise to positions of responsibility, free blacks in a way represented more of a threat. If they acquired craft skills, they could compete directly with white artisans for jobs.

The profile of northern slavery altered drastically after mid-century. Before 1740 or so, northern blacks acculturated rapidly and easily to white culture. They lived in families and achieved demographic stability and a natural population increase more quickly than slaves in any other region. Beginning in the 1730s, however, northerners began to import blacks directly from Africa, rather than from the West Indies or the southern colonies. The sex ratio now swung heavily in favor of the males, and normal family patterns were disrupted. The death rate among newly arrived slaves also increased, since blacks imported directly from Africa were not used to the harsh winters and were more susceptible to the ravages of New World diseases.

This shift had a major impact on black social life. Northern black culture became increasingly Africanized in ritual practices, singing, dancing, and folklore. Since blacks had already achieved considerable autonomy, they were able to maintain these new practices relatively free from white interference. Blacks conducted spring ceremonies in New York City and Albany, for instance, called the Pinkster, a name derived from the Jewish and Christian feast of Pentecost. Slaves in Albany performed Congo dances, which a white observer described with curiosity: "They had a chief, old King Charley. . . a prince in his old country. . . . The music consisted of a sort of drum. . . upon which Old Charley did most of the beating, accompanied by singing some queer African air."[12] Blacks also began to refer to their churches as African, calling themselves "Sons of Africa." Negro Election Day was easily the most impressive of these new borrowings. Blacks from the countryside came to the cities for a series of feasts and parades, during which they dressed in their masters' clothes and exacted tribute from them to finance the feasts. They elected their own "kings" and "governors" and satirized their white masters. The celebratory nature of the events is evident in one white description of the day in

Newport, Rhode Island: "All the various languages of Africa, mixed with broken and ludicrous English filled the air, accompanied with the music of the fiddle, tambourine, the banjo [and] drum."[13]

Music and dance were essential elements of early black culture. Blacks played fiddles, xylophones, flutes, tambourines, and drums, drawing upon African technology in their construction. They played to celebrate and to mourn, and they sang during work and worship. Storytelling filled leisure hours, and dancing provided physical release and joy at holidays. Ring dances, drawn from African traditions, were loud and noisy, much to the dismay of whites. William Grimes, who lived in New Bedford, Connecticut, lost the lease to his home because his neighbors complained of the dancing that took place there late at night. In music and dance, blacks preserved the complex rhythms and percussive qualities of their African heritage. They also influenced white culture, as military bands adopted black percussive sounds in their cymbals, tambourines, triangles, and drums. This was only one of many ways in which African and African-American cultural traits helped shape the eighteenth-century colonial American cultural mosaic.

Black Resistance

For many years, historians noted the relative infrequency of organized, violent rebellions by slaves and assumed that blacks more or less accepted their fate, if not happily, at least with a degree of resignation. Indeed, only a handful of revolts occurred during the eighteenth century. But whites lived in constant fear of slave uprisings and violence. Slave codes limited group meetings, forbade weapons, kept blacks off the streets after dark, and outlawed the use of African drums, which whites feared were used to carry messages of revolt. Even Benjamin Franklin noted of Philadelphia's blacks in 1770: "But the Majority are of a plotting Disposition, dark, sullen, malicious, revengeful and cruel in the highest Degree."[14] Masters and overseers generally inflicted their own punishments of branding, flogging, amputating, and executing, and colony governments executed blacks for arson, poisoning, and frequent theft, as well as insurrection. In 1698, South Carolina castrated two blacks caught attempting to escape to North Carolina. Typical, perhaps, were the cases listed in the records of Middlesex County, Virginia, for the first twenty-five years of the eighteenth century. They included selling eight slaves to the West Indies for "frequent disorderly behavior"; the castration of one slave and the beating to death of another (by a minister) for running away; the cutting off of a slave's toes for "lying out and doing Severall Misdemeanors";[15] the amputation of the ears of yet another for stealing for a second time. On another occasion, the court executed and dismembered a slave for treason and displayed one of his limbs in public.

The spirit of resistance was strongest among those blacks recently arrived from Africa. These slaves often ran away in groups and with others from their own countries. As blacks assimilated, however, overt rebelliousness decreased. They turned, as we have seen, to feigning illness, dragging out tasks, pretending ignorance, breaking tools, destroying crops, theft, arson, poisoning, and murder. Skilled slaves—carpenters and boatmen, for instance—were still more imaginative in resisting and often more successful. More independent in their movements, they generally escaped as individuals and headed for towns where they could perhaps pass as free blacks or for the North Carolina frontier or Spanish Florida. In 1728, a group of runaways built a village near present-day Lexington, Virginia, complete with homes like those in Africa, a tribal governor who had been a prince in Africa, and African farming techniques. It took local whites a year to destroy the village and return the slaves to their owners. The largest number of runaways, though, left only to visit kin or friends. More than a quarter of the runaways in southern Maryland during the middle of the eighteenth-century fell into this category. A slave named Page traveled forty miles between Piscataway and South River in 1749 without being caught; Kate, who eventually ran away from her master at Georgetown and was hidden by friends, was known as "a great Rambler" who often visited friends in Calvert and Anne Arundel counties and frequently went to see her husband at West River.

Individual acts of resistance were common. Slaves sometimes lashed out from desperation. Jemmy, a slave belonging to Capt. Elias Ball, was sentenced for death in 1724 "for striking and wounding one Andrew Songster."[16] Ball saved Jemmy's life only by promising to deport him within two months. Blacks often murdered or attempted to murder masters and overseers, as evidenced in a 1733 case in South Carolina in which a slave was hanged for murdering an overseer with an ax. Verbal insolence—what they called "uppityness"—was particularly threatening to whites. In 1737, the South Carolina Assembly debated a law that would have allowed whites "to kill any resisting or saucy Slave. . . ."[17]

Poisoning and arson were two of the most common, and most feared, forms of resistance. In 1751, Rev. William Cotes of St. George's parish in South Carolina noted that five or six blacks had recently been condemned for poisoning their masters. In response, the assembly passed an addition to the 1740 Negro Act that provided for the conviction of any blacks who procured, conveyed, or administered poison or were even aware of such acts. Three additional clauses denied blacks access to medicines, drugs, and herbs and forbade them to give medicine even to other slaves except under white direction.

Blacks often resorted to arson against cruel masters, since the act was relatively difficult to prove and struck at the whites' most vulnerable point, their property. Newspapers noted frequent barn burnings between October and January as rice production increased during the first few decades of the century. Whenever blacks burned buildings in other colonies, the Charleston newspaper carried news of the event, usually commenting on the fears of such a conspiracy in its own colony. The Great Fire of 1740 destroyed three hundred buildings in the city and led the government to execute an accused black arsonist. In August 1741, several slaves attempted to burn the city, and in late 1741, two were executed for trying to set fire to the city's powder magazine. In 1754, the colony sentenced a slave named Sacharisa to burn at the stake for setting fire to her owner's house. Not surprisingly, the South Caroline militia routinely turned out, armed, for all fires.

More organized resistance, as we have noted, was relatively uncommon in the mainland colonies. The reasons for this are not all that mysterious. The chances of success were slim; the whites, after all, had the guns. Equally important, though, was black perception of the consequences of both success and failure. As kin and family networks grew, blacks had more to lose—wives, children, and others could be punished for their actions. Considering the minimal chances of success, it is not surprising that so few attempted it. Nor is it surprising that rebellions throughout the empire were most frequent where black-to-white ratios were six to one or higher. Still, several waves of unrest swept through the eighteenth century every generation of so. Three in particular stand out.

In New York City in 1712, more than twenty slaves set fire to a building and waited for the whites who came to extinguish the blaze. With knives, axes, and guns, they killed nine whites and injured several others. The whites responded quickly and without ambivalence: thirteen blacks were hanged, one starved to

❧ *Documents* ❧
White Dread of Black Rebellion

The fear of rebellion was pervasive among slave owners in the north and the south. The first selection is a description of a planned rebellion in Charleston, South Carolina; the second is taken from the trial records of the 1741 New York slave conspiracy. The New York account in particular reflects whites' expressed shock at the ingratitude of African-Americans for all that had been done for them.

> I shall give an Account of a bloody Tragedy which was to have been executed here last Saturday night (the 15th Inst.) by the Negroes, who had conspired to Rise and destroy us, and had almost brought it to pass: but it pleased God to appear for us, and confound their Councils. For some of them porposed that the Negroes of every plantation should destroy their own Masters; but others were for Rising in a Body, and giving the blow at once on surprise, and thus they differed. They soon made a great Body at the back of the Town, and had a great Dance, and expected the Country Negroes to come & join them; and had not an overruling providence discovered their Intrigues, we had been all in Blood. . . .
> The Chief of them, with the others, is apprehended and in Irons, in order to a Tryal, and we are in Hopes to find out the whole Affair.

Boston Weekly New-Letter, 22 October, 1730.

> Gentlemen, the monstrous ingratitude of this black tribe, is what exceedingly aggravates their guilt. Their slavery among us is generally softened with great indulgence; they live without care, and are commonly better fed and clothed, and put to less labour, than the poor of most christian countries. They are indeed slaves, but under the protection of the law, none can hurt them with impunity; they are really more happy in this place, than in the midst of the continual plunder, cruelty, and rapine of their native countries; but notwithstanding all the kindness and tenderness with which they have been treated amongst us, yet this is the second attempt of the same kind, that this brutish and bloody species of mankind have made within one age.

> [The court later addressed the defendents, Quack and Cuffee, upon their sentencing:] What then could prompt you to undertake so vile, so wicked, so monstrous, so execrable and hellish a scheme, as to murder and destroy your own masters and benefactors? Nay, to destroy, root and branch, all the white people of this place, and to lay the whole town in ashes.

Quoted in Thomas J. Davis, ed., *A Rumor of Revolt: The "Great Negros Plot" in Colonial New York* (Boston: Free Press, 1985), 92–3.

death in chains, three were burned at the stake, and one was broken on the wheel. Six others killed themselves rather than undergo torture and execution. The colony passed a new slave code, stripping blacks of most of the rights that had, until then, distinguished them somewhat from their southern brethren, and neighboring northern colonies passed similar acts.

A generation later, a second wave of unrest spread across the northern seaboard. Several barns were burned in New Jersey in 1740, and two slaves were executed. A few months later, New York City was hit by a series of thefts and fires. A white tavern keeper, his wife, and a young, indentured servant woman who worked as a prostitute in the tavern were all indicted. Prompted by some mild torture, the servant confessed that her master was involved with several blacks in a conspiracy to burn down the city and kill all the whites. Two slaves were tried for thefts and possible conspiracy, though they were hanged for theft only. The tavern keeper and his wife denied the charges but were hanged for treason, and the servant was hanged for conspiracy. She died renouncing her confession. The court threatened other blacks with torture and execution if they did not reveal the identities of the conspirators. Sixty-seven confessions were extracted. One hundred and fifty slaves and twenty-five whites were imprisoned in all, eighteen slaves and four whites tortured and hanged, thirteen slaves burned at the stake, and seventy transported to the West Indies. Authorities blamed the conspiracy not only on the blacks but also on the nefarious influence of religion (particularly Whitefield's preaching); they were strongly suspicious of a Catholic plot, having been warned by Gen. James Oglethorpe that the Spanish had sent out priests disguised as schoolteachers and physicians to worm their way into trusted positions. Four of those questioned in court were "suspicious school-masters," and the judges believed one John Ury to be a "Romish Priest."[18]

The most famous of all colonial slave rebellions, and one that left no doubt about the intent or who was involved, was the Stono Rebellion in South Carolina in 1739. It is significant in part because it triggered several other smaller rebellions in subsequent years. Led by a black named Jemmy, a group of newly arrived Africans who lived on the Stono River broke into a store and stole small arms and gunpowder, killing and decapitating the storekeepers. As they moved south toward Georgia, apparently hoping to escape to Spanish Florida, they killed whites (sparing a tavern keeper known for his kindness to blacks) and burned houses. By noon of the same day, their ranks had grown to fifty or sixty men. They then met William Bull, South Carolina's lieutenant governor, on his way to Charleston, and he barely escaped with his life. At mid-afternoon, the group halted and "set to dancing, Singing and beating Drums to draw more Negroes to them."[19] A group of armed planters succeeded in dispersing the group, now almost one hundred strong, but it took almost a week for the militia to capture the largest group, and a few individuals remained free for several months. In all, thirty whites and forty-four blacks died. Thereafter, South Carolina viewed all blacks as dangerous and passed the harshest slave code of the mainland colonies. The Stono rebellion occurred during a period of particular rapid economic growth in St. Paul's Parish. The parish had only 1,634 slaves in 1720 and more than three thousand by 1742. Carolinians were paying the price for their growing prosperity; wealth bought at the expense of human life and happiness did not come without its dangers.

Slavery continued to expand as the colonial period neared its end. By 1750, more than forty thousand slaves lived in the Virginia Piedmont alone, and the institution there was an extension of contemporary tidewater slavery, *not* a replication of an earlier phase. Sex ratios were even almost from the beginning, and the population began to reproduce itself almost immediately. Still, family life was not easy to maintain in an area where migration was almost constant, and blacks fought to counter the pain of separation here as much as anywhere else. A planter sold Butcher Will and his wife, Venus, together with their infant girl to one planter but their two sons to another. Apparently, planters commonly promised particular slaves to their own sons or daughters at the slaves' birth. The Methodist minister James Meacham once observed a woman's daughter being taken from her to be given to a planter's heir, her cries "enough to move the heart of the most obdurate."[20] As in the Chesapeake, blacks struggled successfully to maintain kinship connections. The elderly couple Tony and Phyllis found themselves sold twice in their old age, taking them progressively farther away from their children. But they maintained their extensive family ties, so that when they ran away in 1770, their current master did not know which child or grandchild or other relative they might be hiding with. Like most immigrants to America, blacks in the Piedmont recreated Old World (African) personal and institutional networks as rapidly and as extensively as they could.

Europeans who came to the American colonies during the eighteenth century did so with hope and in search of opportunity; Africans came involuntarily, torn from a culture that was whole and prosperous. Europeans came in groups, with families and neighbors, and reestablished Old World networks as soon as possible. Africans came alone, and whites continued to divide them from each other once they landed. Blacks thus faced a more difficult struggle to establish a cultural identity; while they retained as many African traditions as their experience and memory allowed, they created a new, multihued culture forced from their interactions with each other. They established family, community, and kinship networks as soon as demographic conditions allowed. Europeans and Africans, though, shared one element in this migration: black or white, those who retained Old World contacts kept their Old World cultures the longest. Germans abandoned their language and customs only slowly, while blacks in New York and South Carolina, infused with fresh African presence regularly, embraced African culture fully and joyfully. Over time, though, all groups grew farther away from their Old World origins, retaining their old cultures only as elements in a new, hybrid cultural framework.

❧ *Chapter Nine* ❧

Wealth, Work, and Society in Early America

In 1733, Boston merchants proposed to create a public market. They had failed twice before (in 1696 and 1714) to overcome resistance from Boston laborers, who preferred to patronize street vendors and itinerant traders and viewed the merchants' efforts as an attempt by the wealthy to enhance their own power. Now, amidst rising food prices, the debate reached a new level of intensity. The merchants argued that a market would promote industry, prevent idleness, and stimulate productive competition—all modern economic and social values. Ordinary Bostonians felt differently. Led by women, who did most of the household purchasing, Bostonians boycotted the new, regulated market. In 1737, they took their opposition one step further. A midnight mob demolished the building donated by merchant Peter Faneuil for use as a market house, firmly expressing their support for a more traditional moral economy.

This incident reflects the disruptive effects of rapid and dynamic economic growth in eighteenth-century America. From 1650 to 1750, the colonial economy multiplied about twenty-five times over. As productivity exploded and standards of living improved, the American colonies became one of the most attractive centers of economic opportunity in the British Empire. Beneath the surface of rapid statistical growth, however, economic life changed little for the majority of Americans. Most colonists were farmers. Even those who grew some of their crop for market would have noticed little difference in their daily affairs, and those who did often expressed resentment at the changes that threatened their traditional lives.

How modern was the colonial economy? To what extent did market considerations dictate economic activity, and to what degree did traditional attachments to community continue to restrain the pursuit of self-interest and individual gain? While answers to these questions remain elusive, we can search for clues by examining the basic components of the eighteenth-century economy and exploring the various ways in which Americans made their livings.

Wealth And Trade In Colonial America

By the 1770s, Americans had the highest standard of living in the Western world. Taxes were low, and the average colonist could afford to spend about a quarter of his or her income on foreign imports. Many ordinary Americans were positively affluent compared to their European counterparts. Most colonial families were now at least comfortable, owning some earthenware, bed and table linens, and knives and forks. The rich had better clothes and furniture and even china, works of art on the walls, and a variety of luxury goods, while the wealthiest owned the ultimate status symbol, a carriage. The colonists benefited most obviously from their improved diet. They consumed a significant amount of livestock, the average male adult farmer devouring as much as two hundred pounds of meat a year (comparable to today's consumption rate). Americans ate more vegetables than Europeans did and enjoyed more diverse and appetizing meals.

Though wealth statistics from colonial America are scarce, it is clear that the colonies experienced three broad cycles of economic growth. From the early to the mid-seventeenth century, the Chesapeake and New England profited from rapid income growth, high savings rates, and an impressive rate of capital formation. This was followed by several decades of relative economic stagnation. Then, after 1740, living standards rose again, overseas demand for American products increased, and the American population boom created a growing domestic market. The exact timing of these cycles varied by region and colony. Connecticut underwent a recession in the 1730s and 1740s, then a strong recovery from 1750 to 1765. Pennsylvania saw slow economic growth from 1715 to 1730, with a long, sustained recovery from 1730 to 1750. And the Chesapeake experienced its most rapid period of growth between 1755 and 1775, following a long cycle of depressed tobacco prices.

While agriculture was the backbone of the economy, overseas trade was a vital element in maintaining the high American standard of living and a critical factor in the fluctuation of economic cycles. Small farmers often produced a bit of a surplus for the market, and the wealthiest Americans of all were those who depended wholly on overseas trade—merchants and southern planters.

During the second third of the eighteenth century, the American colonies began to occupy an increasingly important position in England's economic empire. England profited in particular from the reexport of colonial goods to other markets. More than four-fifths of the tobacco entering English ports, for instance, was reshipped to other countries. The colonies played an equally significant role as a market for English manufactured goods. In 1774, nearly half of British-produced copperware, ironware, glassware, earthenware, silk goods, and printed cotton and linen goods were sold in America, while more than two-thirds of the cordage and iron nails were shipped to the colonies. The importation of raw materials and unprocessed foodstuffs from the colonies gave rise to new industries in England— sugar refining, tobacco processing, and later, cotton weaving. In addition, increased food demand from southern Europe stimulated American food production. A burgeoning American trading sector emerged from all this activity. Many colonial merchants became independent exporters who owned their own ships and engaged in extensive overseas trade.

We can develop a fuller picture of these activities by examining the regional economies of the mainland British colonies. New England did not fit easily into the mercantilistic system, since most of its products competed directly with identical or similar ones produced in England. The region's merchants did export whale oil, potash, and flaxseed to the parent country, but for the most part, they were forced to look elsewhere for markets—and this they did energetically and with a good deal of success. New England ships carried wheat, fish, and wood products to southern Europe in exchange for wine, fruits, salt, and other commodities. Wheat, fish, and wood went to the West Indies in return for molasses and specie. Rhode Island vessels in particular also engaged in the famous triangular trade, though only a few specialized merchants followed this path on a regular basis. In this trade, colonial ships brought rum and manufactured goods to Africa in exchange for slaves, gold, and ivory, which were then traded in the West Indies for molasses, coin, and bills of exchange. Overall, the bulk of New England exports went to the West Indies, while 66 percent of its imports came from England and 23 percent from the West Indies.

The remaining British colonies fit much better into the mercantilistic system. The middle colonies produced the greatest variety of products for export, and their proximity to the West Indies gave them an increasing advantage there over New England traders. The region sent 44 percent of its exports to the Indies, 33 percent to southern Europe, and 23 percent to England; it received 76 percent of its imports from England and 21 percent from the Indies.

The south was the region most suited to the British system. Since tobacco and rice both were enumerated, the region sent more than 75 percent of its exports to England—and these two products alone comprised more than two-thirds the value of all colonial exports. Other important southern exports included deerskins, indigo, and naval stores, the most valuable export from North Carolina. Turpentine was used for lamps, rosin for candles and soap, tar to preserve wood and ropes from the salt air at sea, and pitch to coat ships' hulls. Foodstuffs comprised the fastest growing southern export sector. The northern Chesapeake was well on its way to shifting production to wheat and corn by mid-century, and the newly opened Shenandoah Valley was much more suited to growing such products than it was to

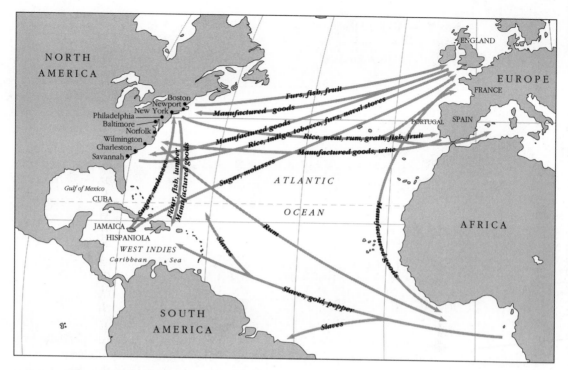

MAP 9.1: Atlantic Trade Routes ❧

tobacco. Ironically, more acres were planted for food, especially corn, throughout the south than for tobacco. The region received more than 85 percent of its imports from England.

Historians have long debated whether this system benefited the colonies or hindered their development. While the persistent imbalance of trade surely drained potential wealth out of the colonies, the lack of statistical information makes this a difficult question to answer, and it is all but impossible to picture the direction the colonial economy might have taken under different circumstances. New Englanders in particular had to deal with a continual drain of specie from the region to pay for their imports, and all colonists had to learn to live with the complex myriad of customs regulations. Still, the present consensus is that the system cost only about 1 percent to 2 percent of the total colonial income in any year during the eighteenth century.

Colonial merchants profited from the system in a variety of ways. Most obviously, they could count on the protection of the British navy, a critical factor in a century plagued by international warfare. Northern shippers benefited from protection against European competition, indigo producers received bounties, and even tobacco growers, who complained loudly about being excluded from direct trade with the profitable European market, received advantageous merchandising services from English and Scottish merchants. Merchants who sought to evade the system, moreover, apparently had little difficulty in doing so. The highly profitable West Indies molasses trade depended on successful smuggling, which New Englanders conducted with little danger of being caught.

Colonial merchants were able to make up much of the trade deficit by providing shipping and commercial services to exporters and by investing in the highly profitable shipbuilding trade; ships remained a major export of colonial builders

Table 7 ⪧ Regional trading statistics, 1700–1760

	New England		New York		Pennsylvania	
	Exports	Imports	Exports	Imports	Exports	Import
1760	37,802	599,647	21,125	480,106	22,754	707,998
1750	48,455	343,659	35,634	267,130	28,191	217,713
1740	72,389	171,081	21,498	118,777	15,048	56,751
1730	54,701	208,196	8,740	64,356	10,582	48,592
1720	49,206	128,767	16,836	37,397	7,928	24,53
1710	31,112	106,338	8,203	31,475	1,277	8,594
1700	41,486	91,918	17,567	49,410	4,608	18,529

U.S. Bureau of the Census, *Historical Statistics of the United States from Colonial Times to 1970*, 2 vols. (Washington, DC: Government Printing Office, 1975), 2:1176–77.

throughout the century. Merchants also profited from the business generated by British troops stationed in the colonies during the various eighteenth-century wars. In the end, the total colonial trade deficit averaged about forty thousand pounds annually, a relatively small sum readily made up through direct specie payments to England.

Economy And Society In Eighteenth-Century New England

Despite the rapid pace of economic growth, New England agriculture remained predominantly traditional in practice and economic goals throughout the eighteenth century. Beginning around 1700, farmers made a smooth transition from mixed-crop agriculture to one based on corn, cattle, and hogs. Instead of wheat, which grew poorly in the thin New England soil, they sowed rye for bread. They relied on apple orchards for cider and grew large amounts of corn, which could also be fed to livestock. They butchered cattle and hogs and salted the meat for the winter. Around mid-century, they began to grow more potatoes, a high-yield and nutritious crop, and a variety of English grasses (timothy, red clover) as summer forage for livestock and for their high nitrogen yield that nourished the soil. They also began to export more surplus salted and pickled meat to the West Indies.

These adjustments took place within a local economic network that remained largely traditional in function and structure. Neighborhood and kin groups continued to work together, exchanging and lending tools, animals, grazing land, and a whole range of labor and resources. Women maintained the central role they had always held in this network, they and their children spinning, sewing, and producing goods to be shared with their neighbors. Indeed, most nonagricultural work outside of cities focused primarily on producing a bit of extra household income. Farmers tried to acquire skills in several areas and enough flexibility to cover emergencies and harvest shortfalls. Tenant farmers spread their work out between wage labor, semiskilled artisanal tasks, and family farming. Artisans traded off their

Table 7 ✺ Regional trading statistics, 1700–1760 (continued)

	Virginia and Maryland		Carolina		Georgia	
	Exports	Imports	Exports	Imports	Exports	Imports
1760	504,451	605,882	162,769	218,131	12,198	—
1750	508,939	349,419	191,607	133,037	1,942	2,125
1740	341,997	281,428	266,560	181,821	924	3,524
1730	346,823	150,931	151,739	64,785	—	—
1720	331,482	110,717	62,736	18,290	—	—
1710	188,429	127,639	20,793	19,613	—	—
1700	317,302	173,481	14,058	11,003	—	—

U.S. Bureau of the Census, *Historical Statistics of the United States from Colonial Times to 1970,* 2 vols. (Washington, DC: Government Printing Office, 1975), 2:1176–77.

products and services against present or future obligations, most retaining some connection with the land and farming and many keeping livestock. Merchants and wealthy millers often had large landholdings in the countryside, which they leased to tenants. Work was done at a slow pace in this world, compared to today's standards, and it differed little from the daily range of activities we examined for the seventeenth century.

But while the rising and setting of the sun and the changing seasons still set the general rhythms of life, historians differ over the extent to which early American farmers were guided by marketplace considerations. The controversy involves more than just pounds and pence. A greater or lesser degree of market orientation tells us much about the attitudes of farmers toward modern economic activity and values—whether, for instance, they were more accepting of the pursuit of self-interest and less interested in serving the needs of the community. Most farmers produced for market to some degree, and they commonly sold food to local artisans and shipped produce to regional towns and cities. In Rhode Island, some landholders raised horses for export to the West Indies, a market-driven activity that was also common in the lower Delaware Valley. Historians must simply accept the fact that contradictory tendencies were common and that farmers rarely acted from any pre-planned orientation toward one side or another. Most continued to consciously embrace communal and family values over individualism and the maximization of profits, but they also sought to improve their standard of living and to willingly enter the marketplace when doing so was to their advantage. Local exchange networks, in which goods and services were bartered informally, were not necessarily incompatible with market sales.

The rapid rate of population growth also had a profound effect on individual involvement in the market. Much evidence exists that increasing pressure on the available land supply plagued the New England colonies, creating a crisis in the balance of resources and people. With population increasing at an annual rate of up to 5 percent, children in third- and fourth-generation towns faced an uncertain future. Available land doubled and tripled in price, and the gap between the rich and poor increased significantly. Family considerations limited out-migration, and adequate employment alternatives did not yet exist in the still undeveloped economy.

Though most New England towns had reached this stage of development by the mid-eighteenth century, some safety valves were available. The northern New England frontier drew large numbers of settlers, though the warfare that plagued the first part of the century often made this alternative less attractive. After the Seven Years War, migration to frontier areas in Maine, New Hampshire, and Vermont increased significantly. The Connecticut economy also offered a growing range of choices. Farming here was becoming more specialized and commercialized, and meat and dairy production were increasing; merchants were becoming increasingly involved in the Atlantic trade. Even much of the poverty that characterized rural Connecticut was directly age-related. Young adult males had to wait several years to inherit land or wealth from their fathers, while older adults often spent the last years of their lives dependent on their children, having dispersed much of their wealth to the next generation.

Poverty was a real problem throughout the rural north. Perhaps 10 percent of the adult males did not fall into one of the above categories; when we add slaves and indentured servants to the total, the numbers grow. The Connecticut countryside did not even remotely resemble the ravaged fields of much of Europe, but neither did it come close to the agricultural utopia of American historical mythology. Still more problematic are questions of attitude and perspective. Did the prospects of future prosperity alleviate young adults' concerns about poverty? Or did economic pressure create a bleak outlook for them? And did prosperity come only at the expense of a difficult struggle, forced relocation, or movement into undesirable occupations?

The answers to these questions can be found only if we consider them within a broader social context. In small towns such as Canterbury, Connecticut, and Chebacco, Massachusetts, rural farmers spent the early part of their adult lives accumulating resources, primarily land, which they then used to provide for their childrens' futures. At least one son would receive a minimum of forty acres and a house, while others got frontier lands that were then sold to finance an apprenticeship, the start of a career in a trade, or perhaps a university education. Widows retained their dower rights, while few daughters received any land. New Englanders were thus able to cope with the growing land shortage, but at a certain cost in family stability. The structure of agriculture life remained traditional. Most farmers maintained livestock for consumption only, and even sawmills, gristmills, tanneries, and taverns were family businesses that catered to the needs of the community. In a larger sense, though, the ideal of a tightly knit, agricultural community was inevitably subverted, as settlements scattered and more and more sons were forced to pursue nontraditional occupations. Most sons remained dependent on their fathers until the latters' death; two-thirds received no property until that time, and more and more men began to postpone marriage until their late twenties. The number of young, unmarried, and landless workers was on the rise, and economic and psychological independence became an elusive goal for many of the young men of Canterbury and Chebacco.

Elsewhere, simple economic survival was difficult. The farmers of Concord, Massachusetts, faced the same problems that disrupted life in most small New England towns. By 1750, crowding was a serious problem there, and one in four taxpayers left the town every decade. To some extent, the frontier provided an outlet. Concord residents had begun moving as early as the 1720s to the Connecticut and Rhode Island borders and northwest to New Hampshire. Benjamin Barrett became a proprietor of Grafton in Worcester County and Peterborough in New Hampshire, intending to use this frontier land or proceeds from its sale to provide for his four sons. When he died in 1728, he left his sons James and Thomas land from the family estate and the two younger sons farms in Paxton, Worcester County. Barrett had provided well for his family, and James started his life in a far more comfortable position than most of his contemporaries. He and fifteen other Concord residents continued the practice initiated by Benjamin's generation when in 1764 they purchased "Township #4" in Berkshire County, Massachusetts. On his own land, James grew oats for market and kept a large herd of cattle, along with oxen that he often rented out to neighbors.

Contrast Barrett's situation with that of two other Concord residents. David Brown was forty-two years old when he captained a minuteman company at Concord in 1775; he had nine children and a total of thirteen people living in his house. The eldest, seventeen-year-old Purchase, probably shared a bed with a younger brother or an uncle. David had served three terms as a Concord select-man, came from an established family, and was well-respected in the town and county. But he had only a twenty-acre homestead and eighty additional acres scattered around the town, most of it suitable only for grazing. Concord land was wearing out, and a farm of this size provided only the barest subsistence. A family could count on bread and milk for breakfast and dinner and a meat-and-vegetable stew for lunch. The father, and perhaps some of the older children, would have to work for others to get enough money to buy cloth, salt, sugar, and a few other necessities. The family farm was small enough so that only the youngest son, if anyone, would inherit it whole. David had, however, speculated in frontier lands and had enough capital from their sale to provide a small stake for each of his children.

But even that was better than the fate of poor Ezekiel Brown (a distant relation). Ezekiel's father, head of a family with five children, never owned more than a small parcel of land; the family spent much of their time wandering around Middlesex County searching for work and opportunity. But there were many other families and individuals doing the same, and most towns took pains to "warn out" these "strolling poor," since they would have to provide for them if they could not support themselves. Ezekiel himself finally achieved a modest level of success in the late 1760s and early 1770s as proprietor of a country store. By 1772, he had married and owned a house, barn, and six acres of prime land in the center of town. He held a minor office in the town and was gaining the respect of his fellow citizens. But like many other New Englanders, the credit crunches that preceded the Revolution wiped him out. At age thirty-one in 1775, Ezekiel found himself in debtor's prison. He eventually joined the army as the only way out of his predicament. The Ezekiel Browns of New England were never more than a small minority of the population. But they were an ever-present reminder to the David Browns of what could befall their own families if things got worse and a constant source of irritation and embarrassment to the Barretts and other gentry families.[1]

Economy And Society In The Middle Colonies

At mid-century, the middle colonies were the most economically dynamic region in British North America. This area combined the best features of the other regions— extensive commercial activity and staple crop production. It was blessed with fertile farmlands, and its wheat production made it the breadbasket of the American colonies. In the first half of the century, a family working with hand sickles could harvest about ten acres of wheat a year with a yield of about 120 bushels. After mid-century, farmers began to use the cradle, a scythe with a long handle and wooden figures above the blade, which was a more balanced and effective cutting tool. Productivity doubled and surpluses grew. The average farm encompassed about 125 acres, about fifty of which remained uncleared. About half of the rest was used for crops and half for meadow and pasture. Even in this highly profitable region, agricultural practices were conservative. Six-year crop rotation was common, with a year each for wheat, barley, and corn and then three fallow years. Farmers turned to clover and grasses (to restore nitrogen to the soil) only after 1750 (a century behind the English).

The region's economy profited from the rising demand for foodstuffs in Europe and the West Indies. The price of wheat alone in the Philadelphia market rose more than 50 percent from 1720 to 1750, and by 1770, wheat exports from the middle colonies and from Maryland and northern Virginia accounted for 20 percent of all colonial exports. But it was not wheat alone that brought profits to middle colony farmers and merchants. Shippers carried corn, pork, flour, and staves to the Indies; bread and flour to the Carolinas and Newfoundland; wheat, flour, and pipe staves to Portugal; flax seed, flour, oak and walnut planks, and barrel staves to Ireland; and animal skins, tobacco, beeswax, staves, oak and walnut planks, pig iron, tar, pitch, turpentine, bills of exchange, and even ships to England. The resultant prosperity meant that many farmers could provide their children with enough property to maintain the same level of farming over the generations—this at a time when Massachusetts had to import food to feed its people.

New York

The Dutch had emphasized trade from the earliest days of New Amsterdam, and when the English took over, they sought to take advantage of Dutch mercantile connections. New York merchants had excellent contacts with European financial centers and traded extensively in flaxseed and other products. The colony's early trade was small but diverse, and for a while, it was the only northern colony to have a favorable balance of trade with England. After 1713, merchants expanded to trading naval stores, lumber, wheat, flour, and livestock; by 1721, they were sending out an average of 215 ships a year. New bridges, roads, and markets helped fuel the growth. The predominance of land speculators and powerful landowners in the colony, though, hindered further development.

New York's landlord-tenant system was unique. The Dutch had granted extensive tracts of lands to patroons in the seventeenth century, and hundreds of thousands of acres continued to be controlled by a few individuals throughout the colonial period. The Van Rensselaers, Johnsons, Livingstons, Schuylers, Philipses, and Morrises lived in a far grander style than their tenants, forming an important segment of the growing colonial elite. At the very least, their control of vast tracts of land hindered the growth of the colony's population. In 1756, New York had only ninety-seven thousand inhabitants (compared to Pennsylvania's 220,000). For the first few decades of the century, wars, threats from Indians and the French, and a pervasive scarcity of labor forced landlords to offer generous terms to attract tenants. In 1714, the Manor of Rensselaerwyck had only eighty-two tenants, but it had attracted 345 by 1752 and almost a thousand by 1779. Most of these people were recent arrivals from Europe, too capital-poor to purchase farms of their own. The Rensselaers and other manor lords offered these new immigrants attractive terms to induce them to settle on their estates: long leases, the right to sell improvements to the next tenants, free access to gristmills and roads, initial rent-free periods and low rents thereafter, equipment, seeds, livestock, and often even a year's worth of free provisions. A tenant who wanted to sell out and leave his lease, however, would often have to pay the landlord one-third of the purchase price. Landlords also required tenants to give them first option on their crops and to grind their grain at their mills. While manor lords like the Philipse family sought to create a caring, paternalistic environment, keeping rents low and attending to their tenants needs, the system ultimately served the landlords' wealth most of all.

The life of Adolph Philipse illustrates many of these developments. Philipse's father, Frederick, died in 1702, leaving Adolph with a healthy inheritance that included several businesses. Adolph became involved in overseas and slave trade and managed ninety thousand acres of land in the Hudson Valley. His tenants grew in number from two hundred to eleven hundred, and he owned twenty-three slaves. Philipse's tenants brought their barley, wheat, and corn to his mills to be processed, and he sent his flour to New York City, overseas, or a bakery he had established to produce ship biscuits. By 1720, he had prospered enough that he could double the size of his father's manor house. Philipse aspired to, and reached, the equivalent of English gentry status.

Albany's independent prosperity gives further evidence of the diversity of New York's economy. Situated on the frontier, Albany County's population grew dramatically after the end of warfare in 1713. A real estate boom ensued, and the region began to export significant amounts of grain and lumber. Albany merchants also added a unique twist to the ever-essential West Indian trade. These men retained their strong Dutch connections, and they imported most of their finished goods from Amsterdam. To pay for them, they sent flour, butter, and grain to the Dutch West Indies, receiving bills of exchange as payment, which they then sent to their merchant correspondents in Amsterdam. Albany entrepreneurs also established successful businesses in masts and bricks, and by 1744, at least twenty-four ships of fifty or more tons commuted regularly to New York City carrying the region's products. Even merchants involved in the fur trade adjusted successfully to the trade's move westward, establishing partnerships with merchants closer to the frontier and diversifying their own enterprises.

Pennsylvania

Freeholders peopled most of the middle colonies, working medium-sized farms assisted by wage, indentured, and slave labor. Pennsylvania was the most prosperous of these colonies. It had better farmland, more egalitarian land policies, and more ethnic and religious diversity. Even where tenancy was common, as it was in Chester County in the southeastern section of the colony, middle-class prosperity prevailed. As in New York, tenants and landlords reached a variety of mutually beneficial arrangements. New arrivals and recently freed indentured servants in particular benefited because the system gave them an opportunity to accumulate enough capital to purchase their own farm. Life was modestly comfortable. Most of the early homes had only one or two rooms with a few spartan pieces of furniture—a bench, some stools, a bed in the loft. Only the wealthiest in the early years of settlement had pewter utensils and ceramic plates; most used wooden plates and cups.

This relatively egalitarian society changed gradually during the first decades of the new century, but after 1750, the pace of economic growth quickened dramatically. Sixteen new towns were founded in the 1750s, twenty-two in the 1760s. As population pressure grew, land prices in heavily settled areas began to increase. The export trade expanded impressively. Before 1750, Philadelphia had been home to a large community of small merchants, few of them really prosperous enough to venture outside West Indies coastal trade or the relatively restricted trade to southern Europe. After 1750, the picture changed dramatically. The British spent heavily in Philadelphia during the Seven Years War, and cereal and grain prices in Europe, affected by war and poor harvests, shot up. Philadelphia merchants exploited new markets in the Mediterranean, France, and England, and they became more specialized and more economically stratified.

A growing trend toward inequality was felt in both urban and rural areas. By 1760, as many as one-third of the families in some of the older counties did not own their land. In Chester County, the wealthiest 10 percent of the population claimed 30 percent of the wealth, while the poorest 30 percent only had 6 percent. Entrepreneurs made small fortunes supplying newcomers with land and equipment. Still, the overall level of prosperity remained far higher than that of New England towns and villages. During the 1750s and 1760s, trading vessels sailed between Philadelphia and small villages along Delaware Bay and its tributaries, exchanging local goods and products from England. Just the requirements of land transport to keep Philadelphia supplied with agricultural products for export greatly stimulated local economic activity—at least ten thousand wagon trips, for example, were needed to move the 370,000 bushels of wheat and corn and sixteen thousand barrels of flour exported annually from the Maryland eastern shore. Pennsylvania certainly deserved its reputation as a prosperous, relatively egalitarian colony. Many farmers could boast of a small annual cash income. "In this province," Gottlieb Mittelberger noted, "even in the humblest or poorest houses, no meals are served without a meat course; and no one eats bread without butter or cheese."[2]

The experiences of two families from Chester County illustrate the daily routines of the prosperous people in this region. Samuel Swayne farmed in East Marlborough, a township with the assortment of mills and artisans typical of Chester County. He and his neighbors—shopkeepers, joiners, shoemakers, and others—complemented each other in a complex, reciprocal relationship of services and debts.

Swayne married Hannah in 1756, and his brother William, administrator of their parents' estate, gave him a ninety-one acre farm. Swayne grew wheat and some rye, oats, hay, corn, and barley. He was a skilled saddletree maker and was widely known for his nursery (apple and peach trees) and the butter and cheese Hannah made and sold. From their starting place in the bottom quarter of the town's taxpayers, the Swaynes moved up slowly until they ranked in the second third in the early 1770s. In 1772, they purchased thirty-five more acres, jumping to the upper third, and by the time Samuel died in 1808, he owned a decanter and wineglasses, a clock, a substantial library of Quaker books, sixteen hundred pounds in credits from his neighbors, and more than one hundred acres of valuable land.

Like most Pennsylvania farmers, Swayne relied on both his neighbors and occasional wage labor to work his farm. He hired temporary workers during harvest and for other jobs, such as ditching, preparing the fields, and collecting firewood. The laborers commanded good wages, but Swayne's returns were even higher, and he often paid them at least part of their wages in goods and services. He even set a few up with cottages on his property while they worked for him. After 1770, when his children were old enough to help out, he relied less on outside assistance.

Daniel Burk worked for Swayne for two years in 1768 and 1769, and his experiences provide insight both into Swayne's business and the lives of the lower class in a prosperous economy. Swayne provided Burk with a cottage and land on which to plant a small garden and keep two or three head of livestock, as well as access to a plow, cart, and horses. Burk also had enough free time to supplement his income with artisanal work. He did not make enough to buy his own farm, but he did pay more than the minimum tax in 1770.

William and Elizabeth Smedley lived in Middletown, a typical Chester County community where farms averaged about 158 acres and rural industries were common—there were several mills, two taverns, and a tanyard in the town. Smedley was a farmer and a carpenter, beginning his career in 1751 after completing an apprenticeship with a local carpenter. He worked at his craft for most of the year, leaving it to hire out as a laborer during harvest. He married Elizabeth in 1753, and his father gave him a sixty-eight acre farm in Middletown, including some livestock and basic farm implements. He, too, hired day laborers during harvest and also received help from his neighbors, which he later repaid in kind. The Smedleys sent their leather out to be tanned, paid cash for shoes, and sold small farm surpluses, and William continued to work in his neighbor's fields for the customary wages.

By the mid-1750s, the couple was prosperous enough to hire domestic servants. During the late 1750s, they became more extensively involved in market activity. Smedley invested in brick making when his carpentry business slowed, and when trade picked up again, he and his workmen sold almost sixty thousand barrel staves to local and Philadelphia merchants. By 1759, he had purchased 148 additional acres of land and hired several more free laborers. From 1757 until he died in 1766, Smedley's home always had at least one domestic servant, an apprentice, a laborer, a bound servant, and a family living in the small cottage he provided. The number was larger than usual, but the mix was typical of middle-colony farm families. Few of these workers, it seems, ever acquired enough capital to buy their own land. But cottagers certainly lived in more favorable conditions than the live-in servants. Cottager status was a definite step up the social ladder.[3]

Quakers

Quaker society, as always, was somewhat different. Like all American colonists, Quaker families were concerned with providing for their children's futures, both spiritually and materially. The unusual degree to which they pursued these goals, though, led them to exert much more control over childrens' marriages and behavior. Elders formed special oversight committees to spy on young Quakers during fairs and market days to ensure they did not get too acquainted with each other before consulting with their parents. As a result, most children married within the meeting. Quaker parents made their children financially independent at or soon after their marriage, with fewer restrictions than New England farm families imposed on their children. Thomas Minshall's son Isaac married in 1707; three months later, Thomas gave his son, free of restrictions, 380 acres. Son Jacob married at twenty-one in 1706 and received six hundred acres and a stone house.

These numbers were typical for prosperous Quaker families, but Pennsylvania was a prosperous colony that simply had more land available. Poverty, however, was not unknown, even among close-knit Quakers. In the early years of the century, the children of poorer families married much later than those of the well-off. Because the poor could not provide as well for their children, Quakers regarded them as less successful in protecting their children from the temptations of the carnal world. But even prosperous Quakers soon found that wealth did not necessarily bring happiness. More and more children began to marry outside the meeting, and meetings began to complain of "shooting matches, singing, and dancing, and the like disorders which too many youth fall into. . . ."[4]

After 1740, the Quakers finally began to run out of land. The first generation had provided their children with an average of 701 acres; these, in turn, provided an average of only 400 acres for their own children. Inflationary land prices meant that poor Quakers who owned land could not afford the high price of labor necessary to increase their agricultural output and accumulate capital. Thus, parents were forced to set up their children more often as tradesmen and in other nonfarm occupations, and their sons in turn began to marry more non-Quakers. Forced to rely on commercial opportunities or trades to make a living, these children found themselves free of the control of their parents. Some migrated to the frontier; movement into the southern backcountry increased dramatically in the 1760s. But most chose to remain near Philadelphia and to start life with whatever patrimony their parents could leave them.

Quaker meetings made these burdens even more difficult to bear, since they enforced the requirements to marry within the meeting mercilessly and held parents responsible for their childrens' actions. Richard Ormes, a minister and recognized Quaker leader, was not asked to serve his monthly meeting for five years after his daughter married while pregnant. Any parents who stood up for their children against the meeting's discipline found both themselves and their children dismissed. While Quaker families were more overtly loving toward their children than their New England counterparts and while they were able to provide for them materially far more successfully, they were heartless toward those who broke the code of behavior and unsympathetic to those who simply had bad luck.

The Chesapeake

Southern agriculture differed significantly from its northern counterpart, and a society dominated by a handful of large planters took some time to emerge.

The critical turning point for Chesapeake society came between 1680 and 1720. Until 1700, only a few areas contained fully developed plantation systems. For much of the seventeenth century, the region was characterized by scattered outposts surrounded by Indian villages and peopled by English settlers who learned how to survive from the Indians and then took their land. Freedmen traveled widely in search of the best opportunities, and for some time, most of them succeeded in accumulating enough capital to buy some land and start a family. Large planters had not yet set themselves off through education, family, and private societies, and most women still had to labor in the fields alongside their husbands.

During the early years of the eighteenth century, however, while opportunity for poor and ordinary planters all but disappeared, wealthy Chesapeake planters created a ruling elite with a success unparalleled elsewhere in the mainland colonies. A series of developments made this transformation possible: the expansion of the slave trade, which alleviated the perennial labor shortage and allowed wives to return to their homes; the decline of white immigration, equalizing sex ratios and aiding the establishment of stable families; and an increase in life expectancy, leading to longer marriages and clearer lines of patriarchal authority through family and kin networks.

In the 1680s, the dominance of small planters that had characterized much of the early Chesapeake experience began to disappear. A severe depression in tobacco prices sorted out the wealthier planters who could weather economic decline from the smaller ones who could not. During the 1690s, more people left the Chesapeake than migrated to it. As the supply of white labor grew perilously short, large planters began to buy more and more black slaves—about three thousand between 1695 and 1700, or the same number as during the prior twenty years. By 1700, most unfree workers in the Chesapeake were black.

It became clearer than ever during this change that inheritance was crucial to accumulating wealth—and the poor, of course, lacked this advantage. Children of the large planters could count on receiving not only money and land but also many slaves. At the very least, a well-off father would leave one son land, another the slaves, and another property and cash from the other two, providing the younger sons with at least enough capital to buy some land and a slave or two. These inheritances became particularly critical during the cyclical depressions that began to characterize the Chesapeake tobacco industry. High output, stagnating productivity, and growing labor costs produced low tobacco prices during the first half of the century. Thus, only the largest planters could hope to turn a profit, and even the sons of wealthy Virginians found it increasingly difficult to match their parents' standard of living. Some turned to wheat and corn, others migrated to the frontier. Those who could afford to expanded their cultivated acreage. Exports increased during this period, but at a price—the purchase of more and more slaves, which stripped the planters of potential profits.

Those who remained in the tidewater exerted considerable effort to enlarge and consolidate their social and economic powers. Robert "King" Carter, the richest man in early eighteenth-century Virginia, inherited one thousand pounds and a thousand acres from his father. Carter expanded his activities into the slave trade, ran the Fairfax proprietary lands on the colony's Northern Neck, and took advantage of his unique situation there to patent three hundred thousand acres of his own. He made sure that his children married into other prominent Virginia families. Thomas Addison inherited most of his father's estate, consisting of eighteen hundred pounds and sixty-five hundred acres of land. He saw that his eldest son John married well, and he left him most of his estate. He arranged for another son, Henry, to receive a clerical education as his share of the inheritance, and he provided financially for two other sons who remained single. Chesapeake fathers, like their New England and middle colonies counterparts, gave each child a fair share while keeping the family estate as intact as possible. But there was much more at stake here. After 1720, only planters who consolidated their holdings, acquired slaves, and became members of the House of Burgesses succeeded in becoming wealthy.

In an attempt to centralize the tobacco trade, some of the larger planters convinced the burgesses to pass legislation in 1703 and again in 1713 to establish towns that could serve as regional market centers. The efforts failed. The burgesses tried again during a subsequent depression between 1727 and 1732, again with no success. The planters pursued a new course when they took steps to lessen the tobacco supply and force prices upward. The 1730 Virginia Tobacco Inspection Act limited the number of plants a worker could tend, but the regulations proved difficult to implement and even harder to enforce. Small planters were the most directly threatened, and they protested, at one point burning down four warehouses that were part of the new inspection system. The large planters, frightened by such a complete rejection of their patriarchal system, smoothed over their own differences and banded together to back the plans implemented by Gov. William Gooch.

Under Gooch's leadership, the burgesses amended and renewed the 1730 act. Tobacco regulation became a fact of life in Virginia, another tool of a united planter class designed to protect their own economic and social hegemony. Even Maryland, after flirting briefly with paper money to counter the falling prices, passed an inspection act in 1747 and repeatedly renewed it. Opponents burned tobacco and put trash tobacco in the hogsheads in attempts to fool the inspectors, all in vain.

Full relief came to the Chesapeake after 1740. European (particularly French) demand for tobacco rose dramatically, prices reached new heights, and planters gained easier access to almost unlimited credit. The benefits of this new wealth, however, flowed mostly to the wealthiest planters, and the division of wealth in the region became more uneven than ever. The gentry comprised up to 10 percent of all adult males and owned up to 75 percent of the wealth. Those who owned some land and

✦ *Documents* ✦
Life in the Chesapeake

Life in the eighteenth-century Chesapeake was far more varied than traditional myths about a slave-based, tobacco plantation society would allow. The first selection is from the journal of Philip Vickers Fithian, tutor to Robert Carter's children. It reports on a conversation between Fithian and Mrs. Carter and indicates that she was aware that slavery was not an unmixed blessing; it also suggests the roots of Virginians' paternalistic belief that they cared for African-Americans from the goodness of their hearts rather than from any economic motives. The second excerpt is from George Washington's diary for 1760; it shows how involved Washington was in the daily affairs of his plantation. The third selection is from Rev. Hugh Jones' 1724 description of tobacco cultivation.

> We both concluded, (& I am pretty certain that the conclusion is just) that if in Mr Carters, or in any Gentlemans Estate, all the Negroes should be sold, & the Money put to Interest in safe hands, & let the Lands which these Negroes now work lie wholly unculti-vated, the bare Interest of the Price of the Negroes would be a much greater yearly income than what is now received from their working the Lands, making no allowance at all for the trouble & Risk of the Masters as to the Crops, & Negroes. How much greater then must be the value of an Estate here if these poor enslaved Africans were all in their native desired Country, & in their Room industrious Tenants, who being born in freedom, by a laudable care, would not onlyly inrich their Landlords, but would raise a hardy Offspring to be the Strength & the honour of the Colony.

Hunter Dickinson Farish, ed., *Journal & Letters of Philip Vickers Fithian, 1773–1774: A Plantation Tutor of the Old Dominion* (Williamsburg, VA: Colonial Williamsburg, Inc., 1957), 92.

> Tuesday April 8th. What time it began Raining in the Night I cant say, but at day break it was pouring very hard, and continued so, till 7 oclock when a Messenger came to inform me that my Mill was

worked at most with a servant or two made up 20 to 30 percent of the population. The rest of Virginia's males owned no land and little property and eked out a meager living as tenant farmers. Below them were laborers, servants, and black slaves.

Middling planters were able to maintain or improve their status through easy access to credit. Comprising about three-fifths of the region's families, they generally had about two hundred acres and a few slaves and by 1776 claimed about half of the total debt owed British merchants. John Pines, a freeholder from Lancaster County, owned a horse, a cupboard, a cedar chest, two tables, and five chairs in the 1720s. By

in great danger of blowing. I immediately hurried off all hands with Shovels &ca. to her assistance and got there myself just time enough to give her a reprieve for this time by Wheeling dirt into the place which the Water had Washd. . . .

Friday Apl. 11th. Set one Plow to Work again in the Morning the other about 10 Oclock in the Clover Field.

Tryd the new Plow brot. Yesterday, found she did good Work and run very true but heavy-rather too much so for two Horses, especially while the Gd. was moist.

Abt. 11 Oclock set the People to Hauling the Sein and by Night and in the Night Catchd and dressd [ ] Barrels of Herring and 60 White Fish.

Donald Jackson, and Dorothy Twohig, eds., *The Diaries of George Washington,* 6 vols. (Charlottesville, VA: U. Press of Virginia, 1976), 1:264–6.

When it is grown up they top it, or nip it off the head, succour it, or cut off the ground leaves, weed it, hill it; and when ripe, they cut it down about six or eight leaves on a stalk, which they carry into airy tobacco houses; after it is withered a little in the sun, there it is hung to dry on sticks, as paper at the paper-mills; when it is in proper case, (as they call it) and the air neither too moist, nor too dry, they strike it, or take it down, then cover it up in bulk, or a great heap, where it lies till they have leisure or occasion to stem it (that is pull the leaves from the stalk) or strip it (that is take out the great fibres) and tie it up in hands, or streight lay it; and so by degrees prize or press it with proper engines into great hogsheads, containing from about six to eleven hundred pounds. . . .

Hugh Jones, *The Present State of Virginia,* Richard L. Morton, ed. (Chapel Hill, NC: University of North Carolina Press, 1956), (London: 1724), 77.

the 1750s, he had acquired ceramics, bed and table linens, chamber pots, and warming pans. But even moderately prosperous planters like Pines found their opportunities declining. By the early 1760s, the poorer tidewater planters could improve their opportunities, and those of their children, only by moving to the frontier.

As land prices rose, opportunities for tenants also declined precipitously. They relied completely on their landlords for tools and housing, paid some of their crop for rent, and, unlike their counterparts to the north, had little opportunity to accumulate capital. They rarely owned more than a horse and some livestock, and they moved frequently. The widow Ann Kitchen, with two children, rented land from Joseph Chew in Prince George's County, Maryland, in 1729 and quickly found she had no legal recourse when Chew refused to fix the tobacco house as he had promised and let his horse run freely through her fields, substantially reducing her crop yield. He even rejected her tobacco when she came to pay her rent, claiming that it was of too low a quality. She petitioned the court but with no success.

Servants had fewer rights than ever. When hard times hit them during the tobacco depression of the 1740s, Humut Godfrey and his wife, Margaret, indentured themselves for seven years to John Cook, a justice and gentleman planter in Prince George's County. When Godfrey hurt his back, Cook reduced his rations because he could not work as hard. The planter did nothing to help Margaret when she miscarried, and he provided no assistance to their children when they fell ill. In April 1748, the ailing Humut and Margaret confronted Cook's wife and the planter's overseer. The overseer called Margaret a "damned bitch" for complaining of Mrs. Cook's demands on Humut and threatened to beat her. Margaret responded that she was not a slave and did not deserve such treatment, so the overseer did in fact beat her with a hickory switch and called her a bitch again. She answered him, "I no more look like a B--ch than you look like the son of one."[5] He bound her and beat her again, while Humut watched helplessly. When Humut tried to untie her, the overseer caught him and beat him as well. The sadistic hireling beat Margaret twice more. When Humut told his story to the county court, it listened and did nothing. The Godfrey's experiences were not typical of servant life in the eighteenth century, but they do remind us of the powerlessness of poor whites in a society that relied on forced labor and where violence always lay close to the surface.

While ordinary Virginians were struggling or living in poverty, the tidewater elite—and later their counterparts in the Piedmont—dramatically increased their imports of European consumer and luxury goods, purchased largely with British credit. London merchants served as agents, or intermediaries, for Virginia planters. They sold their tobacco and shipped them the goods they ordered, holding the balance in bills of exchange. The booming economy (and the disadvantages of distance that relying solely on agents created) also attracted "factors," or resident agents who lived in the Chesapeake and represented British merchant houses. London factors dominated the tidewater, while Scottish factors moved into the Piedmont. By providing liberal credit to middling-level planters in particular, the Scots helped finance both expansion into the frontier and the many small villages and towns that now began to appear at crossroads throughout the region. Most of these "towns" were little more than small tobacco ports, and the majority of urban inhabitants in the Chesapeake lived in one of the nine small cities that had more than one thousand inhabitants each. Alexandria, Fredericksburg, Richmond, and Petersburg were at the head of navigation of several rivers and served as focal points for products coming from the hinterland. Norfolk, Portsmouth, and Baltimore exported grain and provisions to the West Indies and southern Europe. Annapolis and Williamsburg were the social and cultural centers for the Chesapeake elite.

At mid-century, just when a renewal of opportunity seemed to be on the economic horizon, tobacco prices began to fall again. British merchants and banking houses periodically contracted their credit lines to Chesapeake planters in the years after 1760, with devastating effect. The credit crisis of 1772, for instance, was particularly damaging and played an important role in crystalizing a united planter opposition to British imperial policy.

The dominant characteristic of the Chesapeake economy in the years approaching the Revolution was declining, not increasing, opportunity. Population growth continued to put pressure on the supply of land, and tenancy became common among poorer planters. Anxious parents postponed giving their sons land in fear of losing their own independence (not unlike New England parents); in Prince George's County, Maryland, fewer than one-fifth of the fathers under seventy gave land to their sons, and only half of those over seventy had begun to distribute their property. Some children postponed marriage, and others turned to more intensive cultivation techniques—but more and more turned to the frontier.

The Chesapeake was increasingly divided between a tobacco-producing core and a horseshoe-shaped periphery that grew wheat and corn in response to expanding markets in southern Europe and the West Indies. By the 1770s, Virginia alone exported four hundred thousand bushels of wheat a year. Planters and entrepreneurs in the northern Chesapeake also moved into milling, iron production, and shipbuilding, and after mid-century, Norfolk and Baltimore emerged as the region's first true urban centers. Part of the reason for this transition can be found in tobacco. Tobacco rapidly exhausted the land, and planters rotated fields rather than fertilizing or rotating crops. They moved from one piece of land to another, a few acres at a time. Typically, a planter could count on only three tobacco crops in twenty years from any given acreage. With wheat, he could expect twelve. He could grow wheat even in fields left fallow from tobacco. Tobacco brought six times the price of wheat, but when prices were low and land scarce, grain seemed a viable, even desirable alternative.

The Piedmont and the Shenandoah Valley began to draw growing numbers of migrants from the tidewater during the second quarter of the eighteenth century. A diverse cross-section of adults from the older tidewater area moved in as squatters soon after the Indians were driven out, followed by speculators who patented thousands of acres of land. Eager planters then established themselves, and the best land was generally taken within a decade or two. Speculators were particularly critical in this process. Men like William Byrd II used their positions as members of the House of Burgesses and political insiders to gain information about the best available land. In the Southside (south of the James River), they owned about a quarter of the land patented between 1703 and 1753. A few ambitious individuals grabbed enormous tracts—Byrd patented one hundred thousand acres in 1735 along the Roanoke River, one hundred miles from the nearest settlement.

A homogeneous ruling elite emerged much more quickly in these communities than it had in the tidewater. Within only a single generation, patriarchy and wealth polarization made the region a close, if different, cousin of its eastern parent. Sex ratios were even from the beginning, and by the eighteenth century, Indians posed less of a threat to community formation than they had a few generations earlier. Planters quickly established a tobacco monoculture and rapidly became dependent on slave labor, and the same land and population problems soon emerged. At that point, the middling and poor planters seeking opportunities moved to still another new frontier. By the time of the Revolution, the Piedmont and the valleys of the James and Potomac rivers had replaced those of the York and the Rappahanock as the leading tobacco producing areas of the Chesapeake. While the output along the latter two almost doubled from 1714 to 1774, their share of the total output actually decreased from 59 percent to 31 percent. The James River area alone produced about half of the total Virginia crop.

The Lower South

Like the Chesapeake, Georgia and the Carolinas were an economically diverse region. North Carolina had few large plantations and produced a variety of foodstuffs, including corn, wheat, meat, and livestock, as well as tobacco. Its main contributions to the British Atlantic economy were naval stores and wood products.

South Carolina, on the other hand, developed a wealthy, staple-based economy. Early settlers had achieved some economic success with furs and deerskins, both in high demand among the European elite. The colony also exported wood products and naval stores to England and grain and meat products to the West Indies. In 1705, Parliament introduced bounties for tar, pitch, resin, turpentine, hemp, masts, yards, and bowsprits. By the mid-1720s, Charleston was exporting about sixty thousand barrels of tar and pitch a year. But the trade rapidly declined thereafter. High wages forced colonial producers to introduce crude labor-saving techniques, producing inferior tar and pitch, and in 1729, Parliament substantially reduced the bounties. The emergence of rice as the dominant crop in the low country undermined the possibility of any true economic diversity.

Like tobacco, the demands of rice cultivation shaped the contours of the South Carolina social landscape. At first, planters tried to grow the crop on dry land, but they soon discovered that irrigation stimulated growth and controlled weeds and insects. The problem was to find land that could be readily flooded; slaves could then construct the necessary dams, dikes, ditches, sluices, gates, and reservoirs that controlled the flow of water. Inland swamps, subject to unpredictable flooding, were far from ideal for the task. So the planters increasingly turned to tidal culture. The proper use of dikes and gates helped keep salt water out of the fields. More important, this was a far more efficient method of cultivation, doubling the number of acres one man could handle from three or four to seven. Still, rice remained a labor-intensive crop. Cutting and threshing was easy, but pounding the grain in wooden mortars (to remove the inner husk) was demanding work.

In 1710, South Carolinians produced 147 pounds of rice exports per head (four hundred thousand total). By 1730, that figure rose to 626 pounds; by 1740, it was more than nine hundred pounds (43 million total). By mid-century, rice exports accounted for almost 90 percent of the output of the colony's labor force. The industry also brought the demographics of the Caribbean islands to South Carolina. Production units rose in size, wealth inequality increased dramatically, and it became all but impossible for the poor and those without substantial capital to find true economic opportunity. Absentee ownership increased, and as most capital flowed into rice and indigo production, the colony had to import more and more of its food. African-Americans comprised a far higher percentage of the population, particularly in the coastal lowlands, than in the Chesapeake.

The rice boom ended in 1740. Overproduction, wartime disruption of European markets, and increasing shipping rates all conspired to drive the price of rice down 70 percent between 1741 and 1746. In 1759, South Carolina exported less than half the total of 1740. Though the trade recovered in the early 1750s, the depression encouraged South Carolinians to seek another staple to guarantee the colony's economic stability. The English textile industry eagerly sought safe supplies of indigo, a plant whose leaves produced a richly colored copper or purple dye. Before mid-century, English traders relied on supplies from the Spanish and West Indies. After that time, South Carolina stepped in and filled the textile industry's needs. Eliza Lucas, who arrived in the colony at the age of sixteen to manage three of her deceased father's plantations, almost single-handedly mastered the difficult problems involved in growing this valuable crop.

Lucas spent two decades experimenting with various strains and growing methods. Indigo grew most readily on dry land almost anywhere, so it also provided a useful off-season alternative to rice cultivation. Slaves boiled the indigo leaves in large vats in a complex chemical process. Though a single slave could cultivate

A view of Charleston, SC, in the late 1730s. 🌢

only about two acres of indigo plants a year, the high value of the crop produced a greater profit per acre than any other staple in British North America. The British government established a bounty on it in 1748, and in 1750, the colony exported sixty-three thousand pounds of indigo to England. In 1760, it sent a half million pounds and during the first six months of 1775, more than 1 million pounds.

The popular picture of low-country plantations peopled only by slaves, with white land owners living in Charleston for most of the year, is only partly true. Rice plantations were considerably smaller than the West Indian plantations, and their owners were less wealthy. Owner absenteeism was much less extensive. Growers had direct control over their lands for most of the year and generally went to Charleston or Newport for only short periods in the late summer, when the weather became truly oppressive in the swampy, unhealthy low country. They invested much of their income locally. The South Carolina ruling class was thus truly unique in British North America—they were the wealthiest group of mainland entrepreneurs but a group loyal to their own colony.

The economy was more diversified outside of the rice belt. Farms in the back-country and in Georgia and North Carolina supplied food for the core and farm products for export and served as markets for manufactured goods. Such diversity helped spur the growth of Charleston. By 1760, the city had eight thousand people; by 1775, twelve thousand. It prospered at first from the deerskin trade and as a supplier of provisions and timber to the West Indies. In the eighteenth century, it depended increasingly on the rice, indigo, and slave trade and prospered as they did, eventually monopolizing the region's trade. But the British in turn dominated Charleston's trade. The city lacked a shipbuilding industry or an indigenous business community and became more of a shipping point than a true commercial center, a consumer city catering to the needs of merchants and those planters who lived there part of the year. It was, nonetheless, the only true urban center of the south.

❧ *Documents* ❧
The Stormy Emergence of Commercial Capitalism

New England's growing involvement in the Atlantic economy brought drastic changes to the region's social structure and spawned dozens of pamphlets on economic issues. Generally, such comments emerged in the midst of heated political struggles: the land bank debates, the public market dispute, and the endless battle for political power between governors and the House of Representatives. But the messages these heated diatribes contain reach beyond immediate political issues and offer much insight into how the participants—farmers, smaller colonial merchants, and wealthy, British-connected traders—felt about the emergence of commercial capitalism in Massachusetts.

The first selection is by a supporter of a 1714 *private* land bank, attacking the *public*, or government, bank proposed by Paul Dudley, the colony's attorney general and brother of the governor. It reveals the writer's awareness of the political and economic power of the colony's British-connected elite. The second excerpt is from the extensive debate over the 1720 land bank proposal. It seems almost hysterical in tone, but it reflects a realistic awareness of the need for a circulating currency in a specie-starved economy. The final two selections, taken from the debate over the 1740 land bank, portray Massachusetts merchants as public servants and villains, respectively.

> The Tendency of a Publick Bank, as have been proposed, is to Unite the Power of the Country and the Cash together, which all wise people have endeavoured to keep asunder, in order to preserve their Liberties; it tends to bring all the People into a dependency upon the Court Interest; and Consequently to redner them Abject and Servile. . . .

A Letter from One in Boston to His Friend in the Country. . .(Boston: 1714), 28–9.

> That as Merchants and Farmers, are the Grand Pillars of the Flourishing State of this Common Wealth, so being joyned together

Money And Markets In Early America

The American colonies were uniquely blessed with natural resources, but they lacked the one gift of nature most valued in the mercantilist world—precious metals. This was no great drawback during most of the seventeenth century, when barter and book credit sufficed for local exchange. Urban merchants enjoyed

are the Atlas which bears up the Great Globe of our Temporal Business: But without a Medium [of exchange] you place your Feet on a Vacuum: or your Standing is but upon Fluid Air. . . . without a *Medium,* all things will jumble, Run Retrograde, and Rubble into Chaos; and this must needs fill us with many Evils both of Sin, and Misery; as Murmurings, Revilings of Governments, Injustice, Oppressions. . . .

Amicus Patrius, *A Word of Comfort.* . . (Boston: 1721), 1–2.

I must observe, that by the *Vulgar* and *Populace,* I always mean the unthinking Part of Mankind, who are not capable of consulting their own Interest; the *Mobility* who do not reason for themselves. . . . *The Industrious and the Frugal,* [are] our considerable foreign Traders and rich Men; who because of their great Substance deposited in the Country, are obliged to have the Interest of the Country most at Heart. . . .

Postcript to a Discourse Concerning the Currencies. . . . (Boston: 1740), 50, 60.

As the sinking of the Credit of our Province Bills, has in a great Measure subverted commutative Justice thro' the Land; so those who have been the Sufferers by it, have been ready to complain of the Legislature, and too rashly to lay the Blame at their door. I say too rashly, for the State of our Trade and Mechandise abroad has been such, that unless we could suppose our Merchants to act with a due Regard to the publick Weal, and the Cause of common Justice and Equity, as well as their private personal Gain, 'tis hard to conceive how it could have been in the Power of any Laws whatsoever to have kept up the Credit of our Bills.

A Letter Relating to a Medium of Trade. . . . (Boston: 1740), 3.

extended terms from their London creditors, and they generally earned enough specie from the West Indian trade to pay their bills.

As the pace of economic activity quickened in the eighteenth century, the demand for a circulating medium increased. So the colonists turned to paper money. The first method of issuing paper money, adopted by every colony at one time or another except Virginia, was the land bank. In public land banks, the legislature printed "bills of credit" that were then lent to farmers at interest rates (from 5 percent to 8 percent) well below those charged by merchants and planters. The loans were secured by mortgages on the borrowers' land. As the borrowers repaid their loans, the currency was removed from circulation—though new banks were often started almost immediately. Occasionally, particularly in Massachusetts in 1714 and 1740, private groups attempted to form their own land banks.

Another way of issuing paper money originated as a method of financing colonial wars. The colonial government printed bills of credit that were used to pay its expenses. At the same time, the legislature also levied special taxes due at some point in the future that could be paid off in the issued bills. In this way, the bills would be removed from circulation, though new issues often immediately followed the old. These bills were also accepted as legal tender, thus forcing merchants and other creditors to accept them in payment of debts. They usually came with a 5 percent "premium" that gave the creditors some compensation for being forced to accept them.

Whatever its origin, paper money aroused considerable controversy. The Board of Trade, fearful of inflation and believing only in the solid value of gold and silver, instructed governors not to approve paper as legal tender. Governors usually ignored such instructions, though, since they needed the money to finance colonial wars and were often pressured by the legislatures to approve currency emissions; in Massachusetts, the House of Representatives threatened to withhold governors' salaries unless they approved paper money bills. British merchants and the larger colonial merchants also opposed paper money and accepted only specie from their colonial debtors. They did extend credit to Chesapeake planters, but these were desirable customers who paid in tobacco or through ledger sheet financing, both acceptable and reliable methods of payment.

Most colonists, though, energetically supported frequent emissions. The first came in Massachusetts in 1690, when a financially strapped legislature successfully used paper money to pay off its soldiers. The colony issued even larger sums frequently during the next few decades, particularly during the 1720s and 1730s, when intermittent warfare and declining economic opportunity ravaged its economy. Other colonies, such as Pennsylvania during the 1720s, deliberately used paper money to stimulate a stagnating economy. And occasionally, as was done in Maryland in 1733, legislatures emitted moderate sums simply because paper provided a more convenient form of payment. In all of these cases, paper money made economic transactions easier to negotiate and provided capital for new investment, particularly by the middling merchants whose primary economic ties were local and regional, not to England.

The British, however, could not allow Americans to extend credit to themselves, since this threatened their own monopoly in colonial trade. Colonial merchants most often attacked paper money because they believed it spurred inflation, causing creditors to be repaid in money worth less than the sum they had originally loaned out. But historians now agree that this situation was greatly exaggerated. Only in Massachusetts from the 1730s through the 1740s did inflation seriously erode the value of paper money. In most cases, depreciation was spread over several years and did not cause undue loss to any individual. Another difficulty was the uncertain rate of exchange between paper money and specie, creating financial instability that the British preferred to do without. Colonial economies suffered far more from English credit contractions and the larger slowdowns in the Atlantic economy than from any particular currency problems.

A more volatile source of the controversy over colonial paper money can be found in social relations. In a world were the gap between the rich and the poor was growing and where easy access to specie indicated a close identification with London and all it stood for, paper money carried meaning beyond its economic use. One such case emerged during the controversy over the Massachusetts Land Bank of 1740. Like earlier proposals in 1714 and 1720, this proposal was designed to provide currency for moderately wealthy colonial merchants and farmers; subscribers were most common in areas experiencing rapid economic growth. The plan provided for bills of credit at 3 percent interest, backed by mortgages on land or personal bonds. Loan repayments would be placed in a general fund, which would also be loaned out and provide dividends for the bank's subscribers. Almost immediately, a rival bank sprang up, known as the Silver Bank. Chartered by a small group of wealthy merchants, this bank was to function in essentially the same fashion, except that the notes were secured by bonds rather than land, and repayment would be accepted only in silver bullion.

Until the Board of Trade declared both efforts illegal, these banks were at the center of a storm of class rhetoric. Land bank supporters attacked the merchants for seeking personal gain at the expense of community needs and for betraying the colony by trying to increase their own wealth by importing excessive luxuries. For their part, the merchants viewed the land bank and its accompanying rhetoric as a conspiracy against their own interests and against those who worked hard and lived within their means.

Cities In Colonial America

By 1760, a sizable minority of the colonial population lived in urban areas. The largest city was Philadelphia, with 23,750 inhabitants. New York City followed with about eighteen thousand residents, Boston with 15,630, Charleston with eight thousand, and Newport with seventy-five hundred. Important regional towns of smaller size included Salem; New Haven; Providence; Perth Amboy, New Jersey; Baltimore; Norfolk; and Savannah. Smaller but significant regional economic centers included Hartford, Connecticut; Springfield, Massachusetts; and Albany in the north. In Virginia, Richmond, Fredericksburg, and Alexandria served the Piedmont and the backcountry. Camden, South Carolina, was a significant center of trade with the Catawba Indians and was located on important routes to Charleston and Philadelphia. Cross Creek, North Carolina, was a center for the backcountry trade in wheat and flour. County seats and secondary centers comprised the final level of urban life in colonial America.

South East Prospect of the City of Philadelphia by Peter Cooper. ❧

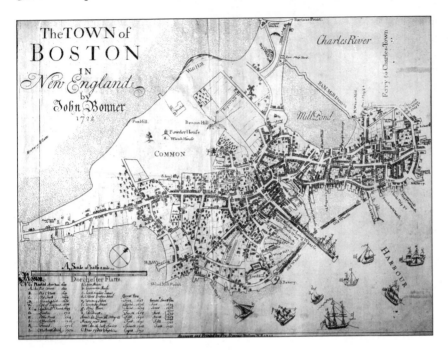

Plan of Boston, 1722 by John Bonner. ❧

The streets of Boston, according to legend, were laid out along cow paths winding down from Beacon Hill and elsewhere to the commons. New York City was similarly unplanned and crowded with houses jammed tightly together, many in a deteriorating condition. Planners laid out other cities more carefully and often with a deliberate sense of harmony, providing for broad straight avenues, open spaces, and public squares. The founders of Charleston constructed the city around a gridiron design, with sixty-foot wide streets and, initially, an open square in the center. William Penn's initial plan for Philadelphia sought to replicate the design implemented in London after the Great Fire of 1666, with wide streets and houses of stone or brick. The city bore little resemblance to this plan by mid-century, though, as the press of population created a crowded mass of buildings and narrow streets.

Northern cities generally had the same sort of public and private buildings. These included a town hall and jail, an almshouse, hospitals, schools, warehouses, and customshouses. As the century progressed, certain kinds of buildings and businesses became concentrated in particular areas of cities. From the beginning, for instance, warehouses lined the waterfronts. By 1750, specialized shops and services were grouped together near Boston's commercial zone, and wealthier citizens had begun to move farther away from the business center, seeking privacy, quiet, and safety.

Businesses and services were concentrated in the center of these towns, easily accessible to event the casual walker. But in most other respects, life in these cities bore little resemblance to our contemporary urban experiences. Sanitation was primitive. While Boston and New York City contracted for garbage disposal in the 1680s, Philadelphia did not do so until 1762. Only a few streets were paved with stones or gravel, and even those were filled with rubbish and horse manure. Paved streets were crowned in the middle, with gutters on the sides. Some underdrains were eventually built, and cities levied penalties on those so inconsiderate as to leave dead animals in the streets. Disease was an ever-present danger, as sailors from foreign ports introduced every variety of illness. Smallpox was especially common, and

Table 8 ❧   Population growth in largest colonial cities

Populations of Boston, New York, and Philadelphia

	Boston	New York	Philadelphia
1720	12,000	7,000	10,000
1740	15,601	10,451	12,654
1760	15,631	18,000	23,750

Adapted from information in R. C. Simmons, *The American Colonies: From Settlement to Independence* (New York: W. W. Norton and Company, 1976), 178.

the colonists faced waves of typhoid, measles, influenza, and diphtheria. Legislatures eventually passed quarantine laws, requiring the inspection of all those on board a ship. Street lighting was not introduced until the early 1760s, when whale oil lamps were set at fifty-foot intervals along the main thoroughfares. Fire was a constant concern. Cities passed regulations prohibiting wooden chimneys and requiring new buildings to be constructed of brick or stone. Fire engines appeared by 1700, and at mid-century, New York City had two engines and twenty-four firemen. Benjamin Franklin founded the Union Fire Company in the 1730s in Philadelphia. The mechanisms employed were crude but somewhat effective; water was poured into a trough and jetted out as high as seventy feet. City governments were also constantly concerned with prostitution. By 1770, about five hundred to six hundred prostitutes regularly worked the battery area of New York City. Philadelphia's "Hell Town" along the river contained brothels and taverns that catered to sailors. Even small towns such as Fredericksburg had brothels on their outskirts. Enforcement against prostitution was lax, with only an occasional whipping meted out against the women, despite citizens' constant complaints about declining morality.

Changes in the colonial social structure, in the division of wealth, and even in types of occupation frequently appeared first in cities, and it was in cities that Americans first and most openly embraced the commercial ethic of self-interest. Late seventeenth-century port towns were relatively traditional places where merchants still depended on kinship connections for business and paid at least lip service to the importance of community. The division of wealth was relatively equitable, and poverty was relatively rare. Most residents were still confident in the real possibility of upward social and economic mobility. Even Boston, which had acquired a diverse, contentious, crime-ridden population soon after its founding, had few of the hallmarks of economic modernism in 1700.

By the middle of the eighteenth century, though, cities were characterized by greater geographic mobility, a more uneven distribution of wealth, greater poverty and larger numbers of poor, more bound and wage labor, and a modern credit system. About half of all urban workers were slaves or indentured servants. By mid-century, about 10 percent of the population controlled 70 percent of the wealth, while 60 percent held no property at all. In contrast, the wealthiest 10 percent of the inhabitants in northern farming communities controlled only 40 percent of the wealth, only about 30 percent had no property, and less than a quarter of the workers were enslaved or indentured. In Massachusetts, land scarcity forced many propertyless young males to seek opportunity in Boston, with little hope of success.

Some of this change stemmed from the unsettling effects of colonial warfare. The Wars of the League of Augsburg (1689–1697) and the Spanish Succession

A Northeast View of Boston, ca. 1723 (attributed to Wm. Burgis). ❧

(1702–1713) produced some economic benefits to Boston, particularly to those involved in shipbuilding. But they also increased the concentration of wealth in the industry and brought only impressment for many of the poor. Taxes rose, wages stagnated, and trade suffered. Estate inventories clearly show that at the end of these two wars, the Boston poor had much less to leave their survivors.

New York City did not participate in these campaigns and benefited significantly from wartime trade—even with the French. Merchants supplied foodstuffs to the British fleet fighting in the West Indies, a trade that easily compensated for the dangers from French war vessels and the outlawing of American trade to the Spanish islands. New York governors welcomed pirates as a source of specie. Here, as in Boston, the wealthy profited from military commerce and grew richer still. Only Philadelphia was uninvolved and generally unaffected by these wars. It prospered from its growing Caribbean trade and suffered little from poverty—only fourteen residents sought aid from the city's Board of Overseers in 1709.

Both Boston and New York continued to have economic problems even during the twenty years of relative peace between 1720 and 1740. Poor relief rose dramatically in Boston during these years, and as many as 25 percent of the city's taxpayers received tax abatements to relieve their suffering. In contrast, a few lucky individuals became even wealthier. As we have seen, attempts to stimulate the economy through currency emissions only heightened tensions between rich and poor.

Boston was forced to devise a virtual "war on poverty" during the 1740s, binding out poor children, warning hundreds of wanderers to go elsewhere, calling for charity from the wealthy, appealing for tax relief to the General Court, and establishing workhouses for the idle, the alcoholic, and prostitutes. The legislature also established the United Society for Manufactures and Importation, an attempt to employ the poor at textile manufacturing. The poor resisted, refusing to leave their homes for the less hospitable environs of the workhouse. Low output and a smallpox epidemic ultimately destroyed the project. New York City was far less imaginative, establishing a single building that served as a poorhouse and a house of correction in 1736.

Poor relief served a variety of people in these cities, including orphans, disabled war veterans, the unemployed, war refugees, accident and fire victims, the diseased, and the elderly. In the earliest days of relief, the poor received money, firewood, food, clothing, and medical care. The government often paid to board the elderly and the ill with other families, and it helped arrange apprenticeships for

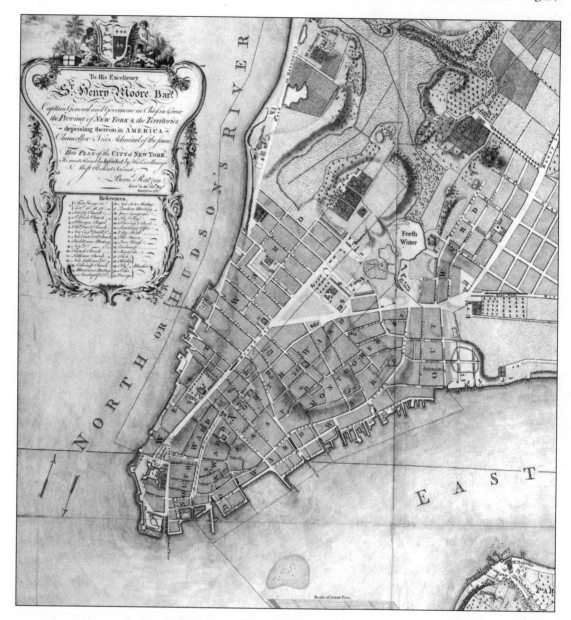

New York City, 1767 by Bernard Ratzer. ❧

orphans and children of the poor. Over time, though, relief became increasingly institutionalized, as cities established almshouses for the blind, lame, and ill. Even these were overcrowded by mid-century, and many of the poor never stayed in one place long enough to benefit from these solutions. "Warned out" by towns and cities, single men and women in Essex County seaports, for instance, traveled throughout the county in search of work.

The Seven Years War (1756–1763) worsened conditions still further. All three major cities experienced economic problems during the early 1750s, and it seems that only the wealthy benefited from wartime spending. Privateering brought gain to some, particularly in New York, and Pennsylvania Gov. William Denny sold flags of truce to merchants who engaged in trade with the French under the pretext of prisoner exchange. By war's end, the number of poor in Boston had doubled and even skilled artisans had lost ground, as food prices rose far more rapidly than their wages. During the 1760s, Americans faced credit contraction, the Sugar Act, and severe blows to the West Indian trade. Bankruptcies became common. New York and Philadelphia now suffered the most debilitating economic problems in their histories, as the British customs service cracked down on smuggling, prices continued to rise (the cost of living had doubled in both cities during the war), and the demands on the public relief system escalated. Life in American cities could be very dismal indeed in 1763.

Work And Culture In Eighteenth-Century America

Merchants and Self-Interest

In northern cities, merchants stood at the top of the status ladder. They worked as both retailers and wholesalers in proprietorships or partnerships. For most of the colonial period, their businesses were rarely specialized, and they often engaged in barter when they moved down the credit ladder and sold goods to smaller merchants in the hinterland. Particularly after 1750, though, small to medium-sized merchants in the cities tended increasingly to specialize in a particular kind of trade or geographical area. In Philadelphia, one group of merchants imported dry goods from England, and another exported provisions to southern Europe and the West Indies. At the same time, more and more merchants were extending their economic ties deeper into the colonial economy. They began to provide a variety of financial services essential to the community, to rapidly expand the coastal trade and their control over it, and to improve the internal trading networks and infrastructures. Many merchants accumulated enough capital to purchase their own ships, and they owned well more than half of the vessels engaged in colonial trade by the time of the Revolution. Others owned a variety of industries associated with shipbuilding, including chandleries, ropewalks, and sail lofts; their business generated capital for enterprises connected to colonial trade, such as food processing, flour mills, meat-packing, and wood, iron, and potash production.

Socially and economically, merchants were rapidly coming to have much more in common with each other than with other members of their town or colony. Their relationships with smaller merchants and country storekeepers were increasingly market-oriented; while the lower ends of the credit chain continued to rely on book credit and barter, urban merchants did not hesitate to demand specie when their own credit needs required it. Merchants sat on colony councils and drew closer to royal governors who could provide them with the metropolitan influence they sought, and they cultivated a wide range of social and financial correspondents in London. By 1750, a daughter of the New York DeLancey family had married a knighted British admiral, and one of the family's sons was close to the archbishop of Canterbury. The changing social mores of these merchants were more immediately visible, and perhaps objectionable, to ordinary Americans. They now openly and proudly wore satin coats, powdered wigs, and knee breaches, all marks of English gentry and to farmers and artisans, symbols of corrupting luxury.

A few examples illustrate this increasingly segregated class. Thomas Hancock (uncle and benefactor of John) was a minister's son who began his career as a Boston bookseller. He married the daughter of a prosperous merchant and gained access to enough capital to invest in several overseas trading ventures; he was also involved extensively in smuggling tea. By 1735, he had a mansion on Beacon Hill. Like many wealthy merchants, he made even more money as a result of the eighteenth-century colonial wars. Hancock used his connections with Gov. William Shirley to win military supply contracts in Britain's wars against Spain and France in the 1740s and profited still more from his investments in privateers. When peace came, he ordered a carriage from London with a heraldic shield on the doors.

The Brown family of Providence, Rhode Island, entered the New England mercantile elite when James married the daughter of a leading shipowner in the 1720s and became captain of a family vessel trading in the Caribbean. He rose rapidly through the firm's ranks, and his brother Obadiah soon joined him. The two expanded the firm's business to include the importation of finished goods from England, which they then resold to inland storekeepers at markups of 60 percent to 75 percent on four months' credit at 6 percent interest. They dabbled unsuccessfully in the slave trade, then moved into manufacturing, opening a small slaughterhouse to provide beef and pork for their crews and a candle factory. In the 1760s, they went into iron production, perhaps the colonial manufacturing enterprise of the largest scale. Their Hope Furnace, located close to Providence, employed up to seventy-five men, half of whom spent their time gathering the huge amounts of wood required to stoke the furnace's fires. They marketed the product through three distribution channels: they sent pig iron on consignment to New York and English firms; they sold some to local merchants who then traded it abroad; and they sold the rest to merchants who owned small, independent forges throughout New England.

Successful, specialized merchants began to emerge even in the predominantly agricultural landscape of the Chesapeake. Earlier, moderate planter-merchants such as Tobias Mickleburrough were common in the tidewater. A county merchant, Mickleburrough established a store in Middlesex County in the 1680s that served customers largely within a three-mile radius. When he died, he had grown wealthy enough to own a silver-handled cane and three gold rings. Yet he was but one of several customers of William Churchill, a true metropolitan merchant who maintained close relationships with English merchants. Churchill arrived in Middlesex in 1675 at the age of twenty-five, and he exploited his kinship with two London merchants to set himself up in business. He wholesaled goods to men such as Mickleburrough throughout the county and bought, sold, and rented large amounts of land. Churchill married the planter Ralph Wormeley's widow when Wormeley died in 1703 and moved onto his Rosegill estate. Even Churchill, it seems, aspired to planter status.

Artisans and Other Nonfarm Workers

Most American workers were farmers who led tradition-bound lives. A growing number of individuals, however, pursued occupations and lives that cast at least a glance toward the modern world. Rural and urban laborers, maritime laborers, and artisans of all sorts shaped a culture on the periphery of early American society that was distinct from the experiences of farming men and women.

Propertyless and landless laborers led a precarious existence, often sinking into poverty and rarely rising far above their original status. They sought work where they could find it, often spending much of their lives moving from town to town. A look at working-class Philadelphians during the second half of the eighteenth century reveals much about these peoples' lives. Shoemakers, tailors, laborers, and merchant seamen made up one-third to one-half of the free adult males in the city during this time. For the most part, they lived near the bottom of the city's economic ladder—though they were better off than the really poor. About one in five had moderate amounts of property—a house perhaps, an indentured servant or a slave, or some land they could rent out for income. But the vast majority held little or no property, and two-thirds held no assets at all during their entire lives. Unlike their rural farm cousins, these workers failed to materially improve their lives over time. They also moved more frequently; had not so many left the city on a regular basis, the number of poor might have been even greater. Even those with some skills changed jobs often. About a quarter of the laborers embarked on a new occupation every decade without developing any new skills. They simply rotated among such jobs as bricklayer, soldier, painter, potato picker, and bartender.

Tax records offer a more intimate glance at the lives of some of these people. Hugh Nelson, a tailor, paid more than the minimum tax in 1767. Even though he had no property, at the time he was earning more than the average tailor. Five years later, his pitiful prosperity had vanished, and he was paying only the minimum tax. The laborer John Burns did not acquire property or increase his wealth at all over a sixteen-year period ending in 1772. During one eight-year period, as many of 60 percent of the journeymen artisans did not succeed in rising to the level of master. Tailors, the wealthiest of these people, were nonetheless near the bottom of the wealth hierarchy in Philadelphia. While about one in four were indeed in the top third of the tax structure (these catered to wealthy clients), almost half of all tailors were assessed only the minimum tax rate in 1772. Printer Benjamin Franklin's success was not at all typical. Franklin, we must remember, benefited from a profitable partnership with Hugh Meredith, an alcoholic who knew little about the printing industry but whose father provided financial backing for the business. Franklin also borrowed from his friends and carefully bargained for a marriage that brought him still more wealth.

Food was plentiful, but it was also expensive—Philadelphia's booming export trade tended to drive prices up, and they went even higher during depressions. Many families changed their eating habits when times were bad, subsisting on high-calorie foods, such as flour and cornmeal, while some also tended gardens or kept hogs. Most lived in small, narrow houses. Philip Mager, a sailor with a wife and four children, rented a two-story tenement twelve feet wide and eighteen feet deep. He lived fairly comfortably compared to others, since many were forced to take in boarders or to double up with another family. The most unfortunate lived in the back-alley hovels and rooming houses that were scattered throughout the city. Wood was essential for fuel and expensive in any city, particularly during the winter.

The overall family budget of laborers, mariners, cordwainers, and tailors for food, rent, fuel, and clothing averaged slightly more than sixty pounds in 1762. Yet this did not include the ever-present rum, medical treatment, child-bearing costs, candles, soap, brooms, or furniture. If employed six days a week, the average worker would have earned slightly less than sixty pounds a year. But regular employment was rare in Philadelphia—particularly when prices were at their highest, such as during the winter.

So how did they manage? Some did not. Illnesses (often caused by weakness from malnutrition), job-related injuries, and the almshouse population all increased during that season. Others coped only because every member of the family contributed. Women often worked as nurses, clothes washers, chimney sweeps, potato diggers, cooks, maids, soap makers, and bakers. Children tended cattle and carried wood and dairy products throughout the city. But women were paid only half the wages of men, and children less than that. Even with the extra work, such families barely broke even.[6]

Poor Richard's values of hard work and thriftiness, as expressed by his creator, Benjamin Franklin, were undoubtedly essential elements of success but by themselves could guarantee nothing. Pure luck did more than anything else to determine

❧ *Documents* ❧
Poor Richard's Formula for Success

Benjamin Franklin's formula for success, as recommended by "Poor Richard," may have worked for him, but many Philadelphia artisans found success elusive even when they did follow his advice. Diligence and savings, we should also note, would also help promote the accumulation of capital and thus encourage investment in the colonies. "Poor Richard" was very much a spokesman for American economic independence.

> If time be of all things the most precious, *wasting Time* must be, as *Poor Richard* says, *the greatest prodigality,* since, as he elsewhere tells us, *Lost time is never found again.* . . . *Sloth makes all Things difficult, but Industry all easy* . . . , *and He that riseth late must trot all Day, and shall scarce overtake his business at Night; While Laziness travels so slowly, that Poverty soon overtakes him.* . . . *Drive thy Business, let not that drive thee; and Early to Bed, and early to rise, makes a Man healthy, wealthy, and wise,* as Poor Richard says. . . .

> If you would be wealthy . . . , *think of Saving as well as of Getting: The Indies have not made* Spain rich, *because her* Outgoes *are greater than her* Incomes.

> Away then with your expensive Follies, and you will not have so much Cause to complain of hard Times, heavy Taxes, and chargeable Families; for, as *Poor Dick* says,

> *Women and Wine, Game and Deceit,*
> *Make the Wealth small and the Want great.*

> *Poor Richard Improved . . . An Almanack for 1758 . . .* (Philadelphia, 1758).

whether or not a working class family survived in eighteenth-century Philadelphia. Weather, disease, epidemics, seasonal unemployment, economic fluctuations—all these were far beyond the ability of the average family to predict or to cope with. Those who could avoid them most successfully lived in comfortable poverty. Those who could not sunk lower in the social scale and farther away from the American myth of prosperity.

Sailors lived under even more precarious conditions. By 1700, ships operated with a clear division of labor that emphasized cooperation and discipline. A typical crew included master, mate, carpenter, boatswain, gunner, quartermaster, cook, and four to five able (ordinary) seamen. Larger ships might also have a surgeon and caulker. Tasks were graded and specialized; a crew of twelve was divided into five or six different ranks and pay stations. Everyone worked at certain general duties, such as loading and securing the cargo.

These men daily faced the possibility of being washed overboard, suffering hernias, breaking or losing fingers from rolling casks, or breaking arms and legs in loading and moving cargo. Physical harm also came at the hands of masters and mates, who enforced ship's discipline by violent means. As the century wore on, technical improvements brought larger ships that carried more cargo but were manned by smaller crews. As captains required more work of each sailor, the men came to believe they were being exploited.

In response to the danger and the exploitation, seamen sought to exert some control over their fate. They engaged in work stoppages over safety issues and reserved the right to unilaterally terminate their contracts. They deserted when they entered waters or ports where they were likely to be impressed into the British navy or to escape excessive cruelties of masters or mates. The competition between the British navy and merchant service for sailors made such resistance possible. In true market fashion, captains were often forced to pay higher wages to keep their sailors on board. Merchants and ship masters sued in court to keep their crews, but seamen retained considerable control over their mobility. They could, after all, count on at best 250 days of work a year.

In the end, this industry introduced a relationship between owner and worker that was far more modern than the traditional patriarchal ones that dominated most of colonial society. Sailors created a cooperative form of community that rebelled against the growing power of wealthy merchants and sought to maintain an independence of action amidst the uncertainty and suffering of some of the worst working conditions of their time.

Pirates, too, shared this sort of communal bond. In the seventeenth century, buccaneers had sailed the West Indies, commissioned by their governments to prey on the shipping of enemies. When they began to assault American ships as well in the early eighteenth century, American colonists became less accepting of their activities. Boston executed eight pirates in 1717, Virginia six in 1720. Rhode Island hanged twenty-seven of Edward Low's crew. The pirates became crueler and more predatory as the decades progressed, partially in reaction to this treatment. Low, for instance, sliced off one of his victim's ears and made the poor soul eat it.

Yet pirates also created a fraternal and collective bond stronger than any other in the Atlantic world. They elected their own captains and officers and distributed their plunder equally among the crews. There were only three pay stations for a typical crew of eighty—the men considered themselves partners in a business venture rather than hired laborers. Pirate ships were also overmanned, often having five times as many crew members as a merchant vessel of the same size, so the daily work requirements were far less than those imposed on British and American sailors. Pirates lived in a true egalitarian society, surrounded by a world that vigorously pursued hierarchy and order.[7]

Skilled Artisans

Like farmers, artisans found their work shaped by weather or the amount of available daylight, but they also had to cope with far more of the less concrete forces of an international market economy. Both mariners and dockworkers, for instance, generally found themselves unemployed at the onset of winter ice. Leather workers' supplies might be delayed by inclement weather that prevented cattle from being delivered to the city. Wars disrupted the supplies of pelts for those who worked in the fur trade. In short, the lives of artisans were increasingly shaped by forces beyond their immediate personal control.

Artisans worked at a bewildering variety of jobs, possessed a wide range of skills, and cannot be comfortably fit into any single social grouping. Their dress identified them as workers: leather work aprons, plain hair (no wigs), and long trousers. On the other hand, their drive for self-improvement has become legendary, epitomized in Franklin's "Poor Richard" essays. Men like the silversmith Paul Revere were ambitious and proud, but part of their pride was in their very status as workers. Revere could afford to have John Singleton Copley paint his portrait, but he posed in work clothes and with his tools at his side.

Skilled artisans learned their trade in roughly the same way their English counterparts did. They began as apprentices, serving until they reached twenty-one, or for seven years. They worked twelve to sixteen hours a day, with the master required (in theory) to provide board, training, and sometimes basic education. The next steps in the profession were journeyman, then master. But while these two steps were clearly distinguished in Europe, the scarcity of labor in the colonies veiled such differences. In practice, the only significant difference between a journeyman and a master was that the journeyman did not set up his own business.

American artisans could count on making anywhere from 20 percent to 100 percent more income than their European counterparts. They worked at home or in small shops. Many invested heavily in their tools and equipment, and they kept their own account books. Most owned enough property to qualify as voters. Metal workers were the highest paid, specializing in domestic hardware, horseshoes, and farm implements. Artisans pursued a wide variety of specialties. They were shoemakers, weavers, carpenters, metal workers, masons, and porters; coopers, tailors, blacksmiths, and mast and sail makers. The elite artisans were millers, tanners, silversmiths, and lock makers. Yet most did not limit themselves to one skill. Revere also worked as a coppersmith, engraver, and dentist besides making branding irons

Shipbuilding in Philadelphia; William Birch, "Preparation for War to Defend Commerce." ❧

for hatters and implements for surgeons. Most artisans also farmed or had another occupation. Only about 10 percent to 15 percent of all artisans, in fact, made more than half of their income from their principal trade.

Both skill and regional specialization became increasingly common. Certain metal workers came to specialize in locks and cutlery. Lancaster, Pennsylvania, was the site of many woolen and linen weavers and gunsmiths. Lynn, Massachusetts, was a center for the shoe industry by mid-century. Shoemaking was still a family activity that was run under a putting-out system, but by 1768, the city was producing about eighty thousand pairs of shoes annually. In Philadelphia, shipbuilding provided work for a number of different artisans. Shipbuilders worked under contract and produced no more than two ships a year, working little in winter. They were so successful, however, that about one-third of all British-owned ships by the end of the colonial period were built in the colonies. Specialization also occurred in the south. Tailors, carpenters, shoemakers, blacksmiths, and weavers, all of whom did not have to struggle against competition from English imports, were common in most Chesapeake counties. Few plantations enjoyed complete self-sufficiency. Robert Goldborough, a leading Maryland planter and political figure, used almost four dozen Talbot County craftsmen during the early eighteenth century, providing them in turn with his services as an attorney and a merchandiser for their products. Black artisans filled many of a plantations' daily needs, but whites readily turned to free labor when the demand arose.

Colonial artisans, particularly those who lived in cities, were fiercely proud of their status. While many did not achieve any real degree of economic success, some came to epitomize the American story of going from rags to riches—as exemplified by one Pennsylvanian family. Francis Richardson, a Quaker mariner, migrated to Pennsylvania in the 1680s. By the time of his death in 1688, he had acquired some land and several slaves. His widow married a wealthy Quaker merchant, and Richardson's son Francis, Jr. became a silversmith and married the daughter of a wealthy Quaker landowner. By the time he died, in 1729, his sons Francis III and Joseph could comfortably claim a place among the Philadelphia elite. Francis III, also a silversmith, invested in a variety of real estate and commercial ventures and retired in gentlemanly wealth at the age of fifty-four.

Americans in 1763 lived and worked in a world that was rapidly becoming part of the transatlantic economic order. Rapid economic growth, increased urbanization, growing scarcity of land, greater specialization of labor, and more extensive involvement in the Atlantic market economy combined to transform the face of the colonial economy. There were often profound differences in the way in which various areas in the colonies experienced these changes, but there were also common elements. Rural Americans everywhere faced a growing demand for land, and all looked to the frontier for a solution. Settlers throughout the colonies reacted with, at best, ambivalence to the rising importance of money and markets in their lives. The increasing disparity between rich and poor and the multiplying numbers of poor led people everywhere to question the direction their world was taking.

❧ *Chapter Ten* ❧

Religion in Eighteenth-Century America: A Clash of Cultures

Historians have traditionally portrayed the eighteenth century as one dominated by political concerns and a gradual but distinct abandonment of the seventeenth-century religious impulse. The phrase "From Puritan to Yankee",[1] for instance, has been applied to such a process in New England. Within this framework, the Great Awakening stands as the century's dominant religious event, an oasis of religiosity amidst a world of unyielding materialism. In reality, religion remained far more pervasive in colonial life during these years than we have been willing to admit. What changed was its form. It did become more responsive to political concerns, but it also became more ordered, more reasoned, and more institutionalized—more genteel. Eighteenth-century religion sought to control emotional expression and to limit and institutionalize doctrinal diversity. In this context, the Awakening emerges as a conservative attempt by the laity and their allies among the clergy to regain a feeling of spiritual intimacy, communal identity, and emotional intensity. Those who participated in the revivals felt they were communing with an earlier, purer version of religious experience, a sacred moment in time where community and spiritual concerns were dominant. Revivalists rejected the growing dominance of self-interest and secular refinement. They spurned Old World gentility in favor of a more direct, honest New World piety.

The Growth of Religious Diversity

The proliferation of religious sects was one of the clearest characteristics of religion in eighteenth-century America, the result both of European emigration and a growing toleration within the colonies. Church buildings dominated the American landscape as never before. Few churches had served seventeenth-century New

Significant Dates

1689	James Blair appointed commissary of Virginia
1690s	Keithian schism
1693	College of William and Mary founded
1700	Sixty Anglican clergy service entire American colonies
1701	SPG founded
1706	Francis Makemie forms first American presbytery in Philadelphia
1707	Philadelphia Baptist Association established
1708	Connecticut adopts the Saybrook Platform
1718	William Tennent, Sr. migrates to the New World
1720	Rev. Theodorus Jacobus Frelinghuysen arrives in New Jersey
	Conrad Beissel arrives in the New World
1722	Rev. Timothy Cutler announces his conversion to Anglicanism at Yale commencement
1726	Log College established
1727	First Amish immigrants arrive in Pennsylvania
1727–40	Massachusetts grants tax exemption to dissenters
1729	Presbyterian factions compromise over subscription issue
1734	First Moravian immigrants arrive in Georgia
1735	Northampton, Massachusetts, revival
1739	George Whitefield arrives in the American colonies
1740	Rev. Michael Schlatter arrives in the New World
	Gilbert Tennent delivers sermon *The Danger of an Unconverted Ministry*
1740–43	Peak of Great Awakening in New England
1741	Jonathan Edwards delivers sermon *Sinners in the Hands of an Angry God*
1742	Rev. Henry M. Muhlenberg arrives in Pennsylvania
	James Davenport begins preaching in Boston
	South Carolina restricts evangelical activity
1742–43	Connecticut passes anti-itinerant legislation
1743	Charles Chauncey publishes *Seasonable Thoughts*
	Revivalism in Hanover County, Virginia
1747	Samuel Davies licensed to preach in Virginia
1753	Dutch Reformed ministers create the American Classis
1755	Revision of Quaker disciplinary code
1756	Isaac Backus founds Baptist church in Middleboro, Massachusetts
1758	Philadelphia Yearly Meeting forbids slaveowners from participating in Society business
	New and Old Light Presbyterians conciliate
1776	Philadelphia Meeting condemns all Quaker ownership of slaves

Yorkers, for instance (in 1695, the only English church was in Fort George), and most of the colonists there had seemed to follow no religion at all. The first church in the Carolinas was not built until 1698, and the first minister there, Atkin Williamson, was famous for baptizing bears when he was drunk. Things changed after 1700. Rural churches became common in the Chesapeake, New England churches became larger and more ornate, and impressive Anglican churches were built in New York, Charleston, and Boston that reflected the growing material wealth of these cities.

One reason for the proliferation of church buildings was a substantial increase in the number of clergy, particularly outside of New England. The church now functioned as a basic institution of provincial life in every colony. Folk religion became secondary to the ritual of regular churchgoing and formalized ceremony, a decided contrast to the volatility of seventeenth-century religious expression. Most religious groups experienced a gradual but inexorable tightening of church structure and discipline, an institutional maturation that brought some resentment among the laity and some of the clergy.

Anglicans

New World Anglicans had received little support from London in the seventeenth century. Except in New Hampshire, the church was all but invisible in New England; in the other colonies, the laity exerted considerable control over church affairs, and ministers were few and far between. In South Carolina, for instance, lay commissioners administered the colony's ten churches, and parishioners elected ministers. Virginia had only ten clergy for forty-eight parishes in 1662, and in 1700, there were only sixty Anglican clergy in all of British North America.

At that point, London made a conscious decision to alter this embarrassing situation. Rev. Thomas Bray established the Society for the Propagation of the Gospel in Foreign Parts (SPG) in 1701, which sent more than three hundred missionaries to labor in the New World vineyards between 1702 and 1783. During the same period, the Anglicans founded three hundred new parishes in the colonies. The commissaries, personal representatives of the bishop of London, began to expand their activities and intensify their oversight of the American clergy. James Blair, the commissary of Virginia for fifty-three years, was the most successful of these individuals. Appointed in 1689, Blair arrived in the New World with ambitions to centralize all church authority and administration in the commissary's hands. He founded the College of William and Mary, which allowed the gentry to educate their children in Virginia rather than England, and he served on the colonial council. Although the gentry jealously guarded their own powers in the vestries and resisted his centralization plans, Blair presided over a remarkable expansion of the Anglican presence in the colony. Membership in the vestry became an even more important element of the gentry's political power, and Anglican ceremony became a central element of communal ritual in the Chesapeake. Services consisted of prayers and a sermon, with communion before the sermon four times a year. The only requirements for receiving communion were confirmation and sound moral character. The gentry paraded their social superiority before the congregation, and the clergy taught reading and writing with an eye toward moral lessons for a reasonable people and moral order for a patriarchal society. Still, only about two-fifths of Chesapeake families attended services regularly in the early eighteenth century, and by the 1770s (after the emergence of the Baptists and Methodists), the number fell to slightly more than one-third. The law required adults to attend monthly and dissenters every two months, but constables did little to enforce these requirements.

The quality of Anglican clergy improved markedly during Blair's tenure. From 1723 to 1776, largely as a result of reforms he implemented, only 10 percent of the clergy had charges of misconduct brought against them. In 1726, more than half of the forty-two ministers had attended a university, twelve at Cambridge or Oxford. By 1750, twenty-three of seventy-four clergy had attended one of these universities, and another thirteen held degrees from William and Mary. Maryland noted similar improvements, and the church made comparable progress in both of the Carolinas. The South Carolina Assembly passed the Establishment Act of 1706 that enfranchised dissenters and established the Church of England, creating ten parishes in the process. By 1750, the colony had almost twice as many churches per capita as Maryland or Virginia, including the elegant Anglican church of St. Philip's in Charleston. North Carolina followed with a 1715 act that also provided for toleration, included a statement of vestry powers, and established several new parishes. New York established the church with the 1693 Ministry Act, authorizing vestries to elect and pay ministers. While dissenters remained in the majority here, the law put in place the structure for a future Anglican establishment. By the 1760s, the city had eighteen Anglican churches, including Trinity Church, a capacious house of worship that was 148 feet long and seventy-two feet wide.

SPG missionaries preached to Indians and blacks as well. They brought their message to the Yamasees in 1703 and the Iroquois in the 1720s and 1730s, though with little success. They blamed their failure on the barbarous trickery of the French and Spanish and believed that the Indians would have willingly and gladly embraced Protestant Christianity had it not been for Catholic perfidy. They also baptized blacks in small but regular numbers. Even before the Great Awakening, men such as Rev. Francis Le Jau, based in Goose Creek, South Carolina, enjoyed steady success. Elias Neau ministered to slaves in New York City from 1703 to 1722, mostly in the evenings. The government, though, blamed his work in part for the 1712 uprising; the council stripped him of his appointment and prohibited blacks from being out at night without their master's consent. Neau was later reinstated, and other ministers continued his work in later years.

The church spent its greatest energy in New England, where eighty-four ministers worked under SPG auspices to dispel the hegemonic power of Puritanism. George Keith arrived in the region in 1702, but as late as 1722, there was not a single full-time Anglican minister in all of Connecticut. One dramatic success, however, gave hope. Yale's rector, the Reverend Timothy Cutler, had been moving toward Anglicanism for some time. At the 1722 commencement exercises, he concluded his prayer with a phrase from the *Book of Common Prayer,* shocking the assembled crowd and sending a shudder through the New England clergy. Cutler and three others joined the Anglican church, and within twenty years, there were seven Anglican ministers (all Yale graduates) and more than two thousand communicants in Connecticut alone.

Most colonial Anglicans were not British officeholders or wealthy merchants (though most such individuals were Anglican); rather, they were small landholders and their families. Christ Church in Boston's north end, for instance, ministered to the needs of tradesmen, artisans, and mariners. The parishioners of St. Michael's in Marblehead, also a seafaring town, were generally poor. In the composition of its congregations, the Anglican church was typical of the American religious experience. Church membership and religious belief generally transcended wealth and poverty.

Anglican parishes reflected the New World experience in their huge geographical expanses. The English parish averaged less than five square miles. Southern parishes in the colonies ranged from sixty to one hundred square miles; one on the

South Carolina frontier encompassed more than ten thousand square miles that had only seven hundred white inhabitants. Most New World ministers became itinerants by necessity, traveling thousands of miles in a year. In rural areas, they preached in small chapels, barns, or private homes. The rector would generally preach two Sabbaths a month in the main church of his parish and one Sabbath every three to four weeks in the outlying chapels. Even in the middle colonies, distance was often a trying burden. Rev. William Beckett traveled 1,632 miles in southern Pennsylvania in one year in the early 1730s. And in Connecticut, SPG missionary Samuel Johnson rode a circuit of more than sixty miles between Stratford, Fairfield, Newtown, and West Haven during the 1720s.

Life became somewhat easier for these ministers during the second quarter of the century. More ministers came to the colonies, settling permanently in eastern parishes and working as occasional itinerants on the frontier and salaries became more generous. Virginia law now required a salary of sixteen thousand pounds of tobacco and a glebe of at least two hundred acres with a house and outbuildings. Some Maryland clergy were able to live as gentlemen. The wealth of parishes varied considerably, though. Most ministers presided over a parish that contained a central church and several outlying chapels; small brick or wooden churches perhaps thirty feet square were common. On the frontier, clergy were generally forced to board in private homes. Ironically, the English were impressed by the vitality of the colonial Anglican establishment, discouraged as they were by the declining religiosity of eighteenth-century England.

Presbyterians

Presbyterians were the fastest growing religious group in eighteenth-century America. The basic Presbyterian beliefs were contained in their statement of faith, the Westminster Confession. New England Puritans believed that each parish was independent and could ordain its own minister. The laity had an equal role in church governance, but only the elect could become full members. In contrast, Presbyterians adopted a more hierarchical conception of the church, somewhere between radical Puritanism and traditional Anglicanism. Presbyteries, or regional groups of ministers, had power over individual churches. Above presbyteries came synods, or regional meetings of presbyteries, and then a general assembly, the final authority of the church. Both ordained and lay elders met at each level, functioning as church courts. The higher courts possessed authority usually ascribed to bishops in the Anglican church. Presbyterians did not believe they could tell who was or was not saved, so they allowed everyone except the most openly blatant sinners to join the church and receive the sacrament, which they believed could help effect salvation in those so inclined. They also stressed the power of the ministry over the laity and believed that only presbyteries could ordain clergy. Presbyterians were generally overshadowed by Puritans in early New England, but Connecticut did adopt a Presbyterian policy when ministers approved the Saybrook Platform in 1708.

Presbyterianism found its true American home in the middle colonies. In 1700, there were only twelve Presbyterian churches in the colonies, including five in Maryland. By 1758, there were two hundred churches and ninety-eight ministers. Francis Makemie was a critical figure in laying the groundwork for this growth. Makemie, a Scotch-Irish minister ordained in Glasgow in 1681, brought together disparate Puritan churches from Long Island, Delaware, and New Jersey under the Philadelphia Presbytery in 1706, based loosely on the principles of the Westminster Confession. This first presbytery had seven ministers, all but one from Scotland or Ireland. In 1716, another group established the Synod of Philadelphia along with four subordinate presbyteries. The synod claimed responsibility for congregations throughout the middle colonies. At about the same time, the Scotch-Irish migration began in earnest, and most of these new arrivals were Presbyterians who dispersed in large numbers throughout the backcountry in small, widely scattered communities. The church thus faced a persistent shortage of clergy from its inception. Even wealthy parishes had to do without their minister for part of the year, as he traveled to tend to other congregations. Student ministers often served as licensed "visitors" to frontier parishes. Since Presbyterian theory gave considerable power to lay elders, the laity in these remote areas began to increase their role in enforcing moral discipline in their church communities.

Scotch-Irish and Scottish immigrants tended to adhere more strictly than others to the Westminster Confession. They were most numerous in the New Castle Presbytery, and by 1724, this group required subscription to the confession. A few of the Scotch-Irish ministers and most of the New England-trained ministers (who dominated the Philadelphia Synod) objected, arguing that the Bible alone was sufficient guide to faith and practice. The two sides reached a compromise in 1729. The agreement separated essential from unessential articles of faith and required that members subscribe only to the former. It also made the synod an administrative rather than a legislative body. Though the compromise left many questions unresolved, it did mark a victory for the antisubscription party. While Presbyterian congregations experienced new conflict during the Great Awakening, they succeeded in redressing the shortage of ministers and in extending the sect's organizational structure. By 1763, eight presbyteries supervised the clergy, ensuring their quality and overseeing their ordination, and intervened regularly in congregational disputes.

The Dutch Reformed Church

The Dutch church continued to grow even after the English took over New Amsterdam. In particular, it remained a vehicle for the preservation of Dutch vernacular culture and a source of influence and social power for Dutch women. But the arrival of Lord Cornbury as New York governor marked the beginning of the end of the church as an Old World institution. Until then, the church retained control over the education of its youth, instructing them (especially girls) in the Dutch language. In 1702, Cornbury initiated a strict licensing policy for all teachers (designed to limit the number of Dutch instructors), established a city school that provided instruction only in English from 1704 to 1712, and supported the establishment of a charity school by the SPG. By 1730, the Dutch had lost control over education, and by mid-century, many had joined the Anglican Trinity Church.

A number of the Dutch ministers began to adopt an Anglicized high church liturgy, with preaching, sacraments, and segregation of the sexes in church. A new infusion of the radical pietist tradition slowed this process among the New Jersey Dutch, though it had little impact in New York or in the Netherlands itself. Theodorus Jacobus Frelinghuysen arrived in New Jersey in 1720, responding to a call from the Raritan Valley church. He and two other pietist preachers spurred a series of Dutch revivals in 1735, marked by spontaneous prayer, preaching in the Dutch language, and a minimum of ritual. Frelinghuysen claimed he could recognize the unregenerate (the worldly and profane) immediately, and he often barred them on the spot from receiving communion. Most of the converted were among the poor and outcast of the Dutch congregations, and they responded to the pietists' suspicion of the outside world and their emphasis on family and kin.

In 1740, there were sixty-five Dutch churches in New York and New Jersey but only twenty ministers. Despite repeated appeals, the Amsterdam Classis, the governing body of the church, refused to allow Americans the right to examine and license their own ministers. A group of American conservatives who wanted to maintain their separate Dutch identity supported this decision. As intermarriage with other faiths and ethnic groups increased, however, so did the pressure to allow greater independence. The Dutch Classis began to allow American ordinations in 1748, supervised by a subsidiary body known as a coetus (synod).

The Americanizers went too far in 1753, though, when they proposed the creation of an autonomous American Classis, and a schism ensued. The older conservative leaders, who were born in Holland and Dutch-trained, insisted on maintaining doctrinal purity and continuing to use the Dutch language. The coetus group (the Americanizers) was more pietistic and younger, and many of these ministers had been educated in America. Time and numbers were on the side of the reformist group. The Dutch acquiesced to forming an American Classis in 1755 and allowed English-language preaching and services.

The German Reformed Church

Germans who migrated after 1720 were usually members of either the Lutheran or the German Reformed churches. The Heidelberg Reform Group oversaw the German Church until 1740, a role then assumed by the Amsterdam Classis of the Dutch Reformed Church. Despite a scarcity of ministers, German churches became community centers, helping the newcomers maintain contact with their Old World customs. In church buildings or in private homes, settlers gathered to sing and pray, and one of their number read the sermon. Schoolmasters and pious laymen often provided leadership for these early communities. John Philip Boehm, for instance, was a schoolmaster who arrived in 1720 and was asked to serve as a church reader five years later. He rode a sixty-mile circuit and ministered to three churches, sharing authority in each with the founding elders and the deacons. Dutch ministers from New York finally ordained him in 1729 to protect his status against a challenge from a minister who had been sent over by the German Church of the Palatinate. Such leadership was typical until 1746, when the Dutch sent Michael Schlatter to establish a more comprehensive New World organization for the church.

Schlatter was a Swiss minister who offered to minister to the German Reformed churches in Pennsylvania for the Dutch synods. Immediately upon his arrival, he showed an amazing ability to conciliate quarreling factions and brought together the region's ministers to form a coetus in 1747. Though the Dutch synods in Amsterdam retained a veto power over the new synod's actions, the establishment of the American coetus was a major step forward for the German church. Schlatter was untiring in his missionary efforts, in four years traveling eight thousand miles and delivering more than six hundred sermons. By 1753, there were some thirty thousand members in fifty-three churches, and Schlatter had garnered additional financial and ministerial support from Amsterdam. At this point, however, he began to work with the British Society for the Promotion of the Knowledge of God among the Germans and quickly saw his influence wane. The reasons are not difficult to fathom: this society shared the common English abhorrence of German culture, portraying Germans in insulting terms in its religious propaganda. Schlatter eventually resigned his position in the society after only two years.

German Lutherans

The Lutherans first established a New World presence in New Sweden and New Netherland in the seventeenth century. But as late as 1719, there were only fourteen congregations in the colonies and only one minister. In 1725, the Reverend William Berkenmeyer arrived and began to extend the church organization. Still, deacons and overseers remained responsible for most church affairs, and the early congregations often had no resident pastor for years at a time. When ministers finally began to arrive in greater numbers during the second quarter of the century, the laity often resisted their attempts to take over control of the parishes. These conflicts remained relatively low-key, though, until the mainstream of Lutheran migration began after 1735.

The most influential Lutheran figure in early America came as part of this new wave of emigrants in late 1742. Born in Germany and educated at the university in Gottingen, Henry M. Muhlenberg was a Halle pietist with strong missionary zeal. He landed in Charleston in September, reaching Philadelphia two months later. Within a month, he had become the spiritual leader of the colony's three congregations. In August 1748, he oversaw the establishment of the Pennsylvania Ministerium, which served thereafter as the synodical organization for German Lutherans in the New World. Six pastors and twenty-four lay delegates attended this first meeting. By 1765, there were 133 Lutheran congregations, reflecting the vitality and growth of the denomination and the continued emigration of its members from Europe. There were, however, only thirty-three pastors. The continued lack of an adequate ministry remained the church's principal weakness in America. Ongoing lay dominance also meant that Lutheran services remained simple, consisting of a sermon, prayer, hymns, a scripture reading, and a benediction.

Catholics and Jews

The story of Roman Catholicism in eighteenth-century America centers primarily in the Spanish and French colonies. There were about six thousand Catholics in Pennsylvania and another ten thousand in Maryland by the 1760s, many of them immigrants from southern Ireland who were seeking refuge from English rule there. But English colonists associated Catholics with religious and political tyranny, and these fears limited both the size and significance of Catholic settlements. There were even fewer Jews. About two or three thousand Sephardic Jews worked predominantly as merchants and in various trades in the northern port towns, and a few settled in Savannah during the early years of the Georgia settlement. They worshipped in their own synagogues and organized their own charitable organizations and religious schools. Only in the nineteenth century would these two groups have a major cultural impact on the American mosaic.

German Pietists

Eighteenth-century German pietism represented a less formalized tradition of worship than that favored by the "high church" groups we have discussed thus far. Pietism emerged in Europe during the last part of the seventeenth century as an effort to revitalize Christian piety and to pursue greater religious purity; it was a protest against the growing intellectualism and formalism that was coming to dominate many Reformation churches. Pietism stressed the heart, ethics, and emotion of religion rather than its formal services, and it emphasized a return to the Bible for inspiration. It rejected religious hierarchy and the need for an educated clergy.

Philip Jacob Spener is generally credited with beginning the pietist movement in the late seventeenth century, influenced by the more mystical and "spiritual" elements of Puritan, Dutch, and German Reformed traditions. He and his successors became increasingly occupied by one central question: "How do I know I am saved?" This was, of course, a central concern of early New England Puritans, but the pietists arrived at a somewhat different resolution of this vexing problem. They accepted the importance of spiritual regeneration, or new birth, and prohibited a wide range of secular, corrupt behaviors, such as card playing and dancing. But they also pursued more voluntaristic and charitable concerns. They engaged in much philanthropy, founded schools, orphanages, and hospitals, and provided crucial impetus to the Protestant missionary movement.

Moravians

The Moravians, or Church of the Brethren, were the remnants of the earlier Hussite movement in Moravia and Bohemia in Germany. In 1722, a group of them took refuge on the Saxony estate of the Lutheran Count Nicholas von Zinzendorf. The first Moravians to migrate to the New World landed in Georgia in 1734. As pacifists, they were soon forced to leave the colony. In 1740, they moved north to Pennsylvania, founding Bethlehem and Nazareth. Over the course of the next decade, some moved south to North Carolina, following the familiar backcountry route, and founded the towns of Wachovia, Bethany, and Salem. By mid-century, there were thirty-one Moravian congregations, though with only a thousand or so members.

Zinzendorf, meanwhile, was expelled from Saxony. Trained at Halle in his youth, the count had developed his own unique brand of Lutheran pietism on his estate. After giving refuge to the Moravians, he found himself increasingly drawn to their doctrines. He came to envision a pan-Protestant union that would bring together Lutherans, Calvinists, Moravians, and even sympathetic Anglicans. Migrating to the New World, he took charge of Moravian operations here, founding the First Moravian Church in Philadelphia and organizing congregations in Nazareth, Bethlehem, and elsewhere.

Moravians revived such early Christian practices as the love feast and foot-washing. At first, New World Moravians lived by a social framework called the "General Economy" (which was dissolved in 1762). Members held land and property in common and worked at their various jobs organized in sex and age cohorts known as choirs. Women had significant power in this community. They did the laundry and prepared the food, but they also produced linen, helped with the harvest, and made cotton. They led the Bible studies that began and ended the day and composed some of the hymns that the community sang.

Moravians were evangelical from the beginning and focused particularly on the Indians. Their missionaries were ordinary people, farmers and artisans, who were motivated solely by religious zeal. Christian Rauch, for instance, traveled deep into the Mohawk Valley and converted more than sixty Indians at Shekomeco. But Rauch was not unusual. Of Bethlehem's 1,062 settlers, forty-eight were Indian missionaries and fifty-four taught school or preached in other colonies. Again, women held a place of honor in these activities. Jeanette Rau was the best known of the female missionaries and spoke several Indian dialects. Bethlehem lent constant support to these efforts, serving as the hub of an extensive missionary network. By 1748, the Moravians had settled some five hundred Indian converts at a missionary station called Gnadenhuetten, about thirty miles from Bethlehem. Their most famous convert was the Delaware warrior Teedyuscung, who moved his family to Gnadenhuetten, confessed his sins, and was baptized on March 12, 1750. He reluctantly accepted the new name the Moravians gave him—Gideon.

❧ *Documents* ❧
A Moravian Missionary's Life

Many Moravians, including women, wrote religious autobiographies. This excerpt from the account of Martha Powell (1704–1774) shows clearly how arduous the life of a Moravian missionary could be.

> In the year 1746 we were at Dansbury. In the year 1748 we were sent to Shemoho, where I had a hard fitt of illness, and returned to Bethlehem in November where the office of servant of the Church was committed to my charge. In the year 1751 we was sent to Long Island and after a 7 Months stay there, was sent a 2nd time to Dansbury. There we staid one year, and then returnd to Bethlehem, where my Husband began Storekeeping. In the year 1755 we were sent to Gnadenhutten on the Mahony, where we staid 9 Months untill the Terrible Attack of the Indians. . . .
>
> In the Year 1759 we received a call to assist in the world of God among the Negroes in Jamaica and after a stay in Bethlehem of 9 Weeks we satt out on our Journey thither on my Birth day the 12th. of February. I lookd upon it as a peculiar Favour to serve the poor Negro Slaves. I loved them, and they loved me, but the excessive heat of the climate weakned my poor Tabernacle greatly. After we had been there near 6 Years we received our call to return home.

The life story of Martha Powell (1704–1774). Personals of our dear Sister Martha Powell who entered the Joy of her Lord the 6th of May 1774. The Moravian Archives, Bethlehem, Pennsylvania; printed in Rosemary Radford Ruether and Rosemary Skinner Keller, eds., *Women & Religion in America,* vol. 2: *The Colonial and Revolutionary Periods* (New York: Harper & Row, 1983), 296.

In the long run, such commitment generated only hostility from other colonists. The Moravians were active participants in Gilbert Tennent's revivals, but Tennent, reacting to accusations of extremism, later attacked their fanaticism and portrayed them as dangerous and deluded. When war broke out with France in 1744, colonists questioned the Moravians' motives for preaching to the Indians and their refusal to take oaths of allegiance. The New York legislature passed a 1744 act that required oaths and licensing for Indian preachers and stipulated that Moravians register their churches with the colony government. The colony also submitted a report to the Board of Trade recounting alleged subversive activities by the Moravians, connecting them with the 1741 slave rebellion and an alleged Catholic plot. Persecution eased with the end of the war, and Parliament thereafter even encouraged their migration and offered them exemption from oaths and service in the colonial militia. Even Benjamin Franklin, noted for his scathing commentary on German immigrants, changed his mind after Moravians gave him a warm reception at Bethlehem in 1755 and after hostile Indians attacked the Moravians at Gnadenhuetten, killing eleven missionaries. Thereafter, in fact, Moravians armed themselves in defense. The more they behaved like ordinary British colonists, it seems, the more the English were willing to accept them.

Other Pietistic Groups

Mennonites first migrated to Pennsylvania in 1683, settling in Germantown. There, they fell under the influence and leadership of the Lutheran pietist and mystic Francis Daniel Pastorius. Pastorius served as mayor, schoolmaster, clerk, and assembly representative of the town and penned the first formal American protest against slavery, submitting a petition to the Quaker Monthly Meeting in 1688. Generally, however, the Mennonites kept to themselves, were little involved in politics, and participated in the general movement westward, settling in Lancaster County and points further west.

They were joined in the late colonial period by the Amish, an even more conservative religious group founded by the former Mennonite preacher Jacob Amman. The first Amish landed in Pennsylvania in 1727 and came in larger numbers during the 1740s. They, too, gravitated farther west, adopting the conservative life-style in dress, manners, and language that now sets them apart. The Amish even opposed the use of church buildings, meeting in barns or homes instead. They refused to establish any church organization and even today insist on educating their own children.

Johann Conrad Beissel left the German Palatinate in 1720, intending at first to join a group called Women in the Wilderness, a pietistic mystical community founded in the Pennsylvania forest to await the millennium. By the time he got there, most of the members had died or scattered. He joined the Dunkers in 1724, leaving to established the Ephrata community in Lancaster County in 1732. Beissel began his community with some thirty celibate men and an equal number of women. He adopted the German writer Jacob Boehme's notion of a female principle of wisdom (called Sophia) that existed prior to the male divine principle and continued to coexist with it. Together, the two created Adam, who at first was androgynous, without sexual organs or digestive functions. Carnal appetites appeared only when Eve was created from Adam. Thus, in this view, only by transcending sexuality could humans return to unity with God.

The community was partly monastic; those who were not full members of the group were allowed to join as "outdoor members." The core group held property in common, and men and women lived in separate houses. The women lived by a rule known as the Rose; they spun, quilted, and made baskets, sulfur matches, paper lanterns, and artificial flowers. But they also chopped their own wood and cared for their household—though not that of the men. As late as 1750, the community had only three hundred members. They operated several successful businesses, pioneered in the German-American printing industry, and produced beautifully illuminated manuscripts. Internal dissension eventually destroyed the community.

The Dunkers, or Church of the Brethren, were another of the many small sects that dotted the Pennsylvania countryside. These people believed in complete immersion during adult baptism but otherwise were similar to the Mennonites. Fleeing religious persecution in Germany, they arrived in Pennsylvania in 1719 and established their first church in Germantown in 1723. By 1770, there were fourteen Dunker congregations in Pennsylvania and one in New Jersey.

The Schwenckfelders followed the teachings of the Reformation figure Kaspar Schwenckfeld von Ossig, who had taught an inward, mystical faith, concerned with the invisible rather than the outward apostolic church. In the eighteenth century, his followers survived in scattered German communities, unorganized and under pressure from the Roman Catholics. They came to Pennsylvania in 1734 at the request of Count Zinzendorf, were joined by other, even more obscure small groups, and continued to pursue their founder's emphasis on inner spirituality. They showed no interest in building churches, establishing a polity, or undertaking evangelical work of any kind, and thus their influence on the colonial world was slight.

The Rosicrucians were undoubtedly among the strangest of these groups. These highly educated Germans arrived in Germantown in 1694, having come to the New World to await the Second Coming and to serve the religious needs of both the white colonists and the Indians. Nominally they were Lutherans, but they did not agree among themselves on the main points of doctrine. They preached a generalized theology of love and benevolence, with a little science, medicine, alchemy, and astrology mixed in for good measure. Their diverse, loosely structured beliefs serve as a metaphor for the Pennsylvania religious landscape itself.

Baptists

Baptists experienced a surge of growth during the eighteenth century; by 1776, they had about one hundred congregations with more than twenty-five thousand members. All Baptists shared beliefs in congregational independence, adult baptism, and lay leadership. But like most eighteenth-century religious groups, they also suffered internal dissent and produced a variety of sectarian offshoots. The Particular Baptists were those who had first emerged in New England. In 1652, they split into a Calvinist and a Six Principle (Arminian) wing. Free Will Baptists, who appeared in North Carolina and Virginia in the 1720s, also embraced a more Armenian doctrinal position. In 1707, several Pennsylvania and New Jersey churches formed the Philadelphia Baptist Association, which solved church disputes and supported Baptist religious activities. By 1762, the association presided over twenty-five congregations with 1,318 adult members. The members also adopted the London Confession in 1741, a Particular Baptist platform with a strong Calvinist bent.

The Great Awakening split the Regular Baptists just as it did other religious groups. Isaac Backus emerged as the leader of the prorevival group. A Congregational pastor in Norwich, Connecticut, Backus founded a Baptist church in Middleboro, Massachusetts, in 1756. From there, he organized New England Baptists into the Warren Association, based in Warren, Rhode Island, and led the church to a more active evangelical position. He is perhaps best remembered for his vigorous support of religious freedom and the separation of church and state, adopting a belief in personal moral autonomy based on his reading of John Locke's *Letter on Toleration:* "[T]o give laws, receive obedience, and compel by the sword belong to none but the civil magistrate; and upon this ground I affirm, that the magistrate's power extends not to the establishing of any articles of faith, or forms of worship, by force of laws. . . . true and saving religion consists in the inward persuasion of the mind. . . ."[2]

The final significant group, the Separate Baptists, experienced their fastest growth in the south. Awakened by George Whitefield, Shubal Stearns (1706–1771) served as pastor of the Baptist church in Tolland, Connecticut, then moved south with his brother-in-law Daniel Marshall to organize Baptist congregations in Virginia and North Carolina that were strongly democratic and stressed emotional preaching. They and others played a critical role in the religious revolution that swept the southern backcountry during the late colonial period.

Quakers

Quakers, too, experienced decisive changes in their polity and theology during this century. William Penn had given some indication of the direction in which the group would eventually move. While he remained an enthusiast, he was decidedly less jarring in his beliefs and actions than men such as George Fox. He even admired early eighteenth-century Puritans as less bigoted than their predecessors, who had persecuted and martyred early Quaker missionaries. Still, Penn ardently clung to an oral, traditional view of religious knowledge. He made a virtue of anti-intellectualism—meditation, he argued, was certainly more rewarding in the search for truth than reading.

Early Quaker beliefs covered a wide spectrum. A group know as the Ranters were centered at Oyster Bay, Long Island, and appeared briefly in New Jersey, Connecticut, and New Hampshire. They were libertines and antinomians, convinced they were sinless and that their thoughts and lives were directly controlled by Christ. George Keith and his followers stood at the other end of the spectrum, attacking mainstream Quakers for embracing too much enthusiasm. Quaker leaders recruited Keith to come to America because of his university education and learning; they named him head of the Quaker school in Philadelphia in 1689 and gave him a mansion and fifteen hundred acres of land.

Keith believed that knowledge of the historical Christ was necessary for salvation and that Quakers could *not* assume that infants who died before acquiring it were justified; their fate, he argued, remained uncertain. Quakers, we have seen, loved their children to an extraordinary extent, and Keith's arguments were, at the least, unsettling. But he went even further. He attacked the Quaker's exclusive reliance on holy conversation in child rearing, admonishing them that catechizing and the Bible were also essential sources of religious truth. In 1690, he proposed an organizational reform that would require an open confession of faith not only from those who wanted to join the sect—this was standard—but also from Quaker children. He accused Quaker leaders of denying the importance of the historical Christ, attacked them as "spiritual and carnal whoredoms," and described Pennsylvania as "a strumpet cohabiting in the wilderness."[3]

Keith drew his strongest support from the poor and the landless, the small freeholders and the tenants; more than half of the Philadelphia artisans supported him. While the colony's leaders accused him of "downright Popery" for his more intellectual orientation, it seems clear that Keith had exposed a weakness in the Quaker utopia. Over time, we know, wealthier Quakers acquired disproportionate power in the meeting, and even at this early date, there were signs that not everyone was pleased with the distribution of power within the colony. Keith eventually left the colony and returned to England, becoming an Anglican early in the next century. He was the first missionary the SPG sent to America; while he did not convert any mainstream Quakers, he did bring quite a few former Keithians into the fold.

As the eighteenth century wore on, most Quakers developed concerns that were not terribly different form those of their Puritan counterparts. By the third decade of the century, Quaker meetings commonly expressed their worry about the rising delinquency among the young. Others voiced their conviction that doctrinal conformity was growing more important than a true experience of the inner light. A movement toward more rigorous religious discipline began around 1740, as increased pressure on available land led more Quakers (particularly the poor) to marry outside the meeting. Quakers also reaffirmed their opposition to military spending and opened a political rift with the proprietary party. Eventually, many leading Quakers simply withdrew from the colony's political life.

In strictly religious terms, the crisis came in 1755. The September Philadelphia Yearly Meeting appointed a Committee of Fourteen to revise the society's disciplinary code, and a Committee of Thirty-One to inspect quarterly and monthly meetings to ensure that the code was being observed. It also required monthly meetings to appoint a select meeting of ministers and elders to report to the quarterly meeting. The results were immediate and profound. Between 1755 and 1776, the Pennsylvania meetings disowned 3,157 of their members, more than 20 percent of their total membership in 1760. The most common offense was marrying outside of the Society, a decision we have already noted was directly connected to the growing disparity in wealth among Quakers.

Quaker spirituality found unique expression in the Society's attitudes toward women. Quakers expected a good woman to control her sexuality and become an embodiment of holy conversation, selflessly sacrificing her own needs for those of her children and the Society. Though Friends isolated women from economic activity and rarely allowed them to handle money, Quaker women enjoyed unusual spiritual—and ultimately social—power. Margaret Sakew Fell, George Fox's wife, was the role model for female activity in the Society. Early organizing activity for the Society took place at Fell's manor, and she wrote hundreds of letters and tracts supporting Quaker missionary efforts. The authorities imprisoned her several times for refusing to swear the oath of allegiance to the Crown, and while in jail, she wrote *Women's Speaking Justified, Proved and Allowed of by the Scriptures,* the pamphlet that provided the spiritual justification for women's active role in Society affairs.

While women and men met together at the weekly local meetings, they met separately at monthly, quarterly, and yearly meetings. Women's meetings inspected marriages, talked with girls about sexual offenses, helped in child rearing, and in general monitored the moral behavior of the women's community. Martha Awbrey Thomas inspected thirty-three women for marriage between 1695 and 1727; the meeting gave her an assistant for each inspection and allowed her a month to complete it. Women's meetings also helped mothers with problem daughters and oversaw courtships, and they disowned unrepentant young women—such as the woman in 1720 "who was overtaken with strong drink late last harvest and was seen dancing with a man's jacket on."[4] Philadelphia Quaker women also did much to aid the poor and provide money and services to the elderly, ill, orphaned, deserted, and widowed.

Female elders tended to be in their fifties and from the wealthiest Quaker households. Ministers, on the other hand, were often poor, talented women who frequently married up the social ladder after receiving their calling. Both female elders and ministers relied heavily on personal charisma. They spoke of receiving visions, led Bible readings and silent devotions, and told their daughters of visitations they had received from the Lord. Some Quaker women, in short, had a real outlet for their talents and ambitions, one that was rudely closed to Puritan women as early as the 1630s. The quiet majority, however, undoubtedly experienced the same material and emotional frustrations that plagued other women of their time. As Anne Cooper Whitall noted: "I am like a pelican in the wilderness. I am like an owl of the desert. . . and am as a sparrow alone upon the housetop. . . . My days are like a shadow that declineth. I am withered like the grass. . . . "[5]

Perhaps the most perceptive questioning of Quaker materialism came from the growing antislavery movement among the Friends. The New Jersey Quaker John Hepburn wrote *The American Defence of the Christian Golden Rule,* an attack on the cruel treatment of slaves. Three years later, the Long Island merchant William Burling urged Quakers to free any slaves they owned, and several other Quakers condemned slavery in the years that followed. Individual Quakers began to free their slaves in the 1740s. In 1753, the Philadelphia yearly meeting stated bluntly that slavery was a sin, and in 1758, it ordered that any Quaker who bought or sold a slave could not participate in the business of the Society unless he repented. The meeting required that slaveholders prepare their slaves for freedom with religious and secular education and declared that they could continue to hold their slaves only for the same length of time as indentured servants. In 1759, Anthony Benezet emerged as the leading publicist of the antislavery movement when he wrote *Observations on the Enslaving, Importing, and Purchase of Negroes,* which used eyewitness accounts to press home the suffering of slaves. In 1776, the meeting condemned *all* Quaker ownership of slaves.

John Woolman was perhaps the most perceptive of all Quaker critics of slavery. In 1754, he published *Some Considerations on the Keeping of Negroes,* in which he argued that the desire to protect Quaker children from poverty—the central concern of Quaker society—had in fact itself caused the moral problems that so disturbed Quakers. Hard (even excessive) work and the drive to accumulate wealth inevitably produced luxury, the root of all social and economic problems. He contended that Quakers should instead "live comfortably on honest employments, without having that temptation they are often under of being drawn into schemes to make settlements on land which have not been purchased of the Indians, or of

❧ *Documents* ❧
"Real Cause for Sorrow"

John Woolman's attack on slavery remains a powerful statement of the best of the Quaker spirit.

> Negroes are our fellow-creatures, and their present condition amongst us requires our serious consideration. We know not the time when those scales in which mountains are weighed may turn. The Parent of mankind is gracious, his care is over his smallest creatures, and a multitude of men escape not his notice. And though many of them are trodden down and despised, yet he remembers them; he seeth their affliction, and looketh upon the spreading increasing exaltation of the oppressor. He turns the channels of power, humbles the most haughty people, and gives deliverance to the oppressed at such periods as are consistent with his infinite justice and goodness. And wherever gain is preferred to equity, and wrong things publicly encouraged to that degree of wickedness takes root and spreads wide amongst the inhabitants of a country, there is real cause for sorrow to all such whose love to mankind stands on a true principle and who wisely consider the end and event of things.

John Woolman, "Considerations on the Keeping of Negroes," *The Journal and Essays,* Amelia M. Gummere, ed. (New York: The Macmillan Company, 1922), 318.

applying to that wicked practice of selling rum to them." Luxuries "masqueraded as moral imperatives" and became part of the childrearing process itself, leading Quakers away from the simplicity of Christ's truth. Friends should leave their children only wise instructions, he told his fellow Quakers, and the knowledge of an honest profession, rather "than laying up treasures for them, which are often a snare, than any real benefit."[6] He closed down his prosperous New Jersey haberdashery shop in 1756 and lived the rest of his life as a simple tailor.

For Woolman, the greatest sin of all was slavery, which deprived other humans of their basic freedom. The Quaker drive for accumulation was irrefutably tied to this horrid crime and the resultant murders and destruction of human souls. So Woolman refused to eat sugar or wear dyes because of their connection to the slave trade, and when he traveled by ship, he did so in steerage, in protest against the use of English ships in the West Indian trade. He traveled through Virginia in 1746 and 1747, confronting slave owners and embarrassing them, reminding them that their use of the Bible to justify slavery was surely false, that "the love of ease and gain are the motives. . . of keeping slaves." "Did not He that made us," he later wrote, also "make them?"[7]

Congregationalists

The vibrant energy of early Puritanism had spent its course by the early decades of the eighteenth century. While Calvinism remained the guiding force of New England theology, it found expression in a broad range of practices that defy easy generalization. The majority of New England parishes adopted the half-way covenant, becoming regional churches that welcomed all who wished to worship. Many rural parishes, however, clung to traditional guidelines for church admission and rejected any relaxation of membership requirements. Some congregations required personal testimony for admission to full membership, while others did not. Solomon Stoddard of Northampton, Massachusetts, admitted all community members to communion, hoping the sacrament itself would somehow spur them to sanctity. Finally, there were others, such as the church in Canterbury in eastern Connecticut, that rejected all innovations in church governance and admission. The Canterbury members worshipped under the Cambridge Platform of 1648, rejecting the half-way covenant and the Presbyterian innovations of Connecticut's Saybrook Platform (1708) and stressing lay control of parish affairs.

Diversity was even more obviously reflected in the growing presence of non-Puritan parishes throughout New England. These dissenters—Anglicans, Quakers, Baptists, Presbyterians, and others—pressured the religious and political establishment to exempt them from taxes levied to maintain Congregational churches. Despite persistent resistance, they succeeded in winning such relief in a series of decisions between 1727 and 1740.

The status of Puritan ministers also underwent considerable transformation during these years. In Massachusetts, some, such as Ipswich's John Wise and later Chebacco's John Cleaveland, sought to preserve the independence of the local congregation and resisted any attempt to consolidate ministerial power. Others began to meet in ministerial conventions, or consociations. In 1705, several of these associations proposed that they take upon themselves the power to screen ministerial candidates before recommending them for vacancies. But the Congregational establishment was not willing to embrace reforms that smacked of Presbyterianism.

Connecticut was another story. Here, the movement toward a more hierarchical, presbyterial form of church government was much more successful. In 1722, the colony and its ministers adopted the Saybrook Platform. Under its structure of church governance, regional associations of ministers and elders were to meet twice a year and choose delegates for an annual General Association. Each county would have standing ministerial councils with the power to ordain and discipline church members. Dissenters were not welcome here. Though the Connecticut Assembly passed legislation in 1708 and 1729 that, on the face of it, exempted dissenters from parish rates, as late as 1730, only one Baptist and one Anglican congregation had been recognized.

Ministers in both colonies had one thing in common, though—their status was on the decline. Though the ministry continued to attract the best college graduates, it provided them with far less social and financial security than in the past. Towns were often frugal with salaries, reluctant to renew contracts with ministers they were dissatisfied with, and not at all hesitant about engaging them in doctrinal debates. Congregational parishes now had as much of a social as a religious function, and ministers were required to pursue pastoral duties—counseling, visiting the sick—more than they were expected to ponder the intricacies of Puritan theology. Finally, the laity continued to define their own sense of religiosity, persisting in their belief in the power of magic and folklore. New England was still a sacralized land; it had 140 churches in 1700, almost three hundred by 1730, and more than 450 by 1750. But institutionalized religion no longer wielded the intensely spiritual power it had once possessed.

Indeed, more liberal, rational religious beliefs made significant inroads during the first decades of the century. The establishment of the Brattle Street Church in 1698 was particularly disturbing to the Puritan establishment. Members of some of Boston's leading families, all religious liberals, helped found the church, of which Benjamin Colman was pastor. The congregation adopted the Westminster Confession and allowed all children to be baptized. They required no public examination of faith and opened communion to all.

Brattle Street marked the first serious breach in the New England Calvinist facade; other representatives of religious rationalism soon poured through. Their enemies often identified them as Arminians. Jacobus Arminius (1560–1609) was a Dutch theology professor who reacted against the conservative Calvinism of the Dutch Reform church. New Englanders used the term *Arminian* to describe religious rationalism of all kinds. American Arminians taught that people could attain salvation through their own actions—by performing good deeds, for instance—and that humans were not permanently tainted by original sin. Charles Chauncey, one of the most forceful critics of the Great Awakening, and Jonathan Mayhew, the first American clergyman to explicitly endorse John Locke's political theory of the right of rebellion, were the best known American ministers to adopt the argument that reason itself could lead individuals to salvation. Ministers such as Ebenezer Gay believed that individuals could discover religious truth from the "Constitution of Things, in their respective Natures and Relations."[8] Scripture, Gay believed, only confirmed what men were fully able to discover for themselves. A major controversy over the appointment of an openly Arminian minister, Robert Breck, erupted in Springfield, Massachusetts, in 1736 (Jonathan Edward's Northampton parish was just a few miles upriver), providing an important backdrop for the enthusiastic resurgence of Calvinism in the Great Awakening.

In all of this variety, one element became characteristic of almost all congregational churches—women comprised the vast majority of the membership. Women continued to join the churches in their twenties, generally just before or after marriage. But men increasingly delayed joining until their thirties or forties, often until shortly before taking political office, and single men rarely became full church

members at all. Men tended to regard membership in the church as closely connected with their status in the community—a secular rather than a spiritual rite of
passage.

The Great Awakening

The Great Awakening was the primary religious event of eighteenth-century
America. Though it did not occur at the same time and with the same intensity in
all places and its particular causes varied from region to region, the wave of revivalism that swept through the British mainland colonies during the middle decades of
the century profoundly affected everyone it touched. And certain common themes
emerged wherever it appeared: an emphasis on emotion and faith rather than reason; a belief in the power of the spirit rather than in the efficacy of good works; a
renewed emphasis on rebirth as central to conversion; and a belief in both human
sinfulness and the power of God's mercy. While isolated figures such as Jonathan
Edwards sought to return to an earlier, harsh vision of God, most Awakening
preachers pointed ahead to a more voluntaristic church and a more forgiving God.
They promised to free participants from guilt, shame, and sin and to initiate them
into a close, loving, and holy community through conversion. In this, the
Awakening spoke above all to a laity that anxiously sought emotional assurance in
a rapidly changing world.

From 1730 to 1760, most of Western Europe was swept by an outpouring of
religious emotionalism—Germany, Holland, Switzerland, France, England, and
Scotland all experienced revivals. Ordinary people, it seems, found little solace in
the scientific, rational explanations offered for personal and natural disasters. For
most, divine intervention continued to be a more logical explanation for such mysterious and seemingly unpredictable events as earthquakes and sudden death. Even
in the American colonies, where literacy was unusually high, most people clung to
a more traditional, oral folk culture and rejected the rational, literate culture of the
educated ministry and elite.

The Middle Colonies

The phrase "Great Awakening" no longer automatically evokes images of New
England only. Indeed, the first ripples of revivalism appeared among the
Presbyterians in the middle colonies, close on the heels of a large Irish migration in
the 1730s. Early controversies among the Presbyterians, such as that over the adoption of the Westminster Confession in 1728, were largely limited to the clergy; the
laity still believed that their ministers could be trusted to protect and maintain the
proper sense of religiosity. Clergy and laity acted together several times in the ensuing decade to keep unorthodox ministers out of Presbyterian congregations.
Ministers often sponsored large communion rituals that brought several congregations together and lasted for days. But the potential for conflict between laity and
clergy remained and indeed intensified as the church prospered and the number of
ministers grew.

The clergy gradually split into two opposing groups. The more conservative
ministers, known as Old Lights, supported academic training for all ministers,
encouraged the laity to study both the Bible and the Westminster Confession, and
downplayed an active role for the laity in seeking a conversion experience. Their
opponents, known as New Lights, put much greater emphasis on the necessity of
true piety in ministers, stressed a more emotional religious experience, and

encouraged church members to actively strive toward a conversion experience. A large majority of the laity supported the New Lights. It was in this environment that the Tennent family rose to influence.

William Tennent, Sr. was ordained an Anglican minister in Ireland but became uncomfortable with Episcopal church structures. After he migrated to the New World in 1718, the Philadelphia synod granted his request to be licensed as a Presbyterian minister, accepting his explanation that he had become disillusioned by the Arminian doctrines, Episcopal hierarchy, and the "ceremonial way of worship" that permeated the Anglican church. Tennent quickly gained a reputation as an excellent preacher and a serious scholar and teacher. By 1733, three of his sons had joined him in his vocation (Gilbert, John, and William, Jr.). While William, Sr. was noted for his calm, humble presence, his sons acquired a somewhat different reputation. Gilbert, who studied at Yale and was ordained to the New Brunswick, New Jersey, pastorate in 1726, was described as "a son of thunder who does not fear the faces of men,"[9] an emotional man who physically confronted the laity with their sinfulness. He was, another observer noted, "a burly, salty, downright man" who preached "like a Boatswain of a Ship, calling the Sailors to come to Prayers and be damned."[10] Gilbert became the true symbol of radical revivalism during the Awakening.

Gilbert Tennent, probably by Gustavus Hesselius. ❧

Tennent and his sons were influenced to some degree by the Dutch Reformed minister Theodorus Jacobus Frelinghuysen, who emphasized personal conversion and holiness as the necessary components of a true religious life and enforced strict standards for admission to communion. As with Jonathan Edwards after him, his doctrinal preferences had much in common with the first generation of Puritan ministers. The revivals Frelinghuysen led at Raritan, New Jersey, were forerunners of the greater revivalism of the Awakening. By the late 1720s, Tennent's own churches had shown similar signs of new religious life.

Tennent gave further impetus to his movement in 1726 by establishing the famed "Log College" at Neshaminy, a seminary that began to turn out pietistic revivalist preachers. But ministers were still more interested in changing members' lives and bringing them under their pastoral wings than in effecting any mass revival. Their activities, and the small revivals they did preside over, remained confined to individual churches.

Then in 1739, the Philadelphia Synod ruled that all ministers must have a degree from either a British or European university or from Harvard or Yale and must submit to an examination by the synod. The evangelical faction saw these restrictions as an attempt to control them—and they were right. They had accepted the earlier compromise over the Westminster Confession with reluctance, but here, they drew the line. William Tennent, Sr. and his sons now began a movement that was to have profound implications for the American religious experience.

The Tennents established a rival presbytery at New Brunswick with responsibility for parishes in northeastern Pennsylvania and eastern New Jersey. They assumed this would give them the power to license their own ministerial candidates, and they proceeded to recognize John Rowland, a graduate of the Log College, as their first licensed preacher. The Philadelphia Synod, firmly in the grip of the Old Lights, refused to accept Rowland unless he submit to its own examination. It admonished the parish of Maidenhead for calling Rowland to its ministry and reproved the New Brunswick Presbytery for not properly examining him. But the synod also proposed a compromise. It retained the right to evaluate candidates for membership in the synod itself but agreed to accept the power of subordinate presbyteries (that is, New Brunswick) to license and ordain ministers. The most divisive—and prophetic—point in this controversy was the New Light insistence that ministers show evidence of conversion *beyond* mere academic training. The Old Light demand for university degrees struck at the heart of the evangelical movement. Ironically, the education of Tennent and his followers was actually superior to that of their opponents. William, Sr. spoke Latin and was a Greek master; the Log College's alumni founded many academies. The real issue was not education or adequate intellectual preparation. Differences over the role of the laity in the church and over the nature of the conversion process drove the two sides apart. Tension was heightened when New Light itinerant preachers began to operate without permission from resident pastors or the higher authorities, as custom dictated.

George Whitefield's arrival at Philadelphia in November 1739 broke the deadlock. Whitefield had come to America once before, preaching briefly in the new Georgia colony in 1737. Now, a mere twenty-five years old, he returned to the New World to embark on a mission that seemed, to his followers, divinely ordained. He was the son of an English tavern keeper and had worked his way through Oxford on his way to becoming an Anglican minister. He stressed the concept of the "New Birth" and an immediate, emotional conversion experience; he was a master of outdoor preaching, attracting thousands to his sermons.

On his arrival, Whitefield preached first in the Anglican church, then on the steps of the courthouse to a much larger crowd. He toured Presbyterian churches

George Whitefield preaching, 1741. ❧

throughout the region, drawing thousands and greatly strengthening the evangelical party. And while earlier revivals had been confined to particular churches, people of all denominations came to hear Whitefield. The revivalist noted the effect on Samuel Blair's New Jersey congregation: "The bitter cries and groans pierced the hardest heart. Some of the people were as pale as death; others were wringing their hands; others lying on the ground; others sinking into the arms of friends; and most lifting up their eyes to Heaven and crying to God for mercy."[11] Though the revival had less impact in neighboring New York (where few ministers invited Whitefield to their pulpits), Whitefield did preach there to thousands in open fields, returning the following spring with similar success.

Four short months after Whitefield's arrival, Gilbert Tennent delivered the sermon that served as the clarion cry to arms for the New Lights—*The Danger of an Unconverted Ministry*. Speaking to a congregation at Nottingham, Pennsylvania, on March 8, 1740, Tennent underlined the importance of true conversion among the ministry. He referred to unconverted ministers as "Caterpillars" who "labour to devour every green Thing. . . "[12] and compared them with the proud and conceited Pharisees. They were ineffective preachers and provided security to the wicked; their emphasis on legal rather than gospel obedience left their congregations

❧ *Documents* ❧
Awakening Dead Souls

It is easy to see from the following selection why many ministers bristled at Gilbert Tennent's defense of itinerancy and his attack on their own spiritual integrity.

> But possibly some may again object against Persons going to hear others, besides their own Ministers;. . . Again it may be objected, That the aforesaid Practice tends to grieve our Parish-Minister, and to break Congregations in Pieces.
>
> If our Parish-Ministers be grieved at our greater Good, or prefers his Credit before it; then he had good Cause to grieve over his own Rottenness and Hypocrisie. And as for Breaking of Congregations in Pieces, upon the Account of People's Going from Place to Place, to hear the Word, with a view to get greater Good; that spiritual Blindness and Death, that so generally prevails, will put this out of Danger. It is but a very few, that have got any spiritual Relish; the most will centure their Souls with any Formalist, and be well satisfied with the sapless Discourses of such dead Drones. . . .

Gilbert Tennent, *The Danger of an Unconverted Ministry Considered in a Sermon on Mark VI, 34* (Philadelphia: 1740), 17–8.

Even Benjamin Franklin, the giant of the American Enlightenment, could not resist the spiritual charms of the "Grand Itinerant," George Whitefield. The following excerpt records Franklin's reaction to Whitefield's preaching in 1739 in Philadelphia.

spiritually dead. People should be able to listen to any minister they desired, he argued, provided that he was godly and converted. Tennent thus combined an Old World emphasis on emotion and personal spirituality with a New World conception of religious voluntarism. His sermon culminated a decade of accusations by Log College graduates against the Scotch-Irish clergy.

Though Whitefield departed for New England in the fall of 1740, the revival continued unabated in his absence. In June 1741, the Log College organized a team of six evangelists to travel to the remote parts of the middle colonies, and Tennent himself left for Boston in early 1741. Old Lights, meanwhile, sought to further restrict New Lights' preaching and travels. The crisis came to a head in the synod of 1741, when the traditionalists demanded that the revivalists be expelled from the synod. The New Lights withdrew voluntarily, forming their own presbyteries and, in 1741, the Synod of New York.

The differences between the ministers in these two opposing camps are instructive. Old Light ministers were, on average, in their early forties and had come to the colonies late in their careers. They had been educated in Scotland and

The Multitudes of all Sects and Denominations that attended his Sermons were enormous and it was matter of Speculation to me who was one of the Number, to observe the extraordinary Influence of his Oratory on his Hearers, and how much they admir'd & respected him, notwithstanding his common Abuse of them, by assuring them they were naturally half Beasts and half Devils. It was wonderful to see the Change soon made in the Manners of our Inhabitants; from being thoughtless or indifferent about Religion, it seem'd as if all the World were growing Religious. . . .

I happened . . . to attend one of his Sermons, in the Course of which I perceived he intended to finish with a Collection [to support the proposed orphanage in Georgia], & I silently resolved he should get nothing from me. I had in my Pocket a Handful of Copper, Money, three or four silver Dollars, and five Pistoles in Gold. As he proceeded I began to soften, and concluded to give the Coppers. Another Stroke of his Oratory made me asham'd of that, and determin'd me to give the Silver; & he finish'd so admirably, that I empty'd my Pocket wholly into the Collector's Dish, Gold and all.

The Autobiography of Benjamin Franklin, Louis Masur, ed. (New York: Bedford Books of St. Martin's Press, 1993), 107–8. Copyright © 1993. Reprinted with permission of St. Martin's Press, Incorporated and Bedford Books.

were professionally settled. The typical New Light minister was thirty-two years old, at the beginning of his career, and was either native-born or had arrived in the colonies at a young age. New Lights were far more likely to resort to popular appeals, spoke derisively of "the Noble & Mighty" elders, and readily identified with the poor and the common people. Tennent attacked "the Grandees" and warned that men "grow in Wickedness in Proportion to the Increase in their Wealth."[13] He and others emphasized individual values over hierarchical ones, encouraged lay participation and mass meetings, and, in their emotionalism, promoted physical closeness. They were indeed a more popular religious force, one that pointed clearly toward the American future of voluntaristic, participatory religion. New Lights proved more responsive to the needs and demands of the laity.

Yet Old and New Lights found common ground when confronted by radical pietists, such as the Moravians. Gilbert Tennent's 1742 meeting with the mystical Count Zinzendorf caused him no small concern. The count embraced the idea of universal salvation, contending that the saved could rest assured of their eternal reward and need not spend the rest of their lives in doubt, striving for this security.

He also used itinerant laymen as missionaries. Zinzendorf's teachings, together with the growing success of James Davenport's emotionally extreme preaching, eventually led Tennent to reject some of the more disruptive expressions of the revivals. In 1758, New and Old Lights reached a reconciliation. They agreed to adopt warnings against the public criticism of ministers, accept the Awakening as a work of God, embrace the notion of conversion as a complete change of life and heart, and reject the more bizarre physical responses of revivalism. They had finally achieved the unity each had long been seeking.

New England

The roots of the Awakening in New England extended deeper than ecclesiastical disputes. The laity here were rebelling not only against clerical control of the religious experience but also against the modern social, economic, and intellectual trends that we have examined in the last few chapters—developments that pointed clearly toward a society that would more resemble the poverty-stricken Old World that settlers had fled a century earlier than the idealized New World of the Puritan past. Here too, though, was considerable opposition to the more radical expressions of revivalism, and disagreements over the validity of this more "enthusiastic" approach to conversion created permanent divisions in many towns and churches. In the end, the Great Awakening in New England failed to stem the tide of secularization that it had so anxiously sought to counter.

The economic and social trends that had troubled Increase Mather and others during the late seventeenth century had accelerated and intensified during the early decades of the eighteenth century. Boston streets seemed filled with petty criminals, orphans, bastards, and indigent children. The Awakening was particularly powerful in such areas as southeastern Massachusetts, where land shortages forced more and more young men and women to postpone their entry into adult society. Market towns and regional economic centers, the rural areas most exposed to impersonal economic forces, were more likely to be involved in large-scale revivals. The majority of new church admissions in these areas were young people in their twenties, landless and unmarried. New Light ministers also predominated in Worcester County towns that had supported the land bank, particularly those in the developing southeast corner of the county where artisans flocked to the revivals and later to dissenting churches.

Town residents pursued bitter, contentious court battles over attempts of Awakening supporters to separate from the main parish, and the General Court found itself forced to intervene in a growing number of such disputes. Ministers and laity contended with each other for power over financial and doctrinal issues. In rural parishes, such as Canterbury, Connecticut, the laity remained committed to the conservative Puritan ideal of independent, self-governing congregations. Canterbury and other eastern Connecticut churches rejected the Presbyterian innovations of the Saybrook Platform and spurned the half-way covenant. Other parishes, characterized more by religious apathy than commitment to an ideal, fought with their ministers over salary, contracts, and other issues that defined ministerial status. Many ministers began to push for the organization of professional associations in an attempt to increase their status and power. Those who studied at Harvard began to read such Anglican theologians as Archbishop John Tillotson and to adopt the vocabulary and style of English literature in their writing and preaching.

Amidst all this change, the moral standard of the Puritan forefathers constantly haunted New Englanders' lives. Ministers glorified John Winthrop, John Cotton, and the other Puritan divines beyond all sense of reality. They spoke of the early years of New England as a spiritual paradise and contrasted them with their own society, torn by contention and cursed by religious apathy. The world around them was "abounding with Temptations, to our Young People in Special, to desert the Interest of Pure Religion, and betray the Cause of God, in which our Forefathers were engaged."[14] New England youth were squandering their time away: "*Mammon* is their *God*, and *they* mind earthly Things."[15]

Awakening preachers here, as they had in the middle colonies, emphasized matters of the heart in things religious, and they exhorted their listeners to accept their sinfulness, welcome God's grace into their souls, and be redeemed. They urged communicants to seek happiness in the love of God and their neighbor. But New England revivalism also harped on the idealized New England past, "when the grace of God had abounded in the hearts of his people."[16] The ritual or rebirth, so essential to all eighteenth-century revivalism in its emphasis on inner renewal through divine grace, served a special role here. In being reborn, Puritans could put themselves in touch with that earlier period of their sacred history; they could feel they were again walking the earth with the giants of the Puritan experiment.

The giant of the New England revival was Jonathan Edwards. Perhaps the major intellectual figure of eighteenth-century America, Edwards had graduated from Yale in 1720 and become a colleague of his grandfather, Solomon Stoddard, in Northampton, Massachusetts, in 1726; he succeeded him as parish minister in 1729. Edwards was a true Calvinist, a Puritan of seventeenth-century cloth who preached justification by faith alone and upheld a belief in strict predestination. God's sovereignty was unquestioned in Edwards's mind, a mark of divine perfection in sharp contrast with human depravity. All humans could do was pray for God's grace and salvation. Yet Edwards was also fully conversant with Enlightenment trends in philosophy and science. And his most famous sermon, *Sinners in the Hands of an Angry God*, gives little indication of his belief in the power of love as a unifying force in the universe and in human life or of his wonderful use of light as an image for the beauty of God.

The first signs of renewal came in Northampton in 1735, in Edwards's own parish. A young boy died suddenly, spurring the conversion of "a young woman who had been notorious as a leader in scenes of gayety and rustic dissipation." The two events, Edwards noted, "seemed to be like a flash of lightning upon the hearts of the young people. . . and upon many others."[17] This emphasis on the conversion experiences of youth was characteristic of the Awakening throughout the colonies but nowhere more so than in New England. And as the revival spread, "the minds of people were wonderfully taken from the *world*, and it was treated among us as a thing of very little consequence."[18] People seemed to become better wives, husbands, parents, children, masters, and servants.

This first revival spread rapidly up and down the Connecticut River Valley, to South Hadley, Suffield, Hatfield, Springfield, West Springfield, Long Meadow, and Enfield, and up to thirty miles east of the valley in Connecticut, but it disappeared as suddenly and mysteriously as it had appeared. Then a diphtheria epidemic swept through the region in 1737 and 1738, taking many young lives with it. In 1739, the War of Jenkins Ear and the beginning of the War of Austrian Succession had a disastrous impact on the New England economy and cost two thousand Massachusetts volunteers their lives. The final blow seemed to come with the humiliating suppression of the land bank of 1740.

The New England Awakening now exploded in an intense wave of religious frenzy between 1740 and 1743, then rapidly fizzled out. In addition to Edwards's published sermons, Gilbert Tennent's works were republished in Boston and received wide circulation. Whitefield arrived in Boston in September 1740 and

❧ *Documents* ❧
"Oh Sinner! Consider the Fearful Danger. . . ."

Jonathan Edwards, despite his brilliance as an American philosopher, embraced a decidedly Calvinist view of the universe. The first selection below, from his famous sermon, *Sinners in the Hands of an Angry God,* reflects his use of powerful imagery (and of John Locke's theories of sensation) to overwhelm the listener with the power of a righteous God. The second selection is from Edwards's defense of the revival against the conservative, Old Light ministers who decried the physical manifestations of conversion; Edwards wrote this piece, though, before the arrival of James Davenport in Massachusetts.

> The God that holds you over the Pit of Hell, much as one holds a Spider, or some loathsome Insect, over the Fire, abhors you, and is dreadfully provoked: his Wrath towards you burns like Fire; he looks upon you as worthy of nothing else, but to be cast into the Fire; he is of purer Eyes than to bear to have you in his Sight; you are ten Times so abominable in his Eyes, as the most hateful venomous Serpent is in ours. You have offended him infinitely more than ever a stubborn Rebel did his Prince; and yet 'tis nothing but his Hand that holds you from falling into the Fire every Moment. . . .

> O Sinner! Consider the fearful Danger you are in: 'Tis a great Furnace of Wrath, a wide and bottomless Pit, full of the Fire of Wrath, that you are held over in the Hand of that God, whose

preached to a crowd of fifteen thousand on Boston Common. In less than a week, he preached to additional crowds of five, six, and eight thousand. He delivered his farewell sermon on October 12 to a gathering of about thirty thousand, then toured Massachusetts and Connecticut towns before leaving for Rye, New York, on October 29. By now, his rapid movements had earned him the name of the "Grand Itinerant," a title portentous enough to strike fear into the heart of any Old Light believer. Throughout his New England tour, Whitefield attacked the "dead" preachers who were responsible for the lack of true religion—"For how can dead Men beget living Children?"—and he ridiculed the "Darkness" of the universities.[19] As the comments of Connecticut farmer Nathan Cole reveal, Whitefield's teachings struck home: "And a sweet, solomn Solemnity sat upon his brow, and my hearing him preach gave me a heart wound, by god's blessing. My old foundation was broken up and I saw that my righteousness would not save me."[20] Whitefield thus prepared already fertile ground for the arrival of Tennent in December 1740.

Tennent preached in a number of parishes throughout the early months of 1741. The New Lights formed nearly thirty private religious societies in Boston alone, each meeting one evening a week to discuss matters of the spirit. The flood

Wrath is provoked and incensed as much against you as against many of the Damned in Hell. You hang by a slender Thread, with the Flames of divine Wrath flashing about it, and ready every Moment to singe it, and burn it asunder. . . .

Jonathan Edwards, *Sinners in the Hands of an Angry God* (Boston, 1741), 15–6.

Besides those that are overcome with conviction and Distress, I have seen many of late, that have had their bodily Strength taken away with a Sense of the glorious Excellency of the Redeemer, and the Wonders of his dying Love; with a very uncommon sense of their own Littleness, and exceeding Vileness attending it, with all Expressions and Appearance of the greatest Abasement and Abhorrence of themselves; And not only new Converts, but many that were, as we hope, formerly converted, whose Love and Joy has been attended with a Flood of Tears, and a great Appearance of Contribution and Humiliation. . . ; with a far greater Sight of their Vileness, and the Evil of their Hearts than ever they had. . . .

Edwards, *The Distinguishing Marks of a Work of the Spirit of God* . . . (Boston: 1741), 66–9.

of revivals continued through the summer of 1741 and into 1742. In particular, ministers noted the change in behavior that seemed to accompany youthful conversions: *"Tavern-Hauntings* and *Night-Assemblings* of *Young People* for wanton Pastime seem'd at once to disappear."[21]

Eastern Connecticut also found itself set afire by the flames of religious enthusiasm. Here, too, a growing shortage of land and decreasing economic opportunity provided fertile ground for discontent with the febrile religious establishment. And it was particularly here that parishes remained under lay control and resisted any relaxation of admission standards. The church at Canterbury adopted only a very limited version of the half-way covenant (at this time, most of rural New England was approaching universal baptism). It also rejected the Saybrook Platform and any hint of a conciliar structure. Here and throughout eastern Connecticut, revivalist preachers spoke to the lay hunger for a more traditional, intense spirituality.

Late in 1741, Rev. James Davenport's arrival in Boston signaled the emergence of a more radical phase of the Awakening. Davenport had been ordained in Southold, Long Island, in 1738. He met Whitefield in Philadelphia in 1740 and spent the summer of 1741 preaching in Connecticut. He garnered considerable support

❧ *Documents* ❧
The Awakening Message

Some who received the Awakening message were more susceptible than others. The Reverend Thomas Prince, one of the great publicizers of the revival, included his own daughter's story in his accounts. Though Deborah found spiritual peace on her death bed in 1744, Gilbert Tennent's preaching in 1740 seemed only to plunge her into despair; she remained unaffected by her father's kind words of assurance.

> From the Beginning she was much more apprehensive of *Danger* than any else: And though concerned about her Soul; yet complained of her Stupidity, Hardness of Heart, Blindness of Mind, Impenitence and Unbelief; censuring and condemning herself of all Good, denying she had any sanctifying Grace, but judging she had been deceiving Herself with the counterfeit Resemblance of it. . . .
> "O Dear Father, (said she) you have better Apprehension of me than you should have: You don't know what a vile Creature I am: I have dreadfully apostatized from CHRIST, have grown exceeding negligent of religious Duties, and was returning to the World again." I told her, we did not perceive it; that I could not see those Decays she spoke of, to be inconsistent with a regenerate State, though they were Matter of deep Abasement, and she should have a Care she denied not the gracious Word of GOD within her. . . .

Thomas Prince, *The Sovereign God Acknowledged and Blessed. . .* (Boston: 1744), 25–6.

there, but his extremism aroused much concern among the Old Lights. When he began to personally attack other ministers as unconverted, blind guides to salvation, even some New Lights spoke out against his tactics. In May 1742, two laymen filed a complaint against him with the General Assembly, which arrested him and another minister and charged the two with disturbing the peace and order of the town of Stratford under the guise of the revival they had conducted there. The assembly found Davenport guilty, "disturbed in the rational Faculties of his Mind,"[22] and ordered him sent back to Long Island.

Uncowed, Davenport simply moved farther north, arriving in Boston in the summer of 1742. Boston ministers refused to open their pulpits to him, so he preached on the Common and on Copp's Hill, in the rain, to throngs of thousands. At times, he tore his clothes off above the waist in the emotion of the moment. He also identified by name twelve of the city's ministers who, he said, were unconverted. With these comments, he succeeded in galvanizing the Old Lights into more concerted action.

Lay exhorting (preaching) had become increasingly common in eastern Massachusetts during 1742. Ministers and the upper class alike reacted strongly against this untutored lay preaching, regarding it as a threat to their social status and their own hegemonic control of Massachusetts literary culture—in effect, as an attempt to resurrect the more popular, traditional oral culture of an earlier day. Davenport seemed to symbolize this entire movement. The clergy referred to his followers as "chiefly made up of the idle or ignorant Persons, and those of the lowest Rank."[23] A grand jury indicted him "on the charge of having said that Boston's ministers were leading the people blindfold to hell. . . ."[24] The court jailed him and then ordered him to leave the colony. The *Boston Evening Post* offered the perspective of the city's ministers and elite when it commented, "Were you to see him in his most violent Agitations, you would be apt to think, that he was a Madman just broke from his Chains; But especially had you seen him returning from the Common after his first preaching, with a large Mob at his Heels, he with his Hands extended, his Head thrown back, and his Eyes staring up to Heaven, attended with so much Disorder, that they look'd more like a Company of *Bacchanalians* after a mad Frolick, than sober Christians who had been worshipping God. . . ."[25] Davenport attracted the poor, indentured servants, seamen, even slaves, and told them, as Whitefield had done, that they could attain their own salvation without the assistance of ministers, merchants, or other members of the upper class.

But Davenport was not finished. He returned to Connecticut in 1743 and focused his efforts on the seaport town of New London. Here, he took advantage of a widespread discontent with the Congregational ministry and a population that had already been "awakened" by a visit from Tennent in 1741. Again, Davenport preached outdoors, and Old Lights complained about his followers parading through the streets at night singing loudly. Music, in fact, had become one of Davenport's favorite emotional tools—but not the traditional Puritan psalms. Rather, he encouraged songs that were more Christocentric and decidedly otherworldly in their implications. As before, he preached extemporaneously and in a style his opponents considered vulgar: "His *Gestures* in preaching are *Theatrical,* his *Voice tumultuous,* his whole Speech and Behavior discovering the *Freaks of Madness,* and wilds of "Enthusiasm."[26]

Then came his crowning achievement. Davenport arrived in New London on March 2. On March 6, the Sabbath, he presided over a bonfire that devoured dozens of books, including Puritan classics by such ministers as Increase Mather and Benjamin Colman. The next day, he built another bonfire of "wigs, cloaks and breeches, Hoods, Gowns, Rings, Jewels and Necklaces. . . ."[27] The whole experience seemed like a nightmare to the Old Lights, and Davenport immediately left town and expressed penitent shock at his own behavior. He ultimately recanted all of his revivalistic activities and settled down to a less obtrusive ministerial career.

Frightened by Davenport and by the spread of the revival in the eastern portion of the colony, the Connecticut Assembly passed legislation in 1742 and 1743 forbidding uninvited ministers to preach in parishes under threat of fines and even expulsion from the colony. The laws also instituted a requirement that all ministers have degrees from Harvard or Yale and forbade separatist preachers from baptizing or presiding at weddings—indeed, some were jailed for overseeing marriage ceremonies in their own churches. The colony also removed justices of the peace who did not enforce the legislation and denied legally elected New Light supporters their assembly seats. Still, the laity of eastern Connecticut did not lessen their commitment to the revival. The courts jailed dozens in Windham County for refusing to pay rates to support the established churches in their towns.

One of the principal results of the Awakening, ironically, was to *increase* the amount of contention and dissent within New England religious society. Ministers commonly complained of the divisive contention that arose within their communities and churches. Ultimately, the only recourse left to those struck by the spirit of the revival and saddled with an unsympathetic minister was to form their own congregation. And, appropriately, one of the Awakening's more impressive legacies was the emergence of a large number of such Separatist churches. New Lights formed their own congregations during the 1740s, then found themselves disagreeing over the issue of infant baptism during the 1750s—those who rejected the concept either joined Baptist congregations or formed new parishes yet again. By the 1770s, there were more than 120 Separatist congregations in New England. Amidst contention and disagreement, voluntarism emerged as the dominant principle New England churches. Individuals grew increasingly confident in their ability to determine their own religious beliefs. In a few short years, they would acquire the same confidence in shaping their political futures.

The formation of the Sturbridge, Massachusetts, Baptist Church exemplifies the post-Awakening separation process. The church's Old Light minister, Rev. Caleb Rice, had barred Whitefield and other itinerants from his pulpit, and in November 1747, the parish's dissidents decided they had had enough and applied for separation. Like other Baptists and Quakers of southeast Worcester County, these people were generally prosperous artisans excluded from the county elite; none, for instance, ever became justices of the peace. Closely tied to the region's emerging commercial economy, they chafed under the economic control maintained by the Old Light establishment. They, too, would eventually seek greater political and economic control over their own lives.

Such developments were particularly upsetting to the rationalist preachers who were beginning to fill many New England pulpits, particularly those in the commercial port towns, who stressed order, balance, morality, and duty in their preaching. These ministers questioned the ability of the lower class to fully appreciate the message of Christ. As Jonathan Mayhew put it, "Those of the lower class can go but a little way with their inquiries into the natural and moral constitution of the world."[28] Charles Chauncey emerged as the group's principal spokesman and critic of the Awakening, attacking Edwards's contention that this was a true work of God. Edwards argued that God worked *through* the emotions to effect salvation; Chauncey felt otherwise. His description of an Awakening service in his antirevival tract *Seasonable Thoughts* (1743) appropriately dramatizes the rationalists' fears: "Shriekings and Screamings; convulsion-like Tremblings and Agitations, Strugglings and Tumblings, which in some Instances have been attended with Indecencies I shan't mention."[29] The revivals seemed only to promote promiscuity and destroy property, "to make all things common, *wives* as well as *goods*."[30]

Yet it is misleading to read the Awakening solely in such terms. When young John Cleaveland of Canterbury, Connecticut, entered Yale, he brought with him a heritage of Calvinistic, lay-oriented Puritanism. His commitment to these beliefs only deepened when he heard Whitefield, Edwards, Tennent, and Davenport all preach there. Yale's rector, Rev. Thomas Clap, reacted angrily and firmly against the revival and forbade students to attend meetings with those who had separated from the local New Haven church. Cleaveland struggled to resolve the conflict between his spiritual needs and his academic ambitions. Family, community, and spiritual longing won out; Clap expelled Cleaveland from Yale for attending a Separatist meeting while at home during term break. Now unqualified to preach in Connecticut, Cleaveland eventually found a spiritual home in Chebacco, a district of Ipswich, Massachusetts. His new congregation had supported the Awakening and separated from the main parish. These men and women were religious moderates leading modest lives in an isolated rural environment. Cleaveland stressed conversionism and lay participation and based his evangelical ministry solidly upon the rock of predestination. It was a pure church ideal that prevailed in many other small parishes scattered about the New England landscape, one that reminds us of the inertial power of tradition in many New England byways. The extremes of enthusiasm that so frightened Chauncey and others were far removed from the sober religiosity that guided the people of Chebacco.

Revivalism In The South

By mid-century, Virginia's gentry had built a patriarchal society that ruled over a seemingly stable, prosperous society. The Anglican church was an integral part of this system, and on the surface, it seemed to function smoothly as one of many venues for the gentry to parade and assert their social superiority. Beneath these calm waters, however, deeper currents of unrest were threatening to break through to the surface.

One area of contention centered around the clergy. Anglican ministers sought to become more professionalized—to gain better salaries and greater security and to enhance their professional status through more frequent ministerial conventions. They rejected the assembly's right to adjust their salaries as it saw fit and chafed under the repressive control of local planters. The clergy first voiced their concerns during the clericalist movement of the mid- and late-1750s, appealing in vain to the House of Burgesses to help attract more educated and disciplined ministers by raising salaries.

The laity formed a second area of stress. Even in the Chesapeake, small planters and the poor did not docilely accept their social positions. The planter class may have successfully imposed political and social control over them and certainly the vast majority of poorer whites embraced the racism that held Chesapeake society together. But these same people did not so readily accede to the lack of prominence their own religion accorded them. They complained about the shortage of clergy, the distance they had to travel to church buildings, and the formalistic services the gentry demanded and the ministry readily provided. Indeed, the majority of the poor rarely attended services. Gentry and ministry had to face the growing diversity of Virginia's population, as immigrants moved down the western valleys to settle in the backcountry.

Whitefield had preached in Williamsburg in December 1739 to little effect. The first real signs of a revival came in Hanover County, Virginia, in 1743, when a group of ordinary people (nongentry) "began reading religious tracts and absenting themselves from church."[31] The small group soon built a meetinghouse to accommodate their rapidly growing membership; their leader, the brick-layer Samuel Morris, began to receive invitations to preach elsewhere in the colony. In mid-1743, a Presbyterian missionary from a Scotch-Irish settlement in the southwestern part of the colony preached to the group, and from then on, they identified themselves as Presbyterian. Revivalists now began to preach to larger meetings, warning their listeners of the decay of the church and clergy. Only when the groups got still larger did the authorities denounce itinerancy, and only in 1745 did the burgesses bring a few dissenting laymen to Williamsburg for trial and fine them "for unlawful assembly."

Then Samuel Davies appeared upon the scene. Davies received a license to preach in 1747 and established four meetinghouses in Hanover County. At first, even Gov. William Gooch described him as "dignified and courteous in manner."[32] The gentry, though, expressed alarm about the growth of itinerancy and dissent, and in 1750, the council revoked a license for a new meetinghouse in New Kent County. It argued that the English Toleration Act did not extend to the colonies,

❧ *Documents* ❧
The Revival in the South

The revival in the southern colonies occurred later and was less general than in New England or the middle colonies. It nonetheless aroused equal levels of enthusiasm among the converted and equally powerful fears among the elite. The first excerpt, from the journal of Charles Woodmason, an Anglican missionary who spent six years traveling through the backcountry, describes the actions of itinerant preachers in the South Carolina backcountry. The second selection provides a vivid description of an extreme gentry reaction in Virginia.

> Tis these roving teachers that stir up the minds of the people against the Established Church and her ministers and make the situation of any gentleman extremely uneasy, vexatious, and disagreeable. I would sooner starve in England on a curacy of 20 per annum than to live here on two hundred guineas, did not the interests of religion and the Church absolutely require it. I find them a set of rhapsodists, enthusiasts, bigots; pedantic, illiterate, impudent hypocrites, straining at gnats and swallowing camels, and making religion a cloak for covetousness, detraction, guile, impostures, and their particular fabric of things.

Charles Woodmason, *The Carolina Backcountry on the Eve of the Revolution: The Journal and Other Writings of Charles Woodmason, American Itinerant,* Richard J. Hooker, ed. (Chapel Hill: IEAHC, University of North Carolina Press, 1953), 42.

despite an opinion to the contrary from the Lords of Trade. Davies himself probably helped deflate the issue a bit through his personal charm and his avoidance of extremes. The burgesses were still relatively unconcerned and seemed to have been more permissive than their counterparts on the council.

Presbyterians eventually became more acceptable, and respectable, after the emergence of an even more serious threat, the Baptists. Gentry culture stressed personal honor, self-assertion, pride, physical courage, and a social life that revolved around drinking, gambling, and dancing—all designed to impress the superiority of their values onto the rest of the population. On court, election, and muster days and in church on Sundays, they proudly paraded their social and personal superiority.

The Baptists created what historian Rhys Isaac has aptly termed a counterculture during the 1760s and 1770s. They lived in a solemn fellowship in comparative equality, and members addressed each other as "brother" and "sister." Theirs was an emotionally supportive community, in stark contrast to the competitive aggressiveness of gentry culture. Baptist preachers emerged from obscurity and led their congregations in a life that stressed austere sobriety and called upon church members to reform their conduct and reject meaningless affluence and violence. Guilt was a major component of this culture. Members were expected to internalize true Christian values and norms, and they embraced even slaves as brothers and sisters—

Brother Waller Informed us . . . [that] about 2 Weeks ago on the Sabbath day Down in Caroline County he Introduced the Worship of God by Singing [.] . . . While he was Singing the Parson of the Parish [who had ridden up with his clerk, the sheriff, and some others] would Keep Running the End of his Horsewhip in [Waller's] Mouth, Laying his Whip across the Hum Book, &c. . When done Singing [Waller] proceeded to Prayer. In it he was Violently jerked off of the Stage, [they] Caught him by the Back part of his Neck [,] Beat his head against the ground, some Times Up [,] Sometimes down, they Carried him through a Gate that stood some Considerable Distance, where a Gentleman [the sheriff] Give him. . . Twenty Lashes with his Horse Whip. . . . The B[rother] Waller was Released, Went Back Singing praise to God, Mounted the Stage & preached with a Great Deal of Liberty.

Quoted in Rhys Isaac, *The Transformation of Virginia, 1740–1790* (Chapel Hill, NC: IEAHC, University of North Carolina Press, 1982), 162–3.

a belief that truly threatened the Chesapeake hierarchy. By 1774, as much as 10 percent of the population worshipped at fifty-four Baptist churches—not an impressive figure until one contemplates the dramatic challenge that the Baptists' culture presented to the violent, affluent world of the gentry. They were concentrated primarily on the frontier—in the Piedmont to the west of Alexandria and Fredericksburg and in the newer areas along the North Carolina border. These were the fastest growing areas of the colony and those most in need of social control. They also tended to have less extreme divisions of wealth than the older tidewater regions, and the gentry were less able to immediately impose their discipline on this society.

By the time of the Revolution, dissenters of all sorts outnumbered Anglicans in Virginia. The threat they represented to the controlled, hierarchical world of the gentry forced the upper class to look inward. Facing economic depression and British intervention in their political lives, the chastened planters adopted a more private, less ostentatious life-style. In doing so, they effectively answered the dissenters' attack on their privileged status.

The Awakening caused barely a ripple in the rest of the south, but it is worth noting again the brief surge of evangelicism that did pass over South Carolina. Inspired by Whitefield and supported by Jonathan Bryan and his brothers, the

Miller Creek (or Mauck's) Meeting House in Delaware—a German or Separate Baptist Church. ❧

revival in Carolina's southern county stirred as much fear as it had farther north. Planters welcomed evangelical preachers at first but became alarmed when they heard their message—a rejection of established churches and educated, ordained ministers—and frightened when they witnessed the appeal such preachers had for the common people. Whitefield maintained that Carolina society rested upon a bed of corruption: "Anyone who has lived in London may have seen and heard some abominations; but [in South Carolina] they have reached the highest peak."[33] The fault, he argued, lay with slavery and the horrible treatment whites accorded blacks. We have seen how the Carolina gentry quickly moved to suppress such ideas. Perhaps because the threat was less portentous, they proved unwilling to make the kinds of changes their Virginia neighbors had embraced.

The Great Awakening was the most obvious expression of a far-reaching cultural struggle in the eighteenth-century colonies. Drawing strength from a disgruntled laity buffeted by disruptive social and economic change, the revival reflected a deeply felt need for social cohesion and the lost comforts of an emotionally satisfying communal life. At the same time, it clearly encouraged a sense of individualism and a questioning of traditional authority. Perhaps these seemingly contradictory explanations can be resolved by viewing the Awakening as a struggle between laity and clergy, between the more spontaneous, physical expressions of popular culture and the more controlled, disciplined, and rational preaching of an American elite that was moving closer to its European counterpart. It was at once a last, failed attempt to restore the harmony of traditional society and a gateway to the secular liberalism of the modern world.

The Awakening also furthered the emergence of a religious landscape that was far more diverse and complex than its counterpart of a century earlier. No colony

Interior view of Miller Creek Meeting House in Delaware. ❧

retained an effective religious establishment; the proliferation of sects reflected the growing diversity of the population itself. Economics, residence, and now even religion divided Americans and often set them in conflict against each other. Revivalism was one attempt to counter these divisions, but it brought only temporary respite while further eroding the unifying power of religion. Americans at mid-century were still seeking some common belief that would help bind a splintering society and offer a coherent explanation of the changes rapidly coursing through their lives.

❧ *Chapter Eleven* ❧

Political Culture
in the
American Colonies

By the 1750s, the American colonies possessed a political culture that reflected a growing uniformity of experience, practice, and belief, a culture that was also part of a broader Anglo-American political system. Colonists believed their government was explicitly based on the English constitution, an unwritten framework widely praised for its uniquely successful balance of monarchy, nobility, and the people. By themselves, each of these elements—represented by the king, the House of Lords, and the House of Commons—would tend to tyranny. An overbearing monarchy would lead to despotism; an overpowerful Lords, to oligarchy; a dominant Commons, to mob rule. In the British system, each checked the other, preserving to an unparalleled degree the benefits of liberty for English people across the world. Underlying it all was a belief in the paternalistic, personal basis of authority. The family provided the model; the king was father to his people, and his subjects owed him the same obedience as children owed their parents.

As the century progressed, American colonists began to drift away from this monarchical conception of government. Patriarchal leaders failed to address pressing economic and social concerns, and colonists turned to participatory politics in search of solutions. The pursuit of self-interest became more common, but it was constrained by ideals of community and public interest. Colonists began to construct their own political language, the language of republicanism. They drew upon a diverse and potentially explosive range of intellectual and moral influences, and they developed a political ideology distinct from the traditional language of patriarchal government.

Significant Dates

1691	John Locke publishes *Two Treatises on Government*
1705	England expands list of enumerated goods
1711	First White Pines Act
	Boston women raid Andrew Belcher's warehouse
1714–27	Reign of George I
1714, 1720	Attempts to establish Massachusetts land banks
1720	Trenchard and Gordon begin publishing *Cato's Letters*
1727–60	Reign of George II
1732	Hat and Felt Act
1733	John Peter Zenger trial
	Molasses Act
1740	Massachusetts Land Bank
	New London Society for Trade and Commerce
1747	Boston impressment riot
1750	Iron Act
1752	Pistole fee controversy
1753	Susquehanna Company established
1755, 1758	Twopenny Acts

British Background

The reality of British politics differed from its ideal. Though Parliament had become sovereign with the Glorious Revolution, the king retained considerable influence and real power. He chose his own ministers and exerted significant legislative influence. He also dispensed considerable patronage through peerages and government and church positions and actively interfered in the affairs of the House of Commons. The House of Lords continued to speak for the interests of the British nobility. And though political theory suggested that the Commons represented the interests of ordinary English men and women, its members often came from the same social background as the Lords. They were often members of the landed gentry, lesser nobles who served as justices of the peace and were an integral part of the British ruling class. In 1761, more than half of the members of the Commons were related to the upper aristocracy.

The House of Commons had 558 members—eighty knights of the shire from forty counties, four representatives from Oxford and Cambridge, and 405 members from 203 cities and towns. Of these, the Crown directly controlled 30 percent to 35 percent, and it could readily influence another 40 percent or so by appealing to patriotism and the glorious empire. Two-hundred and ninety-three of these representatives lived in districts with fewer than five hundred voters, and only a few districts had enough voters to create real political contests. The wealthy used bribery and patronage to control the outcome of contests in these districts; so-called pocket boroughs were small enough to remain "in the pocket" of a single person or family. The Duke of Newcastle controlled seven such pocket boroughs. The Crown freely used its extensive patronage powers to exert a decisive influence on the outcome of many elections. Representation in the Commons was also extremely uneven. London and the newer industrial areas of the north were dramatically underrepresented or not represented at all, while areas of shrinking population continued to receive the same representation they had been allotted centuries earlier (these were known as rotten boroughs). One borough had six voters choosing two representatives, while the rapidly growing industrial town of Manchester had none.

A labyrinthian bureaucracy governed the empire itself, and its policies reflected the relative power of political and economic interests in Britain. Mercantilism was the only unifying theory, emphasizing the complete subordination of the colonies to the mother country. Yet the colonies produced a tremendous amount of wealth for the empire, and men such as Robert Walpole were reluctant to disrupt the flow of trade and specie. As chief cabinet minister under George I and George II from 1721 to 1742, Walpole developed a policy historians have dubbed "salutary neglect." He believed it would be foolhardy to kill the goose that laid the golden egg—to disrupt the flow of colonial wealth for the sake of the few pounds sterling to be gained by enforcing the Navigation Acts more rigidly. Distance further weakened British power and the ability of colonial governors to enforce the imperial will.

Parliament was particularly reluctant to become involved in the internal administration of the colonies, preferring to concentrate on regulating trade and colonial economic activity. Thus, the Board of Trade alone bore the brunt of policy and enforcement responsibilities, and it coordinated the involvement of other agencies, such as the treasury and admiralty boards. Unfortunately, political appointees dominated the Board of Trade, and their general ignorance of American conditions mirrored that of Parliament.

Not everyone in Parliament agreed with Walpole's policy. The Board of Trade consistently pushed for more rigorous enforcement of colonial trade legislation, and the government began to listen after 1748. Before then, the board succeeded in convincing Parliament to pass only a few measures. The government expanded the list of enumerated goods to include tar, turpentine, hemp, masts, and other naval stores in 1705 and added copper and furs in 1722. The White Pines Act of 1711 (expanded in 1722 and 1729) prohibited the colonists from felling any whites pines on public lands, reserving the trees for use as masts by the British navy. It proved all but impossible to enforce. The Hat and Felt Act of 1732, which sought to protect the slumping British hat industry, prohibited the export of hats from the colonies and established stringent regulations for their production. The Sugar Act of 1733 placed prohibitively high duties on imported rum, molasses, and sugar in an effort to stop the illegal trade between New England and the French West Indies. The colonists ignored the legislation with impunity. Finally, Parliament passed the Iron Act of 1750 to protect the iron manufacturing industry of the Midlands. The act removed British duties on American pig and bar iron, but it forbade the construction of any more American slitting mills, plating forges, and steel furnaces. The colonists were not really ready to produce finished iron products on a large scale, and they profited from the stimulus to the production of unwrought iron. By 1776, they were producing more than thirty thousand tons annually.

The ineffective morass that passed for colonial regulation meant that by mid-century, there were really three constitutions in the empire: one for the central British state and its immediate dependencies, another for the provinces, and yet another for the empire in general. The last was largely undefined and failed to specify the distribution of authority between the center (London) and the peripheries (for example, North America). While parliamentary power was in theory unlimited, its implementation was in practice constricted. The colonists had developed an attitude toward parliamentary rule based on a theory of "customary restraints," which assumed people could ultimately limit *all* sorts of power. They believed that only English common law and parliamentary laws that specifically mentioned the colonies applied to them.

Structures Of American Government

The colonial governor occupied the key position in the administration of this empire. Given the vast distances involved and the inherent communication difficulties, the person who bridged the gap between England and the colonies bore burdensome responsibilities indeed. He was, ostensibly, the most powerful and most visible representative of royal authority in the colony he ruled; socially, he was the physical embodiment of the system of dependency and patronage that dominated British politics. At the same time, he had to be acutely aware of the particular needs of the colony if he were to achieve any political success at all, and he had to parry the ambitions of a colonial elite that was rapidly growing in wealth and self-confidence. The office thus called for extraordinary talents in politics and diplomacy. Unfortunately, these qualities often did not figure in the selection process. Colonial governors were chosen through a system that emphasized political connections above all other qualifications. The governor's tenure, moreover, hinged completely on the fortunes of his patron in England. A decline in that individual's influence, a change of administration at Whitehall, or even successful intriguing by the governor's enemies in the colony or in England could abruptly end his tenure. Occasionally, this process resulted in the selection of outstanding administrators. More commonly, the governors were simply competent or mediocre.

A few brief examples will illustrate the nature of the problem. George Clinton, governor of New York from 1743 to 1753, was perhaps typical. He was an inept naval officer who was given a governorship to get him out of England. He ignored the needs of the colony during his term of office, preferring to retire to his country home whenever possible. Sir Danvers Osborn succeeded Clinton, and he committed suicide one week after his arrival. Sir William Phips (1691–1694), the first royal governor of Massachusetts in the late seventeenth century, had a true rags-to-riches story. Born in the colonies as the twenty-sixth child of his mother, he worked as a boy as a shepherd and then a ship's carpenter. His fortunes changed when he married a rich widow and discovered a sunken treasure. The king later knighted him and appointed him to his post, where he served with minimal distinction. Jonathan Belcher became governor of Massachusetts in 1730 through the influence of Robert Walpole's brother-in-law. He was forced out in 1741 because his successor, William Shirley (1741–1757), was acquainted with the Duke of Newcastle (Secretary of State for the Southern Department of the Board of Trade) and was able to take advantage of an active anti-Belcher movement in England. Shirley was one of the few success stories; able to forge a wide-ranging coalition with the help of extensive war contracts, he successfully negotiated his way through the mines of early Massachusetts politics for almost two decades.

Some governors ruled in more than one colony. Sir Edmund Andros began his American career in New York, moved on to preside over the short-lived Dominion of New England, and then served as governor of Virginia. Sir Francis Nicholson was governor of five different colonies. Many governors never came to the colony to

Edward Hyde, Lord Cornbury. ✰

which they were appointed, preferring to pay part of their salary to a lieutenant to govern for them. The Earl of Orkney served as governor of Virginia from 1705 to 1737 without setting foot in the colony. Some, finally, had their own unique claim to fame. Edward Hyde, Viscount Cornbury (1702–1708) did all he could as governor to encourage the growth of the Anglican Church in New York, and he granted hundreds of thousands of acres of land to his political cronies. He is best remembered, though, for making public appearances—and having his official portrait painted—in the garb of his cousin, Queen Anne. William Smith, Jr. later noted, "It was not uncommon for him to dress himself in a woman's habit and then to patrole the fort in which he resided. Such freaks of low humour exposed him to the universal contempt of the people."[1]

Governors were appointed by the king in royal colonies and by proprietors in proprietary colonies; they were elected by popular vote in the two corporate colonies of Rhode Island and Connecticut. Governors' legal powers were extremely broad, surpassing even those of the Crown in the British government. They could call and dismiss the legislature and veto all acts without being overruled. They served as commander-in-chief of the military and naval forces and could appoint subordinate officers. They were a member, with the council, of the colony's highest court and could grant pardons and reprieves to criminals. They could appoint and dismiss judges, justices of the peace, and other officers. They were responsible for regulating the colony's trade according to the Navigation Laws, for conducting all diplomatic affairs, and for exercising supervisory power over religion.

In practice, this imposing authority was severely limited in a variety of ways. Naval commanders tended to ignore the governor and the colony's courts, and after 1702, the governors lost all control over the activities of royal ships in their waters. After 1755, a British military commander-in-chief controlled all military decisions and powers. The governors' lack of patronage power was even more critical. British social and political thought stressed the importance of the master-dependent relationship between ruler and ruled, gentry and commoner. Kings and governors were, in this view, fathers who cared for their children in a loving, paternal way. In England, extensive patronage powers supported the king's use of this authority. Colonial governors lacked any significant appointing powers. London retained the more prestigious and lucrative royal positions as patronage plums, and after 1752, Lord Halifax distributed all colonial patronage, except those positions controlled directly by the treasury and admiralty boards. Finally, colonial assemblies secured control over several important positions during the course of the eighteenth century. Governors had no pocket boroughs, no assembly seats "owned" by the administration.

Governors' instructions allowed them little flexibility. There were two sets: one for general matters and one for trade. By the eighteenth century, there were more than a hundred such instructions, drawn up mostly by the Board of Trade, approved by the secretary of state and the Privy Council, and endorsed by the king. The colonists tended to see these instructions as general guidelines for the governors and assumed they would be overlooked in certain situations. Particularly after 1760, the Crown viewed them as having the force of law.

The colonial councils, which had seven to twelve members, were less essential to the governing process. The council was appointed or elected, depending on the particular colonial charter, and theoretically possessed extensive judicial and legislative powers. All bills required its consent, and it served as the colony's supreme court. The council also had concurrent power with the governor in many of his duties, such as the granting of lands and the appointment of lesser officials. Council members were generally wealthy colonials, often with substantial economic ties to England, whose personal and political ambitions encouraged cooperation with the governor. Unwilling to question imperial policy, they found their powers emasculated by the growing dominance of the colonial assemblies.

For the most part, the elected assemblies embodied the political beliefs and wishes of the colonial population. London claimed that all colonial representative bodies exercised power only at the sufferance of the Crown and were in no way comparable to the Commons. The colonists insisted that their assemblies existed by virtue of inherent British rights, in turn guaranteed by the colonial charters, and that their legislative procedures and powers were the same as those of the House of Commons. All colonial legislatures followed the same general procedural rules. The assembly speaker dominated the sessions and appointed committees, which in turn controlled the power structure. Bills passed through three readings; if approved, they were sent on to the council for its action. If the two houses failed to agree, a conference committee of three members from each would attempt to iron out the differences. When the governor signed it, the bill became law. The only significant exception to this procedure was with bills that were required to contain a suspending clause; that is, if a bill was of questionable legality, such a clause suspended the

❧ *Documents* ❧
A Delicate Balance

The first selection, from the *Journals* of the House of Representatives in Massachusetts, is the House's response to a request from Gov. William Burnet for a fixed salary. It reflects the representatives' belief in the importance of the colony's charter for preserving the delicate balance of constitutional power in the colony. The second selection, from the Pennsylvania Assembly, is a more detailed explanation of a similar belief that also reflects the continued importance of patriarchy in colonial political thinking.

> Therefore we conceive that it is against the Design of Power vested in us by the CHARTER to pass any Acts pursuant to the Instruction Your Excellency has laid before us, foreasmuch as passing such Acts. . . has a direct tendency to weaken if not destroy our happy Constitution, by giving away the great and almost only Privilege that gives weight to the House of Representatives, which is the making Grants of Moneys as the Exigencies of Affairs requires. . . .

Journals of the House of Representatives of Massachusetts, 55 vols. (Boston: The Riverside Press, 1919–1980), 8:279.

> If therefore the Freeborn Subjects of *England* have this Right [to grant moneys], we have it by our Charter, and our Laws. And if we

law until the Crown approved it. Except in Rhode Island and Connecticut, all laws required final approval by the Privy Council, and even in those two colonies, appeals could be heard in London.

As the eighteenth century progressed, almost all of the colonial assemblies increased their powers and brought their status closer to that of the House of Commons. Even in the seventeenth century, the lower houses had begun to lay claim to the traditional rights of English legislatures: the right of free discussion on the house floor, members' immunity from arrest while in session, and the right to make their own procedural rules, to settle contested elections, and to elect their own speaker. They now successfully claimed the right to initiate money bills, and in several colonies, the council lost its right to amend such bills. To varying degrees, the legislatures also gained the right to appoint important colonial officials, such as the treasurer and the attorney general, the power to control the disbursement of public funds and their auditing, and the right to conduct military and Indian affairs.

Most assemblies also won the battle to control the governors' salaries. The British demanded a locally derived permanent revenue for all royal governors; in Maryland and Virginia, governors were paid by a tax on tobacco exports. Elsewhere, the assemblies successfully resisted royal pressure and voted the governors an annual salary. At times, they were able to withhold this salary to pressure

had it not by our Charter and Laws, we should nevertheless have it; for the Freeborn Subjects of *England* do not lose their essential Rights by removing into the King's Plantations, extending the *British* Dominions at the Hazard of their Lives and Fortunes, and encreasing the Power, Wealth, and Commerce of their Mother Country; they have, on the contrary, particular Privileges justly granted and added to their native Rights, for their Encouragement in so useful and meritorious an Undertaking. . . . In one Thing, indeed, it is our Misfortune, that our Constitution differs from that of *England*. The King has a natural Connection with his Subjects. The Crown descends to his Posterity; and the more his People prosper and flourish, the greater is in the Power, Wealth, Strength, and Security of his Family and Descendants. But Plantation Governors are frequently transient Persons, of broken Fortunes, greedy of Money, without any Regard to the People, or natural Concern for their Interests, often their Enemies, and endeavoring not only to oppress but defame them. . . .

Pennsylvania Archives (1852–1935) 8th ser., vol. 5, 4176–77, reprinted in Jack P. Greene, ed., *Settlements to Society, 1607–1763: A Documentary History of Colonial America* (New York: W. W. Norton and Company, 1975 [c. 1966]), 367–8.

governors to compromise or give in on certain crucial issues. The colonists believed that the lower house had to protect itself from the corrupting influence of the governor and at the same time keep the governor properly dependent upon it, thus assuring the proper balance suggested by the English constitution.

Broad public support backed the assemblies' powers. The franchise was generally based on land ownership, and land was abundant in America. Throughout the colonies, 50 percent to 80 percent of adult white males could vote. In New England, a man only needed to own land taxable at forty shillings—a modest requirement met by the majority of the male inhabitants. In Pennsylvania, Maryland, and Delaware, the requirement was only fifty acres of land; in New Jersey, land or property valued at fifty pounds. In Virginia, one hundred acres of unsettled or twenty-five acres of settled land sufficed, while in North Carolina and Georgia, it was fifty acres of settled or unsettled land. New York mandated a freehold of forty pounds, while South Carolina required ownership of three hundred acres of land or other real estate valued at sixty pounds in local currency, which was liberalized in 1759 to ownership of one hundred acres or payment of an annual tax of ten shillings. Over time, inflation eased even these requirements in all the colonies.

But this was not a democratic society, at least not in the sense that we use the term today. The concept of deference dominated social and political values in eighteenth-century America. Deference denoted an acceptance on the part of ordinary colonists that their social and economic superiors possessed both better skills of governance and the economic well-being to make independent political judgments, free from the lures of bribery or other corrupting influences. This did not mean that people simply followed whatever decisions their representatives made. Voters often instructed their representatives on how to vote on specific issues or voted them out of office when they ignored their constituents' wishes.

Still, colonial politicians were a class apart. They proved themselves in lower-level offices before moving up to the assembly, and they were differentiated from the rest of the population by their wealth, family connections, education, and other measures of social status. Southern political leaders tended to be the most elitist. A small number of families dominated Virginia politics and monopolized the most powerful and remunerative offices—the Fitzhughs, Randolphs, Byrds, Carters, Cookes, Harrisons, Lees, and Washingtons. Many seats in the South Carolina legislature stayed in the same family for generations—in 1760, 55 percent of the assembly were grandsons, sons, or brothers of former members. The situation in New England was a bit more complicated. In small towns, most eligible males held some office, while in larger towns, a much smaller percentage of eligible voters controlled political affairs. There were also two types of leaders in New England: substantial yeomen who served only a few terms in office and gained little colonywide prominence and wealthy gentlemen who dominated provincial political offices and often controlled access to the credit they provided to small yeomen farmers.

Many of these gentlemen served in county government. County courts became a common avenue of upward mobility for the colonial gentry in every region. During the eighteenth century, as colonial governments issued paper money on a large scale, the population became more mobile, and intertown disputes were more common, local vehicles of conflict resolution broke down. The courts became the logical place to turn. By mid-century, the clear outlines of a specialized legal profession began to appear, and more careful attention was paid to the details of court procedure. In seventeenth-century Connecticut, merchant-storekeepers simply brought their ledgers to court, and the justice compared the entries with the claims of the defendant. Now, debt litigation became technical and formalistic, following strict guidelines and uniform procedures and ignoring individual characteristics of the case.

While deference prevailed throughout this system, colonists still felt justified in protesting the actions of their leaders, even in taking control of the situation if circumstances so dictated. In most cases, this meant electing or defeating representatives depending upon their stand on particular issues. Increasingly during the eighteenth century, people also acted collectively within a long-standing Anglo-American tradition of extralegal political action. Rural land riots occurred in several northern colonies, with the most violent and bitter arising in New Jersey over complex title problems. There were even occasional food riots. The women of Boston took to the streets in 1711, taking much-needed grain from Andrew Belcher's warehouse and accusing the merchant of hoarding it for greater profits in the intercolonial market. In their view, Belcher was ignoring his primary obligation of maintaining the health and well-being of his own community.

The best-known such incident occurred in Boston in November 1747, when Commodore Charles Knowles attempted to impress Bay colonists into the British navy. Impressment was a common practice throughout the empire. It involved British military commanders "volunteering" unsuspecting (and often drunk) citizens for service in His Majesty's army or navy. High desertion rates in the British navy (due to the terrible conditions) and the growing demands of the mid-century intercolonial wars made British and American ports common sites of such events.

American colonists never took kindly to the practice; Massachusetts passed a law in 1707 that prohibited the impressment of any of its citizens, which the British refused to recognize, and Bostonians resisted violently several times during the 1740s. This time, when the press gangs marched through town grabbing ship-builders, servants, slaves, and any other unfortunates who happened to be in the wrong place at the wrong time, a huge crowd gathered in opposition. Suddenly, the hunters became the hunted. The town's sheriff and deputies were attacked, the militia refused to obey orders by Governor Shirley to put down the uprising, and a royal barge was burned in front of the governor's house. While the town's conserv-ative citizens portrayed the incident as the actions of "Foreign Seamen, Servants, Negroes, and other Persons of Mean and vile Condition. . . ,"[2] the crowd's leaders defended their actions as their legal and "natural right." They attacked the wealthy leaders of the House of Representatives for failing to protect the rights of the colonists and caring more about their own riches than for the rights of the people. As we will see, this implied conflict between poor and rich had become an impor-tant component of Massachusetts politics. Here and in other colonies, it foreshad-owed the decay of deferential politics and the rise of a more modern notion of political and social equality.

English government was largely limited to maintaining order and conducting war and foreign affairs; all other issues were left in private hands. American colo-nial governments were far more interventionist and participatory, and leaders were expected to respond to the needs of the community. But there was another, more emotionally explosive component of colonial political culture that seems almost alien from our twentieth-century perspective. Americans perceived their world with-in a uniquely moral framework. Colonists reacted to governors' vetoes, restrictive British legislation, impressment, and a host of other secular events with a sense of fear and moral urgency that bears closer examination.

Republican Ideology

During the seventeenth century, religion shaped the daily perceptions of most Europeans and Americans. Religion orders experience. It gives meaning to reality and legitimizes social arrangements, ensuring their continuance by requiring certain behaviors. Most important, religion promises an emotional, transcendental experi-ence, personal contact with the sacred. This spirituality provides the ultimate sense of security for individuals confronting the chaos of the world.

Ideology serves many of the same purposes. It, too, provides people with a portrait of their social world and their place in it, with a set of assumptions that define the parameters of their identity and their external world. Ideology differs from religion in its essentially secular orientation. Ideologies offer a sociopolitical program that promises to transform society into a utopia and to unify disparate groups under a common belief, such as patriotism. In most cases, ideologies cannot escape the tenacious hold of the religious past; they use much of the same lan-guage and continue to offer the same hope of communion with the sacred. The ideology of civic humanism, or classical republicanism, that unified eighteenth-century Americans offered such assurances. Colonists at every level of society embraced its beliefs in pamphlets, private papers, and newspapers. Artisans, entre-preneurs, merchants, planters, and farmers discovered in its portrait of the eighteenth-century world a persuasive explanation of the moral failings of contem-porary society. At the same time, each of these groups interpreted this ideology in its own way, their use and understanding of its language shaped by their own particular social and economic worlds.

The North American colonists were the most literate people in the Western world. Through pamphlets, newspapers, and private correspondence, Americans gained a widespread awareness of world affairs. In schools and churches, moreover, they received and interpreted messages about the nature of man, society, and politics that helped shape their distinctive world view. The Greek and Roman classics profoundly influenced educated colonists, particularly such writers as Cicero and Tacitus who stressed the corruption of the Roman Empire as opposed to the virtue, simplicity, and liberty of the earlier republic.

Enlightenment radicalism was another crucial influence. Montesquieu and his admiration of British liberty and the unique genius of the mixed British constitution, Voltaire and his writing on church oppression, Grotius and Pufendorf on natural law—all were significant influences on colonial thought. Puritanism continued to influence Americans even into the eighteenth century, particularly through its oft-transformed vision of the New World as a special place, the site of a unique divine mission to the world's sinful people. Equally formative was its tendency to view the world in Manichean terms—in rigid divisions of good and evil.

The many writers who composed the civic humanist tradition were still more important. A number of Italian authors, including Nicolai Machiavelli, sought to understand and explain the instability of republics in history. Inevitably, it seemed to these writers, governments of virtuous, politically involved citizens were ravaged all too quickly by corruption and self-interest. These authors developed a conception of human nature and government that sought to preserve republican experiments, islands of universal principles (virtue, or *virtù*), against the ravages of particular time (corruption, or *fortuna*). This literature, which deliberately excluded women, who were regarded as incapable of political involvement, argued that men fulfilled their humanity best in self-governing republics where citizens remained virtuous and subordinated self-interest to the public good. This was the language of republican virtue, based on the assumption that man was a political being who realized himself only in civil life. Its roots were in Aristotle and Cicero as well as in Machiavelli. Virtuous behavior came with autonomous participation in politics and self-denial in private life. Corruption emerged when the constitutional balance was upset or unearned luxury dominated the lives of the citizenry. In the end, liberty prevailed when individuals could exert virtuous control over their appetites, stemming the tide of *fortuna* that came with the predominance of private interests.

A second strain of this civic humanist tradition can be found in the writings of John Locke and other liberal thinkers. Locke provided the foundations for eighteenth- and nineteenth-century liberalism, which stressed the free pursuit of self-interest in the form of contracts between government and citizens and between individuals. Ultimately, this line of thought would result in the free-market concepts of Adam Smith, wherein the pursuit of self-interest was believed to be the only effective means of achieving the public good. In the eighteenth century, however, the power of community values and the negative connotations attached to the notion of self-interest were far too forceful to allow such untrameled liberalism to dominate; few Americans accepted the legitimacy of private interests at this time. Hence, colonists embraced Locke's philosophy more for its political implications. In his *Second Treatise on Government* (1691), Locke argued that humans had once lived in a state of nature and enjoyed natural rights such as life, liberty, and property. But even here, dangers lurked, and the inhabitants of this state soon realized they needed protection for their rights. So they formed a contract to establish a government. The contract placed obligations on both sides: the government would protect people's rights, and the people would obey the government so long as it did so. If the government failed to carry out its obligations, the people could form a new government, since they, not God, had chosen their ruler. Locke's theory rejects the patriarchal notion of authority and embraces the idea of choice that would become critical to the colonial version of republicanism.

A final strain of republican thought can perhaps be best characterized as the language of virtuous republicanism. The relevant authors included a wide range of

❧ *Documents* ❧
The Lockean Influence

Historians no longer view John Locke as the only, or even the primary, intellectual influence on the revolutionary generation. But the following excerpts indicate that the American colonists were thoroughly familiar with his contract theory of government. The first selection is from John Wise, an early eighteenth-century Ipswich, Massachusetts, minister who was widely versed in European political theory and philosophy. The second excerpt is from a well-known sermon by Jonathan Mayhew.

> Consider Man in a state of Natural Being, as a Free-Born Subject under the Crown of Heaven, and owing Homage to none but God himself. It is certain Civil Government in General, is a very Admirable Result of Providence, and an Incomparable Benefit to Man-Kind, yet must needs be acknowledged to be the Effect of Humane Free-Compacts and not of Divine Institution; it is the Produce of Mans Reason, of Humane and Rational Combinations, and not from any direct Orders of Infinite Wisdom, in any positive Law wherein is drawn up this or that Scheme of Civil Government.

John Wise, *Vindication of the Government of New-England Churches. . .* (Boston: 1717), 33.

> For, please to observe, that if the end of all civil government, be the good of society; if this be the thing that is aimed at in constituting civil rulers; and if the motive and argument for submission to government, be taken from the apparent usefulness of civil authority; it follows, that when no such good end can be answered by submission, there remains no argument or motive to enforce it; if instead of this good end's being brought about by submission, a *contrary end* is brought about, and the ruin and misery of society effected by it, here is a plain and positive reason against submission in all cases, a regard to the public welfare, ought to make us with-hold from our rulers, that obedience and subjection which it would, otherwise, be our duty to render to them.

Jonathan Mayhew, *A Discourse Concerning Unlimited Submission and Nonresistance to the Higher Powers. . .* (Boston: 1750), 29.

❧

writers in the English country-Whig tradition, such as James Harrington and Algernon Sidney from the seventeenth century and John Trenchard and Thomas Gordon, and Henry St. John, Viscount Bolingbroke from the eighteenth century. Trenchard and Gordon, particularly in their famed "Cato's Letters" and in *The Independent Whig,* are the best known of this group; their essays were widely published in American newspapers as early as the 1720s. These writers looked back nostalgically to an almost mythical past of gentlemen and yeomen farmers who were morally and economically independent. They feared the emergence of centralized power and the commercialization of English life—the rise of banks, mercantile firms, stock markets, and market-driven agriculture and the creation of a public debt. Such developments, they argued, introduced luxury, corruption, and commercial values into a virtuous English society, releasing a rampage of corruption and vice that would reduce freedom-loving English people to slavery. Armies, placemen, and excise plots were among the most visible arms of this conspiracy, led by members of the "court" faction, such as Sir Robert Walpole, who lived in luxury while enslaving the people. The forces of liberty had to bolster the English constitution and strengthen the moral fiber of the English people to resist this onslaught. Men of independent property, the "country," would provide the leadership against the corrupt "court." Such men would be ever-vigilant, aided by frequent elections and an uncorrupted electorate. Civic-minded English people must show qualities of industry, economy, temperance, and frugality, avoiding extravagance and luxury and establishing self-sufficiency and self-reliance—subdue the earth, in short, and realize themselves through their work. Change had to extend even to the top of society. Bolingbroke argued for a Patriot King, somewhat analogous to Machiavelli's prince, who would dedicate himself to the preservation of English liberty and Protestantism and take the lead against the forces of luxury and corruption.

Out of this diverse and seemingly chaotic range of moral and literary influences, Americans created their own version of republicanism. Its key concepts embraced natural rights, the contractual basis of society and government, and the uniqueness of England's liberty-preserving constitution. The colonists believed that the English constitution, their own charters, and the liberties guaranteed by the Glorious Revolution provided them with institutional and moral guarantees for the preservation of liberty and English Protestantism. Power—the dominion of some people over others—continually threatened liberty, becoming evil as it expanded beyond its legitimate boundaries. "Power is like fire. . . ," Cato warned, "it warms, scorches or destroys according as it is watched, provoked, or increased."[3] Power "turns Men that have it into Monsters. . . " who become victim to their passions, "which being boundless and insatiable, are always terrible when they are not controuled. Who was ever satiated with Riches, or surfeited with Power, or tired with Honours?"[4] The colonists valued the English constitution precisely because its balanced governmental structure was able to check such forces. The constitution countered individual interests and desires and helped control riches and power to an extent unparalleled since the days of Rome and Sparta. It could even contain the negative influences of commerce, harnessing them into public service.

The colonists viewed history as the perennial struggle between the forces of power and corruption and those of liberty and virtue. They feared that a conspiracy was at work to destroy liberty and that the course of this plot could be clearly observed in the pages of history. To counter this "design," English people everywhere would have to sacrifice individual interests to the common good. Simplicity, frugality, virtue, and public-spiritedness would be the hallmarks of the true liberty-loving citizen: "He is the Honourable Man who is Influenc'd and Acted by a

❧ *Documents* ❧
The Dangers of Power and Luxury

"Cato's Letters," by the English writers John Trenchard and Thomas Gordon, were reprinted over and over again in colonial newspapers and quoted extensively in many pamphlets. Sentiments such as those expressed in this excerpt, from Saturday, Feb. 18, 1720, undoubtedly made American colonists sensitive to the connection between power, luxury, and dependence.

> They [traitors] will be ever contriving and forming wicked and dangerous Projects, to make the People poor, and themselves rich; well knowing that Dominion follows Property; that where there are Wealth and Power, there will be always Crowds of servile Dependents; and that, on the contrary, Poverty dejects the Mind, fashions it to Slavery, and renders it unequal to any generous Undertaking, and incapable of opposing any bold Usurpation. They will squander away the publick Money in wanton Presents to Minions, and their Creatures of Pleasure or of Burthen, or in Pensions to mercenary and worthless Men and Women, for vile Ends and traiterous Purposes. . . .

> They will promote Luxury, Idleness, and Expence, and a general Depravation of Manners, by their own Example, as well as by Connivance and publick Encouragement. They will not only divert Mens Thoughts from examining their Behaviour and Politicks, but likewise let them loose from all the Restraints of Private and publick Virtue. From Immorality and Excesses they will fall into Necessity; and from thence into a servile Dependence upon Power.

The English Libertarian Heritage: From the Writings of John Trenchard and Thomas Gordon in *The Independent Whig* and *Cato's Letters*, David L. Jacobson, ed. (NY: The Bobbs-Merrill Co., Inc., 1965), 53–5.

Publick Spirit, and fir'd with a Generous Love to Mankind in the worst of Times; Who lays aside his private Views, and foregoes his own Interest, when it comes to competition with the Publick."[5]

To a great extent, the American Revolution was a response to the colonists' fear that England had succumbed to this conspiracy. But different people responded to the ideology of civic humanism in different ways. Rural farmers sought to defend a vision of organic community; many of them felt more comfortable in the traditional world of social deference and personalized economic relations (*if* the gentry fulfilled their obligations) than they did in a cold, impersonal world controlled by morally neutral market forces. On the other hand, farmers in areas increasingly drawn into the international market were unhappy with the growing inequalities in the division of wealth and resentful of the British-connected gentry who controlled the sources of credit. The fear of luxury and corruption, together with strong antimerchant feelings, dominated ideological discourse in such areas.

Americans who lived in cities tended to have the most complex views. Many embraced a more individualistic ethos, attacking the gentry for blocking their own upward mobility. Others defended a more traditional image of community, supporting restrictions on economic activity and stressing the obligation of all citizens to put the needs of the community above their self-interest. Even for the individualists, the image of an artificial economy driven by the pursuit of gain and self-interest was a frightening specter. In response, they resorted to traditional language to describe modern economic activity. Corruption became idleness and unproductivity; virtue was industry and economic productivity. Only gradually did a small minority come to accept the validity of private gain as the best way of working for the common good. Even after the Revolution, most shied away from openly embracing such tenets.

The gentry supported an older, more traditional conception of society, but with a significant difference from the one embraced by yeomen farmers. The American gentry aspired to recreate in the colonies their own version of the English culture they deeply admired. They yearned for a society bonded by patronage, personal influence, and dependent relationships reciprocal in their obligations and duties. This was a vision based on order, harmony, and unity—on a belief in the "rightness" of a society that functioned as an organic, familial whole. People would know what to expect from each other in this world, and they would happily accept their proper place in the social order.

Clearly, civic humanism was an ideology firmly based in the economic and social loyalties of the various groups in American society. In the end, it was the conflict between these competing ideological visions that drove American society to revolutionary change and enshrined, for a brief time, a more radical version of republicanism. More immediately, it allowed and encouraged Americans of all persuasions to choose their political allegiances. To understand how this came about, we must explore the nature of political life in several representative American colonies.

The Southern Colonies

Virginia

During the first part of the eighteenth century, the Virginia gentry shaped a patriarchal political system that brought an extraordinary degree of civil peace to the colony. There were disputes, of course, but to a considerable extent, the gentry embodied the essential social and political values of their society, successfully extended and defended their political privileges within the empire, and accommodated and gave voice to the concerns of most white Virginians. Even during these decades of relative consensus, though, this system was based on black slavery, a form of labor that depended on violence for its very existence. And after mid-century, religious and social dissent from lower-class whites forced the gentry to alter their lives in profound ways.

Patriarchy   Between 1680 and 1720, as we have seen, wealth in Virginia became increasingly concentrated in the hands of a small, elite ruling class. By mid-century, the gentry had created a landscape dotted by churches, mansions, and courthouses, a landscape that approximated as much as possible the English society they desired to emulate. They viewed themselves as patriarchs; fathers to their families and to the dependents who lived on their plantations, they believed in their obligations to further the public good and to sacrifice their own interests to those of the community. William

Byrd II spent his entire life seeking to achieve the level of cultural refinement he had grown up with during his education in England. He dominated his wife in every way, and he looked at his slaves as "my people." Indeed, Byrd's attitudes toward the blacks who did his work reflect how deeply Virginians needed their slaves for reasons not entirely economic. He beat them when they disobeyed, cared for them when they were sick, raped the women when he felt the urge, and seemed to spend as much or more time with them than he did with whites. The same sense of patriarchy characterized his militia service—"Everybody respected me like a king. . .,"[6] he noted proudly, comparing himself to the ultimate patriarch.

In 1726, as Byrd was embarking on the construction of his beautiful mansion at Westover, he bemoaned that "[l]ike one of the Patriarchs, I have my Flocks and my Herds, my Bond-men and Bond-women. . . so that I live in a kind of Independence on every one but Providence. However this Soart of Life is without expence, yet it is attended with a great deal of trouble. I must take care to keep all my people to their Duty, to set all the Springs in motion and to make every one draw his equal Share to carry the Machine forward."[7] One can almost hear him sighing under the weight of his duties. Landon Carter felt much the same way, though he tended to complain about his patriarchal duties. When a lightning bolt hit the main house at Sabine Hall, for instance, striking four people (three of them black), he described the situation thus:

> Reader, whoever thou art, picture to yourself this dismal sum. Grandchildren many, though unhurt, with every sorrowful countenance, though ignorant of the consequences. Yet crying with Concern. A mother calling but for her babies though in her

William Byrd II. ✿

company, and going from place to place to be safe, through some confused expecta-
tion; and Poor slaves crowding and following their master, as if protection only came
from him, and yet quite void of senses enough to assist me.[8]

Carter's carping aside, Virginia patriarchs took their status seriously and were at
great pains to select those who were best suited to take on these burdens in the larger
society. They sought out leaders when they were young. Wealth, education, and family
background were the essential qualifications, though exceptions were sometimes made.
Virginians generally began their political careers as justices of the peace, served as militia officers and vestrymen, and moved up the ladder to the House of Burgesses, where
the most skilled and gifted moved on to positions of leadership and the chairmanships
of important committees. This was a small, tightly knit ruling hierarchy. In the twenty
years before the Revolution, Virginia had sixteen hundred justices, 420 of whom came
from only fifty-five families. Patrick Henry's father was presiding justice of Hanover
County Court and a militia colonel and vestryman; his uncle was an Anglican clergyman. Thomas Jefferson's father married into the Randolph family and served as a justice,
sheriff, surveyor, vestryman, and militia lieutenant. George Washington's father, grandfather, and great-grandfather were all justices, and his father was a churchwarden and
sheriff. Many justices served for twenty or thirty years, and the governor added new
ones only on the recommendation of those already serving.

In these various roles, young gentrymen learned to rule in a responsible and
accountable manner. As vestry members, they levied taxes to pay for church expenses
and administered the parishes' poor relief system. As justices, they settled debt suits,
licensed and controlled taverns, safeguarded illegitimate and orphaned children, fixed
local tax rates, and often served as one of twelve church vestrymen. Collectively, they
comprised the Court of Quarter Sessions. They also chose other county officials—clerks,
coroner, militia officers, tobacco inspectors, and sheriffs. A ranking justice generally
served as sheriff, the most crucial of these positions, for a year or two. Rotating service
in this office provided more justices with an opportunity to gain valuable experience
and kept any one individual from acquiring too much power.

By mid-century, the gentry made it a habit to seek the advice of the yeomen they
ruled. They asked them to serve on juries, supported them in forming new parishes or
counties, gathered with them for various public rituals and family celebrations, and
sought their votes. Petit jurors, for instance, decided criminal and civil cases at the Court
of Quarter Sessions, while once a year, grand jurors returned indictments in criminal
cases. The gentlemen of the county had to be sure they had loyal, responsible yeomen
sitting in those seats. Yeomen could even get sheriffs or tobacco inspectors to relax the
laws on tax collection or tobacco inspection when prices were low, and they could
occasionally convince the planters to appoint a yeoman planter as justice to better service their own needs. Most gentry, in fact, had yeomen in their wider kin group, and
few small planters or farmers were completely isolated from the ruling hierarchy.

One of the most important bonds between gentry and yeomen and among gentry
themselves was the credit system that regulated financial exchange in the Virginia countryside. Planters who needed to buy slaves or land or to pay off debts after a bad harvest often mortgaged their plantations or slaves to a merchant or large planter. Yeomen
and gentlemen traded back and forth constantly, so that estate accounts often resembled those of their northern counterparts—the deceased owed many and was owed by
many others. An individual's social position determined his place in the credit hierarchy.
The justices were responsible for regulating this system, and they rarely sent debtors to
prison. After all, they could find themselves in a similar position at any time.

The gentry further strengthened their patriarchal dominance by participating in a
number of public rituals. Election day was perhaps the most important of these affairs.
The governor issued the writ calling for a new election. The county sheriff decided the

time and location, as well as when to open and close the polls. On election day, county voters cast their ballots orally in front of the candidates, who sat at a long table as voters filed by. The successful candidate then rewarded his loyal supporters by "swilling them with bumbo," or providing them with the local version of a potent rum punch. Thus, the politically powerful paraded their patriarchal dominance but also symbolically noted their obligations to the community that elected and supported them—their dependents.

The system was rife with opportunities for things to get out of hand, of course. Candidates were expected to provide refreshments for everyone present, and many even held a sort of open house before election day so that those traveling a distance could stop for sustenance or spend the night. The sheer amount of food and drink dispensed must have given some pause. At a July 1758 election in Frederick County, George Washington's agent supplied twenty-eight gallons of rum, fifty gallons of rum punch, thirty-four gallons of wine, forty-six gallons of beer, and two gallons of cider royal for a crowd of 391 voters and various others. Could anyone have been left standing at the end of the day? Violence in such circumstances was not unknown; a riot put an end to one 1755 election, "the Sheriff being thrown on the Table, which broke under him, and the Clerks fled to the Bench; and during the Tumult *Lapsley* [one of the instigators] called out, 'Lads, Stand by me. I'll pay the Fine, cost what it will: You know I am able.'"[9] The gentry could serve as final arbiters of such disturbances only because they sat on the House Committee of Privileges and Elections and heard any disputes concerning election irregularities.

On court days, the gentlemen justices dressed in wigs and robes to hear the cases, a practice borrowed from English custom and no doubt designed to enhance their patriarchal roles. The courthouse was centrally located at a convenient crossroads, giving ready access to all and highlighting its symbolic importance; an ordinary (tavern) and a store were usually next door. The highly impressive ritual of oath taking pervaded the day's events—in legal transactions, in the calling and swearing of jurors, and in giving testimony. Before, during, and after the legal proceedings, gentry and yeomen engaged in all sorts of business transactions outside the courthouse and in the adjacent buildings.

On militia days, while the wealthiest gentlemen were exempt from the muster, all other men over the age of sixteen were required to drill, after which their gentlemen officers invited them back to their plantations for refreshments and sometimes imbibed with them, heightening the patriarchal presence. The Sabbath was an occasion for playing out the roles of patriarch and dependent, as gentlemen gathered before the service to socialize and exchange news, then entered the church after everyone else. Even their seating was arranged to maximize their visibility to the entire community. Robert "King" Carter highlighted the importance of the building itself when he paid for the construction of Christ Church in Lancaster County and laid out a special road from his plantation to it. He decorated his own pew with damask curtains on brass rods and reserved the entire north transcept for his servants and tenants.

Willing and generous hospitality was expected of the gentry, as indeed it was of all Virginians; even ordinary planters would spend a night sleeping on the floor to provide comfort for a traveling guest. Gentlemen mixed with all social ranks at taverns and cockfights. They kept to themselves, though, at the horse races and gaming events that were the exclusive preserve of the wealthy; these events fed their sense of danger and competitiveness and offered them a way of reaffirming their masculine, patriarchal roles.

The House of Burgesses   The gentry extended their power to the highest levels of society through their control of the House of Burgesses. As the eighteenth century progressed, the assembly gained full control over money bills, fees, the creation of counties and boroughs and representational apportionment, and the appointment of most of its own officials. Only certain officials, those who had demonstrated their superiority and possessed the proper combination of family background, education, and wealth, could hope to become speaker, clerk, or treasurer, or a member of the crucial Committee of Elections and Privileges. The rewards for these few were substantial. John Robinson served as both speaker and treasurer from 1738 until his death in 1766 and amassed a huge personal fortune along the way. Peyton Randolph succeeded Robinson as speaker and served for ten years. Seven men monopolized the chairs of the six standing committees between 1761 and 1774; Randolph had been chair of the two most important committees, Privileges and Elections and Propositions and Grievances.

The assembly began to make serious inroads into royal power during the administration of Gov Alexander Spotswood (1710–1723). Spotswood attempted to initiate a more restrictive land grant policy, and in reaction, the burgesses cut off funds for his planned expeditions against western Indians. The governor twice tried to use the Tobacco Inspection Act as a vehicle for appointing assembly favorites as inspectors, thereby enhancing his own political power. Both times the small planters, who stood to lose the most from any limitation on the tobacco crop, voted out of office almost every burgess who accepted appointment as an inspector. In the end, Spotswood simply gave up trying to carry out royal policy and allied himself with the gentry. He thereby brought political peace to the colony and enriched himself by participating in the rush to patent new lands.

A relatively uneventful administration under Gov. Hugh Drysdale was followed by that of William Gooch (1727–1740), who proved to be the best politician among the governors of this period. The colony faced a continued depression in tobacco prices during these years, and the planters sought to deal with the problem in the same way they had always had—by expanding westward. But Gooch and the assembly also cooperated in the passage of the Tobacco Inspection Act of 1730, which was designed to bolster prices by securing high quality in the product that went to market. Gooch aided the effort by relinquishing any patronage that might come to his office through the act. He did a superb job of shepherding the bill through the maze of London imperial politics, and the gentry closed ranks on the measure; they feared mass popular uprisings by the smaller planters, who again stood to lose the most through such inspection procedures. Short crops for the next two years gave the measure at least a semblance of success, as prices temporarily rose again. The burgesses continued tobacco inspection over the next two decades, and they extended the franchise to allow landowners to vote in any county where they owned the requisite property, further extending their electoral power.

Expansion westward during the 1730s and 1740s deflected attention from the economic problems that were endemic to the Chesapeake. The population skyrocketed: in 1730, Virginia had 115,000 people; in 1740, 180,000; and in 1760, 340,000. During these three decades, the House of Burgesses created twenty-two new counties (of a total of fifty-two), adding administrative burdens that severely tested the government. Rapid economic growth also exacerbated the rising stress of racial relations. The Chesapeake had completed the process of moving from white to black bound labor by 1720. The black population grew as rapidly as white did during the middle of the century, and Virginians faced problems on a new scale in guarding against slave revolts. By 1750, the strain had reached a crisis point.

Threats from Within, Dangers from Without   Two major disputes scarred Virginia politics at mid-century and accentuated domestic stress. The first was the 1752 pistole fee controversy. When Gov. Robert Dinwiddie, (1751–1758) a typical career bureaucrat, arrived in the colony in 1751, he immediately cast about for ways to augment his income. Faced with a backlog of land patents for the newly exploited western regions, he decided to charge a fee (one pistole, a Spanish coin worth about sixteen shillings) for their validation. The burgesses objected to the fee as a tax. The Crown upheld Dinwiddie's action but seemed to understand its unpopular nature, since so many exceptions were noted that they made the fees meaningless. The burgesses reacted by labeling Dinwiddie "a betrayer of the rights of the people. . . ,"[10] a suspicion confirmed in their minds when he unsuccessfully sought to extend his control over church appointments and to limit the assembly's powers to apportion representation and regulate country courts.

The second and more significant controversy was the so-called Parson's Cause. The Virginia Anglican clergy finally achieved a degree of economic security in 1748, when the burgesses passed a law fixing their salary at the value of sixteen thousand pounds of tobacco annually. Then in 1755 and 1758, the legislature passed the Two Penny Acts. In both of these years, the tobacco crops were short and prices high. Limited to only ten and twelve months' duration, respectively, the acts commuted payments to the clergy to two pence per pound of tobacco—in effect, drastically cutting their salaries. The lawmakers also deliberately omitted the suspending clause in both of the new laws, since they had to take effect immediately if they were to have any relevance. When Lt. Gov. Francis Fauquier signed the 1758 measure, he knew he was breaking his instructions, but his predecessor (Dinwiddie) had signed the 1755 law with no repercussions from London. Now, though, the clergy began to resist its enforcement. Rev. John Camm, a divinity professor at William and Mary College and rector of Yorkhampton Parish in York County, led the opposition. Camm even sailed to England to seek the Crown's intervention, asking that Parliament declare the acts null and void from the time of their passage—opening the way for legal recovery of back salaries. Though the Privy Council disallowed the measures and criticized the burgesses, it did not make the appeal retroactive, and the laws thus served their purpose. The clergy brought four lawsuits to recover damages, but all four failed.

The gentry reacted bitterly at this challenge to their authority. Landon Carter and Richard Bland accused the ministers of deceit, greed, and complicity in the Catholic conspiracy to undermine Protestant liberty. The notion of a Roman Catholic conspiracy had deep roots in English culture, and it would receive further affirmation during the Seven Years War. The accusations of moral failure were even more significant, though, since these issues mirrored concerns of the gentry themselves.

As we have seen, the Baptists in particular created a world that directly challenged the morality of gentry life. Baptist preachers stressed sobriety, community, and a solemn fellowship of equals that rejected the secular, celebratory nature of gentry society. The economic crisis of the 1750s and 1760s added a new dimension to the situation. Virginia gentlemen evaluated themselves and each other at least partly in terms of their success and skill in growing fine tobacco. These large planters, little involved with the Scottish factors who monopolized the trade of the smaller planters, viewed credit relations as a special form of friendship through which they could maintain their personal autonomy. They embraced an "etiquette of debt" that stressed the spirit of reciprocity and viewed credit in distinctly anticapitalist terms—as a means of creating links between men rather than driving them apart.

As tobacco prices continued to decline and as the length of the economic cycle grew shorter, depressions became deeper and more frequent than before. During boom times, planters increased their importation of luxuries from England, enlarging their personal debt. British merchants failed to share the Virginians' traditional view of credit relations. As their London creditors called in debts with growing urgency in the 1760s and 1770s, Virginians saw their world crumbling. The planters felt betrayed and concluded that their English connections were plotting against them to gain their property for themselves. Planters viewed this as a real threat to their personal autonomy; many reacted by promising to reform and lead simpler lives. Such feelings remained largely personal until the late 1760s, when the issue took over the public forum. By that time, the gentry had long been expressing their concerns in private diaries and letters, bemoaning their descent into factionalism and vice and complaining about their lack of virtue and their pursuit of luxury and extravagance. Worry over growing debt became a major theme of these expressions, together with a self-accusatory concern over the gentry's lack of a sense of responsibility for the common good. As the *Virginia Gazette* noted, "Luxury poisons a whole nation. . . ."[11] Responding to criticism from religious dissidents and to their own precarious economic situation, the Virginia gentry eagerly embraced republican ideology during the 1760s and 1770s. A closer look at the experiences of a few individuals will help us understand why they did so.

George Washington's friend and neighbor, Capt. John Posey, was a planter whose drinking and hunting habits contributed to his downfall. By 1767, he owed Washington at least seven hundred pounds, but he kept asking for more. Washington scolded him for his behavior but never thought to cut him off—he apologized to Posey for not being able to come up with five hundred pounds more. Washington wanted to help his friend: "'Twas done to serve your family and if possible to save your Estate from dispersion."[12] Posey, however, was too far gone; he eventually died in debtor's prison in Maryland.

Robert Beverley noted that if he was going to live in such an isolated place as Virginia, he might as well make his life as "commodius" as possible—so he spent heavily to keep up with the latest in British luxury. He knew he was in trouble financially as early at 1761, yet that year, he ordered a "chariot" from London at a cost of eighty-five pounds. In 1764, his British merchant correspondent told him he was cutting back on Beverley's credit. Beverley felt betrayed and, more important, condemned to a life of want: "I dread very Much from the Appearances of this Day that I will be condemned forever to a state of *Vassalage & Dependence*."[13] He finally confronted his situation in 1766, swearing to live a simple and virtuous life if he could only regain his credit and independence. Washington himself was in debt by 1761 to the tune of two thousand pounds to Robert Cary and Company, and when Cary began to pressure him for payment, the future president complained that the Londoner had ignored the etiquette of debt. Washington was all too aware that he, too, was losing the valued economic independence that made him a proper guardian of English virtue and liberty. As the British traveler Andrew Burnaby observed in 1760, Virginians "are haughty and jealous of their liberties, impatient of restraint, and can scarcely bear the thought of being controuled by any superior power."[14] For some planters, finally, the concerns were not so very different from those of prosperous farmers in the middle colonies or even the hard-pressed ones of New England. Henry Fitzhugh pleaded his situation to an English creditor in 1764: "I have [a] large family, & the chiefest of my estates [is] entailed on a few of my children so that I [am] under a necessity of purchasing Lands for the Others. . . ."[15]

As London creditors began to pressure their Virginia debtors for payment, they also lobbied the British government to do something about a Virginia currency that was falling dramatically in value against the British pound. The passage of the Currency Act of 1764, which forbade any new issues of paper money as legal tender, left the planters feeling betrayed. The government's action convinced them that British merchants were plotting against Virginia interests in a conspiracy of "designing men." Those merchants "who draw their Subsistence, as it were, from our very Vitals"[16] were working to deprive the gentry of their independence and liberty.

Slavery, an economic system that performed crucial social functions, ultimately made this political system uniquely functional. Slavery provided the wealth that gentlemen relied upon for their claims of independence, accentuated the notion of patriarchy that gave the system its foundation, and buttressed the psychological unity that brought whites together despite their social and economic inequalities. Ironically, slavery also created the wealth and consumption habits that contributed to a growing sense of unease among Virginia's gentlemen, and it was slavery that made them ever more aware of the ideological danger of their lives of dependence, luxury, and exploitation.

South Carolina

South Carolina was the wealthiest British colony on the mainland, and its merchants and planters forcefully expanded their control over its political affairs during the first decades of the century. The lower house began its battle with the council and the governor even before royal government was instituted in 1719. After the Crown took control, the assembly defended its newly won control over its internal governance, retaining the right to appoint and pay the colony's officers and to apportion new seats. In the late 1720s, the collapse of the naval stores market precipitated a further series of clashes between the colonists and Britain that proved intractable until Gov. James Glen (1738–1756) arrived in 1743. Even the politically skilled Glen was unable to stop the erosion of royal power, and by mid-century, the governor retained only the power to veto legislation and to prorogue, or dissolve, assembly sessions.

From 1743 to 1763, governors and the assembly battled over the control of defense spending, Indian trade policy, and paper money issues; by mid-century, the representatives had gained considerable control over the framing of money bills and the supervision of expenditures. London, though, was not about to endanger the flow of wealth from Carolina's indigo and rice production. When Gov. Thomas Boone (1761–1764) attempted in 1762 to challenge the results of an assembly election, he succeeded only in getting himself removed from office by the Crown for disrupting political life in a colony of crucial economic importance to the empire.

Economic prosperity was the key to the colony's political and social unity. From 1730 to 1760, rice production almost doubled, and returns on invested capital skyrocketed. Rice and indigo produced enough wealth to provide economic opportunities for everyone and help alleviate economic conflict. Merchants and planters lived in political and social harmony, religious toleration prevailed, and Charleston's urban values permeated the entire culture. The gentry served on local committees that provided for community needs, such as building bridges, and as churchwardens and vestrymen, controlling church affairs and administering poor relief. Most of the ruling elite were careful not to alienate those who accorded them political and social deference. In 1769, when considering a ban on the importation of British goods after the passage of the Townshend Acts, the gentry argued that the artisans were "the bones and sinews of society; and in any general plan, are as much to be regarded, where their liberties and properties are equally at stake, as any others whatever."[17]

Between 1738 and 1742, Indian problems, the Stono Rebellion, a major fire in Charleston, the threat of Spanish invasion, and the disruptive emotionalism of the Great Awakening together strengthened this sense of solidarity among those in the white upper class, giving pause to all malcontents. When wealthy planters became politically apathetic, merchants and professionals willingly stepped in to take up the burden. All were well-schooled in the tenets of classical republicanism. They were familiar with *"Cato's Letters"* and *The Independent Whig,* and they pursued lives that consciously emulated those of English country gentlemen. The colony remained free of serious conflict among whites until the Regulator movement of the 1760s, when the gentry's failure to address the governmental and judicial needs of the growing frontier population finally caught up with them.

The Middle Colonies

Different patterns emerged in the middle colonies. While the lower houses here modeled themselves after the House of Commons and fought with general success to have similar, and even greater, powers, northern elites found it far more difficult to maintain control over the burgeoning and more diverse populations in their colonies. In some cases, they were forced to deal with economic difficulties more severe and pervasive than those anywhere in the south. The resulting political configurations have led some historians to regard the middle colonies as the birthplace of the modern American political system, a region dominated by a variety of particular interests seeking satisfaction through active and widespread participation in government, with little regard for larger communal values. Nowhere in this area do we find the social unity so characteristic of the southern colonies or the lingering utopian impulse so dominant in New England. If we define modern political liberalism as the pursuit of self-interest through political means, the middle colonies were indeed the prototypes for the American political future.

New York

The growth of New York City, large numbers of immigrants, and the persistence of Dutch-English conflict combined to create a pattern of divisive political conflict and expanding popular involvement in eighteenth-century New York government. Even in New York City, which had a less participatory governmental structure than Boston, involvement in political affairs broadened as the century progressed.

Various types of town and county governments provided order and addressed the daily concerns of rural New Yorkers. Township government emerged rapidly after England took the colony from the Dutch. Annual spring elections chose six to twelve trustees and several constables and assessors. Town meetings passed local ordinances, but trustees decided which matters to place before the larger meetings. Residents also elected road surveyors, fence viewers, overseers of the poor, and other officials as needed. The assembly divided less populated areas, such as Duchess and Orange Counties, and parts of Ulster and Albany counties, into precincts, and residents there elected supervisors, assessors, and collectors. At first, the governor controlled county governments and appointed justices of the peace, sheriffs, and county clerks, but an elected board of supervisors gradually took over the justices' executive duties, leaving them a strictly judicial function. Middling sort of men, constrained by a provincial vision, held most local and county offices and were less powerful than the New England or southern elites, weakening the influence of patriarchal power in New York.

The assembly garnered powers similar to those won in other colonies. By 1709, it had almost total control over specific financial appropriations, and in 1755, the Crown completely abandoned attempts to secure a regular salary for the governor. The lower house also succeeded in requiring that money allocated for emergency military defenses be physically lodged with the colony's treasurer, whom it appointed. The representatives also won a decisive role in regulating military affairs, a significant matter for a colony so critically situated.

Politics in New York were deeply rooted in social conflict. Well into the eighteenth century, factional allegiances continued to center on the Leisler/anti-Leisler split of the 1690s. Though individuals occasionally switched sides to suit their personal needs, these factions remained relatively stable and functioned remarkably like future political parties. An organizational structure began to emerge when the merchant elite, composed of a number of powerful families, such as the DeLanceys, Van Cortlands, Schuylers, Livingstons, and Philipses, gained power under Gov. Benjamin Fletcher (1692–1698).

City artisans often relied on the merchants for their jobs, so there was a certain natural reluctance to express resistance to their policies. Nonetheless, in the 1695 municipal elections, the Leislerians, with Dutch and artisan support, carried the city. Their fortunes grew when Richard Coote, Earl of Bellomont (1698–1701) became governor. Bellomont allied himself with the Leislerians, cracked down on smuggling and piracy, and sought to recoup many of Fletcher's expansive land grants to the elite. He reburied Leisler and Milbourne in a Dutch church, a symbolically crucial ceremony attended by more than a thousand mourners.

Bellomont's policies obviously upset the power structure. Political clubs began to emerge. These groups organized, wrote pamphlets, and formed election tickets; huge voter turnouts became common. In the 1702 election, Nicholas Bayard circulated petitions criticizing Bellomont for pursuing pro-Dutch policies. The governor ordered Bayard arrested and charged with "incitement to mutiny and conspiracy against the government."[18] A public trial led to Bayard's conviction for treason, and only an official reprieve saved him from hanging.

Edward Hyde, Viscount Cornbury (1702–1708) succeeded Bellomont and allied with the anti-Leislerian forces. Gov. Robert Hunter (1710–1719) brought a brief respite from political strife by building a broad coalition. He appealed especially to artisans and shopkeepers with a program of fixed interest rates and protective duties, established a government monopoly over the fur trade, and introduced a patronage system in an attempt to extend royal influence throughout the colony. Even Hunter, though, could not free himself completely from the complexities of the colony's politics. James DeLancey and the Philipse family, cut off from the Canadian trade that had enriched them, created a powerful antiadministration faction and won a series of off-year elections. After this faction prevailed in the 1727 assembly elections, DeLancey reopened the colony's trade with Canada.

The appointment of Gov. William Cosby (1732–1736) led to renewed factionalism and political conflict. Cosby found himself embroiled almost immediately in political infighting with Lewis Morris, the colony's chief justice. Morris ruled against the governor in Cosby's attempt to collect half of the salary paid to Dutch merchant Rip Van Dam, who had been acting governor for the preceding thirteen months. In the newly established *New York Weekly Journal,* journalist John Peter Zenger attacked Cosby for arbitrarily ignoring the law. The government brought Zenger to trial for seditious libel, but a jury acquitted him in one of the most celebrated court cases in early America. In some ways, the trial was merely another episode in the long and complex history of New York political factionalism. It was also, however, one of many opportunities for colonists to embrace the language of classical republicanism. Zenger defended freedom of the press and openly contrasted the Whig principles of liberty with Cosby's attempts to deprive citizens of their property and political independence and reduce them to slavery.

The trial released the few remaining restraints on political factionalism. Morris and his supporters began enlarging the political community by appealing specifically to the artisans' self-interests. They called for secret ballots, for making the offices of sheriff and other major positions elective, and for government stimulation of the economy. Under Cosby's successor, Lt. Gov. George Clarke (1736–1743), the assembly introduced measures to eliminate the governor's influence in elections, make all appropriations annual, and eliminate fees for Crown officials. In all of this, the political literature paraded the language of English rights and liberties and specifically attacked the wealthy for their disdain of the rights of the community. In the 1733 and 1734 New York City municipal elections, a number of artisans and laborers won city offices. Pseudonymous writers such as "Timothy Wheelwright" called for government by honest workers, maintaining that "[a] poor honest Man [is] preferable to a rich Knave."[19] In the 1739 assembly election,

❧ *Documents* ❧
"Unspeakably Calamitous" Factionalism

New York was the sight of some of the most ferocious and bitter political factionalism in the American colonies. Many writers drew heavily from the tradition of classical republicanism to help make sense of these events, as the following excerpts reveal.

> Unspeakably calamitous have been the Consequences of Party-Division. It has occasioned Deluges of Blood, and subverted Kingdoms. It always introduces a Decay of publick Spirit, with the Extinction of every nobel and generous Sentiment. The very Names of Things are perverted. On Fury and Violence it bestows the Appellation of Magnamity and Opposition, and stiles Resentment and Rancour, Heroic Ardor, and Patriot-Warmth. Nor is it ever at a Loss for Pretences to bubble the Mob out of their Wits, and give its wildest Ravings a plausible Colour. . . .
>
> THUS as the designing Party-Man always appears in the Mask of publick Spirit, and conceals the most selfish and riotous Disposition, under the venerable Pretext of asserting Liberty, and defending his Country; so the ministerial Scribbler, taking Advantage of this fre-

one slate of candidates published its stands on various issues, a distinctly modern approach to political campaigning. Deference faded as more ordinary New Yorkers became politically involved, and specific interests were often the deciding factors in determining political affiliation.

Traditional values of community and public interest, though, continued to dominate political rhetoric. Practice may have been modern, but beliefs and attitudes remained cast in traditional language. Proponents of laws designed to service the artisan and laboring classes, such as those calling for the establishment of public schools, a lowering of the legal interest rate, and the issuance of paper money, couched their arguments in the language of community interest and contrasted their efforts with the private, selfish interests of the mercantile elite.

By the 1740s and 1750s, even the political conservatives had turned to the press to conduct their campaigns, and in 1752, the *Independent Reflector* appeared, the first American paper devoted exclusively to politics. The chief issue during these years concerned Gov. George Clinton's (1743–1753) desire to meet the French threat head-on in the colonies and to halt the Albany-Montreal fur trade. But this meant the colony would have to become involved in the Seven Years War, which promised higher taxes on the mercantile elite. As always, James De Lancey opposed such a policy and supported continuation of the illegal trade. De Lancey had powerful British connections, control of the council, and considerable influence in the assembly. While Clinton succeeded in laying

quent Prostitution, gives a sinister Turn to the most laudable Views, and stigmatizes every Man who opposes the Encroachments of the Court.

William Livingston, John Morin Scott, and William Smith, *The Independent Reflector,* Milton M. Klein, ed. (Cambridge, MA: Harvard University Press, 1963), 146–7.

There have been *Nicholsons, Cornburys, Cootes, Burringtons, Edens, Lowthers, Georges, Parkes, Douglases* and many more, as very bashaws as ever were sent from Constantinople; and there have not been wanting under each of their administrations, persons the dregs and scandal of humane nature *who have kept in with them,* and used their endeavors to enslave their fellow subjects, and persuaded others to do so too. . . . an ill governor not only enslaves the present generation, but makes slavery hereditary to latest posterity. . . .

New York Weekly Journal, 21 January, 1733.

the basis for New York's later participation in the war, De Lancey's opposition cost the governor his English support; the Board of Trade, in fact, scarcely even wrote to him. Both Clinton and De Lancey made extensive use of the press and courted the middle and lower classes, further expanding popular participation in New York's political culture.

The difficulty of making even a marginal living created bitter feelings among many ordinary New Yorkers; as one urban artisan noted, "[T]he Expence of living in the most frugal Way has increased so exorbitantly, that I find it beyond my ability to support my Family with my utmost Industry. . . . "[20] The alternative, he bemoaned, was to "starve or be dishonest." But there was a third option available to the urban poor—to vie for political power themselves. This movement would become integral to the radicalization of American politics over the next two decades.

Pennsylvania

By the early eighteenth century, Pennsylvania was the most ethnically diverse colony in North America. Its constant need for military defense, stemming partly from the push for land by western settlers, created unusual problems for an assembly dominated by Quaker pacifists. The colony's proprietary status also produced a divisive issue that would eventually culminate in a movement to establish a royal government. The Penn family provided fodder for much of the dissension by, among other things, continuing to own much untaxed land.

County government was stronger than town government in Pennsylvania. At first, justices of the peace presided over an English county system similar to that of Virginia. Then between 1718 and 1725, the colony created a unique county commission system. The people elected three commissioners, one each fall for a three-year term, and county assessors each year; these officials levied local taxes. The electorate also chose nominees for sheriff and coroner. There was no upper house in Pennsylvania, only a council that had no legislative powers, and the assembly accrued governing powers similar to those of legislatures in other colonies. Its first victory came in 1701, when it forced Penn to greatly enlarge its legislative powers in the Charter of Liberties. The proprietor also extended greater power to county courts, including the right to judge land disputes.

Pennsylvania had escaped the trauma of the Glorious Revolution, but as we have seen, Penn faced strong antiproprietary feelings from the first days of the colony. The Keithian controversy showed shopkeepers, master artisans, and others that they could make their voices heard through political involvement, as hundreds of them signed petitions supporting the reformer's cause. Developments during the early eighteenth century further extended popular participation in government.

David Lloyd, a former Penn protege and the colony's attorney general, emerged as the influential leader of the antipropietary movement after Penn removed him from all offices in 1699. Lloyd believed that government should be an arm of the people's will, and he led the fight against Penn's newest personal representative, James Logan. Both individuals accumulated much political power by holding a wide variety of offices. With Penn's attention focused on his troubled personal affairs in England, Lloyd's faction won control of the assembly for five years running by extending political involvement to middle- and lower-class Philadelphians. Lloyd believed in the ability of ordinary people to think for themselves and to control their own destinies, and he began to publish the assembly's proceedings as a means of providing his supporters with the knowledge necessary to act. Thus by 1701, there were two distinct factions in Pennsylvania politics: the country party of rural farmers and artisans and the proprietary party of Philadelphia merchants and the Penn family.

As yet, no street demonstrations or violent displays of animosity toward the wealthy arose in Pennsylvania, because economic prosperity and a relatively equitable distribution of wealth helped postpone disruptive political controversy for some time. Pennsylvania was far removed from the main theaters of the early eighteenth-century colonial wars and thus escaped heavy taxation, and it contributed no men to the military efforts. It even survived the recessions of the 1720s without serious harm. Nonetheless, the seeds of political opposition continued to germinate, this time under the leadership of Sir William Keith (1717–1726).

Keith arrived in the colony in 1717 as Penn's appointed governor, but his loyalties shifted after the proprietor's death. As the colony's economic fortunes began to change, he forged an alliance with David Lloyd. The two spurred the development of an antiproprietary radical press that called for a host of economic and political reforms, including the issuance of paper money, the reduction of interest rates, a curb on lawyers' fees, and restrictions on the imprisonment of debtors. The welfare of the community, Keith argued, was no longer served by the leadership of the wealthy and educated. Though the colony as a whole prospered, many commoners suffered. As one pamphleteer noted, "How deplorable are the Lives of the Common People. . . . The ship Builder & the Carpenter starve for want of Employment . . . the usurer grinds the Face of The Poor so that Law suits multiply, our Gaols are full, and we are justly apprehensive of falling into debt."[21] His solution? Paper money. In response to rising political pressure, the assembly issued large sums of paper money in 1723 and 1724, effectively lifting the recession.

During the late 1720s, Keith and Lloyd formed political caucuses, recruited immigrant Germans and Scotch-Irish to the cause, and made direct appeals to the electorate

through the press and outdoor rallies. "Roger Plowman" attacked the aristocratic pretensions of the wealthy when he argued that "the principal Reason why you are angry with
Paper-money, is because People who are in your Debt can raise money to pay you,
without surrendering up their Lands for one half of what they are worth."[22] The poor
were poor because the rich had abandoned their obligations to society; as "Plowman"
more crudely put it, "It is an old Saying with us, that we must never grease the fat Sow
in the Arse, and starve the Pigs."[23] Keith's party also succeeded in uniting rural farmers
and urban artisans in a coalition that promoted private interests while appealing to the
well-being of the whole community. James Logan felt the sting of these forces when he
voiced the traditional arguments that the rich were the industrious and frugal of society,
while the poor were so because of their own failings and idleness. An angry crowd
responded by attacking his house. During the 1728–1729 depression, street gangs pressured hard-money proponents and convinced the assembly to pass another generous
paper money bill.

Economic prosperity throughout the 1730s restored a degree of political peace.
Artisans and dockworkers prospered, continued immigration stimulated a building
boom, and rising demand from the West Indies helped fuel economic growth. But with
the onset of King George's War, Quakers (now a minority of the population) reaffirmed
their opposition to military spending. Both the Quakers and proprietor Thomas Penn
actively courted the German vote. During the 1742 assembly elections, the proprietary
party spread rumors that the Quakers were planning to import unnaturalized Germans
to vote, and the Quakers reported that the proprietary leader William Allen had hired
armed sailors to keep Friends away from the polls. The Quakers won overwhelmingly,
and a riot begun by Allen's sailors cast a cloud over the proprietary party for the next
decade. Gone were the days of William Penn's quiet pacifism.

Some Quakers, meanwhile, were beginning to question the Society's commitment
to pacifism in a time of war. Benjamin Franklin argued in *Plain Truth* (1747) that the
colony simply had to defend its western frontiers and eastern shoreline—that war
endangered trade and that artisans, shopkeepers, and farmers deserved to be defended
and had been too long neglected by the rich. He himself was allied with the Quaker
party and passed no judgment on the Friends, simply noting that Quaker principles
need not prevail when Friends were a minority of the population.

By 1750, the majority of Quaker politicians, led by Isaac Norris, supported some
sort of compromise; some favored defensive warfare, while others backed Franklin's
idea of a voluntary militia. The minority peace faction, under the leadership of Israel
Pemberton, Jr., rejected both options. As the Seven Years War approached, it became
increasingly difficult for Quakers to avoid the issue, particularly after seven hundred
angry Germans marched on Philadelphia in November 1755, demanding that the assembly raise a militia and allocate money for defense.

The conflict between Quakers and the proprietary party continued until the two
sides reached a compromise in 1756. Pemberton and five other Quakers resigned their
assembly seats, unable to justify their participation in a government that supported military action. They organized the Friendly Association for Regaining and Preserving Peace
with the Indians by Pacific Measures, hoping to keep Quaker pacifistic principles alive.
Shortly thereafter, the remaining Quaker representatives agreed to voluntarily leave the
assembly during wartime only, satisfying both their religious beliefs and the needs of
the empire.

Franklin assumed leadership of the assembly-based party after the Quakers left
office, and both he and the proprietary party continued to court the German vote.
Franklin orchestrated the general election of militia officers, and the proprietary party
responded by organizing their own militia. The proprietary party tried, to no avail, to
convince the city's residents that Franklin was giving the people "Anarchical Notions"
and "levelling Principles."[24] Between 1754 and 1760, the ordinary people of

Pennsylvania consistently defeated the more aristocratic interests of the proprietary party.

Penn, meanwhile, continued to refuse to pay taxes on the family's proprietary estates, and in 1757, a frustrated assembly sent Franklin to England to try to change Penn's mind or to convince London to overrule him. Franklin failed. Instead, he initiated a movement to bring royal government to Pennsylvania. But Pennsylvania politics were beyond the point where the colony could accommodate the patriarchal presence of British rule.

New England

At least in popular consciousness, the New England town meeting remains the proto-type for American self-government. The tradition of participatory self-government was older and stronger here than in any other region of the British empire. All adult white males could attend town meetings, and nearly everyone did when critical issues arose. Even franchise requirements were commonly ignored on such occasions, as townsmen sought to create a consensus of opinion that would present a united front to the outside world and avoid the bitter factionalism of modern interest politics. But New England political life was much more than the town meeting. The growth of power in the lower houses, the emergence of political factionalism and conflict with royal governors, and the divisive impact of economic and social change were all as common in the New England colonies as they were elsewhere.

Connecticut

Connecticut had more internal political unity and economic equality than did other colonies, but even here, unsettling economic and social changes eroded traditional lines of authority and spurred broader and more intense political involvement. During the first half of the eighteenth century, the colony experienced rapid population growth. As the economy expanded to serve the needs of more people, merchants extended their activities and the aggregate level of wealth in the colony grew. But the increase was not evenly distributed.

Population growth had its most serious impact in the newly settled eastern section of the colony. Here, the money supply failed to keep pace with the boom in economic activity, and farmers, artisans, and merchants anxiously sought a more fluid currency to help finance land purchases and to create economic alternatives to farming; debt-ridden farms were becoming an all-too common feature of the rural landscape. Merchants were also frustrated by their long-standing reliance on Boston, New York, and Newport merchants as middlemen with London traders. Paper money seemed the best solution. Twice during the 1720s, the lower house passed bills establishing land banks, and twice the upper house defeated them. In 1740, New London merchants established the New London Society for Trade and Commerce, hoping to issue their own currency. The governor shut the society down. But public pressure forced the assembly to issue substantial public loans throughout the 1730s and 1740s, though even these were markedly limited in comparison to issues in Massachusetts and Rhode Island.

Eastern political leaders and frustrated merchants eventually forged an alliance with religious New Lights against their common enemies, Old Lights and political conservatives. In 1753, they organized the Susquehanna Company, a private company that claimed for the colony a portion of northern Pennsylvania under the original Connecticut charter, sold lots to speculators and settlers alike, and eventually settled the area. The result was a military conflict with Pennsylvania in the 1760s and several decades of legal wrangling before the issue was finally settled. Since the company seemed to offer a solution to the economic difficulties of the easterners, it received widespread support even from an initially reluctant assembly. Many of the individuals involved in this venture were also central to the New Light political coup of 1766, when the group swept conservatives from office and finally took control of the colony. Seventeenth-century Connecticut had developed a reputation as a "land of steady habits." A century after its founding, it had joined other American colonies by rebelling against patriarchal authority and embracing a new, more republican conception of society.

Rhode Island

For most of the seventeenth century, Rhode Island had been a small, isolated collection of semi-independent towns, characterized by little economic development and much religious freedom. Politically and economically, it began to mature under the administration of Gov. Samuel Cranston (1698–1727). Cranston centralized the government, strengthened and systematized the legal system, and directed the rapid economic growth that characterized the next three decades. Much of his reorganization effort was directed toward supporting Newport's commercial goals: he connected the hinterland to the port through a new series of roads, passed laws to regulate trade to the city's advantage, and established the Rhode Island tradition of paper money to supply the medium of exchange necessary for trade. His political skills ensured that local interests remained under control and did not become overly resentful of Newport's privileged place.

Cranston also successfully resisted British pressures to modify the colony's independent government, and he succeeded in winning the struggle with Connecticut for control of the Narragansett country. The colony became trustee for the tribe, taking most of its land as compensation for military defense and relegating the remaining Indians to a small reservation. Most significant, though, was Cranston's complete overhaul of the colony's system of government. He helped establish the assembly's tax power, codify laws, and peacefully resolve land conflicts and town boundary disputes. At his urging, the assembly regularized town government, increasing the number of local officials and giving town councils responsibility for caring for the local poor and controlling blacks and Indians. The assembly became a true legislature, referring to the colony's charter as its constitution and imitating the Commons procedurally. Because of Cranston, the colony was able to avoid internal conflict during the middle of the century and concentrate on economic growth and development.

Even Rhode Island, though, could not escape the emergence of a politics of self-interest. Indeed, ordinary people exerted an extraordinary influence on political affairs here. They elected the lower house twice a year and the ten assistants annually, as well as the governor, deputy governor, secretary, treasurer, and attorney general. Town meetings were frequent and well-attended. A tradition of political involvement was thus firmly in place when the political rivalry between Samuel Ward and Stephen Hopkins emerged in 1757 to dominate the colony's affairs for the next decade. Historians disagree as to the causes of this rivalry that paired two men of similar interests and wealth off against one another, each relying on an assortment of political, religious, and economic grievances to galvanize their supporters. What remains most important is the explosion of political activity that ensued. Candidates held caucuses and raised money, and ordinary Rhode Islanders voted in unprecedented numbers and wrote pamphlets and newspaper articles advocating their particular causes. Every election during these ten years was narrowly and bitterly contested, as the voters began to realize how important government was to fulfilling their own interests. As it was in many other colonies, war proved to be the decisive catalyst to this realization; someone had to protect the colony's trade and deal with the currency and taxation problems that inevitably accompanied colonial involvement in international conflict. Tiny and vulnerable, this independent colony did not hesitate to embrace the political future of self-interest and democratic liberalism.

Massachusetts

After the imposition of the charter of 1691, most Massachusetts inhabitants were both relieved at the establishment of political stability and anxious about the future. The charter destroyed the independent government that had guided the colony through most of the seventeenth century. The Crown now appointed the governor, the franchise was based on property rather than religion, and the governor appointed sheriffs, county court justices, and justices of the peace. Yet the House of Representatives hardly missed a beat in the transition to royal government, continuing to assert its identity with the British Commons and embracing anew its role as advocate for the colony's interests. Early in the 1690s, for instance, the General Court passed an act that contained several sections copied directly from the Magna Carta, while other passages vigorously asserted the colony's rights and privileges and claimed complete control over financial legislation and taxation. While England disallowed the act, its passage was prophetic of the future dominance of the House of Representatives in the colony's political life.

As in other colonies, the lower house increasingly differentiated itself from the council during the early decades of the century while greatly expanding its own legislative and regulatory powers. It oversaw seemingly endless conflicts within towns concerning tax payments and petitions for separation, often leading to the formation of precincts or of entirely new towns, and it helped settle numerous boundary disputes between towns. The House provided financial support for frontier ministries, arbitrated ministerial salary disputes, offered aid to disabled veterans, and controlled the entire process of land grants, particularly in offering rewards to veterans and in settling the Maine frontier.

Throughout this period, the lower house fought continuously to expand its constitutional powers at the expense of the council and governors. At various times, it succeeded in expanding the paper money supply, limiting the governor's salary to annual grants, claiming the right to control the appointment of the colony's treasurer and attorney general, and expanding its voice in the coordination of military affairs. A small group of ambitious entrepreneurs led the representatives' drive to control the colony's affairs. As elsewhere, they consistently worked to expand the involvement of ordinary colonists in political affairs.

As the seventeenth century came to a close, the colony was embroiled in almost constant warfare with both the French and the Indians. Military expeditions necessitated heavy taxation and led to a growing burden of debt. And war affected the population unequally. Those at the top grew wealthier from war contracts and artisans benefited from the military spending boom, but indentured servants, apprentices, and immigrants found their well-being increasingly threatened. They were most often the ones who did the fighting. Paper money fueled inflation, and wages failed to keep pace. Mariners and widows in particular were devastated. The colony was involved in military expeditions in 1691, 1704, 1707, 1709, and 1711; during these years, up to one-fifth of adult Bay Colony males served in the fight against Canada, and perhaps a quarter of these perished. Only once, in 1711, did England fulfill its promise of military assistance.

The colony's relations with the royal governors were no more fruitful. William Phips (1691–1694) was rude and intolerant of the colonists, perhaps because so many of them reminded him of his own humble beginnings. William Stoughton (1694–1697) complained to the Crown that the colonists insisted on passing laws repugnant to those of England and destructive of imperial trade and that they refused to transmit such acts to England for approval. He recommended that the colony's new charter be revoked.

Stoughton was friendly with the pre-Andros moderates and had nothing but contempt for the popular faction within the House. Only Richard Coote, the Earl of Bellomont (1697–1701), proved sympathetic to colonial rights, establishing friendly relations with the popular party and the legislature.

Bellomont's successor, Joseph Dudley (1702–1715), proved to be the worst of the lot. Strongly pro-empire, Dudley consolidated the support of wealthy merchants through a judicious allocation of military contracts, and he challenged and criticized the House constantly. The representatives fought back, refusing Dudley's request for a permanent salary and arguing that it was their right and privilege as native English subjects to control such disbursements as they saw fit. Dudley's rule eventually ended amidst accusations that he traded with the French and sought to bribe and corrupt the legislature.

Spurred on by such conflicts and by the continued strains of war and widespread economic dislocation, Elisha Cooke, Jr. led a small number of influential politicians in fashioning the outlines of the political organization that would eventually become known as the Boston Caucus. Cooke and his followers built substantial personal fortunes through a variety of economic ventures, but they were shut out from the more lucrative imperial trade and were seeking alternative means of expanding their wealth. They had already begun to support expansion of the currency supply and the establishment of more lenient bankruptcy laws. The group's proposal for a private land bank in 1714 was defeated, countered by a Dudley proposal for a similar public bank. The latter did increase the currency supply, but under much stricter regulation and to the benefit of Dudley's own political allies—including his brother Paul, the colony's attorney general. The private bankers argued that their own proposal would restrain the influence and spending power of the government, encourage domestic manufactures and discourage the importation of English luxuries, and help correct the persistent trade imbalance with England. Such measures were essential, they argued, since "Poverty, Misery, and Oppression. . . is breaking in upon us. . . . "[25] Cooke also attacked Dudley's proposal to reorganize Boston's government as a municipal corporation, thereby eliminating town meetings. One writer portrayed the plan's advocates as "Great Fish" seeking to extend control over the lives of ordinary people. "Then," the writer argued, "the Great Men will no more have the Dissatisfaction of seeing their Poorer Neighbors stand up for equal Privileges with them."[26]

During the following decades, Cooke and his allies formalized the organization of the popular party and extended its influence into the countryside. Cooke first incited local resistance in Maine to the White Pine Acts, while at the same time acquiring several thousand acres of valuable property for himself. He and his supporters than introduced a new land bank proposal in 1720, designed specifically to appeal to farmers. The Boston Caucus extended its hold on a variety of city offices, including those of representative, selectman, assessor, collector, town meeting moderator, treasurer, and clerk. The organization created slates of candidates, mobilized voters through the liberal use of taverns, alcohol, and the press, and directed its appeals to artisans, shopkeepers, and, increasingly, farmers. The group supported more liberal paper money issues (to feed their own economic needs as well as to supply the currency that the colony lacked), greater control over the governor's powers and his patronage, and public works projects to provide jobs for the growing poor and, again, to further their own economic ambitions. Throughout this process, Cooke, and his assistants conjured up images of an oligarchical plot by the rich who were seeking to deprive Bostonians of their English rights and corrupt, designing politicians who were plotting to undermine the liberty-preserving balance of the constitution—"like a design to inslave a People and make a few Lords and the rest Beggars."[27]

The Boston economy continued to worsen during the 1720s. Poor relief increased, tax abatements became more common, and per capita imports and exports decreased.

The House forced frequent emissions of paper money, but depreciation and the resultant inflation meant that the working class continued to suffer from the rising cost of living while merchants and landowners prospered. The representatives clashed with Governors Samuel Shute (1716–1722) and William Burnet (1727–1729) over currency issues, control of the settlement of the Maine woods, and their desire to completely control the colony's expenditures. The leaders charged the governor with "the subversion of the constitution," but they also won a number of significant legislative victories, including the right to appoint their own speaker. War veterans emerged as another important pressure group during the 1720s and 1730s; the *Journals* of the House of Representatives are filled with petitions from disabled men or their widows seeking varying forms of relief from the government, and the House granted many of these petitioners land on the frontier.

Gov. Jonathan Belcher (1730–1741), a native of the colony, began the next decade in a conciliatory fashion, but his aristocratic demeanor and exceptional stubbornness identified him with the growing specter of Crown influence. As the House continued to assert its claims to legislative control, the governor lost his patience and became embroiled in disputes over his salary and control of the treasury. Economic antagonisms exploded again when merchants tried to establish a public market in 1733.

The Boston economy, meanwhile, sank deeper into recession. By 1742, in a population of slightly more than seventeen thousand there were 146 residents of almshouses and workhouses and at least a thousand nonrateable or destitute widows. Between 1734 and 1751, some 247 pauper children were apprenticed in the city. No longer was the family or the local village able to care for its own. In this context, currency issues attained greater urgency, and the House sent an agent to London to plead its case.

The king was not sympathetic. Instead, acting on the advice of London merchants involved in the New England trade, the Crown proposed conservative, strictly controlled emissions. In response, the Cooke's popular party made a final attempt to wrest economic and political control from London-based merchants, proposing yet another land bank. While the first such proposal in 1714 had drawn only nine subscribers, this one drew 395 from sixty-four towns. The wealthy merchants supported the Crown's position. In areas such as Worcester County, these men used the existing credit and court structure to maintain their economic and social hegemony. A land bank would bypass such structures by making credit far more widely available without recourse to the British-connected elite. The support of Dr. Jabez Upham of Brookfield, in the southeast corner of Worcester County, was typical. Upham was a militia officer who later became a Baptist and a member of the House opposition to the governor in the late 1750s. He may have had some status in his community, but he controlled no patronage and had few financial resources; he thus remained outside the patriarchal lines of royal authority and gentry credit.

Merchants chartered a silver bank that issued currency redeemable only in silver, and they refused to accept land bank notes in daily business. Belcher fired or dismissed all those government officials who subscribed to the land bank and purged all justices of the peace who showed any signs of supporting the effort. While bank supporters succeeded in solidifying their control of the House in the next election, their efforts were in vain. England declared the bank illegal. The crisis galvanized popular opinion into a coherent explanation of the colony's economic ills. Just as paper money was seen as a way for ordinary citizens to keep out of debt and as a means of encouraging economic growth, so the refusal of merchants and the royal government to cooperate reflected their alienation from the public needs of the colony. Land bank supporters portrayed merchants as duplicitous, selfish, and traitorous enemies of true British rights, more concerned with importing corrupt luxuries than protecting the colony's "Charter Rights" and English liberties. Such men were moved, one pamphleteer argued in 1750, by "a love of Power, love of *Prerogative,* love of Money. And as these are the killing Causes of our CONSTITUTION, we never again can possibly be made whole, until these Instruments and Causes are finally removed. . . . "[28]

After the defeat of the land bank and the religious convulsions that swept the colony during the Great Awakening, Massachusetts continued to experience profound economic and social dislocation. Social violence rose sharply, with a dramatic increase in court cases involving riot, assault, burglary, and theft. Only the skillful, tactful admin-istration of Gov. William Shirley (1741–1757) preserved some degree of social peace. Appointed through his impressive English connections, Shirley proved to be a master politician, skillfully compromising with the colonial opposition and using defense spending and patronage to create a wide-reaching alliance among the different political and economic factions within the colony. He also guided the colony through a long and acrimonious settlement of lawsuits over the land bank and a bitter controversy concern-ing rising legal fees. He even survived the popular anger and unrest that swept through Boston during the impressment riots. That Shirley succeeded in rising above all these difficulties and in ruling Massachusetts until 1757 is a tribute to a man who could bridge the roles of imperial administrator and protector of the colony's interests.

Even Shirley, though, could not stem the tide of resentment, and indeed he inad-vertently encouraged it. Naturally sympathetic to a patriarchal view of society, the gov-ernor forged a close political alliance with Thomas Hutchinson (speaker of the House) and other gentry leaders. Angered by continued economic problems and by Hutchinson's attack on Bostonians' resistance to impressment in 1747, opposition lead-ers established their own newspaper in 1748, the *Independent Advertiser,* and a new popular party led by Samuel Adams, Jr. and others renewed attacks on the gentry: "Is it a Crime to be rich? Yes, certainly. At the Publick Expense."[29] They portrayed war profi-teers as a few men driven by "Lust of Power, Lust of Fame, Lust of Money. . . ."[30] "Phileleutheros" addressed Boston artisans in 1751, reminding them that it was their

---

❧ *Documents* ☙
A Conspiracy Against Liberty

The belief in a conspiracy against virtue and liberty was central to the colonial world view, as the following selection makes clear.

> It is impossible that a *whole* nation should be ruin'd *all* at once, or when they behold the Engines of their Ruin at *Work.* This must be brought about by a Succession of *Acts* adapted to the unnumber-able Weaknesses of our Make, which render the Incautious and Honest the Prey of *those* who make Mankind their *Study,* in Order to make them their *Property.* It has always been the Subtlety of ambitious Men to affect Generosity and Publick Spiritedness, Humility and Self-Denial, 'till they have attained a Degree of *Power,* that stands in no Need of Reputation of any Virtue to support it.

Boston Independent Advertiser, 1 February, 1748.

labor that provided the rich with their wealth: "Gentry, Clergy, Lawyers, and military officers, do all support their Grandeur by your Sweat, and at your Hazard."[31]

Despite the prestige and wealth of Hutchinson and his political allies, the power of patriarchal authority in the colony continued to erode. In 1760, Hutchinson and his merchant and lawyer supporters decided to launch an assault on the town meeting system of government. Dubbed the "junto" by the popular opposition, this "court" party believed that the common people were ruled by passion and that only men like themselves could be legitimate rulers. The artisans and laborers of Boston organized to resist the junto's attack. The confrontation between the two sides in the 1760 elections was indecisive, but the incident proved to be the beginning of a brief but influential career for James Otis as leader of the colony's popular party in the early 1760s.

The great variety of political activity and conflict in these colonies would seem to make any significant generalizations impossible, but certain patterns are worth stressing. The representative assemblies of most colonies greatly increased their power during the eighteenth century. At the same time, members of the upper class enlarged their share of colonial wealth and began to consciously emulate their English counterparts. The community of interest between rich and poor, a precarious balance even in the best of times, disappeared. Those in between found themselves shut out from the most profitable investment opportunities. The poor turned to the legislatures to seek redress for their grievances, while the middle class did so as a means of increasing its own political and economic power. Even in the south, where the local gentry maintained a firm grip on legislative power, the elites were forced to contend with serious threats to their social control. Republicanism depended upon social harmony, and at mid-century, most colonies maintained only a precarious social and political stability. It was a delicate balance that could survive only if Americans avoided further economic disruption, retained their relative political independence, and somehow healed the painful emotional wounds that so bitterly divided them. None of these possibilities was in the cards. Ordinary Americans abandoned deferential politics and moved to make the political system more amenable to their needs. This was not, however, a mere political decision. The moral imperatives of republicanism made the pursuit of self-interest in America a righteous cause and allowed the political opposition to claim theirs as the only true course of public interest and the common good.

❧ *Chapter Twelve* ❧

Enlightenment and Popular Culture in Eighteenth-Century America

The Great Awakening exposed critical fault lines in eighteenth-century American culture. Clearly, many colonists felt threatened by the growing dominance of an elite, hierarchical, and rational culture that was more genteel than their own. These people continued to embrace a vibrant folk culture in rituals, popular entertainments, and a magical view of the world, and they rejected what they viewed as dangerous excesses of luxury and extravagance. Other Americans, though, welcomed the rationalism of Enlightenment philosophy and eagerly sought to emulate contemporary European manners. In science, philosophy, literature, the arts, and in their expectations of the family and of women, educated Americans grew closer to their European counterparts. Elites on both sides of the ocean applied reason and the scientific method to all of life in search of a better, more civilized world.

Culture, Behavior, And Social Decay

Before 1700, most Europeans questioned whether North America was yet sufficiently civilized for habitation. In the second quarter of the eighteenth century, New Yorkers' boorish behavior shocked the peripatetic Dr. Alexander Hamilton. One individual he met "exceeded everything I had seen for nastiness, impudence, and rusticity. He told us he was troubled with the open piles and with that, from his breeches, pulled out a linnen hankercheff all stained with blood and showed it to the company just after we had eat dinner."[1] Yet by the end of the American Revolution, Europe was eagerly studying the young United States to see what it could learn from "The American, this new man?"[2]

The roots of this transformation can be traced in part to the American elite's adoption of what historians have termed the "metropolitan standard" of behavior.

These individuals embraced polite behavior and its accompanying rituals to mediate the harshness of the emerging capitalist economy and to enhance their own sense of status in the immature social environment of the New World. Many found guidance in French and British reprints of books on manners and proper behavior. Eleazar Moody's *School of Good Manners* went through thirty-three editions by 1750. Originally published in 1564 as a guide to behavior for French children, it now served as an instructional manual for Americans who feared they were children in the international forum of decorous behavior. "Smell not of thy meat nor put it to thy nose. . . ," Moody advised, and "[p]ut not thy hand in the presence of others to any part of thy body not ordinarily discovered." He counseled the expectorating gentleman to "[s]pit not in the room but in the corner, or rather go out and do it abroad."[3] An adolescent George Washington read a French Jesuit book called *Rules of Civility and Decent Behavior* that was originally published in 1595 and learned not to spew another's face with spit by speaking too close and to clean his teeth with toothpicks, rather than napkins, knives, or forks.

A number of factors lent urgency to these attempts to achieve cultural gentility. Colonial society lacked the extensive patronage and ties of social obligation that bonded English society; even the traditional restraints of social and political deference were decaying. The growing importance of individualistic market values in American society heightened the need for new social bonds. Finally, by the mid-eighteenth century, many Americans accepted a view of history and of the evolution of societies that fed their growing sense of unease. They believed that over time, societies moved from relatively simple agricultural forms toward more complex, hierarchical structures that brought both greater sophistication and subtle dangers. Wealth and worldliness exposed people to the dangers of luxury and social decay that figured so prominently in the conspiracy theories of republican ideology.

Americans feared they were moving rapidly through these stages of development—and many believed too rapidly. But a few believed they could, with care, avoid the dangers of corruption and deceit that seemed to accompany the final stages of development, that they could combine the virtue of the new continent with the refinement of the old and create a society that would embody the best of Enlightenment ideals.

The Enlightenment In America

"Dare to Know!": Have the courage to use your own intelligence."[4] Thus did the philosopher Immanuel Kant dramatically summarize Enlightenment beliefs. Isaac Newton, John Locke, and the French philosophes created a system of thought that preached the application of reason and the scientific method to the understanding of life itself. The world was as a machine, and Enlightenment intellectuals believed they could discover the natural laws of politics, economics, and even morality in the same way that Newton had bared the immutable laws of nature. Locke argued that by changing the environment, humans could change society and the people in it. Evil lay not in men and women but in the institutions that shaped them. In abandoning the constraints of the past, humans could move toward a better society of hope and progress.

Seventeenth-century colonists embraced an essentially medieval view of the universe. Mystery held sway and God's intervention remained a daily possibility. By the mid-eighteenth century, most Americans had abandoned this view. To be sure, they had not yet adopted an entirely modern sense of causation. Their knowledge of many natural and human events was limited, and they tended to explain the unknown, particularly in human affairs, by resorting to tales of conspiracy and deceit. In exploring natural phenomena, though, more and more Americans turned to a scientific, rational approach. They viewed the universe as a machine, governed by laws that could be studied and understood. Deism was the most extreme form of this belief. Deists believed that God had essentially would up the universe at the beginning of time, like a clock, and then sat back and watched events unfold without interfering. Thus, the universe remained divine but subject to human understanding and even manipulation.

While many Americans accepted a more scientific view of the universe, few contributed in any meaningful way to the speculative side of philosophy; only a handful of names stand out. Jonathan Edwards was perhaps the greatest of these. Some of his earliest works, such as *Notes on the Mind* and *Notes in Natural Science,* explored complex issues in epistemology and showed a mastery of Newtonian science. His *Treatise Concerning Religious Affections* (1746) was a profoundly original study of the psychology of religious feeling; Edwards understood that the preacher could arouse the emotions in a most calculating way. But though he saw himself as a rationalist, Edwards was essentially a traditional thinker. Enlightenment explanations of reality were useful only in so far as they served as vehicles of his Calvinistic condemnation of human sinfulness. Human existence remained ephemeral, the individual a speck of dust in God's universe. Edwards saw nature as a symbolic system that humans must interpret to seek the truth of divine revelation. God created beauty in nature, he argued, to help humans understand the operations of the Holy Spirit. All the universe was no more than a revelation of the Divine Will. Light, the symbol of reason for the European Enlightenment, was for Edwards a way of reaching the heart. Indeed, his writings on light are reminiscent of the medieval, mystic adulation of God's presence in the glorious light of the Gothic cathedrals. For Edwards, the purpose of life in the New World was not to mimic the corruption of the Old but to prepare for the day when the kingdom of God would appear in America to guide the blinded Old World to salvation.

Most Americans influenced by the Enlightenment were more practically minded, gatherers and observers of natural and human phenomena rather than speculators. The world scientific community appreciated and honored their discoveries and writings. The British Royal Society, a clearing house for scientific information, admitted fifty-three Americans as fellows between 1663 and 1783. The society's official publication, the *Philosophical Transactions,* printed 260 articles by Americans. Americans in 1743 founded the American Philosophical Society, which grew out of a smaller group begun by Benjamin Franklin in 1727. In 1750, another group founded the American Society for Promoting and Propagating Useful Knowledge, a quintessential American organization.

Eighteenth-century scientists divided their field into two broad categories: natural philosophy, which included the physical sciences and mathematics, and natural history, which included botany and zoology. Americans made important contributions in both areas. Cadwallader Colden was one of the best-known names in both political and scientific circles in early America. Colden received a master's degree from the University of Edinburgh and tutored medicine privately in London; he later became lieutenant governor of New York and widely known—and condemned—for his strongly loyalist views. Colden attempted to formulate an original theory of gravity, arguing that it was caused by the exertion of ether on planets and stars, its force inverse to the square of the distance between any two bodies. William Small, British-born and educated and a professor at the College of William and Mary, founded a society to encourage scientific experimentation and to promote interest in the arts and manufactures. He taught Jefferson and later became his patron and correspondent.

❧ *Documents* ❧
Of Magnets, God, and Smallpox

In the first excerpt below, Cotton Mather relates how he came to believe in the validity of inoculation as a preventative for smallpox. His comments reflect the Enlightenment emphasis on practical experimentation and empirical knowledge. The second selection is drawn from Mather's discussion of magnetism and follows an earlier, scientific description of how a magnet works. In this paragraph, he puts his explanation in a more traditional religious context. The combination serves to remind us that the Enlightenment, though powerful, made only partial inroads into American society.

> There has been a wonderful practice lately used in several parts of the world, which indeed is not yet become common in our nation. I was first instructed in it by a Guramantee servant of my own, long before I knew that any European or Asiatics had the least acquaintance with it, and some years before I was enriched with the communications of the learned foreigners, whose accounts I found agreeing with what I received of my servant, when he showed me the scar of the wound made for the operation, and said that no person ever died of the smallpox in their country that had the courage to use it.

> I have since met with a considerable number of these Africans, who all agree in one story: that "in their country grandy-many die of the smallpox, but now they learn this way: people take juice of small-

In New England, the strong religious emphasis in the curriculums at Harvard and Yale delayed scientific exploration. But by the beginning of the eighteenth century, European currents of thought began to make significant inroads in the books read and courses taught at both schools, and New Englanders emerged as significant contributors to Anglo-American scientific discourse. Though some of Cotton Mather's beliefs were almost medieval in their mysticism, the Puritan divine was open to all varieties of scientific investigation and maintained an extensive correspondence with leading figures in the Western world. His advocacy of smallpox inoculation is just one example of his willingness to question accepted wisdom.

Men such as Isaac Greenwood were even more in the mainstream of modern scientific thought. Greenwood graduated form Harvard in 1721 and studied mathematics and natural philosophy in England. He returned to Harvard and actively promoted Newtonian science. His most important student was John Winthrop IV, who provided an appropriate bookend to the Winthrop dynasty in Massachusetts. A professor of mathematics and natural and experimental philosophy at Harvard, Winthrop's interests could not have been farther removed from those of his illustrious ancestor. While the first John Winthrop studied the heavens for hints of divine signs and portents, John IV observed them for entirely naturalistic reasons. He

pox and cutty skin and put in a drop; then by 'nd by a little sicky, sicky; then very few little things like smallpox; and nobody die of it; and nobody have smallpox any more." Thus in Africa, where the poor creatures die of the smallpox like rotten sheep, a merciful God has taught them an infallible preservative. 'Tis common practice and is attended with a constant success. . . .

Cotton Mather, "The Angel of Bethesda," in Richard H. Shryock and Otho T. Beall, Jr., eds., *Cotton Mather, First Significant Figure in American Medicine* (Baltimore: Johns Hopkins University Press, 1954), 175–6.

Once for all, gentlemen philosophers, the magnet has quite puzzled you. It shall then be no indecent anticipation of what should have been observed at the conclusion of this collection, here to demand it of you, that you glorify the infinite creator of this, and of all things, as incomprehensible. You must acknowledge that human reason is too feeble, too narrow a thing to comprehend the infinite God. . . . They have done well to call it the loadstone, that is to say, the lead-stone: *May it lead me unto Thee O my God and my Saviour!* magnetism is in this like to gravity, that it leads us to God and brings us very near to Him. When we see magnetism in its operation, we must say, This is the Work of God!

Cotton Mather, *The Christian Philosopher* (Charleston, MA: J. M. Kown, 1815), 112.

specialized in astronomy, accumulated a large scientific library, conducted experiments in electricity and meteorology, and led an expedition to Newfoundland in 1761 to observe the transit of Venus across the face of the sun.

Pennsylvania was the most fecund source of American scientific ingenuity. Clock maker David Rittenhouse studied the transit of Venus and built a refracting telescope. He is best known for his orrery, a mechanical device that showed the relationship of the bodies in the solar system, and his astronomical observatory, a mechanical planetarium. But Rittenhouse's star shone weakly in comparison to that of his contemporary and colleague, Benjamin Franklin.

Franklin was born in Boston in 1706, the youngest son of a poor tallow maker. Apprenticed at twelve in his father's shop, he left home at seventeen and was a wealthy man by the age of forty-two. His accomplishments are legion. After leaving the tallow shop, he worked for a time at his brother's Boston newspaper, the *New England Courant,* and wrote witty essays that offered advice on how to get ahead in the world—immature versions of his later, more famous, Poor Richard essays (*Poor Richard's Almanac* was published between 1733 and 1758). Franklin's words of wisdom were typical of the practical, earthy advice that characterized the American Enlightenment, advocating thrift, hard work, and virtuous behavior. The

Ben Franklin at 54; engraving
by James McArdell after
Benjamin Wilson. ❧

Puritan influence, without the religious context, is obvious, but so is Franklin's acceptance of one of the key Enlightenment beliefs—the use of reason to govern the passions. Enlightenment thinkers everywhere believed that individuals who could so control themselves could readily achieve worldly success. Franklin also wrote his *Autobiography* as a guide for his son, in imitation of Lord Chesterfield. He portrayed his own life as a quest for moral perfection *and* social achievement, again stressing the virtues of thrift and industry. It was a tale of upwardly mobile adventure; but while Edwards's self-reflections traced a path toward God, Franklin's followed the road to material success.

Franklin's scientific interests dominated his life for only a brief period of time, from the late 1740s to the early 1760s, but during these years, he drew worldwide attention to himself and the American colonies. His interests reflected the uniquely pragmatic approach that characterized the American Enlightenment—the belief that philosophy was worthy of study only if it could be put to some practical use. For six years, beginning in 1748, Franklin directed his attention to electricity. The Dutch scientist Pieter van Musschenbroek had recently developed the Leyden jar, a device that condensed electricity in a glass bottle; he also produced electrical sparks by attaching a conductor to the bottle's sides. Franklin devised a number of experiments using Leyden jars in his Philadelphia home, leading to several important theoretical discoveries. He publicized his findings in a 1751 book, *Experiments and Observations on Electricity,* that created a sensation in European scientific circles.

Franklin is best known for his 1752 kite experiment. He designed this experiment to prove empirically that lightning produced by thunderstorms was, in fact, a form of electricity. He constructed a primitive kite of a large silk handkerchief on two crossed wooden sticks and added a tail and a wire to the top. At the end of the string leading down from the kite, he attached a metal key and from the key to his hand a silk ribbon. He theorized that lightning would strike the wire, electrifying the kite; rain would wet the kite and string, which would then conduct electricity to the key. The experiment was a success. Franklin's name became a household word among the greatest European minds, and he was awarded the Copley Medal by the Royal Society in 1753. Three years later, he became one of the few Americans to be elected a fellow of the Royal Society.

Franklin pursued studies in other scientific areas, particularly in heat conductivity. He designed the Franklin stove, which forced heat to descend before escaping through the chimney, thereby warming the room at all levels. He did a good deal of tinkering as well, inventing bifocals and the famed glass harmonica, an instrument for which Mozart wrote a charming concerto. He maintained an active interest in astronomy, meteorology, oceanography, optics, botany, medicine, phonetics, and music. In addition to his involvement with the American Philosophical Society, he was director of the first American fire insurance company, helped finance the first American ship to explore the Arctic, and formed the colonial postal service. He was also extensively involved in colonial and imperial politics. Franklin undoubtedly deserves his reputation as America's preeminent Enlightenment figure.

Americans also made notable contributions in the natural sciences, particularly in the field of natural history. European Enlightenment thinkers looked to America for new discoveries, and a number of colonists were central figures in an international group of collectors of fauna and flora in England, France, Holland, Sweden, Germany, and Italy. The London merchant Peter Collinson maintained an extensive American correspondence and did much to popularize American plants in Europe. William Byrd II sent many samples of plant life to England, and his diaries are filled with observations of American nature. Mark Catesby, known as "the colonial Audubon," was a skilled illustrator who did extensive fieldwork and wrote *The Natural History of Carolina, Florida, and the Bahama Islands* (1731). John Banister, Alexander Garden and John Lining were other noble figures who did important fieldwork in the southern colonies. In the middle colonies, the politician James Logan collected insects, birds, and fossils. Cadwallader Colden collected plants, and his daughter Jane continued his work after his death, compiling *Flora of New York*, a work with 340 illustrations that was placed in the British Museum. John Bartram sent seeds and plants to London, Holland, and even to Carolus Linnaeus, the famed Swedish naturalist who developed the modern species classification system. Linnaeus was so impressed by his work that he called Bartram "the greatest natural botanist in the world."[5]

At first, colonial medicine was most primitive, generally practiced as a sideline by men in other fields. Physicians generally believed that illness resulted from impurities in the bodily fluids (humors) or from nervous or vascular disorders. Common treatments included bleeding, induced vomiting, blistering, and purging, all just as likely to kill as cure the patient. Remedies included a mixture of boiled and pounded snakes, white wine, herbs, and opium for whooping cough, eagle brain mixed with wine for jaundice, and eagle dung for tremors.

After 1700, a medical profession of sorts began to emerge, and by 1776, there were about thirty-five hundred physicians in the colonies. But only about five hundred of these had any formal training, and only twenty-five held medical degrees, mostly from schools in Scotland. Medical societies began to appear in cities after mid-century, and medical departments were established at the College of Philadelphia and King's College. Two hospitals were also established before the Revolution, in Philadelphia (1752) and New York (1769).

❧ *Documents* ❧
The Broad Impact of the Enlightenment

The following selections indicate the breadth of the impact of Enlightenment beliefs on American thought. The first three are from Benjamin Franklin's writings on deism, his proposed curriculum at the Philadelphia Academy, and the Pennsylvania Hospital. The final selection is from William Livingston's *The Independent Reflector;* it suggests the connection between Enlightenment rationalism and Anglo-American patriotism.

> I grew convinc'd that *Truth, Sincerity & Integrity* in Dealings between Man & Man, were of the utmost Importance to the Felicity of Life, and I form'd written Resolutions. . . to practise them ever while I lived. Revelation had indeed no weight with me as such; but I entertain'd an Opinion, that tho' certain Actions might not be bad *because* they were forbidden by it, or good *because* it commanded them; yet probably those Actions might be forbidden *because* they were bad for us, or commanded *because* they were beneficial to us, in their own Natures. . . .

The Autobiography of Benjamin Franklin, Louis P. Masur, ed. (New York: Bedford Books of St. Martin's Press, 1993), 70. Copyright © 1993. Reprinted with permission of St. Martin's Press, Incorporated and Bedford Books.

> Thus instructed, Youth will come out of this School fitted for learning any Business, Calling or Profession, except such wherein Languages are required; and tho' unacquainted with any ancient or foreign Tongue, they will be Masters of their own, which is of more immediate and general Use; and withal will have attain'd many other valuable Accomplishments; the Time usually spent in acquiring those Languages, often without Success, being here employ'd in laying such a Foundation of Knowledge and Ability, as, properly

In the early years of the eighteenth century, European improvements in microscopes allowed scientists to study bacteria. Perhaps the best-known American application of their findings came when Cotton Mather championed smallpox inoculation. Mather had read of the inoculation procedure in a Royal Society of London publication. Ironically, when smallpox ravaged Boston in 1721, the most "enlightened" scientific minds of the colony opposed inoculation, arguing against the logic of curing a disease by injecting it into a patient. They were joined in their opposition by the more conservative religious elements in the colony, who contended that only God had power over life and death and that man was tempting fate by interfering. Mather and two Boston physicians observed that there were far fewer deaths elsewhere among those who were inoculated than among those who were not and

improv'd, may qualify them to pass thro' and execute the several Offices of civil Life, with Advantage and Reputation to themselves and Country.

Benjamin Franklin, *Idea of the English School* in Leonard W. Labaree and William B. Willcox, eds., *The Papers of Benjamin Franklin* 26 vols. to date, (New Haven: Yale University Press, 1959–), 4:108.

Experience has more and more convinced all concerned of the great usefulness of this charity. The careful attendance afforded to the sick poor; the neatness, cleanness, and regularity of diet with which they are kept in the hospital are found to contribute to their recovery much sooner than their own manner of living at home, and render the physic they take more effectual. . . . In short, there is scarce any one kind of doing good which is not hereby in some manner promoted; for not only the sick are visited and relieved, but the stranger is taken in, the ignorant instructed, and the bad reclaimed.

Benjamin Franklin, *Some Account of the Pennsylvania Hospital* (Philadelphia: 1754), 38.

Let us abhor Superstition and Bigotry, which are the Parents of Sloth and Slavery. Let us make War upon Ignorance and Barbarity of Manners. Let us invite the Arts and Sciences to reside amongst us. Let us encourage every thing which tends to exalt and embellish our Characters. And in fine, let the Love of our Country be manifested by that which is the only true Manifestation of it, a patriotic Soul and a public Spirit.

William Livingston, John Moris Scott and William Smith Jr., *The Independent Reflector. . .* , Milton M. Klein, ed. (Cambridge, MA: Harvard University Press, 1963), 220.

argued that this evidence warranted adopting the practice. In accepting the inviolability of empirical evidence, the trio acted as early American champions of the Enlightenment emphasis on scientific experimentation and reason.

Literacy And Culture In Eighteenth-Century America

Print culture dominated American society by the mid-eighteenth century. By the time of the revolution, 85 percent of white adult males could read and write in New England, 60 percent in Pennsylvania and Virginia. Though in the early eighteenth century about 60 percent of American women could write their names, the comparative figure for England was closer to 25 percent—and probably most American women could read. Print culture introduced colonists to the wider world and exposed them to international events and European cultural practices and ideas. It did so through the various institutions and mechanisms that dominated the educational process in the eighteenth-century world: schools, colleges, newspapers and other popular print forms, and literature.

Schools

As population grew and settlement spread, the family lost some of its ability to socialize the next generation into the culture's religious beliefs and social customs. The church took on some of this burden; by the end of the seventeenth century, church-sponsored catechism and religious societies were responsible for religious education. Local schools assumed many of the other burdens of socialization, and selectmen and even the General Court began to intervene to ensure that towns established and maintained their schools at a minimum level. Town precincts and districts often fought for the right to use taxes to establish and support their own schools.

The structure of local schools was essentially unchanged from the previous century. The people of Chebacco, a precinct of Ipswich, Massachusetts, supported their local school by rental income, taxes, and tuition (two shillings, three pence a child in 1742). Schoolmasters moved among the town's parishes, and only in the late 1750s were individual district schools established. Classes were held for only four months a year, and the teachers generally lacked college degrees. Generally, only instructors who taught in the higher grammar schools had college degrees. And parents did not always heed the desires of town and colony officials—only twenty-four parents, or 16 percent of Chebacco's families, sent their children to school in 1760.

Education in the middle colonies was generally in private hands. The Germans sent their children to church-related schools or taught them the basics of reading and writing at home. By mid-century, the Pennsylvania Quakers' seventeen monthly meetings supported forty schools, relying on voluntary subscriptions and tuition and offering free education for the poor. There were also a few small, church-supported charity schools, but these were never very successful. Night schools emerged as particularly important institutions in this region, offering practical subjects in business, engineering, surveying, and other needed skills, including a wide variety of foreign languages. The classes were offered by individuals who often taught them, for a fee, in their own homes. The career of at least one teacher, Anthony Benezet, spanned several of these pedagogical forms. Benezet left France for Philadelphia in 1731. He taught at the Germantown School from 1739 to 1742, then at the Philadelphia Friends School, and then became master of a Quaker girls' school in the city. He also established a night school for blacks. From all accounts, he showed compassion for his students and taught anyone who sought instruction—old and young, black and white, rich and poor. More than fifty schoolmasters worked in Philadelphia between 1695 and the Revolution. If they even approximated the character and skill of Benezet, the city was rich in educational opportunities.

The southern colonies were not so lucky. Few formally organized schools existed in the south; wealthy planters sent their sons to England or hired private tutors. Daughters were educated along with sons until the age of ten, then given two or three years of instruction in music, dancing, and social graces. Robert Carter of Nomini Hall, for instance, hired a number of private tutors for his children, as well as music and dancing masters and governesses. Private schoolmasters became more common after mid-century. Prince George's County, Maryland, had a dozen or so schoolmasters by 1755, each teaching eighty-five to one hundred families. Most ran simple reading schools, though there were also a Latin school, one in which math as well as reading and writing was taught, and two in which girls learned sewing, knitting, and French. The clergy ran parish schools in Virginia, which also had several endowed charity schools. The wealthier the planter, the more likely he was to provide for his childrens' education in his will. Male orphans could generally count on at least a year or two of formal education after their parents' deaths. Private schools and tutors, finally, dominated education in South Carolina, despite the assembly's attempts to encourage public efforts such as the Charleston Free School, where only those who could afford it paid tuition.

At the time of the Revolution, the colonies had nine colleges. Harvard (1636), William and Mary (1693), and Yale (1701) were all well established, but the Great Awakening stirred an even greater interest in higher education. Several colleges emerged out of the controversies surrounding the revival, founded by particular denominations to further their own interests. New Light Scottish Presbyterians founded the College of New Jersey in 1746 in Elizabethtown. In 1754, the college merged with a smaller academy and moved to Princeton, eventually becoming interdenominational. The Baptists established the College of Rhode Island (later Brown University) in 1754. Dutch New Light preachers of the Reformed Church founded Queen's college (later Rutgers University) in 1766, and New Light Congregationalists established Dartmouth College in 1769. Other efforts were more in keeping with the practical nature of the American Enlightenment. Benjamin Franklin helped establish the College of Philadelphia in 1755 (later the University of Pennsylvania) and left his indelible mark on the curriculum; the school did not require a religious test for admission. The Anglicans established King's College (later Columbia University) in 1754, but the colony's religious diversity ensured an interdenominational student body and a relatively broad curriculum.

Franklin, the champion of a uniquely American culture and education, viewed most colleges as little more than assemblages of pompous, useless individuals, noting that the students at Harvard learned "little more than how to carry themselves handsomely, and enter a room genteely, (which might as well be acquir'd at a Dancing-School,) and from whence they return, after Abundance of Trouble and Charge, as great Blockheads as ever, only more proud and self-conceited."[6] Still, it is worth examining the content of the formal curriculum at these schools, for it says much about the direction of elite intellectual culture in America and suggests the direction in which even popular culture was moving.

In general, a medieval curriculum predominated, though the emphasis differed from school to school. Students studied the trivium (grammar, logic, rhetoric) during their first two years, then the quadrivium (arithmetic, geometry, astronomy, music) as juniors and seniors. Science and math occupied increasingly prominent positions. Much like today, students heard lectures and took notes, delivered oral presentations on particular subjects, and wrote essays. Individual institutions and presidents put their own stamp on the course of study. Rev. Samuel Johnson, president of King's College, catered to the college's wealthy Anglican and Dutch Reformed students by emphasizing languages, writing and reasoning, surveying and navigation, and a variety of other practical subjects. The Reverend William Smith, the first president of the College of Philadelphia and a graduate of Aberdeen College in Scotland, recommended a course of study that focused on the science of moral philosophy popularized by the Scottish Enlightenment yet also addressed the practical demands of the Philadelphia economic milieu. Students at Philadelphia thus studied ethics and moral philosophy, as well as math, natural history, geography, surveying, geometry, astronomy, politics, trade, commerce, rhetoric, and the classics. Fully a third of the curriculum was devoted to math and the natural sciences, and in 1765, the college established a medical department. John Witherspoon, president of Princeton, synthesized Calvinist piety and the Scottish commonsense philosophy to offer a viable alternative to the theological liberalism that dominated many college curriculums. Like Smith, he promoted the idea of an internal human sense that could perceive moral excellence in a way similar to the manner in which external senses perceived sound and color. But he also stressed the rights of the laity in religious congregations, the pastoral responsibilities of ministers, and high personal standards for the clergy.

The age of admission to these schools varied, with some students entering as young as eleven or twelve, others at seventeen or even older. In some respects, students' personal lives differed little from those of students today. At Yale, Jonathan Edwards wrote home of students' "Unseasonable Nightwalking, Breaking People's windows, playing at Cards, Cursing, Swearing, and Damning, and Using all manner of Ill Language."[7] In this behavior, at least, Edwards saw little difference between the elite culture of Yale students and the popular folk entertainments of Northampton youth. He rejected both, even while drawing from each for his intellectual powers and religious fervor.

Literature

Only forty-four hundred Americans graduated from college between 1715 and 1775. These individuals spearheaded the adoption of continental ideas and philosophies and were the intellectual leaders of the emerging gentry culture. But most colonists were exposed to wider concerns through more mundane sources. Almanacs were particularly popular at all levels of society. About two hundred of these collections of literature and all-purpose information were published before 1800, and they were used by all members of the family. The best known almanac publisher was Nathaniel Ames, whose *Astronomical Diary and Almanack* (1725–1764) sold more than fifty thousand copies annually. Benjamin Franklin's *Poor Richard's Almanack* sold about ten thousand copies each year of its publication, from 1733 to 1796. Ames was a physician and tavern keeper from Dedham, Massachusetts. His almanac contained poems, moralistic essays, proverbs, adventure stories, popularized science, calendars, astrological predictions, tidal phases, moon charts, and weather predictions for the entire year. He offered cures and health diets for all varieties of illnesses. It is clear that these publications were expressions of the popular culture that continued to dominate much of the colonial experience. Much almanac humor was directed at artisans, city dwellers, and anyone who acquired pompous, "genteel" habits. Anti-Catholicism became common after mid-century, and stories of Catholic atrocities and Jesuit plots appeared often.

Newspapers were the next level of information and cultural dispersion in the colonies. Between 1704 and 1775, seventy-eight newspapers appeared in the colonies, with thirty-seven publishing when the Revolution began. The first true paper was the *Boston News-Letter*, initially published in 1704. Other noteworthy efforts included the *Pennsylvania Gazette*, the *American Weekly Mercury*, the *Virginia Gazette*, Zenger's *New York Weekly Journal*, and the irreverent *New England Courant*, which mercilessly mocked Cotton Mather and other New England clergy. Most papers were published weekly or biweekly, consisted of four pages, and were dominated by ads and shipping notices. Foreign and colonial news appeared on the first and second pages. Most reprinted poems, essays, and letters from their readers, but they also openly and frequently borrowed articles and essays from European papers and magazines. Increasingly, these items were intended as direct commentary on events in England, the colonies, and the world, reflecting colonial concerns with power, liberty, and corruption. Like many other publications, newspapers also offered guidelines to colonists about how to live their lives, emphasizing virtuous behavior and the avoidance of luxury and political corruption. A glance at any issue of these publications reveals a blend of popular and genteel culture that helps explain their popularity. Articles from prestigious London magazines shared space with homegrown medical remedies, astrological predictions, and accounts of strange omens in the skies.

Magazines were a rare commodity in the colonies. The first, *The American Magazine,* was not published until 1741 and lasted only three months. In 1752, William Livingston published the first issue of *The Independent Reflector,* and it proved both longer-lasting and more influential. Drawing heavily from its English models, the *Reflector* was a vehicle for the Whig principles of virtue and liberty and became a focus for attacks on local British officials. Livingston argued that Anglican culture brought only corruption; he insisted that politics, science, and religion be explored solely with an eye toward social betterment. "The most intimate acquaintance with the classics," he noted, "will not remove our oaks; nor a taste for the *Georgics* cultivate our lands."[8]

The men who printed these newspapers and magazines, as well as the books and pamphlets published in America, occupied a position that has no counterpart in the publishing world today. Printers imported books and sold them; they were also political figures whose allegiances were well known within the community. Their advocacy of particular political beliefs or causes was instrumental in creating an educated electorate in Boston, Philadelphia, New York, and elsewhere. James Parker of the *Connecticut Gazette* and Timothy Peters of the *South-Carolina Gazette* made their papers vehicles for controversial opinions and printed numerous essays extolling the value of a free press in protecting English liberties. As Parker noted, "The press has always been an Enemy to Tyrants, and just so far as Tyranny prevails in any Part of the World, so far the Liberty of the Press is suppressed."[9]

The colonists also relied heavily on libraries for access to literature. Personal libraries were generally practical; lawyers, doctors, clergy, and even wealthy planters who dabbled in law or commerce had fairly large collections. Estate inventories of Maryland planters reveal much about who read what. By 1770, two-thirds of the inventories had books—but one-sixth of them had only a Bible, and three-quarters had fewer than ten books. A sixth of these estates could boast of a small library, and a few had several hundred volumes. Books on religion and morality were widespread; apart from the Bible, for instance, the most common book was the semireligious guide to daily life, *The Whole Duty of Man* (1657). Lewis Bayly's *Practice of Piety* (1613) also appeared often. Besides these religious guides, planters were most likely to own such volumes as Jethro Tull's *Horse-Hoing Husbandry* and Giles Jacob's *Every Man His Own Lawyer.* Cotton Mather and William Byrd II had two of the largest private libraries in the colony; Mather owned almost four thousand titles, Byrd more than thirty-six hundred. The content of these collections, moreover, was amazingly similar, reflecting a growing convergence of intellectual interests among all members of the colonial upper class.

As the century progressed, both private and public lending libraries became increasingly common throughout the colonies, serving the goals of social advancement and practical learning that dominated American learning in this century. Thomas Bray, head of the SPG, left many libraries during his years in North

America. In 1696, he financed a library of 1,095 volumes in Annapolis, Maryland—the earliest lending library in the colonies. By 1700, there were more than thirty such libraries. Generally, the books in these collections covered a great variety of topics, intended to serve the laity as well as the clergy.

Town and parish libraries also became more common. The subscription library was the most important innovation, first established in 1731 by Benjamin Franklin in Philadelphia. This library was based on an association of subscribers, each of whom would contribute a certain amount (forty shillings for the Franklin library) for the initial purchases and an annual contribution (ten shillings for the Franklin library) to enlarge the collection. Franklin collected fifty signatures for his first subscription, and the first selection of books included works by Homer, Plutarch, and Sidney. Atlases, histories, and personal handbooks were also prominent. Connecticut alone had more than half a dozen such libraries, including the Book Company of Durham (established in 1733) and the Philogrammatical Library in Lebanon (founded in 1739 by Rev. Solomon Williams and a group of neighbors). Abraham Redwood set up the Redwood Library in Newport, Rhode Island, in 1747, and seventeen leading citizens established the Charleston Library Society in 1748. New York's first permanent circulating public library—the New York Society Library—was founded in 1754.

Private clubs also served a critical role in spreading knowledge and establishing forums for intellectual discussion. The most famous of these was the Tuesday Club, started by Alexander Hamilton in Annapolis in 1745. Hamilton was a cultured physician who found Maryland summers unbearable—hence, his extensive travels and famous account thereof, the *Itinerarium* (1744). He served as secretary of the club and wrote a satirical mock epic, the *History of the Tuesday Club*. The group thrived on witty presentations, speeches, and mock trials. In 1748, New Yorkers also established a discussion club called the Society for the Promotion of Useful Knowledge, followed later by a medical society, a society for the arts, and a debating club.

Many Americans may have read extensively; some few may have even become intimate with the classic works of Western literature. But very few produced great works. One such accomplishment was Thomas Hutchinson's three-volume *History of the Massachusetts Bay Colony*. The colonists, of course, regarded history as one of the essential sources of human truth, but this was the first modern history written in the colonies, and it was based on Hutchinson's own extensive source and manuscript collection. Ironically, the Anglophile Hutchinson showed some sympathy to the plight of Indians and dissenters in the colony's past.

New England's ministers remained the most prolific of colonial writers. The vast majority of their work consisted of published and unpublished sermons, most of it bearing little permanent literary value—though we have already examined two exceptions in the writings of Cotton Mather and Jonathan Edwards. Ministers became more concerned with secular events by mid-century, as if they were rushing to compete for influence with the flood of political literature appearing in newspapers, pamphlets, and broadsides.

The power of the written word remained weak in the south, but the level of immersion in British literary culture was sufficient to spawn several works of distinction. William Byrd II knew Latin, Greek, Hebrew, French, and Italian. He studied law and science in England and explored drama with the London playwrights William Wycherley and William Congreve; his circle of friends included Jonathan Swift and Alexander Pope. His three main works, though not published until 1841, were stylishly written and captured the urbane sophistication of a perceptive observer. *The History of the Dividing Line Betwixt Virginia and North Carolina Run in the Year 1728, A Progress to the Mines in the Year 1732,* and *A Journey to the*

Land of Eden in the Year 1733 all provide fascinating details about life among white frontier settlers and Indians. He portrayed his own plantation existence as ideal for the rural gentleman-philosopher, his own mansion as a temple and refuge from the demands of the external world. More humorous, perhaps, and equally valuable as literature are the three surviving fragments of his secret diary, from the years 1709 to 1712, 1717 to 1721, and 1739 to 1741. These journals provide intimate portraits of Byrd's family life, his patriarchal immersion in the lives of his slaves, and above all his endless search for sexual conquest. Byrd eagerly bedded servants and slaves, as well as his wife; though he occasionally expressed a bit of guilt, more often he seemed to regard it as his due.

Then there was Ebenezer Cooke, an English tobacco merchant who emigrated to Maryland. In 1708, he published a humorous epic poem titled *The Sot-Weed Factor* that satirized Maryland settlers as uncouth drunks, bent only on increasing their fortunes. That was likely a fairly accurate description in 1708. By 1763, though, even Marylanders eagerly embraced the genteel culture of metropolitan London. Cooke would have found more familiar territory on the frontier.

The Arts

The creative arts in the colonies reflected an inevitable tension between a New World orientation and the growing preference for genteel Old World models. In furniture, Americans modified European styles to suit their needs, developing a

John Singleton Copley, "Paul Revere" (Gift of Joseph W., William B., and Edward H. R. Revere. Courtesy, Museum of Fine Arts, Boston). ❧

"Rachel Weeping," by Charles Wilson Peale. ❧

plainer and simpler style, less decorative and with a cleaner line and form. Individual craftsmen added their own touches. Many became skilled carvers, while others painted such figures as sunflowers and tulips on their products or inlaid different woods in desks and chests.

The art of decorative silversmithing began in the late seventeenth century with the production of communion cups and porringers. Silversmiths were craftsmen, who like Paul Revere, Jr., started off their careers as lowly apprentices and became among the most skilled and creative of all American artisans, producing beautifully scrolled handles, cherub motifs, and decorative fluting. Revere, Jr. apprenticed in his father's shop, but he progressed far beyond the elder's basic products of various drinking vessels, tankards, and porringers. The son was strongly influenced by the European rococo style. A lavishly decorated sugar and creamer set he produced in 1762 was typical. Such skills allowed silversmiths to earn handsome livings in Philadelphia, New York, and other American cities.

Puritan folk culture found expression in funerary art. Skeletons and figures of Father Time with an hourglass were popular on gravestones, and certain motifs were common: a grapevine represented Christ, a dove devotion, and a cherub hope and resurrection. Gravestones grew increasingly ornate as the years went on. Other forms of folk art went through similar stages of transformation, including German glass and earthenware, weather vanes, and ship carvings.

Artists known as limners dominated painting in the seventeenth century; many of these actually began their careers as house or sign painters. They produced two-dimensional portraits with black and brown the dominant colors, idealizing their subjects and generally portraying them as somber, serious individuals. By the 1680s, at least in New England, merchants commissioned works portraying themselves with more gentry-like features and with more color and attention to detail. During the early decades of the eighteenth century, limners in the upper Hudson Valley in New York used bright colors in full-length portraits of their wealthy subjects.

Limners generally reflected the folk traditions of a region in their work. Their efforts contrasted sharply with the British emigrant artists who were often trained in baroque or rococo techniques and sculpted busts with a self-conscious technique.

American painting began to acquire its own identity during the second third of the eighteenth century, when the colonies produced several portrait painters of note. John Smibert began his career as a house painter in Edinburgh and came to America in 1728. He lived in Newport and Boston, producing 241 portraits in all. He is best known for his *Dean George Berkely and his Family,* a three-dimensional portrait with careful attention to detail and bright colors in the subjects' clothing. Gustavus Hesselius from Sweden, lived in the Delaware Valley and is known for his paintings of two Delaware Indians, Tishcohan and Lapowinsa. He also did religious scenes, landscapes, and portraits of planters. Henrietta Johnston did pastel portraits of upper-class Charlestonians.

The most important figures in early America painting appeared as the colonial upper-class grew in numbers, wealth, and social stature and began to embrace European customs in more than just their material lives. Many commissioned their portraits as European aristocrats did. The arrival of John Wollaston from England in

John Singleton Copley, "Mrs. James Smith" (Elizabeth Murray), 1769 (Gift of Joseph W. R. and Mary C. Rogers. Courtesy, Museum of Fine Arts, Boston). ❧

New York City in 1749 inaugurated a new era; during his two-year stay, he painted about one hundred individual portraits. A number of other European painters followed him to these shores. But America was producing its own artists. John Singleton Copley, born in Boston in 1738, averaged twenty portraits a year from 1762 to 1774 before he moved to London. Pennsylvania's Benjamin West, who also moved to England in 1760, pioneered an heroic style and was an important teacher of other American artists. Charles Wilson Peale became the most popular portrait painter in America, particularly noted for his rich textures.

American architecture also became more elaborate. The wealthy commonly sought to adopt the new Georgian styles of England: two stories and four rooms, a central hall, symmetrical floor plans and facades, and many graceful touches characteristic of Georgian architecture. Individuals commonly bought English design books and painstakingly duplicated the styles. In the Chesapeake, many mansions had large interior halls and elaborate stair balustrades, with high, white plaster ceilings that cooled the interiors. The typical Virginia great house had four large rooms on the first floor, with paneling, marble fireplaces, pedimented doorways, and elaborate cornices in the main rooms. The gentry placed particular emphasis on broad, open stairways as marks of wealth and prestige and on first-floor parlors that served as private entertainment rooms; these heightened their sense of separateness from the ordinary people of Chesapeake society and provided a convenient center for their ritualistic, upper-class entertainments.

The gentry placed equal weight on the external appearance of their estates. When Byrd II planned his new mansion in the early 1730s, he included formal gardens, gravel paths, fruit trees, and hedges. The Burnwell family's mansion had two stories, each sixty-one feet by forty feet, flanked by two brick buildings, each twenty-two feet by forty-five feet, that housed kitchens, plantation offices, and slaves. The plantation also had several other separate slave quarters, ranging from a forty-foot-by-eighteen-foot cabin with two rooms to a tiny eight-by-eight-foot shack. Annapolis became a center of such homes, planters and merchants competing with one another in accommodating to the latest style and in importing the best in English luxury. Gardens were particularly important components of these homes, serving as beautiful landscapes within which the genteel could stroll and engage in polite conversation. Even many middle-level farmers and artisans in the Chesapeake adopted the Georgian style. Carolina farmers, for instance, often lived in one-story houses with two rooms and symmetrical facades, though they added a steep roof to counter the hot southern summers.

Merchants and artisans in Pennsylvania and New England built their own great houses, which signaled the emergence of a tradition of formal entertainment by the upper-middle class, a marked contrast to the villagewide entertainments of traditional colonial society. Merchants such as Samuel Powell and John Cadwalader built three-story mansions in the 1760s and 1770s and spent summers in comfortable summer homes only ten miles from Philadelphia. When Swan's *British Architecture* became available in Philadelphia in 1775, 172 of the 186 subscribers were carpenters eager to satisfy their style-conscious customers. Eighteenth-century New England great houses appeared most frequently in the port towns and followed an English townhouse pattern, complete with pedimented door frames and classical pilasters. But even moderately prosperous members of the New England gentry built homes with enlarged entryways and stairways with handrails and balusters. If they were not as impressive as their great house counterparts, they still declared to visitors their residents' claim to genteel status.

Americans imported furniture from England and bought still more from skilled domestic craftsmen who made exact copies from English design books. The Boston

Some examples of colonial craftsmanship: A mahogany kneehole chest, made in New York ca. 1760 (Gift of Mr. and Mrs. Maxim Karolik for the M. and M. Karolik Collection of 18th Century American Arts. Courtesy, Museum of Fine Arts, Boston) and a creampot and sugar bowl, by Paul Revere, 1761 (Pauline Revere Thayer Collection. Courtesy, Museum of Fine Arts, Boston). ❧

merchant Robert Oliver possessed a mahogany tea table, damask linen, a bed with curtains, and plates and beds for each member of the family. In the 1740s, a typical New York City merchant might have the following in his sitting room: an armchair or two; sturdy side chairs that could be used for dining; a wall cupboard with some stoneware, pewter, and silver tankards; a game table; some porcelain dishes from Japan; a rug and damask curtains; and a looking glass. The merchant Metcalf Bowler of Portsmouth, Rhode Island, had his chimney inlaid with blue-and-white delft tiles and a special cabinet built over the fireplace to display his collection of fine plates.

All of this served a purpose beyond mere ostentation. The American gentry believed it their duty to spend and consume and to engage in polite, refined behavior that would help buttress fragile social relations in a market-oriented society. They were constantly concerned with appearance, with how they seemed to others. Thus, they sought to refine their manners, to beautify their environment, and to make a positive impression on all who watched them. They were, in a sense, performing a role.

Nowhere was this concern with appearances more evident than in the gentry's new-found love affair with the theater during the eighteenth century. Colonists had earlier shared a widespread distrust of theater. Puritans in particular had attacked acting and actors as duplicitous and somehow in league with the devil for portraying someone other than themselves. Even secular New York forbade "play-acting" in 1709. But theaters were common in American cities by mid-century. Colonial cities had become places where identity was mobile and changeable, much like the economic marketplace that was replacing traditional economic structures. Theater dealt with problems of authenticity, accountability, and intentionality—the same issues that urban merchants and artisans confronted everyday in the marketplace. In acting, the self became a commodity, completely changeable.

Williamsburg, New York City, Philadelphia, and Charleston had their own playhouses, though most of the actors were members of British traveling companies. One such group, the American Company, made its first American tour between 1758 and 1761 and performed forty plays in a single season, including thirteen of Shakespeare. British farces and political allegories were repertoire mainstays. A

New York company staged the first American production of Shakespeare in 1730 with a performance of *Romeo and Juliet*. In 1750, the Murray-Kean company arrived in New York from Philadelphia and began a sixteen-month run, including an opening production of *Richard III* in a converted warehouse seating 280 people. Throughout that decade, resident and visiting companies put on comedies, ballad operas, and concerts of all sorts. Despite continued resistance by some (in 1753, William Livingston argued that "a troupe of comedians would be injurious to public morals. . . ."[10]), the theater became an accepted part of American life. By the 1750s, even remote Annapolis was the scene of many productions, including *Othello*.

Music was also an important part of colonial culture, and it too reflected the division between genteel and folk culture. The Puritans had always used song in their worship, drawing from both the *Book of Psalms* and the *Bay Psalm Book*. But apparently the quality of singing deteriorated through the seventeenth century. Clergy began to complain about out-of-tune singing, and ministers established singing schools in the early eighteenth century and published instructional books to guide the laity to a more euphonious expression of joy in their worship of God. But by 1720, others had concluded that studying singing was close to witchcraft, and a debate ensued over the validity of formalized song as opposed to the more spontaneous customs of old. Thomas Symmes published his *First Essay of the Reasonableness of Regular Singing* in 1720, arguing that the saints and angels in their heavenly world sang rhythmically and in tune. Even Cotton Mather supported this group when he wrote *The Accomplished Singer* in 1721. The argument for practice won out in the end, culminating in the work of William Billings, perhaps the most original of early American composers. Billings published *The New England Psalm Singer* in 1770 and wrote more than three hundred musical compositions.

Other colonial religious groups also used music in their worship. The Moravians were particularly fond of it, even using trombone choirs, and Conrad Beissel wrote a number of hymns. Colonial secular music was even more widespread. The Puritans brought with them English nursery songs, ballads, and sea chanties, and their children played singing games. Southern planters regarded music as a sign of gentility; plantation families and slaves often came together for musical performances. Robert Carter owned a number of musical instruments, including a harpsichord, a piano forte, a glass harmonica, and a two-stop organ. Itinerant music masters traveled throughout the colonies, and both singing schools and choral societies became common. Concert subscriptions began to appear in the cities by the 1760s, and songs and dances almost always accompanied theater performances. In 1735, Charleston witnessed the first opera presented in the colonies, a work called *Flora*. Gay's *The Beggar's Opera* was presented in Williamsburg and elsewhere. As in Europe, these productions were attended by the upper class, who dressed for the occasion, and the lower class, who sat in the pit. On a less exalted level, ballads provided widespread entertainment for the less genteel. Songs such as "Kiss Me Quick, My Mother's Coming," "Bonny Lass under a Blanket," and "Sweetest When She's Naked" were widely popular.

Women And The Family In A Genteel World

European cultural influences also began to effect changes in the lives of colonial women and their families, though here the nature and degree of change varied according to class, region, and whether a woman lived in an urban or rural setting. In the northern and middle colonies, drudgery and boredom filled the days of women who lived on farms. Women performed the same duties day after day and did seasonal work in the fields. Girls helped their mothers by baking pies, making candles, washing floors, making cheese, doing laundry, and spinning and weaving.

Urban wives did not have to spin or weave, but they still had to cook; they often cultivated small gardens and raised poultry, and they were held to higher standards of cleanliness than their rural counterparts. Many city women who traveled, in fact, expressed shock at the dirty farmhouses they saw. Middle- and upper-class women in the cities shared a common routine. They got up early and did their morning chores, which included baking, washing and ironing, cooking, sewing and knitting, and occasionally seasonal work, such as preserving fruit or salting pork and beef. They served dinner at two and perhaps visited friends or read in the afternoon. Child care was interspersed through all of these chores. Their daughters were the only females who had any sort of leisure. They could sleep late, learn dancing, and spend time with their friends. Even when they did sewing for the family, a common chore, they worked with their friends in small social groups.

Mary Vial Holyoke of Salem, Massachusetts, was married to Edward, a gentleman physician. Despite her upper-class status, Holyoke washed and ironed like other women and had to polish the brass, hang the pictures, and prepare the food for the many guests who frequented her home. Like many women of moderate-sized cities, she also had to care for the family's barnyard animals. Unlike her poorer counterparts, she had more free time to spend at teas and to remodel her clothing to keep up with the latest fashions.

Mary Gilman of Exeter, New Hampshire, was an evangelical churchgoer who felt her life constantly threatened by the sort of gentility Holyoke took for granted. Her son Joseph, a clerk in a Boston counting house, kept writing home for more clothes, specifically noting, "I do not desire you to send my homespun Cloth coulerd Jacket if you do I shall not wear it. . . . "[11] Joseph made a particular point of vowing he would not wear shoes made in Exeter; they simply did not measure up to the cosmopolitan standards of Boston culture. His comments, and the frustrated responses of his mother, reflect both the increasing divergence of material culture between rural and urban colonists and the moral judgments frequently attached to those differences.

Some women in northern cities gained significant legal rights and a certain degree of economic freedom during the eighteenth century. They could board lodgers, run taverns, make clothes for upper-class women, take in sewing or do housework for others, and work as midwives. Artisans' widows often took charge of their husband's shop. So-called she-merchants frequently ran corner stores, and a few were even experienced traders. Elizabeth Murray Smith of Boston was so successful that she bragged she was able "to live and act as I please"[12] and had John Singleton Copley paint her portrait.

Women in eighteenth-century New York, on the other hand, seemed to be losing ground. Dutch law had been unusually liberal in its provisions for women's legal and property rights, guaranteeing widows an equal division of assets. These principles continued to influence English practice for some time, and before 1750, women in New York often actively participated in the economic and legal systems. Martha Smith ran a lucrative whaling business early in the century while she was married and without declaring herself a *femme sole* trader. Gradually, however, change began to set in during the eighteenth century, stemming partly form lawyers' efforts to make colonial practices conform to British law and partly from the American gentry's spreading view of women as ornaments to the household. Husbands increasingly gave their wives less control over property and restricted their uses of power of attorney. Widows began to receive smaller portions of their husband's estate or only a life interest; by 1750 in New York, more than two-thirds of bequests to widows were for life interest only. A common pattern emerged by mid-century: the widow received the use of all property until the eldest son, or even all the children, came of age but then retained only the use of the house or a part of it.

Attitudes toward children seemed to soften throughout the colonies during these years. Family life became more private, and parents developed more trusting relations with their children. As standards of living rose and upper- and middle-class families acquired more leisure time, children gained greater control over their lives and futures. These changes were apparent even among evangelicals. Hannah Eaton, a guilt-plagued Connecticut New Light Calvinist, lived out a tempestuous relationship with her husband, whom she regarded as an unconverted Old Light. But her powerful love of her children and her concern for their souls softens our picture of her character and gives pause to the contention that evangelicals sought to break the wills of their children. Her grief at the death of two children before the age of two was great but not as profound as her suffering over the "irreligious" behavior of her sons Jonathan and Calvin. Jonathan eventually became a minister, but Eaton continued to express dismay and sorrow at the failure of Calvin to find God. Except for a brief resurgence during the Awakening, the image of a powerful, inflexible God gave way to that of a loving, conciliatory Christ.

As southern family life stabilized during the middle decades of the eighteenth century, marriages of twenty years of more became typical rather than exceptional. Fewer orphans appeared as burdens before the county courts, and children lived with both of their parents for a much longer time. The disease-fostering environment of the tidewater, however, meant that about one-fifth of all children still died before their first birthdays, and most still lost one parent before they themselves reached maturity.

After mid-century, a further transformation occurred. Emotional relations between husbands and wives softened, and a more openly affectionate family emerged. Children claimed more choice and autonomy in their lives and exerted more control over their marriages. The family began to pull inward, fashioning a greater sense of privacy. But husbands and wives also began to express their affection in a more restrained fashion, seeking above all to maintain peace and domestic tranquility.

Certainly these late eighteenth-century planters were far removed from their earlier counterparts. William Byrd II, though undoubtedly unusual, probably reflected to some degree the more open emotionality that persisted among wealthy planters in the first decades of the century. He and his wife enjoyed an active and often athletic sexual life and quarreled frequently and violently, but they also shared many moments of deep, quiet affection. They cared for each other when one was ill and offered comfort when grief struck, as when their young son died.

Ironically, women seem to have lost status in this new environment, which was increasingly dominated by the emerging patriarchal, authoritarian family structure. A husband now expected his wife to be submissive, "agreeable, affable, amenable, and amiable; she should practice charity and benevolence to her neighbors and the poor; and she should always behave virtuously."[13] Men rarely informed their wives of major economic transactions ahead of time, even if it involved the sale of plantation land. At the same time, women continued to perform more than their share of work on the plantation. Operations here were on a far larger scale than in homes or on small farms in the north. Simply doing the laundry could take an entire week or two on some plantations. Women oversaw the distribution of food for the entire plantation, and early in the century, they often helped with plowing, seeding, and harvesting, in addition to their daily and seasonal household chores.

In other, more concrete ways, the status of southern women continued to decline. During the early part of the century, husbands generally appointed their wives executors of their estates, guaranteeing that they would control all the property as the estate passed through probate. They also left enough land to their wives to allow them to live a comfortable, even profitable, life. But after mid-century, more and more men appointed their eldest sons as executors. While women often received more than the dower third in their inheritance, husbands began to leave land to particular children, removing from the widow's hands the right of dividing the estate herself as she saw fit. It was the sons, in fact, who held the real power—as they came of age, most simply took their portions and left. In 1776, three-quarters of the widows in Prince George's County, Maryland, lived with sons or neighbors, unable to support themselves any longer. In almost every case, unmarried sons who remained at home took over as head of the household upon reaching the age of twenty-one.

To be sure, there were exceptions to these somewhat dismal generalizations; a few individual women succeeded in seizing much greater control over their lives. Perhaps the best example is Eliza Lucas Pinckney (1722–1793). Pinckney began to run her father's South Carolina plantation when she was only seventeen; her father was a British army officer stationed in the West Indies, her mother an invalid. She also conducted experiments in growing and processing indigo, succeeding after several years and a number of failures in producing a marketable product and thus greatly enhancing the colony's economic health. She rejected her father's hand-picked suitors, choosing her own mate (Charles Pinckney) at age twenty-two. She proved to be as skilled a wife and mother as a plantation manager and continued to pursue her experimental interests—in silk—during the remainder of her life. Her two sons became important figures in the new nation's politics, while her daughter became a plantation manager herself both during and after her husband's life. And then there was Frances Parke Custis, who was married to Col. John Custis of Arlington. These two quarreled bitterly over anything that struck their fancy but especially over money. She was wealthy in her own right, but her husband retained the legal power to manage her property, obligated only to pass it along intact to her children. Frances Parke did not suffer this loss of power lightly, and she and John refused to speak to each other for long periods of time, communicating only through their slaves. John was apparently so angered during one "discussion" that he drove their carriage off the road and straight into Chesapeake Bay. "Where are you going, Mr. Custis?" Frances asked. "To hell, Madam," he responded. "Drive on," she retorted, "any place is better than Arlington."[14]

The Persistence Of Folk Culture

Even wealthy Americans who actively pursued genteel cultural mores could not, of course, measure up to their aristocratic models. American mansions and fortunes were small, indeed, beside their European counterparts. And not all Americans welcomed a Europeanized, genteel culture. It seemed too closely connected to the dangers of luxury and corruption of which republican ideology warned, somehow insincere and duplicitous. Devereaux Jarrett, rising in the world of the Virginia gentry from humble backcountry origins, resolved consciously *"to act the hypocrite"*[15] to gain the good opinion of his landlady, who could help him in his ascent up the social ladder. For many ordinary Americans, this desire to deceive, to abandon the true inner self, seemed the predominant characteristic of metropolitan culture. They deeply mistrusted the material wealth and culture of the upper class and embraced instead a localized, vernacular culture that changed little over time. To be sure,

New World commoners were generally cut off from Old World traditions and became more dependent on government, clergy, and print for cultural sources. New England ministers, notorious for their attempts to repress popular culture, were often the main source of information about the outside world in rural communities. But the laity resisted the wholesale imposition of a literate culture and continued to cling to their own cultural forms. It was most certainly a losing battle, but events such as cornhusking, apple paring, maple sugar making, sheep shearing, elections, and militia training days brought the people together in ways that stressed traditional, timeless bonds of community.

Most colonial governments sponsored official holidays (such as Christmas) that allowed workers to celebrate community-affirming rituals. Pope's Day (Guy Fawke's Day), observed on November 5 in Boston and New England, celebrated the discovery and suppression of a Catholic plot to blow up Parliament in 1605. Rival gangs (groups from the north and south ends of Boston, for instance) fought to capture the other sides' papal effigies, which they then burned in symbolic victory on a nearby hill. In Boston, the ritual took on the characteristics of European status-reversal celebrations (similar to Election Day among New York City blacks), as the young people and lower-class workers controlled the city's streets and collected "tribute" from the wealthy to finance the food and drink that crowds consumed throughout the day. Not many dared to refuse.

Public hangings also attracted large crowds, as they did throughout the Western world, and offered the opportunity for picnics and conviviality. At one such occasion in Boston, a large crowd filled the banks of the Charles and choked the river itself with boats and canoes. Taverns were popular gathering places throughout the colonies, offering an opportunity for plebeian and patrician culture to meet on common ground. Billiards and dancing were common here, as were indoor games that were also played at home: cards, backgammon, chess, dominoes, and dice. Various sports entertained both the wealthy and the poor. Many people went fishing and hunting, bowled or golfed, and played games that resembled cricket, soccer, baseball, and football. In Boston, an early American version of football could get out of control, played by whole communities and sometimes marked by women taking off their dresses and even their petticoats. Wrestling and bare-knuckle fighting were also fairly common, though they became truly violent on the frontier.

Some colonial governments did their best to discourage these pursuits. Puritan New England tried to suppress several sports, attempted to punish those who played on Sundays, and continued to attack gambling, drinking, card and dice playing, and even shuffleboard. The Quaker government in Pennsylvania banned the theater, prize games of all sorts, dice, cards, cockfighting, and bull- and bear-baiting. Here, the courts had more power than their counterparts in New England to punish rude, crude, and irreligious behavior. Quakers also did their best to discourage any sport that they viewed as idle and a waste of time, including such harmless pursuits as running races. Recreation was suitable only as physical exercise. "The best recreation," William Penn noted, "is to do good."[16]

One thing no colonial government successfully suppressed was an ongoing belief in the occult and the supernatural. Cotton Mather and other ministers noted the prevalence of magic and the occult in New England long after the seventeenth century came to a close. Colonists north and south continued to study astrology, and almanacs with astrological charts became more common than ever. Quaker leaders indicted Robert Roman for "practicing geomancy" and "divineing by a stick,"[17] but they could not stop others from doing the same. Farmers looked to the stars to guide them in their planting, "cunning people" remained common, and seamen and mariners in particular continued to use magic in an effort to predict and control the dangerous natural forces they faced daily. None of these practices was anywhere near as common or influential as it had been a century earlier. In a sense, colonial ministers and governments could afford to look the other way, since a rational print culture was in fact slowly moving across the colonial landscape.

The Chesapeake offers a rather unique picture, since here more than anywhere else, genteel and popular culture met in public entertainments and influenced each other. This was particularly true early in the century, before the gentry began to carve out their own specialized cultural niche, but it remained so even after that time. Horse racing was the most prestigious pursuit of the Virginia gentry, and all classes participated to some extent. At first, quarter races dominated—quarter-mile sprints with horses going all out, jockeys whipping each other as well as their horses. Things were a bit more controlled later on, as gentlemen laid out specific courses and staged a series of five-mile heats. In both cases, betting was common and heavy; wagers of hundreds of pounds were not unknown. For the gentry, this was another test of manhood. Steeds vied with tobacco and the size of wagers as measures of success and masculinity. After formalized races became the norm, the commoners and smaller planters continued to stage their own quarter races, heightening the growing split between gentry and popular culture.

Cockfighting started off as the preserve of common planters, but large planters joined the ritual before mid-century. Again, heavy betting was common, and these events became opportunities for gentlemen and commoners to literally rub elbows; the size of the bet was meant to impress on lower-class whites—and the many slaves who attended the fights—the power and wealth of the ruling class. Ironically, the gentry looked down on the New England ball games, arguing that they were too violent for true gentlemen to pursue. They preferred riding, shooting, and hunting deer, fox, and other small game in their desire to mimic the lives of the English privileged. But they did not shrink from the violence of cockfighting or slavery or from the gouging and no-holds-barred fighting that was common in much of the south. One traveling Englishman observed a fighter renowned for his gouging abilities "who constantly kept the nails of both his thumbs and second fingers very long and pointed. . . [and] hardened them every evening in a candle."[18]

Virginians developed a culture that subtly—and unknowingly—integrated not only the values of popular yeoman culture but also some of those of traditional African and African-American culture. Gentry dances, for instance, could be graceful, refined minuets, though even these were intensely competitive. But they could also be common jigs and other more rhythmic steps influenced by white observation of black dances. At most of these affairs, moreover, the musicians were black, and they undoubtedly brought their own sense of rhythm even to the staid, square movements of ordered, baroque steps.

As we have seen, blacks retained many traditional West African attitudes toward religion, time, and work, and the gentry often expressed fears that whites would succumb to the temptations of seasonally paced black work patterns. William Byrd II was obsessed with spending time productively and berated those on his plantation who did not do so, including his first wife. The constant complaining by the plantation owners seems to support the conclusion that the pace of work was indeed slowing down in the south, to a rhythm that was more accommodating to African work patterns. Blacks and whites came together constantly, at work, in entertainment, at holiday celebrations, and even in crime, and it was inevitable that cultural cross-fertilization would occur. Thus, black beliefs in magic and the occult, in the use of talismans and amulets to ward off illness and physical harm, and in divining to foretell the future all reinforced similar practices and beliefs in the popular culture of ordinary white Virginians.

❧ *Documents* ❧
A Lewd and Wanton Country

The Reverend Charles Woodmason, an Anglican minister and former South Carolina planter, spent several years traveling through the Carolina backcountry in the 1760s. His journal contains many complaints about the widespread drunkenness, swearing, and promiscuity that appalled him. The first two selections below are typical of the eastern elite's attitudes toward backcountry culture. The final excerpt suggests that backcountry settlers certainly did not lack a sense of humor, especially when they could enjoy themselves at Woodmason's expense.

> Nor is this a Country, or place where I would wish any Gentleman to travel, or settle, altho' Religion and the State requires a number of Ministers—Their Ignorance and Impudence is so very high, as to be past bearing—Very few can read—fewer write—Out of 5000 that have attended Sermon this last Month, I have not got 50 to sign a Petition to the Assembly. They are very Poor—owing to their extreme Indolence for they possess the finest Country in America, and could raise but ev'ry thing. They delight in their present low, lazy, sluttish, heathenish, hellish Life, and seem not desirous of changing it. Both Men and Women will do anything to come at Liquor, Cloaths, furniture, &c. &c. rather than work for it—Hence their many Vices—their gross Licentiousness Wantonness, Lasciviousness, Rudeness, Lewdness, and Profligacy they will commit the grosses Enormities, before my face, and laugh at all Admonition.

Popular culture survived best on the frontier and in the backcountry. Migrants to these areas resisted change and consciously maintained ties to their "ancestral ways," including evangelical religion and a dominant loyalty to clan and family. They lived at first in earthen cabins, but as soon as possible, they built log cabins that duplicated their Old World homes—one-room buildings sixteen or seventeen feet long with earthen floors. Even those who prospered built larger homes that often consisted of smaller ones connected by breezeways. They preserved traditional sex roles. Women were workers in this world; they joined men in slaughtering large animals and clearing forest land. Men were warriors and dominated their families more than men anywhere else in the northern colonies. Like the world of northern England, this was a sensual culture. There was little concern for sexual privacy, and premarital pregnancy rates were very high. But the culture also condemned seduction and abandonment, imposing a strong sense of male responsibility in sexual relationships.

Families reared their children permissively. They sought to strengthen the child's will and to build a sense of pride, personal independence, and courage in the face of death and the uncertainty of life. Fueled by tradition, anger, and alcohol,

The Young Women have a most uncommon Practise, which I cannot break them off. They draw their Shift as tight as possible to the Body, and pin it close, to shew the roundness of their Breasts, and slender Waists (for they are generally finely shaped) and draw their Petticoat close to their Hips to shew the fineness of their Limbs—so that they might as well be in Puri Naturalibus—Indeed Nakedness is not censurable or indecent here, and they expose themselves often quite Naked, without Ceremony—Rubbing themselves and their Hair with Bears Oil and tying it up behind in a Bunch like the Indians—being hardly one degree removed from them—In few Years, I hope to bring about a Reformation, as I already have done in several Parts of the Country.

The people took up two others for entering the house where I was when in bed—stealing my Gown—putting it on—and then visiting a Woman in Bed, and getting to Bed to her, and making her give out next day, that the Parson came to Bed to her—This was a Scheme laid out by the Baptists—and Man and Woman prepared for the Purpose.

Richard J. Hooker, ed., *The Carolina Backcountry on the Eve of the Revolution: The Journal and Other Writings of Charles Woodmason, Anglican Itinerant* (Chapel Hill, NC: IEAHC, University of North Carolina Press, 1953), 52, 61, 45.

this was a violent world even in its games; men engaged in wrestling and fighting with an intensity and cruelty unknown anywhere else in the New World. One particular game, known as "rough and tumble," had no rules at all, and some emerged from such contests maimed or blinded. Courage and virility were admired above all else. Blood feuds were common, retributive justice prevailed, and crimes against people far outnumbered those against property. The potential brutality of this culture was graphically illustrated when unidentified robbers seized a Carolina man named Davis in 1767 and "tortured him at his own hearth with red-hot irons until he told them where his money was hidden."[19] Men and women alike often acted out of blind rage, even within their own families. Strong personal leadership prevailed, and government institutions were weak.

Backcountry settlers were fiercely hostile to organized religion and its clergy, and they especially derided Anglican priests for lacking piety. Emotional, often violent conversions were the norm in the Old World camp meetings that dominated backcountry religion. Charles Woodmason's description of one Carolina frontier revival in the 1760s remains classic: "Extravagancies—One on his knees in a Posture of Prayer—Others singing—some howling—These Ranting—Those

Crying—Others dancing, Skipping, Laughing and rejoycing. Here two or 3 Women falling on their Backs, kicking up their Heels, exposing their Nakedness to all Bystanders."[20] Woodmason's description calls to mind some of the accounts of revivals led by the New England itinerant James Davenport, an earlier proponent of an oral, popular religious culture.

Sorcery and witchcraft fascinated these people. Charms, potions, omens, spells, and belief in astrology were all pervasive, and specialists dispensed rituals and charms for every need and occasion—disease, the health of crops, or trouble with animals. "A cure for homesickness," one such purveyor noted, "is to sew a good charge of gunpowder on the inside of the shirt near the neck." "To cure a fever," another adage went, "climb a tall tree with your hands (do not use feet), and jump off."[21] Most cures were harmless—such as washing one's face in cobwebs to remove freckles. All of these beliefs reflected the backcountry conviction that time and causation were beyond human control or understanding; like many of their seventeenth-century counterparts, these people still believed that things just happened.

Average schooling levels in the backcountry were the lowest in the British Colonies; northern Ireland and England and parts of rural Scotland, from where most of these settlers had come, had been almost untouched by the Reformation and Enlightenment. Backcountry communities relied on small neighborhood schools taught by itinerant schoolteachers for a few weeks a year and supported by private subscriptions. The teachers were poorly educated and came from the lowest levels of society, and schools suffered from high turnover rates. Only the dozen or so short-lived Presbyterian Academies that emerged out of the Awakening to prepare ministerial candidates provided more sophisticated schooling. Learning was thus another area where popular, oral culture predominated. Devereaux Jarrett learned to repeat songs from memory when he was growing up, and he could listen to the Bible and repeat it aloud word for word. Parents encouraged a certain amount of literacy but only enough to allow their children to function in the economic marketplace. The marketplace of ideas, a concept acquiring greater force in the eastern sections of most colonies, was a foreign notion here.

Agricultural techniques remained primitive in the backcountry; swine grazed freely, and cattle roamed in herds of up to a thousand and were driven to market once a year. Wealth distribution here followed the strangest patterns in the British colonies. There was a very large underclass of tenants and squatters, a small middle class, and only a few very rich large landowners, often absentees. Many families remained landless for generations. There was more inequality here than anywhere else in the mainland British colonies, a pattern that closely resembled the Old World society of the northern British borderlands. As it approached the Revolution, the backcountry was divided to a considerable extent into two groups. The proprietors and large landowners, who were either representatives of the eastern elite culture or desired to be so, wanted to tie the area into the international marketplace. The small landowners, renters, and squatters had no such ambitions. They did not grow commercial winter wheat but rather cultivated a mix of grains that better served their own needs, and they participated in the marketplace only when it did not interfere with their traditional cultural practices.

Yet there was also an unusual equality of esteem—rich and poor interacted as social equals and even wore similar clothing. All seemed to be equally insolent and rude, with unrefined, crude manners that were far removed from the growing genteel culture of the more settled areas of the colonies. Status in this world had nothing to do with "airs" or clothing or fancy carriages. It came from wealth alone, which in turn did not make one individual better than anyone else. People moved constantly, though usually only a few miles at a time. Families lived on isolated farms in valleys, replicating their North Britain settlement patterns. Yet friends and relatives visited one another often, frequently staying overnight. Even here, it seems, community was an essential, viable goal.

These characteristics go far to explain the attitudes easterners held toward residents of the frontier. The English tended to view their colonies as existing on the periphery of true civilization, despite the attempts of colonists to mimic metropolitan standards of behavior. In the same way, colonial elites viewed the backcountry and its people as barbaric and uncivilized, often drawing no distinction between white settlers and Indians. They wanted the right kind of people to live there. Woodmason saw only what most other easterners saw when he complained about "the licentiousness of the People. . . swopping their Wives as Cattle and living in a State of Nature more irregularly and unchastely than the Indians."[22] Easterners thus welcomed the growth that integrated frontier areas more extensively into the market economy and encouraged closer ties between backcountry leaders and the eastern gentry. Only Virginians, though, seemed to have mastered the art of cultural accommodation and compromise. In most other cases, conflict continued to plague east-west relations in the colonies.

The American colonies were moving haltingly toward a semblance of cultural unity in 1763, but the process was incomplete and marked by often bitter, and perhaps unresolvable, conflicts. Popular versus elite culture, rural versus urban, backcountry versus eastern seaboard interests, rich versus poor, black versus white— these were only the most obvious of the divisions threatening the stability of colonial society. They were not so much resolved as subsumed under a broader, more encompassing political culture that found greater evils and more imminent dangers elsewhere. Americans perceived France, and then England, as the overriding threat, and it certainly would not be the last time they would seek to resolve internal conflict by fighting an external enemy.

Chapter Thirteen

Empires Collide

Between 1700 and 1763, the British mainland colonies grew not only in population and wealth but also geographically, as land-hungry settlers pushed the frontiers farther and farther west. At the same time, French settlers to the north extended their occupation of Canada, though at a far slower rate. While the English population in North America had reached one and a half million by 1760, a mere sixty-five thousand hardy French settled the vast reaches of New France.

It seems almost ludicrous that, given such an abundance of land for relatively few people, the British and the French in the New World should come to blows several times during the eighteenth century. Yet that is exactly what happened. The following pages will detail the causes and events of three major intercolonial wars and several smaller ones, conflicts that also involved the declining Spanish empire and were both American and international in scope. These wars were equally significant for their impact on the lives of American Indians. Indians fought for both the French and the English but with their own motives and in ways that reflected the transformation of their cultures by European contact. The Iroquois, for instance, maintained their sovereignty and protected their lands from French and English invasion. They possessed the largest fighting force in North America at the end of the seventeenth century—twenty-eight hundred warriors, well-armed and knowledgeable in the ways of woodland warfare. While the wars centered on issues of prestige and economic and political power for the European nations, they involved issues of survival for the Indians. Their lands, their cultures, and their very lives were at stake in ways that Europeans simply failed to imagine.

In sum, fur traders and land speculators, farmers and merchants, politicians and Indians all went to war for their own reasons. The interaction of the four protagonists—the English, the French, the Indians, and the Americans—created a series of conflicts that reverberated throughout the world.

Significant Dates

1701	Louis XIV orders establishment of colony of Louisiana and other settlements in interior
1702–13	War of Spanish Succession (Queen Anne's War)
1704	Attack on Deerfield
1711	Walker Expedition
1713	Treaty of Utrecht
1715	Yamasee War
1720	French construct Fort Niagara
1722	Tuscarora Indians join Iroquois Confederation
1723–27	Grey Lock's War
1727	British construct fort at Oswego
1732	Crown grants trustees territory of Georgia
1735	Walking Purchase
1739	War of Jenkin's Ear
1740–48	War of Austrian Succession
1740	Cartegena expedition
	Gen. Oglethorpe's failed attack on St. Augustine
1744	Lancaster Treaty
1744–48	King George's War
1745	New England troops capture Louisbourg
1748	Ohio Company founded
	Treaty of Aix-la-Chapelle
	Treaty of Logstown
	French-Choctaw Treaty
1752	Georgia becomes a royal colony
	French destroy Pickawillany
1753	Susquehanna Company established
	George Washington's first mission to the Ohio Valley
1754	French build Fort Duquesne
	Albany Conference
	Washington constructs Fort Necessity
1755	Braddock's defeat
	British capture Forts Beauséjour and Gasperau
1756	French capture Fort Oswego
	Earl of Loudoun assumes command of British colonial forces
1757	French take Fort William Henry
	Gen. James Abercromby replaces Loudoun
1758	British capture Louisbourg and Forts Frontenac and Duquesne
1759	Iroquois agree to aid British forces
	British take Quebec
1760	British capture Montreal
1763	Peace of Paris

The Spanish Empire

The Spanish empire in the eighteenth century was a bloated giant, constantly trying to adapt to declining trade and Spain's weakening position in the world. As early as 1648, the Treaty of Munster forced Spain to recognize Dutch possessions in the West Indies. The 1670 Treaty of Madrid did the same for England's possession of Jamaica and its occupation of most of North America. Florida by now was an impoverished outpost, a weak link in a chain of other weak links that served primarily to protect Spanish shipping in the Bahama Channel. In 1700, there were only 323 soldiers at St. Augustine and in other parts of Florida, and the colony's other two forts were in disrepair; at mid-century, slightly more than three thousand Hispanics lived in the entire colony. Texas and New Mexico remained on the periphery of Spanish concerns, sparsely populated by Hispanic settlers and protected only by a handful of military posts built in reaction to threats of French expansion.

Ironically, Spain's central colonies in the New World experienced tremendous economic growth during the eighteenth century; silver production, for instance, rose to new heights. But this prosperity did not translate into wealth for Spain or security for its colonial borders, as overall revenues and trade declined throughout the early part of the century. The Spanish monarchy sought to counter these problems in a variety of ways. It granted the French access to its colonial trade, a measure that freed Spanish ships to service the country's European needs. It extended the *asiento,* or the right to supply the colonies with slaves, to England in the 1713 Treaty of Utrecht. It introduced monopoly trading companies for a variety of products, including Cuban tobacco. Register ships, or single ships sailing to specified American ports, became more common as a faster and more dependable mode of transportation; the fleet system was completely eliminated in 1789. Spain was a factor in several of the wars between France and England, but its economic and military might in the New World was a thing of the past.

The War Of The Spanish Succession (Queen Anne's War) (1702–1713)

While the lure of the beaver and its more exotic cousins, such as the otter, continued to draw coureurs de bois westward in New France, there were still those who advocated that the government leave the west to the Indians and consolidate settlement in a more developed east. In particular, these individuals supported abandoning the area around the Mississippi River and the southwestern portion of the empire. But Louis XIV had his own ideas, dictated in part by his European ambitions. He had begun to cast jealous eyes on Spain's enormous American empire. Charles II had no heir, and when he died in 1700, William of Orange and Louis were already negotiating for control of Spain. Unfortunately, Charles had the temerity to leave a will! He ceded the throne to Louis—but through Louis's grandson, the duc d'Anjou—and if Louis refused the arrangement, the throne would pass to the son of the Hapsburg emperor. Louis accepted, d'Anjou became Charles V, and William immediately created the Grand Alliance. England, Holland, Hapsburg Austria, and some German states united to prevent a potential union of France and Spain under the same dynastic family.

Louis now finalized a plan he had begun to fashion as early as 1689—an attempt to keep the English American colonies east of the Alleghenies by constructing a cordon of forts from Montreal to the mouth of the Mississippi River. The

French monarch understood that if the English populated the region west of the Appalachians, their numbers would swell and increase the wealth and power of England, thus upsetting the European balance of power. So the king made the fur trade the handmaiden of French imperial policy; from this point on, economic goals would be secondary in French planning. Louis ordered missionaries sent throughout the west to forge anew a strong economic and military alliance with the Indians. After hearing rumors that the English were planning to establish a colony at the mouth of the Mississippi, Louis ordered in 1701 a new colony created in Louisiana and other settlements established at Detroit (between Lake Erie and Lake Huron) and at Kaskasia and Cahokia in Illinois country. All of these remained tiny agricultural outposts; the largest, Louisiana, had a population of only forty-one hundred as late as 1746. The French also built a series of fur-trading posts throughout the region, but these consisted only of three or four log buildings surrounded by a palisade. The Indians welcomed their guests but reminded the French that they had not given up title to their land. Fur traders were never quite certain of their safety from Indian attack while traveling through this remote country.

The Iroquois remained neutral as they had promised, and the French assured them that they would conduct war only "in the direction of Boston."[1] The French had to deal with a more delicate situation in Acadia. The English had gone out of their way to improve relations with the Abenaki, in hopes of preventing the terrifying attacks on frontier towns that had become the hallmark of New World warfare. This arrangement seriously threatened the French, who relied heavily on the Indians for defense of the region. So to prove their strength and value to the Abenakis, the French launched an attack on Deerfield, Massachusetts.

Indians had attacked the village of Pocumtuck, as it was then known, in 1664 and 1675. By 1704, the town was home to 260 people, but it remained isolated on the frontier, forty miles from the nearest English town to the east and fifty miles from New York settlements to the west. A small Indian raiding party captured two men in October 1703, but the town strengthened its fortifications and the General Court sent soldiers to help in its defense. But on February 29, 1704, in the early hours of the morning while the inhabitants slept inside the town's fort, two to three hundred French and Indians launched their attack. The night watchman had fallen asleep, and high drifts of snow piled up against the fort's walls helped the attackers quickly make their way inside. They killed fifty-six men, women, and children and captured another 109. To the settlers on the frontier, this was yet another terrifying event in the history of English-Indian warfare. To the French, it was a critical step in solidifying their northeastern frontier. To eighteenth-century New Englanders, Deerfield became a cause célèbre, immortalized in Rev. John Williams's account, *The Redeemed Captive Returning to Zion* (1707). As both jeremiad and captivity narrative, Williams's book kept alive the spirit of the Puritan mission in the same way Mary Rowlandson had done a generation earlier.

Organized warfare between French and English forces began when nine hundred Apalachee Indians, with Spanish assistance, invaded South Carolina. A force of Carolina militiamen, aided by their allies the Creeks, defeated the Apalachees at Flint River. In 1703, Governor Moore led a force of Indians against the Apalachees west of St. Augustine and captured about a thousand as slaves. The Spanish, aided by the French, attempted a reprisal against Charleston, but the colonists fought them off. In the summer of 1707, the English retaliated with an attack on the Spanish settlement at Pensacola, but the French came to the aid of the town and drove the English force off. In the end, though, their own persistence and attrition among the Spanish gave the English control of most of the southeast outside of the Florida peninsula.

New Englanders, meanwhile, anticipated substantial military assistance from the British. But as always, English military aid proved to be illusory and a source of much bitterness among the colonists. In 1709, a planned assault against Quebec was called off when the British decided not to send a support fleet, even though Massachusetts had billeted soldiers and constructed fortifications at great expense. The following year, a force of four hundred British marines and fifteen hundred colonial militia men succeeded in capturing Port Royal, and in 1711, the British planned another two-pronged invasion of Quebec—the Walker Expedition—and a British naval force of sixty-five hundred men actually entered the St. Lawrence River. But the British called off the expedition after six ships ran aground on the rocks, killing 884 soldiers. British and colonial complaints reflected the disillusionment each side felt with the other's efforts. The British commander argued that his troops were plagued by high desertion rates among the American troops and a lack of supplies and cooperation from the colonists. The colonists, on their part, had reached the limits of their patience. They pointed out that a fifth of their inhabitants fit for military service had already served in the conflicts between the English and the French and that one-fifth of those had died; they noted "the heavy pressures of a long calamitous war under which we are languishing and have suffered the loss of so much blood and treasure. . . ."[2] Thomas Hutchinson later estimated that from 1675 to 1713, more than five thousand Massachusetts troops were killed in the various wars.

The Treaty of Utrecht (1713) ended this phase of the Anglo-French conflict. The French held their own militarily in the New World, their only real losses coming in Acadia. In Europe, however, they were not so lucky, and they were forced to make concessions at the peace table. They gave up Hudson Bay, Acadia, and Newfoundland, recognized English lordship over the Iroquois Confederacy, and opened trade with the western tribes to the English traders. Still, they could easily hem in the Hudson Bay post, and they retained fishing rights off the Newfoundland coast—the key issue at that time. They also kept Cape Breton Island. The real victims of this peace were the Acadians. Most of the five thousand French settlers could not bring themselves to take an oath of allegiance to the British Crown. Both sides procrastinated on resolving this issue, since an Acadia without settlers was of little immediate use to the British.

The French also retained certain advantages inherent in the different colonizing systems of French and British North America. The Canadians were far more politically centralized and thus better organized, and they were more skilled at leading small war parties of Europeans and Indians. Montreal's emissaries controlled the vast majority of the continent's Indian trade—even the English merchants at Albany cared little for the Crown's claims to the interior. They were just happy to get affordable furs from the French and profit from their trade.

Almost three decades of formal peace between the French and the English followed the Treaty of Utrecht. But while the European powers may not have been at war, their American colonists continued to struggle over control of the vast hinterland and to engage in sporadic warfare with the Indians they sought to displace. In the north, the most significant of these conflicts was Grey Lock's War (1723–1727), more commonly known as Dummer's War (after Massachusetts's lieutenant-governor). This struggle engaged the Abenakis and the New Hampshire and Massachusetts colonies. New York and Connecticut sympathized but contributed little more than diplomatic aid (New York) and a few soldiers (Connecticut). Massachusetts tried to get the Iroquois to attack their traditional rivals, the western Abenakis, with little success, since the confederation did not want to alienate its French allies. The French also stayed out of the conflict, though they contributed considerable financial aid to their Abenaki allies.

Grey Lock was a leader of the Missisquoi Abenakis who lived at the northern end of Lake Champlain, though he seems to have originally been a member of the Woronoke tribe from western Massachusetts. By 1723, he had formed a composite community of disgruntled refugees near the main Indian village at Missisquoi, what the English referred to as his "castle." Over the next few years, this location remained his base for frequent strikes south. The war began in the spring of 1723, when Dummer attempted unsuccessfully to conciliate Grey Lock and his followers. The Indians staged a series of raids, including one on August 13 on the north-central Massachusetts settlement of Northfield in which they killed two white settlers. They

❧ *Documents* ❧
French and Indian
Views of the Wars

England and its colonists viewed the eighteenth-century wars as a struggle to preserve Protestant liberty from the tyranny of French Catholicism and Indian barbarism. The French and the Indians, as these documents illustrate, had their own perspectives. The first selection reflects the continuing Jesuit dedication to American missionary work. The second is a Penobscot Indian's comment in 1727 on the treaty ending Grey Lock's War.

> Father Rasles, the missionary of the *Abnakis,* had become very odious to the english. As they were convinced that his endeavors to confirm the savages in the Faith constituted the greatest obstacle to their plans of usurping the territory of the savages, they put a price on his head; and more than once they had attempted to abduct him, or to take his life. At last they have succeeded in gratifying their passion of hatred, and in ridding themselves of the apostolic man; but, at the same time, they have procured for him a glorious death, which was ever the object of his desire—for we know that long ago he aspired to the happiness of sacrificing his life for his flock.

Reuben Gold Thwaites, ed., *The Jesuit Relations and Allied Documents,* 73 vols. (New York: Pageant, 1959), 67:231.

> He again said to me—But do you not recognize the King of england as King over all his states? To which I answered—Yes, I recognize him King of all his lands; but I rejoined, do not hence infer that I acknowledge thy King as my King, and King of my lands. Here lies my distinction—my Indian distinction. God hath willed that I have no King, and that I be master of my lands in common.

E. B. O'Callaghan, ed., *Documents Relative to the Colonial History of the States of New York,* 46 vols. (Albany, NY: Weed, Parsons and Company, 1853–1887), 9:966.

struck the Northfield region again in early October, leading the Massachusetts legislature to establish a blockhouse near Brattleboro, Vermont, named Fort Dummer. The two opposing sides now faced each other from northern and southern Vermont, across vast forests that gave the Indians a distinct advantage.

By this time, both Massachusetts and New Hampshire were growing uneasy under a claustrophobic sense of siege; New Hampshire's governor complained that 10 percent of the population was on constant guard duty. Raids continued back and forth in 1724 and early 1725, the most significant battle occurring when the colonists defeated the eastern Abenakis at Noridgewock, Maine, and killed the French priest Sebastian Rasle, a Jesuit who had led the Abenakis in a series of attacks on northern new England outposts.

The eastern Indians and the colonists signed a tentative peace at Boston in December 1725, but Grey Lock refused to cooperate. He remained an elusive, if less dangerous, force on the frontier as warfare abated; he did not even attend the July 1727 conference where the Canadian and Maine Indians signed a formal peace. While the colonists turned to other matters, Grey Lock disappeared into the shadows of history, last noted in the records in 1744 and dying some time before 1753. His legacy certainly outlived him. As a result of the extended, sporadic warfare of the 1720s, life on the northern New England frontier remained a tenuous proposition at best, and the influx of refugees and disabled war veterans from the frontier strained the Massachusetts treasury.

Quakers And Indians

Pennsylvania provided a last refuge for many eastern Indians in the early eighteenth century. William Penn's benevolent policies attracted tribes from the south and west who came seeking only the opportunity to live their lives free from the pressure of European settlement and fraud or from Iroquois encroachment on their hunting grounds. Many of the new arrivals settled in the Susquehanna River Valley. The Indians who had originally lived in the region had, like many others, suffered a demographic catastrophe; those who were there when whites began to arrive had all come from elsewhere. The Susquehannocks were the most numerous. They were originally from a territory in the north that was also claimed by the Iroquois. In the mid-seventeenth century, they established peaceful relations with Maryland in an attempt to gain allies in their struggle against the Iroquois, but the Marylanders abandoned their brief alliance with the tribe to side with the Iroquois. The Susquehannocks were constantly on the move for several years, fleeing both English and Canadian attacks. Eventually, the Iroquois invited them to move back into the Susquehanna Valley, but the Indians dispersed as they moved, many joining Iroquois or Delaware bands. The remaining Susquehannocks eventually established a town at Conestoga, where Pennsylvania frontiersmen killed the last of their number in 1763.

The Iroquois had invited several other bands to move to the Susquehanna Valley, hoping to maintain control over them while using their presence to stave off white settlement. By mid-century, the valley had a number of multitribal communities; Otsiningo, for instance, was a cluster of villages inhabited at separate times by Indians from eight different tribes. The culture of these newly formed bands differed little from that of other northeastern tribes, and they suffered the same process of destabilization through trade. Though these Indians maintained their agricultural orientation, disease and alcohol wreaked their familiar havoc, and the Indians became dependent on white products and technology. Alcohol became a particularly valuable staple of this region; Indians traveling through from the west exchanged liquor with the valley Indians for the food they no longer grew, having abandoned farming for fur trading.

White settlement would not reach the Susquehanna Valley until the 1750s. The Pennsylvania government, meanwhile, was busily clearing out the remaining Indian villages in the eastern part of the colony. Ill, disillusioned, and plagued by creditors, William Penn had placed his estate and the colony into receivership and returned to London in 1712. His respect for and fair treatment of the Indians did not survive him. During the ensuing decades, land-hungry Europeans, fleeing economic depression in their homelands, anxiously sought homesteads at any cost. The lure of furs, essential to the economic survival of the colony, increased the pressure on colony officials to reverse Penn's policies of accommodation and respect. Still, the Indians might have held out even longer had it not been for the genius and persistence of one man—James Logan.

As Penn lay dying in London, his creditors gave Logan the power to raise the money needed to release the colony from receivership. Logan raised much of it through a combination of land sales and the Indian trade. He served as secretary of the colony and commissioner of property and had a friend appointed surveyor-general; in one way or another, he was personally involved in all Pennsylvania land transactions. His power made him a critical figure from the Indian point of view, both economically and diplomatically. The Shawnee had moved into the Susquehanna Valley at the end of the seventeenth century, but the Iroquois controlled the valley's fur trade, particularly after the Agreement of 1701. Logan became deeply involved in this trade, importing European goods and selling them at a markup of more than 100 percent to traders, who in turn sold them to Indians in exchange for furs. He increased his personal worth fivefold in only eight years. Logan's control of land sales also brought him considerable wealth when large numbers of immigrants began to flock to the colony.

In the late 1720s, Logan became embroiled in a dispute with Gov. William Keith over control of the remaining Indian lands in the eastern part of the colony. After the proprietors replaced Keith as governor, Logan picked up the pieces at a tidy profit to himself. He was most imaginative in devising a notorious scheme to remove the Lenape and Shawnee from the Lehigh Valley. The valley was located along the Delaware River, and by the early 1730s, it was the only remaining Indian land in eastern Pennsylvania. There was considerable dispute over legal title to the land (though certainly not from the Indian perspective), and the Lenape and Shawnee refused to negotiate with Logan, insisting on dealing only with a member of the Penn family. Penn's two sons, John and Thomas, arrived in the colony and agreed that the Indians had to be removed. They produced a copy of a contested (and fabricated) 1686 deed, insisting, with Logan, that the document granted Penn's heirs all the land from a specified point in Bucks County westward, as far as a man could walk in a day and a half. The Penns helped send secret scouting parties ahead to blaze a trail, and on September 19, 1737, three specially trained walkers, operating as a relay team, forged sixty miles into Delaware territory, defining what became known as the "Walking Purchase." The Indians were all but helpless; the Iroquois, who could perhaps have aided them, were more interested at the time in courting a Pennsylvania alliance. Viewing the contradictory and perplexing actions of the Penn dynasty, Christianized Indians who had come to Pennsylvania seeking refuge might very well have noted the biblical injunction, "The Lord giveth, and the Lord taketh away."

Penn was loving and respectful, Logan greedy and ambitious. No such easy generalizations characterize the life of Conrad Weiser. When he was only sixteen years old, Weiser's family sent him to a Mohawk village to master their language, and he there learned respect for Mohawk culture. Throughout the 1730s, he maintained his Indian contacts while developing a close relationship with Logan. Weiser suffered pangs of conscience after the Walking Purchase, and he spent some time at a religious cloister at Ephrata. But by 1741, he was again working with Logan, and a year later, he was interpreting the Walking Purchase to the Iroquois. In 1744, Weiser presided over the Lancaster Treaty meeting with officials from Maryland, Virginia, and Pennsylvania. This treaty renewed the covenant chain with the Iroquois, who now allied with the English and ceded them their claims to the Ohio Valley. In exchange, the English gave the Iroquois free passage through the Virginia backcountry. Weiser and the fur trader George Croghan negotiated another treaty at Logstown in 1748 that opened a trading route through the Ohio country. Croghan built trading posts at Pickawillany (1748) and several other locations, as Pennsylvania traders moved to match the growing Virginia interest in the region.

Good relations with the Iroquois lasted only a short while, and Weiser soon began to advise that the colony bypass the confederation and deal directly with the Ohio tribes. But in 1752, the French broke their earlier pledge not to settle in the Ohio Valley without permission from the Six Nations. The French had taken the first step toward renewed international conflict, and the Iroquois now regained their former value to the English.

Indians And Whites In The Southern Colonies
Yamasees and Creeks

Carolina settlers had misled and mistreated the region's Indians from the earliest days of European settlement. The Tuscaroras, for instance, had suffered through fraudulent trade practices and slave raids for decades, and Swiss and German immigrants encroached relentlessly on their lands. Tuscarora representatives even met with Pennsylvania officials in 1710 in hopes of migrating to the friendlier colony, but the Pennsylvania government withdrew its initial offer. Frustrated, the Tuscarora and other area tribes attacked southern backcountry settlers. The South Carolina Indian trader Col. John Barnwell retaliated with an army of five hundred, composed mostly of rival Indians. Barnwell's forces, depleted by desertion, soon agreed to a truce after capturing one Indian fort. Barnwell, however had taken only thirty Indian slaves, so he broke the truce and moved through the countryside in search of more victims. The Tuscaroras responded in kind, and a second colonial expedition moved into the area, headed by the slave merchant James Moore. Moore led an army of almost a thousand Indians against the Tuscarora fort at Hooherooka in March 1713. The colonists burned hundreds of Indians alive, slaughtered 166 males, and sold 392 women and children into slavery. Over the course of the war, some sixty English and seventy German settlers died; about a thousand Indians lost their lives, and another seven hundred were enslaved.

The westward expansion of South Carolina cattle raisers threatened the Yamasees as well. The colony decided to restrict the Indians to reservations, but whites soon encroached on these lands. At the same time, white traders continued to steal from and enslave Indians, and many of the Yamasees fell deeper and deeper into debt. They had allied with the English against the Tuscaroras, and their experience had convinced them that the Europeans were weak and divided. On April 15, 1715 (Good Friday), the Yamasees attacked, coordinating their efforts with the Creeks inland, who in turn were spurred on by the French. Several other smaller tribes joined in the fray. The Indian attacks were so successful that refugees began pouring into Charleston; Francis Le Jau wrote fearfully to England that "If this Torrent of Indians continue to fall Upon us, there is no resisting them. . . ."[3] The colony hurriedly opened negotiations to establish an alliance with the Cherokees. The Cherokees had four thousand warriors, but they hesitated to commit their forces to a clearly questionable cause. In the end, however, their dependence on English trading goods overcame their concerns. The English-Cherokee counterattacks soon had the desired effect. Military pressure forced the Creeks to abandon their eastern Carolina towns and to pursue new links with the French and the Spanish; the remaining Yamasees fled to the Spanish. Nonetheless, the Yamasees had led a pan-Indian uprising that came remarkably close to wiping out a European colony.

The Creeks adapted much more successfully than the Yamasees. They used their access to English trade to establish substantial influence in a wide area coveted by France, Spain, and England, and they succeeded in playing the three European powers off against each other for some time. Like the Iroquois, they learned the wiles of European diplomacy to good effect. Seeking to counter the English attempts to drive out the French and the Spanish, the Creeks made overtures to the Spanish after the war, inviting them to construct a fort in the Lower Creek town of Coweta. They also opened negotiations with the Senecas to the north and with the English. English threats and trade embargoes forced them to end their continued support of the Yamasees, but the Creeks resisted later English pressures to attack French and Spanish settlements.

Cherokee Diplomacy

By mid-century, the English regarded the twelve thousand Cherokees as essential allies who provided security for the southern English frontier against both the Spanish and the French. But abuses by English traders led many Cherokees to question English motives, and the German mystic missionary Gottlieb Priber convinced others that they could successfully avoid dependence on the European invaders. Priber began living among the Cherokees in 1736, showing an unusual respect for Indian culture and encouraging them to reject the temptations of corrupt European society. He taught the Cherokees the use of weights and measures so they could avoid being cheated by the traders and even encouraged them to establish trading connections with the French so they would not be completely dependent on the English. He hoped to establish a confederacy of southern tribes that would resist all European intrusion and maintain a balance-of-power strategy between the French, the English, and the Spanish.

South Carolina authorities sought to arrest Priber without success, but the Creeks finally captured him and turned him over to the English in 1743. He died in a Georgia prison. The Carolinians further antagonized the Cherokees by refusing, despite a treaty agreement, to defend them from an attack by the Upper Creeks in 1748. The Cherokees retaliated by attacking Carolina traders. They also continued to make overtures to the French, intent on showing the English that they were an independent people, not lackeys of English policy and whim. At the same time, English authorities recognized that both Creeks and Choctaws were essential buffers against a group of Choctaws allied with the French and throughout the 1750s plied both tribes with a wealth of gifts.

Still, white contact inevitably drew Indians into a larger cultural orbit, and their political skill at manipulating European powers eventually transformed their society in both direct and subtle ways. Early in the century, Cherokees still lived in autonomous villages. But conflict with the English and growing tensions with the rival Creeks necessitated greater coordination in their reactions, and by 1750, they had formed their villages into a loose confederation and selected an "emperor" from among the village chiefs. As military resistance became a more appealing option, warriors began to garner more power than civil leaders. Most Cherokees, however, retained many of their traditional cultural practices. They continued to believe that their own culture was superior to that of the English in law, religion, education, family, and child rearing. In the end, though, they suffered the same depredations as other Indians—disease, warfare, a growing scarcity of game animals, and increasing integration into a white-dominated trading network.

Both Creeks and Cherokees saw their cultural and political independence slowly compromised by the debilitating encroachment of white culture. Upper and Lower Creek towns split their loyalties, the former moving to the French trading orbit, the latter to the English. The Overhill Cherokees were more closely drawn to the French, the Middle and Lower Cherokees to the English. Both Creeks and Cherokees centralized tribal leadership and formed loose political confederacies so the tribes spoke with one voice to the European powers. The nature of political succession itself was transformed in this process. The tribes switched to patrilineal succession, and chiefs now passed power to their own sons rather than to those of their sisters. Europeans sometimes intruded farther into Indian power relations by supporting one candidate or another for headman, using favored headmen to distribute their gifts, and intermarrying to increase their influence in particular villages. Mary Musgrove Bosomworth, a niece of Chief Brims, successively married three Englishmen who attained considerable status within the Creek nation.

The Catawba Nation

The Catawba nation consisted of a group of villages on the border between the Carolinas. The region was unique because of its broad mixture of Indian cultures; many Piedmont Indians migrated to the area as white settlement spread westward, and the Catawba nation became an important center of Indian life in the early eighteenth century. Though they remained somewhat protected from direct interaction with whites, the Catawbas could not resist the inevitable progression of European contact: disease, traders and material goods, and finally settlers seeking land. European diseases appeared even before the Spanish explored the region, and the Indians suffered major epidemics in 1698, 1718, 1738, and 1759.

As the home of so many different tribes, the Catawba nation had unique forms of cultural interaction and adaptation. When migrating Indians arrived, they had to establish a new subsistence cycle in a new environment and lay out fields and hunting territories in a way at least comparable to the divisions in the old territory. They even had to decide what language they would speak. The diversity of settlement was so great that as late as 1741, more than twenty dialects were spoken in the region. Over time, though, old traditions weakened. Intermarriage, joint war parties and hunting expeditions, and the homogenization of daily contact all tended to create a more unified Indian nation.

Like all other Indians, the inhabitants of the Catawba nation incorporated English trading goods into their traditional cultures. Alcohol, for instance, became a part of ceremonial life. Indians used it to facilitate visions and entry into the spirit world. The closer the particular tribe was to the whites, the more European goods—tools, cloth, and weapons—became necessary parts of the members' lives. Those farther away continued to operate within a precontact framework and were content with ornamental items, such as mirrors or beads, which probably had some logical relationship to Indian religious beliefs.

Inevitably, tribes fought with each other over European products. The demand for deer pelts, much like the demand for beaver and other furs in the northern colonies, engendered conflicts over hunting territories—though here, the struggles lasted well into the eighteenth century, due in part to the wider expanse of territory and the somewhat smaller European populations. The white demand for Indian slaves was even more destructive. This trade encouraged tribes to expand their warfare and introduced an element of cruel irony into Indian adaptations to white culture.

The Catawbas participated in the Yamasee War, invading South Carolina with Yamasee assurances of support and guarantees that the Virginians would not come to their neighbor's aid. The result illustrated clearly how dependent Indians had become on white culture and trading goods. The Carolinians shut off the flow of goods during the war to the Catawbas, who could get neither ammunition nor essential supplies. Eventually, white traders bypassed the Catawbas entirely. They no longer needed Indian slaves, and deer had become too scarce to make the effort worthwhile. Still, the Indians were valuable guardians of the frontier, so the South Carolina government continued to provide them with ammunition and other trading goods.

Then whites began to settle the Carolina uplands in the 1730s. Unlike their predecessors the traders, landowners and planters had little use for Indians and viewed them only as obstacles to settlement. Whites built farms next to villages, trampled burial grounds, and ignored Indian rules of hospitality. Even friendly settlers furthered conflict by building fences and bridges and erasing the less visible (to white eyes) Indian signatures on the land. Catawba youths finally reacted in frustration, raiding farms and hunting cattle and horses. But by 1759, disease and the pressures of white settlement had reduces the Catawbas to fewer than five hundred. Those who remained abandoned all resistance. Ironically, they later fought along with and supplied the colonists during the Revolution, and Americans cast them in the image of republicans and patriots.

The Founding Of Georgia

While the English succeeded in neutralizing Indian resistance, the Spanish remained a serious nuisance. The South Carolina government took a series of steps to counter the threat. In 1720 and 1721, it constructed forts on the colony's southern border. In 1728, the Carolina militia retaliated against Yamasee raiding parties on the Altamaha River and moved into Spanish territory, attacking a village close to St. Augustine with impunity. The founding of Georgia, though, represented the most ambitious attempt to counter the Spanish presence.

The area that came to be Georgia was originally part of the Carolina grant of 1663, though from the end of the seventeenth century to the first half of the eighteenth, both Spain and England claimed the region. In 1729, Gen. James Oglethorpe chaired a parliamentary commission investigating conditions in British prisons, and he became convinced that it was poverty more than anything else that led many down the road to prison—the poor simply could not pay their debts and so were either imprisoned or resorted to illegal activities to fend off creditors. Oglethorpe saw the abundance of land in America as the solution to this problem. Not coincidentally, he also supported an aggressive military policy against Spain in the New World. The Associates of Thomas Bray, a group of influential philanthropists interested in missionary work in the New World, backed the proposal for a new American colony and became the Trustees of Georgia.

❧ *Documents* ❧
The Founding of Georgia

The founding of Georgia was, at least in part, an attempt to deal with the continued problem of poverty and landlessness in England. The following excerpt, from the introduction to Gen. James Oglethorpe's promotional pamphlet, emphasizes that motive and also indicates once again the Anglo-American awareness of the importance of history. The second selection, from a 1741 pamphlet, recounts the experiences of the early colonists and shows that the trustees had learned little from the previous century's experiences with the land and climate of the New World south. Since slavery was well established in the British colonies, they were able to turn quickly to a convenient solution.

In *America* there are fertile lands sufficient to subsist all the useless Poor in *England,* and distressed Protestants in Europe; yet Thousands starve for want of mere sustenance. The distance makes it difficult to get thither. The same want that renders men useless here, prevents their paying their passage; and if others pay it for 'em, they become servants, or rather slaves for years to those who have defrayed the expense. Therefore, money for passage is necessary, but is not the only want; for if people were set down in America, and the land before them, they must cut down trees, build houses, fortify towns, dig and sow the land before they get in a harvest; and till then, they must be provided with food, and kept together, that they may be assistant to each other for their natural support and protection.

The Romans esteemed the sending forth of Colonies, among their noblest works; they observed that Rome, as she increased in power and empire, drew together such a conflux of people from all parts that she found herself over-burdened with their number, and the government brought under an incapacity to provide for them, or

King George II granted the trustees a charter for the lands between the Savannah and Altamaha rivers and west to the Pacific Ocean. The group would have control of the colony for twenty-one years, with no profit to themselves, after which the Crown would have the option of taking control. Oglethorpe became the "President," while the charter gave the trustees the power to make laws without a legislature and to appoint a governor and all colony officials. The group envisioned Georgia as a model society, a refuge for paupers and ex-convicts, financed by charitable contributions and Parliament. They prohibited Catholics from settling but otherwise granted full religious freedom.

The trustees advertised for recruits extensively in the English and European press, and the first 113 settlers arrived in 1733. In their own way, the group's plans

keep them in order. Necessity, the mother of invention, suggested to them an expedient, which at once gave ease to the capital, and increased the wealth and number of industrious citizens, by lessening the useless and unruly multitude; and by planting them in colonies on the frontiers of their empire, gave a new strength to the whole; and *This* they looked upon to be so considerable a service to the commonwealth, that they created peculiar officers for the establishment of such colonies, and the expense was defrayed out of the public treasury.

James Oglethorpe, *Some Account of the Designs of the Trustees for Establishing the Colony of Georgia* (London, 1733), reprinted in Peter Force, ed., *Tracts and Other Papers . . . ,* 4 vols. (Washington, DC: Peter Force, 1836–1846), 1:4.

The felling of timber was a task very unequal to the strength and constitution of white servants; and the hoeing the ground, they being exposed to the sultry heat of the sun, insupportable. And it is well known that this labor is one of the hardest upon the Negroes, even though their constitutions are much stronger than white people, and the heat no way disagreeable nor hurtful to them. But in us it created inflammatory fevers of various kinds, both continued and intermittent wasting and tormenting fluxes, most excruciating colics. . . , And the yearly sickness of each servant, generally speaking, cost his master as much as would have maintained a Negro for four years. These things were represented to the trustees in the summer of 1735 in a petition for the use of Negroes, signed by about seventeen of the better sort of people in Savannah.

Patrick Tailfer, et al., *A True and Historical Narrative of the Colony of Georgia in America* (London, 1741), reprinted in Peter Force, ed., *Tracts and Other Papers . . . ,* 4 vols. (Washington, DC: Peter Force, 1836–1846), 1:22.

and hopes were as naive as those of the early Chesapeake settlers. They envisioned a settlement of small farms and intended to establish a population that would both produce its own food and defend itself and the Carolinas from the Spanish. Most of the early colonists received up to fifty acres of land, tools, and a year's worth of supplies, and no one was allowed to own more than five hundred acres of land. In 1735, the trustees forbade slavery; they believed the institution would invite Spanish subversion and weaken the colony's defense. They disallowed rum, fearing its use in trade would bring about poor relations with the Indians, which in turn would also expose the colony to threats from the Spanish. Finally, the trustees expected that the colony would support a prosperous fur trade and produce silk, wine, flax, and hemp, products that England could not make. Between 1733 and 1744, another twenty-five hundred settlers arrived in Georgia, mostly poor artisans and laborers from London, German Lutherans, Moravians, and Scottish Highlanders. Those who could not pay their own passage came as indentured servants and were promised twenty acres of land after they completed their terms of servitude. Few convicts ever migrated to the colony. The colonists founded Savannah and Augusta, the latter serving as the center for the early Indian trade. They also established military outposts on the Altamaha and St. Johns rivers, provoking conflict with the Spanish in early 1740.

The best-laid plans of the trustees came inevitably to naught; their understanding of the political and environmental requirements of New World settlement had progressed little beyond those of their early seventeenth-century counterparts. The only profitable agricultural product seemed to be rice—and this endeavor would require slaves, since the whites refused to perform the necessary labor. The trustees also soon realized that they could earn quick profits from the fur trade, but this required more involvement, and hence more conflict, with the Indians. The colonists themselves demanded more of a say in making laws. More concretely, they also wanted land and rum. In 1738, the settlers demanded the right to own slaves and land outright. Two years later, the trustees eliminated the last restrictions on land ownership. In the late 1740s, large planters petitioned the trustees for the right to establish slavery; in fact, they had already smuggled in more than a thousand slaves. In 1750, the antislavery law was repealed. Georgia became a royal colony in 1752, and an assembly was established in 1755. These measures apparently provided the spark for an economic and population boom. The Savannah area had thirty-five hundred slaves and six thousand whites in 1760; by 1775, it had fifteen thousand slaves and twenty-four thousand whites.

Oglethorpe saw his original vision vanish like the early-morning Georgia mist. The settlers refused to cooperate with his plans, the Spanish put steady pressure on the settlement, and South Carolina protested Georgia's intrusion into the Indian trade. The general finally resigned his position. He married an heiress and lived out his life in genteel fashion in the best London social circles.

The Renewal Of International Conflict

New France Expands

New France continued to formulate diplomatic and military strategies to counter the expansion of Spain and England in the New World. It now turned to the lower Mississippi Valley. In 1717, the French established Fort Toulouse on the Alabama River and another fort among the Natchez tribe. In 1718, they settled New Orleans with seven thousand whites and five thousand African slaves. Disease eroded this population, and an uprising by the Natchez in 1729 discouraged further migration, but New Orleans survived as a plantation-based society. Slaves produced wood products, indigo, rice and other crops; the settlers also bought wheat from French farming villages in the Illinois territory and beef from herds in the Mobile River valley and acquired deerskins and pelts from the Indians. A governor and a small appointed council ruled the colony without an assembly or elections of any sort. Since the colony was home base for a substantial military force, the king supported the effort financially.

After years of trying, the French succeeded in affirming a friendship pact with the Choctaws at a 1745 conference in Mobile. Choctaw territory had been the focus of rivalry between French and South Carolinian traders and the source of an abundant supply of deerskins. Though the superior English trading goods continued to draw some Choctaws, the French were now in a position to pose a considerable threat to both the Spanish and English settlers to the east. They also built a half-dozen or so small villages around Kaskasia that would supply French outposts with wheat and serve as communications links with the Illinois territory, itself connected to the main French settlements by a series of small forts.

The government also expanded its efforts in an area to the northwest of the Illinois territory, a fur-rich region that was essentially unexplored by Europeans. Here, the French hoped to redirect the flow of pelts away from the English at Hudson Bay and channel the profits into their own coffers. They built a fort at Detroit to block English passage to the Great Lakes basin and established posts at Niagara and on the south shore of Lake Ontario to provide a variety of services to the Iroquois. English presence in the region was minimal. The British constructed a trading post at Oswego, but the French frequently used this station to exchange their furs for the superior English trading goods. As early as 1720, the French had ringed the Great Lakes basin with fur trading posts, all at very little monetary cost and with fewer than a thousand men total between 1719 and 1750. The English simply conceded French control of the western tribes.

French traders worked aggressively to undercut the sole English advantage in the backcountry wilderness, the posts at Hudson Bay. Montreal fur merchants launched exploratory expeditions as far west as the Rocky Mountains, seeking both furs and a passable route to the Pacific and Asia beyond. In 1730, the Sieur de la Verendtrye, with his sons and a nephew, began the long trek to the western Great Plains in Canada, establishing a series of trading posts along the way and building the network that would in the future siphon off furs to Montreal and away from Hudson Bay.

The transformation of French colonial society also shaped imperial policy. By the time the Treaty of Utrecht was signed in 1713, the French were in dire straits economically and simply could not afford another war. Fur prices rose, thanks in part to the moths and rats that disposed of the glut in French warehouses. But furs were also becoming scarcer, and traders had to trek farther and farther west to find them. Luckily, the economy was diversifying. Wheat was the main crop. Though shipbuilding was the only industry of any size, there were also tanneries, sawmills, and brick and tile works that catered to local needs. Ordinary citizens (habitants) appear to have been fairly well off. Taxes were low, and France expended large sums of money to supply and maintain its troops.

Socially, the settlers developed a strong sense of independence, often ignoring laws and directives they did not agree with. But there was little violence aside from tavern brawls, and government control over Indian access to liquor lessened the possibility of white-Indian conflict in Canadian towns. When Iroquois and western Indians came to Montreal and other towns during the summer, the government granted them special privileges and even established different taverns for different nations, hoping to prevent tribal disputes. The white fur traders, too, gave Canadian cities a unique look and feel. In the spring, they left for the west burdened with detailed contracts drawn up by the authorities. In late summer and early fall, the canoes returned with their furs, sometimes from places so distant that two groups of voyageurs were required, meeting and transferring furs at a half-way point at the western end of Lake Superior. The Frenchmen who were the first leg of this return voyage were called the *hommes du nord*—men of the north—and many of them married Indians and became more Indian than French. Their lives remind us of the extent to which New France remained a river empire.

English Expansion

Neither England nor its colonies were willing to sit idly by and accept complete French control of the west. The colonists were eager to stake claims to the western lands to ease the growing pressure on available land supplies. In every region, colonial population had begun to push up against the Appalachians by the beginning of the Seven Years War. Most important, colonial governments oversaw this expansion and gave every encouragement to entrepreneurs and land speculators.

Southerners were both ambitious and organized in their expansion. Virginia began exploring western territory as early as 1650, when two traders reached the Cherokee in the Great Smokey Mountains; by 1675, fur traders had reached the Ohio Valley. The government actively encouraged settlement by both Virginians and European immigrants. As early as 1714, Governor Spotswood brought in German-Swiss immigrants to work in his iron foundries in the Piedmont, and the government settled both German and Scotch-Irish families in the Shenandoah Valley after 1727, granting one thousand acres of land per family.

Meanwhile, land-hungry Virginians had begun to push south and west into the Piedmont; the population in the Southside, for instance, almost quadrupled between 1727 and 1745. Speculators, as they did in many other colonies, controlled the process to maximize their profits. They held about one-quarter of the land patented in the Southside between 1703 and 1753, and they sold their holdings only slowly in order to maximize profits. The one hundred thousand acres along the Roanoke River that William Byrd II purchased in 1735 (a hundred miles from the nearest settlement) remained largely unsold even in 1750.

The Virginia Council distributed large land grants to important families throughout the century. Robert Carter and a friend received fifty thousand acres in the Shenandoah Valley in the 1720s. In 1736 alone, William Beverley, Sir John Randolph, and John Robinson, the colony's treasurer, patented 118,491 acres. Individuals or groups commonly received grants of one hundred thousand acres or more. On one fine July day, the council issued land grants of more than 1 million acres. Much of this land lay in the remote northwestern corner of the colony, or in present-day West Virginia. By 1749, only the most remote and less attractive lands remained available for expansion. Many Virginians even moved into North Carolina, where land was cheaper and more abundant.

By the 1760s and 1770s, frontier migrants began to move into the central Piedmont, the rest of the Southside, and the Shenandoah Valley, and the speculators began to reap their rewards. The first arrivals were usually the poorest, squatters who had little they could call their own. Once they had established the basic infrastructure of roads, bridges, and so on, tenants and laborers moved in and pushed them off the land. These people had usually moved westward in small steps, working as field laborers or temporarily renting land along the way and accumulating as much capital as they could. Once settled, of course, they still had to buy livestock, food, and land, and many failed; in Amelia County on the Southside, more than two-thirds of the original settlers left the region between 1736 and 1759, seeking opportunity still farther to the west or south. But those who stayed did achieve some success, accumulating several hundred acres on the average. Most of them, though, never had more than one slave and the barest of material possessions. The real winners were the wealthy eastern planters, who settled their sons in the region. By the 1750s and 1760s, wealthy, landed slave owners dominated much of the Southside and had begun to reproduce the tightly knit network of kin and neighborhood relationships that characterized the tidewater.

The colony's leading families, though, had ambitions that extended far beyond their own boundaries. Council President Thomas Lee organized the Ohio Company in 1748. The Board of Trade granted the company two hundred thousand acres in the Ohio River valley outright and rights to another three hundred thousand if it maintained a fort and settled a hundred families there within seven years. Most of the members of the company came from Virginia's northern neck and later included George Washington, Richard Henry Lee, George Mason, and Gov. Robert Dinwiddie. The group appointed Christopher Gist its agent and in 1751 sent him to explore the region and build a trading post. In 1749, the House of Burgesses granted eight hundred thousand acres to a rival group headed by Speaker John Robinson. They appointed Dr. Thomas Walker to investigate the area, and in 1750, he reached the Cumberland Gap, later the principal route for the settlement of the Kentucky bluegrass country.

New England, too, was experiencing land problems, though of a somewhat different sort. As they subdued the remaining Indians, New Englanders began to push their frontiers farther north and west. By 1760, the frontier already extended from the middle of New Hampshire east to the Maine coast, and anyone hardy enough to settle north of this line faced serious problems—agriculture was limited and transportation undeveloped, and the opportunity for accumulating real wealth, or even making ends meet, was questionable at best. The farmers of eastern Connecticut, as we have seen, moved to control their own fate by establishing the Susquehanna Company in 1753. Their audacious claim to a substantial portion of Pennsylvania was the most blatant colonial attempt to seek relief from internal economic pressures through western expansion.

New York expansion was limited in the west. The manorial land grants, though unsuccessful in creating a landed nobility, had stifled population growth, and the Iroquois Confederation presented an obstacle unmatched by Indians in other colonies. Thus, the colony's western frontier extended only about seventy-five miles west of Albany. To the east, migrants from Connecticut and Massachusetts settled on land claimed by manorial lords in the Hudson River valley, and riots broke out on manors owned by the Livingstons, the Van Cortlandts, and the Van Rennselaers. The Green Mountain boys—settlers and speculators from New Hampshire and Massachusetts migrants—also challenged New Yorkers for control of the area that would later become Vermont, along the upper Hudson River valley.

Warfare Resumes

As the English colonists pressed west toward their seemingly inevitable confrontation with Indians and the French, international conflict resumed with the War of Jenkin's Ear (1739–1742). The founding of Georgia, together with continued conflict over the Indian trade and alleged English abuses of the *asiento,* created the background for this brief war. The Spanish insisted on the right of search and seizure of English ships trading with their colonies. On April 9, 1731, a Spanish captain captured the *Rebecca,* an English trading vessel, and cut off the ear of the sailor Robert Jenkins. The episode was forgotten (except by Jenkins) until it became a convenient rallying cry for a war party in Parliament. The Spanish refused to give up their claims to search, and the English declared war on October 19, 1739. The British recruited Americans for an expedition against Cartegena in the Spanish West Indies and promised adventure, glory, and booty. New Englanders in particular, eager for relief from the region's growing economic problems, signed up by the thousands. The invasion failed; scores lost their lives, and the New Englanders were again deeply disillusioned with the commitment of the British to their well-being.

☙ *Documents* ☙
The Siege of Louisbourg

To New Englanders, the capture of Louisbourg seemed an event of divine origin. To the soldiers who fought in the siege, it was also a traumatic experience. The following excerpts from their journals and letters indicate the intensity of the campaign and reflect the despair that seems to have afflicted officers and troops alike. The final selection clearly shows the disbelief that followed the return of the fortress to the French at the Treaty of Aix-la-Chapelle.

> Never was a place so mauled with cannon and shells...; neither have I read in history, of any troups behaving with more courage, when I consider the difficulty we had in landing our cannon, provision, &c., by reason of the sea filling on shore in an open bay, the miserable swamps and hills in transporting the cannon to the several batteries we erected so near their fortifications, in doing which we had several of our men killed and wounded, with small arms, that when I look back, it is a matter of surprise to me to think of the hardships and difficulties we have gone through in a cold, foggy country; the Almighty of a truth has been with us. . . .

William Pepperrell to William Shirley, "Pepperrell Papers," Massachusetts Historical Society, *Collections*, ser. 1, 1:52.

> My dear wife; it is be the Will of God, I hope to see your pleasant face again, but if God in his sovereign Providence has ordered oth-

King George's War (1744–1748)

The War of Jenkin's Ear evolved into King George's War in the colonies. This was itself an extension of the War of the Austrian Succession, which had begun in 1740 in Europe. Austrian Emperor Charles VI spent a good deal of his later life negotiating an agreement with other European leaders called the Pragmatic Sanction, which secured his daughter Maria Theresa's accession to the Austrian throne after his death. But when the time came, Frederick II of Prussia invaded Austrian Silesia, and the French soon joined him. Maria Theresa quickly made an alliance with England. This time, the war was global, extending to the newly established colonial outposts in India.

Despite the disastrous Cartegena expedition and the long-remembered disappointments of earlier experiences, this war aroused more enthusiasm in New England than any previous British effort. Ironically, few major battles were fought in the colonies. The Abenakis again rejected an English alliance and attacked frontier settlements in Maine, New Hampshire, and northwest Massachusetts during the first two years of the war. The Iroquois remained neutral. The only major American conflict took place at Louisbourg. The Canadians struck the first blows this time,

erwise, I hope to have a glorious meeting with you in the Kingdom of Heavan, where there are no wars nor fatiguing marches, no roaring cannon, nor screeching bombshells, not long campaigns, but an eternity to spend in peace and perfect harmony.

"Journal of Seth Pomeroy," in Louis DeForest, ed., *Louisbourg Journals, 1745* (New York: Society of Colonial Wars in The State of New York, 1932), 52.

Upon the whole, it is impossible for any Man who truly loves his Country to be unaffected with the present melancholly Situation of its Affairs. To behold the Fruits of all our Labours, Toils, and Hazards, given up at once to our proud ensulting Enemies. . . . The Mind opprest with Grief, anxious and fearful, cannot help raising to itself most frightful Prospects. Who can tell what will be the Consequence of this Peace in Times to come? Perhaps the goodly Land itself- Even *this* beloved Country, may share the same Fate with its conquest. . . . I conclude, therefore, that *New-England* under all these Distresses, must be reduc'd to a very low Ebb, being drain'd of its Inhabitants; its Trade and fishery ruined; the Gentlemen and Officers and common People humbled and impoverished; whilst they have all been exerting themselves, with uncommon Zeal, to promote the Interest of the *British Empire*.

The Independent Advertiser, 27 June, 1748.

capturing a small English outpost in Acadia and attacking the naval base at Annapolis Royal. But it was the fortress at Louisbourg that presented the greatest threat to New Englanders and to colonial commerce. A haven for privateers, the city was the origin of dozens of destructive raids on New England shipping. This activity seemed to validate American fears of a Catholic plot against English liberties, one led by the French with assistance from their "pagan" Indian allies. When Massachusetts Gov. William Shirley proposed an expedition against the town, New Englanders responded with both religious and economic fervor.

In late March 1745, a British naval squadron and four thousand New England militia men, commanded by William Pepperrell, a Maine militia chief and merchant, began the siege. Their timing was perfect. The French had only 455 regulars and eight hundred or so sailors and fishermen in the fort, at which a mutiny had recently occurred. The colonial force lost three hundred lives in a naval assault but in the end wore down the garrison. Fifteen hundred cannonballs were used on the fort, and the terms of surrender were quickly forgotten once the troops entered the walls. They drove citizens from their homes and looted houses and businesses. The siege also had a powerful psychological impact on the New England troops. The protracted effort led to great suffering among many unused to the rigors of warfare;

the journals some left behind bespeak a sadness and despair unmatched in previous colonial experience. Victory, however, brought a paroxysm of joyful expectations, both secular and religious. New England's trade would now be safe, and good Protestants everywhere could be thankful that "in this fashion has been smitten one faction of the power of Anti-Christ, and the visible kingdom of Christ thereby gains in strength."[4] Such comments make it easier to understand the despair of New Englanders when Louisbourg was returned to the French at the Treaty of Aix-la-Chapelle (1748), simply a pawn of international politics.

Interwar Strategy

The Treaty of Aix-la-Chapelle was no more than a temporary truce in the ongoing struggle between Great Britain and France for supremacy in the Western world.

MAP 13.1: European and Indian Territories in North America, 1750
By mid-century, French and English colonists in particular had extended their settlements far into the American interior. Their claims conflicted both with each other and with those of the Indians, creating a shifting and volatile diplomatic mosaic. ❧

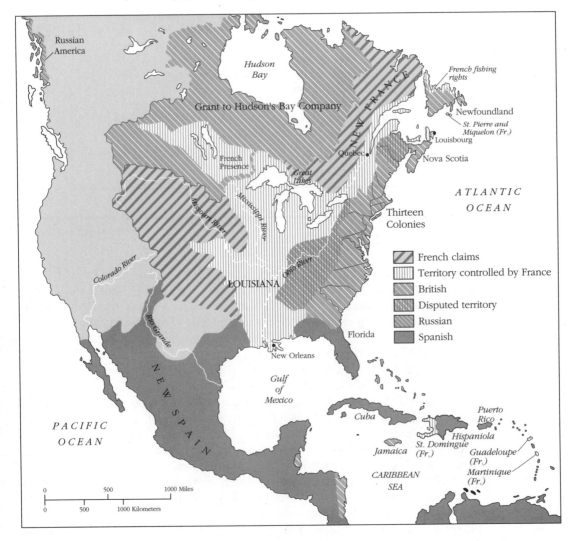

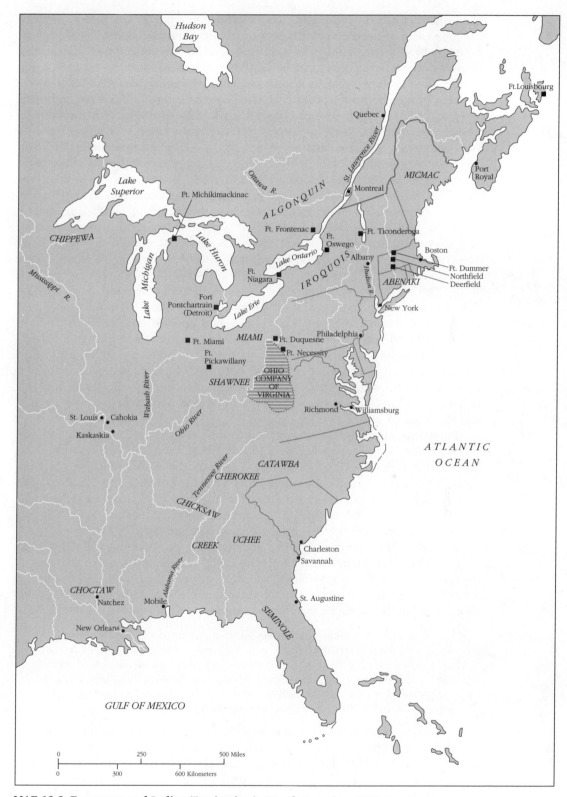

MAP 13.2: European and Indian Territories in North America, 1750 ❧

The French actually desired peace, hoping for time to regroup. The British commercial community, headed by Lords Newcastle and Pitt, argued that if peace was good for the French, it was bad for the British. American planters and land speculators supported this point of view. Ultimately, the French were forced to confront reality—the growing British colonial population, coupled with an aggressive expansionist policy, would eventually threaten French dominance in the fur trade and even sever communications between French Canada and Louisiana. For the French, whose population advantage in Europe had swung the balance of power there in their favor, such a shift would be catastrophic. After 1748, they redoubled their efforts to increase their power in North America. The governor-general at the time, the comte de La Galissonière, proposed a string of garrisoned forts in the Ohio Valley and a concerted effort to bring the region's Indians into a firm French alliance. Since the American militias appeared incapable of countering such a threat, the French expected that the British would be forced to commit much of their navy to the mainland colonies, thus opening the West Indies to French control. With relatively few men, the French hoped to tie down a much larger British army and navy.

In 1749, de La Galissonière sent an expedition to the Ohio Valley to officially claim the region for France and to drive out English traders. Here, the French discovered a situation much worse than they had anticipated. American settlers, traders, and land speculators had begun to move into the region in large numbers. Benjamin Franklin and other Pennsylvania merchants were pressuring Indians to grant them extensive tracts of land, and both the Virginia and Ohio companies were stepping up their activities. By 1750, Americans were actively trading with the Delawares, Miamis, Shawnees, Mingos, and Wyandots and making serious inroads into the French dominance in the region.

In response, the new Canadian governor, the marquis Duquesne, built and garrisoned a new chain of western forts and strengthened the post at Louisbourg. The governor of Louisiana, the Marquis de Vaudreuil-Caragnal, went even further, strengthening posts in the Illinois territory and constructing Fort Chartres near Kaskasia. Even after reinforcements arrived from France in 1751, though, Vaudreuil had only two thousand regulars to occupy the entire Mississippi Valley. Strong Indian alliances were clearly essential to French success.

A 1750 British report noted that members of the Onondaga, Cayuga, and Seneca tribes had abandoned their neutrality and joined the French, and it expressed the fear that the Mohawks would also break their traditional ties to the English. A 1753 report by the earl of Halifax, president of the Board of Trade, reveals the British understanding of the situation:

> Should the French establish themselves here, which no doubt but that they will, unless soon and vigorously opposed, they will have completed their favourite Plan, and will be in possession of near two thirds of the very best unsettled land on this side of the Mississippi and St. Lawrence, while Great Britain will not only lose near one half of the territory, to which it is undisputably entitled, but in case of a future Rupture will find it extremely difficult to keep the other half.[5]

Hostilities began when French troops led an Indian assault in June 1752 that destroyed the British post at Pickawillany, and Gov. Duquesne proceeded to build a road from Lake Erie to the headwaters of the Ohio River, protected by a chain of forts. In the summer of 1753, London warned colonial governors that the French were planning to begin hostilities and ordered them to take whatever steps were necessary to stop the construction of additional French forts. The Board of Trade specifically instructed Gov. Dinwiddie of Virginia to build two forts on the Ohio River. Dinwiddie was only too glad to comply, since he viewed the French forts as

George Washington, painted by Charles Willson Peale in 1772. ❧

intrusions on Virginia territory. He sent twenty-one-year-old George Washington and seven others with a letter protesting French occupation of lands they claimed as their own. The French, predictably, "contemptuously rejected" Washington's ultimatum.

In September 1753, the board also ordered the governor of New York to call an intercolonial Indian conference and negotiate a treaty with the Iroquois. This was the famous Albany Conference, which met during June and July 1754. Representatives of New York, New Hampshire, Pennsylvania, Massachusetts, Connecticut, and Rhode Island attended. Separate colonies made individual agreements with the small number of Indians who were there, and the Indians left with thirty wagon-loads of gifts, having affirmed their loyalty to the British but making no commitment to fight against the French. They were perhaps more impressed with the bickering and disagreements among the colonists. Typical was the debate over the draft plan (the Albany Plan) submitted by Benjamin Franklin, proposing a union of the colonies under a president-general appointed by London, with a grand council of colonial representatives that would be concerned with such common issues as Indian affairs, western lands, and defense. The conference recommended the plan be considered by the colonial legislatures, to little effect. Even Massachusetts, the home of Gov. William Shirley, one of the plan's strongest proponents, failed to offer any support. Franklin's famous cartoon of a chopped-up snake with the motto "Join or Die" had little impact. As Franklin himself noted, "Everyone cries a union is necessary, but when they come to the manner and form of the union, their weak noodles are perfectly distracted."[6] Given the profound disagreements between the colonies over such issues as western lands, it would have been even more surprising if they had supported this premature attempt at unity.

In 1754, the Virginia militia built a fort at the juncture of the Ohio and Monongahela rivers, but a five-hundred-man French force pushed them out and constructed Fort Duquesne on the site. Dinwiddie stubbornly sent Washington back with a militia to drive the French from the region. Unfortunately, Washington ambushed a French diplomatic party, killing nine and taking twenty-one prisoners. Having aroused the enemy, the future president now suffered the consequences. With only 350 men, he took a stand at a place called Great Meadows, building Fort Necessity. The tiny outpost was not even large enough to hold his small force, and only an earthen parapet protected most of the men. Bushy hills surrounded the site, giving the French and their Indian allies ideal vantage points. The battle dragged on for hours. Washington ran around giving orders, stepping over bodies and slipping on the blood. Rain set in during the afternoon, and the fort became a quagmire of mud, blood, and water. But Washington refused to surrender, breaking open the rum rations and urging his men on. By the end of the day, he had lost one-third of his force. On July 4, he finally signed a surrender document that stipulated that the French had acted only to avenge the "assassination" of their diplomat, Jumonville, in Washington's earlier attack. The Indians flocked to the French side in ever greater numbers, giving New France full control over the Ohio region.

While the colonists called for war in the press and private correspondence, their own responses left something to be desired. Throughout 1754, Pennsylvania, Maryland, and South Carolina refused to supply any troops, while New York and North Carolina sent only a few hundred poorly equipped men to aid Virginia. Then, in the autumn of 1754, London decided to send two regiments to America and raise two additional regiments of colonial troops—a bold move that was an entirely new element in British military policy for North America.

Major Gen. Edward Braddock was appointed commander-in-chief of the expedition. Braddock arrived in Virginia in February 1755, and in April, he met with several colonial governors to discuss the coming campaign. The British intended to clear out the French from the Ohio, Niagara, and Lake Champlain areas. Braddock himself would lead the first effort against Fort Duquesne. Second-in-command Shirley would direct the second, against Niagara. William Johnson, Indian commissioner for the northern colonies, would lead the third, against the French fortress at Crown Point. Braddock also planned to come to Shirley's assistance after he had completed his mission.

Geography and the forces of nature, together with the naive British planning, conspired against the campaign from the beginning. Against Washington's advice, Braddock chose a route that led him cross-country with siege guns, artillery, and horse-drawn wagons; with twenty-two hundred men, he cut a road through the wilderness, covering only about two miles a day. Then in mid-June, he divided his forces, taking about half of his men with him as he forged ahead. By July 9, this much smaller force stood only about nine miles from Fort Duquesne. Unfortunately, Braddock lowered his guard at this point and neglected to secure a neighboring hill, and a French force flanked the British troops. In the ensuing debacle, 456 British soldiers were killed and 421 wounded; sixty-three of eighty-six officers were killed or wounded, and Braddock died as he was being carried back to the other half of his force. Washington had two horses shot from under him, and his clothes were filled with bullet holes. The British retired immediately to Fort Cumberland, burning many supplies as they hastily fled. The Ohio remained in the hands of the French. Braddock had not sought Indian support, and his decision to ignore Washington's advice proved fatal.

William Johnson led an army of New England and New York troops against the French positions at Champlain. He established a camp at the southern end of Lake George and on September 8 drove off a French attack. But Johnson failed to follow up his victory and allowed the French to continue to construct a fort at Crown Point (Ticonderoga), only twelve miles away. He completed his own Fort William Henry, hoping to use both it and Fort Edward, on the upper Hudson River, as defensive barriers against further French advance.

Meanwhile, Shirley found himself competing with Johnson for supplies and Indian allies. New York Gov. James De Lancey worsened matters by using his connections in England and the colonies to stir up hostile feelings against New England. De Lancey was reluctant to get New York involved in the war in any way, preferring to have the colony maintain its profitable trade with the French and the Indians. Shirley finally abandoned his original plans and settled for refortifying Fort Oswego.

After Braddock's defeat, French-supplied Indians attacked settlers throughout the Virginia and Pennsylvania backcountry; indeed, most of the tribes north of the Ohio River were now convinced that the French held the winning cards. Only in Nova Scotia did the English achieve any measure of success. There, they focused on the Chignecto Isthmus. This strategically crucial strip of land linked the Nova Scotia peninsula with the mainland and in turn with the principal French settlements by a recently completed road. A series of inconsequential confrontations between French and English had occurred during the preceding decade, resulting in the construction of the British Fort Lawrence and the French Forts Beauséjour and Gasperau.

A joint Anglo-American force captured both forts in mid-June and took more than four hundred prisoners. The French, who had not expected a major British effort that year, had simply been unprepared. Some of the region's Acadian residents came to Fort Beauséjour's assistance, but they insisted that the commander sign a written order requiring them to bear arms under pain of death—if captured, they could then claim coercion. Most of them had disappeared back into the surrounding countryside by the time of the surrender. Ironically, the terms of surrender stipulated that Acadians who had taken up arms would be pardoned, but the British commander, Gov. Charles Lawrence of Nova Scotia, meant only that they would not be put to death. Thus, the British put them to work reconstructing the forts, before scattering them in colonial ports throughout North America.

The Seven Years War (French And Indian War) (1756–1763)

France Gains the Early Advantage

Both the English and the French now renewed their efforts to draw Indians into their diplomatic webs. The French attempted to convince the Iroquois, as well as the Shawnees, Delawares, and other Ohio tribes, that an alliance was essential to Indian survival. The English, the French asserted, planned to deprive the Indians of their

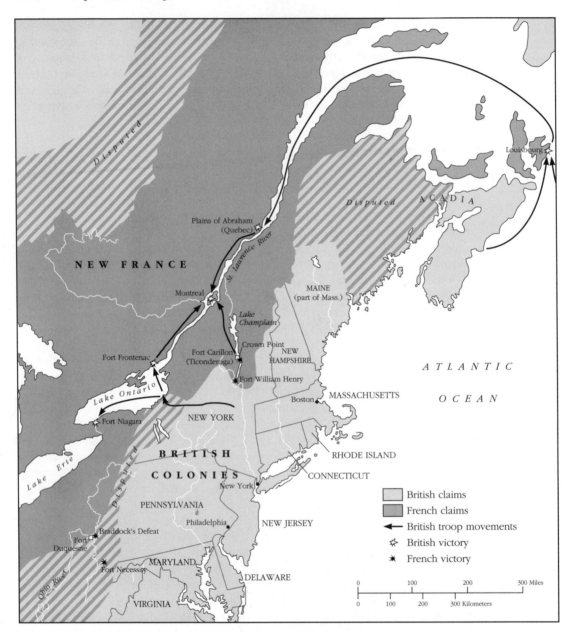

MAP 13.3: Major Battles in the American Theater of the Seven Years War ❧

independence. So successful were the French in these initial efforts that by 1755, they had driven the English from the Ohio Valley. Throughout the summer of 1755, the Delawares and other French-allied Indians terrorized the Pennsylvania and Virginia backcountry. Revenge must have been sweet for the Delawares; settlers had driven them from their tribal homelands in eastern Pennsylvania years earlier.

As French victories mounted, English hopes came to rest on winning support or neutrality from the Iroquois, Cherokees, Creeks, and Choctaws. Iroquois society had undergone dramatic changes in the early decades of the century. Many Iroquois now lived in communities with Delawares, Shawnees, and other Indians;

some moved west into the Ohio region, while still others migrated north of the Great Lakes. Those who remained behind began to abandon many of the traditional patterns of village life, even moving into single-family cabins and abandoning their longhouses, now used largely for ceremonial purposes. By the 1740s, Iroquois from all of the six nations were working for wages as scouts, porters, guides, and construction laborers. Still, many of the traditional practices—matrilineal patterns of descent, clan membership, and the sexual division of labor—remained strong wherever Iroquois lived.

The members of the confederation also retained their fearsome reputation and their tenacious desire for independent action. The English failed to impress them at the Albany Conference, though the Mohawks did fight for the English as mercenaries in 1757. Only in October 1758 did the Iroquois finally agree to halt the Delaware attacks on the Pennsylvania settlements. In exchange for a promise of neutrality, the English returned land the confederation had ceded at Albany. But the Indians still made no military commitment to the English; the Senecas, in fact, allied with the French in 1757 and 1758. Otherwise, confederation members changed their policy only in 1759, when they saw the fortunes of war shifting in favor of the English. In April 1759, the Iroquois promised the English eight hundred warriors for

The Marquis de Montcalm. ❧

the planned attack on Fort Niagara. Once again, the Iroquois Confederation had successfully navigated the tortuous seas of European diplomacy.

After Braddock's defeat and death, Shirley remained optimistic in planning the 1756 campaign. London, however, was not as sanguine. It replaced the Massachusetts governor as commander in March 1756 with a sixty-one-year-old Scot, the Earl of Loudoun. He too began optimistically, but after receiving word of the French capture of Fort Oswego, Loudoun abandoned his planned attack on Fort Ticonderoga. In 1757, he called off an attack on Louisbourg after a French fleet arrived at the port with reinforcements. Then on August 9, the French besieged and captured Fort William Henry, the culmination of a long string of humiliating and discouraging defeats for the English.

At this point, the French made a surprising and fatal decision. They abandoned the forts in the interior and fell back to the settlements in the St. Lawrence River valley. The fate of all of New France now hinged on holding Quebec and defeating the growing English armies to the south and west of Montreal. The French hoped only to retain control over some of the territory until the end of the war, anticipating that they would be in a better bargaining position than if they took a chance and lost everything.

What caused this dramatic shift in policy? Gov. Vaudreuil had developed the original optimistic policies. In contrast, the French military commander, Louis Joseph, marquis de Montcalm, painted a bleak picture for the French ministry. England had only now officially declared war on France, and events in Europe began to heavily influence French policy decisions in North America. Maria Theresa had convinced France to abandon Prussia and ally with Austria. England completed the diplomatic revolution by moving to the side of the Prussians. France was in the decidedly weaker position, forced to confront the fact that the struggle was truly global this time—extensive fighting took place in Europe, India, and North America. British war minister William Pitt decided to rely on Prussian strength in Europe and concentrate England's forces in the colonial phase of the war. As Pitt noted, "America would be conquered in Germany."[7]

The French suffered from other problems as well. With most of its farmers in the militia, New France was short of food. A disastrous crop failure in 1757 worsened conditions, and the government cut daily bread rations from two pounds to one-quarter of a pound. The final blow came from a smallpox epidemic. Weakened and chastened, the French made the fateful decision to abandon the forts in the west. Their last victory came with the heroic defense of Fort Ticonderoga against a nine-thousand-man British force, three times the size of the garrison.

The Tide Turns

Pitt now took full control of Britain's war effort. In December 1757, he replaced Loudoun with Gen. James Abercromby and personally drew up the plans for the 1758 campaign. The key element, both for England and for the Americans, was the decision to bring the full force of Britain's military might to bear in North America. This included complete support for colonial troops. England would pay for a force of twenty-five thousand British regulars and an equal number of provincial troops. The plan called for three separate campaigns. First, Abercromby would invade Canada by way of Lakes George and Champlain, taking Forts Ticonderoga and Crown Point on the way. Second, Lord Jeffrey Amherst would take Louisbourg. Finally, Gen. John Forbes would reopen the Ohio River valley by capturing Fort Duquesne. Amherst would move on to Quebec to join forces with Abercromby, and together the two would move through the heartland of New France to the lower Mississippi. Pitt was determined to avoid earlier mistakes and began to assemble his troops early in the year.

Abercromby was a fifty-two-year-old staff officer who was given little leeway by the confident but cautious Pitt. He did not reach Lake George until the end of June, much later than anticipated, and with sixteen thousand rather than the planned twenty-seven thousand troops. Montcalm, though, had only three or four thousand French forces to defend Fort Ticonderoga, so Pitt had every reason to be confident. Abercromby assaulted the fort on July 8 but retreated with high casualties at the end of the day. The French were as amazed as Pitt would be; they expected the attack to be renewed the following day and surely anticipated defeat in a relatively short time. But they failed to count on the incompetence of the British military. Abercromby never attacked again, and London recalled him within the month.

A more determined but equally short-sighted Forbes ignored advice by Washington and other colonists and chose a route to Fort Duquesne farther north than Braddock's. He advanced slowly, constructing blockhouses and supply depots along the way, and did not arrive at the fort until mid-September. Forbes had a much larger force and had convinced a number of Indians to abandon the French cause. The British had also taken Fort Frontenac, a strategically critical staging post that controlled Lake Ontario and served as a center for the fur trade, ensuring that the French could not count on reinforcements. Before the siege could begin, the French retreated, blowing up the fort in their wake. Thus, the British scorecard in the midwest was decidedly mixed. Abercromby's failure to take Ticonderoga meant that the British would have to postpone their planned invasion for another year, and the onset of winter delayed the move down the Mississippi. To the east, however, Amherst won England's greatest victory of the war thus far.

Louisbourg was located on a rugged promontory on the east coast of Cape Breton Island, just south of a spacious, sheltered harbor. The town depended heavily for its defense on the presence of a large and powerful French fleet. Economically, it was an important trade depot for products from both the French northlands and the northern British colonies and a center for the fishing industry. As we have noted, it also was a fruitful embarkation point for French privateers preying on New England shipping. Massachusetts colonists harbored bitter memories of Britain's decision to return the fortress to the French at Aix-la-Chapelle and had submitted several proposals for another attack on the city since that time; thus, the new plans aroused considerable enthusiasm in the Bay Colony.

Montcalm anticipated that the year's chief effort would be against Louisbourg, and he increased the size of the naval squadron stationed there, reinforced the garrison, and stocked the fortress with provisions. The British faced a force of more than two thousand officers and men in the fortress and thirty-six hundred marines and seamen. The French also took precautions against an amphibious landing, building extensive land defenses and stationing troops at a variety of sites around the harbor and fortress.

It was not enough. The vastly superior British navy kept most of the French fleet hemmed up in Europe. Other warships, with two thousand sailors and nineteen hundred guns, blockaded the Louisbourg harbor in early spring. The army gathered a force of 13,200 officers and men for the invasion. Amherst divided his force into three brigades, commanded by Brig. Gen. James Wolfe, Gov. Charles Lawrence of Nova Scotia, and Brig. Gen. Edward Whitemore. The plan was simple. Each of the three brigades would embark and reassemble at a designated place on shore. Support ship guns would pound the shore defenses, and the main forces would then land, headed by Wolfe's brigade.

The attack began at 2 A.M. on June 8. The French shelling, though, was so heavy that Wolfe ordered his force to withdraw. Fortuitously, three of the boats drifted off to the west and found a small beach, protected from sight by a rocky headland, that the French had overlooked in their defensive preparations. The three boats landed unopposed and notified the rest of the division, which quickly followed. The British forces took the French defenders completely by surprise, and by 8 A.M., they had driven the French back within the town's walls. Both sides suffered during the ensuing siege. The British were hit by smallpox, while the French commander hanged soldiers who sought to evade their duties. On June 22, a lucky artillery hit set the French barracks on fire and destroyed a large part of the fort. The surrender was arranged on July 26.

Amherst found himself something of a hero after this victory, arriving in Boston in September to a tumultuous reception. New Englanders were fully aware of the economic benefits they could now expect to enjoy. Their shipping was safer than it had been in years, their insurance rates fell by more than half, and England had gained full control of the Atlantic fisheries. But the colonists learned other lessons from this siege as well. They were appalled by the strict, cruel discipline of the British army; regulars seemed mere slaves to the officers, who appeared to be products of a culture seemingly lacking in moral or religious commitment. The experience sowed strong seeds of doubt about the British suitability to serve as the leaders of the Protestant cause.

The British Take Quebec and Montreal

The length of the Louisbourg siege, together with British defeats in the midwest, forced the ministry to postpone its planned attack on Quebec for another year. As 1759 dawned, both Amherst and Pitt realized that a two-pronged attack on Canada held the greatest chance of success. Pitt appointed Wolfe to command the principal expedition up the St. Lawrence River against Quebec, while Amherst would invade from the south on the route followed earlier by Abercromby. Leading sixteen thousand troops, Amherst carefully moved north, stockpiling supplies, laying out encampments, and constructing boats. He also showed a commendable concern for his men's health. Instead of liquor, he encouraged them to drink spruce beer, what he called a "wholesome beverage" of "melasses and the tops of spruce fir, boiled together in a proper quantity of water. . . ."[8] This unappetizing concoction was designed to prevent scurvy and to relieve hangovers.

Amherst arrived at Lake George on June 22, a month behind schedule, and spent another month rebuilding Fort William Henry. It was almost the end of July before he embarked on the final push, stopping regularly to build more forts and feeling his way ahead for French-allied Indians. On October 18, he received news that Quebec had fallen a month earlier. His dilatory march negated any chance Britain had of striking a final blow that year.

Only thirty-two years old, James Wolfe was a brilliant tactician but a poor strategist. He led eighty-five hundred of England's best troops and commanded a strong naval force of forty-nine ships, supported by 150 transports and merchant vessels. The force moved up the St. Lawrence River unopposed early in the summer of 1759, and Wolfe established his headquarters on the island of Orleans, which divided the river just below the town. Quebec sat high atop steep bluffs, and the French had further buttressed the city's defenses by building a series of impenetrable entrenchments around the walls. They beat back the first English assault, but Wolfe set up bombardment batteries on a cliff just across the river, turning homes, convents, and other buildings into rubble. He also sent raiding parties above the

Destruction of the lower town, Quebec, by English bombardment, 1759;
Martin Shortt. ❧

city to ravage the countryside, forcing Montcalm to send out troops to defend the area. But victory continued to elude the English forces.

Wolfe wanted to avoid an all-out frontal assault, and he even considered a winter-long siege. In his frustration, he ordered all homes and villages on the river burned. But he still could not force Montcalm to surrender, and time was running out. Though he was ill, Wolfe attempted one last assault. He accepted a plan proposed by his subordinates to stage a landing west of the city. Against their advice, though, he chose a steeply inclined site less than two miles from the city on which to land and deploy his forces. During the night of September 12 and 13, Wolfe led four thousand British troops up the slope, quickly disposing of a very surprised and very small French guard. When Montcalm awoke the next morning, he faced a British army on the Plains of Abraham. He had not believed the English could achieve what had seemed to be impossible. The British took the field in a fifteen-minute battle. Though the main body of French troops was able to retreat into the city, the starving French surrendered five days later. Each side had about six hundred wounded and fewer than sixty killed, but both Montcalm and Wolfe were among the dead.

It was too late in the season and Amherst was too far away to launch a final attack on Montreal; the British would have to wait one more year to make their control of North America official. Pitt's plans for 1760 called for a three-pronged attack on Montreal. James Murray was to move up the river with the Quebec garrison; Brig. Gen. William Haviland would march from Crown Point up Lake Champlain; and Amherst would move down the St. Lawrence from Lake Ontario. For once, the British forces moved successfully and with relative synchronization. By early September, Governor Vaudreuil faced seventeen thousand British troops with a mere two thousand men of his own. He realized resistance was futile, and Montreal surrendered on September 8. The French still controlled Louisiana and outposts on the Great Lakes and in the Illinois country, and Amherst was to lead subsequent expeditions against the French Caribbean Islands and Newfoundland. But the war was over.

The Treaty of Paris (1763) redrew the map of North America. The British ministry briefly debated whether it should take Canada or the recently conquered sugar

❧ *Documents* ❧
"We Dream'd of Your Times"

By the time the Seven Years War had begun, Americans had developed a clear, almost millennial vision of their future on the North American continent. The selections below illustrate the power of such beliefs and the American desire to extend the blessings of Protestantism westward in the ever-expanding search for gold, glory, and land. Ames's comments are from his almanac for 1757, a popular purveyor of popular culture in North America; James Horrocks was an Anglican minister and a future president of the College of William and Mary. In their vision of the American future, at least, these representatives of popular and elite culture were one.

III. Thirdly, of the Future State of NORTH AMERICA—Here we find a vast Stock of proper Materials for the Art and Ingenuity of Man to work upon:—Treasures of immense Worth; conceal'd from the poor ignorant aboriginal Natives! The Curious have observ'd, that the Progress of Humane Literature (like the Sun) is from the East to the West; thus has it travelled thro' Asia and Europe, and now is arrived at the eastern Shore of America, As the Coelestial Light of the Goepel was directed here by the Finger of G O D, as it will doubtless, finally drive the long! long! Night of Heathenish Darkness from *America:*—So Arts and Sciences will change the Face of Nature in their Tour from Hence over the Appalachian Mountains to the Western Ocean; and as they march thro' the vast Desert, the Residence of Wild Beasts will be broken up, and their obscene Howl cease for ever,—Instead of which the Stones and Trees will dance together at the Music of *Orpheus,*—the Rocks will disclose their hidden Gems,—and the inestimable Treasures of Gold & Silver be broken up. Huge Mountains of Iron Ore are already discovered; and vast Stores are reserved for future Generations: This Metal more useful than Gold and Silver, will imploy Millions of Hands, not only to form the martial Sword, and peaceful Share, alternately; but an Infinity of Utensils improved in the Exercise of Art, and Handicraft amongst Men. Nature thro' all her Works has stamp'd Authority on this Law, namely, "That all fit Matter shall be improved to its best

islands of Guadeloupe and Martinique from the French; it decided to take Canada. The French retained the sugar islands and fishing rights off Newfoundland and received two small islands off the coast, St. Pierre and Miquelon. The treaty also awarded the British Spanish Florida, which they immediately divided into East and West Florida; the Spanish received Cuba and the Phillipines as compensation. Spain also received Louisiana west of the Mississippi River, a confirmation of the secret 1762 Treaty of Fontainebleau it had negotiated with France.

Purposes."—Shall not then those vast Quarries, that teem with mechanic Stone,—those for Structure be piled into great Cities,—and those for Sculpture into Statues to perpetuate the Honor of renowned Heroes; even those who shall NOW save their Country.—O! Ye unborn Inhabitants of America! Should this Page escape its destin'd Conflagration at the Year's End and these Alphabetical Letters remain legible,—when your Eyes behold the sun after he has rolled the Seasons round for two or three Centuries more, you will know that in Anno Domini 1758, we dream'd of your Times.

Nathaniel Ames, *An Astronomical Diary;* or *An Almanack for . . . 1758* (Boston, 1757), 16.

The first Thing that will naturally present itself to us in our reflecting upon the happy Consequences resulting from the Blessing now given us, is the Security of our Civil Liberty, a Happiness we justly glory in; For Britons have preserv'd it pure and uncorrupted thro' all the Struggles of Ambition and the most dangerous Attacks of Power: They have set the World a fair Example that the highest Ambition of Princes shou'd be to govern a free People, and that no People can be great or happy but such as are so; whilst other Nations have bow'd their Necks to the Yoke of Power and have basely given up this indisputable Right of Man deriv'd to Him from the first Law of Nature, and daily feel that Misery, which every waits on Slaves. Oh Liberty! Thou are the Author of every good and perfect Gift, the inexhaustible Fountain, from whence all Blessings flow. Without Thee, what avails the Sweetness of Climate, or the most delightful Situation in the World? what avail all the Riches of Nature, the various Production of the Earth, the Mine bringing forth a thousand Treasures, the Olive and the Vine blooming upon the Mountains, if Tyranny usurps the happy Plains, and proud Oppression deforms the gay-smiling face of Nature. . . .

James Horrocks, *Upon the Peace . . .* , (Williamsburg: 1763), 7.

The American colonists reacted to the end of the war with unbounded joy. Beginning with the fall of Quebec, pamphlets and newspapers throughout the colonies wrote glowingly of the prosperous, glorious utopia awaiting British-Americans in the years head. The colonists had increasingly identified the French with the Antichrist and the war as a struggle between the forces of liberty (English Protestantism) and those of slavery (French Catholicism). The Anglo-American victories at Quebec and Montreal convinced Americans that the millennium was at hand.

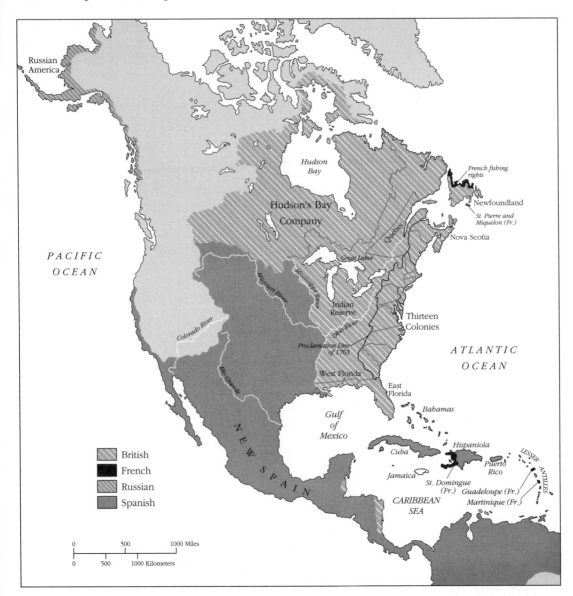

MAP 13.4: North American Claims after the Peace of Paris, 1763 &*

  Even as the dazzling light of victory shone on the colonists' horizons, there were rumblings of discontent closer to home. The British officers made little attempt during the war to hide their disdain for their American counterparts, and they complained constantly of the lack of support from the colonists. Colonial soldiers always seemed reluctant to enlist and serve but eager to leave their regiments for home. Disputes over providing winter quarters for British soldiers arose in New York and Massachusetts, convincing some British officials that they would have to permanently station troops in the colonies to ensure that America remained a loyal part of the empire. Colonists migrating westward continued to ignore the rights of Indians and to risk unwarranted and expansive wars with the tribes whose lands they stole. And colonial merchants, potentially England's greatest allies in imperial governance, seemed more than willing to overlook British restrictions on trade, even engaging in exchanges with Canadians and French Caribbean colonies whenever it was profitable. As Loudoun noted in 1757, Rhode Islanders in particular seemed "a lawless set of smugglers, who continually supply the Enemy with what Provisions they want, and bring back their goods in Barter for them. . . ."[9] Such concerns led the British to institute the Writs of Assistance in 1761—blanket search warrants that the British hoped would help control smuggling and that the colonists saw as an unjustified violation of their political and civil liberties.

Americans reacted angrily to the arrogant condescension that British officers, particularly Loudoun, showed toward them and objected bitterly to the lower pay and rank they received when the colonial militias were incorporated into the British army structure. But while royal governors warned American politicians of belt-tightening times ahead and while the British planned ways of increasing their American income, Americans themselves could only talk of the coming millennial empire, a time "when these *American* Desarts which for Ages unknown have been Regions of Darkness, and Habitations of Cruelty, shall be illuminated with the Light of the Glorious Gospel! And when this part of the World, which, till the later Ages, was utterly unknown, be the Glory and the Joy of the Whole Earth. . . !" With the evil French defeated, Americans could now "push out in Safety on all Sides. . . A VAST and fertile Country is now subjected to the *British* Sovereignty. . . . May it prove a happy Seat of the Redeemer's Kingdom. . . ."[10]

Conclusion

In 1763, white Americans were united in their expectations that the Anglo-American defeat of the French forces had opened the door to unlimited expansion and boundless prosperity. Many, perhaps a majority, also shared a moral vision of a future utopia shaped by the religious and civic dictates of republicanism and British protestantism.

But this was a precarious unity, threatened by the very processes that generated prosperity and opportunity. American society was gradually becoming more modern, its social institutions more complex and stable. At the same time, geographic mobility remained high and unsettling, and material wealth was unevenly shared. Americans were divided by conflicts of every kind—between rich and poor, cities and countryside, east and west, north and south, and popular and elite cultures. Urban artisans and laborers, for instance, feared poverty and exploitation by an unresponsive native aristocracy; farmers and agricultural workers feared tenancy and resented a rural gentry often unresponsive to their economic and social needs. Western settlers often reacted violently against the unresponsive eastern elite that dominated colonial legislatures. Even religion, once a common source of unity, now divided Americans more often than it brought them together. As Gordon Wood has noted, revolutions are caused by "sources lying deep within the social structure. . . ."[1] Almost thirty years after Wood's observation, scholars are only beginning to understand the relationship between these sources and political revolution. But it has become clear that the convulsive changes shaping American society continued in the years immediately preceding the Revolution and that they were often intimately preceding the Revolution and that they were often intimately connected to American resistance to British rule. A few brief examples will suggest the ways in which these changes pointed the way toward rebellion and eventual independence.

Massachusetts

The bitter dispute between Thomas Hutchinson and James Otis during the early 1760s in Boston galvanized the polar extremes of elite and popular culture into a dance of death. Hutchinson, perhaps better than anyone else, represented the Old World concept of patriarchy in its most honorable sense. He was confident of the superior moral and intellectual abilities of his own social class, but he also believed the gentry had a responsibility to serve society. He saw himself as a "father to his people," a benevolent parent responsible for providing for the less fortunate and able simply because of his superior position and abilities. And though he questioned the wisdom of many of the measures the British were to take in the coming years, he never doubted the legitimacy of parliamentary power and the superiority of the British empire. He held several high offices; he was appointed lieutenant-governor in 1758, and he also served as a probate judge, militia officer, and council member. In 1760, Governor Bernard appointed him chief judge to the superior court, a position Otis felt had been guaranteed to his own father.

Many of the colony's inhabitants already held Hutchinson in contempt, both for his defense of British imperial interests and for his earlier attack on the town's system of government. Then, in 1761, customs officials asked the Superior Court to renew the writs of assistance, general search warrants that allowed the officials to enter any residence, without specific cause, to search for contraband. The writs had already aroused much antagonism in the colony, and if the court ruled that they were still in force, they would continue to be so while the reigning monarch lived.

Otis, a lawyer from Barnstable, represented a group of Boston merchants who opposed the extension. Some of these men were undoubtedly smugglers, but the issue soon expanded beyond the mere economics of trade. Otis delivered a speech before the court arguing the Parliament did not have the authority to authorize the writs because they violated the fundamental principles of the English constitution. He did not question parliament's right to govern the colonies, but he did raise a standard of measurement that would ultimately guide the colonists to rebellion and independence. Hutchinson sought advice from London, and in November, he ruled the writs were legal.

The two sides continued their dispute in the newspapers over the next three years, Otis and Samuel Adams seeking the support of Boston artisans and laborers and reenergizing the popular party by tapping into the hatred and suspicion of Hutchinson and his vast wealth. Speaking as a mechanic in a Boston newspaper article in 1762, Otis argued: "I am forced to get my living by the labour of my hand; and the sweat of my brow; as most of you are and obliged to go thro' good report and evil report, for bitter bread, earned under the frowns of some who have no natural or divine right to be above me, and entirely owe their grandeur and honor to grinding the faces of the poor, and other acts of ill gotten gain and power."[2] As he said of Hutchinson on another occasion, "I have seen him twice or thrice in the pomp and puff of an American barrister. Nay, his cloven foot has peep'd from under the summer flowing black, white, and gray, and the gorgeous winter scarlet."[3] In 1763, Hutchinson and the Junto launched yet another attack on the popular party and the Boston town meeting, seeking to dismantle this venerable institution of self-government. The people responded resoundingly, electing Otis moderator of the meeting. The conflict between popular and elite cultures, between artisans and gentry, would continue to shape Boston's resistance to British measures throughout the years leading up to American independence.

New York

While Hudson Valley landlords had long granted concessions to prospective tenants, there was always the potential for discontent. The manor lords did own the land, after all, and controlled its sale. They retained first option on tenants' crops and could dictate what crops were grown and insist on a variety of other obligations. As land grew scarcer throughout the northeast after mid-century, migrating New Englanders squatted on some of these manor lands east of the Hudson River, lands that were also claimed by both Massachusetts and Connecticut. Some landlords, such as Henry Beekman, were tolerant of the invading New Englanders and flexible in their lease arrangements. Others insisted on maintaining their traditional manor rights; New England town meetings and communal traditions did not sit well with paternalistic landlords.

Problems first appeared in 1753, when a group of Massachusetts land speculators laid out a tract of land on the Livingston manor and even built a house on it, which Robert Livingston promptly tore down. The speculators rebuilt the house twice, but Livingston eventually had the intruders jailed. Violence spread during the following year, between Massachusetts and Connecticut settlers ensued in 1757, with three dying in the conflict.

Revolt became more widespread a decade later. Roger Morris and Beverly Robinson, sons-in-law of the Philipse family, touched off this more dangerous uprising when they issued eviction orders to New England tenants on their land, some of whom had lived there for over two decades. The case went to the courts, which supported the landlords and ordered the New Englanders off the land. Instead, in the spring of 1766, the settlers revolted, and for almost a year, they controlled much of the Hudson River valley, burning barns and crops and threatening tenants loyal to the proprietors. Two British regiments finally succeeded in putting the uprising down, and William Pendergast, the leader, was convicted of high treason, though later pardoned by the king. Once again, economic difficulties had disturbed the traditional social and political relationships between rulers and ruled.

Pennsylvania

In 1763, both whites and Indians on the Pennsylvania frontier were unhappy with their status. Settlers in western Pennsylvania had long complained of unequal representation in the colony's assembly. By the early 1760s, the eastern and western counties had almost equal population, but the three eastern counties had over twice as many delegates as the five western counties. The end of the Seven Years War, meanwhile, gave the English an unprecedented monopoly over the Indian trade in the Ohio Valley. British traders raised their prices, abandoned the rituals of gift-giving that had always accompanied the trade, and stopped the traditional policy of paying rent to the Indians for forts. The Pennsylvania government also allowed settlers to move onto Delaware and Iroquois land in the Monongahela and Susquehanna River valleys.

In response, the Delaware prophet Neolin urged Indians to repudiate white culture and return to their own cultures, and he converted the Ottawa war chief, Pontiac, to his cause. In the spring of 1763, Pontiac created an alliance of Ottawas, Shawnees, Delawares, Hurons, Chippewas, and Potawatomis. He attacked and captured British forts throughout the Ohio Valley, and Indian forces roamed through the Virginia and Pennsylvania backcountry at will all summer. Forts Detroit, Niagara, and Pitt, though, held out, and in August, British troops defeated a combined Indian force at the battle of Bushy Run in Pennsylvania. Pontiac ended his failed siege of Detroit in late October, British troops reasserted control of the frontier, and the two sides negotiated a treaty ending the war in 1766.

Indian raids had pushed back white settlement in Pennsylvania hundreds of miles, and frontier settlers vented their rage against any Indian they could find. A group of Scotch-Irish settlers from Paxton Township attacked the village of

Conestoga Manor, home to twenty peaceful Conestoga Indians, and killed six of them, scalping and mutilating their bodies. The whites later attacked the workhouse where the survivors of the raid were sheltered and hacked fourteen more Indians to death. In February 1764, hundreds of frontier settlers, known as the Paxton Boys, marched on Philadelphia to insist that the government provide them protection against future Indian attacks. Benjamin Franklin met the Paxtons at the edge of town; they presented him with a *Remonstrance,* complaining about the assembly's Indian policy and calling for more equitable representation for the western counties. The beleaguered assembly promised to consider their petitions, and the frontiersmen returned peacefully to their homes. Again, westward expansion created potentially explosive tensions in colonial society, threatening the fragile relationships between government and frontier settlers.

The Carolinas

The Carolina backcountry was the scene of endemic conflict, between blacks and whites and between whites and Indians. Since squatters' rights were common there, conflict also arose within the white community, between speculators and ordinary settlers. Unlike the Virginia ruling class, the Carolina gentry, North and South alike, chose not to address the demands of ordinary white settlers for greater responsiveness from their rulers and more equitable representation in the assemblies. As did most Americans, western settlers expected their rulers to speak for broader community interests, not just gentry concerns, and they acted accordingly.

The western counties of South Carolina were administered as extensions of eastern parishes, but the gentry were often lax in their governmental duties and failed to provide such essential services as schools, roads, and bridges. Without local courts, settlers had to travel all the way to Charleston to pursue legal grievances. When a crime wave swept through the area in the mid-1760s and eastern officials failed to respond, frustrated vigilantes took things into their own hands and formed an "association" to bring the guilty to justice. Though the leaders of this group were members of the elite, they had the support of thousands of ordinary farmers and planters. These "regulators" burned the thieves' homes and whipped or banished other suspects. More moderate westerners recoiled from these actions and formed a countergroup, and the two sides exchanged shots in 1769. The regulators finally disbanded later that year when the legislature passed the Circuit Court Act, establishing courts, jails, and sheriffs in the backcountry. The rebels simply wanted to bring a greater sense of authority to the region, to make the area safe for economic development and secure for others like themselves. The assembly hesitated to use force against the group, fearing slave uprisings if the militia were sent to the west. In the end, the two sides found common ground in their desire to preserve a prosperity that rested on the backs of African-Americans.

The North Carolina gentry had created new counties for backcountry settlers, but they appointed their own eastern neighbors to courts and other positions, and they pursued their own interests rather than those of the frontier community. Lawyers and land speculators acquired huge tracts of land, closing off opportunities for the poor and middle class. German, Irish, Scotch-Irish, and Scottish tenants and farmers complained of corruption, favoritism, high fees, and unfair taxation. They rose in protest, and after they failed to reach a resolution through peaceful means, turned to organized violence. They closed the courts to prevent debt collection and attacked the homes of unpopular judges. Governor William Tryon responded with force, and the two sides clashed at the Battle of the Alamance in May 1771. Twenty regulators died, one hundred were wounded, and six were tried and executed by the victorious government. The movement collapsed in failure.

American society thus continued to experience conflict and division as it grew economically and expanded westward, even as colonists were more united in their expectations of a glorious Anglo-American future. The British understood little of this and cared not at all; they had their own problems. England's victory in the Seven Years War won it military dominance in western Europe and North America, but at a cost. The British national debt in 1763 was 146 million pounds, with annual interest payments of 5 million pounds. The very size of its new empire created serious governance problems for the British. The territory gained from France, to the north and west of the original thirteen colonies, demanded immediate attention. Not only did the British have to find a way of peacefully ruling over the French population, but they also had to control the alarming predeliction of Americans for westward expansion, with the costly consequence of frequent Indian wars. Pontiac's Rebellion had alarmed others besides the Pennsylvania frontiersettlers; it was a warning bell to the British ministry.

To find solutions to these problems, George III, who had acceded to the throne only in 1760, appointed George Grenville first lord of the Treasury in April 1763. Grenville harbored bitter resentment at what he viewed as the American reluctance to cooperate with the British effort during the Seven Years War. The Board of Trade pointed out, for instance, that most colonial assemblies had refused to appropriate funds for troops and supplies unless they retained some control over appointments and operations. Grenville also understood that the English landed class would not accept higher taxes to pay off the war debt. Thus, he looked to the American colonies for the solution to the debt problem, as a matter of simple justice. While Otis and others believed that English rights, including the right of self-taxation, had followed them to American shores, Grenville, Parliament, and George III never doubted the supremacy of Parliament over the colonies. Colonists enjoyed only those rights, they believed, that Parliament was willing to accord them.

The full story of the subsequent attempts of Grenville and others to impose new regulations and taxes on the colonies belongs to another volume, and here we can only point the way. In October 1763, the British resolved the long-debated problem of what to do about the American west. The ministry issued the Proclamation of 1763, which prohibited governors from granting lands beyond the headwaters of rivers flowing to the Atlantic Ocean. Americans viewed it as a temporary measure only, and many ignored it. The British, moreover, continued to argue among themselves over its implementation, and the Crown never did implement a coherent western lands policy.

The following year, Grenville introduced the Revenue, or Sugar Act of 1764. Among other things, this measure sought to combat American smuggling in the West Indies by reducing the duty on molasses from six to three pence per gallon, reasoning that colonial merchants would no longer find it worthwhile to risk the dangers of smuggling and would thus steer their trade through legal channels. Grenville, like most Englishmen, failed to anticipate American objections to the revenue goals of the act. Otis and many others argued that Americans retained the right of all Englishmen to raise their own taxes. When the British tried again the following year with the Stamp Act, Americans found themselves united, perhaps surprisingly, in their opposition to the intrusive British measure.

When colonial representatives met in the Stamp Act Congress, they took the first step on the road to political independence. But this was not yet their goal; they still considered themselves loyal members of the British empire. And in some ways the American Revolution was simply a way station, albeit a highly significant or on the economic and social road of modernization that the colonies had long been traveling. For too long, we have seen the colonial period as only a prelude to the revolution. It is time, perhaps, to see these years as part of a larger, and more significant, transformation of the Western world.

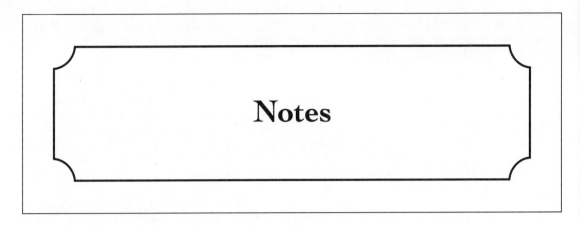

Notes

Chapter One

1. Quoted in L. S. Stavrianos, *Man's Past and Present,* 2d ed. (Englewood Cliffs, NJ: Prentice-Hall, 1975), 215.
2. Francis Jennings, *The Invasion of America: Indians, Colonialism, and the Cant of Conquest* (Chapel Hill, NC: IEAHC, University of North Carolina Press, 1976), 162.
3. Pierre de Charlevoix, *Journal of a Voyage to North America* (London, 1761); quoted in James Axtell, ed., *The Indian Peoples of Eastern America: A Documentary History of the Sexes* (New York: Oxford University Press, 1981), 16. I am indebted to Axtell's work for the "life cycle" approach.
4. Robert H. Fuson, trans., *The Log of Christopher Columbus* (Camden, ME: International Marine Publishing Company, 1987), 76.
5. Quote in Zvi Dor-Ner, *Columbus and the Age of Discovery* (New York: William Morrow & Company, 1991), 213.
6. Quoted in J. H. Parry, *The Discovery of South America* (New York: Taplinger Publishing, 1979), 59.
7. Christopher Columbus, *The Four Voyages of Columbus,* Cecil Jane, trans. and ed., 2 vols. (London, 1929, 1932; reprinted New York: Dover, 1988), 2:28.

Chapter Two

1. Quoted in James Axtell, *Imagining the Other: First Encounters in North America* (Washington, DC: American Historical Association, 1991), 27.
2. Bernal Diaz del Castillo, *The Conquest of New Spain,* J. M. Cohen, trans. (Baltimore, MD: Penguin Books, 1963), 214.

3. Reprinted in David Quinn, ed., *New American World: A Documentary History of North America to 1612,* 5 vols. (New York: Arno Press and Hector Bye, 1979), 1:427.
4. Quoted in Gregory Cerio, "The Black Legend," *When Worlds Collide* (*Newsweek,* 1991), 50.
5. Quoted in Marvin Lunenfeld, ed., *1492: Discovery, Invasion, Encounter* (Lexington, MA: D.C. Heath and Company, 1991), xxxvi.
6. Zvi Dor-Ner, *Columbus and the Age of Discovery* (New York: William Morrow and Company, 1991), 220.
7. Quoted in J. H. Elliott, *The Old World and the New, 1492–1650* (New York: Cambridge University Press, 1970), 48.
8. Quoted in E. Brooks Holified, *Era of Persuasion: American Thought and Culture, 1521–1680* (Boston: Twayne Publishers, 1989), 69.
9. H. P. Biggar, ed., *The Voyages of Jacques Cartier,* in David B. Quinn, ed., *New American World: A Documentary History of North America to 1612,* 5 vols. (New York: Arno Press and Hector Byye, 1979), 1:300.
10. Quoted in James Axtell, *The Invasion Within: The Contest of Cultures in Colonial North America* (New York: Alfred A. Knopf, 1985), 46.
11. *Ibid.,* 50.
12. *Ibid.,* 65.
13. *Ibid.,* 80.

Chapter Three

1. Robert Crowley, "Advice to a Yeoman," in Asa Briggs, *A Social History of England* (New York: The Viking Press, 1983), 105.
2. Quoted in Briggs, *Social History,* 127.

3 Richard Hakluyt, "Discourse of Western Planting," in E. G. R. Tayolor, ed., *The Original Writings & Correspondence of the Two Richard Hakluyts* (London: The Hakluyt Society, 1935), 318.

4 Quoted in Nicholas P. Canny, "The Ideology of English Colonization: From Ireland to America," *William and Mary Quarterly,* 3d Ser., 30 (1973), 588.

5 *Ibid.,* 583.

6 Quoted in David Hawke, *The Colonial Experience* (New York: Bobbs-Merrill, 1966), 33.

7 Quoted in David B. Quinn, *The Roanoke Voyages,* 2 vols. (London: The Hakluyt Society, 1955), 1:108.

8 John Smith, *Generall Historie of Virginia, New-England, and the Summer Isles* (London, 1624, in Philip L. Barbour, ed., *The Complete Works of Captain John Smith,* 3 vols. (Chapel Hill, NC: University of North Carolina Press, 1986), 2:113.

9 "Nova Brittannia," in David B. Quinn, ed., *New American World: A Documentary History of North American to 1612,* 5 vols. (New York: Arno Press and Hector Bye, 1979), 5:240.

10 *The Proceedings of the English Colonie in Virginia* (1612), in Philip L. Barbour, ed., *The Complete Works of Captain John Smith,* 3 vols. (Chapel Hill, NC: IEAHC, University of North Carolina Press, 1986), 1:237.

11 James Axtell, *After Columbus: Essays in the Ethnohistory of Colonial North America* (New York: Oxford University Press, 1988), 28.

12 Quoted in James Kirby Martin, et. al., *America and its People* (Glenview, Ill.: Scott, Foresman, and Company, 1989), 31.

13 Quoted in James Axtell, *After Columbus: Essays in the Ethnohistory of Colonial North America* (New York: Oxford University Press, 1988), 207.

14 Quoted in Gary Nash, *Red, White, and Black: The Peoples of Early America,* 2d ed. (Englewood Cliffs, NJ: Prentice-Hall, 1982), 51.

15 Quoted in James Axtell, *After Columbus: Essays in the Ethnohistory of Colonial North America* (New York: Oxford University Press, 1988), 214.

16 Quoted in Edmund S. Morgan, *American Slavery, American, Freedom: The Ordeal of Colonial Virginia* (New York: W. W. Norton and Company, 1975), 127.

17 Quoted in Robert Brugger, *Maryland: A Bicentennial History* (Baltimore, MD: The Johns Hopkins University Press, 1988), 3.

18 *Ibid.,* 9.

Chapter Four

1 Quoted in Douglas R. McManis, *Colonial New England: A Historical Geography* (New York: Oxford University Press, 1975), 21.

2 William Bradford, *Of Plymouth Plantation,* Harvey Wish, ed. (New York: Capricorn Books, 1962), 70.

3 *Ibid.,* 69.

4 John Dane, "A Declaration of Remarkable Providences in the Course of My Life," in John Demos, *Remarkable Providences: Readings on Early American History,* rev. ed. (Boston: Northeastern University Press, 1991), 60–70.

5 From "The First Massachusetts Charter," in Jack P. Greene, ed., *Settlements to Society, 1607–1763: A Documentary History of Colonial America* (New York: W. W. Norton and Company, 1975), 22.

6 Quoted in Kenneth Lockridge, *A New England Town: The First Hundred Years* (New York: W. W. Norton and Company, 1970), 29.

7 *Ibid.,* 31.

8 From trial excerpts printed in Rosemary Radford Ruether and Rosemary Skinner Keller, eds., *Women & Religion in America,* vol. 2, *The Colonial and Revolutionary Periods* (New York: Harper & Row, 1983), 166, 168, 172.

9 Quoted in James Axtell, *The Invasion Within: The Contest of Cultures in Colonial North America* (New York: Oxford University Press, 1985), 137, 148.

10 Quoted in Alden T. Vaugan, *New England Frontier: Puritans and Indians, 1620–1675* (Boston: Little, Brown, 1965), 104.

11 William Bradford, *Of Plymouth Plantation,* Harvey Wish, ed. (New York: Capricorn Books, 1962), 296.

Chapter Five

1 Quoted in Michael Garibaldi Hall, *Edward Randolph and the American Colonies, 1676–1703* (Chapel Hill, NC: IEAHC, University of North Carolina Press, 1960), 22.

2 Quoted in Philip D. Morgan, "British Encounters with Africans and African-Americans," in Bernard Bailyn and Philip D. Morgan, eds., *Strangers Within the Realm: Cultural Margins of the First British Empire* (Chapel Hill, NC: IEAHC, University of North Carolina Press), 174.

3 *Ibid.*

4 *Ibid.,* 175.

5 Quoted in Gary Nash, *Red, White, and Black: The Peoples of Early America,* 2nd ed. (Englewood Cliffs, NJ: Prentice-Hall, 1982), 91.

6 *Ibid.,* 92.

7 *Ibid.,* 91.

8 Quoted in Michael Kammen, *Colonial New York: A History* (New York: Scribner's, 1975), 88.

9 David Hackett Fischer, *Albion's Seed: Four British Folkways in America* (New York: Oxford University Press, 1989), 426.

[10] *Ibid.,* 458.

[11] Quoted in Joseph E. Illick, *Colonial Pennsylvania: A History* (New York: Scribner's 1976), 20.

[12] *Ibid.,* 26.

[13] David Hackett Fischer, *Albion's Seed: Four British Folkways in America* (New York: Oxford University Press, 1989), 523.

[14] Quoted in Robert A. Divine, T. H. Breen, George M. Frederickson, and R. Hal Williams, *America: Past and Present,* 3d ed., 2 vols. (New York: Harper-Collins, 1991), 1:58.

[15] Quoted in Robert M. Weir, *Colonial South Carolina: A History* (Millwood, NY: KTO, 1983), 33.

Chapter Six

[1] Quoted in Darrett B. Rutman & Anita H. Rutman, *A Place in Time: Middlesex County, Virginia, 1650–1750* (New York: W. W. Norton and Company, 1984), 136.

[2] Quoted in Gary Nash, *Red, White, and Black: The Peoples of Early America,* 2d ed. (Englewood Cliffs, NJ: Prentice-Hall, 1982), 151.

[3] Quoted in Warren Billings, John Selby, and Thad Tate, *Colonial Virginia: A History* (Millwood, NY: KTO, 1986), 91.

[4] Bacon's Manifesto," *Virginia Magazine of History and Biography,* 1 (1893), 55–8.

[5] Quoted in Stephen Innes, *Labor in a New Land: Economy and Society in Seventeenth-Century Springfield* (Princeton, NJ: Princeton University Press, 1983), 130. I have drawn my analysis of Springfield from Innes's excellent book.

[6] *A Discourse in Explanation of the Bank of Credit. . .* (Boston, 1687), in Andrew W. Davis, ed., *Colonial Currency Reprints,* 4 vols. (New York: Burt Franklin, 1971, [c. 1910]), 1:122.

[7] *Ibid.,* 1:124.

[8] Nathaniel B. Shurtleff, ed., *Records of the Governor and Company of Massachusetts Bay in New England,* 5 vols. (Boston: W. White, 1853–4), 4:59.

[9] Quoted in Harry S. Stout, *The New England Soul: Preaching and Religious Culture in Colonial New England* (New York: Oxford University Press, 1986), 75.

[10] Quoted in Seymour Van Dyken, *Samuel Willard, 1640–1707: Preacher of Orthodoxy in an Era of Change* (Grand Rapids, MI: William B. Eerdmans, 1971), 179–80.

[11] Quoted in Harry S. Stout, *The New England Soul: Preaching and Religious Culture in Colonial New England* (New York: Oxford University Press, 1986), 68.

[12] Increase Mather, *An Earnest EXHORTATION To the Inhabitants of NEW ENGLAND. . .* (Boston, 1676), in Richard Slotkin & James K. Folsom, eds., *"So Dreadful; a Judgement": Puritan Responses to King Philip's War, 1676–1677* (Middletown, CT: Wesleyan University Press, 1978), 174–5.

[13] This series of quotations is taken from Ronald P. Dufour, *Modernization in Colonial Massachusetts, 1630–1763* (New York: Garland, 1987), 84–6.

[14] Quoted in R. C. Simmons, *The American Colonies: From Settlement to Independence* (New York: W. W. Norton and Company, 1976), 138.

[15] Quoted in Michael Kammen, *Colonial New York: A History* (New York: Scribner's 1975), 116.

[16] Quoted in W. J. Eccles, *France in America* (New York: Harper & Row, 1972), 72.

Chapter Seven

[1] David Hackett Fischer, *Albion's Seed: Four British Folkways in America* (New York: Oxford University Press, 1989), 7.

[2] Darrett B. Rutman and Anita H. Rutman, *A Place in Time: MiddleSex County, Virginia, 1650–1750* (New York: W. W. Norton and Company, 1984), 12.

[3] Quoted in Helena M. Wall, *Fierce Communion: Family and Community in Early America* (Cambridge, MA: Harvard University Press, 1990), 18.

[4] *Ibid.,* 25–6.

[5] David Hackett Fischer, *Albion's Seed: Four British Folkways in America* (New York: Oxford University Press, 1989), 190.

[6] Quoted in Helena M. Wall, *Fierce Communion: Family and Community in Early America* (Cambridge, MA: Harvard University Press, 1990), 38.

[7] *Ibid.,* 39.

[8] *Ibid.,* 90.

[9] Quoted in David Hackett Fischer, *Albion's Seed: Four British Folkways in America* (New york: Oxford University Press, 1989), 194.

[10] *Ibid.*

[11] Quoted in David Thomas Konig, *Law and Society in Puritan Massachusetts: Essex County, 1629–1692* (Chapel Hill, NC: University of North Carolina Press, 1979), 48.

[12] Quoted in Helena M. Wall, *Fierce Communion: Family and Community in Early America* (Cambridge, MA: Harvard University Press, 1990), 38.

[13] *Ibid.,* 40.

[14] Quoted in Edmund S. Morgan, *American Slavery, American Freedom: The Ordeal of Colonial Virginia* (New York: W. W. Norton and Company, 1975), 152.

[15] *Ibid.*

[16] David Hackett Fischer, *Albion's Seed: Four British Folkways in Early America* (New York: Oxford University Press, 1989), 585.

[17] James Merrell, "Indians and Colonists in Early America," in Bernard Bailyn and Philip D. Morgan, eds., *Strangers Within the Realm: Cultural Margins of the First British Empire* (Chapel Hill, NC: IEAHC, University of North Carolina Press, 1991), 127.

[18] *Ibid.,* 129.

[19] *Ibid.,* 132.

[20] Bruce Trigger, "Early Native North American Responses to European Contact: Romantic versus Rationalistic Interpretations," *Journal of American History,"* 77 (1991), 1201.

[21] James Axtell, *The Invasion Within: The Contest of Cultures in Colonial North America* (New York: Oxford University Press, 1985), 137.

[22] Quoted in James Merrell, "Indians and Colonists in Early America," in Barnard Bailyn and Philip D. Morgan, eds., *Strangers Within the Realm: Cultural Margins of the First British Empire* (Chapel Hill, NC: IEAHC, University of North Carolina Press, 1991), 151.

[23] Quoted in James Axtell, *The Invasion Within: The Contest of Cultures in Colonial North America* (New york: Oxford University Press, 1985), 228.

[24] *Ibid.,* 52.

[25] *Ibid.*

[26] *Ibid.,* 307–8.

[27] *Ibid.,* 311.

[28] *Ibid.,* 312.

[29] *Ibid.,* 314–5.

[30] *Ibid.,* 316.

[31] *Ibid.,* 325.

[32] *Ibid.,* 327.

[33] Quoted in Helena M. Wall, *Fierce Communion: Family and Community in Early America* (Cambridge, MA: Harvard University Press, 1990), 59.

[34] *Ibid.,* 99.

[35] *Ibid.,* 103.

[36] Quoted in Edmund S. Morgan, *The Puritan Family: Religion and Domestic Relations in Seventeenth-Century New England,* rev. ed. (New York: Harper & Row, 1966), 61.

[37] *Ibid.,* 60.

[38] *Ibid.,* 64.

[39] Quoted in David Hackett Fischer, *Albion's Seed: Four British Folkways in America* (New York: Oxford University Press, 1989), 483.

[40] Quoted in Barry Levy, "Tender Plants: Quakers, Farmers and Children in the Delaware Valley, 1681–1735," *Journal of Family History,* 3 (1978), 117.

[41] Laura Thacher Ulrich, *Good Wives, Image and Reality in the Lives of Women in Northern New England, 1650–1750* (New York: Alfred A. Knopf, 1982), 9.

[42] *Ibid.,* 130.

[43] Quoted in David Hackett Fischer, *Albion's Seed: Four British Folkways in America* (New York: Oxford University Press, 1989), 299.

[44] *Ibid.,* 125.

[45] Richard Godbeer, *The Devil's Dominion: Magic and Religion in Early New England* (New York: Cambridge University Press, 1992), 9.

[46] *Ibid.,* 42–3.

[47] *Ibid.,* 67.

[48] *Ibid.,* 206.

[49] Quoted in Carol F. Karlsen, *The Devil in the Shape of a Woman: Witchcraft in Colonial New England* (New York: W. W. Norton and Company, 1987), 53.

[50] *Ibid.,* 85.

[51] W. Elliot Woodward, ed., *Records of Salem Witchcraft Copied from the Original Documents* 2 vols. (Roxbury, MA: Privately Printed, 1864), 1:44–8.

[52] Quoted in John Demos, *Entertaining Satan: Witchcraft and the Culture of Early New England* (New York: Oxford University Press, 1982), 100–1, 130.

[53] Nathaniel B. Shurtleff, ed., *Records of the Governor and Company of Massachusetts Bay,* 5 vols. (Boston: W. White, 1853–1854), 2:203.

[54] Quoted in David Hackett Fischer, *Albion's Seed: Four British Folkways in America* (New York: Oxford University Press, 1989), 530.

[55] David D. Hall, *World of Wonder, Days of Judgment: Popular Religious Belief in Early New England* (New York: Alfred A. Knopf, 1989), 57.

[56] Quoted in David D. Hall, "Literacy, Religion, and the Plain Style," in Jonathan L. Fairbanks and Robert F. Trent, eds., *New England Begins: The Seventeenth Century,* 3 vols. (Boston: Museum of Fine Arts, 1982), 2:104.

[57] William Bradford, *Of Plymouth Plantation,* Harvey Wish, ed. (New York: Capricorn Books, 1962), 61.

[58] Edward Johnson, *The Wonder-Working Providence of Sion's Savior in New England* (London, 1654), in Perry Miller and Thomas H. Johnson, eds., *The Puritans: A Sourcebook of Their Writings,* rev. ed., 2 vols. (New York: Harper & Row, 1963), 1:160.

[59] Quoted in Jonathan L. Fairbanks and Robert F. Trent, eds., *New England Begins: The Seventeenth Century,* 3 vols. (Boston: Museum of Fine Arts, 1982), 1:123.

[60] *Ibid.,* 1:125.

[61] Alan Heimert and Andrew DelBanco, eds., *The Puritans in American: A Narrative Anthology* (Cambridge, MA: Harvard University Press, 1985), 130.

62 Quoted in Richard Ruland and Malcolm Bradbury, *From Puritanism to Postmodernism: A History of American Literature* (New York: Viking Penguin, 1991), 7–8.

Chapter Eight

1 Gottlieb Mittelberger, *Journey to Pennsylvania* (1756), Oscar Handlin and John Clive, trans. and eds. (Cambridge, MA: Harvard University Press, 1960), 15.

2 *Ibid.*, 14.

3 Quoted in Richard Hofstadter, *America at 1750* (New York: Vintage Books, 1970), 26.

4 Quoted in Maldwyn A. Jones, "The Scots-Irish in British America," in Bernard Bailyn and Philip D. Morgan, eds., *Strangers Within the Realm: Cultural Margins of the First British Empire* (Chapel Hill, NC: IEAHC, University of North Carolina Press, 1991), 296.

5 Quoted in Winthrop Jordan, *White Over Black: American Attitudes Towards the Negro, 1550–1812* (Chapel Hill, NC: IEAHC, University of North Carolina Press, 1968), 7.

6 Olaudah Equiano, *The Interesting Narrative of the Life of Olaudah Equiano, or Gustavus Vassa, the African, Written by Himself* (London, 1789), 72.

7 *Ibid.*, 106.

8 Quoted in Gary Nash, *Red, White, and Black: The Peoples of Early America,* 2d ed. (Englewood Cliffs, NJ: Prentice-Hall, 1982), 168.

9 *Ibid.*, 191.

10 Quoted in Peter Wood, *Black Majority: Negroes in Colonial South Carolina from 1670 to the Stono Rebellion* (New York: W. W. Norton and Company, 1974), 135.

11 Quoted in Ira Berlin, "Time, Space, and the Evolution of Afro-American Society," *American Historical Review,* 85 (1980), 44.

12 Quoted in Bruce Levine, et. al., *Who Built America?: Working People and the Nation's Economy, Politics, Culture, and Society,* 2 vols. (New York: Pantheon Books, 1989), 1:106.

13 Quoted in Ira Berlin, "Time, Space, and the Evolution of Afro-American Society," *American Historical Review,* 85 (1980), 47.

14 Quoted in Gary Nash, *Red, White, and Black: The Peoples of Early America,* 2d ed. (Englewood Cliffs, NJ: Prentice-Hall, 1982), 181.

15 Quoted in Donald R. Wright, *African Americans in the Colonial Era: From African Origins Through the American Revolution* (Arlington Heights, IL: Harland-Davidson, 1990), 99.

16 Quoted in Peter Wood, *Black Majority: Negroes in Colonial South Carolina from 1670 to the Stono Rebellion* (New York: W. W. Norton and Company, 1974), 286.

17 *Ibid.*, 287.

18 Quoted in David S. Lovejoy, *Religious Enthusiasm in the New World: Heresy to Revolution* (Cambridge, MA: Harvard University Press, 1985), 204.

19 Quoted in Donald R. Wright, *African Americans in the Colonial Era: From African Origins through the American Revolution* (Arlington Heights, IL: Harlan-Davidson, 1990), 102.

20 Quoted in Philip D. Morgan, "Slave Life in Piedmont Virginia," in Lois Green Carr, Philip D. Morgan, and Jean B. Russo, eds., *Colonial Chesapeake Society* (Chapel Hill, NC: IEAHC, University of North Carolina Press, 1988), 449.

Chapter Nine

1 I have drawn the information on Concord from Robert Gross's superb study, *The Minutemen and Their World* (New York: Hill and Wang, 1976), ch. 4.

2 Gottlieb Mittelberger, *Journey to Pennsylvania* (1756), Oscar Handlin and John Clive, trans. and eds. (Cambridge, MA: Harvard University Press, 1960), 49.

3 I have drawn these biographical sketches from Paul G. E. Clemens and Lucy Simler, "Rural Labor and the Farm Household in Chester County, Pennsylvania, 1750–1820," in Stephen Innes, ed., *Work and Labor in Early America* (Chapel Hill, NC: IEAHC, University of North Carolina Press, 1988), 109–27.

4 Gwymmed Meeting, quoted in Barry Levy, *Quakers and the American Family: British Settlement in the Delaware Valley* (New York: Oxford University Press, 1988), 234. This section draws heavily from Levy's work.

5 Quoted from Allan Kulikoff, *Tobacco and Slaves: The Development of Southern Culture in the Chesapeake, 1680–1800* (Chapel Hill, NC: IEAHC, University of North Carolina Press, 1986), 296. I have been influenced by Kulikoff's work throughout this section.

6 I have taken this material from two articles by Billy G. Smith: "The Vicissitudes of Fortune: The Careers of Laboring Men in Philadelphia, 1750–1800," in Stephen Innes, ed. *Work and Labor in Early America* (Chapel Hill, NC: IEAHC, University of North Carolina Press, 1988), 221–51; and "The Material Lives of Laboring Philadelphians, 1750–1800," *William and Mary Quarterly,* 3d Ser., 38 (1981), 163–202.

7 I have taken this material from Marcus Rediker, "The Anglo-American Seaman as Collective Worker, 1700–1750," in Stephen Innes, ed., *Work and Labor in Early America* (Chapel Hill, NC: IEAHC, University of North Carolina Press, 1988),

252–286. Also see his excellent book, cited in the bibliography.

Chapter Ten

1 Richard L. Bushman, *From Puritan to Yankee: Character and the Social Order in Connecticut, 1690–1765* (Cambridge, MA: Harvard University Press, 1967).

2 Quoted in John L. Brooke, *The Heart of the Commonwealth: Society and Political Culture in Worcester County, Massachusetts, 1713–1861* (New York: Cambridge University Press, 1989), 82.

3 Quoted in David Hackett Fischer, *Albion's Seed: Four British Folkways in America* (New York: Oxford University Press, 1989), 469.

4 Quoted in Barry Levy, *Quakers and the American Family: British Settlement in the Delaware Valley* (New York: Oxford University Press, 1988), 212.

5 Quoted in David Hackett Fischer, *Albion's Seed: Four British Folkways in America* (New York: Oxford University Press, 1989), 496.

6 Quoted in Barry Levy, *Quakers and the American Family: British Settlement in the Delaware Valley* (New York: Oxford University Press, 1988), 260.

7 Quoted in Mechal Sobel, *The World They Made Together: Black and White Values in Eighteenth-Century Virginia* (Princeton, NJ: Princeton University Press, 1987), 238.

8 Quoted in Patricia U. Bonomi, *Under the Cope of Heaven: Religion, Society, and Politics in Colonial America* (New York: Oxford University Press, 1986), 140.

9 Quoted in Marilyn J. Westerkamp, *Triumph of the Laity: Scots-Irish Piety and the Great Awakening, 1625–1760* (New York: Oxford University Press, 1988), 160.

10 Quoted in Gary Nash, *The Urban Crucible: The Northern Seaport Towns and the Origins of the American Revolution,* abridged ed. (Cambridge, MA: Harvard University Press, 1986), 129.

11 Quoted in Marilyn J. Westerkamp, *Triumph of the Laity: Scots-Irish Piety and the Great Awakening, 1625–1760* (New York: Oxford University Press, 1988), 186.

12 Gilbert Tennent, *The Danger of an Unconverted Ministry, Considered in a Sermon on Mark VI. 34* (Philadelphia, 1742), 2.

13 Quoted in Gary Nash, *The Urban Crucible: The Northern Seaports and the Origins of the American Revolution,* abridged ed. (Cambridge, MA: Harvard University Press, 1986), 136.

14 Thomas Foxcroft, *Observations Historical and Practical. . .* (Boston, 1730), 1.

15 Jacob Bucknam, *Ability to, and Fidelity in, the Ministry* (Boston, 1743), 38.

16 David S. Lovejoy, *Religious Enthusiasm in the New World: Heresy to Revolution* (Cambridge, MA: Harvard University Press, 1985), 179.

17 Jonathan Edwards, *Narrative of Surprising Conversions. . .* (Boston, 1738), in Jack P. Greene, ed., *Settlements to Society, 1607–1763: A Documentary History of Colonial America* (New York: W. W. Norton and Company, 1975), 323.

18 *Ibid.,* 324.

19 Quoted in Edwin S. Gaustad, *The Great Awakening in New England* (New York: Harper & Row, 1957), 27.

20 "The Spiritual Travels of Nathan Cole," excerpted in Darrett B. Rutman, ed., *The Great Awakening: Event and Exegesis* (Huntington: NY: Robert E. Krieger Publishing Company, 1977), 45.

21 Thomas Prince, *The Christian History, containing Accounts of the Revival and Propagation of Religion in Great-Britain & America. For the Year 1744* (Boston, 1745), 164–5.

22 *The Boston Evening-Post,* 5 July, 1742.

23 *Ibid.*

24 *Ibid.*

25 *Ibid.*

26 Quoted in Harry S. Stout and Peter Onuf, "James Davenport and the Great Awakening in New England," *Journal of American History,* 71 (1983), 568–9.

27 *Ibid.,* 557.

28 Quoted in Harry S. Stout, *The New England Soul: Preaching and Religious Culture in Colonial New England* (New York: Oxford University Press, 1986), 223.

29 Charles Chauncey, *Seasonable Thoughts on the State of Religion in New England, a Treatise in Five Parts. . .* (Boston, 1743), 77.

30 Quoted in David S. Lovejoy, *Religious Enthusiasm in the New World: Heresy to Revolution* (Cambridge, MA: Harvard University Press), 196.

31 Quoted in Rhys Isaac, *The Transformation of Virginia, 1740–1790* (Chapel Hill, NC: IEAHC, University of North Carolina Press, 1982), 148.

32 Quoted in Patricia U. Bonomi, *Under the Cope of Heaven: Religion, Society, and Politics in Colonial America* (New York: Oxford University Press, 1986), 181.

33 Quoted in Alan Gallay, *The Formation of a Planter Elite: Jonathan Bryan and the Southern Colonial Frontier* (Athens, GA: University of Georgia Press, 1989), 37.

Chapter Eleven

1 Quoted in Michael Kammen, *Colonial New York: A History* (New York: Scribner's, 1975), 156.

2 William H. Whittemore, ed., *Reports of the Record Commissioners of the City of Boston,* 39 vols. (Boston, 1876–1908), 8:217.

3 From *Cato's Letter,* quoted in Bernard Bailyn, *The Origins of American Politics* (New York: Alfred A. Knopf, 1968), 41.

4 *New England Courant,* 9–16 April, 1722.

5 *Ibid.,* 26 March–2 April, 1721.

6 Quoted in Rhys Isaac, *The Transformation of Virginia, 1740–1790* (Chapel Hill, NC: IEAHC, University of North Carolina Press, 1982), 13.

7 Quoted in J. William T. Youngs, *American Realities: Historical Episodes,* 2 vols. (Boston: Little, Brown, 1981), 1:66.

8 *Ibid.*

9 Quoted in Charles S. Sydnor, *American Revolutionaries in the Making: Political Practices in Washington's Virginia* (Chapel Hill, NC: IEAHC, University of North Carolina Press, 1952), 25–6.

10 Quoted in Jack P. Greene, "Society, Ideology, and Politics: An Analysis of the Political Culture of Mid-Eighteenth-Century Virginia," in Richard M. Jellison, ed., *Society, Freedom, and Conscience: The Coming of the Revolution in Virginia, Massachusetts, and New York* (New York: W. W. Norton and Company, 1976), 59.

11 Warren M. Billings, John E. Selby, Thad W. Tate, *Colonial Virginia: A History* (White Plains, NY: KTO, 1986), 268.

12 Quoted in Timothy H. Breen, *Tobacco Culture: The Mentality of the Great Tidewater Planters on the Eve of the Revolution* (Princeton, NJ: Princeton University Press, 1985), 100.

13 *Ibid.,* 134.

14 *Ibid.,* 89.

15 *Ibid.,* 145.

16 *Ibid.,* 139.

17 Quoted in Robert M. Weir, *Colonial South Carolina; A History* (Millwood, NY: KTO, 1983), 219.

18 Quoted in Gary Nash, *The Urban Crucible: The Northern Seaports and the Origins of the American Revolution,* abridged ed. (Cambridge, MA: Harvard University Press, 1986), 56.

19 *Ibid.,* 89.

20 *Ibid.,* 162.

21 *Ibid.,* 74.

22 *Ibid.,* 94.

23 *Ibid.*

24 *Ibid.,* 170.

25 *The Second Part of South-Sea Stock. . .* (Boston, 1720), 20.

26 Quoted in Gary Nash, *The Urban Crucible: Northern Seaports and the Origins of the American Revolution,* abridged ed. (Cambridge, MA: Harvard University Press, 1986), 49.

27 *Ibid.,* 52.

28 Vincent Sentinel, *Massachusetts in Agony. . .* (Boston, 1750), 3, 12–3.

29 *Boston Independent Advertiser,* 25 January, 1748.

30 Vincent Sentinel, *Massachusetts in Agony. . .* (Boston, 1750), 8.

31 *An Address to the Freeholders and Inhabitants of Massachusetts-Bay* (Boston, 1751), 5–6.

Chapter Twelve

1 Quoted in Michael Kammen, *Colonial New York: A History* (New York: Scribner's, 1975), 271.

2 [Crevecoeur, M. G. St. J. de.] J. Hector St. John, *Letters from an American Farmer. . .* (New York: E. P. Dutton and Company, 1912 [1782]), 43.

3 Quoted in John F. Kasson, *Rudeness and Civility: Manners in Nineteenth-Century Urban America* (New York: Hill and Wang, 1990), 13.

4 Quoted in Jackson J. Spielvogel, *Western Civilization* (St. Paul, MN: West Publishing Company, 1990), 595.

5 Quoted in Harry M. Ward, *Colonial America, 1607–1763* (Englewood Cliffs, NJ: Prentice-Hall, 1991), 291.

6 *Ibid.,* 327–8.

7 *Ibid.,* 328.

8 Quoted in Michael Kammen, *Colonial New York: A History* (New York: Scribner's, 1975), 243.

9 *The Connecticut Gazette,* February 7, 1756.

10 Michael Kammen, *Colonial New York: A History* (New York: Scribner's, 1975), 243.

11 Quoted in Laura Thacher Ulrich, *Good Wives: Image and Reality in the Lives of Women in Northern New England, 1650–1750* (New York: Alfred A. Knopf, 1982), 80–1.

12 Quoted in Bruce Levine, et. al., *Who Built America? Working People and the Nation's Economy, Politics, Culture, and Society,* 2 vols. (New York: Pantheon Books), 1:113.

13 Quoted in Allan Kulikoff, *Tobacco and Slaves: The Development of Southern Cultures in the Chesapeake: 1680–1800* (Chapel Hill, NC: IEAHC, University of North Carolina Press, 1986), 176.

14 Quoted in David Hackett Fischer, *Albion's Seed: Four British Folkways in America* (New York: Oxford University Press, 1989), 292.

15 Douglass Adair, ed., "The Autobiography of the Reverend Deveraux Jarrett, 1732–1763," *The William and Mary Quarterly,* 3d Ser., 9 (1952), 370.

16 Quoted in David Hackett Fischer, *Albion's Seed: Four British Folkways in America* (New York: Oxford University Press, 1989), 555.

17 *Ibid.,* 528.

18 Quoted in Rhys Isaac, *The Transformation of Virginia, 1740–1790* (Chapel Hill, NC: IEAHC, University of North Carolina Press, 1982), 98.

19 David Hackett Fischer, *Albion's Seed: Four British Folkways in America* (New York: Oxford University Press, 1989), 770.

[20] Charles Woodmason, *The Carolina Backcountry on the Eve of the Revolution,* Richard J. Hooker, ed. (Chapel Hill, NC: IEAHC, University of North Carolina Press, 1953), 101–2.

[21] Quoted in David Hackett Fischer, *Albion's Seed: Four British Folkways in America* (New York: Oxford University Press, 1989), 711, 713.

[22] Charles Woodmason, *The Carolina Backcountry on the Eve of the Revolution,* Richard J. Hooker, ed. (Chapel Hill, NC: IEAHC, University of North Carolina Press, 1953), 15.

Chapter Thirteen

[1] Quoted in Richard I. Melvoin, *New England Outpost: War and Society in Colonial Deerfield* (New York: W. W. Norton and Company, 1989), 225.

[2] Quoted in Thomas Hutchinson, *The History of the Colony and Province of Massachusetts Bay,* Lawrence S. Mayo, ed., 3 vols. (Cambridge, MA: Harvard University Press, 1936), 2:150–1.

[3] Quoted in James H. Merrell, *The Indians' New World: Catawbas and Their Neighbors from European Contact through the Era of Removal* (Chapel Hill, NC: IEAHC, University of North Carolina Press, 1989), 68.

[4] Quoted in W. J. Eccles, *France in America* (New York: Harper & Row, 1972), 114.

[5] Quoted in W. J. Eccles, *The Ordeal of New France* (Toronto: Canadian Broadcasting Company, 1967), 116.

[6] Quoted in Joseph E. Illick, *Colonial Pennsylvania: A History* (New York: Scribner's, 1976), 209–10.

[7] Quoted in W. J. Eccles, *The Ordeal of New France* (Toronto: Canadian Broadcasting Company, 1967), 127.

[8] Quoted in Douglas Edward Leach, *Arms for Empire: A Military History of the British Colonies in North America, 1607–1763* (New York: Macmillan, 1973), 448.

[9] Quoted in R. C. Simmons, *The American Colonies: From Settlement to Independence* (New York: W. W. Norton, 1976), 291.

[10] Nathaniel Appleton, *A Sermon Occasioned by the Surrender of Montreal. . .* (Boston, 1760), 36.

Conclusion

[1] Gordon Wood, "Rhetoric and Reality in the American Revolution," *William and Mary Quarterly,* 3d Ser., 23 (1966), 26.

[2] *Boston Gazette,* 11 January, 1762.

[3] Quoted in Malcolm Freiberg, *Prelude to Purgatory: Thomas Hutchinson in Provincial Massachusetts Politics, 1760–1770* (New York: Garland, 1990), 46.

Bibliography

Given the vast amount of literature on the colonial period, some selectivity in listing important works is unavoidable. For a complete bibliography, see David L. Ammerman and Philip D. Morgan, comps., *Books about Early America* (Williamsburg, VA: The Institute of Early American History and Culture [hereafter IEAHC], 1989). For reviews of more recent works, see *The William and Mary Quarterly*. The IEAHC has published many of the best works in the field, and the *Quarterly* remains a gem among scholarly journals. I recommend in particular the various essays and forums that have been published over the past decade surveying the "state of the literature" in various subspecialties of early American history.

General Books

Many of the the books cited in this bibliography discuss material covered in more than one chapter, but a few warrant particular mention. Jack P. Greene and J. R. Pole, eds., *Colonial British America: Essays in the New History of the Early Modern Era* (Baltimore: Johns Hopkins University Press, 1984) contains essays by the most eminent scholars in the field, surveying the literature on various thematic topics. Milton M. Klein and Jacob E. Cooke have served as general editors for a series of histories of the thirteen original colonies. They are: Warren M. Billings, John E. Selby, and Thad W. Tate, *Colonial Virginia: A History* (White Plains, NY: KTO, 1986); Kenneth Coleman, *Colonial Georgia: A History* (New York: Scribner's, 1976); Jere R. Daniell, *Colonial New Hampshire: A History* (Millwood, NY: KTO, 1981); Joseph E. Illick, *Colonial Pennsylvania: A History* (New York: Scribner's, 1976); Sydney V. James, *Colonial Rhode Island: A History* (New York:

Scribner's, 1975); Michael Kammen, *Colonial New York: A History* (New York: Scribner's, 1975); Benjamin W. Labaree, *Colonial Massachusetts: A History* (Millwood, NY: KTO, 1979); Aubrey C. Land, *Colonial Maryland: A History* (Millwood, NY: KTO, 1981); Hugh T. Lefler and William S. Powell, *Colonial North Carolina: A History* (New York: Scribner's, 1973); John A. Munroe, *Colonial Delaware: A History* (Millwood, NY: KTO, 1978); John E. Pomfret, *Colonial New Jersey: A History* (New York: Scribner's, 1973); Robert J. Taylor, *Colonial Connecticut: A History* (Millwood, NY: KTO, 1979); and Robert M. Weir, *Colonial South Carolina: A History* (Millwood, NY: KTO, 1983).

Jack P. Greene, *Pursuits of Happiness: The Social Development of Early Modern British Colonies and the Formation of American Culture* (Chapel Hill, NC: University of North Carolina Press, 1988) is a particularly valuable analysis of colonial culture. David Hackett Fischer, *Albion's Seed: Four British Folkways in America* (New York: Oxford University Press, 1989) is a far reaching, controversial interpretation; see the critiques in "*Albion's Seed: Four British Folkways in America*—A Symposium," *William and Mary Quarterly*, 3d Ser., 48 (1991), 224–308; and Greene, "Interpretive Frameworks: The Quest for Intellectual Order in Early American History," *William and Mary Quarterly*, 3d Ser., 48 (1991), 515–30. Gary Nash, *Red, White, and Black: The Peoples of Early America,* 3d ed. (Englewood Cliffs, NJ: Prentice-Hall, 1992) remains an excellent introduction to Indian and African-American cultures in particular. Also see Michael Kammen, *People of Paradox: An Inquiry Concerning the Origins of American Civilization* (New York: Alfred A. Knopf, 1972); Donald W. Meinig, *The Shaping of America:*

A Geographical Perspective on 500 Years of History, Vol. 1, *Atlantic America, 1492–1800* (New Haven, CT: Yale University Press, 1986); and Richard D. Brown, *Modernization: The Transformation of American Life, 1600–1865* (New York: Hill and Wang, 1976).

David D. Hall, John M. Murrin, and Thad W. Tate, eds., *Saints and Revolutionaries: Essays on Early American History* (New York: W. W. Norton and Company, 1984) and James A. Henretta, Michael Kammen, and Stanley N. Katz, *The Transformation of Early American History: Society, Authority, and Ideology* (New York: Alfred A. Knopf, 1991) both contain several valuable essays, while Stanley N. Katz, John M. Murrin, and Douglas Greenberg, eds., *Colonial America: Essays in Politics and Social Development*, 4th ed. (New York: McGraw-Hill, 1993) remains the best reader in the field.

Several excellent collections of primary sources are available. They include: Karen Ordahl Kupperman, ed., *Major Problems in American Colonial History: Documents and Essays* (Lexington, MA: D. C. Heath and Company, 1993); Jack Greene, ed., *Settlements to Society, 1584–1763* (New York: W. W. Norton and Company, 1975); W. Keith Cavanagh, ed., *Foundations of Colonial America: A Documentary History*, 3 vols. New York: Chelsea House, 1973); and John Demos, ed., *Remarkable Providences: Readings on Early American History*, rev. ed. (Boston: Northeastern University Press, 1991).

William H. Goetzmann and Glyndwr Williams, *The Atlas of North American Exploration: From the Norse Voyages to the Race to the Pole* (New York: Prentice Hall General Reference, 1992) is a remarkable example of cartographic excellence and an essential source for following the exploration of the North American continent.

Chapter One

On American Indians in general, see Wilcomb E. Washburn, *The Indian in America* (New York: Harper & Row, 1975); Gary Nash, *Red, White, and Black: The Peoples of Early America*, 3d ed. (Englewood Cliffs, NJ: Prentice-Hall, 1992); Alvin M. Josephy, Jr., *America in 1492* (New York: Alfred A. Knopf, 1991); and James Axtell, ed., *The Indian Peoples of Eastern America: A Documentary History of the Sexes* (New York: Oxford University Press, 1981). Inga Clendinnen, *Aztecs: An Interpretation* (New York: Cambridge University Press, 1991) and Michael D. Coe, *The Maya*, 5th ed. (New York: Thames-Hudson, 1993) are excellent introductions to Central American Indian culture. For the southeast, see Charles Hudson, *The Southeastern Indians* (Knoxville: University of Tennessee Press, 1976) and Helen C. Roundtree, *The Powhatan Indians of Virginia: Their Traditional Culture* (Norman: University of Oklahoma Press, 1989). For the northeast regions, begin with William C. Sturtevant, gen. ed., *Handbook of North American Indians*, vol. 15, *Northeast*, ed. Bruce G. Trigger (Washington, DC: Smithsonian Institution Press, 1978). Trigger's other writings are also essential. See especially Bruce G. Trigger, *The Children of the Aataentsic*, 2 vols. (Montreal: McGill-Queen's University Press, 1976). On the Iroquois, see Anthony F. C. Wallace, *The Death and Rebirth of the Seneca* (New York: Alfred A. Knopf, 1970) and especially Daniel K. Richter, *The Ordeal of the Longhouse: The Peoples of the Iroquois League in the Era of European Colonization* (Chapel Hill, NC: IEAHC, University of North Carolina Press, 1992). For New England Indians, consult Howard S. Russell, *Indian New England before the Mayflower* (Hanover, NH: University Press of New England, 1980).

On the Vikings, see Gwyn Jones, *The Norse Atlantic Sage, Being the Norse Voyages of Discovery and Settlement to Iceland, Greenland, and America*, rev. ed. (New York: Oxford University Press, 1986) and Erik Wahlgren, *The Vikings and America* (New York: Thames and Hudson, 1986). See the following general works on exploration: J. H. Parry, *The Age of Reconaissance: Discovery, Exploration, and Settlement, 1450–1650* (Cleveland: World, 1963); Parry, ed., *The European Reconnaissance: Selected Documents* (New York: Harper & Row, 1968); David Beers Quinn, *North America from Earliest Discovery to First Settlements: The Norse Voyages to 1612* (New York: Harper & Row, 1975); and Samuel Eliot Morison, *The European Discovery of America*, 2 vols. (New York: Oxford University Press, 1971–74).

The best biography of Columbus is Felipe Fernandez-Armesto, *Columbus* (New York: Oxford University Press, 1991). On Spain and its exploration of the New World, see J. H. Elliott, *Imperial Spain, 1492–1716* (New York: Penguin, 1990); J. H. Parry, *The Discovery of South America* (New York: Taplinger, 1979); Parry, *The Spanish Searborn Empire* (Berkeley: University of California Press, 1990); Jerald T. Milanich and Susan Milbrath, *First Encounters: Spanish Explorations in the Caribbean and the United States, 1492–1570* (Gainesville: University Presses of Florida, 1989); and William D. Phillips and Carla Rahn Phillips, *The Worlds of Columbus* (New York: Cambridge University Press, 1992). The Columbus Quincentennial spawned a bounty of studies on the cultural contact of Old World and New. The reader should begin with older classics, such as J. H. Elliot, *The Old World and the New, 1492–1650* (Cambridge: Cambridge University Press, 1970); Carl O. Sauer, *Sixteenth-Century North America: The Land and the People as Seen by the Europeans* (Berkeley: University of California Press,

1971); and two seminal works by Alfred W. Crosby, *The Columbian Exchange: Biological and Cultural Consequences of 1492* (Westport, CT: Greenwood Press, 1972) and Ecological Imperialism: The Biological Expansion of Europe, 900–1900 (New York: Cambridge University Press, 1986).

Among the newer works, the following are most valuable: Fredi Chiapelli, ed., *First Images of America: The Impact of the New World on the Old*, 2 vols. (Berkeley: University of California Press, 1976); Tzvetan Todorov, *The Conquest of America: The Question of the Other*, trans. Richard Howard (New York: Harper & Row, 1984); Urs Bitterli, *Cultures in Conflict: Encounters Between European and Non-European Cultures, 1492–1800*, trans. Ritchie Robertson (Stanford, CA: Stanford University Press, 1989); David Hurst Thomas, ed., *Columbian Consequences* (Washington, DC: Smithsonian Institution Press, 1989); William Brandon, *New Worlds for Old: Reports from the New World and Their Effect on the Development of Social Thought in Europe, 1500–1800* (Athens: Ohio University Press, 1986); Herman J. Viola and Carolyn Margolis, *Seeds of Change: A Quincentennial Commemoration* (Washington, DC: Smithsonian Institution Press, 1991); P. J. Marshall and Glyndwr Williams, *The Great Map of Mankind: Perceptions of New Worlds in the Age of Enlightenment* (Cambridge: Harvard University Press, 1982); and Anthony Grafton, with April Shelford and Nancy Siraisi, *New Worlds, Ancient Texts: The Power of Tradition and the Shock of Discovery* (Cambridge: Belknap Press, Harvard University Press, 1992). Particularly valuable are the brief American Historical Association pamphlet by James Axtell, *Imagining the Other: First Contacts in North America* (Washington, DC: American Historical Association, 1991) and Axtell, "Columbian Encounters," *William and Mary Quarterly*, 3d Ser., 49 (1992), 183–360. Axtell's *Beyond 1492: Encounters in Colonial North America* (New York: Oxford University Press, 1992) contains several excellent essays. Stephen Greenblatt has mapped out challenging new directions in his *Marvellous Possessions: The Wonder of the New World* (Chicago: University of Chicago Press, 1991), a path also explored by Jeffrey Knapp, *England, America, and Literature from Utopia to the Tempest* (Berkeley: University of California Press, 1992).

Chapter Two

David B. Quinn, ed., with Alison M. Quinn and Susan Hillier, *New American World: A Documentary History of North America to 1612*, 5 vols. (New York: Arno Press and Hector Bye, 1979) is a superb collection of documents on New World exploration and the early Spanish, French, and English empires. Marvin Lunenfeld, ed., *1492: Discovery, Invasion,*

Encounter (Lexington, MA: D. C. Heath and Company, 1991) is an excellent shorter collection John E. Kicza, "The Social and Ethnic Historiography of Colonial Latin America: The Last Twenty Years," *William and Mary Quarterly*, 3d Ser., 45 (1988), 453–88 is a useful survey of recent literature, while Leslie Bethell, ed., *The Cambridge History of Latin America*, vols. 1–3 (Cambridge: Cambridge University Press, 1984–85) contains authoritative essays by a variety of scholars. Charles Gibson, *Spain in America* (New York: Harper & Row, 1966) remains valuable, but James Lockhart and Stuart B. Schwartz, *Early Latin America: A History of Colonial Spanish America and Brazil* (New York: Cambridge University Press, 1983) and Mark A. Burkholder and Lyman L. Johnson, *Colonial Latin America* (New York: Oxford University Press, 1990) are the best modern surveys. Also see Lyle McAlister, *Spain and Portugal in the New World, 1492–1700* (Minneapolis, MN: University of Minnesota Press, 1984); Colin M. Macachlan, *Spain's Empire in the New World* (Berkeley: University of California Press, 1991); and James Lockhart, *Spanish Peru, 1532–1560: A Colonial Society* (Madison, WI: University of Wisconsin Press, 1966).

David J. Weber, *The Spanish Frontier in North America* (New Haven: Yale University Press, 1992) is a recent work that promises to become a classic on an often neglected area of the Spanish Empire. On the Spanish in the American southeast, see Paul E. Hoffman, *A New Andalucia and a Way to the Orient: The American Southeast during the Sixteenth Century* (Baton Rouge: Louisiana State University Press, 1990). C. R. Boxer, *The Portuguese Seaborne Empire, 1415–1825* (London: Hutchinson, 1968) remains an essential study of the Portuguese overseas empire.

On Indians under Spanish rule, see the following works: Samuel N. Wilson, *Hispaniola: Caribbean Chiefdoms in the Age of Columbus* (Tuscaloosa, AL: University of Alabama Press, 1990); Ramon A. Gutierrez, *When Jesus Came, the Corn Mothers Went Away: Marriage, Sexuality, and Power in New Mexico, 1500–1846* (Stanford, CA: Stanford University Press, 1991); Nancy M. Farriss, *Maya Society under Colonial Rule: The Collective Enterprise of Survival* (Princeton, NJ: Princeton University Press, 1984); Inga Clendinnen, *Ambivalent Conquest: Maya and Spaniard in the Yucatan, 1517–1570* (New York: Cambridge University Press, 1987); James Lockhart, *The Nahuas after Conquest* (Stanford, CA: Stanford University Press, 1992); Charles Gibson, *The Aztecs under Spanish Rule: A History of the Indians of the Valley of Mexico, 1519–1810* (Stanford, CA: Stanford University Press, 1964); and Miguel Leon-Portilla, ed., *The Broken Spears: The Aztec Account of the Conquest of Mexico,* trans. Angel Maria Garibay and Lysander Kemp (Boston: Beacon Press, 1962). Nathan Wachtel, *The Vision of the Vanquished: The Spanish Conquest of Peru through Indian Eyes, 1530–1570*, trans. Ben and Sian Reynolds (New York: Barnes and Nobel, 1977) contains useful primary sources.

There are several outstanding surveys of the early years of the French empire: W. J. Eccles, *Canada under Louis XIV, 1663–1701* (New York: Oxford University Press, 1964), *The Canadian Frontier, 1534–1760* (New York: Holt, Rinehart, and Winston, 1969), and especially *France in America* (New York: Harper & Row, 1972); Marcel Trudel, *The Beginnings of New France, 1524–1663*, trans. Patricia Claxton (Toronto: McClelland and Stewart, 1973) and *Introduction to New France* (Toronto: Holt, Rinehart and Winston, 1968); Gustave Lanctot, *A History of Canada*, trans. Josephine Hambleton and Margaret M. Cameron, 3 vols. (Cambridge: Harvard University Press, 1963–65). James Axtell, *The Invasion Within: The Contest of Cultures in Colonial North America* (New York: Oxford University Press, 1985) is one of the best of the new ethnohistorical studies, an essential beginning point along with the Trigger volumes cited earlier. On particular topics, consult the following: Denys Delage, *Bitter Feast: Amerindians and Europeans in the American Northeast, 1600–64*, trans. Jane Brierley (Vancouver: University of British Columbia Press, 1993) and Cornelius J. Jaenen, *The Role of the Church in New France* (Toronto: McGraw-Hill Ryerson, 1976) and *Friend and Foe: Aspects of French-Amerindian Cultural Contact in the Sixteenth and Seventeenth Centuries* (New York: Columbia University Press, 1976).

Chapter Three

There are a number of excellent surveys of English political, social, and religious affairs during the Tudor-Stuart period. See, in particular, John Guy, *Tudor England* (New York: Oxford University Press, 1988) and the briefer study by Guy and John Merrill, *The Tudors and Stuarts* (New York: Oxford University Press, 1992). G. R. Elton, *Reform and Reformation, England 1509–1558* (Cambridge: Harvard University Press, 1977) is a traditional but reliable work. On Elizabeth's reign, consult Wallace T. MacCaffrey, *Queen Elizabeth and the Making of Policy, 1572–1588* (Princeton, NJ: Princeton University Press, 1991) and *Elizabeth I: War and Politics, 1588–1603* (Princeton, NJ: Princeton University Press, 1992). On the Reformation in England, see the classic A. G. Dickens, *The English Reformation* (New York: Shocken Books, 1964); Patrick Collinson, *The Elizabethan Puritan Movement* (Berkeley: University of California Press, 1967) and *The Birth of Protestant England* (New

York: St. Martin's Press, 1988); and Rosemary O'Day, *The Debate on the English Reformation* (London: Methuen, 1986).

The Understanding of English society under the later Tudors and the early Stuarts has benefited from an explosion of creative scholarship over the last two decades. Begin with Mark Kishlansky, "Community and Continuity: A Review of Selected Works on English Local History," *William and Mary Quarterly*, 3d. Ser., 38 (1980), 139–46, and the most satisfying overall survey, Keith Wrightson, *English Society, 1580–1680* (New Brunswick, NJ: Rutgers University Press, 1982). Also consult D. C. Coleman, *The Economy of England, 1450–1750* (New York: Oxford University Press, 1977); the seminal study by Peter Laslett, *The World We Have Lost: Further Explored* (New York: Scribner's, 1984); and for an illuminating look at life at the local level, Margaret Spufford, *Contrasting Communities* (Cambridge: Cambridge University Press, 1974).

The story of England's early involvement in America receives authoritative treatment in David B. Quinn, *England and the Discovery of America, 1481–1620* (New York: Harper & Row, 1974). On the Irish background to Colonization, see Quinn, *The Elizabethans and the Irish* (Ithaca, NY: Cornell University Press, 1966) and Nicholas P. Canny, "The Ideology of English Colonization: From Ireland to America," *William and Mary Quarterly*, 3d ser., 30 (1973), 575–98. For the Roanoke colony, see David Quinn, ed., *The Roanoke Voyages, 1584–1590*, 2 vols. (London: Hakluyt Society, 1955) and the standard secondary account, David B. Quinn, *Set Fair for Roanoke: Voyages and Colonies, 1584–1606* (Chapel Hill: University of North Carolina Press, 1985), as well as the briefer study by Karen Ordahl Kupperman, *Roanoke: The Abandoned Colony* (Totowa, NJ: Rowman & Allanheld, 1984). John White's remarkable drawings are reproduced in Paul Hulton, *America, 1585: The Complete Drawings of John White* (Chapel Hill, NC: University of North Carolina Press, 1984).

The standard work on early Virginia is now Edmund S. Morgan, *American Slavery, American Freedom: The Ordeal of Colonial Virginia* (New York: W. W. Norton and Company, 1975), but also see the following: Karen O. Kupperman, "Apathy and Death in Early Jamestown," *Journal of American History*, 66 (1979), 24–40; Alden T. Vaughan, *American Genesis: Captain John Smith and the Founding of Virginia* (Boston: Little, Brown and Company, 1975); and Jon Kukla, "Order and Chaos in Early America: Political and Social Stability in Pre-Restoration Virginia," *American Historical Review*, 90 (1985), 275–98. James R. Perry, *The Formation of a Society on Virginia's Eastern Shore, 1615–1655* (Chapel Hill, NC: IEAHC, University of North

Carolina Press, 1990) offers a persuasive challenge to the picture of uniform chaos that dominates our vision of the early Chesapeake. A number of excellent articles on Chesapeake society are found in two volumes from the Institute of Early American History and Culture, Thad W. Tate and David M. Ammerman, eds., *The Chesapeake in the Seventeenth Century: Essays on Anglo-American Society* (Chapel Hill, NC: IEAHC, University of North Carolina Press, 1979) and Lois Green Carr, Philip D. Morgan, and Jean B. Russo, eds., *Colonial Chesapeake Society* (Chapel Hill, NC: IEAHC, University of North Carolina Press, 1989). Many of the works cited here discuss the early colonists' relations with Indians, but also see Bernard W. Sheehan, *Savagism and Civility: Indians and Englishmen in Colonial Virginia* (Cambridge: Harvard University Press, 1980); Wesley Frank Craven, *White, Red, and Black: The Seventeenth-Century Virginian* (Charlottesville: University of Virginia Press, 1971); several of the essays in James Axtell, *After Columbus: Essays in the Ethnohistory of Colonial North America* (New York: Oxford University Press, 1988); and Helen C. Roundtree, ed., *Powhatan Foreign Relations, 1500–1722* (Charlottesville: University Press of Virginia, 1993). Finally, Warren M. Billings, ed., *The Old Dominion in the Seventeenth Century: A Documentary History of Virginia, 1606–1689* (Chapel Hill, NC: IEAHC, University of North Carolina Press, 1979) is an exceptional documentary collection, and Anita H. Rutman, "Still Planting the Seeds of Hope: The Recent Literature of the Early Chesapeake Region," *Virginia Magazine of History and Biography,* 95 (1987), 3–24, is a useful survey of much of the recent literature. For particular studies of early Maryland, see David B. Quinn, ed., *Early Maryland in a Wider World* (Detroit: Wayne State University Press, 1982) and Aubrey C. Land, Lois Green Carr, and Edward C. Papenfuse, eds., *Law, Society, and Politics in Early Maryland* (Baltimore: Johns Hopkins University Press, 1977).

Chapter Four

Information on the English background to settlement in New England can be found in many of the works cited for chapter three, as well as in a number of the volumes below. For early Plymouth, see John E. Pomfret and Floyd Shumway, *Founding of the American Colonies, 1583–1660* (New York: Harper & Row, 1970), which is also excellent on all of the colonies founded during these years, and George D. Langdon, Jr., *Pilgrim Colony: A History of New Plymouth, 1620–1691* (New Haven: Yale University Press, 1966). For Massachusetts, begin with Edmund S. Morgan, *The Puritan Dilemma: The Story of John Winthrop* (Boston: Little, Brown and Company, 1958). Puritan migration is studied in T. H. Breen

and Stephen Foster, "Moving to the New World: The Character of Early Massachusetts Immigration," *William and Mary Quarterly,* 3d Ser., 30 (1973), 189–222; David Grayson Allen, *In English Ways: The Movement of Societies and the Transferral of English Local Law and Custom to Massachusetts Bay in the Seventeenth Century* (Chapel Hill, NC: IEAHC, University of North Carolina Press, 1981); David Cressy, *Coming over: Migration between England and New England in the Seventeenth Century* (New York: Cambridge University Press, 1987); and especially Virginia DeJohn Anderson, *New England's Generation: The Great Migration and the Formation of Society and Culture in the Seventeenth Century* (New York: Cambridge University Press, 1991). Also see the essays in David D. Hall and David Grayson Allen, eds., *Seventeenth-Century New England* (Boston: Colonial Society of Massachusetts, distributed by University Press of Virginia, 1984).

The study of American Puritanism continues to yield an abundance of exceptionally creative scholarship. For historiographical overviews, see Michael McGiffert, "American Puritan Studies in the 1960s," *William and Mary Quarterly,* 3d Ser., 27 (1970), 36–67, and David D. Hall, "On Common Ground: The Coherence of American Puritan Studies," *William and Mary Quarterly,* 3d ser., 44 (1987), 193–229. Perry Miller's works continue to reward a close reading; see, for instance, the title essay of *Errand into the Wilderness* (New York: Harper & Row, 1956). Francis J. Bremer, *The Puritan Experiment: New England Society from Bradford to Edwards* (New York: St. Martin's Press, 1976) is a comprehensive survey of both the settlement process and Puritan religious beliefs. The following are among the best recent works: Andrew Delbanco, *The Puritan Ordeal* (Cambridge: Harvard University Press, 1989); Stephen Foster, *The Long Argument: English Puritanism and the Shaping of New England Culture, 1570–1700* (Chapel Hill, NC: IEAHC, University of North Carolina Press, 1991); Philip F. Gura, *A Glimpse of Sion's Glory: Puritan Radicalism in New England, 1620–1660* (Middletown, CT: Wesleyan University Press, 1984); David S. Lovejoy, *Religious Enthusiasm in the New World: Heresy to Revolution* (Cambridge: Harvard University Press, 1985); Theodore Dwight Bozeman, *To Live Ancient Lives: The Primitivist Dimension in Puritanism* (Chapel Hill, NC: IEAHC, University of North Carolina Press, 1988); and Charles Lloyd Cohen, *God's Caress: The Psychology of Puritan Religious Experience* (New York: Oxford University Press, 1986). The following studies continue to be valuable: Michael McGiffert, ed., *God's Plot: The Paradoxes of Puritan Piety, Being the Autobiography and Journal of Thomas Shepard* (Amherst: University of Massachusetts Press, 1972); Edmund S. Morgan,

Visible Saints: The History of a Puritan Idea (New York: New York University Press, 1963); E. Brooks Holified, *The Covenant Sealed: The Development of Puritan Sacramental Theology in Old and New England, 1570–1720* (New Haven: Yale University Press, 1974); Norman Pettit, *The Heart Prepared: Grace and Conversion in Puritan Spiritual Life* (New Haven: Yale University Press, 1966); and David D. Hall, *The Faithful Shepherd: A History of the New England Ministry in the Seventeenth Century* (Chapel Hill, NC: IEAHC, University of North Carolina Press, 1972).

On Roger Williams, see Edmund S. Morgan, *Roger Williams: The Church and the State* (New York: Harcourt, Brace and World, 1967) and Edwin S. Gaustad, *Liberty of Conscience: Roger Williams in America* (Grand Rapids, MI: William B. Eerdmans, 1991). For Anne Hutchinson, begin with Emery Battis, *Saints and Sectaries: Anne Hutchinson and the Antinomian Controversy* (Chapel Hill, NC: IEAHC, University of North Carolina Press, 1962); also see Amy Schrager Lang, *Anne Hutchinson and the Problem of Dissent in the Literature of New England* (Berkeley: University of California Press, 1987) and David D. Hall, ed., *The Antinomian Controversy, 1636–1638: A Documentary History*, 2d ed. (Durham, NC: Duke University Press, 1990). Finally, Alan Heimert and Andrew DelBanco, eds., *The Puritans in America: A Narrative Anthology* (Cambridge: Harvard University Press, 1985) tells the New England story through a judicious use of excerpts from primary sources.

On the social cohesion of early New England, see T. H. Breen, "Persistent Localism: English Social Change and the Shaping of New England Institutions," *William and Mary Quarterly*, 3d Ser., 32 (1975), 3–28; Breen and Stephen Foster, "The Puritans' Greatest Achievement: A Study of Social Cohesion in Seventeenth Century Massachusetts," *Journal of American History*, 60 (1973/4), 5–22; and Foster, *Their Solitary Way: The Puritan Social Ethic in the First Century of Settlement in New England* (New Haven: Yale University Press, 1971). Town studies provide particularly revealing insights into early Puritan society. See the following works: Darrett B. Rutman, *Winthrop's Boston: Portrait of a Puritan Town, 1630–1649* (Chapel Hill, NC: IEAHC, University of North Carolina Press, 1965); Sumner Chilton Power, *Puritan Village: The Formation of a New England Town* (Middletown, CT: Westleyan University Press, 1963); Kenneth A. Lockridge, *A New England Town, the First Hundred Years: Dedham, 1636–1736* (New York: W. W. Norton and Company, 1970); and Philip Greven, *Four Generations: Population, Land, and Family in Colonial Andover, Massachusetts* (Ithaca, NY: Cornell University Press, 1970). These early studies are per-

ceptively summarized in John Murrin, "Review Essay," *History and Theory* 11 (1972), 226–75. See, however, a challenging and thoughtful contrary view in John Frederick Martin, *Profits in the Wilderness: Entrepreneurship and the Founding of New England Towns in the Seventeenth Century* (Chapel Hill, NC: IEAHC, University of North Carolina Press, 1991). Douglas R. McManis, *Colonial New England: A Historical Geography* (New York: Oxford University Press, 1975) is a useful overview of the colonies, while Charles E. Clark, *The Eastern Frontier: The Settlement of Northern New England, 1610–1763* (New York: Alfred A. Knopf, 1970) is an invaluable survey of a relatively neglected area.

On the settlers' relations with Indians, see Neil Salisbury, *Manitou and Providence: Indians, Europeans, and the Making of New England, 1500–1643* (New York: Oxford University Press, 1982) and Francis Jennings, *The Invasion of America: Indians, Colonialism, and the Cant of Conquest* (Chapel Hill, NC: IEAHC, University of North Carolina Press, 1975). A contrasting view is presented in Alden T. Vaughan, *New England Frontier: Puritans and Indians, 1620–1676*, 2d ed. (New York: W. W. Norton and Company, 1979).

Chapter Five

The literature on the English Civil War is vast, and the reader would do best to start with the following general works: Derek Hirst, *Authority and Conflict: England, 1603–1658* (Cambridge: Harvard University Press, 1986); Lawrence Stone, *The Causes of the English Revolution* (New York: Harper & Row, 1972); G. E. Aylmer, *Rebellion or Revolution? England, 1640–1660* (New York: Oxford University Press, 1986); David Underdown, *Revel, Riot, and Rebellion: Popular Politics and Culture in England, 1603–1660* (New York: Oxford University Press, 1986); and Conrad Russell, *The Causes of the English Civil War* (New York: Oxford University Press, 1990). Also see the excellent local study William Hunt, *The Puritan Moment: The Coming of Revolution in an English County* (Cambridge: Harvard University Press, 1983) and J. G. A. Pocock, ed., *Three British Revolutions: 1641, 1688, 1776* (Princeton, NJ: Princeton University Press, 1980).

On English attempts to regulate the empire, see J. M. Sosin, *English America and the Restoration Monarchy of Charles II: Transatlantic Politics, Commerce, and Kingship* (Lincoln: University of Nebraska Press, 1981); Robert M. Bliss, *Revolution and Empire: English Politics and the American Colonies in the Seventeenth Century* (New York: St. Martin's Press, distributed for Manchester University Press, 1990); Joyce Oldham Appleby, *Economic Thought and Ideology in Seventeenth-Century England* (Princeton, NJ: Princeton University Press,

1978); K. G. Davies, *The North Atlantic World in the Seventeenth Century* (Minneapolis, MN: University of Minnesota Press, 1974); Ralph Davis, *The Rise of the Atlantic Economies* (Ithaca, NY: Cornell University Press, 1973); and the early chapters of Thomas C. Barrow, *Trade and Empire: The British Customs Service in Colonial America, 1660–1775* (Cambridge: Harvard University Press, 1967).

On the Caribbean colonies, see Richard S. Dunn, *Sugar and Slaves: The Rise of the Planter Class in the British West Indies, 1624–1713* (Chapel Hill, NC: IEAHC, University of North Carolina Press, 1972); Richard B. Sheridan, *Sugar and Slavery: An Economic History of the British West Indies, 1623–1775* (Baltimore: Johns Hopkins University Press, 1973); Michael Craton, *Searching for the Invisible Man: Slaves and Plantation Life in Jamaica* (Cambridge: Harvard University Press, 1978); Hilary McD. Beckles, *White Servitude and Black Slavery in Barbados, 1627–1715* (Knoxville: University of Tennessee Press, 1989); Jerome S. Handler, *The Unappropriated People: Freedmen in the Slave Society of Barbados* (Baltimore: Johns Hopkins University Press, 1974); Handler and Frederick W. Lange, *Plantation Slavery in Barbados: An Archaeological and Historical Investigation* (Cambridge: Harvard University Press, 1978); Richard B. Sheridan, *Doctors and Slaves: A Medical and Demographic History of Slavery in the British West Indies, 1680–1834* (New York: Cambridge University Press, 1985); and Michael Craton, *Testing the Chains: Resistance to Slavery in the West Indies* (Ithaca, NY: Cornell University Press, 1982).

Wesley Frank Craven, *The Colonies in Transition, 1660–1713* (New York: Harper & Row, 1968) is a excellent introduction to the founding of the Restoration colonies and their subsequent development. Also see Douglas Greenberg, "The Middle Colonies in Recent American Historiography," *William and Mary Quarterly,* 3d Ser., 36 (1979), 396–427, for a good overview of the literature. On New Amsterdam and New York, consult Oliver A. Rink, *Holland on the Hudson: An Economic and Social History of Dutch New York* (Ithaca, NY: Cornell University Press, 1986); Robert C. Ritchie, *The Duke's Province: A Study of New York Politics and Society, 1664–1691* (Chapel Hill, NC: IEAHC, University of North Carolina Press, 1977); Thomas E. Burke, Jr., *Mohawk Frontier: The Dutch Community of Schenectady, New York, 1661–1710* (Ithaca, NY: Cornell University Press, 1991); and Thomas J. Archdeacon, *New York City, 1664–1710: Conquest and Change* (Ithaca, NY: Cornell University Press, 1976).

On William Penn, see Richard S. Dunn, *William Penn, Politics and Commerce* (Princeton, NJ: Princeton University Press, 1967); Richard S. Dunn and Mary Maples Dunn, eds., *The World of William Penn* (Philadelphia: University of Pennsylvania Press, 1986); Mary Maples Dunn, *William Penn: Politics and Conscience* (Princeton, NJ: Princeton University Press, 1967); and Melvin B. Endy, Jr., *William Penn and Early Quakerism* (Princeton, N.J.: Princeton University Press, 1973). On early Pennsylvania, see Gary Nash, *Quakers and Politics: Pennsylvania, 1681–1726* (Princeton, NJ: Princeton University Press, 1969) and the wide-ranging interpretation in David Hackett Fischer, *Albion's Seed: Four British Folkways in Early America* (New York: Oxford University Press, 1989). Jean R. Soderland, et al., eds., *William Penn and the Founding of Pennsylvania, 1680–1684: A Documentary History* (Philadelphia: University of Pennsylvania Press, 1983) is a valuable documentary collection. For East Jersey, Ned C. Landsman, *Scotland and Its First American Colony, 1683–1765* (Princeton, NJ: Princeton University Press, 1985) is excellent.

On early Carolina, consult Robert M. Weir, *Colonial South Carolina: A History* (Millwood, NY: KTO 1983); Timothy Silver, *A New Face on the Countryside: Indians, Colonists and Slaves in South Atlantic Forests, 1500–1800* (New York: Cambridge University Press, 1990); and M. Eugene Sirmans, *Colonial South Carolina: A Political History, 1663–1763* (Chapel Hill, NC: IEAHC, University of North Carolina Press, 1966).

Chapter Six

On Virginia under Governor Berkeley, see the controversial interpretation in David Hackett Fischer, *Albion's Seed: Four British Folkways in Early America* (New York: Oxford University Press, 1989) and the contrasting view expressed in Martin H. Quitt, "Immigrant Origins of the Virginia Gentry: A Study of Cultural Transmission and Innovation," *William and Mary Quarterly,* 3d Ser., 45 (1988), 629–55. Also see Warren M. Billings, "The Growth of Political Institutions in Virginia, 1634 to 1676," *William and Mary Quarterly,* 3d Ser., 31 (1974), 225–42; the excellent selection of documents in Billings, ed., *The Old Dominion in the Seventeenth Century: A Documentary History of Virginia, 1606–1689* (Chapel Hill, NC: IEAHC, University of North Carolina, 1979) and Wilcomb E. Washburn, *The Governor and the Rebel: A History of Bacon's Rebellion in Virginia* (Chapel Hill, NC: IEAHC, University of North Carolina Press, 1957). The relevant portions of Edmund S. Morgan, *American Slavery, American Freedom: The Ordeal of Colonial Virginia* (New York: W. W. Norton and Company, 1975) remain essential. For Maryland, see Russell R. Menard, "From Servant to Freeholder: Status Mobility and Property Accumulation in Seventeenth-Century Maryland," *William and Mary Quarterly,* 3d Ser., 30

(1973), 37–64, and Lois G. Carr and David W. Jordan *Maryland's Revolution of Government, 1689–1692* (Ithaca, NY: Cornell University Press, 1974).

On social and economic change in New England, see Bernard Bailyn, *The New England Merchants in the Seventeenth Century* (Cambridge: Harvard University Press, 1955); Richard S. Dunn, *Puritans and Yankees: The Winthrop Dynasty of New England, 1630–1717* (Princeton, NJ: Princeton University Press, 1962); Kenneth A. Lockridge, "Land, Population, and the Evolution of New England Society, 1630–1780," *Past and Present*, 39 (1968): Philip J. Greven, *Four Generations: Population, Land, and Family in Colonial Andover, Massachusetts* (Ithaca, NY: Cornell University Press, 1970); Stephen Innes, *Labor in a New Land: Economy and Society in Seventeenth Century Springfield* (Princeton, NJ: Princeton University Press, 1983); and David Thomas Konig, *Law and Society in Puritan Massachusetts: Essex County, 1629–1692* (Chapel Hill, NC: University of North Carolina Press, 1979).

On the breakdown of the Puritan religious consensus, see Perry Miller, *The New England Mind: From Colony to Province* (Cambridge: Harvard University Press, 1953); Robert G. Pope, *The Half-Way Covenant: Church Membership in Puritan New England* (Princeton, NJ: Princeton University Press, 1969); Michael G. Hall, *The Last American Puritan: The Life of Increase Mather* (Middletown, CT: Wesleyan University Press, 1987); Carla Gardina Pestana, *Quakers and Baptists in Colonial Massachusetts* (New York: Cambridge University Press, 1991); Sacvan Bercovitch, *The American Jeremiad* (Madison: University of Wisconsin Press, 1978) and *The Puritan Origins of the American Self* (New Haven: Yale University Press, 1975); and Robert Middlekauf, *The Mathers: Three Generations of Puritan Intellectuals, 1596–1728* (New York: Oxford University Press, 1971).

There are several excellent studies of King Philip's War, from a variety of perspectives. Contrast, for instance, Douglas E. Leach, *Flintlock and Tomahawk: New England in King Philip's War* (New York: W. W. Norton and Company, 1958) with Francis Jennings, *The Invasion of America: Indians, Colonialism, and the Cant of Conquest* (Chapel Hill, NC: IEAHC, University of North Carolina Press, 1975). Also see Michael J. Puglisi, *Puritans Besieged: The Legacies of King Philip's War in the Massachusetts Bay Colony* (Lanham, MD: University Press of America, 1991); Richard Slotkin, *Regeneration through Violence: The Mythology of the American Frontier, 1600–1860* (Middletown, CT: Wesleyan University Press, 1973; Colin G. Calloway, *The Western Abenakis of Vermont, 1600–1800: War, Migration, and the Survival of an Indian People* (Norman: University of Oklahoma Press, 1990); and Richard Melvoin, *New England Outpost: War and Society in Colonial Deerfield* (New York: W. W. Norton and Company, 1989).

On British plans to consolidate the political governance of the colonies and American reactions, see David S. Lovejoy, *The Glorious Revolution in America* (New York: Harper & Row, 1972); Philip S. Haffenden, *New England in the English Nation, 1689–1713* (Oxford: Oxford University Press, 1974); J. M. Sosin, *English America and the Restoration Monarchy of Charles II* (Lincoln: University of Nebraska Press, 1980), *English American and the Revolution of 1688: Royal Administration and the Structure of Provincial Government* (Lincoln: University of Nebraska Press, 1982), and *English America and Imperial Constancy: The Rise of Provincial Autonomy, 1696–1715* (Lincoln: University of Nebraska Press, 1985); Richard R. Johnson, *Adjustment to Empire: The New England Colonies, 1675–1715* (New Brunswick, NJ: Rutgers University Press, 1981); and Michael G. Hall, *Edward Randolph and the American Colonies, 1676–1703* (Chapel Hill, NC: IEAHC, University of North Carolina Press, 1960). Michael G. Hall, Lawrence H. Leder, and Michael G. Kammen, eds., *The Glorious Revolution in America: Documents on the Colonial Crisis of 1689* (Chapel Hill, NC: IEAHC, University of North Carolina Press, 1964) offers an excellent selection of documents. Note the controversial interpretation advanced by Stephen S. Webb in *The Governors-General: The English Army and the Definition of Empire, 1569–1681* (Chapel Hill, NC: IEAHC, University of North Carolina Press, 1979) and *1676: The End of American Independence* (Cambridge: Harvard University Press, 1985) and the critical response by Richard R. Johnson, "The Imperial Webb: The Thesis of Garrison Government in Early America Considered," *William and Mary Quarterly*, 3d Ser., 43 (1986), 408–30.

Finally, for the British context, consult Richard R. Johnson, "Politics Redefined: An Assessment of Recent Writings on the Late Stuart Period of English History, 1660–1714," *William and Mary Quarterly*, 3d Ser., 35 (1978), 691–732; J. R. Jones, *Country and Court: England, 1658–1714* (Cambridge: Harvard University Press, 1979); and W. A. Speck, *Reluctant Revolutionaries: Englishmen and the Revolution of 1688* (New York: Oxford University Press, 1988).

Chapter Seven

Many of the studies cited in chapters three, four, and five discuss the concept of community, but also see Darrett B. Rutman, "Assessing the Little Communities of Early America," *William and Mary Quarterly*, 3d Ser., 43 (1986), 163–78, and Darrett B. Rutman and Anita H. Rutman, *A Place in Time: Middlesex*

County, Virginia, 1650–1750 (New York: W. W. Norton and Company, 1984). On settlers' interaction with Indians and the environment, begin with William Cronon, *Changes in the Land: Indians, Colonists, and the Ecology of New England* (New York: Hill and Wang, 1983), and see Carolyn Merchant, *Ecological Revolutions: Nature, Gender, and Science in New England* (Chapel Hill, NC: University of North Carolina Press, 1989) and Timothy Silver, *A New Face on the Countryside: Indians, Colonists, and Slaves in South Atlantic Forests, 1500–1800* (New York: Cambridge University Press, 1990). Bruce G. Trigger, "Early Native North American Responses to European Contact: Romantic versus Rationalistic Interpretations," *Journal of American History,* 77 (1991), 1195–1215, is a thought-provoking analysis of Indian adaptations to European cultural borrowings. The following are excellent specialized studies: Alden T. Vaughan and Edward W. Clark, eds., *Puritans among the Indians: Accounts of Captivity and Redemption, 1676–1724* (Cambridge: Harvard University Press, 1981); Yasuhide Kawashima, *Puritan Justice and the Indian: White Man's Law in Massachusetts, 1630–1763* (Middletown, CT: Wesleyan University Press, 1986); and Kenneth M. Morrison, *The Embattled North-East: The Elusive Ideal of Alliance in Abenaki-Euroamerican Relations* (Berkeley: University of California Press, 1984). James Axtell, *The European and the Indian: Essays in the Ethnohistory of Colonial North America* (New York: Oxford University Press, 1981) contains several important essays.

On the family, see Helena M. Wall, *Fierce Communion: Family and Community in Early America* (Cambridge: Harvard University Press, 1990); John Demos, *A Little Commonwealth: Family Life in Plymouth Colony* (New York: Oxford University Press, 1970); Edmund S. Morgan, *The Puritan Family: Religion and Domestic Relations in Seventeenth Century New England,* rev. ed. (New York: Harper & Row, 1966); Daniel Blake Smith, "The Study of the Family in Early America: Trends, Problems, and Prospects," *William and Mary Quarterly,* 3d Ser., 39 (1982), 3–28; Gerald R. Moran and Maris A. Vinovskis, *Religion, Family, and the Life Course: Explorations in the Social History of Early America* (Ann Arbor: University of Michigan Press, 1992); Moran and Vinovskis, "The Puritan Family and Religion: A Critical Reappraisal," *William and Mary Quarterly,* 3rd. ser., 39 (1982), 29–63; and John J. Waters, "Family, Inheritance, and Migration in Colonial New England: The Evidence from Guilford, Connecticut," *William and Mary Quarterly,* 3d Ser., 39 (1982), 64–86.

On the status of women and the nature of witchcraft, begin with Carol F. Karlsen, *The Devil in the Shape of a Woman: Witchcraft in Colonial New England* (New York: W. W. Norton and Company, 1987). Also see the following interpretations: John P. Demos, *Entertaining Satan: Witchcraft and the Culture of Early New England* (New York: Oxford University Press, 1982); Paul Boyer and Stephen Nissenbaum, *Salem Possessed: The Social Origins of Witchcraft* (Cambridge: Harvard University Press, 1974); Richard Godbeer, *The Devil's Dominion: Magic and Ritual in Early New England* (New York: Cambridge University Press, 1992); and Keith Thomas, *Religion and the Decline of Magic* (New York: Scribner's, 1971). David D. Hall, ed., *Witch Hunting in Seventeenth Century New England* (Boston: Northeastern University Press, 1990) is an excellent selection of documents. Also see Lois Green Carr and Lorena S. Walsh, "The Planter's Wife: The Experience of White Women in Seventeenth-Century Maryland," *William and Mary Quarterly,* 3d Ser., 34 (1977), 542–71.

On the material culture of the seventeenth-century colonies, see the stimulating study by James Deetz, *In Small Things Forgotten: The Archaeology of Early American Life* (Garden City, NY: Doubleday, 1977) and the following works: Jonathan L. Fairbanks and Robert F. Trent, *New England Begins: The Seventeenth Century* (Boston: Museum of Fine Arts, 1982); Robert Blair St. George, ed., *Material Life in America, 1600–1860* (Boston: Northeastern University Press, 1988); A. L. Cummings, *The Framed Houses of Massachusetts Bay, 1625–1725* (Cambridge: Harvard University Press, 1979; Allan I. Ludwig, *Graven Images: New England Stonecarving and Its Symbols, 1650–1815* (Middletown, CT: Wesleyan University Press, 1966); and the comprehensive survey by Louis B. Wright, *The Cultural Life of the American Colonies* (New York: Harper & Row, 1957).

For education, contrast Bernard Bailyn, *Education in the Forming of American Society: Needs and Opportunities for Study* (Chapel Hill, NC: IEAHC, University of North Carolina Press, 1960) with Lawrence A. Cremin, *American Education: The Colonial Experience, 1607–1783* (New York: Harper & Row, 1970). Also see Samuel Eliot Morison, *Harvard College in the Seventeenth Century,* 2 vols. (Cambridge: Harvard University Press, 1936) and James Axtell, *The School upon the Hill: Education and Society in Colonial New England* (New Haven: Yale University Press, 1974). For literature, begin with Philip F. Gura, "The Study of Colonial American Literature, 1966–1987: A Vade Mecum," *William and Mary Quarterly,* 3d Ser., 45 (1987), 193–229. Also see David D. Hall, *Worlds of Wonder, Days of Judgment: Popular Religious Belief in Early New England* (New York: Alfred A. Knopf, 1989); Norman S. Grabo, *Edward Taylor,* rev. ed. (Boston:

Twayne Publishers, 1988); and Elizabeth Wade White, *Anne Bradstreet: "The Tenth Muse"* (New York: Oxford University Press, 1971).

Chapter Eight

For a general overview of colonial migration, see Bernard Bailyn, *The Peopling of British North America: An Introduction* (New York: Alfred A. Knopf, 1986). Bailyn's *Voyagers to the West: A Passage in the Peopling of America on the Eve of the Revolution* (New York: Alfred A. Knopf, 1986) is a magisterial, evocative study of migration during the latter part of the century. A. Roger Ekirch, *Bound for America: The Transportation of British Convicts to the Colonies, 1718–1775* (Oxford: Oxford University Press, 1987) is the standard study of convict migration. The essays in Bailyn and Philip D. Morgan, *Strangers within the Realm: Cultural Margins of the First British Empire* (Chapel Hill, NC: IEAHC, University of North Carolina Press, 1991) offer a glimpse of the best of recent scholarship. Also see the following: A. G. Roeber, *Palatines, Liberty, and Property: German Lutherans and Colonial North America* (Baltimore: Johns Hopkins University Press, 1993); Jon Butler, *The Huguenots in America: A Refugee People in New World Society* (Cambridge: Harvard University Press, 1993); Ned C. Landsman, *Scotland and Its First American Colony, 1683–1765* (Princeton, NJ: Princeton University Press, 1985); Duane Meyer, *The Highland Scots of North Carolina, 1732–1776* (Chapel Hill, NC: University of North Carolina Press, 1953); James G. Leyburn, *The Scotch-Irish: A Social History* (Chapel Hill, NC: University of North Carolina Press, 1962); Daniel B. Thorp, *The Moravian Community in Colonial North Carolina: Pluralism on the Southern Frontier* (Knoxville: University of Tennessee Press, 1989); and Gillian Lindt Gollin, *Moravians in Two Worlds: A Study in Changing Communities* (New York: Columbia University Press, 1967).

There are several excellent surveys of British North American slavery. Begin with the brief but comprehensive overview, Donald R. Wright, *African-Americans in the Colonial Era: From African Origins through the American Revolution* (Arlington Heights, IL: Harland Davidson, 1990), and see the essays in Philip D. Curtin, *The Rise and Fall of the Plantation Complex: Essays in Atlantic History* (New York: Cambridge University Press, 1990). Curtin's *Africa Remembered: Narratives of West Africans from the Era of Slave Trade* (Madison: University of Wisconsin Press, 1968) is a valuable collection of primary sources, while Peter H. Wood, "I Did the Best I Could for My Day: The Study of Early Black History during the Second Reconstruction, 1960–1976," *William and Mary Quarterly,* 3d Ser., 35 (1978), 185–225, provides a perceptive

assessment of the literature to that date. On African society, also see Philip D. Curtin and Paul Bohannon, *Africa and Africans,* 3d ed. (Prospect Heights, IL: Waveland Press, 1988) and Patrick Manning, *Slavery and African Life: Occidental, Oriental, and African Slave Trades* (New York: Cambridge University Press, 1990).

On British-American racial attitudes, begin with Winthrop Jordan's classic *White over Black: American Attitudes toward the Negro, 1550–1812* (Chapel Hill, NC: IEAHC, University of North Carolina Press, 1968). Also see A. Leon Higginbotham, Jr., *In the Matter of Color: Race and the American Legal Process. The Colonial Period* (New York: Oxford University Press, 1978) and Jan Nederveen Pieterse, *White on Black: Images of Africa and Blacks in Western Popular Culture* (New Haven: Yale University Press, 1992).

On the slave trade, begin with Philip Curtin, *The Atlantic Slave Trade: A Census* (Madison: University of Wisconsin Press, 1969), which remains remarkably accurate despite years of further research. Also see Herbert S. Klein, *The Middle Passage: Comparative Studies in the Atlantic Slave Trade* (Princeton, NJ: Princeton University Press, 1978); Daniel Pratt Mannix, *Black Cargoes: A History of the Atlantic Slave Trade, 1518–1865* (New York: Viking, 1962); James A. Rawley, *The Transatlantic Slave Trade: A History* (New York: W. W. Norton and Company, 1981); and Jay Coughtry, *The Notorious Triangle: Rhode Island and the American Slave Trade, 1700–1807* (Philadelphia: Temple University Press, 1981).

On African-American culture and slavery in the Chesapeake, begin with the superb article by Ira Berlin, "Time, Space, and the Evolution of Afro-American Society on British Mainland North America," *American Historical Review,* 85 (1980), 44–78. Also see the innovative work by Leland Ferguson, *Uncommon Ground: Archaeology and Early African America, 1650–1800* (Washington, DC: Smithsonian Institution Press, 1992) and the following studies: T. H. Breen and Stephen Innes, *Myne Owne Ground: Race and Freedom on Virginia's Eastern Shore, 1640–1676* (New York: Oxford University Press, 1980); Mechal Sobel, *Trabelin' On: The Slave Journey to an Afro-Baptist Faith* (Princeton, NJ: Princeton University Press, 1979) and *The World They Made Together: Black and White Values in Eighteenth Century Virginia* (Princeton, NJ: Princeton University Press, 1987); Philip D. Morgan and Michael L. Nicholls, "Slaves in Piedmont Virginia, 1720–1790," *William and Mary Quarterly,* 3d Ser., 46 (1989), 211–51; Thad W. Tate, *The Negro in Eighteenth Century Williamsburg* (Williamsburg: Colonial Williamsburg, distributed by University Press of Virginia, 1965); Gerald W. Mullin,

Flight and Rebellion: Slave Resistance in Eighteenth Century Virginia (New York: Oxford University Press, 1972); and especially Allan Kulikoff, *Tobacco and Slaves: The Development of Southern Cultures in the Chesapeake, 1680–1800* (Chapel Hill, NC: IEAHC, University of North Carolina Press, 1986). For an argument that differs with Kulikoff regarding the emergence of community among Chesapeake slaves, see Jean Butenhoff Lee, "The Problem of Slave Community in the Eighteenth Century Chesapeake," *William and Mary Quarterly,* 3d Ser., 35 (1986), 333–61.

For the Carolinas and Georgia, begin with Philip D. Morgan, "Work and Culture: The Task System and the World of Lowcountry Blacks, 1700–1800," *William and Mary Quarterly,* 3d Ser., 39 (1982), 563–99, and Peter H. Wood, *Black Majority: Negroes in Colonial South Carolina from 1670 through the Stono Rebellion* (New York: Alfred A. Knopf, 1974). Also see Daniel C. Littlefield, *Rice and Slaves: Ethnicity and the Slave Trade in Colonial South Carolina* (Baton Rouge: Louisiana State University Press, 1981) and Betty Wood, *Slavery in Colonial Georgia, 1730–1775* (Athens: University of Georgia Press, 1984). Gwendolyn Midlo Hall, *Africans in Colonial Louisiana: The Development of Afro-Creole Culture in the Eighteenth Century* (Baton Rouge: Louisiana State University Press, 1992) and Daniel H. Usner, Jr., *Indians, Settlers, and Slaves in a Frontier Exchange Economy: The Lower Mississippi Valley before 1783* (Chapel Hill, NC: IEAHC, University of North Carolina Press, 1992) are path-breaking studies of an often-ignored area of North American colonial society.

For slavery in the northern colonies, consult Wiliam D. Piersen, *Black Yankee: The Development of an Afro-American Subculture in Eighteenth Century New England* (Amherst: University of Massachusetts Press, 1988); Thomas J. Davis, *A Rumor of Revolt: The "Great Negro Plot" in Colonial New York* (New York: Free Press, 1985); and Gary Nash, *Forging Freedom: The Formation of Philadelphia's Black Community, 1720–1840* (Cambridge: Harvard University Press, 1988).

Chapter Nine

Any study of the colonial economy must begin with the essays in John J. McKusker and Russell R. Menard, *The Economy of British America, 1607–1789* (Chapel Hill, NC: IEAHC, University of North Carolina Press, 1985). Edwin J. Perkins, *The Economy of Colonial America,* 2d ed. (New York: Columbia University Press, 1988); James F. Shepherd and Gary M. Walton, *The Economic Rise of Early America* (London: Cambridge University Press, 1979); and Marc Egnal, "The Economic Development of the Thirteen Colonies, 1720–1775,"
William and Mary Quarterly, 3d Ser., 32 (1975), 191–222; are solid surveys.

Richard Hofstadter, *America at 1750: A Social Portrait* (New York: Alfred A. Knopf, 1971) remains an evocative portrait of American life at mid-century. On daily life, also see David F. Hawke, *Everyday Life in Early America* (New York: Harper & Row, 1988) and Stephanie Grauman Wolf, *As Various as Their Land: The Everyday Lives of Eighteenth-Century Americans* (New York: Harper-Collins, 1993). Alan Kulikoff, *The Agrarian Origins of American Capitalism* (Charlottesville: University Press of Virginia, 1992) is a controversial but soundly argued interpretation of rural American life. Also see Daniel Vickers, "Competency and Competition: Economic Culture in Early America," *William and Mary Quarterly,* 3d Ser., 47 (1990), 3–29; Stephen Innes, ed., *Work and Labor in Early America* (Chapel Hill, NC: IEAHC, University of North Carolina Press, 1988); James Henretta, "Families and Farms: *Mentalité* in Pre-Industrial America," *William and Mary Quarterly,* 3d Ser., 35 (1978), 3–32; Michael Merrill, "Cash Is Good to Eat: Self-Sufficiency and Exchange in the Rural Economy of the United States," *Radical History Review,* 4 (1977), 42–69; and Bettye H. Pruitt, "Self-Sufficiency and the Agricultural Economy of Eighteenth-Century Massachussetts," *William and Mary Quarterly,* 3d Ser., 41 (1984), 333–64. Many of these scholars, particularly those who see continued resistance to the early stirrings of capitalism, have been profoundly influenced by the essays of E. P. Thompson, which have been recently collected in *Customs in Common* (New York: New Press, 1991).

On wealth and trade in the colonies, see Alice H. Jones, *Wealth of a Nation to Be: The American Colonies on the Eve of the Revolution* (New York: Columbia University Press, 1980): Carole Shammas, *The Pre-Industrial Consumer in England and America* (New York: Oxford University Press, 1990); T. H. Breen, "Baubles of Britain: The American and Consumer Revolutions of the Eighteenth Century," *Past and Present,* 109 (1988), 73–104; James F. Shepherd and Gary M. Walton, *Shipping, Maritime Trade and the Economic Development of Colonial North America* (London: Cambridge University Press, 1972); Thomas M. Truxes, *Irish-American Trade, 1660–1783* (New York: Cambridge University Press, 1989); Richard Pares, *Yankees and Creoles: The Trade between North America and the West Indies before the American Revolution* (Cambridge: Cambridge University Press, 1956); John J. McCusker, *Rum and the American Colonies: The Rum Trade and the Balance of Payments in the Thirteen Continental Colonies* (New York: Garland, 1989) and *Money and Exchange in Europe and America, 1600–1775: A Handbook* (Chapel Hill, NC: IEAHC,

University of North Carolina Press, 1978).

On New England society and economy, consult the following works: James A. Henretta, "Economic Development and Social Structure in Colonial Boston," *William and Mary Quarterly*, 3d Ser., 22 (1965), 75–92; Bruce C. Daniels, "Economic Development in Colonial and Revolutionary Connecticut: An Overview," *William and Mary Quarterly*, 3d Ser., 37 (1980), 429–50; Robert A. Gross, *The Minutemen and Their World* (New York: Hill and Wang, 1976); Christopher Jedrey, *The World of John Cleaveland: Family and Community in Eighteenth-Century New England* (New York: W. W. Norton and Company, 1979); Toby L. Ditz, *Property and Kinship: Inheritance in Early Connecticut, 1750–1820* (Princeton, NJ: Princeton University Press, 1986); Jackson Turner Main, *Society and Economy in Colonial Connecticut* (Princeton, NJ: Princeton University Press, 1985); Christine L. Heyrman, *Commerce and Culture: The Maritime Communities of Colonial Massachusetts, 1690–1750* (New York: W. W. Norton and Company, 1984); and Edward Byers, *The Nation of Nantucket: Society and Politics in an Early American Commercial Center, 1660–1820* (Boston: Northeastern University Press, 1986).

On the middle colonies, see Sung Bok Kim, *Landlord and Tenant in Colonial New York: Manorial Society, 1664–1775* (Chapel Hill, NC: IEAHC, University of North Carolina Press, 1978); Jessica Kross, *The Evolution of an American Town: Newtown, New York, 1642–1775* (Philadelphia: Temple University Press, 1983); James T. Lemon, *The Best Poor Man's Country: A Geographical Study of Early Southeastern Pennsylvania* (Baltimore: Johns Hopkins University Press, 1972); Stephanie G. Wolf, *Urban Village: Population, Community, and Family Structure in Germantown, Pennsylvania, 1683–1800* (Princeton, NJ: Princeton University Press, 1976); Sharon V. Salinger, *"To Serve Well and Faithfully": Labor and Indentured Servants in Pennsylvania, 1682–1800* (New York: Cambridge University Press, 1987); Mary M. Schweitzer, *Custom and Contract: Household, Government and the Economy in Colonial Pennsylvania* (New York: Columbia University Press, 1987); Lucy Simler, "Tenancy in Colonial Pennsylvania: The Case of Chester County," *William and Mary Quarterly*, 3d Ser., 43 (1986), 543–69; Thomas M. Doerflinger, *A Vigorous Spirit of Enterprise: Merchants and Economic Development in Revolutionary Philadelphia* (Chapel Hill, NC: IEAHC, University of North Carolina Press, 1986); and Barry Levy, *Quakers and the American Family: British Settlement in the Delaware Valley* (New York: Oxford University Press, 1988).

In addition to Kulikoff's work on the Chesapeake, see the following: T. H. Breen, *Tobacco Culture: The Mentality of the Great Tidewater Planters on the Eve of the Revolution* (Princeton, NJ: Princeton University Press, 1988); Jacob M. Price, *Capital and Credit in British Overseas Trade: The View from the Chesapeake, 1700–1776* (Cambridge: Harvard University Press, 1980); Price, *France and the Chesapeake: A History of the French Tobacco Monopoly, 1674–1791, and of Its Relationship to the British and American Tobacco Trades*, 2 vols. (Ann Arbor: University of Michigan Press, 1973); Lois G. Carr, Lorena S. Walsh, and Russell R. Menard, *Robert Cole's World: Agriculture and Society in Early Maryland* (Chapel Hill, NC: IEAHC, University of North Carolina Press, 1991); Gloria L. Main, *Tobacco Colony: Life in Early Maryland, 1650–1720* (Princeton, NJ: Princeton University Press, 1982); Paul G. E. Clemens, *The Atlantic Economy and Colonial Maryland's Eastern Shore* (Ithaca, NY: Cornell University Press, 1980); and Gregory A. Stiverson, *Poverty in a Land of Plenty: Tenancy in Eighteenth Century Maryland* (Baltimore: Johns Hopkins University Press, 1977).

On paper money, see Joseph Ernst, *Money and Politics in America, 1755–1775* (Chapel Hill, NC: IEAHC, University of North Carolina Press, 1973) and Leslie V. Brock, *The Currency of the American Colonies, 1700–1764: A Study in Colonial Finance and Imperial Relations* (New York: Arno Press, 1975). On life in the cities, begin with the classic work by Gary B. Nash, *The Urban Crucible: Social Change, Political Consciousness, and the Origins of the American Revolution* (Cambridge: Harvard University Press, 1979). Also consult Joyce D. Goodfriend, *Before the Melting Pot: Society and Culture in Colonial New York City, 1664–1730* (Princeton, NJ: Princeton University Press, 1992); G. B. Warden, *Boston, 1689–1776* (Boston: Little, Brown and Company, 1970); and Lynne Withey, *Urban Growth in Colonial Rhode Island: Newport and Providence in the Eighteenth Century* (Albany: State University of New York Press, 1984). On seamen, pirates, and urban workers, see Marcus Rediker, *Between the Devil and the Deep Blue Sea: Merchant Seamen, Pirates, and the Anglo-American Maritime World, 1700–1750* (New York: Cambridge University Press, 1987); Robert C. Ritchie, *Captain Kidd and the War against the Pirates* (Cambridge: Harvard University Press, 1986); Billie G. Smith, *The "Lower Sort": Philadelphia's Laboring People, 1750–1800* (Ithaca, NY: Cornell University Press, 1990); and Ian M. G. Quimby, *The Craftsman in Early America* (New York: W. W. Norton and Company, 1984).

Chapter Ten

The first part of Sidney E. Ahlstrom, *A Religious History of the American People* (New Haven: Yale

University Press, 1972) is an excellent overall survey of religion in early America. Also see Patricia U. Bonomi, *Under the Cope of Heaven: Religion, Society, and Politics in Colonial America* (New York: Oxford University Press, 1986). Jon Butler, *Awash in a Sea of Faith: Christianizing the American People* (Cambridge: Harvard University Press, 1990) argues that religion became more pervasive, not less so, in the daily life of eighteenth-century Americans. For Anglicanism in the colonies, see John Frederick Woolverton, *Colonial Anglicanism in North America* (Detroit: Wayne State University Press, 1984); S. Charles Bolton, *Southern Anglicanism: The Church of England in Colonial South Carolina* (Westport, CT: Greenwood Press, 1982); and Dell Upton, *Things Holy and Profane: Anglican Parish Churches in Colonial Virginia* (Cambridge: Harvard University Press, 1987). On the Dutch Reformed church, see Randall H. Balmer, *A Perfect Babel of Confusion: Dutch Religion and English Culture in the Middle Colonies* (New York: Oxford University Press, 1989). On the Baptists, consult William McLoughlin, *New England Dissent, 1630–1833: The Baptists and the Separation of Church and State* (Cambridge: Harvard University Press, 1991), *Soul Liberty: The Baptists' Struggle in New England, 1630–1833* (Hanover, NH: University Press of New England, 1991), and *Isaac Backus and the American Pietistic Tradition* (Boston: Little, Brown and Company, 1967).

On the Quakers and on religion in Pennsylvania, see Arthur J. Worrall, *Quakers in the Colonial Northeast* (Hanover, NH: University Press of New England, 1980); Jack D. Marietta, *The Reformation of American Quakerism, 1748–1783* (Philadelphia: University of Pennsylvania Press, 1984); Sydney V. James, *A People among Peoples: Quaker Benevolence in Eighteenth-Century America* (Cambridge: Harvard University Press, 1963); Jean R. Soderland, *Quakers and Slavery: A Divided Spirit* (Princeton, NJ: Princeton University Press, 1985); Sally Schwartz, *A Mixed Multitude: The Struggle for Toleration in Colonial Pennsylvania* (New York: New York University Press, 1987); and Jon Butler, *Power, Authority, and the Origins of American Denominational Order: The English Churches in the Delaware Valley, 1680–1730* (Philadelphia: American Philosophical Society, 1978).

There are a daunting number of excellent studies of eighteenth-century congregationalism, but the following can serve as guides to this impressive literature: Perry Miller, *The New England Mind: From Colony to Province* (Cambridge: Harvard University Press, 1953); Kenneth Silverman, *The Life and Times of Cotton Mather* (New York: Harper & Row, 1984); Ralph J. Coffman, *Solomon Stoddard* (Boston: Twayne Publishers, 1978); Paul R. Lucas, *Valley of Discord: Church and Society along the Connecticut*

River, 1636–1725 (Hanover, NH: University Press of New England, 1976); James W. Jones, *The Shattered Synthesis: New England Puritanism before the Great Awakening* (New Haven: Yale University Press, 1973); J. William T. Youngs, Jr., *God's Messengers: Religious Leadership in Colonial New England, 1700–1750* (Baltimore: Johns Hopkins University Press, 1976); Harry S. Stout, *The New England Soul: Preaching and Religious Culture in Colonial New England* (New York: Oxford University Press, 1986); Amanda Porterfield, *Female Piety in Puritan New England: The Emergence of Religious Humanism* (New York: Oxford University Press, 1992); Norman Fiering, *Jonathan Edward's Moral Thought and Its British Context* (Chapel Hill, NC: IEAHC, University of North Carolina Press, 1981; Joseph A. Conforti, *Samuel Hopkins and the New Divinity Movement: Calvinism, the Congregational Ministry, and Reform in New England between the Great Awakenings* (Grand Rapids, MI: Christian University Press, 1981); Robert J. Wilson, III, *The Benevolent Deity: Ebenezer Gay and the Rise of Rational Religion in New England, 1696–1787* (Philadelphia: University of Pennsylvania Press, 1984); and Conrad Wright, *The Beginnings of Unitarianism in America* (Boston: Beacon Press, 1955).

On George Whitefield, see Harry Stout, *The Divine Dramatist* (Grand Rapids, MI: William B. Eerdmans, 1991), and Frank Lambert, "Subscribing for Profits and Piety: The Friendship of Benjamin Franklin and George Whitefield," *William and Mary Quarterly*, 3d Ser., 50 (1993), 529–54. In addition to the general works listed above, William G. McLoughlin, *Revivals, Awakenings, and Reform: An Essay on Religion and Social Change in America, 1607–1977* (Chicago: University of Chicago Press, 1978) provides a good introduction to the Awakening. Also see David S. Lovejoy, *Religious Enthusiasm in the New World: Heresy to Revolution* (Cambridge: Harvard University Press, 1985) and two collections of primary sources: Richard L. Bushman, ed., *The Great Awakening: Documents on the Revival of Religion, 1740–1745* (Chapel Hill, NC: IEAHC, University of North Carolina Press, 1989) and Alan Heimert and Perry Miller, eds., *The Great Awakening: Documents Illustrating the Crisis and Consequences* (Indianapolis: Bobbs-Merrill, 1967).

For the middle colonies, also see Marilyn J. Westerkamp, *Triumph of the Laity: Scots-Irish Piety and the Great Awakening, 1625–1760* (New York: Oxford University Press, 1988); Leigh Eric Schmidt, *Holy Fairs: Scottish Communions and American Revivals in the Early Modern Period* (Princeton, NJ: Princeton University Press, 1989); and Milton J. Coalter, *Gilbert Tennent, Son of Thunder* (Westport, CT: Greenwood Press, 1986). For New England, begin with Edwin Scott Gaustad, *The Great*

Awakening in New England (New York: Harper & Row, 1957). Also see J. M. Bumsted, "Religion, Finance, and Democracy in Massachusetts: The Town of Norton as a Case Study," *Journal of American History,* 57 (1971), 817–31; Michael J. Crawford, "The Spiritual Travels of Nathan Cole," *William and Mary Quarterly,* 3d Ser., 33 (1976), 89–126, and *Seasons of Grace: Colonial New England's Revival Tradition in its British Context* (New York: Oxford University Press, 1991); Patricia J. Tracy, *Jonathan Edwards, Pastor: Religion and Society in Eighteenth-Century Northampton* (New York: Hill and Wang, 1980); and Nathan O. Hatch and Harry S. Stout, eds., *Jonathan Edwards and the American Experience* (New York: Oxford University Press, 1988). For the south, consult Rhys Isaac, "Religion and Authority: Problems of the Anglican Establishment in Virginia in the Era of the Great Awakening and the Parsons' Cause," *William and Mary Quarterly,* 3d Ser., 30 (1973), 3–36. Also see Harvey H. Jackson, "Hugh Bryan and the Evangelical Movement in Colonial South Carolina," *William and Mary Quarterly,* 3d Ser., 43 (1986), 594–614, and Alan Gallay, "The Origins of Slaveholders' Paternalism: George Whitefield, the Bryan Family, and the Great Awakening in the South," *Journal of Southern History,* 53 (1987), 369–94.

Alan Heimert, *Religion and the American Mind from the Great Awakening to the Revolution* (Cambridge: Harvard University Press, 1966); Patricia U. Bonomi, *Under the Cope of Heaven: Religion, Society, and Politics in Colonial America* (New York: Oxford University Press, 1986); and Nathan O. Hatch, *The Sacred Cause of Liberty: Republican Thought and the Millenium in Revolutionary New England* (New Haven: Yale University Press, 1977) all explore the relationship between the Awakening and the Revolution.

Chapter Eleven

There are a number of excellent works on English politics and British imperial policy during the first half of the eighteenth century. Begin with the broad interpretations in J. H. Plumb, *The Origins of Political Stability, England 1675–1725* (Boston: Houghton-Mifflin, 1967); W. A. Speck, *Stability and Strife: England, 1714–1760* (Cambridge: Harvard University Press, 1977); and John Brewer, *Party Ideology and Popular Politics at the Accession of George III* (New York: Cambridge University Press, 1976). On imperial policy, see James A. Henretta, *"Salutary Neglect": Colonial Administration under the Duke of Newcastle* (Princeton, NJ: Princeton University Press, 1972); Michael G. Kammen, *Empire and Interest: The American Colonies and the Politics of Mercantilism* (Philadelphia: Lippincott, 1970); and I. K. Steele, *Politics of Colonial Policy: The Board of Trade in Colonial Administration, 1696–1720* (New York: Oxford University Press, 1968). On the political ties between England and the colonies, begin with the general issues raised in Jack P. Greene, *Peripheries and Center: Constitutional Development in the Extended Politics of the British Empire and the United States, 1607–1788* (Athens: University of Georgia Press, 1986), and then move on to these more specific studies: Alison Gilbert Olson, *Making the Empire Work: London and American Interest Groups, 1690–1790* (Cambridge: Harvard University Press, 1992); and Ian K. Steele, *The English Atlantic, 1675 to 1740: An Exploration in Communication and Community* (New York: Oxford University Press, 1986); and Michael G. Kammen, *A Rope of Sand: The Colonial Agents, British Politics, and the American Revolution* (Ithaca, NY: Cornell University Press, 1968).

On local and colony-wide government, see Bruce C. Daniels, ed., *Town and County: Essays on the Structure of Local Government in the American Colonies* (Middletown, CT: Wesleyan University Press, 1978); Michael Zuckerman, "The Social Context of Democracy in Massachusetts," *William and Mary Quarterly,* 3d Ser., 25 (1968), 523–44; and Jack P. Greene, *The Quest for Power: The Lower Houses of Assembly in the Southern Royal Colonies, 1689–1776* (Chapel Hill, NC: IEAHC, University of North Carolina Press, 1963). On eighteenth-century crowd activity, see Pauline Maier, "Popular Uprisings and Civil Authority in Eighteenth-Century America," *William and Mary Quarterly,* 3d Ser., 27 (1970), 3–35. There are several good studies of colonial governors. See Sheila Skemp, *William Franklin: Son of a Patriot, Servant of a King* (New York: Oxford University Press, 1990); John R. Alden, *Robert Dinwiddie: Servant of the Crown* (Williamsburg, VA: Colonial Williamsburg Foundation, 1973); and John A. Schutz, *William Shirley, King's Governor of Massachusetts* (Chapel Hill, NC: IEAHC, University of North Carolina Press, 1961).

Republicanism remains a somewhat elusive concept, and historians disagree on how colonists interpreted and used its language. The student should begin with the classic works: Bernard Bailyn, *The Ideological Origins of the American Revolution* (Cambridge: Harvard University Press, 1967) and *The Origins of American Politics* (New York: Alfred A. Knopf, 1968); J. G. A. Pocock, *The Machiavellian Moment: Florentine Political Thought and the Atlantic Republican Tradition* (Princeton, NJ: Princeton University Press, 1975); the essays by Pocock in *Virtue, Commerce, and History: Essays on Political Thought and History, Chiefly in the Eighteenth Century* (New York: Cambridge University Press, 1985); Caroline Robbins, *The*

Eighteenth Century Commonwealthman: Studies in the Transmission, Development, and Circumstance of English Liberal Thought from the Restoration of Charles II until the War with the Thirteen Colonies (Cambridge: Harvard University Press, 1959); Gordon S. Wood, *The Radicalism of the American Revolution* (New York: Alfred A. Knopf, 1992); and Wood's articles, "Rhetoric and Reality in the American Revolution," *William and Mary Quarterly,* 3d Ser., 23 (1966), 3–32, and "Conspiracy and the Paranoid Style: Causality and Deceit in the Eighteenth Century," *William and Mary Quarterly,* 3d Ser., 39 (1982), 401–41. These authors generally contend that republicanism, while containing elements of liberal thought, was essentially a traditional ideology that rejected the initial appearances of capitalism. The essays in Joyce Appleby, *Liberalism and Republicanism in the Historical Imagination* (Cambridge: Harvard University Press, 1992) argue that American republicanism was far more liberal and accepting of modern economic values. For an historiographical analysis of debate, see Daniel T. Rodgers, "Republicanism: The Career of a Concept," *Journal of American History,* 79 (1992), 11–38. Also see Isaac Kramnick, *Republicanism and Bourgeois Radicalism* (Ithaca, NY: Cornell University Press, 1992) and "Republican Revisionism Revisited," *American Historical Review,* 87 (1982), 629–44. It is also worth consulting Wood's first book, *The Creation of the American Republic, 1776–1787* (Chapel Hill, NC: IEAHC, University of North Carolina Press, 1969) and Forum, "*The Creation of the American Republic, 1776–1787*: A Symposium of Views and Reviews," *William and Mary Quarterly,* 3d Ser., 44 (1987), 550–640, where the major disputants in the controversy summarize their views. Richard R. Beeman, "Deference, Republicanism, and the Emergence of Popular Politics in Eighteenth-Century America," *William and Mary Quarterly,* 3d Ser., 49 (1992), 401–30, is a recent, and persuasive, attempt to move toward a new synthesis. Finally, see Jack P. Greene, *Imperatives, Behaviors, and Identities: Essays in Early American Cultural History* (Charlottesville: University Press of Virginia, 1992); Edmund S. Morgan, *Inventing the People: The Rise of Popular Sovereignty in England and America* (New York: W. W. Norton and Company, 1988); and Melvin Yazawa, *From Colonies to Commonwealth: Familial Ideology and the Beginnings of the American Republic* (Baltimore: Johns Hopkins University Press, 1985) for somewhat different perspectives.

On politics, society, and gentry values, in Virginia, see Charles S. Sydnor, *Gentlemen Freeholders: Political Practices in Washington's Virginia* (Chapel Hill, NC: IEAHC, University of North Carolina Press, 1952); Jack P. Greene, *Landon Carter: An Inquiry into the Personal Values and Social Imperatives of the Eighteenth Century Virginia Gentry* (Charlottesville: University of Virginia Press, 1965); A. G. Roeber, "Authority Law, and Custom: The Rituals of Court Day in Tidewater Virginia, 1720–1750," *William and Mary Quarterly,* 3d Ser., 37 (1980), 29–52, and *Faithful Magistrates and Republican Lawyers: Creators of Virginia Legal Culture, 1680–1810* (Chapel Hill, NC: University of North Carolina Press, 1981); Kenneth A. Lockridge, *The Diary, and Life, of William Byrd II of Virginia, 1674–1744* (Chapel Hill, NC: IEAHC, University of North Carolina Press, 1987); and especially Rhys Isaac, *The Transformation of Virginia, 1740–1790* (Chapel Hill: IEAHC, University of North Carolina Press, 1982). On the Virginia frontier, consult Richard R. Beeman, "Social Change and Cultural Conflict in Virginia: Lunenberg County, 1746–1774," *William and Mary Quarterly,* 3d Ser., 35 (1978), 455–476; and his longer study, *The Evolution of the Southern Backcountry: A Case Study of Lunenburg County, Virginia, 1746–1832* (Philadelphia: University of Pennsylvania Press, 1984); and Albert Tillson, *Gentry and Commonfolk: Political Cultures on a Virginia Frontier, 1740–1789* (Lexington: University of Kentucky Press, 1991). For a view that stresses consensus in pre-Revolutionary Virginia society, see Jack P. Greene, Richard Bushman, and Michael Kammen, *Society, Freedom, and Conscience: The Coming of the Revolution in Virginia, Massachusetts, and New York,* ed. Richard M. Jellison (New York: W. W. Norton and Company, 1976). Finally, for an informed discussion of the early career of the future first president, see John R. Alden, *George Washington: A Biography* (Baton Rouge: Louisiana State University Press, 1984) and Thomas A. Lewis, *For King and Country: The Maturing of George Washington, 1748–1760* (New York: Harper-Collins, 1993).

For politics in the Carolinas and Georgia, consult the following: A. Roger Ekirch, "*Poor Carolina*": *Politics and Society in Colonial North America, 1729–1776* (Chapel Hill, NC: IEAHC, University of North Carolina Press, 1981); Robert M. Weir, "'The Harmony We Were Famous for': An Interpretation of Pre-Revolutionary South Carolina Politics," *William and Mary Quarterly,* 3d Ser., 27 (1969), 473–501; Richard Maxwell Brown, *The South Carolina Regulators* (Cambridge: Harvard University Press, 1963); and Alan Gallay, *The Formation of a Planter Elite: Jonathan Bryan and the Southern Colonial Frontier* (Athens: University of Georgia Press, 1989).

For political affairs in New York, see Patricia U. Bonomi, *A Factious People: Politics and Society in Colonial New York* (New York: Columbia University Press, 1971); Stanley Nider Katz, *Newcastle's New York: Anglo-American Politics, 1732–1753*

(Cambridge: Harvard University Press, 1968); Cynthia A. Kierner, *The Livingstons of New York: 1675–1790* (Ithaca, NY: Cornell University Press, 1992); Lawrence H. Leder, *Robert Livingston, 1654–1728, and the Politics of Colonial New York* (Chapel Hill, NC: IEAHC, University of North Carolina Press, 1961); and Mary Lou Hustig, *Robert Hunter, 1666–1734: New York's Augustan Statesman* (Syracuse, NY: Syracuse University Press, 1983).

Alan Tully, *William Penn's Legacy: Politics and Social Structure in Provincial Pennsylvania* (Baltimore: Johns Hopkins University Press, 1977) and James H. Hutson, *Pennsylvania Politics, 1746–1770* (Princeton, NJ: Princeton University Press, 1972) provide thorough accounts of Pennsylvania politics in the decades preceding the Revolution, while Thomas L. Purvis, *Proprietors, Patronage, and Paper Money: Legislative Politics in New Jersey, 1703–1776* (New Brunswick, NJ: Rutgers University Press, 1986) and "Origins and Patterns of Agrarian Unrest in New Jersey, 1735–1754," *William and Mary Quarterly,* 3d Ser., 44 (1982), 600–27, are useful guides to the complex political affairs of New Jersey.

Edward M. Cook, Jr., *The Fathers of the Towns: Leadership and Community Structure in Eighteenth Century New England* (Baltimore: Johns Hopkins University Press, 1976) is a landmark study of political leadership in New England, while Richard L. Bushman, *King and People in Provincial Massachusetts* (Chapel Hill, NC: IEAHC, University of North Carolina Press, 1985) and Ronald P. Dufour, *Modernization in Colonial Massachusetts, 1630–1763* (New York: Garland, 1987) explore the role of ideology in the colony's political life. Consult William Pencak, *War, Politics, and Revolution in Provincial Massachusetts* (Boston: Northeastern University Press, 1981) for a detailed study of political conflict in the colony between the House of Representatives and the royal governors. Gregory H. Nobles, *Divisions throughout the Whole: Politics and Society in Hampshire County, Massachusetts, 1740–1775* (New York: Cambridge University Press, 1983) is a path-breaking analysis of political attitudes in rural towns in the years leading to the Revolution; his findings confirm those of Robert Gross, *The Minutemen and Their World* (New York: Hill and Wang, 1976). John L. Brooke, *The Heart of the Commonwealth: Society and Political Culture in Worcester County, Massachusetts, 1713–1861* (New York: Cambridge University Press, 1989) provides the most thorough analysis of local political culture available and suggestively explores the long-term relationship between eighteenth- and nineteenth-century ideological structures. Paul S. Boyer, "Borrowed Rhetoric: The Massachusetts Excise Controversy of 1754," *William and Mary Quarterly,*

3d Ser., 21 (1964), 328–351; is the standard analysis of a revealing political controversy. Two works examine Johathan Mayhew's political philosophy: Charles W. Akers, *Called unto Liberty: A Life of Jonathan Mayhew, 1720–1766* (Cambridge: Harvard University Press, 1964) and John Corrigan, *The Hidden Balance: Religion and the Social Theories of Charles Chauncy and Jonathan Mayhew* (New York: Cambridge University Press, 1987). John J. Waters, Jr., *The Otis Family in Provincial and Revolutionary Massachusetts* (Chapel Hill, NC: IEAHC, University of North Carolina Press, 1968) and David S. Lovejoy, *Rhode Island Politics and the American Revolution, 1760–1776* (Providence, RI: Brown University Press, 1958) fruitfully explore the relationship between local political conflicts and the coming of the Revolution in their respective colonies.

Chapter Twelve

There are many rewarding studies of the American Enlightenment. Begin with Henry F. May, *The Enlightenment in America* (New York: Oxford University Press, 1976) and *The Divided Heart: Essays on Protestantism and the Enlightenment in America* (New York: Oxford University Press, 1991); Donald H. Meyer, *The Democratic Enlightenment* (New York: Putnam's, 1976); Esmond Wright, *Franklin of Philadelphia* (Cambridge: Harvard University Press, 1986); Wright, ed., *Benjamin Franklin: His Life as He Wrote It* (Cambridge: Harvard University Press, 1990); Ormond Seavey, *Becoming Benjamin Franklin: The Autobiography and the Life* (University Park: Pennsylvania State University Press, 1988); I. Bernard Cohen, *Benjamin Franklin's Science* (Cambridge: Harvard University Press, 1990); Brooke Hindle, *The Pursuit of Science in Revolutionary America, 1735–1789* (Chapel Hill, NC: IEAHC, University of North Carolina Press, 1956); Raymond Phineas Stearns, *Science in the British Colonies of America* (Urbana: University of Illinois Press, 1970); Richard H. Shryock, *Medicine and Society in America, 1660–1860* (New York: New York University Press, 1960); and George E. Frick and Raymond P. Stearns, *Mark Catesby: The Colonial Audubon* (Urbana: University of Illinois Press, 1961).

In addition to Lawrence Cremin, *American Education: The Colonial Experience, 1607–1783* (New York: Harper & Row, 1970), see the following for education in the eighteenth-century colonies: Robert Middlekauf, *Ancients and Axioms: Secondary Education in Eighteenth Century New England* (New Haven: Yale University Press, 1963); David W. Robson, *Educating Republicans: The College in the Era of the American Revolution, 1750–1800* (Westport, CT: Greenwood Press, 1985); Howard Miller, *The Revolutionary College: American*

Presbyterian Higher Education, 1707–1837 (New York: New York University Press, 1976); and Richard Warch, *School of the Prophets: Yale College, 1701–1740* (New Haven: Yale University Press, 1973).

The following works provide discussions of various aspects of eighteenth-century American literature: David S. Shields, *Oracles of Empire: Poetry, Politics, and Commerce in British America, 1690–1750* (Chicago: University of Chicago Press, 1990); Daniel A. Cohen, *Pillars of Salt, Monuments of Grace: New England Crime Literature and the Origins of American Popular Culture, 1674–1800* (New York: Oxford University Press, 1992); Dr. Alexander Hamilton, *The History of the Ancient and Honorable Tuesday Club*, ed. Robert Miklus, 3 vols. (Chapel Hill, NC: IEAHC, University of North Carolina Press, 1990); Robert Miklaus, *The Comic Genius of Dr. Alexander Hamilton* (Knoxville: University of Tennessee Press, 1990); Louis B. Wright, ed., *The Prose Works of William Byrd of Westover: Narratives of a Colonial Virginian* (Cambridge: Harvard University Press, 1966); Carl Bridenbaugh, ed., *Gentleman's Progress: The Itinerarium of Dr. Alexander Hamilton, 1744* (Chapel Hill, NC: IEAHC, University of North Carolina Press, 1948); and three books by Richard Beale Davis: *A Colonial Southern Bookshelf: Reading in the Eighteenth Century* (Athens: University of Georgia Press, 1979) *Literature and Society in Early Virginia, 1608–1840* (Baton Rouge: Louisiana State University Press, 1973); and *Intellectual Life in the Colonial South, 1585–1763,* 3 vols. (Knoxville: University of Tennessee Press, 1978).

Recent studies have focused more on the broader social functions of books and reading. See David D. Hall and John B. Hench, eds., *Needs and Opportunities in the History of the Book: America, 1639–1876* (Worcester, MA: American Antiquarian Society, 1987); William L. Joyce, et al., eds. *Printing and Society in Early America* (Worcester, MA: American Antiquarian Society, 1983); Richard D. Brown, *Knowledge Is Power: The Diffusion of Information in Early America, 1700–1865* (New York: Oxford University Press, 1989); Michael Warner, *The Letters of the Republic: Publication and the Public Sphere in Eighteenth-Century America* (Cambridge: Harvard University Press, 1990); Leonard W. Levy, *The Emergence of a Free Press* (New York: Oxford University Press, 1985); and Jeffrey A. Smith, *Printers and Press Freedom: The Ideology of Early American Journalism* (New York: Oxford University Press, 1988).

The volume of work on the fine arts in early America is imposing, and only a few of the best works can be cited here. See Hugh F. Rankin, *The Theater in Colonial America* (Chapel Hill, NC: University of North Carolina Press, 1960) and the difficult but brilliant analysis by Jean-Christophe Agnew, *Worlds Apart: The Market and the Theater in Anglo-American Thought, 1550–1750* (New York: Cambridge University Press, 1986). Also consult Jonathan L. Fairbanks, et al., *Paul Revere's Boston, 1735–1818* (Boston: Museum of Fine Arts, 1975); Peter Benes, *The Masks of Orthodoxy: Folk Gravestone Carving in Plymouth County, Massachusetts, 1689–1805* (Amherst: University of Massachusetts Press, 1977); Wayne Craven, *Colonial American Portraiture: The Economic, Religious, Social, Cultural, Philosophical, Scientific, and Aesthetic Foundations* (New York: Cambridge University Press, 1986); Robert C. Alberts, *Benjamin West: A Biography* (Boston: Houghton Mifflin, 1987); Jules David Prown, *John Singleton Copley,* 2 vols. (Cambridge: Harvard University Press, 1966); Edgar P. Richardson, Brooke Hindle, and Lillian B. Miller, *Charles Willson Peale and His World* (New York: Abrams, 1983); and Gerald W. R. Ward and William N. Hosley, Jr., eds., *The Great River: Art and Society of the Connecticut River Valley, 1635–1820* (Hartford, CT: Wadsworth Atheneum, 1985). On material culture, start with Richard L. Bushman, *The Refinement of America: Persons, Houses, Cities* (New York: Alfred A. Knopf, 1992), and also see Peter Martin, *The Pleasure Gardens of Virginia: From Jamestown to Jefferson* (Princeton, NJ: Princeton University Press, 1991); Blair St. George, ed., *Material Life in America, 1600–1860* (Boston: Northeastern University Press, 1988); and T. H. Breen, "An Empire of Goods: The Anglicization of Colonial America, 1690–1776," *Journal of British Studies,* 25 (1986), 467–99.

On women and the family, begin with the overviews in the following works: Ronald Hoffman and Peter J. Albert, eds., *Women in the Age of the American Revolution* (Charlottesville: University Press of Virginia, 1989); Mary Beth Norton, "The Evolution of White Women's Experience in Early America," *American Historical Review,* 89 (1984):593–619; and the early chapters of Norton, *Liberty's Daughters: The Revolutionary Experience of American Women, 1750–1800* (Boston: Little, Brown and Company, 1980) and Linda K. Kerber, *Women of the Republic: Intellect and Ideology in Revolutionary America,* (Chapel Hill, NC: IEAHC, University of North Carolina Press, 1980). Though concerned with a limited geographic area, perhaps the best book to appear on women in the American colonies in recent years is Laura Thatcher Ulrich, *Good Wives: Image and Reality in the Lives of Women in Northern New England, 1650–1750* (New York: Alfred A. Knopf, 1982). On particular colonies and topics, consult these works: Nancy F. Cott, "Divorce and the Changing Status of Women in

Eighteenth Century Massachusetts," *William and Mary Quarterly*, 3d Ser., 39 (1976), 586–614; Cornelia Hughes Dayton, "Taking the Trade: Abortion and Gender Relations in an Eighteenth-Century New England Village," *William and Mary Quarterly*, 3d Ser., 48 (1991), 19–49; J. William Frost, *The Quaker Family in Colonial America: A Portrait of the Society of Friends* (New York: St. Martin's, 1973); Firth Haring Fabend, *A Dutch Family in the Middle Colonies, 1660–1800* (New Brunswick, NJ: Rutgers University Press, 1991); Mary Maples Dunn, "Saints and Sisters: Congregational and Quaker Women in the Early Colonial Period," *American Quarterly*, 30 (1978), 582–601; Jean R. Soderlund, "Women's Authority in Pennsylvania and New Jersey Quaker Meetings, 1680–1760," *William and Mary Quarterly*, 3d Ser., 44 (1987), 722–49; Joan R. Gundersen and Gwen Victor Gampel, "Married Women's Legal Status in Eighteenth Century New York and Virginia," *William and Mary Quarterly*, 3d Ser., 39 (1982), 114–34; Marylynn Salmon, *Women and the Law of Property in Early America* (Chapel Hill, NC: University of North Carolina Press, 1986); Joan R. Jensen, *Loosening the Bonds: Mid-Atlantic Farm Women, 1750–1850* (New Haven: Yale University Press, 1986); Jan Lewis, "Domestic Tranquility and the Management of Emotion among the Gentry of Pre-Revolutionary Virginia," *William and Mary Quarterly*, 3d Ser., 39 (1982), 135–49, and *The Pursuit of Happiness: Family and Values in Jefferson's Virginia* (New York: Cambridge University Press, 1983); and Daniel B. Smith, *Inside the Great House: Planter Family Life in Eighteenth-Century Chesapeake Society* (Ithaca, NY: Cornell University Press, 1980).

Philip Greven, *The Protestant Temperament: Patterns of Child-Rearing, Religious Experience, and the Self in Early America* (New York: Alfred A. Knopf, 1977) presents a controversial but suggestive interpretation of attitudes toward child and self in colonial America. Finally, Jay Fliegelman, *Prodigals and Pilgrims: The American Revolution against Patriarchal Authority, 1750–1800* (New York: Cambridge University Press, 1982) is a suggestive interpretation of the connection between changing family values and the revolutionary shift in political beliefs during the "age of revolution."

A creative, if small, body of research in colonial legal history is beginning to accumulate. For an overview of recent literature, see Douglas Greenberg, "Crime, Law Enforcement, and Social Control in Colonial America," *American Journal of Legal History*, 26 (1982), 293–325, and "Explaining the Law in Early American History: A Symposium," *William and Mary Quarterly*, 3d Ser., 50 (1993), 3–50. Also see Peter Charles Hoffer, *Law and People in Colonial America* (Baltimore: Johns Hopkins University Press, 1993); Stephen Botein, *Early American Law and Society* (New York: Alfred A. Knopf, 1983); Douglas Greenberg, *Crime and Law Enforcement in the Colony of New York, 1691–1776* (Ithaca, NY: Cornell University Press, 1974); and the superb social analysis in Bruce H. Mann, *Neighbours and Strangers: Law and Community in Early Connecticut* (Chapel Hill, NC: University of North Carolina Press, 1987).

The most vivid portrayal of daily life in the back-country is found in David Hackett Fischer, *Albion's Seed: Four British Folkways in America* (New York: Oxford University Press, 1989). Also consult Richard R. Beeman, "Social Change and Cultural Conflict in Virginia: Lunenburg County, 1746–1774," *William and Mary Quarterly*, 3d Ser., 35 (1978), 455–76; Alan Taylor, "'A Kind of Warr': The Contest for Land on the Northeastern Frontier, 1750–1820," *William and Mary Quarterly*, 3d Ser., 46 (1989), 3–26; and the suggestive overview by Gregory H. Nobles, "Breaking into the Backcountry: New Approaches to the Early American Frontier, 1750–1800," *William and Mary Quarterly*, 3d Ser., 46 (1989), 641–70. Charles Woodmason, *The Carolina Backcountry on the Eve of the Revolution: The Journal and Other Writings of Charles Woodmason, American Itinerant* (Chapel Hill, NC: University of North Carolina Press, 1953) remains an invaluable and highly enjoyable source, despite its obvious biases.

Chapter Thirteen

There are a number of general studies of the colonial wars. Consult the following: John Ferling, *Struggle for a Continent: The Wars of Early America* (Arlington Heights, IL: Harlan Davidson, 1993) and *A Wilderness of Miseries: War and Warriors in Early America* (Westport, CT: Greenwood Press, 1980); Douglas Edward Leach, *Arms for Empire: A Military History of the British Colonies in North America, 1607–1763* (New York: Macmillan, 1973) and *Roots of Conflict: British Armed Forces and Colonial Americans, 1677–1763* (Chapel Hill, NC: University of North Carolina Press, 1986); Guy Fregault, *Canada: The War of the Conquest* (Toronto: University of Toronto Press, 1969); Don Higgingotham, "The Early American Way of War: Reconnaisance and Appraisal," *William and Mary Quarterly*, 3d Ser., 44 (1987), 230–73; Douglas E. Leach, *The Northern Colonial Frontier, 1607–1763* (New York: Holt, Rinehart and Winston, 1966); and an excellent study of Indian attitudes and resistance, Gregory Evans Dowd, *A Spirited Resistance: The North American Indian Struggle for Unity, 1745–1815* (Baltimore: Johns Hopkins University Press, 1992).

On Queen Anne's War and related events, see Francis Jennings, *The Ambiguous Iroquois: The*

Covenant Chain Confederation of Indian Tribes with English Colonies from Its Beginnings to the Lancaster Treaty of 1744 (New York: W. W. Norton and Company, 1984); Richard Aquila, *The Iroquois Restoration: Iroquois Diplomacy on the Colonial Frontier, 1701–1754* (Detroit: Wayne State University Press, 1983); Colin G. Calloway, *The Western Abenakis of Vermont, 1600–1800: War, Migration, and the Survival of an Indian People* (Norman: University of Oklahoma Press, 1990); and W. J. Eccles, "The Fur Trade and Eighteenth-Century Imperialism," *William and Mary Quarterly,* 3d Ser., 40 (1983), 341–62. On the southern frontier, consult W. Stitt Robinson, *The Southern Colonial Frontier, 1607–1763* (Albuquerque: University of New Mexico Press, 1979); David Corkran, *The Creek Frontier, 1540–1783* (Norman: University of Oklahoma Press, 1967); Kathryn E. Holland Braund, *Deerskins and Duffels: Creek Indian Trade with Anglo-America, 1685–1815* (Lincoln: University of Nebraska Press, 1993); J. Leitch Wright, Jr., *Creeks and Seminoles: The Destruction and Regeneration of the Muscogulge People* (Lincoln: University of Nebraska Press, 1986); John B. Reid, *A Better Kind of Hatchet: Law, Trade, and Diplomacy in the Cherokee Nation during the Early Years of European Contact* (University Park: Pennsylvania State University Press, 1976); David H. Corkran, *The Cherokee Frontier: Conflict and Survival, 1740–1762* (Norman: University of Oklahoma Press, 1966); and James H. Merrell, *The Indians' New World: Catawbas and Their Neighbours from European Contact through the Era of Removal* (Chapel Hill, NC: IEAHC, University of North Carolina Press, 1989).

On colonial Georgia, see W. W. Abott, *The Royal Governors of Georgia, 1754–1775* (Chapel Hill, NC: IEAHC, University of North Carolina Press, 1959); Harold E. Davis, *The Fledgling Province: Social and Cultural Life in Colonial Georgia, 1733–1776* (Chapel Hill, NC: IEAHC, University of North Carolina Press, 1976); Phinzy Spalding, *Oglethorpe in America* (Chicago: University of Chicago Press, 1977); and Clarence L. Ver Steeg, *Origins of a Southern Mosaic: Studies of Early Carolina and Georgia* (Athens: University of Georgia Press, 1975).

On Indians and their relations with European settlers in the upper Ohio River valley, see Michael N. McConnell, *A Country between: The Upper Ohio Valley and Its Peoples, 1724–1774* (Lincoln: University of Nebraska Press, 1992) and Richard White, *The Middle Ground: Indians, Empires, and Republics in the Great Lakes Region, 1650–1815* (New York: Cambridge University Press, 1991). On colonial expansion westward, see Peter C. Mancall, *Valley of Opportunity: Economic Culture along the Upper Susquehanna* (Ithaca, NY: Cornell University Press, 1991) and Alan V. Briceland, *Westward from Virginia: The Exploration of the Virginia-Carolina Frontier, 1650–1710* (Charlottesville: University Press of Virginia, 1987).

For the later colonial wars, see Francis Jennings, *Empire of Fortune: Crowns, Colonies, and Tribes in the Seven Years' War* (New York: W. W. Norton and Company, 1988); Richard Middleton, *The Bells of Victory: The Pitt-Newcastle Ministry and the Conduct of the Seven Years' War, 1757–1762* (Cambridge: Cambridge University Press, 1985). Fred Anderson, *A People's Army: Massachusetts Soldiers and Society in the Seven Years' War* (Chapel Hill: IEAHC, University of North Carolina Press, 1984); Alan Rogers, *Empire and Liberty: American Resistance to British Authority, 1755–1763* (Berkeley: University of California Press, 1974); Harold E. Selesky, *War and Society in Colonial Connecticut* (New Haven: Yale University Press, 1989); and James Titus, *The Old Dominion at War: Society, Politics, and Warfare in Late Colonial Virginia* (Columbia: University of South Carolina Press, 1991) are studies of the impact of war on colonial society.

Nathan O. Hatch, "The Origins of Civil Millenialism in America: New England Clergymen, War with France, and the Revolution," *William and Mary Quarterly,* 3d Ser., 31 (1974), 407–430; and Ruth H. Bloch, *Visionary Republic: Millenial Themes in American Thought, 1756–1800* (Cambridge: Cambridge University Press, 1985) explore postwar colonial expectations. For postwar expansion, see Alan Taylor, *Liberty Men and Great Proprietors: The Revolutionary Settlement on the Maine Frontier, 1760–1820* (Chapel Hill, NC: IEAHC, University of North Carolina Press, 1990) and the controversial interpretation in Marc Egnal, *A Mighty Empire: The Origins of the American Revolution* (Ithaca, NY: Cornell University Press, 1988).

Conclusion

The literature on the coming of the Revolution is daunting in its size, breadth, and diversity; students should consult the bibliographies in the following studies for a more thorough guide. Robert Middlekauf, *The Glorious Cause: The American Revolution, 1763–1789* (New York: Oxford University Press, 1982) is the liveliest and fullest general account; Merrill Jensen, *The Founding of a Nation: A History of the American Revolution, 1763–1776* (New York: Oxford University Press, 1968) provides even greater detail on the years of resistance. Edmund S. Morgan, *The Birth of the Republic, 1763–1789* (Chicago: University of Chicago Press, 1977) and Colin Bonwick, *The American Revolution* (Charlottesville: University Press of Virginia, 1991) are excellent brief accounts. Edward Countryman, *The American Revolution* (New York: Hill and Wang, 1985) is the best brief interpretative history, while all students will profit from Gordon Wood's *The Radicalism of the American Revolution* (New York: Alfred A. Knopf, 1992). Two collections of essays edited by Alfred A. Young are essential reading: *The American Revolution: Exploitations in the History of American Radicalism* (DeKalb: Northern Illinois University Press, 1976) and *Beyond the American Revolution: Explorations in the History of American Radicalism* (DeKalb: Northern Illinois University Press, 1993). Finally, see Richard D. Brown, ed., *Major Problems in the Era of the American Revolution, 1760–1791* (Lexington, MA: D. C. Heath and Company, 1992).

Index

O

W

Photo Credits